TABLE OF CONTENTS

TO HIS EMINENCE JAMES CARDINAL GIBBONS

Archbishop of Baltimore

YOUR EMINENCE: It is most fitting that this biography of Leo XIII, the work of an American priest, should be dedicated to you.

You have shed a new lustre on the See of Baltimore, first filled, a century ago, by John Carroll—an ever dear and honored name among Americans —since adorned by the learning of a Kenrick and the eloquence of a Spalding, and hallowed by the apostolic virtues of the archbishops who preceded and followed them.

Two years have not passed since the Christian world beheld you, at the head of eighty-six prelates, opening the Third National Council of Baltimore, the most important ever held in the New World. We all know now with what exceeding care the Holy Father had prepared and disposed all things for this great assemblage. He would have the work done there to be considered in a special manner his own. In the impossibility of presiding in person, he committed to you the charge of representing him; he followed the proceedings of that August body with absorbing interest, and approved of their acts with often expressed satisfaction.

In raising to the supreme honors of the Roman Purple the Apostolic Delegate who had so admirably presided over these momentous deliberations, Leo XIII has fulfilled the wishes and prayers of the American Church and ratified the judgment of the entire American people.

That Your Eminence may be spared to see Religion extend her sway while our Republic advances in all that constitutes Christian civilization, and that the teachings and examples of the life herein sketched may become to our land the *Lumen in Caelo* foretold long ago, is the prayer of

Your devoted servant,

BERNARD O'REILLY, S.T.D.

Rome, June 3, 1886.

BELOW IS THE REDUCED FAC-SIMILE OF A LETTER FROM
HIS EMINENCE JAMES CARDINAL GIBBONS ARCHBISHOP OF BALTIMORE,
ACCEPTING THE FOREGOING DEDICATION.

Baltimore, Nov. 5th 1886

Rev. Dear Father:

I am deeply grateful to you for your great kindness in dedicating to me the English edition of your Life of Leo XIII., and for associating my name with the distinguished Cardinal Parocchi whom I have had the honor of knowing for several years, and to whom you dedicate the French edition.

I shall naturally take a lively interest in the work, not only on account of my relation to it, but still more on account of the august character of the subject who is today a spectacle of admiration to the world.

I am happy to learn that the Holy Father has been graciously pleased to bestow his approbation and blessing on the work, and that you have been furnished with authentic and valuable documents bearing upon the life of the illustrious Pontiff.

Believe me Yrs. Very sincerely in Xt.

Rev. Bernard O'Reilly. James Card. Gibbons
Archbp. of Balt.

FROM THE AMERICAN CARDINAL

Baltimore, November 5, 1886.

REV. DEAR FATHER: I Am deeply grateful to you for your great kindness in dedicating to me the English edition of your Life of Leo XIII, and for associating my name with the distinguished Cardinal Parocchi, whom I have had the honor of knowing for several years, and to whom you dedicate the French edition.

I shall naturally take a lively interest In the work, not only on account of my relation to it, but still more on account of the August character of the subject, who is today a spectacle of admiration to the world.

I am happy to learn that the Holy Father has been graciously pleased to bestow his approbation and blessing on the work, and that you have been furnished with authentic and Valuable documents bearing upon the life of the illustrious Pontiff.

Believe me, yours very sincerely in Christ,

JAMES CARDINAL GIBBONS,
Archbishop of Baltimore

BELOW IS THE FAC-SIMILE OF A LETTER FROM
CARDINAL LUCIDO MARIA PAROCCHI, VICAR OF HIS HOLINESS LEO XIII.

Monsieur:

Le Révérend Docteur O'Reilly m'a communiqué votre désir de publier la Vie du Saint Père Léon XIII., qu'il vient d'écrire avec l'encouragement l'approbation et la bénédiction de Sa Sainteté, sur documents authentiques et autorisés, avec le concours et la direction de personnes haut-placées près du Souverain Pontife

Je vous en félicite dans l'intérêt de la foi et de la civilisation, auxquelles Léon XIII. consacre toujours son génie avec le dévouement d'un grand Chrétien et d'un grand Pape. En souhaitant à vôtre entreprise si digne du plus heureux succès, les divines bénédictions, j'ai l'honneur de me dire

Rome, 27 avril 1886.

Mr Charles L. Webster

Votre très-dévoué serv.

L. M. Parocchi

Cardinal Vicaire de Sa Saint.

Translation of the letter on the opposite page from Cardinal Parocchi, Vicar of His Holiness Leo XIII

SIR: The Reverend Doctor O'Reilly has informed me of your desire to publish the Life of Our Holy Father Leo XIII, which he has just written with the encouragement, the approbation, and the blessing of His Holiness, from authentic and authorized documents, with the concurrence and the direction of persons high placed near the Sovereign Pontiff.

I congratulate you thereupon in the interest of faith and of civilization, to which Leo XIII ever consecrates his genius with the devotion of a great Christian and a great Pope. While wishing your undertaking, deserving as it is of the greatest success, the divine blessing, I have the honor to be,

Your very devoted servant,

L. M. PAROCCHI,

Cardinal Vicar of His Holiness

Rome, April 27, 1886.

LETTER OF COMMENDATION FROM HIS EMINENCE JOHN CARDINAL SIMEONI,
Prefect of the Propaganda.

S. CONGREGAZIONE DI PROPAGANDA,
Segreteria,
N. 152,
Risposta intorno alla Vita di Leone XIII.

Rome, January 21, 1887.

REVEREND SIR:

I received not long ago your two letters. I am much pleased to learn that the editing of the first volume of your Life of the Holy Father is happily approaching its completion. I congratulate both yourself and Mr. Webster on the activity and energy displayed *to make of this work a splendid one*, in every way worthy of the subject, and in spite of the opposition encountered and of more than one serious difficulty met with, and successfully overcome. I entertain a firm confidence, and I pray with all my heart that your united efforts may be crowned with gratifying results.

Meanwhile, I also pray our Lord to bestow on you every blessing.

Yours affectionately,

JOHN CARDINAL SIMEONI, *Prefect*

✠ D., ARCHBISHOP OF TYRE, *Secretary*

FROM THE ARCHBISHOP OF NEW YORK

452 Madison Avenue
New York

November 29, 1886

Mr. Charles L. Webster:

DEAR SIR,

From your favor, of recent date, I am glad to learn that *The Life Of Pope Leo XIII*, written by the Rev. Dr. O'Reilly, is now completed, and will very soon be given to the public, in the Jubilee Year of the Sovereign Pontiff. From very many points of view the luminous career of Pope Leo XIII is full of interest. In your publication this interest is enhanced, first, by the fact that the narrative is drawn from authentic sources, and next that it is presented in the graceful and polished style already so favorably known to the large circle of Dr. O'Reilly's readers.

I congratulate you, therefore, on the happy thought of this important contribution to the Holy Father's Golden Jubilee, and I trust that your success will be commensurate with your enterprise and your labors in offering to us all a rare gem in a handsome setting.

I am, my dear sir,

Very respectfully yours,

M. A. CORRIGAN
Archbishop of New York

THE AUTHOR'S PREFACE

THE LIFE OF LEO XIII has been devoted, next to the divine interests of souls, to the culture and advancement of letters and science. What he effected by his generous patronage and bright example in Perugia, and wherever he could exercise influence, the following chapters will fully relate. What he has effected in Rome and throughout the Catholic world during his Pontificate we shall also record there.

Leo XIII stands forth even now as one of the most cultivated scholars of the present or of any past century. His Encyclical Letters, apart from their opportuneness, their doctrinal authority, and their wonderful grasp of the moral needs and dangers of Christian society, are acknowledged to be masterpieces of literary composition, models of the purest and most exquisite Latinity.

But superior to all these qualities of intellectual culture is the man's own stainless character, a saintly life lending tenfold authority to his exalted station, and to the recognized abilities of the ruler and the statesman.

The work which is here laid before the public is one that ought to commend itself to every man and woman in both hemispheres.

Even those who most differ from Leo XIII and the Church of which he is the head, are fain to acknowledge that no other teacher in modern centuries has given utterance to such pregnant, needful, and far-reaching words of inspired wisdom.

If Christian society, and with it Christian civilization, are to subsist and endure, it must be—all acknowledge it—on the basis laid down by the Pontiff in his wonderful Encyclical *Immortale Dei.*

But all Christian men and women, to whom, in an age running so fast into the reckless extravagance and furious appetite for luxury and sensual enjoyment of the Imperial Roman world, the return to the Gospel ideals and practices is a cherished dream, must hail the law of Christian living laid down by Leo XIII as a raising anew on high of the banner of Christ.

To scholars of every land, no matter what department of learning they cultivate, the name of Leo XIII must ever be an honored, if not a cherished, name.

It is not so much that he has himself been all his life an unwearied student and an admired publicist, as that, both before and after his elevation to the Pontificate, he has been the consistent advocate and generous promoter of education in its truest and noblest sense, of a thorough education for the people as well as for the leading classes.

This is clearly shown by what he attempted and achieved in Perugia; by what he has strenuously endeavored to accomplish in Rome in the face of the most adverse circumstances; and by the encouragement given and the sacrifices made by him, throughout Italy and the entire Christian world, to found great educational centres worthy of the age and its requirements.

Nor has the world-wide fame of Leo XIII as a scholar failed to help him less wonderfully than his diplomatic skill toward winning the confidence of governments and peoples. It is his reputation for superhuman prudence, for moderation, and for the most varied learning that has enabled him to restore friendly relations between the Holy See and the most hostile non-Catholic Powers; that has helped him to prevent an open rupture with more than one cabinet; that has caused him to be chosen as Arbitrator between Germany and Spain; and that has gained him the happiness of concluding with Portugal a Concordat healing the inveterate and complicated grievances arising out of the Portuguese protectorate over the East-Indian churches.

Enlightened public opinion, founded on the exquisite tact shown by the Pontiff in dealing with ecclesiastical matters in Great Britain, demands even now that British statesmen shall treat the Holy See with the same deference and respect shown by those of Berlin. There are mighty questions threatening the internal peace of the Three Kingdoms, which the far-seeing wisdom of the Head of Christendom and the inviolable sense of justice of the common Parent of Christians can alone solve satisfactorily and once for all.

In this connection we cannot regard as without a providential purpose the fact that Leo XIII is the only Pope who, since the reign of Henry VIII, has set foot on the shores of England, and studied there the great social, political, and religious problems, on the solution of which depends the future of civilization.

Bernard O'Reilly.

Rome, June 7, 1886.

Note.—The authentic manuscript Memoir, placed in our hands by the Vatican to serve us as a guide in our narrative, is designated as *MS.* in our quotations throughout this volume.

Dedicated with grateful devotion to

Mr. Thomas Dickson

Whose generous assistance has made the reproduction of this work possible.

PART FIRST

Early Life of Joachim Pecci Until His Elevation to the Priesthood

March 2, 1810 - December 31, 1837

CHAPTER I

Auguror: Apparent flammantia lumina coelo,
Sidereoque rubens fulget ab axe dies.
—Leo XIII, *Poems.*

ALL through the long Pontificate of Pius IX, especially when troubles thickened around him, people could not help saying that the words *Crux de Cruce*—"Cross upon Cross"—of the celebrated prophecy attributed to St. Malachy, were verified in his bitter and prolonged trials. While writing, in 1878, the *Life* of that Pope, the Author could not help asking himself, Who was to be his successor? For the prophecy depicts the Pontiff taking up the cross laid down by Pius as "Light in the Heavens"— *Lumen in Caelo.*

Truly the unprecedentedly long reign of the late Pope had closed with the darkest days ever known to the Papacy since the times of the early persecutions. The States of the Church had been absorbed by the new kingdom of Italy. In the palace of the Quirinal was throned a power more hostile to everything Catholic than Henry VIII or Elizabeth, and supported by a Parliament whose policy and principles are infinitely more irreconcilable with Catholicism than the policy and principles of Cromwell and his Parliament. The two most powerful empires in Europe, those of Germany and Russia, had broken off all diplomatic intercourse with him who was, in a very true sense, "the Prisoner of the Vatican." Republican France, in the hands of Voltairean sceptics and radical revolutionists, was with difficulty withheld from breaking openly with the Pope. Spain was friendly, but powerless to help him. Austria, like Belgium and Portugal, was secretly ruled by these occult but powerful organizations, which gave the law to the President of the French Republic, as well as to the successor of Victor Emmanuel. Great Britain, which had efficiently aided in despoiling the Pope of his States, never had, since the reign of James II, sent an official representative to the Holy See; and the Republican Congress of the United States had, after our war, and forgetful of the thousands of Catholics who had died for the Union, suppressed the American Legation at the Vatican. It was an ungenerous and impolitic act, which another Congress and President will not fail to undo in the near future.

But meanwhile Pius IX died, seemingly abandoned by all the nations who could help him effectually, and given over to the absolute dominion of the power which had stripped him of everything save the precarious tenure of the Vatican and its garden, with the mockery of a sovereign title, and which at any time could seize the Vatican itself and leave the Pope without a roof in Rome or in all Italy he could call his own.

It was dark indeed. And how and whence was the light to come amid this settled and ever-deepening gloom above St. Peter's and the venerable seat of an authority which had outlived that of the Caesars, of Charlemagne and the Germano-Roman emperors who succeeded to his title?

The bright, solitary star which, in the ancient family-escutcheon of the Pecci,[1] sheds so brilliant a radiance on the earth beneath, might, and doubtless did, to some persons appear an augury of coming dawn, of hope of better things for the Papacy, for Christianity itself.

But, leaving out of the question the prophecy and its suggestions, there is in the brief reign of Leo XIII enough of splendid achievement to justify the pregnant words of the prediction, had it been authentic. Against all seeming hope, against all the most solemn utterances of political prophets in both hemispheres, the moral superiority which Leo XIII established for himself by his noble character, by the firm but gentle dignity of his official letters, and by the incomparable eloquence and elevation of his solemn teachings addressed to the Universal Church, has disarmed prejudice and hostility. As

---

[1] See Coat of Arms of Leo XIII facing the frontispiece.

we write it is hoped that Germany is again renewing with the Holy See the friendly relations of other times, repealing the oppressive laws enacted against Catholics, and paying, in the eyes of the civilized world, the most exalted homage to the personal character and sovereign rank of the Roman Pontiff. At the same time Russia, which had already made approaches toward conciliation, is said to be sending a special envoy to negotiate about the sad condition of Polish Catholics and other delicate and difficult religious matters in the empire.

Great as is this result, brilliant as is, assuredly, the light shed from the Chair of Peter during the eight years already passed of this Pontificate, the life of the man himself, from his childhood to his sixty-eighth year, when chosen to fill the place of Pius IX, is one long, luminous track, marked at its every stage by the gentlest, noblest virtues, by all those qualities which endear a man to all who know and approach him, by those utterances and deeds which all who value still what is most fundamental in Christianity are sure to admire and to praise.

Thus the personage whom we present to the study and admiration of the reader in the following chapters is not merely a great man, a great Pope, a great and eloquent teacher of all Christians and all mankind: he was a good and a true man in every relation of life in which he was placed; a gentle, docile, loving son; a child and a boy pious and thoughtful beyond his years, but a bright, joyous, manly, generous boy. And all the sweet promises which blossomed forth in his boyhood and youth were realized in the rich fruits of maturer years.

It is only by looking well into the life of him who is now Leo XIII, at all its stages, that one sees how beautiful it is. His pure, gentle, but erect figure is one Fra Angelico could have delighted to paint; his life would have been worthy of the pen which wrote the "*Fioriti di San Francesco.*"

CHAPTER II

BIRTHPLACE
PARENTAGE
HOME AND MOTHER

THE subject of this biography was born at Carpineto on March 2, 1810. There are several places in Italy all but identical in name with Carpineto—called sometimes Carpineto Romano, so called because it belonged to the territory immediately surrounding Rome. The most conspicuous of these localities, outside of Latium, is the ancient fortress of Carpineti, on a spur of the Æmilian Apennines, near Reggio, which was a favorite residence of Matilda, Countess of Tuscany, the protectress of Pope Gregory VII and the benefactress of the Papacy.

Our Carpineto—to use the words of the authentic manuscript notes given to us to be our guide in this narrative—"is a populous little town of five thousand inhabitants, situated in a cleft of the Monti Lepini," a portion of the Volscian range nearest to Velletri. "It is an eagle's nest placed for security high above the plain, between two gigantic rocks."[2] In ancient times it was fortified, some parts of the ruined walls and towers still remaining to attest the fact. Within its neighborhood also stood the Volscian city of Cuentra, destroyed by the Romans, and the ancient fortress of Pruni, ruined—so the local traditions say—by the Duke of Alba's soldiery in the sixteenth century. Its remains are still pointed out to visitors.

THE BIRTHPLACE OF LEO XIII

The mediaeval town became a feudal possession of the

[2] Such was the picturesque expression used by the venerable Cardinal Joseph Pecci in describing to the author the mountain-home of his family.

Aldobrandini. Cardinal Pietro Aldobrandini, nephew of Pope Clement VIII (1592-1605), built there at his own expense a monastery for Reformed Franciscan Monks, which we shall have occasion to mention more than once.

Four parish churches, one of them being a collegiate church founded by Pope Clement XIV, himself a Franciscan, ministered to the spiritual needs of the population. Two of these were Gothic structures of the fifteenth century, dating from the Pontificate of Calixtus III (1455-58). All of them, in the year of grace 1810, were in a sad state of dilapidation. The French Republican soldiers had passed there also, committing their wonted sacrilegious pillage and destruction; and the already scanty revenues of the parochial clergy had been reduced to the merest pittance by the Imperial Government in Rome.

The elevated position of Carpineto, and its great difficulty of access from the valley of Latium beneath, are to this day obstacles which all but a few travellers, students, or artists care to encounter. The railroad which sweeps around the eastern flank of the Volscian range leaves wayfarers still far away from the lofty mountain-crest with its rare towns, hamlets, and ruins. And yet in the late autumn or the lovely spring weather a drive from the nearest railway-station in the valley, Segni, up the narrowing defile or cleft in the mountain-side, through which tumbles ever a foaming torrent, is one of unmingled delight. The wild, weird, and ever-changing scenery of the defile, with its lofty walls of rock, its trees and shrubs of every shade of green; the wild flowers that bloom on every side along the path of the stage-coach; the luminous haze which fills the air in November, as well as in March and April, and which, as you look back into the valley or catch a glimpse of the distant hills, shrouds every distant object with a veil of every shade of blue, fading often into delicate purple; the bracing, invigorating mountain-air—all fill one's soul with a sense of deep joy

About a mile from the top your *vetturino* points out, at the top of a sloping green expanse between two lofty acclivities, the country-house of the Pecci family amid clumps of tall chestnut-trees. It is a beautiful position; and one can fancy how happy parents, surrounded by a band of joyous children, could develop mind and heart beneath yonder shades and on that greensward, from which the eye can wander over panoramas of surpassing grandeur.

AN EAGLE'S NEST

But here we are on the unequal rocky plateau of Carpineto—truly an eagle's eyrie fitting in between two enormous crags. No wonder that the first Pelasgi or Etrusci who wandered hither from the East, in quest of a secure and permanent home, should have fixed upon this almost inaccessible and impregnable site. The quaint, mediaeval houses and streets straggle among the inequalities of the surface. And through them, to the very highest point of the plateau, the stage-coach labors along till it leaves you in front of a fifteenth-century palatial pile, with a church adjoining and separating it from the residence of the parochial clergy.

The masters of this palace in 1810 were Domenico Lodovico Pecci, then in his forty-first year, and his wife, Anna Prosperi-Buzi, who was in her thirty-seventh. Their union has been blessed with six children—four boys and two girls—the youngest child being an infant just baptized,, to whom have been given the names of Joachim Vincent Raphael Lodovico (or Louis). He is the subject of this biography. The other children are: Charles, a lad of sixteen; Anna Maria, almost twelve; Caterina, who is in her tenth year; John Baptist, in his eighth; and Joseph, who is just beginning his fourth.[3]

---

[3] Domenico Lodovico Pecci was born June 2, 1769, and died March 8,. 1838. His wife, Anna Prosperi-Buzi, was born December 30, 1773, and died August 5, 1824. Of their seven children, Carlo was born November 25, 1793, and died in Rome August 29, 1879; Anna Maria, born May 25, 1798, died August 27, 1870; Caterina, born November 4, 1800, died June 13, 1867; Giovan Battista, born October 20, 1802; Giuseppe, born February 15, 1807; Gioacchino, born March 2, 1810; Ferdinando, born January 7, 1816, died at college in his

THE PECCI FAMILY

But who are these Pecci in whose fortunes we desire to interest our readers?

The Pecci are of a noble Siennese stock. Since the accession to the Pontifical Chair of Leo XIII travellers in the ancient and most interesting mediaeval city are shown the Pecci Palace, adjoining the Cathedral Square, and in the cathedral itself the tombs of some high dignitaries of that name are pointed out. When the evil days preceding the reign of Duke Cosimo I dei Medici had involved heroic Siena in a deadly but unequal struggle with her old rival and enemy, Florence—or, rather, with the Medici family, which had destroyed the liberties of the latter, and was bent on forcing the republican Siennese to bend their necks to the yoke—it so happened that the Pecci had taken sides against their countrymen.[4] Under the Pontificate of Clement VII (1523-34), therefore, a branch of the Pecci, favored by that Pope, migrated into the States of the Church and settled at Carpineto. No one who has read the thrilling history of the siege of Siena by the Florentines under the Marquis of Melegnano—Giovanni dei Medici—but will easily understand how fierce and indomitable a spirit animated the Siennese women as well as men against their ancient foe, Florence, and how hard they were likely to make the lot of such of their own as had made common cause with the enemy.

---

fourteenth year.

[4] The MS. in our hands thus relates this incident: "Un ramo della nobile famiglia Pecci di Siena, secondo un' antica tradizione domestica, sotto il Pontificato di Clemente VII, si trasferi in Carpineto, costretto ad esulare dalle fazioni di quella repubblica e rifugiarsi negli Stati della Chiesa col favore di Papa Clemente VII della famiglia dei Medici, per la quale, come 6 fama, avevano parteggiato I Pecci." A note in the corrected MS. says: "*Esiste sul proposito una memoria scritta dal Conte Ceccopieri di Modena.*"

THE PECCI OF CARPINETO

In their new home at Carpineto the Pecci were not altogether safe from the warlike bands which in swift succession desolated Italy in the fifteenth century, allowing the land no rest, the scourge of the plague ever following fast the scourge of the sword. Still, apparently at least, the comparative quiet of their mountain solitude weaned their minds from martial pursuits and ambition and turned them to the old peaceful, intellectual avocations and culture so dear to the proudest Italian aristocracy of the Catholic ages. Letters and the law never seemed to the proudest nobles of the Italian republics a profession less honorable than that of arms. The professor's chair in any one of the great mediaeval universities conferred, in public estimation, a higher degree of nobility than that of birth; and distinction in literature and science made its professors the companions and equals of princes and sovereigns.

Therefore it is that we find among the Pecci of Carpineto several who made themselves a name in the learned professions. Ferdinand Pecci was a renowned lawyer in the Pontificate of Benedict XIV (1740-58); John Baptist Pecci, Vicar-General of Anagni, was appointed Bishop of Segni, but death prevented his taking possession of his see; and a Monsignor Joseph Pecci had so great a reputation in the Roman law-courts that Pius VI entrusted to him the law-business of the Braschi family, then involved in a multitude of suits. He held a still higher place under Pius VII, who made him Commissary-General of the Apostolic Chamber, a position to which was attached much power and influence.

Count Domenico Lodovico Pecci—or Count Lodovico, as he was simply styled—to whom we have introduced the reader, had apparently embraced a military career, or was forced into it by Napoleon I, who needed all the soldiers he could get, and drew largely from the Italian populations to recruit his armies. Count Lodovico had married Anna Prosperi-Buzi, the daughter of a noble house of the ancient Volscian city of Cora—the modern Cori—situated on the western crest of the same Monti Lepini, and not very far distant from Carpineto. The Prosperi-Buzi held in the ancient Volscian stronghold and its district the same place which the Pecci held in their own native town. And the Countess Anna brought to her husband a notable increase of property, which their descendants hold to this day in and around the old cyclopean walls made so famous in Roman history.

But she brought to him and to her children a still richer inheritance of Christian virtues and noble womanly qualities.

Her fourth son—destined one day to be Leo XIII—was born on March 2, 1810. As Carpineto belonged to the diocese of Anagni,[5] whose bishop, Joachim Fosi, was a warm friend of the Pecci family, this prelate was invited to baptize the little stranger and to fulfil toward him the office of godfather. He bestowed on his godson the names of Joachim Vincent Raphael Louis. The name of Vincent was given him at the special request of the countess, who had a special veneration for the great Dominican missionary, St. Vincent Ferrer, Archbishop of Valencia; and she never called him by any other name. Indeed, so long as she lived the child and boy was only known by the name of Vincent Pecci. But when that worshipped mother was taken from him, and especially since 1830, he assumed and retained exclusively the name of Joachim. Was this to show still more his reverence for the memory of this admirable woman? Joachim and Anna are the names given, in the unbroken tradition of the Churches of both the East and the West, to the parents of the Blessed Virgin Mary, the Mother of Christ. Her name, those of her parents and relatives, of the persons immediately connected with Him while He was on earth, such as the apostles and disciples, women as well as men, mentioned in the New Testament, and those of the apostolic men and saintly women who continued Christ's work in the first centuries, honored

[5] The native place of Boniface VIII.

His faith by their lives, and bore him glorious witness by their death—have ever been especially dear in Christian households. It was thought, in the firm and universal belief of the real though invisible communion between the spiritual world of the blessed in heaven and their brethren still struggling on earth, that the bestowing of these dear and honored names on children in baptism secured them special protectors in heaven, and it was to them a powerful motive, when grown to manhood and womanhood, to honor by Christian lives the sainted names they bore.

So Joseph, Joachim, Anna, Mary, and all those sweet names so familiar in Catholic countries, are only flowers of Eastern birth, transplanted into the home-gardens of European peoples and shedding their sweet fragrance there.

Of the five sons, one, and he the youngest, died in his fourteenth year and while pursuing his studies in Rome. So that within the tapestried walls of the Pecci Palace in Carpineto, as well as on the greensward and beneath the chestnut groves of their country residence outside of the town, the fond and pious mother saw herself surrounded by a joyous circle of seven doting and happy children. And both she and her husband were such parents as could and would make home a paradise for their dear ones, a sanctuary of peace, piety, hospitality, and charity in the eyes of servants and dependants, of relatives and friends, and of the suffering and the needy far and near.

She must have been not only a lovely and loving wife and mother, but a noble and worshipped Christian woman, this Countess Anna Pecci, whose portrait, taken in the first years of her motherhood, still hangs in the great hall of her palace at Carpineto by the side of her handsome young husband.

For the writer of these pages it was extremely touching to hear her third son, the venerable Cardinal Pecci of today, recount, with a voice not unshaken by emotion, the qualities of the parent taken from her children all too soon.

"She was, in truth, most devoted to the poor," he said. "She was always working for them. In seasons of great distress she had daily supplies of bread baked for them. You know how fond our peasants are of polenta, or rich, nourishing soup. She directed in person and watched the servants while preparing and cooking huge caldrons of this species of pottage. This, as well as the bread, was dealt out under her superintendence to all who needed it. And she took especial care that the sick poor who could not leave their homes should have their supply sent to them; and that the bashful poor who could not bear to have their distress known should receive assistance in such a delicate way as to prevent their being abased thereby in their own eyes.

"She was the soul of every good work of piety and beneficence that was set afoot in the town. Indeed, she started many of them herself. But all this active outside charity never made her neglect her home-duties. She lavished on us all a mother's most devoted tenderness."

Both the count and countess were most earnest Christians. This union of minds and hearts in the knowledge and practice of the holiest and most ennobling duties, this one common hope of the Christian's exceeding great reward, was, in their home as in their life, the light which brightened and warmed everything around them, and filled with joy and bliss the hearts of their children.[6]

We may well believe that the law of home-life, so well proved by experience, held good in the palace of the Pecci, as elsewhere and at all times: that the generous encouragement and co-operation of the husband enable the wife to attempt, and almost to accomplish, impossibilities.

---

[6] In the Church of the Stigmata, where this good woman reposes in death, there is a plain marble slab on the floor, which records her worth: "Anna Alex. F. Prosperia, egenorum altrix, filiorum amantissima, domo Cora, Femina veteris sanctitatis, frugi munifica, H.S.E. Quae omnis matris familiae munere nitide et in exemplum perfuncta, decessit cum luctu bonorum Non. Aug. An. M.DCCC.XXIV.—Vixit dulciss. cum suis An. LI. M.VII. D.XI. Ludovicus Peccius conjux cum liberis mærentibus. Mulieri rarissimae incomparabili M. P. Ave. Anima Candidissima Te in pace."

CHAPTER III

DARKNESS AND STORM, AMID WHICH JOACHIM VINCENT PECCI IS BORN AND REARED

SO PASSED, under the loving and watchful eye of the Countess Anna Pecci, the infancy and childhood of her two oldest sons, amid the serene atmosphere of these lofty Volscian hills, while Pius VII was cruelly hurried, in the last stage, seemingly, of a mortal illness, from one prison to another; while the towering pride of the French emperor, bent on making the Church of Christ an instrument of universal domination and the captive Pope a docile tool of his state policy, shut up his venerable prisoner from all communication with the outside world, and by extreme and unmanly violence, as well as by every art of persuasion and deception, endeavored to extract from him concessions fatal to religion. From the heights around Carpineto both the countess and her husband could listen to the echoes of the mad and unholy wars kindled by the Napoleonic ambition rolling from the Straits of Gibraltar to the shores of the Baltic, and hear of his armies driven back in disastrous rout from the gates of Madrid, Moscow, and Leipzig to those of Paris, while the unquiet spirit of the foiled conqueror and pitiless tyrant broke forth from its prison in the Island of Elba to raise a fresh whirlwind of flame and blood in France; only, however, to be vanquished anew at Waterloo, and sent to fret and pine away amid the torrid rocks of St. Helena.

Then came the return of the care-worn and gentle Pius to Italy and that Rome where all the evil spirits that Voltaire and the Revolution had called up from the pit and let loose in France had been allowed to reign from 1797 till 1814. Nor did the restoration of the Pope to his capital, or of the other Italian princes to their States, put a sudden stop to the propaganda of evil so long carried on in the Peninsula with consummate skill and untiring energy.

What power save the creative power of nature, or rather of nature's God, can restore in a great country, in an entire continent utterly devastated by flame and convulsed by earthquakes, the beauty, the life, the order, the divine harmony of all things destroyed by the blind rage of the elemental forces? What husbandman, though never so skillful and so untiring, can weed out from his field in a day, a month, a single season, the tares which his enemy has sown during the night over the seed-grain cast into the furrows? Besides, the deeper and richer the soil the more rapid is the growth of the noxious weed, and the more difficult the task of ridding the land of its presence.

So is it with man's moral nature. The more privileged a people is in all the rarest gifts of intellect and heart, the more lavish toward them has been the bounty of Providence in the supernatural order, the deeper will be the perversion effected by an anti-Christian propaganda. What ruin, what desolation is comparable to the sowing of the minds of an entire nation with errors, prejudices, passions, which, taking deep root, prevent the possibility of cultivating or planting therein the most necessary and salutary religious notions?

Such had been the process carried on among all classes of the Italian population ever since the days of Voltaire. His works, in the native French, in excellent translations, and in popular editions, had been sedulously circulated from one end of the Peninsula to the other. As in France, so in Italy, scepticism had first tainted the upper classes, and from them and by them the intellectual pestilence had been spread downwards through the ambitious middle classes, reaching at length the laboring population in city and country. And so, when the Revolution of 1789 first startled Europe by its utterances and innovations, every one of its doctrines found a wide echo in Italy, and too willing apostles among the titled and the learned devoted all their energy and influence to the work of popularizing it. When Voltaireanism and Illuminism

had become incarnate in the Revolution of 1793, and sent their armies into Italy a few years later, there were found, unhappily, but too many influential Italians to hail their advent as the hosts of the new Liberty which denied God and declared war on the existing order of things.

Napoleon's inconsistent and spasmodic efforts to restore the altars which his soldiers had polluted and torn down, and to use, in forwarding his own schemes of domination, the mighty moral forces of religion, were productive, in Italy, of more harm than good. From one end of the Peninsula to the other, he, his officers, his soldiers, his co-operators and abettors of every degree and occupation, had for a quarter of a century taught a religious people to despise, to hate, to ridicule, to outrage religion and its ministers; taught Catholics to look upon the August Head of the Church as a usurper in the political order, as an anomaly and an anachronism in the new social order inaugurated by the Revolution. The revenues derived from the Pontifical States—a peaceful principality created and guaranteed by Christendom to the Common Father—were seized. They had ever been devoted to the fostering in Rome and throughout Italy of the Religious Orders and other institutions—the well-springs of education, piety, and the apostolic spirit at home, the nurseries of the missionaries who spread the name of Christ and the blessings of true civilization among the heathen peoples of both hemispheres. All Church property, all establishments of education and beneficence, the houses and revenues of the Religious Orders especially, were seized by the Revolutionary armies. The confiscations, the plunder, the destruction, the violation of the most sacred rights, and the disorder thereby caused in the popular mind and heart, in the most deep-seated notions, beliefs, and customs, constituted a condition of things so chaotic that no length of time, no labor of restoration, no efforts of the discredited ministers of religion to build up anew the material temple or to win back the confidence of the alienated populations, have achieved anything like a real success, even down to our day.

And when the wave of French invasion had retired beyond the Alps, all the germs of evil deposited in the soil of Italy sprang up and brought forth the harvest that we know of. We know, too, how well the second generation of revolutionists have applied their wide-spread organizations to the cultivating in the souls of the people, with a scientific and fatal certainty, of all this growth of evil principles.

Pius VII returned to Rome on May 24, 1814, to find before him, in the political, social, moral, and material ruin wrought by the French occupation, and the action of all the anti-Christian forces which had so long reigned supreme in Italy, a state of things which might well fill the youngest, the strongest, the bravest with dismay and discouragement.

Such was the social and religious condition of their beautiful native land amid which Lodovico and Anna Pecci saw their little family increase and grow up around them. How were they to preserve them from the irreligious indifference, the contempt, the hatred of all things holy, the habit of deriding the past, the false notions about liberty, the seductive theories about philanthropy and equality, which were floating for ever in the atmosphere, and carried on the wings of the wind like germs of intellectual and moral distempers more fatal than the cholera of 1832 or the Black Plague of 1347?

Where should they find for their sons, bright and quick, and eager to learn as these were, masters they could trust, schools without danger to piety and morality?

Count Pecci and his wife, though tenderly attached to their boys, and knowing how much their home and their brothers and sisters would miss them, felt that Carpineto, on its mountain-crest, was not the place in which to find a school fitted to prepare young men for public life. Rome was near at hand; and in Rome the Popes had ever been solicitous to create and maintain the most efficient establishments of Christian education. Indeed, the worst enemies of the Papacy, who do not wilfully shut their eyes to the evidence of historical truth, are wont to confess that the Popes have been as much the generous foster-parents of letters and science as they have, confessedly, been the most liberal patrons of the fine arts.

But the passage of the Revolutionary armies through Rome and Italy had been as destructive to all educational institutions, to all serious intellectual culture, to the monuments with which Christian art had covered Italy, and to the beautiful creations of Christian genius, as had been the invasions of Attila and Genseric. What the blind and impious rage of Bonaparte's Sans-Culottes did not destroy or mutilate was carried away beyond the Alps. Paris, not Rome, was intended to be the center of civilization as of dominion, and the parent of all culture in the new era which had dawned with the year 1793. But that culture and civilization were founded on principles in every way antagonistic to those which had formed and constituted Christendom. Even when General Bonaparte became consul and then emperor, his blundering and inconsistent efforts to reorganize in Italy a system of national education in harmony with the new Revolutionary creed, as well as with his own notions of Christianity, only resulted, as they did in France, in paganizing the spirit and teaching of public schools of every grade.

His war on the Papacy, his usurpation of the States of the Church and of the government of Rome, naturally led him, and those who carried out his will in the patrimony of St. Peter, to infuse into educational establishments of all kinds an anti-papal, an anti-Catholic, and, without his intending it directly, an anti-Christian spirit and tendency which Pius VII and his successors have consistently combated, without being able effectually to exorcize it from the land.

The first great triumph of irreligion, in the last half of the eighteenth century, was to obtain, through the tyrannic influence of the united Bourbon sovereigns, the suppression of the Jesuits—the great teaching body in the Church—and to substitute for their numerous colleges in all Latin countries a thoroughly organized system of national non-religious education, as in Spain and Portugal, where the anti-Christian philosophers had it all their own way, on the "Philosophic" or Voltairean methods which prevailed in France till Napoleon created his National University—the most potent engine, next to the secret societies, ever devised by Caesarism to take the youth of a nation out of the hands of Christian parents and the control of the Church.

The first care of Pius VII, restored to his people, had been to devise adequate means to counteract the effects of this evil teaching, as well as the seductive and demoralizing influence of so many years of horrible scandals, licentiousness, and blasphemy.

He restored, by a solemn bull, the Society of Jesus, suppressed by Clement XIV by an act wrung from him by the threats and obsession of the Bourbon sovereigns, and which the Pontiff believed to be necessary to save the Church from the gravest dangers.

To the Jesuits, tried in the furnace by such long suffering as the innocent alone can bear in silence, and purified by the fires of calumny, by imprisonment, exile, poverty, and starvation, Count and Countess Pecci resolved to entrust their boys.

Joseph and Joachim (or Vincent, as the latter continued to be called till some years after his mother's death) were then respectively in their tenth and eighth years. It was hard, at so tender an age, to leave the warmth and shelter of their mother's wing, the comforts and freedom of their blessed mountain-home. The wise parents began, in the autumn of 1817, by taking their sons with them to Rome, and, after some days spent in making them see and admire what was most attractive in the Eternal City, they were left for some months in the family of their Uncle Antonio. Meanwhile the Jesuits had opened a college at Viterbo, which was soon filled with the sons of the best families of Rome and all Italy. Thither, in the autumn of 1818, Joseph and Joachim Vincent Pecci were sent to begin their long and careful education for public life.

Whatever opinions may be entertained or expressed about the merits or disadvantages of schools in which children of either sex are reared away from their parents and deprived of a mother's loving care, of the examples and the safeguards of a

Christian home, certain it is that these Jesuits of Viterbo, more than one of whom had traveled all the way to Russia to join there the noble band of exiles protected by the czar, were intent on giving to the youth confided to them the benefit of a truly homelike Christian education. They had toiled much, travelled much, sacrificed much, and endured manifold sufferings to gather among the snows and wilds of the Muscovite Empire the fruits of the ripest knowledge and the ripest virtue. They yearned to impart to the children of their native land what they had themselves acquired at such a cost—an equally ardent thirst for knowledge and for moral goodness.

Such were the masters into whose hands Joseph and Vincent Pecci fell at Viterbo.

As our chief concern is with the latter, it is interesting to gather from authentic records how it fared with him during the six years he remained at Viterbo (1818-1824). The tender and enlightened piety to which his admirable mother had formed him was—as became the most beautiful flower in the human soul—still further cultivated and perfected by men who prized moral excellence above all the treasures of mere knowledge. But while guarding and forming the heart, they also formed and developed the boy's mind. They filled him with a love for the ancient language of his native Latium, and for the classic literature come down to us from the Augustan age, which nothing could satisfy but the utmost perfection and the closest resemblance in composition and diction to the prose-writers, the orators and poets of Rome. Ever since the school-boy of Viterbo has become the teacher of the Christian world, European and American scholars have been able to admire and praise the classic taste and exquisite finish of the productions of his pen, in prose and in verse.

He gave early promise of uncommon literary distinction. Just as he had completed his twelfth year a college festival was got up to welcome the Provincial of the Jesuits, Father Vincent Pavani. This gave to Vincent Pecci the first recorded opportunity of showing his proficiency in Latin verse, as well as his admiration for the character of the venerable man who honored the name of Vincent.[7]

His masters, at the same time, bore unanimous testimony to the boy's tender piety and spotless purity of soul. A very serious sickness which he had during the college sessions of 1821 impaired not a little the robust health nourished in the bracing air of his native Volscian hills. But while his gentleness and patience under suffering won the hearts of the rector and professors, their devoted care of him made a deep impression on the little sufferer. The vacations spent at Carpineto beneath his mother's eye, and the thousand soothing and strengthening influences of maternal love, restored the invalid to health, but he never afterward enjoyed the physical vigor of his early boyhood.

This was, indeed, the sweetest season of life for Vincent Pecci and his brother. The countess lived most of her time in Rome, so as to be nearer to her sons while indulging her own pious tastes. Her frequent letters to them continued to foster in their souls the home-virtues she had planted there. She delighted in their progress, and took comfort from the frequent accounts received from the college of their good conduct and proficiency. Thus did she endeavor to find some compensation for the sacrifice made in sending them away from home at an age when boys most need a mother's eye and hand and heart, .and when boys can be to a mother a source of unspeakable joy.

To be sure the sons and daughters who remained at Carpineto were, with the exception of Ferdinando, the youngest, a great comfort to the countess. Her daughters were now her companions, associated with her in all her good works and charities. But the anxious, motherly heart would

[7] In our MS. is the following Latin epigram composed by Vincent Pecci for the Provincial:

> "Nomine Vincenti, quo tu, Pavane, vocaris,
> Parvulus atque infans Peccius ipse vocor.
> Quas es virtutes magnas, Pavane, secutas.
> Oh! utinam possem Peccius ipse sequi!"

busy itself principally about the two boys far away in Viterbo. She had now no fears about their moral conduct; they were both most exemplary, and the piety of both was solidly grounded in a thorough knowledge of the truths and duties of religion, superadded to the principles instilled into their minds by their mother's early culture.

One feature in her training of them at Carpineto was the deep reverence which her example taught them for the much-persecuted Franciscan monks of the neighboring monastery. These belonged to the strictly reformed branch of the great family of St. Francis, whom St. Bernardine of Siena, St. Peter Alcantara, St. John Capistrano, St. Leonard of Port Maurice, and so many other divine men taught to walk firmly and fervently in the arduous path of poverty and self-sacrifice trodden by the pierced and bleeding feet of St. Francis himself. The Franciscan monastery at Carpineto did not escape the vandalism of the first French invasion in 1797-98. The officers and soldiery of the Revolutionary armies everywhere displayed a peculiar animosity against the houses and brethren of that Order. The old Roman nobility were treated little better than the monks and priests; so the Aldobrandini were powerless to prevent the acts of spoliation and cruelty exercised toward the inmates of an establishment they were bound to protect. When Pius VII was restored, and the religious communities suppressed and dispersed by Napoleon were allowed to return to their former homes, they had a hard struggle to face. Even when allowed to take possession of their monasteries—which was far from always being the case—they found their revenues confiscated. They had to depend on the charity of the surrounding impoverished populations for their daily bread; they had not unfrequently to look to the generosity of old friends to build up anew and to render habitable the religious homes pulled down or wantonly wrecked by their temporary masters.

The Countess Pecci and her husband were not backward in giving a helping hand to the brown-coated and barefooted Observantines. The people of the mountainous districts of Italy have always cherished a warm and grateful affection for these sons of St. Francis, who were to them not only models of the most sublime Christian virtue, but benefactors, supporters, comforters in seasons of distress and illness. The monastery always shared with the needy poor the bread its brethren had begged in the neighborhood; there was always a dispensary where the sick got gratuitous advice, medicine, and care; and the brother physician or surgeon, or dispensarian, visited the bed-ridden in their cottages, and brought with them ever balm and healing for the spirit, even when their drugs or simples availed not to restore health to the body.

And the Third Order of St. Francis, embracing men and women of every rank and profession living in the world, communicated to its members the most precious spiritual advantages of brotherhood with the Order, on condition of leading, in each one's respective sphere of duty, a life in conformity with the precepts of the Gospel, a life of ever-helpful charity to the neighbor for the dear love of the Father of all. This formed a close bond of union between every home in the district, whether that of the prince or of the peasant, and the Franciscan monastery.[8]

The Countess Anna was a member of the Third Order, and

---

[8] The Third Order of St. Francis, which spread so rapidly over all Europe and embraced persons of both sexes and of every rank and condition, counted within the lifetime of St. Francis upwards of 500,000 members living in the world, only in a most exemplary manner. In our times many pious Catholic men and women join it, because it is especially intended for them. The rule does not bind them to take a vow of poverty; it only enjoins the practice of works of charity, daily prayer, a regular performance of church duties, confession and communion, and, in their daily lives, bids them to refrain from excess or indulgence in the pomps and vanities of the world. It is a holy conspiracy or brotherhood, in which the members help each other by word and example to live up, in the ordinary walks of life, to the precepts and spirit of the Gospel; the great and the rich restraining themselves from a wrong use of their wealth, and using it generously to help the needy and to encourage the industry of the laboring poor.

It was the Christian communism revived by St. Francis in the thirteenth century, and which we shall see Leo XIII endeavoring to restore.

her example inspired all others to join it, and thereby to pledge themselves to a faithful observance of all the duties of Christian manhood and womanhood. She was most punctual in her attendance at the meetings held in the monastery chapel for purposes of devotion or charity. And she loved to bring her children with her. Thus did the little Vincent become from his earliest years familiar with the brown habit and sandaled feet of the sons of St. Francis of Assisi. From his mother's lips he heard the story of the gentle saint's wonderful and beneficent life, told in the simple way in which true mothers can tell such stories of Godlike virtue and generosity. And the outlines of that life remained imprinted on the bright child's memory, till in after-years he could fill in every detail from his own careful studies. At any rate, the example of both his parents, the ardent and active piety of his mother, and, later on, of his two sisters, but in particular his familiar acquaintance with the humble, self-denying Observantines, the air of poverty and purity which reigned in their church, that "beauty of holiness" which encircled like a halo the men and the place, stamped on the boy's soul such impressions of living faith and piety as nothing ever afterward could weaken.

The year 1823 passed away at Viterbo with the same uniformity of application and uncommon literary success for Vincent Pecci. He was already in the higher Humanities courses, in which he was introduced to all the chief masterpieces of composition in his own native Italian, as well as in the classic Latin and Greek. He revelled in these studies, for which he seemed to have an uncommon aptitude. His masters—the very best classic scholars whom the Society of Jesus had in the Peninsula—knowing what precious material they had in Vincent Pecci, took especial pains to form and perfect his taste. He only needed guidance and moderation. A disposition like his required no artificial stimulus to make him keep up with the most advanced or outstrip them.[9]

The vacations of 1823 were again spent on the sunny heights of Carpineto, the boys and their brothers taking long draughts of the bliss of home-life by the side of such a mother as Anna Pecci was. They were now, respectively, Joseph in his seventeenth year and Vincent in his fourteenth. It was for them the very springtide of existence, the blossoming of the soul into all the beautiful promise of a future carefully prepared for both by the culture of their parents and by the conscientious labor of the masters they had chosen for their sons.

From the healthy amusements and recreations of Carpineto the proud mother sent them once more back to Viterbo. She was never again to gather them round her in that home which she had made to them a paradise.

A fatal sickness had seized upon her, and her husband, at the first serious symptoms of danger, decided that they should go to Rome, so as to be within reach of the best medical skill. But the ripest medical science in Rome could not arrest the progress of the disease. In the prime of life the adored wife and mother felt that she must leave husband and children when she was most needed by them.

It was then that her deep faith and enlightened piety stood her in good stead. She had too long studied to make her own will conform in all things with the Divine not to accept the sentence of her physicians with perfect submission. She had all

---

[9] In the United States very many among both clergy and laity will remember some of Vincent Pecci's schoolmates at Viterbo, and later at the Roman College. The venerable Father Tellier, S.J., who died not many years ago in Montreal, Superior-General of the Mission in Canada, was, by his exquisite taste and the finished literary excellence of all his compositions, a not unworthy rival of him who was destined to produce the Encyclical *Immortale Dei*. Another classmate was the V. Rev. Wm. S. Murphy, whose memory still lives in New York, New Orleans, and St. Louis. A third was the Rev. Paul Mignard, S.J., of St. Xavier's, New York. These men never ceased praising the enthusiastic love of study with which such masters inspired them.

her life sought too earnestly spiritual strength and comfort in their true source not to find them in abundance in her supreme need. Her sons were sent for, and hastened to the bedside of their dying parent. What both Joseph and Vincent there saw and heard made on such minds as theirs indelible impressions, and gave to their course in life a direction which they, perhaps, did not then appreciate. The mother's heart yearned for her little Ferdinand, then in his eighth year. But he would soon follow her.

Her last looks rested on the circle of her loved ones' faces. She died, as die all who live for home and duty, for God and neighbor, blessed of God and men. Her body was arrayed in the brown habit and cord of the Franciscan Tertiaries, and by them taken to the Observantine Church of the Forty Martyrs (SS. Quaranta Martiri), where she was buried amid the tears and prayers of her family, of the poor of Rome, who had learned to love her. Her husband and children were inconsolable; the three youngest were old enough to estimate the greatness of their irreparable loss. To Vincent, whose life we are especially busied with, this church and its treasure have never ceased to be a thing most sacred and most dear. We shall, in a future chapter, relate the special care bestowed by him on this sanctuary, which is the birthplace and the center of activity of one of the most admirable Confraternities of Rome dedicated to works of enlightened charity.

The affectionate heart of the thoughtful and gentle youth yearned long for her who had left her own image on his features, his heart, and his life. People have related to us in Rome touching anecdotes of the tenderness with which, in his now venerable old age and exalted position, he paints to children presented to him the unspeakable privilege of possessing a mother's love and care, and insists on the fulfilment of the sacred duties of filial piety. His voice then assumes an accent of special tenderness, and his delicate, transparent features are overspread with a special light.

Even as we write this our soul is still moved after seeing the Pope, in his seventy-seventh year, surrounded in early morning by families—parents and children from different lands far asunder—kneeling around him, while that great, fatherly heart of his went out in looks and words of love to those who are truly every one his own, confided to him by Christ.

It is an education in itself to follow the progress of such a beautiful life.

CHAPTER IV

JOACHIM VINCENT PECCI FORMS THE ACQUAINTANCE OF LEO XII—1825

WHILE the Countess Pecci, in the last days of her life, was made happy by what she knew herself and heard from others of the love of her sons for all that should excite the noblest ambition of youth, the saintly, meek, and much-tried spirit of Pius VII passed to its everlasting rest. In his place was elected Cardinal Annibale della Genga, who took the name of Leo XII, and who set himself, from the very beginning of his reign, to complete the work of reconstruction inaugurated by his predecessor. The new Pontiff had a perfect consciousness of the spirit and tendencies of the nineteenth century, of the disorder fallen upon the States of the Church during the long, sad years which closed with the life of his predecessor, and of the manifold and urgent needs in the Church itself, which claimed all the zeal of a saint and the authoritative energy of the Supreme Pastor.

Leo XII displayed both the one and the other during his all too brief Pontificate. Feeling that the enemies of religion and society were using education as a mighty and most effective force to de-christianize Europe and the world, Leo applied himself to collect around him in Rome the most accomplished educators. Italy, he thought, ought, by the superior culture and the superior virtues of its inhabitants, to set the example to the rest of the civilized world. Rome, being the center of Catholicity, the seat of the great teaching and governing authority in the Church, should be like an unfailing light set on high and shedding its radiance abroad through the whole earth, like the fountain-head and source of the waters of life for all humanity, ever gushing and ever pure. In Rome, grouped around the Shrine of the Holy Apostles, were the great nurseries of the apostolic and missionary spirit, to which all heathen lands looked for the men who were to evangelize them. There were the splendid seminaries of learning, in which the twin lamps of sacred and secular knowledge had been ever fed by the Sovereign Pontiffs from out the revenues of their narrow principality. There resided the various and admirable administrative bodies who were the Pope's efficient instruments in governing the Church Universal.

Papal Rome and the Papal States had thus the honor of being, in the designs of that Providence whose course the Christian historian marks all through the events of the last two thousand years, the country and the people set apart by Him to help Him in making Christians of all the tribes of earth, and in binding all men in the sweet chains of one common brotherhood. The glorious and exceptional prerogative bestowed of old on Palestine and its chosen people was transferred, in the Christian Dispensation, to Italy and the Roman State; they were to be the great agency, under God, for Christianizing, civilizing, and uniting the entire human family.

Napoleon's genius clearly perceived this truth, and his blind ambition impelled him to endeavor to transfer from Rome to Paris, with the seat of the Sovereign Pontificate, that of this unique and universal moral power, more far-reaching than his imperial sway. But God, who will move the foundations of the earth in order to give freedom to His Church, independence to His Vicar, caused the Napoleonic Empire suddenly to fall and vanish like a splendid dream, and Pius VII returned to his people.

So must it befall, sooner or later, any earthly power which attempts to incorporate with its dominions the principality created by Providence and the accord of Christian nations to secure to the Papacy not only perfect freedom in the discharge of its divinely appointed office, but the indispensable means for fulfilling it.

Leo XII, who had borne his part in the sufferings and sorrows of the seventh Pius, threw his whole energy into reorganizing perfectly every part of the vast administration of the ecclesiastical government, and restoring perfect order, discipline, and observance in the great monastic bodies, and in creating schools of every grade, such as were needed by Christian Rome in presence of new circumstances, new ideas, and the new and irresistible tendencies of the age.

The College of Viterbo was too far away from Rome, where it was the wise policy of the Popes to open great central schools accessible not only to the young students of the great Religious Orders, but to those of the various national colleges sent to the Eternal City to learn the sacred sciences within the shadow of the Vatican, and to all the Roman youth of every class, whose education was the special care of the bishop and clergy of Rome.

Leo XII, in the year 1824, restored the famous Collegio Romano to the Jesuits. Few indeed as were the men who had survived the long period of dispersion, exile, poverty, and proscription consequent upon the suppression of the Society by the Bourbons, their spirit had passed into the noble band nursed among the snows of Russia; and the young men who flocked to the Jesuit novitiates after the restoration of the Society allowed themselves to be moulded to the same heroic generosity and lofty intellectual ideas which had characterized, in their long and cruel trial, the dispersed sons of St. Ignatius.

When, in the autumn of 1825, the Roman College solemnly inaugurated its courses of ecclesiastical and secular teaching, its halls were at once filled by fourteen hundred students. Among these was Vincent Pecci. His brother Joseph, impressed by his mother's death, and attracted by the lofty ideals of self-sacrificing virtue and zeal in the divine service followed by his Jesuit masters, had, with his father's consent, cast his lot with them. The younger brother, reserved providentially for even a higher destiny, gave himself up to his ardor for study, his enthusiasm being constantly fed not only by the genius and methods of his masters, but by the emulation they knew so well how to maintain among their pupils of every degree. The taste for literary excellence developed at Viterbo by the illustrious Father Lionardo Garibaldi was still further cultivated and matured by such renowned men as Fathers Ferdinando Minini and Joseph Bonvicini. Under them he completed what may be considered the middle collegiate course in the Jesuit system—Humanities and Rhetoric.[10]

That, in these very years, the lad of fourteen was earnestly endeavoring to grasp the full significance of the political, social, and religious changes occurring on every side, we have an indication in a Latin oration which he was chosen to deliver before the assembled students and faculty at the end of his year of Rhetoric. Vincenzo Pecci (as he continued to be called by his school-fellows) had taken for his subject, "Pagan Rome as compared with Christian Rome," and pointedly referred to the moral and unbloody triumph of the Holy See, in the person of Pius VII, over the brute-violence of Napoleon's military despotism. The honor of delivering this oration was due to the fact of the young speaker's having won the prize of excellence in Latin prose-composition.

More remarkable still was his success in Latin verse. The rule for all who contended here for the prize of excellence was that they should within the space of six hours, and without

---

[10] The first or lower course in Jesuit colleges, according to Acquaviva's "Ratio Studiorum," consists of the infima, media, and suprema Grammatica, or first, second, and third Grammar classes or forms. Then come the two classes of Humanities and Rhetoric, equivalent to the Sophomore Course in American colleges. To the Undergraduate Course among us corresponds their Philosophy Course, which lasts three years, and comprises, besides Logic, Metaphysics, and Ethics, a course of pure .and applied Mathematics, Physics, Chemistry, Natural History, Geology, Biology, etc.

any external aid whatever, write a certain number of Latin hexameters on a specified subject. This subject happened to be the Feast of Belshazzar. Young Pecci produced one hundred and twenty verses of such unquestionable excellence that the prize was unanimously awarded to him by the judges. This, however, was not his only success: to him were also awarded the first honors in Greek.

Thus was crowned, while he was yet only at the beginning of his Undergraduate Course, the uncommon ardor with which young Pecci had given himself up to the cultivation of the classical literatures of Greece and Rome. The fine taste thereby developed only made him more ambitious to acquire a perfect mastery of his own native Italian. We shall have occasion further on to show that his efforts here were rewarded with no less success.

The masterpieces of these ancient classic literatures must ever be, so long as civilization lasts, the most perfect models of literary composition, of the most beautiful thoughts clothed in language the most beautiful. To public, professional men of every class, whose great instrument of action and influence is human speech, oral and written, a perfect mastery over the resources of one's own native tongue is indispensable. And experience has demonstrated that, in our own days as in the past, the men who in Church and state are the leaders of their fellow-men —like a Newman, a Gladstone, a Leo XIII—are men who have most assiduously and successfully cultivated classic antiquity.

These academic honors were won at the end of the college sessions of 1825. The more serious studies and less inviting subjects comprised in the curriculum of philosophy often prove a source of failure to young men who have distinguished themselves in the pursuit of mere literature. But where imagination and intellect are equally balanced and harmoniously developed, there is no reason why great success in the culture of letters should not be followed by equal success in philosophy and the sciences. Vincent Pecci proved that his faculties were so happily balanced and cultivated.

In the printed list of prizes distributed in the Collegio Romano at the end of the scholar-year 1828 our Pecci's name is mentioned for the first prize in Physics and Chemistry, and for the first *accessit* for mathematical physics. And, in connection with this creditable fact, it should be mentioned here that among the Faculty of Science in the Roman College at that time were such men as John Baptist Pianciani and Andrea Carafa, scientists of European fame. For a brief space, in 1848-49, the United States possessed, together with the illustrious Pianciani, such of his exiled brother-professors as the astronomers De Vico and Secchi. The government of Washington, well aware of the merit of the great scholars whom Mazzini and Garibaldi would not tolerate in Rome, vainly endeavored to secure their services for the observatory of the Federal capital, while the British government were equally anxious to place under their direction the observatory of Calcutta. Father de Vico, returning temporarily to London, caught typhus-fever from a poor Irish emigrant to whom he ministered on shipboard, and died a victim to his charity. Secchi lived to create the science of solar physics; to become, in spite of the disfavor attaching to the name of Jesuit, a foremost authority in the highest walks of science; and to see, before his death, his brethren driven pitilessly forth from the great University School,[11] which had so long been one of the glories of Italy, the nursery of great Popes, great scholars, and great Christian men.

The success which rewarded Pecci's application to philosophy and science at the end of 1828 increased all through the next year. His acknowledged superiority to his fellow-students caused him to be selected, at the close of the curriculum, to defend against all objectors, and in the most public manner, theses so chosen from the subject-matter of the three years' teaching that they would in reality embrace the entire field of philosophy.

---

[11] The Collegio Romano was also called the Gregorian University, from Gregory XIII, who erected the present magnificent building.

This was the highest distinction that could, at that stage of his university career, be conferred upon the young student, then in his twentieth year. Such public disputations on philosophy, canon law, theology, etc., have always been held in high honor in Rome. They were characteristic of the mediaeval universities, and were adopted by the Jesuits in their great schools as one of the most powerful stimulants to the pursuit of excellence in every department of human learning. These solemn academical tournaments, which were frequented by the elite of Roman society, and in which the most learned men and the highest dignitaries, even cardinals themselves, entered the lists, were often graced by the presence of the Papal Court. It required both uncommon ability and uncommon nerve in a young man to face such an audience, and to reply, during six entire hours, to the most formidable and unforeseen objections, urged, too, by men thoroughly versed in the dialectic art.

Our young philosopher threw himself into the work of preparation with his habitual ardor—with too much ardor, indeed; for he had never quite got over the effects of the gastric fever which had brought him to death's door at Viterbo. The mental excitement and fatigue consequent on overwork were soon visible. The family physicians would not hear of his exposing himself to the public ordeal that awaited him. His masters, however, who were perfectly aware of his thorough mastery of the subject-matters to be discussed, had to acquiesce reluctantly in the decision of the physicians. Still, they were unwilling that one who, in the judgment of students and faculty, was pre-eminently distinguished for talent and proficiency, should be deprived, by the accident of illness, of all the honor he so well deserved. The Faculty decreed that a solemn attestation of Pecci's worth in connection with the proposed academical solemnity should be drawn up and given to him.[12]

One of his schoolmates in Viterbo and in Rome wrote in February, 1878, immediately after the election of Leo XIII:

"I can bear witness to the fact that while yet at Viterbo he won our admiration not only by his quick intelligence, but still more by the singular purity of his life. During our Humanities course we were rivals, and there each time I saw him he impressed me as being all life and intellect. All through his studies in Rome he never sought social gatherings, conversazioni, diversions, or games. His worktable was his world; it was paradise to him to be plunged in the study of science. From his twelfth and thirteenth years upwards he wrote Latin prose and verse with a facility and an elegance

---

[12] Here is the document in question, still carefully preserved by the Pecci family:

"COLLEGIUM ROMANUM SOCIETATIS JESU.

"Fidem facimus praestantem juvenem Joachinum Vincentium Pecci per triennium in hoc Athenaeo Gregoriano philosophiae studio vacasse, in eoque adeo profecisse ut judicio Doctorum Decuvialium dignus habitus sit, qui de selectis ex universa Philosophia thesibus, labente anno scholastico 1829, publice disputaret. Cum vero id perficere ab infirma valetudine fuerit prohibitus, rem ipsam nostris hisce literis testatum volumus, atque optimae spei adolescentem promerita laude et elogio prosequimur.

"Datum in Collegio Romano, 30 Octobri, 1830.

"Franciscus Manera, S.J.,

"Praefectus Studiorum."

"ROMAN COLLEGE OF THE SOCIETY OF JESUS.

"We hereby attest that the distinguished young gentleman, Joachim Vincent Pecci, has studied philosophy in this Gregorian University during three years, and that his proficiency therein was such that, in the judgment of the Faculty, he was chosen as fit to maintain a public disputation on a selection of theses from the entire philosophical curriculum at the close of the year 1829. But inasmuch as he has been prevented by illness from so doing, we desire to bear witness to the fact itself by this written attestation, and bestow on a youth of such excellent promise the honor and praise he deserves.

"Given in the Roman College, October 30, 1830.

"Francis Manera, S.J.,

"Prefect of Studies."

that were wonderful in one so young."[13]

During his university studies Joachim Pecci resided with his uncle Antonio in the Muti Palace. He seems to have been singularly drawn to Pope Leo XII, whose life closed in 1829, just as Pecci was terminating his philosophical studies. In 1825 the Holy Father proclaimed a Jubilee for the entire Christian world. The last had been in 1800, just after Pius VI had died, exiled and imprisoned, at Valence, in France, and when Pius VII, elected under the protection of the Russian flag, was beginning his long martyrdom. Much had been done during these twenty-five eventful years to blot out from the souls of the Latin peoples, with the veneration for the religion of their ancestors, the belief in the divinity of Christ and the very notion of a Godhead. Could Leo XII stir what had once been a united Christendom by the proclamation of a Jubilee? And would pilgrims from every Christian land be seen to come, at the Pontiff's call, to kneel once more at the shrines of the Apostles? Such questions did grave men ask each other as they surveyed the wide-spread wreck around them and listened to the sneers of the sceptic press, which were only the echo of the old Voltaireanism.

Leo XII's prophetic soul was deeply moved and comforted by the sight of the throngs of pilgrims, the very elite of Christian countries, who filled Rome and consoled the Vicar of Christ for half a century of persecution, destruction, and blasphemy. He himself gave the example of unaffected piety by visiting the privileged churches of Rome, and joining his own people and the pilgrims of every land in supplicating the divine mercy in the sore need of the Christian world. He also saw to it in person that the preparations he had ordered to be made for the reception of the multitudes of strangers were carried out in the proper spirit. Men who bore a part in these proceedings have put on record their testimony to the living piety and indefatigable charity of the nobles, clergy, and

---

[13] Letter written in February, 1878, to Father Ballerini, editor of the Civiltà Cattolica, and quoted in the "Cenni Storici," c. I. v 9.

people of Rome, animated by the person and examples of their saint like Pontiff.

These were days which made on the young and pure soul of Joachim Vincent Pecci impressions which shaped the whole of his after-life. The spectacle of Leo XII, pale, emaciated, brought back from death's door by a miracle, expending all his energy in purifying the house of God and building up the ruins made by revolution and impiety, dying like a saint and desiring to be buried near the altar-tomb of St. Leo the Great, where he should be under the feet of the multitude, were lessons which the serious-minded and noble-souled son of Countess Anna Pecci was to treasure up for imitation.

The boy—for he was only fifteen in 1825—followed the Pope from church to church, from hospital to hospital, as with naked feet and in penitential garb, amid the chant of penitential psalms and prayers, the Common Father of Christendom taught his people how to turn away the divine anger from the earth torn by convulsions and swept by pestilence and flame. All Rome imitated the conduct of the Supreme Pastor. Nor were the youth of the Roman schools backward in following in the footsteps of their elders. Together with the students of the Collegio Romano, and headed by their respective professors, they imitated the touching precedent set them by the Holy Father, and made the pilgrimage and the visits to all the seven churches in the most edifying manner. Ending with St. Peter's, these thousands of young men of all nations were then ushered into the Belvidere Court in the Vatican, where Leo XII appeared on the middle balcony above and blessed them solemnly.

Joachim Pecci was unanimously selected, young as he was, to head a deputation of students and to present to the Sovereign Pontiff an address of thanks in Latin. This incident, connecting himself personally with a Pope for whom he entertained so deep a veneration, was one of the most cherished memories of his later years.

Thus the springs of religious feeling opened by a Christian mother in the soul of her child, and so carefully fed as he grew up, gave forth their waters all through youth and manhood.

But the memory of that lost mother, so tenderly loved, and the image of her blessed home at Carpineto, haunted Pecci amid the halls of the Gregorian University, his quiet rooms in the Muti Palace, and all the sights of Rome at her busiest and most exciting times. His vacations were always spent among his native hills, the recollections and atmosphere of which never failed to brace up soul and body during the few weeks of occupied repose enjoyed there.

An incident connected with the annual vacation spent among his native hills may be given here as quite characteristic of the student of nineteen. During his fowling and hunting excursions he was fond of resorting to the church of Our Lady of the Annunciation, at some distance from the town, and in which was a painting of the Madonna held in great veneration. It was his custom to pay the homage of his devotion to the Incarnate God and His Mother, and then to rest himself in the shady portico. Having made inquiries about the sanctuary and the painting, he learned that the latter had been brought to its present site from a little oratory built on the banks of the mountain stream, that the ground for the present church had been given by his own family, and the new edifice itself reared by the piety of the people.

He thereupon resolved to place on record the memory of these facts; selected a monumental stone, fashioned it, and then wrote out the following inscription, which he cut into the slab himself. Scholars can judge of the ripe knowledge of the classic lapidary style already acquired by one so young:

MARIÆ SANCTÆ
DEIPARÆ AB ANGELO SALUTATAE
TEMPLUM HOC
QUOD POSITUM INFERIUS SECUS FONTEM
EMINERE OLIM MINUS POTERAT
CAIETANUS PASQUALIUS
FUNDO A GENTE PECCIA TRIBUTO
Ære a Carpinetensibus collato
In elatiori et amoeniori hacic loco
EREXIT
AN. D. MDCCLXXVII

TO HOLY MARY
THE MOTHER OF GOD, SALUTED BY THE ANGEL,
THIS TEMPLE
WHICH, PLACED LOWER DOWN NEAR A STREAM,
WAS THEN LESS CONSPICUOUS,
CAJETAN PASQUALI,
THE GROUND BEING GIVEN BY THE PECCI FAMILY
And the money made up by the Carpinetians,
Here in a loftier and pleasanter place
ERECTED
A.D. 1777.

CHAPTER V

DRAWN TO THE SERVICE OF GOD

IT CANNOT be wondered at if, taught from his earliest years to revere and love the humble sons of St. Francis of Assisi, Joachim Vincent Pecci should have felt secretly drawn to a life of self-denial and sacrifice. The study of the history of that sweet saint, when he was better able to appreciate the divine poetry with which it is filled, and a knowledge of the labors, at home and abroad, of the great family of saints, missionaries, apostles, and scholars founded by the seraphic lover of Christ crucified, could not help to increase this attraction toward the service of God.

Then the apostolic virtues, the eminent learning, and the still more eminent holiness of life of the first generation of restored Jesuits, who were Pecci's admiration at Viterbo and in Rome, together with the never-to-be-forgotten figure of the seventh Pius, surrounded with the halo of suffering and sanctity, and the noble life of his immediate successor, Pope Leo, were more than enough to inspire a nature already religiously inclined to embrace a career of devotion to the good of others. He did not feel called to follow his brother, and selected the ranks of the secular priesthood in which to combat and to labor.

He therefore was matriculated in 1830 among the theological or Divinity students of the Gregorian University, his Alma Mater. Whatever may have been the undisputed excellence of the Jesuits' Faculty of Arts in every department, it is no exaggeration to say that in the sphere of sacred knowledge they surpassed themselves. Their theologians, in 1830, were a galaxy of accomplished men whose fame belongs to both hemispheres. Among them were Perrone, whose works have ever since been classic in the great Catholic schools of all countries, and Patrizi, whose commentaries on Scripture are esteemed even by Protestant Biblical scholars.

It was, in more than one way, an age of religious renovation, a sort of intellectual renaissance after a period of revolution and decay. A noble spirit of emulation under Leo XII and his successors possessed all the great Religious Orders in the Church, and was manifested in the bands of learned professors with whom they filled the chairs in the Propaganda, the Sapienza, the Minerva, and the other celebrated schools of Rome. Leo XII, soon after his accession, in 1824, issued a bull, *Quod Divina Sapientia*, reorganizing Intermediate and University Education throughout the Papal States. A congregation of cardinals was given charge over all these educational establishments; and the great University of the Sapienza,[1] which was, properly speaking, the University of Rome, was renovated and improved in its faculties, methods, and discipline, so as to be thoroughly on a level with the highest requirements of the times.

Joachim Pecci needed no stimulus to urge him to attain in sacred science the degree of excellence reached by him in letters and philosophy. People were then carried onward and upward by the powerful current which had set in, and which was most favorable to all the highest studies. His very first year in the Divinity curriculum was crowned by such a triumphant success as went far to compensate him for his accidental failure of the previous autumn. He was again selected for a solemn public disputation, or "Theological Act," as it was called, embracing select questions from all the

[1] The University of the Sapienza derives its popular name from the text inscribed over its rear entrance by Sixtus V, who was a Franciscan monk, had filled the chair of Theology in it, and became, when Pope, one of its most generous benefactors. The text is: Initium sapientia timor Domini—"The beginning of wisdom is the fear of the Lord." The words are a bitter comment on the principles which now guide the teaching of the sceptic or anti-Christian professors under King Umberto.

matters taught.[2] The University Register merely says that "the young gentleman gave such proof of his talent as to enable one to foresee that he would attain great distinction." But the Annuary, recording the list of premiums and the names of the laureates, goes out of its way to praise his great talent and his no less great industry.[3]

So much, in fact, did he rise above his classmates, and above the level of knowledge to which mere learners generally attain, that he was appointed to repeat the lectures on philosophy to the pupils of the German College. It was a happy selection for him, as it compelled him to put his scientific lore into more perfect form in order to render it profitable to his hearers.

We find also mentioned in our manuscript guide another fact equally creditable to the Faculty of the Gregorian University and to the subject of this history, and one which

---

2 The fact is thus mentioned in the College Register: "Vincentius Pecci de selectis quaestionibus ex tractatu de Indulgentiis, nec non de Sacramentis Extremae Unctionis atque Ordinis, in aula collegii maxima, publice disputavit, facta omnibus in frequenti praesulum aliorumque insignium virorum corona, post tres designatos, arguendi potestate. In qua disputatione idem adolescens tale ingenii sui specimen praebuit ut ad altiora proludere visus sit"—"Vincent Pecci held a disputation in the great hall of the college on selected questions on Indulgences and the Sacraments of Extreme Unction and Order. There was a large attendance of prelates and other distinguished men, who were allowed, after the three regular objectors had done, to present their objections. The young disputant gave such evidence of his ability that one may easily divine to what distinction he is sure to attain" ("Cenni Storici," *ibidem*, n. 3).

3 "Inter theologiae academicos, Vincentius Pecci strenue certavit de Indulgentiis in aula maxima, coram doctoribus collegii, aliisque viris doctrina spectatissimis. Quum vero in hac publica exercitatione, academico more peracta, industrius adolescens non parvam ingenii vim et diligentiam impenderit, placuit ejus nomen honoris causa heic recensere"— "Among the theological students Vincent Pecci well maintained a public disputation in the Great Hall before the college Faculty and other persons greatly distinguished for learning. Inasmuch as in this public act, carried on according to rule, the laborious candidate displayed great talent and learning, it is deemed well to give him here honorable mention" (*ibidem*).

should interest all who are concerned in teaching how to expose and how to defend the entire system of Revealed Truth.

Father Perrone, the eminent professor of theology, and the no less distinguished Father Manera, who was prefect of studies, had established an academy among the theological students for the encouragement of all who wished to acquire more than ordinary skill in expounding the dogmas of Revelation and in defending them against the most formidable objections of science and unbelief. To give this academy a firm standing in the public opinion of the university two solemn disputations were held in the university hall. Four of the cleverest academicians prepared, each on a given line of argument, the most knotty difficulties found against the supernatural order by science, rationalism, materialism; against the Catholic Church by Lutherans, Jansenists, Rationalists, or Caesarists. The person chosen on both occasions to expose the doctrines of Revelation and to detect and refute all possible objections was Pecci. Many of our readers will be familiar with this large freedom of discussion, this thoroughness with which the youth of our great Catholic university schools are trained to the knowledge of theology, and the care taken to familiarize them with the most formidable weapons used by the adversaries of Christianity, as well as with those employed in defending it by its most successful apologists.

Nowhere are truth and error placed side by side and studied in all their bearings with a more conscientious and thorough earnestness than in the Roman schools, and in all those who follow the same well-approved and large-minded methods.

But these same readers will have also appreciated how creditable was the part assigned to Vincent Pecci. And, in fact, the credit by him won was all the greater that he never failed to meet his opponents with victorious arguments couched in language as elegant as it was precise.

The time had now come when he was to lay aside the

name of Vincent, by which he had been known all through his college and university courses. In 1832 he won and received his degree of Doctor in Theology, the highest and most important academical distinction conferred by the Church. Thenceforward he invariably signed his name Gioacchino, or Joachim.

Having determined to cast his lot with the secular priesthood, he found himself, at the end of the year 1832, in the necessity of choosing between a career of parochial duty or the service of the Holy See. With the approval of his father and uncle he resolved on the latter course, and, in consequence, entered the academy or college for noble ecclesiastics, which was the nursery of all who were destined for a diplomatic or administrative career under the Pontifical government. The students of this establishment pursued in the University of the Sapienza the special courses appropriate to their calling. There the Sovereign Pontiffs had secured the services of the most eminent jurists for the schools of civil and canon law, the chairs being won by a public concourse.[4]

Pecci, while applying himself diligently to acquire a thorough knowledge of civil and ecclesiastical jurisprudence, profited also by the great facilities offered in the Sapienza to push still further his studies in theology. Indeed, he gave in public more than one proof of his uncommon proficiency therein. He won, in particular, in 1835, a very enviable intellectual triumph, together with a premium of sixty sequins ($132) offered for the best essay on one from among a hundred given theses. These were numbered, and the contestants had to draw by lot. , The thesis which fell to Pecci was that of "Immediate Appeals to the Roman Pontiff in person."[5]

And so at each stage of his education the young nobleman displayed the same conscientious determination to do well whatever he had to do, to master thoroughly, in order the

---

[4] See further information on the University of the Sapienza in Appendix A.

[5] See Appendix R.

better to serve the Divine Master, whatever branch of sacred or profane science was set before him. Among the young nobles who were his schoolmates in the Ecclesiastical Academy was one to whom he became bound by a life-long friendship—the Duke Sixtus Riario-Sforza, whose saintly life, heroic virtues, self-sacrifice, and unbounded charities have been made known to the whole civilized world by the pens of non-Catholic writers. Appointed Cardinal Archbishop of Naples during the troublous days which beheld so many political and social changes in the Kingdom of the Two Sicilies, as well as in the entire Peninsula, Cardinal Riario-Sforza won the veneration of all by showing himself the man of God, the good shepherd ever ready to lay down his life for his stricken flock.

Such friendships, springing from identity of disposition in two young souls drawn together, honor both the one and the other.

In such holy companionship, and buoyed up by lofty aims, Joachim Pecci labored to make himself worthy of the degree of Doctor in Civil and in Canon Law, which was bestowed on him after the usual examinations.

All these successive academical triumphs, achieved under the eyes of the highest dignitaries and the most learned men in Rome, spread the young doctor's fame among all classes of Roman society, and brought him under the favorable notice of the reigning sovereigns themselves. More than one even among the cardinals, attracted to him by his unaffected piety, his modesty and gentle courtesy, and by the solid and general knowledge which was so rare in one of his years, foresaw that he would render great service to the Holy See, and bestowed not a little pains in counselling and directing him. The venerable Cardinal Sala, in particular, who had been associated with Cardinal Caprara[6] in the disastrous legation to Paris in 1808, and whose soul had been tried, like that of Pius VII

[6] Cardinal Caprara was no match for Napoleon in the crooked ways of diplomacy.

himself, by the six terrible years that followed, conceived a warm attachment for Pecci. In their intercourse the young and inexperienced churchman learned, from one who had been thrice purified in the furnace, many lessons which were soon to be of priceless service to himself in governing men and dealing with governments.

After the death of Leo XII in 1829, the College of Cardinals, moved by the same lofty motives which had directed their choice in the election of the two last saintly Popes, gave their suffrages to another man of equally splendid virtue and uncommon learning. But Pius VIII only shed a brief gleam of brightness on Rome and the Chair of Peter; and then came the stormy reign of Gregory XVI, to be followed by one more stormy still, more disastrous to the liberty of the Sovereign Pontiffs, and protracted beyond all those which had come before it.

Pius VIII, who took in the members of the Ecclesiastical Academy the interest which a sovereign and a parent should take in the principal nursery of his future assistants in Church and state, watched the progress of Pecci, and bestowed on him more than one mark of his regard.

But the illustrious Cardinal Pacca, the friend, counsellor, and fellow-sufferer of the seventh Pius, happened to be the protector of the academy, and took a lively interest in the gentle, pious, refined, and cultivated youth, whom everybody loved and praised because of his retiring, modest, and unobtrusive disposition. When Gregory XVI had succeeded to Pius VIII, Cardinal Pacca warmly recommended to him the young Pecci, in whom his experienced eye had discovered uncommon merit and the promise of a great career. Gregory thereupon, in January, 1837, appointed Joachim Pecci one of his Domestic Prelates. It was a distinction fairly won, not granted to mere nobility of birth, but conferred on the true nobleness of rare virtue united to accomplishments as rare.

His preparatory studies were now completed. He was about to begin his twenty-eighth year, the ordinary age for receiving Holy Orders. He therefore left the academy, and went to reside once more with his uncle Antonio in the Muti Palace, near Ara Cœli. On March 16 he was appointed Referendary to the Court of *Segnatura*—an appointment indicating that the sovereign and his counsellors had discovered in the young prelate administrative talent of a high order. This was made still further manifest by his being given soon afterward a place among the prelates of the Congregation *di Buongoverno*, specially charged with the financial administration of all the communes of the Papal States. Here he came under the immediate control of his friend Cardinal Sala, who was president of the Congregation or Permanent Committee of Government.

Meanwhile the terrible Asiatic cholera had invaded Italy and made its way to Rome. Cardinal Sala was appointed by the Pope to superintend all the cholera hospitals in the city. The mortality was fearful, baffling the skill of the physicians and sweeping away persons of all classes. Monsignor Pecci, not being in priest's orders, could not help in ministering to the spiritual needs and comfort of the plague-stricken. But, possessing, as he did, the entire confidence of the cardinal, he became his right-hand man, displaying not only great practical judgment in providing for the urgent wants of so many thousands, but that indefatigable zeal and that fearlessness of personal danger which came as much from his own ardent piety and his love of the poor as from his natural unselfishness and generosity.

If, during these awful summer months, Monsignor Pecci had often wished that he, too, could be privileged to minister priestly consolation to the dying, his desire was soon to receive a partial fulfilment, at least. He was told to prepare for Holy Orders as soon as, with the cold weather, the plague had subsided.

On November 13 of the same memorable year he received sub-deaconship and deaconship at the hands of Cardinal Odescalchi, the Pope's vicar-general, in the little chapel of St. Stanislas Kostka in the gem-like church of "St. Andrew on the Quirinal."

It will help the reader to understand the hidden springs of the life we have undertaken to describe if he will pause with us a moment in this, one of the most beautiful sanctuaries in Rome itself, one of the sweetest and most restful spots for the traveller and pilgrim in this city so crowded with the monuments of pagan civilization and Christian piety. The author has just returned from a visit to this place—already doomed, with all the edifices which line the same side of the street opposite the grand masses of the Quirinal Palace, to disappear within the next twelve months.

Let us go back together to the 13th of November, 1837, the anniversary of the death of Stanislas Kostka (about 1580), the boy-saint whom Catholic Poland reveres as its patron and protector in heaven. Here he arrived, footsore and exhausted, with the seeds of a mortal disease fast spreading in his frame, after his long and perilous journey from his native land. He had left his brother's lordly halls to cast his lot with the brethren of Bellarmine and Aloysius Gonzaga, of Francis Xavier and Francis Borgia, and give his life to the work of evangelizing the heathen in Asia, America, and Africa. But the light of that young life, after blazing out with surpassing splendor in the novitiate on the Quirinal, went out forever. The sweet odor of his virtues remained; the memory of the angelic youth—reminding one of Samuel at the same age, a bright lamp in God's house shedding unearthly radiance on the holy place for a brief time—remained ever after his death, more potent to kindle in the pure souls of the young and the truly noble an ardent love of supernatural excellence than the examples of a long and eloquent career.

It was the influence of this holy memory that made all that was best in Rome vie with each other in decorating the modest little church where was buried the gentle Polish pilgrim, and attracted the elite of Roman youth to enlist among the soldiers of the cross, whose battles on both hemispheres Stanislas Kostka had yearned to fight.

It was a kindred feeling that made both Cardinal Carlo Odescalchi and Monsignor Pecci select this retired spot, this quiet little sanctuary, as the place best fitted for the latter to give himself to the service of the altar, like Samuel of old, and at the very feet of Stanislas Kostka in his tomb to invoke and receive a share of that Spirit who creates saints and fires apostles.

It is a balmy morning in the golden autumn of Rome, this 13th of November, 1837. The beautiful church is well filled by the friends who are come to see the accomplished son of Count Ludovico and Countess Anna Pecci taking his first irrevocable engagements and devoting his young life to the God who gave it. It is true that he has no thought of laboring among the brethren of St. Stanislas in the missionary fields of the East or West Indies. There is to be fulfilled in Rome and all throughout Italy, in that year of grace 1837, an apostleship no less difficult or important than the conversion of the heathen—an apostleship increasing both in difficulty and importance as the century advances, till, fifty years later, Christianity shall have to put forth all the zeal, the self-sacrifice, the learning, and the devotedness of the apostolic age to stem the tide of evil.

They are a most interesting group toward whom all eyes are directed during the ordination ceremony in the church of Sant' Andrea. The little chapel of St. Stanislas is scarcely more than a large niche in the elliptical circuit of the marble-encrusted walls. Between the railing and the altar beneath which, in his sepulchral urn of lapis lazuli, all that is mortal of St. Stanislas reposes, there is not space for more than a very few persons to move freely. On the platform is seated the cardinal in his priestly vestments—a saintly presence recalling in very deed the person and the virtues of St. Charles Borromeo; before him, at his feet, kneels the levite Joachim Pecci in his simple white alb. You might fancy that both of these figures had just come down from the groups of saintly personages painted or frescoed on the surrounding walls, such an unearthly light is on the features-of both! In a very short time this cardinal will lay aside his high dignity, his princely rank, turn his back on the near prospect of a dignity still higher, and become a novice within these same walls, emulating the humility, the obedience, the poverty practised by Stanislas Kostka, coveting only and gaining all too soon the honor of dying near where he died, clothed with the poor livery Stanislas wore, and happy to be called his brother.

Pecci felt himself called to struggle and triumph in another sphere. But still he, too, felt his soul filled by the spirit of the place. Here had passed the great soldier-saint who yearned to win all souls by persuasion and supernatural holiness to the service of Christ, and to make the cross rule over every tribe of earth. Here, attracted by the magnetism of Ignatius's heroic self-denial, Francis Borgia, Duke of Gandia and Viceroy of Catalonia, had lived, greater in the garb of poverty than when he outshone princes in the imperial court. And here Francis Xavier had fed the sacred fire with which later he set all souls aflame along the coasts of India and the Archipelago to Japan, where the fire of faith still burns inextinguishable.

How often had Pecci meditated on all this during his long years of serious study in the Roman College and the Sapienza, and his frequent visits to these beautiful shrines, which are, to souls touched by the love of things supernal, like shady groves near life's dusty and sun-burnt road with their springs of living water!

Not without its influence on his generous spirit had been the sight of a royal tomb alongside the little chapel of St. Stanislas. Nor can the pilgrim from afar who chances to know the touching story of the king who lies buried there, pass it by without pausing reverently awhile to recall the memory of his trials and those of his saintly queen. He was Charles Emmanuel IV of Savoy, King of Sardinia and Piedmont, and she was Marie Clotilde of France, sister of Louis XVI and a worthy daughter of St. Louis. This royal pair, driven from their throne by the Revolutionary armies under Bonaparte, had to fly from country to country as the wave of French invasion spread. But everywhere they won the admiration and love of all classes by their noble fortitude, their Benefactions, and the sweet fragrance shed by the angelic virtues of the queen.

Scarcely had they been restored to their kingdom when she was called away to her rest, and he, ambitious only to be worthy of her in the better life, laid down his recovered sceptre and became a poor lay brother in this house where St. Stanislas had lived and died.

Little dreamed he, as his last years were spent here in the shadow of the Peace Eternal, that long ere the century had closed princes of his own blood would be enthroned yonder across the way in the Quirinal; that the men whom he called his brothers and served with his royal hands would be pitilessly expelled from their home; and that house and church, the chapel and shrine of St. Stanislas and his own resting-place in death, must disappear before the blind hatred of the new domination.

But we must not anticipate.

On the last day of that same year, 1837, Cardinal Odescalchi, in the private chapel of his residence in the vicariate, conferred the order of Priesthood on Joachim Pecci. As the year 1838 dawned upon the world the young priest was privileged to go up to the Altar of the Lamb, and to offer that Eucharistic oblation which to the priest is the sweetest, dearest, and most unfailing source of comfort, strength, and zeal in the divine service.

How he shall need the light and strength from on high, and to what uses he was to put them, we shall see presently.

Scarcely had they been restored to their kingdom when she was called away to her rest, and he, ambitious only to be worthy of her in the better life, laid down his recovered sceptre and became a poor lay brother in this house where St. Stanislas had lived and died.

Little dreamed he, as his last years were spent here in the shadow of the Peace Eternal, that long ere the century had closed princes of his own blood would be enthroned yonder across the way in the Quirinal; that the men whom he called his brothers and served with his royal hands would be pitilessly expelled from their home; and that house and church, the chapel and shrine of St. Stanislas and his own resting-place in death, must disappear before the blind hatred of the new domination.

But we must not anticipate.

On the last day of that same year, 1837, Cardinal Odescalchi, in the private chapel of his residence in the vicariate, conferred the order of Priesthood on Joachim Pecci. As the year 1838 dawned upon the world the young priest was privileged to go up to the Altar of the Lamb, and to offer that Eucharistic oblation which to the priest is the sweetest, dearest, and most unfailing source of comfort, strength, and zeal in the divine service.

How he shall need the light and strength from on high, and to what uses he was to put them, we shall see presently.

higher, and become a novice within these same walls, emulating the humility, the obedience, the poverty practised by Stanislas Kostka, coveting only and gaining all too soon the honor of dying near where he died, clothed with the poor livery Stanislas wore, and happy to be called his brother.

Pecci felt himself called to struggle and triumph in another sphere. But still he, too, felt his soul filled by the spirit of the place. Here had passed the great soldier-saint who yearned to win all souls by persuasion and supernatural holiness to the service of Christ, and to make the cross rule over every tribe of earth. Here, attracted by the magnetism of Ignatius's heroic self-denial, Francis Borgia, Duke of Gandia and Viceroy of Catalonia, had lived, greater in the garb of poverty than when he outshone princes in the imperial court. And here Francis Xavier had fed the sacred fire with which later he set all souls aflame along the coasts of India and the Archipelago to Japan, where the fire of faith still burns inextinguishable.

How often had Pecci meditated on all this during his long years of serious study in the Roman College and the Sapienza, and his frequent visits to these beautiful shrines, which are, to souls touched by the love of things supernal, like shady groves near life's dusty and sun-burnt road with their springs of living water!

Not without its influence on his generous spirit had been the sight of a royal tomb alongside the little chapel of St. Stanislas. Nor can the pilgrim from afar who chances to know the touching story of the king who lies buried there, pass it by without pausing reverently awhile to recall the memory of his trials and those of his saintly queen. He was Charles Emmanuel IV of Savoy, King of Sardinia and Piedmont, and she was Marie Clotilde of France, sister of Louis XVI and a worthy daughter of St. Louis. This royal pair, driven from their throne by the Revolutionary armies under Bonaparte, had to fly from country to country as the wave of French invasion spread. But everywhere they won the admiration and love of all classes by their noble fortitude, their Benefactions, and the sweet fragrance shed by the angelic virtues of the queen.

St Peter's in Montorio.

Erected on the Spot where St. Peter, the First Pope, was Crucified Head downwards.

PANORAMIC VIEW OF THE VILLAGE OF CARPINETO.

BIRTHPLACE OF LEO. XIII.

The House in which Leo XIII. was Born at Carpineto.

Church of St. Leo, Carpineto.

Pope Leo XII

Pope Gregory XVI

Perugia, Italy

Door of the Municipal Hall,

Cathedral Square Perugia.

Leopold I
King of the Belgians

WALTHÈRE FRÈRE ORBAN

PART SECOND

Joachim Pecci's Administrative and Diplomatic Career January, 1838-1846

CHAPTER VI

MONSIGNOR PECCI'S FIRST SHINING PROOFS OF PRACTICAL STATESMANSHIP; GOVERNOR OF BENEVENTO

1838 to 1841

THE LIFE OF JOACHIM PECCI was thenceforward devoted to the service of the Holy See, although his hope and desire were that he might be allowed to labor for it in Rome and to confine his attention to purely ecclesiastical matters. Cardinal Sala, who was well acquainted with the wishes of his protégée and with his capacity, had taken pains to have him attached to the great congregations of the Propaganda, of Bishops and Regulars, and of the Council.[1] Cardinal Lambruschini, who was the Pope's Secretary of State, or Prime Minister, and who appreciated Monsignor Pecci's rising merit, had him appointed official to several other most important bodies, placing him, in this preparatory stage, under the especial care of the learned prelates (soon to be cardinals) Frezza and Brunelli. This solicitude about his thorough training was an evidence of the great opinion they had of his ability and character.

He must have given more than ordinary satisfaction to the cardinals who watched his conduct so closely during the trying cholera season, and they must have reported to the Holy Father how well fitted the young prelate was to manage the most important public business and to govern men; for Gregory XVI, in February, 1838, appointed him Delegate or Governor of the Province of Benevento, with instructions to repair without delay to his government.

This little principality, which is only forty-six geographical square miles in extent, was given, like other possessions, to the

[1] See Appepdix C.

Popes by the piety of former ages. It is situated in the midst of what was once the kingdom of Naples, a short day's journey from the city of that name, and in the midst of a population which, in 1838, had been rendered utterly reckless of all rule by the preceding political and social changes. Napoleon I, in his hour of undisputed supremacy, had given this little territory, with the title of Prince of Benevento, to his clever and unprincipled minister, Talleyrand. There are writers who say, not without some show of good reason, that Talleyrand, whose wife Pius VII had refused to see during his stay in Paris for the coronation ceremonies, had revenged himself on the Pontiff by urging the crowned soldier to possess himself of the Papal States, and to bestow on him, the apostate ex-Bishop of Autun, a slice of the territory thus sacrilegiously and iniquitously taken away from an unarmed and defenceless sovereign.

This is not the place to show how little such usurpation and spoliation served either the emperor or the minister who was his evil genius. But the French rule in Benevento, as well as the short-lived reign of Murat in Naples, together with the growth and spread, in the south of Italy especially, of Carbonarism, Jacobinism, brigandage, and lawlessness, rendered the government of these populations a matter of almost moral impossibility, once the French had withdrawn and the former rulers resumed their sway.

The men who had been the firmest in their loyalty to the princes expelled by Napoleon, and had been most active in organizing against the French occupiers the guerilla bands which defied the pursuit of the best-disciplined troops, soon became themselves the terror of the entire country. They levied a heavy tax on the towns and hamlets they protected, or pretended to protect, against the foreign invader they blackmailed the rich and powerful, and profited by the fear they inspired to oppress and to plunder friends as well as foes, and to gratify with impunity their greed or their private resentments. Indeed, the powerful and the rich who had, in the beginning of the invasion, been instrumental in getting up these armed bands, and had often led them in their desperate encounters with the French, soon began to feel that brigandage was a powerful weapon for serving their own selfish purposes, even when it had no longer the pretext of serving the public good.

The restoration, therefore, of the Bourbons to Naples and of the Pope to Rome found, in every province of the southern kingdom at least, society in town and country fallen back to the disorders of the feudal times. The wealthy and the nobles had filled their castles with armed retainers, and these had to live on the country.

In the little province of Benevento another evil seriously increased and complicated this state of lawlessness and confusion. The Papal rule was mild and fatherly at all times; the people had no heavy burden of imposts or taxes to bear. Then a small province situated in the very heart of a foreign and quite different government would naturally become the refuge of smugglers and a retreat for evil-doers flying from justice.[2]

There was thus perpetual risk of conflict between the Neapolitan and the Papal authorities, as well as a growing contempt for all law and order among the Beneventini, particularly among the classes interested in maintaining disorder and violence.

Such was the state of things for which it was expected a young priest of twenty-eight years could find a remedy. Gregory XVI and his counsellors must have had a very high opinion of the youthful prelate, and his ability to cope with well-organized bands of desperate men, to think of despatching him on such a mission, when others, far more experienced and of higher dignity, had failed to check the inveterate disorder and had retired, baffled, from their battle with brigandage and smuggling.

But, whether he had taken the seeds of typhoid fever with

---

[2] See the author's "Leo XIII and his Probable Policy," New York, March 1878; MS.

him from Rome, or had contracted the disease during the then long and tedious journey through the Pontine Marshes or his brief stay in Naples, he was taken suddenly ill the third day after his arrival in Benevento. Perhaps, considering the nature of the disorders which he was commissioned to repress, and the numbers of men of all classes interested in their continuance, it was a kindly disposition of Providence which permitted the young Delegate to be thus brought to death's door almost immediately on his arrival amidst the excited population. The Beneventini had been very favorably impressed by the youth, the dignified bearing, the gentle courtesy, and the graceful speeches of their new governor; and while both the lawless among them and the law-abiding were discussing the qualities of the man and his probable course of action, they were startled to hear that his life was in imminent danger. Then people began to speak of the goodness he had displayed toward the poor people during the terrible visitation of the cholera, and the grateful popular heart was moved by the mortal peril of one so young and so accomplished, sent among them, too, on an errand of mercy in favor of the oppressed laboring classes.

The ripest medical skill which Naples could supply was summoned; but the very best physicians could only declare that their skill was powerless, so malignant was the distemper and so rapid the effects of its poison on a frame exhausted by long and severe study, and perhaps weakened by the austerities of ascetic fervor. The case was pronounced hopeless.

Meanwhile public prayers were offered for his recovery in all, the churches of the city. But the ardent southern nature would not be contented with that. As the danger of losing their youthful governor increased hourly, and people could only speak of his goodness, his piety, and his learning, he seemed to them an angel sent to heal all their public ills, and about to be suddenly taken from them in punishment of their own evil doings.

In the outskirts of Benevento is one of those sanctuaries of the Blessed Virgin Mary, one of those chosen spots dear to those who, in the ever-recurring political commotions of the times and the popular suffering they brought in their train, loved to come to the Incarnate Son of God and to supplicate His aid, as it were, in the house of His Mother and through her intercession.

This sanctuary, where the popular belief asserted that our Lord had often heard the cry of bruised hearts and needy souls, was called the Church of the Virgin of Graces, Thither the citizens went in solemn procession to implore Christ's Mother to plead with her Son for a life so dear to them—so precious, though they knew it not, to the Universal Church.

There was also in Benevento at that time a college of Jesuits which did good work in educating the youth of the province and the neighboring country. To them Monsignor Pecci was well known, having been trained in their schools, and reflecting such honor on his masters by his brilliant successes. Their concern was therefore great at beholding him reduced to such sudden extremity by the dreaded fever. The rector of the college, Father Tessandori, was one of that early generation of the restored Jesuits who had sacrificed much, braved persecution, and been purified by the flame of long and malignant obloquy. The people revered him for his saintly life, the educated admired him for his great learning. He was simply a man of God. He joined his prayers with those of the entire population, and had, moreover, recourse to one of those divine men who pass through this world like Isaiah in the days of Achab and Jezabel, appearing in public only to be the interpreters of God's judgments on an offending generation, or to confound His enemies by some unexpected display of His power; who were, in seasons of dire distress, the comfort and the salvation of the famishing and plague-stricken. Such had Francesco de Geronimo been in the last century to the whole kingdom of Naples. And now Father Tessandori invoked his succor in favor of the young prelate, on whose preservation so many mighty issues depended in the designs of Providence.

Certain it is that all these prayers were heard, and that,

against all hope and contrary to the judgment of the physicians, the fever relaxed its hold on the victim.[3] On first hearing of Monsignor Pecci's illness the Pope manifested the deepest concern. He, too, had daily prayers offered up in Rome for the recovery of the sufferer, and demanded' that daily information should be sent him about the progress of the illness.

The recovery, coming as unexpectedly as the malignant fever itself, filled the people of Benevento as well as the Roman Court with sincere joy. No sooner was Monsignor Pecci able to attend to business than he set about making himself thoroughly acquainted with all classes of the people, and took every possible means to repress the inveterate disorders which had until then defied all efforts at reform, as well as to promote education, agriculture, and industry in the province.

His first act, however, was to lay, at the request of the octogenarian Cardinal Bussi, Archbishop of Benevento, the corner-stone of a new church in honor of Our Lady of Graces, destined to replace the venerable but ruinous sanctuary whither the citizens had gone in solemn procession to pray for his own recovery. The new edifice was a votive offering to the Incarnate Word and His Mother in thanksgiving for having been preserved from the cholera the year before. The plague had committed fearful ravages in Naples and its environs, but

[3] The MS., as was to be expected where anything *miraculous* is concerned, is extremely measured in its statement:
"Il Padre Tessandori, Rettore del Collegio dei Gesuiti, uomo di santissima vita, assisteva con cariti ammirabile al letto del Prelato morente, e con una reliquia di San Francesco di Geronimo posta sul corpo dell' infermo, scongiurava con fervidissime preci la grazia della guarigione. Fu meraviglioso l'intervento di questo Santo, e non 6 lecito svelarne il segreto"—"Father Tessandori, Rector of the Jesuit College, a man of most holy life, stood by the bed of the dying prelate with admirable charity, and, by means of a relic of St. Francis de Geronimo placed on the invalid's body, he besought the grace of a perfect cure with the most fervent prayers. The mediation of the saint proved to be miraculous, but we are not allowed to reveal its secret."

spared Benevento.

The entire city and country was represented at the solemn ceremony of blessing the corner-stone. It afforded Monsignor Pecci a most favorable opportunity for making the acquaintance of the people of every class, to whom he now felt so grateful, and whose attachment to him was naturally increased by their own pious interest in his recovery. Happy and graceful at all times in his discourses, his words on this occasion must have had, together with the eloquence of the heart, a peculiar force and appositeness from his own relation toward the people and the province.

The brigands, smugglers, outlaws, and their protectors fancied, at first, that they could be more than a match for the young scholar, pale from the long vigils of his study in Rome, and now sadly debilitated by a dangerous illness. But the knowledge he had previously had, as a high-officer of the Roman government, of the condition of things in Benevento and of the misdeeds of the men who now confronted him, had enabled the delegate to make up his mind to quick, sharp, and decisive measures.

The Pontifical troops at his disposal made a sudden and combined descent on the principal strongholds of the brigands, on the most secret retreats of the outlaws and smugglers. One of the most dreaded chiefs of these lawless bands, who kept the country in perpetual fear, was one Pasquale Colletta, who had his center of operations in the Villa Mascambroni, whence, at the head of fourteen desperadoes like himself, he was in the habit of raiding the country on every side. All had to pay this brigand blackmail in order to save their property, persons, and lives.

It was with equal joy and surprise, therefore, that the Beneventini one morning beheld this dreaded tyrant, with every man of his band, led in chains through their streets by the Pontifical soldiers. Toward men who had stained themselves with innocent blood, and who had set at naught all law and authority, the Delegate was justly severe. No intercession availed to save the murderer, the midnight robber, the oppressor of the weak, the defenceless and inoffensive. But with this inflexible firmness toward the inveterate criminal and law-breaker he joined great patience in examining into the cases referred to him, and great impartiality in weighing the evidence for and against the criminal.

The decision once given, however, was irrevocable.

He was, if anything, more severe toward criminals of high social standing than toward those of inferior rank and education. Nor did it avail the noble, wealthy, or powerful relatives or friends to intercede for high offenders, once the guilt of the latter had been clearly established.

One of the most serious sources of difficulty between the Pontifical and the Neapolitan governments arose from the fact that numbers of political conspirators and others guilty of high political misdemeanors in the kingdom of Naples had long found a safe refuge in the province of Benevento, where they continued to hatch their plots and to defy all pursuit. This had given rise to grave complications.

Monsignor Pecci's firmness toward these refugees forced them to quit the Pontifical territory and to seek an asylum elsewhere. Thereby the difficulty between the two governments was happily terminated, and King Ferdinand expressed his satisfaction and thanks through the Marquis del Carretto, his minister.

In an earlier biography the author related, in substance, the following fact, to which later authentic information permits him to add fuller details.

One day, while the whole province of Benevento and the adjacent Neapolitan districts were excited over the success with which Monsignor Pecci was following up his raids on brigandage and smuggling, a nobleman of the former locality, who had been the most active promoter of all these disorders, had the audacity to complain to the Delegate that the custom-house officers had not respected the privacy of his home, nor the dignity of marquis inherited from his ancestors. Vainly did Monsignor Pecci endeavor to convince his arrogant visitor that the laws are made for all classes in the community without distinction of birth or rank; and that the highest in station owe to those beneath them the example of being law-abiding. The man's pride was up in arms against such reasoning, as well as against the pale, sickly young prelate who had dared to put such an insult on his nobility as to threaten to have his ancestral castle searched by the gendarmerie.

He told the Delegate to his face that he would forthwith set out for Rome, whence he would soon return with an order recalling the man who was turning the country upside down. "You may go on your errand, my lord marquis," was the firm and calm reply. "But I warn you that on arriving in Rome you shall have to pass through Castle Sant' Angelo before carrying your complaints to the Vatican."

The answer completely cowed the blusterer, who had to give up all thought of resistance. Immediately afterward his castle was surrounded and taken by the Pontifical troops, and its numerous garrison of brigands and smugglers carried off to prison.

In this campaign against brigandage and smuggling Monsignor Pecci's right-hand man had been an officer of the name of Sterbini. With his aid he also established customs offices, with an efficient military support, at the most important points of the frontier, giving to Sterbini the superintendence of the whole.[4]

The young Governor did not content himself with ridding the province of all these chronic sources of evil; he had carefully and conscientiously studied its resources and the needs of the population. To develop agriculture and other local industries, roads, good and practical at all seasons, must be opened between Benevento and the adjoining provinces of Molise, Terra di Lavoro, and Avellino. This would make their market-towns easily accessible to his people, and place the markets of Benevento within easy distance of the neighboring Neapolitan populations.

He made a rapid journey to Rome to confer with Gregory

---

[4] MS.

XVI and his ministers on what he purposed doing for the development of the province entrusted to him, and returned with full powers to carry out the plans proposed. So the new roads were at once constructed. Moreover, the taxes and imposts levied by the French during their occupation, and, like all French exaction's in countries held by the sword, wrung from the people in spite of the absence of commerce and local industry, had not been altogether repealed after the restoration of the Papal authority. The young Delegate, who had even then a keen eye for the needs of both country and people, a just and warm sense of the duties more even than of the rights of the government with respect to the governed, had not much difficulty in persuading one so wise and so unworldly as Gregory XVI and his treasurer, Monsignor Tosti.

The people of Benevento were relieved of their burdens; brigandage and smuggling disappeared; the reign of law, with order, peace, and security, was firmly established in town and country; agriculture revived in this atmosphere of true liberty with law and with lightened taxation; industry and commerce sprang into new life with agriculture and the opening of accessible markets. All men went about their business without fear of midnight violence or outrage committed in the open day. It was a transformation; and less than three years of wise statesmanship and true political economy had sufficed to make the change.

Just then the King of Naples was urging the Pontifical government to exchange the province of Benevento for a larger territory adjoining the Papal States, and apparently much more desirable to the Pope. The negotiation was very nearly concluded when the Secretary of State, Cardinal Lambruschini, thought it proper to notify Monsignor Pecci and to ask him to give his advice in writing. This made the latter write at once an energetic remonstrance against the impolicy of such an exchange, accompanied by a detailed report and considerations of a high political and moral order which should forbid the Pope's government from entertaining such a proposition. Among the motives urged against the cession of

Benevento were deep religious reasons. The ecclesiastical province of that name had one metropolitan and fourteen suffragan sees, so that the spiritual needs of the people were far better provided for than they were likely to be under a merely secular government.

The advice of the Delegate prevailed with the Holy Father, and the negotiations were broken off.

So, with the extirpation of brigandage, the expulsion of political conspirators and refugees, and the revival of agriculture and industry, it was now an easy task to govern Benevento. Any delegate would be sure to be welcome and blessed there who would be more anxious to fulfil his duties as the representative of a fatherly sovereign than to stand on his rights as a ruler and a master.

Gregory XVI, whose expectations had been more than justified by the inexperienced young prelate of twenty-eight, had now a wider field for his talent—an administration beset with far more difficulties.

So Monsignor Pecci was suddenly summoned to Rome. But to this day his name is loved and blessed by the Beneventini.

One circumstance unmentioned in our manuscript Memoir occurred soon after Monsignor Pecci's departure for Benevento—that was the death of his father, which took place on March 8, 1838. It was a great grief to the young prelate, and contributed not a little, perhaps, to the utter prostration which at one time threatened to cut off all hopes of his recovery.

CHAPTER VII

PERUGIA AND ALL UMBRIA FIRST BECOME ACQUAINTED WITH JOACHIM PECCI; HOW THE YOUNG STATESMAN DEALT WITH THE CAUSES OF ITALY'S UNREST

May, 1841, to January, 1843

MONSIGNOR PECCI was recalled to Rome from his government in May, 1841, and was immediately appointed Delegate of Spoleto. This was rapid promotion for one so young. But, amid the effervescence which the revolutionary societies were fomenting all through the Papal States—all through the Italian Peninsula, indeed— the Sovereign Pontiff thought that one who had shown so deep and almost intuitive a knowledge of the means of preventing as well as of curing popular discontent should be sent to one of the principal centres of agitation—Perugia.

Perugia, the capital of Umbria, is, like Chiusi and Spoleto, like Orvieto and Siena, like the ancient Etruscan Fiesole, one of those hill-cities with which Central Italy abounds, and whose position above the plain suggests security from predatory warfare, where it has not been chosen also for security against the malaria which ravages the lowlands. It was one of those mediaeval republics whose growth was fostered by the Church, and whose foundation and progress were the joint product of free labor sanctified and sustained by religion. Like its sister-commonwealths of Umbria, Etruria, Emilia, and Lombardy, Perugia had a long struggle against the ambition of the feudal nobles and its own wealthy burgesses, all striving to win the mastery by force of arms or to purchase it by gold. Gold and the military skill of the aristocracy succeeded everywhere in stifling the liberty which the workingmen's guilds had created, in possessing themselves of the rich field cultivated so painfully during long centuries by religion and free labor working side by side, and just as it was ripening into the golden harvest of the most magnificent civilization the world had ever seen.

This beautiful city of Perugia, just as it had passed for ever out of the hands of one set of tyrants to be ruled by the Popes as sovereigns, was made still more beautiful by one of its own adopted sons, Pietro Vanucci (better known as the painter Perugino, the master of the great Raphael). In the latter half of the fifteenth century the tyranny which had sprung up in the Italian free cities on the ruins of mediaeval liberty was half-concealed under the outward forms of self-government still left in the hands of the citizens. The thrift of the labor guilds had literally created Siena and Florence, Pisa and Genoa, Perugia and Arezzo and Assisi, just as they had Milan and Lodi, Crema, Cremona, Mantua, and Verona, with so many others all over the land.

It was the Guild of Merchants who invited Pietro Vanucci to adorn the City Exchange with the masterpieces of art which we admire even in their decay. And the magnificent cathedral, with the numerous churches which shine on the hillside like brilliants in the diadem of a queen—what are they, like those of Florence, Siena, Pisa, and Milan, but the creations of a generous people of workingmen, craftsmen, and merchants?

The important province of which Perugia was the capital possessed many beautiful cities, each sprung from the same forces of labor, magnificent piety, thrift, religion, and liberty. Near at hand was Assisi on its hill-top, with the glorious temple and monastery which had sprung, grown up, and blossomed out of the tomb of St. Francis. Why mention others?

But in the year 1841 the seeds left behind by French Voltaireanism and Jacobinism had been long growing and waxing strong, till they now defied all efforts to uproot them. They had become so thickly mixed with the wheat in the ripening harvest-field that to the wisest husbandry it was a puzzle to know how to prevent them from utterly choking the good grain.

Italy in 1820 counted upwards of one hundred thousand Carbonari, or charcoal-burners. But all the Carbonari of 1820 were, some writers affirm, not hostile to religion, certainly not to the religion of Christ. The more formidable, far more widespread, infinitely better organized societies which covered, like a net from which there was no escape, every province and city, every town and hamlet of the Peninsula, were pledged to the destruction of the existing Church and religion, as to that of the sole barrier which stood between them and the realization of a United Italy, free from foreign domination; of a kingly Italy first, if so it must be, but finally in the constitution of a republic without Church, pontiff, or priest—*a radical centralized democracy.*

Ideas, in our day, are the seed which the great vehicles of thought, the printing-press, journalism, and club oratory, sow all over the face of the earth, and cultivate there with a scientific husbandry matured and perfected by our knowledge of the intellectual past. Illuminism, Voltaireanism, Jansenism, and then the Jacobinic frenzy employed these agencies to destroy the Christian order and the Christendom of our fathers. Mazzini's genius welded all these agencies into one mighty force. His was the brain which conceived, Garibaldi's was the arm which wielded, this mighty weapon; both were taken into the service of Cavour, who also had at his beck the veteran army and fleet of an Italian kingdom.

These were the forces and the men against which the old Italian political and social order was expected to do battle. But, while the aggressors knew their own purpose thoroughly, saw clearly the goal toward which their course was bent, had counted their resources up to a fraction, and were sure to be a unit when the time for action came, and resolved as well to be stopped on their way by none of the old-time forms or scruples, their adversaries were wrapped in a half-dreamy consciousness of approaching danger, trusted implicitly for the preservation of what was most venerable in existing institutions to some intervention of Providence; whereas that Providence, who created the tremendous forces of free human agency, will have communities and their rulers ever wide awake to foresee dangers, and ever prepared and able to avoid them by timely and prompt preventives. They had no unity of purpose or of counsels, these shepherds of the peoples whose houses were undermined beneath their feet. They could not count on each other, and they scarcely counted on themselves.

The Holy See, aware of the falling off among its faithful people in consequence of their being drawn into the net of the secret societies; aware of the spread of revolutionary, anti-social, and anti-Christian pamphlets among the people; alarmed by partial risings here and there, by the utterances of the press at home and the loud and undisguised boastings of the English and the French press, had become fully alive to the danger. But at home and abroad every precaution taken and every effort toward repression were denounced as acts of treason against liberty, progress, enlightenment, and modern civilization.

Perugia, like Bologna, was one of the most active centres of this formidable propagandism and the agitation it inevitably tended to produce; they stirred up the most powerful patriotic passions combined with a passion more terrible still—the hatred of all religion, which is, like the most recently invented explosives, an uncontrollable force, developing with a suddenness that baffles all calculations and precautions, and destroying the man who uses it as well as the man whose destruction is aimed at.

Thither in 1841 was sent Joachim Pecci. He hastened to this new field of labor in order to make immediate preparations for the expected visit to Perugia and its province of Gregory XVI. For this much-abused Pope, whose every act was misconstrued and misrepresented by the anti-Catholic press of England, as well as by the organs of public opinion in the United States, was most anxious to see with his own eyes the condition of his people, and to remedy, so far as he might, the abuses and evils of which they could justly complain. One thing at that time disagreeably struck strangers visiting Perugia. The old mediaeval road leading up from the plain to the city was—as travellers may remember the old road at Laon running straight up to the fortifications at an angle of forty-five degrees—almost impracticable for vehicles of any description. This was a serious drawback to traffic.

The new Delegate saw at a glance what was to be done, and lost not a moment in doing it. Within twenty days a broad and well-paved thoroughfare winding up the hillside gave access to the place. And up this new road the Sovereign Pontiff was escorted by an enthusiastic multitude. It was thenceforward known as the *Strada Gregoriana.*

Monsignor Pecci's reputation had preceded him in Umbria: people expected from him intelligent and salutary reforms. The opening and completion of this new road made on them a very favorable impression, convincing them that their governor was a practical man who had an eye to the popular needs. This also inspired them with no little fervor in preparing for the reception of the sovereign. They took it as an evidence of his fatherly interest in their welfare that he had sent them a Delegate who had sincerely at heart the improvement of the country and the happiness of the people. So Gregory XVI had from Perugia a right hearty welcome. He felt its warmth, guessed to whom he was indebted for all these demonstrations of respect and affection, and thanked Monsignor Pecci for them.

Gregory had a special predilection for the beautiful mediaeval city, and the greeting given him by its people delighted him beyond measure. "During this journey through the provinces," he said to the Delegate in presence of a courtly crowd, "I have been in some places received like a monk; in several others with the ceremony due to a cardinal; in Ancona and Perugia I have had a reception such as truly becomes a sovereign."[1] In Città della Pieve the Pope rested for three days, during which he placed in the hands of the Delegate many

[1] MS.: "Nel mio viaggio in alcuni luoghi sono stato ricevuto da Frate, in molti altri convenientemente, ma da Cardinale; in Ancona e Perugia veramente da Sovrano."

presents and decorations for the most meritorious citizens of Perugia and Umbria. "Before long, Monsignor," he said, "and as soon as I shall have returned to Rome, I shall also remember you."

But the Delegate did not content himself with following the Pope to the principal cities of Umbria and sharing in the triumphal welcome everywhere given to the Holy Father. No sooner had the latter left Umbria for Rome than the Delegate began in good earnest the work he had set himself to accomplish. After doing what was of most pressing urgency for the capital, he resolved to visit every commune of the province in person, examining closely into every detail of local administration, informing himself exactly of the needs of each locality and the grievances complained of, correcting as he proceeded inveterate abuses, removing guilty or incapable officials, and taking note of the reforms to be submitted to the central government in Rome.

His presence was everywhere hailed with real satisfaction by the people. What he did on the spot, and what he promised to obtain from superior authority, contributed largely to remove well-founded popular discontent and to appease the agitation fomented by the secret societies. He was very firm in putting down these pernicious organizations. But he was not satisfied with repression; he left nothing undone to take away from these conspirators against Church and State the very reason of their existence by diminishing the burdens of the people, by fostering—as he had done in Benevento—industry, agriculture, and commerce, by securing an impartial, inexpensive, and prompt administration of justice, thereby making the people love and respect the law and its ministers. Meanwhile he was inexorable in punishing lawlessness and all disturbance of the public peace.

In this way, within the space of one twelvemonth, Monsignor Pecci succeeded in effecting most important and beneficial changes in every department of the public administration. The communal or town councils were entirely remodelled; to cut off all pretexts for delays in terminating law-suits, all the courts of Perugia were united in one great building, and every door was closed against the ruinous custom of adjourning and procrastinating. So active was he in removing all causes of public discontent, and in repressing and punishing private wrong-doing, that there came a time when the prisons of Perugia did not contain a single criminal.

Moreover, to encourage thrift among the laboring classes, and to provide funds at a low interest for industrious tradesmen and farmers, he exerted himself strenuously to establish the Perugia Savings-Bank, contributing a generous share to the necessary capital.

But even then, at the very outset of his public career, the young statesman, who sought to grasp the whole problem of Italy's unrest and aspirations, clearly discerned the fact that there could be for the peoples of the Peninsula neither true political unity nor real and stable social progress and prosperity without a thorough moral renovation accomplished by true religion.

Religion, to fit a people for a new phase of existence, a new period of civilization and national greatness, must descend deeply into minds and hearts, implant there strong convictions, and the generous impulses to great deeds and great sacrifices which can alone spring from strong convictions.

All these springs of greatness in private and in public life had been either entirely obliterated in a great portion of the Italian people or weakened more or less in the remainder by the education given to the nation by the teachings of French infidelity, by the terrible influence of the long-prevalent revolutionary Jacobinism, and by the open or secret action of the anti-Christian societies. The most active and energetic elements of public life in Italy in 1841-42 were the men in whose souls and lives the one absorbing passion was to overthrow religion and utterly to discredit among the masses the principles and practices of ancestral morality.

A scholar himself, and passionately devoted to the pursuit of the highest intellectual culture, Joachim Pecci believed that one of the most potent means of regenerating Italy was to give her leading classes a thoroughly religious as well as a thoroughly superior education. From them, he thought, true enlightenment would descend downward in society, helping the clergy and the most popular teaching orders of men and women to co-operate with Christian parents in thoroughly educating the children of the lower and middle classes. He therefore used all his authority and influence to open schools wherever there were none, to encourage and improve them where they existed. He especially exerted himself to give a new life to the College Rosi of Spello, the Pope appointing him Apostolic Visitor of the same. Its finances were placed on a prosperous and secure footing; a new staff of able professors were attached to the institution; its studies were thoroughly reorganized, and every precaution taken for the maintenance of that severe discipline without which there can be no steady progress in learning.

The Delegate was planning much more for the intellectual and moral advancement of Umbria, for the development of the material resources of that beautiful and classic land, when Gregory XVI recalled him and prepared to send him on a mission of far higher importance and wider utility.

Thus was fulfilled the Pontiff's promise made at Città della Pieve: "Before long I shall remember you also."

CHAPTER VIII

ARCHBISHOP PECCI STUDIES THE WORKING OF FREE CONSTITUTIONAL GOVERNMENT IN BELGIUM

1843 to 1846

THE YOUNG PRELATE, still in his thirty-third year, was not a little surprised to learn from the Holy Father that he had been chosen to fill the post of Apostolic Nuncio in the court of Brussels. This was in the beginning of January, 1843. On the 27th of that month the Pope nominated him to the dignity of titular Archbishop of Damietta. On February 19 his episcopal consecration took place in the ancient church of San Lorenzo in Panisperna, erected on the spot where, according to the constant tradition of Christian Rome, the heroic deacon of the second century was tortured to death. The consecrating prelate was Cardinal Lambruschini, the Secretary of State, who took a fatherly interest in Monsignor Pecci, on whose noble character and splendid abilities he had set a high estimate.

A month later, on March 19, the Archbishop-Nuncio set out for his destination. Traversing France rapidly, he spent a few days in Namur with his old friend and classmate in the Roman College, Canon Montpellier, later Bishop of Liége, and one of the most distinguished prelates of Belgium. In Brussels he was warmly welcomed by Monsignor (afterward Cardinal) Fornari, who had been his professor of canon law in the College of Nobles, and who had just been promoted to the Nunciature of Paris.

The veteran diplomat was able to give his old pupil precious information regarding the duties he was expected to fulfil in Belgium—duties which the division of religious and political parties, and the perpetual intrigues of the already numerous and powerful secret societies, rendered extremely delicate and difficult.

In the separation of Belgium from Holland in 1830 the main directing force had been the love of religious liberty in the Catholic population, to whom the House of Orange refused obstinately the freedom of conscience stipulated by the Congress of Vienna. The union of the provinces, at best, had been a forced and unnatural one. There were irreconcilable antipathies of race as well as of religion—the memory of long historical antagonism, rendering the yoke of Holland still more galling to the Celtic Belgians, who, in race and language and creed, had more affinity to their powerful French neighbors. But it were hard to say which was the greater error, that of the Congress of Vienna deciding by a stroke of the pen the political and religious destiny of five or six millions of Catholics, or that of that other Congress of 1830-31 imposing on emancipated Belgium a form of constitutional government to which the people were strangers. The political quacks who think that the constitutional forms which suit the English race at home or in the United States ought also to suit Belgium, or France, or Spain, or Italy, forget that the institutions of a country are the natural growth and outcome of a people's habits and social life. Where, as in Great Britain and in the American Union, the form of government, with the laws and the judiciary, has ever been a part of the people's existence, it needs no political education to train the masses to the knowledge and exercise of their political rights. They are matters of course, as familiar to the farmer in the country as his implements and methods of agriculture; as handy to the craftsman in the cities as the rules and practice of his trade. How different among the Latin nations of Continental Europe and their offshoots was the use of the suffrage, whether open or secret, in electing to municipal or national offices! What a farce the ballot was from the beginning, and is still, in countries we might name! And what oppression is practised, in the name of liberty and under the sham of constitutional forms, by peoples among whom anti-Christian teachings destroy the religious and moral sense, with the elementary and essential ideas of individual right, making what they call free government the most hideous intolerance and the downright and unrestrained proscription of all opinions, convictions, and acts which differ from their own false and narrow notions!

From the very birth of constitutional government in Belgium the country became, like the little Republic of Geneva, a hot-bed in which sprang up a luxuriant growth of secret associations conspiring against the monarchical institutions of the Continent. All political exiles, all socialistic and anarchical dreamers, found a safe refuge there, and there wrote and published, plotted and planned.

Belgium, Catholic Belgium, became especially the paradise of this Occult Force, not of the purely or professed benevolent and kindly associations which go by different names wherever the English language prevails, but of those bodies of conspirators against Church and State, against the entire social order inherited from the Christendom of the past, who are the legal and legitimate descendants of Weishaupt and his Illuminism. English and American societies long and blindly refused to acknowledge the evidence offered them that this Occult Force on the Continent of Europe, as well as in Spanish and Portuguese America, was a vast and mighty conspiracy against God.

Now our people have opened their eyes, and severed every tie of brotherhood, not of solidarity, with these banded enemies of all religion and of all society, since without religion society is impossible.

The reader, knowing the character, the creed, the aims, principles, and policy of this mighty organization in Europe, will not be surprised at the alarm and consternation of the Belgian Catholics when they found, from the very first day when Belgium elected her representatives to Parliament, that they had for principal adversaries the members of that body.

We have often heard the Belgian hierarchy, as well as Belgian Catholic statesmen, accused of bigotry, intolerance, obscurantism, because of the stand they took and maintained in favor of denominational education, as against the godless schools patronized and advocated by Frère-Orban and his brother-sectarians in the past and present.

But the programmes of late years published both in France and in Belgium by the Occult Force triumphant must convince any impartial reader, if he be a Christian man, that the battle fought in constitutional Belgium from the beginning was between the supporters of Christianity, the advocates of a thorough religious education, on the one hand, and the conspirators against religion, who wanted to get possession of the youth of the kingdom and extinguish in their souls all knowledge or all love of the ancient faith of Christendom.

Such was the battle which raged in Belgium when, in late March, 1843, Archbishop Pecci presented to the Court of Brussels his credentials as ambassador of the Holy See.

Who was the king to whom these letters were presented?

Leopold of Saxe-Coburg, King of the Belgians, has already had biographers and historians, official and unofficial, to tell the story of his life and reign. His character is as well known to American as it is to European readers. The statesmen who had a voice in Continental affairs when the Great Powers decided who would be the constitutional head of the new kingdom decided in favor of this prince, because he was a liberal in politics, a nominal Protestant in religion, a member of this same organization, who had been married to the heiress to the British crown, who was uncle to Queen Victoria and her husband's near relative, and who was soon to become the son-in-law of the French King Louis Philippe. These two men were both cast in the same mould. What the Belgian sovereign was the public has long ago learned from the published memoirs of his intimate friend and chief counsellor, Baron Stockmar, as well as that of Prince Albert and his wife.

King Leopold, thus placed on the throne of Belgium as a checkmate to the Ultramontane tendencies of the men who had created free Belgium, and a man acceptable to the numerous, powerful, and sworn enemies of the Church in that Catholic country, threw the whole weight of his influence from the beginning into the scale against denominational education.

Those among us in America who have always looked upon our public-school system as unimpeachable, because it freely educates the children of all citizens, rich and poor, without any regard to creed, will not see in the conduct of King Leopold anything that is blameworthy. But we in America are beginning to see that the public-school system was from the first open to two serious and unanswerable objections. It levied a heavy tax on those who objected conscientiously to schools where no religion whatever was taught, and refused to grant any share of the school fund to denominations who insisted on a religious teaching in their schools; and it tended practically (as it has now, confessedly, ended in doing) to turn out young men and women indifferent to all religious principle and practice—men and women all the more dangerous to the community that their trained intellect and acquired knowledge are a terrible agency in the service of their passions, whereas no fear of God is there to restrain them from evil courses or to encourage them to well-doing.

Besides, in a country like the United States, where so many sects exist side by side, with equal rights before the law, if the majority must decide the school question like all others of public importance, the minority must perforce submit. Still, that minority will deem it oppression to be taxed for an institution which they cannot approve of or profit by without violating their conscience. But where, as in Belgium in 1843, the immense majority were Catholics, and only demanded to be left free in educating their own children as conscience dictated, it was intolerable in the minority to impose on them a school system condemned by the Church, and which both conscience and .experience proved to be blameworthy and pernicious.

Yet the English-speaking world, through its organ, the public press, has invariably sided with the tyrannical minority, and held up the struggles of the Catholics of Belgium and their clergy as the battle of ignorant and intolerant fanaticism against enlightenment, intellectual progress, and modern civilization.

And the struggle goes on still in the year 1887. It is still the contest between two antagonistic and diametrically opposite forces, that of religion on the one hand and that of irreligion on the other, for the possession of education, the mightiest means ever devised for the moral elevation or the utter destruction of the human race.

Had not the political battles of to-day in Belgium been fought on the same ground and for the same vital issues as in 1843 and the preceding decade, we should apologize to the reader for what might appear a digression of unwarrantable length. But Archbishop Pecci, as Nuncio to Brussels, found himself in presence of the same hostile camps, which at this moment, and from his elevation to the Papal chair, occupy the attention of Leo XIII

On his first appearance at court the new Ambassador of the Holy See made a most favorable impression. It was; evident to all that he was an accomplished scholar, a well-bred and courteous gentleman, whose conversation, while carefully avoiding political subjects and diplomatic questions, could take the widest range. His learning, his education in the capital of Christendom, the historic center of art culture, science, and letters, enabled him to speak on all topics with equal ease and authority. He had also, inherited not a little of Roman wit. None, however, felt its edge save such as, in his presence, presumed to attack religion or trespass against propriety. For such offenders he had little pity. And more than one witty saying of his survives in the court circles of the Belgian capital..

Happily for the court of Brussels, for the entire Belgian people, indeed, the queen was one whose life was a mirror of all womanly virtues. Even over the mind of her sceptical husband she wielded the influence which deep faith accompanied by saintly deeds exercises over all men in whom the moral sense is not quite extinct. Fervently practising the religion taught her by her exemplary mother, she was also devoted to all its interests and would have it preserved to her subjects as the dearest of all treasures. Her own education having been acquired amid the scepticism of French court society and the practical contradiction, in French families, between the faith of one parent and the actions and professions of the other, she prized at its full value the boon of Christian education for every household, every child in her kingdom.

The Belgian archbishops and bishops, in their unceasing struggle for this most precious fruit of the liberty of conscience guaranteed by the constitution, could always count on the sympathy of the queen and her secret advocacy of their sacred cause, even when prudence would not permit her to side with them openly. To the Nuncio her counsels were also of great assistance in the selection of a line of conduct which should protect the inalienable rights of the Church without bringing her authority into conflict with the principles of responsible government.

At any rate, while studying the position of the Belgian Catholics and devising the best means to protect their interests, Archbishop Pecci applied himself to the labor of visiting the great Catholic schools which had rendered the country famous in the past. Instinctively the Belgian clergy felt that, in the struggle for retaining under their own control the education of the youth of the kingdom, the first condition toward success was to make their schools superior to those directed by their antagonists. There could be for the state no decent pretext for interfering with educational establishments which did the work they had to do better than any other of the kind, and which did more of it.

This must be the law for denominational schools the whole world over. The Belgian hierarchy and their educationists made it a rule for themselves.

In the capital itself the College of St. Michael, being immediately under the eyes of king, ministers, and members of the Legislature, was more likely than any other t6 be taken by friends and foes as a measure of comparison in judging the excellence of the other Catholic schools and their methods.

The Nuncio took a lively interest in this important institution, visited it frequently, won the confidence and affection of professors and pupils, and by his tact as well as by his zeal spurred them on to aim at the highest standards of proficiency. Such standards had ever been his own. On them, in every sphere of learning, he had regulated his own studies. And no one could converse with him long, or listen to him on public occasions when he had to honor his office and his reputation by some display of scholarly culture, without perceiving, in the exquisite finish of whatever came from his lips or his pen, how elevated were the literary and scientific ideals which he had successfully pursued.

Such a man, and he a young man, raised already to such eminence by these rare gifts, acquired as well as natural, had invariably great influence over the studious youth whom he addressed—over the most cultivated audiences, indeed.

From the visits he paid to the College of St. Michael, and the active interest he took in its advancement, dates a new period in the existence of that great diocesan school.

But side by side with that college the "Liberals" of Belgium—that is, the adepts of the secret societies, who masked their real purpose in the beginning, and won over to their views very many unsuspecting and not very serious Catholics, fascinated by the spell word of "liberalism"—had succeeded in creating an undenominational school of higher studies, with the name of "University of Brussels." This was solely under state control. The standards, the methods, the irreligious spirit of the French university and its dependent schools were the model after which the Belgian Liberals framed this great national institution. National they affirmed it was, although repudiated by those who had a right to speak and to act for the immense majority of the nation; and national they persisted in calling it and persevered in making it, by supporting it with the moneys taken from the people indiscriminately, and infusing into its teaching a spirit adverse to the religious character of the Belgians, but one which they hoped—and not without reason—to see in due time the spirit of the Belgian masses.

What cannot education do, even when directed to the worst ends, if carried on for a few generations by the public authorities, and with all the agencies and resources that a government can command, and if assisted by the omnipresent modern press?

It was a novel and a momentous contest, that which was carried on in Belgium, and the main strategic position of which was that same University of Brussels.

In 1789, just as the Estates General of France were doing their work of social destruction in liberalizing the kingdom of Saint Louis, the Emperor Joseph II, then sovereign of the Low Countries, was bending all the resources of his sceptic intellect and of the imperial power to de-Christianize education in Belgium. His attempt to create such an anti Catholic school as the modern University of Brussels made the Belgian Catholics rise up like one man and resist him with force of arms. When, in 1830, William of Orange tampered in the same way with the rights of the Belgian people to educate their children in accordance with their ancestral faith, the resistance to his will grew, until it burst into open and triumphant insurrection.

But the men who had drawn up the constitution of 1830 knew well—some of them, at least—that they were shaping an instrument which, under the cover of protecting all the liberties of the nation, would help the unbelieving minority toward confiscating the most precious liberty of all—that of conscience in the right to educate the young.

The University of Brussels had been established in the very dawn of Belgian independence. The men, the heroic Catholics, who had been its parents did not suspect the designs of the promoters of this early scheme of higher studies. The nature and tendency of the great central institution were clearly perceived only when it was an existing fact—a formidable organism working under the sanction of the laws and drawing its support from the public treasury.

What were the leaders of the Catholic majority to do? All efforts made to bring back the University of Brussels to conformity with Catholic principles and practice, to make its teaching such as could be accepted with safety by Catholic parents for their children, were defeated by the resistance of the Chambers and that of the king, supported as these were by the liberal press of the country and by that of France, Germany, England, and the United States.

In 1834 the archbishops and bishops set about' restoring the University of Louvain, which had had a worldwide reputation in the sixteenth and seventeenth centuries. They could not count on state aid. But they knew their people were with them, and they relied on God and themselves in undertaking this unequal contest with the united forces of Continental Liberalism.

Archbishop Pecci, soon after his arrival in Brussels,[1] had an opportunity of visiting Louvain, of beholding in the restored University the élite of the kingdom, and of associating himself with the archbishops and bishops in their laudable endeavor to raise their great national school to the height it occupied in former ages, and to the unquestionable superiority demanded by modern culture.

On Thursday, July 27, 1843, the University of Louvain held a solemn academical session for the purpose of conferring degrees in theology and canon law. All the representative men of Catholic Belgium were present, headed by the Cardinal-Archbishop of Mechlin. The Nuncio was invited to address the graduates, and was delighted to find among the visitors the venerable De Forbin-Janson, Bishop of Nancy, lately returned from his apostolic missions in America, where many still living, from Quebec to New York, from St. Louis to New Orleans, treasure the recollection of his eloquence, his munificence, and his saintly life. It was a deep consolation to this son of the Crusaders of old to witness in Louvain the manifestations of that living faith which refused to yield to the disciples of Voltaire and the apostles of modern scientism the

[1] "Cenni Storici," c. I. n. 5; account extracted from *L'Ami de l'Ordre* of March, 1878.

training of the youth of Christendom.

Of course the representative of the Holy See was received in Louvain with the cordial respect due to his character and mission. The rector and the members of the university faculties waited on him with an address of welcome, to which he replied in suitable and graceful terms. Then came, in the university library, a welcome from the students. One of them, a student in the law school, who at present fills the office of judge in the high court of Namur,[2] delivered a discourse in the name of his fellow-students. To this the Nuncio replied: "I am happy," he said, "to witness here the rapid progress made by an institution that owes in a special manner its birth to the revered clergy of Belgium, whose illustrious head I see before me. This institution is also the creation of its worthy rector, of his learned staff of professors, of the whole body of Belgian Catholics. ... Yes, the traditions of the ancient University of Louvain are still a living thing; and to you, gentlemen, it belongs to perpetuate them by your labors. You have already shown that you know how to continue the work of those who were here before you, henceforth your Church and your country also know what they can expect from you. Follow persistently the path you are pursuing; it will lead, doubt it not, to the most fruitful results. For my part, I cannot help being deeply moved by the sight of this assemblage of noble and dear young men whose souls are aflame with the love of the true wisdom and with devotion to Holy Church. This brilliant youth—I cannot question it—shall be one day the happiness and the honor of Belgium."

The journal from which these details are taken goes on to say that in the course of the afternoon Monsignor Pecci visited and inspected carefully the colleges and other buildings belonging to the university. He could not conceal the extreme satisfaction he felt at seeing all belonging to this great Catholic school in such a flourishing condition.

The position of a representative of the Holy See near a

---

[2] M. Capelle.

court, where powerful and contrary currents of influence were apt to carry even the strongest and best-intentioned beyond the strict boundaries marked by conscience, and where weak men are entirely lifted off their feet to drift helplessly with the tide, is one which demands in him who fills it the rarest gifts of the practical intellect and the upright will.

The kingdom of Belgium was under the protection of the Great Powers; its constitution, hurriedly framed in the hour of national triumph and enthusiasm, was accepted by a Catholic people without too close a scrutiny, in their impatient haste to become an independent people with a regularly constituted government acknowledged by other nations. Be it said to the eternal honor of the Belgian Catholics in sanctioning by their assent the principle of absolute freedom for all forms of religious worship, they fancied they were following the example first set by the people of the United States, and which their practical good sense and true love of liberty have carried out faithfully.

But the United States, happily for its people, never had, as a political party—in a minority, indeed, but active, determined, and perfectly organized—the anti-Christian sects and conspirators who in Continental Europe cloak their principles and designs under the fair name of Liberalism or Freemasonry. If this party were not masters of the situation in 1843, they were powerful and united enough to compel any party in the kingdom to compromise with them or to see the administration of public affairs brought to a dead-lock.

Monsignor Pecci, knowing well that a constitutional sovereign has to govern through his ministers, and that a ministry is only the instrument of the most powerful party, could only exert himself to win the confidence of King Leopold I as well as the good opinion of his ministers. Once trusted and consulted by the king and taken into the confidence of his advisers, he might prevent much evil, albeit much positive good could not be achieved for the time being.

That his youth, his modest and dignified presence, his courtly and reserved address did win him golden opinions from the very beginning we have ample testimony from contemporary writers as well as from the lips of those who bore a personal share in the events we are narrating or pointing to. The young Archbishop-Nuncio was an accomplished scholar and diplomat; but he was also—everybody saw and declared it—a priest of unblemished life. Such a character exercises irresistible ascendency even in royal courts, even in the councils of the most characterless politicians.

"The affability of Monsignor Pecci," says on this head a Belgian biographer, "his exquisite tact, and his deep learning forced Leopold I, who was a discerning connoisseur of men, to form a very high opinion of him. He endeavored to make of him a counsellor and a friend, and induced him to be a frequent visitor at court. The king often conversed familiarly with him, and took pleasure in propounding all sorts of difficult questions. The Nuncio, however, was never taken aback, so that the king would end by saying: 'Really, Monsignor, you are as clever a politician as you are an excellent churchman.'

"Our beloved and regretted queen, Louisa Maria, had a great veneration for the Archbishop of Damietta, and never missed an opportunity to obtain his blessing for herself and her children. This is a fact which Monsignor Pecci still remembers. Not long ago a Belgian priest, who went to Perugia to pay the prelate his respects, heard him recall these incidents. 'Yes,' said the Cardinal-Archbishop, 'I knew well the father of your present king, as well as his pious mother. I was often admitted to the cordial intimacy of the royal family, and I have often had in my arms the little Leopold, Duke of Brabant. I remember, too, that Queen Louisa Maria, who was so good a Christian, used to ask me to bless this her oldest child, ... in order that he might be a good king. And I have often blessed him with the hope that he would.'

"We say it with sincere pleasure, Monsignor Pecci has preserved a grateful remembrance of our country. Every time that one of our countrymen approaches him he never fails to express the sentiments of affection he entertains toward Belgium. In Belgium itself many of our active politicians who then knew him describe the superior intelligence, the delicate grace, the practical tact with which he conducted everything pertaining to the business of his Nunciature in Brussels. In our highest society people still recollect his noble affability of manner, his correctness of judgment, and the elevation of his ideas. In the family of Count Felix de Mérode[3] Monsignor Pecci was a welcome guest, his brilliant conversation adorning that home-circle which has remained celebrated in the history of modern Belgium."[4]

To this testimony we add another, taken from a well-authenticated source: "The fact is that he [Monsignor Pecci] conceived so great an affection for that deeply religious country that he afterwards made of his archiepiscopal palace in Perugia a staying-place for every Belgian citizen who presented himself there. There also, during vacation-time, he was in the habit of welcoming the pupils of the Belgian College in Rome; and in this college he usually lodged when business brought him to the capital of Christendom."[5]

Being the man he was, trusted and respected, if not beloved, by men of all classes and parties, it was natural that his influence and authority were often used to prevent or to extinguish untimely discussions. His moderation was like oil on the troubled waters. And they were rough enough in Belgium in those days. Sometimes there was trouble between the Catholics themselves, and conflicts of rights which it required consummate prudence, as well as great learning, to terminate to the satisfaction of both parties. "In 1845 a very serious dispute arose between the Jesuits and the University of

---

[3] One of the founders of Belgian independence, the father of the Countess de Montalembert and of the late Monsignor de Mérode, Minister of Arms under Pius IX.

[4] From a biographical notice by Count Henri de Condé in Le Courrier de l' Escaut.

[5] *Civiltà Cattolica*, March, 1878; notice by F. Ballarini.

Louvain. It originated in the sudden creation of a special faculty of philosophy in the Collége de la Paix at Namur, the teaching of philosophy having till then been reserved in Belgium to seminaries for clerical students, and for laymen to the Catholic University of Louvain. So the Belgian Catholics thereupon were split into two factions. For the university stood all the bishops and a great portion of the clergy; for the Jesuits sided powerful and influential persons, even in Rome. The Nuncio did all he could to calm the public mind, and succeeded in getting both parties to refer their claims to the supreme judgment of the Holy See. The Pope asked the opinion of all the Belgian bishops, and adopted such a prudential course as effectually restored peace."[6] The Nuncio was thus justified in refusing to give his own decision on the point in dispute.

The law on intermediate education also gave rise to quite a breezy controversy among the Catholics themselves, the Catholic press being divided in opinion, and Bishop Von Brommel, of Liége, taking a very decided stand. But the Nuncio's timely interference and wise words of advice put a stop to the discussion, besides securing to the clergy an unexpected share in the superintendence of intermediate schools.

So was it when the Ronge scandal—the forerunner of the "Old-Catholic" scandal of our own days—broke out in Germany, and threatened to spread the flame of schism through the Rhenish Provinces. Monsignor Pecci at once took the most effective steps to prevent the mischief from crossing the German frontier, although its author was a native of the diocese of Liége. He went, without a moment's delay, to confer with the bishops of Cologne, Treves, and Mayence, and communicated with the nuncio at Munich, securing their co-operation in localizing and isolating this heretical pestilence.

During his stay in Belgium Monsignor Pecci seized upon every opportunity to encourage the prelates of that country in

[6] MS.

their constitutional efforts to obtain from the state a due recognition and support for denominational education. He was, as the reader may have gathered from this and the preceding chapters, more especially zealous in promoting the superior education of the priesthood, judging rightly that, in the march of modern progress, the clergy should lead in intellectual excellence as in holiness of life. And as in Rome, from the earliest Christian ages, had been established schools of sacred and profane learning—centres from which the soundest science in all that pertains to divine things, to the government and discipline of the Church and the relations of all legislation with her laws, is derived for all peoples—so Monsignor Pecci wished that the Belgian bishops should send to be formed thoroughly in Rome the most promising clerics of their respective dioceses. This project was first laid by him before the assembly of the bishops at Mechlin in August, 1844, and met with a unanimous and hearty approval. No time was lost in giving effect to their resolution. The Holy See was but too glad to second the zeal of its Nuncio and the desire of the Belgian hierarchy. An elevated and healthy location for the proposed college was found quite near the Quattro Fontane[7] in a vacant monastery founded in the seventeenth century by Barefooted Carmelites (the reform of St. Teresa), and given by Pius VII to the Nuns of the Perpetual Adoration (called *Sacramentine*). These, having in their turn selected a more desirable site near the Quirinal, left their monastery free for

---

[7] The Quattro Fontane, or "Four Fountains," are placed at the intersection of two of the great thoroughfares in Rome—that leading from the Porta Pia to the Quirinal Palace, and that opened or completed by Sixtus V from St. Mary Major to the church of Trinità de' Monti, on the Pincio, and called from him Via Sistina. The four fountains are situated in niches placed in the opposing angles of the four adjoining blocks. Three of these thus belong to the three neighboring palaces of the Barberini, Albani, and Trugli, the fourth to the little church of San Carlino. The practical old Franciscan monk who was the dreaded Sixtus V wished to give the neighborhood a supply of wholesome water rather than a great work of art. Adjoining San Carlino is the Belgian College.

other purposes. Gregory XVI immediately sanctioned the purchase of this property. And thus the Belgian College in Rome subsists to this day as a monument, and an eloquent one, of the enlightened zeal of the Archbishop of Damietta for the best interests of a country than which, if we except Ireland, none more thoroughly Catholic exists, a country also which is, without exception, the most thrifty and prosperous on the European Continent.

As the autumn of 1845 was drawing to its close Gregory XVI was persuaded to recall Monsignor Pecci from a post which he had filled with such credit to himself and the Holy See, such benefit to religion, and such satisfaction to the Belgian court, clergy, and people.

The causes which moved the Pontiff to this step, though extremely honorable to the Nuncio, may be regretted by the statesman, the reader of this biography and its author, as they were by the most enlightened of Monsignor Pecci's friends and contemporaries.

His recall from Brussels to be made Bishop of Perugia, though intended by Gregory XVI as a reward and a promotion, removed from the great scene of active diplomatic service a young man of surpassing ability to bury him during more than thirty-two years in the obscurity and limited usefulness of a bishop's office in a provincial town. Was this a misfortune?

CHAPTER IX

STUDYING—LONDON, PARIS, AND ROME

1846

LET US FORGET PERUGIA and its expectant people for a few moments longer, and follow Monsignor Pecci, step by step, from Brussels to Rome. He had of his own free will, and at the first intimation of the reigning Pontiff's delicately expressed wish that he should accept the bishopric offered him, at once yielded. It was not in itself a promotion, Perugia was not an archiepiscopal see, while Monsignor Pecci was an archbishop, with only titular rank, it is true, but, bestowed on one who was beginning his regular career of nunciatures, it was sure to lead him ere long to the cardinalate.

It is not going out of our way for remote or deep reasons for the Pope's wishing the Belgian Nuncio to accept the proffered see of Perugia, to say that Gregory, aged, taught by long experience, and near his death, foresaw the fearful storms about to burst on the Pontifical States, and knew that Perugia was, on its hill-top, one of the centres of revolutionary activity. Both he and his sagacious Secretary of State, Cardinal Lambruschini, felt that such a man as Monsignor Pecci was needed. To Perugia, then, he consented to go.

In Belgium, it is not too much to say, court, clergy, and people were filled with deep and sincere regret at the first tidings of their young Nuncio's recall. He had proved that he thoroughly understood the country and its people, the political and social problems involved in this first stage of their independent national existence, and that he was one who could sustain and promote the best of all causes without arraying against it in open warfare the angry passions of its adversaries.

The king and queen, who had seen much of the

Archbishop of Damietta in the intimacy of their private life, were grieved at his approaching departure as at the loss of a dear friend whose counsels had been to them light and: comfort. The ministers were even more pained than the sovereigns. The clergy and the Catholic press of the kingdom were loud in deploring the withdrawal of Monsignor Pecci as a national calamity.

Leopold I seemed unable to testify sufficiently his esteem for a man who had fulfilled his mission at the court of Brussels with such extraordinary satisfaction to all classes. He decorated him in the most solemn manner with the Grand Cross of the order founded by himself, and wrote with his own hand to Gregory XVI:

> "I feel bound to recommend Archbishop Pecci to the kind protection of your Holiness; he deserves it in every respect, for I have seldom seen a more uncommon devotion to duty, more upright intentions and straightforward conduct. His stay in this country must have enabled him to do your Holiness good service. I beg you to require him to give you an exact account of the impressions he takes away with him on Church matters in Belgium. His judgment on all such things is very sound, and your Holiness can trust him wholly."[1]

The Nuncio could not have spent three years in the intimacy of Leopold I without hearing much of his niece, Queen Victoria of England, and of her husband, Prince Albert of Saxe-Coburg-Gotha. Baron Von Stockmar, who had had not a little to do with placing Leopold on the throne of Belgium, had also been instrumental in bringing about a marriage between the Queen of England and her cousin. He had great influence in both courts, all the greater that he carefully abstained from intruding himself upon the public of either country. He had learned to prize Monsignor Pecci, and at the joint solicitation of the king and his confidential adviser the

[1] MS.

Roman prelate consented to visit London.

Of course he was warmly recommended to the queen and her husband, and by them was received as became one who was the friend of so dear a relative, and who had shown such extraordinary qualities in the discharge of his office under the most trying circumstances.

The Anglo-Saxon race, on both hemispheres, was too important a factor in the problem of Christian civilization at its present phase not to have, long before the year 1845, fixed the attention of one so well informed and observant as the Joachim Pecci whose career we have been following. Ireland, for centuries kept in the twofold degradation of enforced ignorance and hopeless, helpless poverty, had, as soon as the terrible yoke was somewhat lightened, flooded with Catholic exiles Great Britain in its length and breadth, her vast colonial empire, and that mightier empire of the United States. Everywhere the still increasing millions of the chronically starving Celtic race at home confronted England with a stern demand for political justice, and as a living assurance that, through the Irish race, Catholicism would, in all future time, be coextensive with the English-speaking world.

These Irish exiles in England in 1845-46 were mainly instrumental in building up and supporting the Catholic churches which began to reappear all over England, Wales, and Scotland; and in 1845 the religious world had already been startled by the issue of the Oxford movement and the Tractarian controversy. The foremost theologians and scholars of which the great Protestant university boasted had braved public opinion and renounced every worldly prospect to join the Church of Rome.

How could the Archbishop of Damietta forego the opportunity of seeing a country where the hand of Providence was so visibly sowing the seeds of a near and mighty religious and political change? At the head of the clergy of his church was then a man whom he had known in Rome—a great scholar like himself; a churchman such as Archbishop Pecci would have all those of his cloth in modern times; foremost in all learning, secular and divine; one looked up to by the men of his nation; one revered as a great teacher by the Christian world. It was consoling to confer with such a man on the religious future of England, on the providential mission entrusted to the down-trodden Irish race, from which Dr. Wiseman himself was descended.

The illustrious visitor was, of course, received at the Court of St. James as the friend of the King of the Belgians could not fail to be. A whole month was thus spent in England, and spent to good purpose, as subsequent events proved. The knowledge and experience derived from the spectacle of the social life of a great and free nation; of the varied activities of the people; of whole populations plunged in hopeless poverty, in the most degrading ignorance and vice, side by side with the most enormous wealth, with upper classes holding the land in their own grasp and distributing among their sons the chief offices of government as if they were an heirloom; of a state Church splendidly endowed, and as alien to the impoverished, ignorant masses as if it and they belonged to different spheres—such contrasts and contradictions forced themselves upon the Bishop of Perugia. They were to occupy much of his thoughts during his long years of retirement and study in the capital of Umbria.

He was at the time unaware of the extreme gravity of the illness from which the Sovereign Pontiff, his friend and benefactor, was suffering. On his way homeward he spent several weeks in Paris, the guest of Monsignor Fornari, and honored by Louis Philippe and his family, to whom the Queen of the Belgians had warmly recommended him.

The social, industrial, and political condition of France at that moment was one which might well excite alarm in the mind of one less enlightened than Monsignor Pecci, and less familiarly acquainted with the attitude and aims of great political parties, with the ambitious designs of European courts, and with the terrible power and the well-defined plans of the secret organizations which were slowly but surely making themselves masters of Europe itself.

Even as the ex-Nuncio conversed with the French king and queen, absorbed at the time in their projects of matrimonial alliances, their throne was like a frame dwelling in the Brazilian forests—though untouched in appearance, all eaten away secretly by white ants, and sure to collapse with the first breath of the storm.

Monsignor Pecci was destined to see more of these terrible workers. He arrived in Rome on May 22, 1846, when Gregory XVI, lying at death's door, could not read or receive the autograph letter of King Leopold. The two months spent in visiting London and Paris had a most serious influence in shaping the course of the Archbishop's after-life. Had he returned to Rome immediately on quitting Brussels, the Pope, who so highly prized his diplomatic services, might have reconsidered and cancelled his nomination to the see of Perugia, and, even if raised to the dignity of cardinal, as requested by the King of the Belgians and half-promised by the Pontiff in recalling him, Joachim Pecci could have rendered the Holy See the most important services at a period when far-seeing statesmanship was more needed in Rome, and in Rome's representatives abroad, than at any period in modern history.

But it is useless to speculate on what might have been. We are now in presence of a momentous change in Rome itself.

The mortal illness of Gregory XVI filled Monsignor Pecci with deep sorrow. The firmness with which this Pontiff repressed the insurrectionary movements, at various points, of the secret societies; the dignity with which he repelled the pretensions of the English ministers and other foreign statesmen to dictate to him a line of policy in administering the States of the Church; and the reputation so easily created for him by the Liberal anti-Catholic press of being narrow-minded, illiberal, intolerant, and a despot, did not affect the judgment of those who approached him, who knew the man and the Pope in his daily life, and who could appreciate the thorough conscientiousness which he brought to the discharge of every duty of his high office, the deep love of his country and his people which formed so salient a feature of his character. Gregory XVI had the misfortune to be the chief obstacle in Italy, in Christendom, to the revolutionary designs of the Occult Force and its allied organizations, "Young Italy" and "Young Europe." Had he been an angel of goodness it was their interest to paint him with the colors of the Pit. And they strenuously labored to do so.

But Gregory XVI, as one who approached him nearly[2] testifies, was, like his immediate predecessor, Pius VIII, one of the most accomplished scholars in Europe. He was not only learned, but a generous patron of learning. His was a life of unwearied labor, self-denial, and self-sacrifice. Placed by the votes of his peers of the Sacred College in the Chair of Peter, his private life was governed by the same simplicity and piety which had distinguished him when only a Camaldolese recluse. Once official business and the cares of his vast administration left him free at the end of his long days of toil, he was only the monk Mauro Capellari, seeking the poverty and solitude of his cell, and the presence of the God who judges popes and emperors, as He does the lowliest priest and the poorest peasant, in the scales of inexorable justice.

To Cardinal Lambruschini, Gregory's great Secretary of State, and no less than his master the detestation of every secret or open conspirator, Archbishop Pecci, on his arrival in Rome, had no need to render a very long account of the .mission he had fulfilled in Belgium. The secretary was well acquainted with all that had been done, and had already expressed his appreciation of it.

But there was one among the members of the Sacred College assembled in Rome in preparation for the conclave to whom the ex-Nuncio was led to open his heart. This was Cardinal Mastai-Ferretti, soon to become Pope Pius IX What the latter's opinion of the Archbishop of Perugia's services at Brussels was, and what he had said to him before the conclave, was expressed anew in the very first audience after his

---

[2] See Cardinal Wiseman, "Recollections of the Four Last Popes."

election to the Pontificate.

"We know you well," he said; "and we wish to reaffirm the pleasure we expressed to you on a former occasion about what you have accomplished in Belgium for the good of the Church."[3]

It fell to the lot of the new Pontiff to reply to the autograph letter of King Leopold addressed to Gregory XVI. "Monsignor Pecci, lately Nuncio near your majesty," wrote Pius IX, "has placed in our hands the precious letter which you wrote to our venerable predecessor on the 14th of May. ... The high testimony which your majesty has pleased to render to Monsignor Pecci, Bishop of Perugia, is most honorable to that prelate, who shall in due time experience the effects of your royal and kindly wishes as if he had continued to fulfil to the end the course of his nunciatures."[4]

The Archbishop of Perugia did not prolong his stay in Rome much beyond the time necessary for completing his official account to the new Secretary of State and visiting Carpineto and the members of his family. Before, however, directing his steps toward Umbria, he had witnessed the exciting scenes which in Rome followed Pius IX's celebrated Act of Amnesty. But he knew all classes of the citizens too well, and was too well acquainted with the plans of the

---

[3] MS.: "Prima di lasciare Roma, *Monsignore Pecci non aveva potuto vedere il Pontefice che lo aveva eletto, Gregorio XVI, perchè passato a miglior vita in quei giorni:* ma essendo sul punto di adunarsi il Conclave volle visitare il Cardinale Mastai-Ferretti, vescovo d'Imola per farne la conoscenza; e ne fu accolto contratto della più squisita e benevola cortesia, e seco lui in confidente colloquio favello dei felici successi della sua nunziatura ai Belgio. Salito poco appresso Pio IX sulla Cattedra Apostolica, lo ricevette a formale udienza con eguali sentimenti di cordiale benevolenza, ed ebbe a dirgli: *Monsignore, ben ci conosciamo, e su quello che ella ha fatto per la Chiesa nel Belgio non abbiamo che a rinnovarle I sensi di vera compiacenza che le esprimemmo nel nostro colloquio."*
We have transcribed this passage as it is in the original, the sentences in italics being exactly left as they were, to convey to the intelligent reader the meaning intended by the writer.

[4] "Cenni Storici," I. 5.

Revolutionists in the Eternal City, throughout the Papal States and all Italy, not to know that the hymns of triumph sung to the new Pontiff always ended by a prayer which sounded very much like a menace.

We must ask the reader to go back with us now to the capital of Umbria, and to learn from the most authentic sources the circumstances which led to the appointment of the Archbishop of Damietta, still only in his thirty-sixth year, to the important pastoral charge he so little expected.

Perugia lost its bishop, Monsignor Cittadini, in April, 1845. It at once occurred to the clergy and people of the diocese that they could have no more desirable successor to their deceased prelate than the man who, during his brief sojourn among them as governor, had won such golden opinions from all classes, and endeared himself to the people by advancing their best interests and by the shining examples of his private life.

"The city magistrates and the most distinguished among the nobility, through the intermediary of Cardinal Mattei, the Protector of Perugia, laid their wishes before the Sovereign Pontiff, who received the petition very favorably. Gregory XVI was gratified to see renewed in the person of Monsignor Pecci what befell St. Ambrose, who, while governing the province of Æmilia, was sent to preside over the canonical election of a bishop for Milan, and was himself chosen by the people. Gregory, therefore, declared himself ready to accede to the prayers of the Peruginese, provided they could obtain the assent of the prelate himself, 'who, created in 1843 Archbishop of Damietta, was then Apostolic Nuncio in Belgium.'[5] The latter, as well to comply with the kind intentions of the Pope as influenced by the affectionate memories and relations which bound him to Perugia, did not hesitate to change his

[5] The MS., which is here quoted, underlines this last sentence, as if it was taken from the text of the Pope's answer to the petition of the Peruginese. We shall see presently that Gregory XVI did consider Monsignor Pecci's prompt obedience to his desire as an act which touched him deeply. It was sacrificing future prospects to the least wish of the Pontiff.

career, and to accept this pastoral mission among a people who had for him so high a regard and asked so earnestly for his return to them. He was preconized[6] as Bishop of Perugia in the Consistory of January 19, 1846, and on July 26 following made his solemn entry into his church, according to the ritual prescribed for such occasions, and amid the general rejoicing.

"Before entering Perugia, however, and taking possession of his see, Bishop[7] Pecci gave another proof of his lifelong devotion to St. Francis of Assisi. He made a pilgrimage to the shrine of the Umbrian saint, poured out his heart in the magnificent church of St. Mary of the Angels, within the exquisite little sanctuary of the Portiuncula,[8] and then tarried near the tomb of St. Francis himself in Assisi.

"Another incident also serves to define the character of Joachim Pecci. He had determined to make his entry into Perugia on July 26, the day on which the Church celebrates the feast of St. Anne, the mother of the Blessed Virgin Mary. This, as we know, was the name of his own mother, so tenderly loved, so unceasingly regretted. From her he had imbibed the deep piety which he ever cherished for the parents of Her who had given birth to the Incarnate Word. It is a sentiment which

---

[6] "Preconizing" is the technical term for proclaiming in solemn Consistory such episcopal appointments.

[7] Perugia was not then an archbishop's see. But as Monsignor Pecci was titular Archbishop of Damietta at the time of his promotion to Perugia, according to Roman rule he was designated as "Archbishop-Bishop." We shall simply style him Archbishop henceforward.

[8] The Porziuncola is so called in the history of the Franciscan Order because it was at first a ruinous little chapel, in the plain below Assisi, which the Benedictines offered as a free gift to St. Francis and his two first companions. The plot of ground it covered, with the crumbling walls and roof, was thus the only portion of God's earth the Saint and his associates could call their own. There they lived during the beautiful period of their earliest growth. Later the chapel was repaired and made a sanctuary by the popular veneration. Around that little sanctuary, later still, a magnificent church was reared, called St. Mary of the Angels. But within this glorious temple, like the Ark of the Covenant in the Temple of Solomon, was preserved the Porziuncola, decorated and beautified by all the artists of Italy.

the Catholic heart in every part of the world has ever instinctively cherished.[9]

"There was an immense concourse of people; and it was said that not less than sixty thousand persons came to Perugia from the neighboring districts and the surrounding country, lining the streets which lead from the Monastery of San Pietro to the cathedral. This happy event was also celebrated by a general illumination, and by literary academies vying with each other in honoring the man."

Under St. Anne's protection, with the holiest filial affections of earth and heaven purifying and elevating his spirit, Joachim Pecci entered the city in which, with his whole heart and soul, he intended to do the work set before him by the Incarnate God, the great Shepherd of souls.

The Perugians were impatiently expecting him. He was their own choice. He loved them and brought to them the devotion of a whole life still in its early prime, already crowned with glorious performance and filled with the promise of many fruitful years. His welcome was an ovation—not so much one distinguished by outward display as by the outpouring of unmistakable popular joy. Display enough there was, assuredly; for they thought they could not do enough for one who, during his brief stay among them, had done so much to better the condition of all classes. The streets were decorated on his passage, as if he were a royal personage whom all delighted to honor. The beautiful cathedral, which he was to beautify still more, was crowded to its utmost

---

[9] In France the national sanctuary of Ste. Anne d'Auray, near Nantes, is well known to all travellers. It has been ever specially dear to seamen. In Canada, below Quebec, on the North Shore and opposite the island of Orleans, is ***La Grande de Sainte Anne,*** scarcely less famous than the church in Brittany, and which is also a national shrine.

In Youghal, Ireland, was once a Convent Church of St. Anne on the beach at the entrance of the harbor, and whose tower only still remains standing. It is the lighthouse—as it ever was in mediaeval times, the nuns being obliged to see that the light was always fed. It was a sanctuary most dear to Irish seamen in Catholic times. Our New Ireland will rebuild it.

capacity as the people conducted him in triumph to it. There were addresses from the civil authorities, from the chapter and clergy, and other bodies, all heartfelt in the sentiments they expressed, and to all of which the Archbishop replied in his happiest vein; for his heart, deeply stirred by all these manifestations, went out to his people and was felt in every sentence he uttered. In the evening the entire city was illuminated; and the country folk from far and near who had flocked in lingered lovingly around the episcopal residence to catch a glimpse of their young prelate's person, to get his blessing or perchance a word of fatherly affection from his lips. And they were not disappointed.

Who that has mingled, in the Italian cities of the north and center at least, with the masses of the common people in street, public square, or church, on any one of those great religious celebrations which are so dear to them, but must remember with emotion how gentle, how orderly, how well-bred, and how courteous toward each other and to strangers this much maligned people are? And who, coming from any part of the English-speaking world, and comparing the conduct of the popular masses in his own land, on days of public festivity, with that of the Italian *contadini*, but must ask, "On which side is true civilization, the result of long Christian culture? Is it not on that of the sober, peaceful, orderly, civil crowds enjoying themselves innocently?"

We know what deep political passions, artfully and scientifically nursed, and let loose and directed with consummate skill, characterized the popular demonstrations in nearly all the Italian cities in the summer of 1846 and afterward. These passions, created and fostered for the most sacred of all earthly purposes—that of securing national liberty and self-government—were a force unhappily set in motion and directed against the religion and the institutions which had been, in Italy, the parent and the nurseries of Christian civilization. The cause and interests of religion, by the long and scientific education given by the Revolution to the people of the cities and towns especially, had been identified with what these were taught to regard as the enemy of liberty and fatherland, as the irreconcilable foe of all amelioration among the laboring masses.

It was so often said, repeated, taught, taught over again, repeated, and said, by every mouth and pen and organ that could reach the popular eye, the popular ear, the popular heart, that, more even than the foreign princes who owned so much of the soil of Italy and held her peoples in bondage, the Pope, the priesthood, the Church were the foes to be beaten down, crushed, and got rid of once and for ever, that many of the laboring masses in the cities began to believe it, and the middle classes, who wanted to climb over their betters into power, feigned to believe it, acted as if they did, and threw themselves furiously into the rising, swelling, rushing current of popular hatred, heading, guiding it, and lashing it into fury.

This the clubs of the secret societies had long been doing in Perugia, as well as elsewhere. They had hitherto done it in secret and dark places. The Amnesty of Pius IX now gave the conspirators an opportunity to come to the surface and the open light of day. Thenceforward no earthly power could destroy them, though it might check them for a brief space.

Who will create and organize a religious, a Christian, a conservative opinion capable of counteracting these passions? Who will call into being, by teaching and example, the mighty moral forces able to confront these powers of evil, and save Christendom and society from the chaos of anarchy toward which it is hastening?

It was, therefore, no undivided, harmonious, one-minded, one-hearted community that the new Archbishop of Perugia was called to govern in spirituals; for in temporals the province was always administered by a prelate-delegate appointed by the Pope.

The Archbishop, from the first day, understood exactly his position, with its perils and its duties. He had grasped all the elements of the European problem, all the tendencies of the age, all the probabilities and possibilities of the coming era, so far as human sagacity, a careful observation of facts, and study of principles could enable a man, brought early into contact with the leaders of men and of human opinion, to understand the present and divine the future.

He lost no time in doing his duty, in educating and preparing his flock to withstand the perils which beset their consciences, their homes, and their country. We shall find him instructing them diligently and solidly; creating churches and schools wherever most needed; promoting piety and education in every parish; raising the standard of education in the seminaries destined for clerical students; renovating the great schools of superior education; lifting his eloquent voice, in pastoral letters, to protest against the outrages and injustice done to religion and its chief, and warning, by writings as admirable for their sound doctrine and exquisite literary forms as they are for their opportuneness, the people of Italy and all Christendom against the errors which unsettle and corrupt men's minds in our age, and against the vices begotten of unbelief, the unbridled love of pleasure, and the loss of faith in the eternal world with its rewards and punishments.

It were hard to say which one may praise most in this laborious episcopate of thirty-two years in Perugia—the works accomplished by the Archbishop to foster faith, education, and piety among his people, or the prophetic writings by which he taught them Christian wisdom, and with them taught also the whole Christian world.

We have now to follow him in his labors.

PART THIRD

Joachim Pecci's Glorious Episcopate in Perugia 1846-1878

CHAPTER X

IN PERUGIA PREPARING FOR THE BATTLE

I. BY EDUCATION

AS WAS to be expected, the Archbishop of Perugia's first care was education. When, in the middle of the sixteenth century, St. Charles Borromeo, younger even in years than Monsignor Pecci, took possession of the see of Milan, his knowledge of the needs of his flock and of the needs of all Italy made him devote himself to the task of organizing not only a perfect system of secular instruction, complete in all the departments of science then known, but a thorough system of religious instruction, beginning with the teaching of the catechism in every parish church, in every elementary school, and ending in the best endowed chairs of theology, canon law, philology, and hermeneutics.

He found already existing, as is attested by a monument placed in the cathedral of Milan, a society of Christian Doctrine, established earlier in the century by a zealous priest whose prophetic mind divined the coming dangers to faith and morals, and who devoted himself, and enlisted others with him in the cause, to the labor of thoroughly grounding the children of the people in the knowledge of the Gospel truth and morality. This was also the primary object to which St. Ignatius Loyola and his first associates gave themselves up after their arrival in Italy, when the Holy See permitted them to evangelize the populations of town and country. They endeavored to make revealed truth penetrate into the popular mind by the most efficient methods ever devised by the mind of man.

Not content with preaching—in language which charmed the most educated by its pregnant simplicity and entered the intelligence of the most unlearned as the light penetrates a sound eye—in the cathedrals and principal churches, they afterward went about the streets ringing a hand-bell and summoning all the children to catechism. The children flocked to the churches at their call, and with them came their parents. There these men broke to the little ones of Christ's flock the bread of the divine word in such a way that not a particle fell to the ground. Thus did Francis Xavier in Rome and elsewhere; thus did he in the capital of Portugal on his way to the East Indies; thus did he everywhere, and almost every day, during his marvellous missionary labors in the East. Bell in hand, he would pass through the streets of the pagan cities and summon the little children to follow him and listen to the word of God. And, as if the bell were some magic instrument which compelled their wills to follow the great modern apostle, they trooped after him to be enlightened and to be baptized, they and their parents with them. Read his method of catechising, and see if anything can be more admirable, more effective in captivating the intelligence and the heart, when wielded by a man or a woman whose soul is earnest in the work of God.

This St. Charles Borromeo saw carried out in Rome by the brethren of Xavier, and this he carried out himself in the vast diocese of Milan. This his cousin and successor, Archbishop Frederick Borromeo, embodied in his wonderful Confraternities of Christian Doctrine, which soon extended to all Italy.

This is what Italy most needed in 1846 and the terrible years which followed. This is what she most needs to-day, January 1, 1887.

Archbishop Pecci was too enlightened, too sagacious, too practical not to have perceived, ere taking charge of the diocese of Perugia, that such was also the need of the Italian populations—a need made all the more imperative by the propaganda of irreligious, immoral, and revolutionary teachings and principles which found means, through the secret agencies of the "clubs," to disseminate their prints among all who could read, to inoculate with their venom the minds and hearts of those who could not. No amount of vigilance on the part of the authorities availed to check the spread of this pestilential apostleship of irreligion and revolt.

The sacred words of country, nationality, independence, and Italian unity were the spell-words used by these ubiquitous and sleepless agents of what was upheld as the cause of the people to catch the ear, move the heart, and enlist the sympathy of the popular masses, especially in the cities.

The growing mischief and the mighty influence of all these admirably organized agencies could only be counteracted by another apostleship—one combining the earnestness, the spirit of self-sacrifice, the devotion to God and God's people which distinguished the first preachers of the Gospel in Imperial Rome and Italy, with the knowledge of the present needs and dangers of the country, and the scientific skill to meet and vanquish in intellectual conflict all the enemies of revelation, who were also the enemies of the faith professed by the Italian people.

Nothing could withstand, baffle, and beat back the wide-spread and well-disciplined forces of Unbelief—who, unfortunately, won their successes in the name of patriotism and Italy—but a clergy fully alive to the dangers and responsibilities of the situation, and fully equipped with the best weapons for the contest; who had, marshalled behind them, partaking of the ardor, the convictions, the knowledge, and the skill of their leaders, the popular masses in city and country.

The people of Italy, it was already evident in 1846, would be lost to religion, and won over, by force, by persuasion, by seduction, by sympathy, to the cause of the Revolution holding aloft the banner of nationality, if the clergy did not hasten to make the people understand that religion never had stood and never could stand in the way of Italy's true freedom or national interests.

At any rate, the people had to be thoroughly grounded in religious knowledge and in the faithful practice of Christian morality, if they were to be saved from all the manifold influences of evil to which they were exposed even then, and which succeeding political events were so to intensify and complicate as to baffle the previsions of all human forethought.

Monsignor Pecci's first care in Perugia was to make every possible provision for the education of his clergy in the first place, then for that of the upper classes; knowing, as he did, that education, like all mighty influences for good or evil, spreads from above downward, from the leading classes to the masses of the people. Indeed, from his first taking possession of his episcopal see his keen, practised eye took in the condition of education among all ranks of his people. And if we mention before all else his labors in behalf of his ecclesiastical and university schools, it is to deal with the subject in logical order much more than in the order of time.

We here quote from our manuscript:

"No praise can do justice to the earnest zeal which he displayed for the diffusion of Christian knowledge and for spreading religious instruction among the people. He promoted this great object by the work of missions, by spiritual exercises, by the teaching of catechism, by the solemn festivities of First Communion celebrations, by the establishment of Christian Doctrine Societies.

"The text of the Diocesan Catechism, which he recast and reproduced in a number of editions; the episcopal decrees and ordinances which he published for regulating in all the parishes of his charge the explanation of the Gospel and of the letter of the Catechism; and the collection of learned and practical pastoral letters which he annually addressed to his diocesans, especially for the Lenten season, all bear witness to the wonderful zeal which he felt for the spiritual welfare of his people, and to the intense desire he had to maintain in its integrity and purity their baptismal faith."

After the Piedmontese occupation of Umbria and "the dispersion of the Monastic Orders, he saw that there would be among the people a dearth of spiritual food on account of the loss of so many preachers. Wherefore, in 1875, he founded a

Union of Preachers of the Word of God, whose object was to extend the benefits of religious instruction to the various classes and quarters of the city and diocese, together with missions, spiritual retreats, catechistical lessons, First Communions; for all which sacred ministrations he had in 1873 established admirable rules, in order to surround them with greater solemnity, to make them more fruitful and more edifying in the city parishes.

"Moreover, he decreed, after consulting with the parish priests and rectors, a fixed regulation for divine services throughout the city. There-were to be stated hours for: these and for sermons on feast-days, so that the people of every quarter could at every hour have the utmost facility for attending to their duties and profiting by the instructions given. In this same year of 1872, as well as by another rule promulgated in 1875, he strongly urged all parish priests and their assistants not to desist from teaching the Christian Doctrine to children, and to have Catechism classes in the afternoon for adults."

The Diocesan Seminary, as being the nursery of the local priesthood, naturally obtained an unusual amount of care. "He was wont to call it the apple of his eye."[1] It had been founded in 1571 by Cardinal Fulvio della Corgna, Bishop of Perugia, and had also been an object of special solicitude to Bishop Napoleone Comitali, one of Monsignor Pecci's immediate predecessors. The Seminary was close by the episcopal palace, and the new prelate conceived at once the design of enlarging the edifice by uniting it with the episcopal residence and giving up to the Seminary the wing which adjoined it. It was a generous conception. But Monsignor Pecci went further, for between 1846 and 1850 he spent six thousand Roman crowns of his own money—and he was not rich—in making all these changes and improvements.

"At the same time," the manuscript goes on to say, "his principal attention was bestowed on raising the standard of

---

[1] MS.

education in the establishment by creating new professorships and appointing to them the best men he could find. Nothing was spared by him that could help to make the zeal for study flourish in the schools, so that the Seminary of Perugia should enjoy the greatest possible fame in Umbria and the neighboring provinces."[2] The mind of the Archbishop-Bishop of Perugia had been from his early years too thoroughly disciplined, and his whole life, even at that time, was too well ordered, that he should not value discipline and perfect order in his great schools, and insist upon their observance by both professors and pupils.

His object in incorporating the Seminary buildings with his own residence was to have the institution and the great work it was doing under his own eye day and night. The pride of the gardener is to see every plant in his nursery thrive and grow, every flowering shrub covered with the loveliest blossoms of spring, every fruit-tree bearing the ripening promise of golden autumn. And the gardener's joy is to see tree and shrub and flower responding to his careful and loving husbandry.

It seemed to be Archbishop Pecci's dearest delight to be among these young plants of the sanctuary, or to watch the habits and growth of each, as if it were indeed the apple of his eye. If he had it at heart that the pupils, all through their classic, scientific, and theological courses, should derive as much benefit as possible from the lessons of their accomplished masters, he was equally anxious that these should omit no pains to make their teaching perfect. They were to be well prepared and punctual in their attendance. The Archbishop, although trusting to the superiors and directors in the discharge of their respective duties, and exacting a full and minute account of the progress made in each department, would not throw upon any one the duty of securing, both in professors and scholars,, a careful fulfilment of their allotted tasks. He could be expected in the schools at any moment, never giving notice of his coming, but entering quietly in the

[2] MS.

midst of a lecture or recitation, seating himself without exciting observation, and listening attentively to the proceedings of the class.

Both master and pupils were sure to profit by these unexpected visits. He knew how to convey to both, with equal tact and delicacy, whatever defects he had noticed, as well as to praise and encourage what was meritorious. It is a rare gift in a superior, that of bestowing aright the due meed of blame or praise.

One anecdote in this relation paints Monsignor Pecci's character and habits to the life. It is told by Professor Geromia Brunelli:

"Neither my scholars nor myself," he says, "are likely ever to forget a remarkable incident connected with Cardinal Pecci. ... I do not know how it happened, but one day I failed to be in my place at the appointed hour in my school of Belles-Lettres. Hastening to repair the delay, with the trepidation of a man who knew that the most likely thing in the world was to meet the Cardinal in the corridor of the college, watchful over the silence and order to be kept there, what was my astonishment, when entering the school without any previous knowledge of the fact, to see the Cardinal seated in my chair and translating for the benefit of my rapt scholars a passage from Cicero's 'Pro Milone,' making them feel and admire, in his own elegant language and with his fine taste, the hidden beauties of the Roman orator's composition and diction!

"Confused at first, but taking courage presently, I sat down on the benches among the pupils, and begged the Cardinal to condescend to continue his lesson. But he left the chair, inviting me graciously to occupy it, and impressing on his young hearers the importance of gathering all the fruit they could from their studies. Perhaps in the smile which lit up his countenance he conveyed to the professor a silent but pleasant reproof."[3]

---

[3] Prolusione letta dal Brunelli per l'anno scolastico 1878-79, e pubblicata nella "Leonis XIII Pont. Max. Carmina," Udine, 1883.

Of course such a man would insist upon testing solidly the quality of the teaching in college and theological seminary, as well as the application of the students, by severe quarterly examinations. He never failed to be present at these, and to be himself one of the examiners. At the end of each scholar-year he made it a rule to have Academies, to which the most cultivated citizens were invited, and in which the students had to read or declaim compositions of their own as specimens of the culture they had received during the year.

All this was after the model of the strong and careful culture which he had himself received at the hands of the Jesuits. From their method, too, he borrowed the admirable practice of having the students in Philosophy and Divinity sustain yearly, and particularly at the end of each of the philosophical and theological curriculums, a great public act embracing all the matters taught. Such a distinction is one that must ever be highly prized and much sought for; the prospect of it is a great stimulus to the noblest intellectual ambition.

Archbishop Pecci gave the utmost solemnity and éclat to these scholastic celebrations and assemblages. The neighboring bishops, Roman prelates famed for their learning, the foremost theologians and scientists in Umbria, all that was distinguished for rank or culture, were invited, and deemed it an honor to encourage by their presence these feasts of the intellect.

It was while he was thus perfecting everything connected with lay and clerical education in his diocese and throughout Umbria that he began to call public attention to the scientific method of that greatest of Italian scholars, St. Thomas Aquinas, who is in truth the greatest luminary of the Catholic Church.

His careful philosophical and theological training in the Collegio Romano, where, as the Jesuits are enjoined by their founder, the works and method of St. Thomas are made the basis of the entire curriculum of Philosophy and Divinity, had filled Monsignor Pecci with a great admiration for him who is known in the Church as the "Angelic Doctor."

In truth, it is impossible to find any intellectual method better fitted, in imparting or acquiring a scientific knowledge of the entire system of Revealed Truth, to place before the mind, side by side, both the errors which are opposed to the various doctrines of Revelation and these doctrines themselves stated in all their native simplicity and supported by every argument which can help to elucidate and convince. In St. Thomas's great "Summa Theologiae," and in his wonderful philosophical "Summa contra Gentiles," every objection ever devised against Revelation as a whole, its separate parts, or the solid array of evidence which natural reason brings to its support, is stated clearly, fairly. Before each proposition embodying a particular theological truth, as before some outwork about to be carried by storm, these objections, gathered from pagan and Christian times, are arrayed in regular order. Each one is heard, discussed, disposed of before the particular doctrine itself is formulated, analyzed, and demonstrated.

In the schools this method imposes on the professor a large and liberal view of the dogma under discussion; it supposes that he has gone round and round the truth, and surveyed it in all its bearings, and that he can guide his hearers in a like survey of the majestic edifice as a whole and in its minutest details. It imposes on the student—who has to attack and defend, by turns, the propositions of Christian theology or philosophy, as the case may be—a like thorough study of both sides in every question. This method of investigation and discussion in use in the great Catholic university schools is necessarily productive of large-mindedness, for it compels the deepest and widest study of all departments of human knowledge. And it begets, at the same time, that liberal and tolerant temper arising from a scientific knowledge of Revealed Truth, from an enlightened and firm conviction of its divine origin and of its unspeakable benefits to mankind, but arising as well from a clear perception of the limits, on every subject, of the truth demonstrated, and a calm tolerance of the doubts and objections created by seeming contradictions and by the vast region of speculation and probability lying outside what is certain or defined as of faith.

These were the large and sure methods which Monsignor Pecci labored, and not without success, to introduce, familiarize, and develop in the great clerical schools. To encourage all who had at heart the progress of a Christian philosophy based on these methods, he drew up in 1858 a constitution and rules for an Academy of St. Thomas Aquinas which was to extend its benefits to the whole of Umbria. The events which convulsed all Italy in 1859, and the Piedmontese invasion of 1860, prevented Cardinal Pecci from carrying out his design. This could only be done in 1872, when the Academy was instituted and limited in its membership to the sole diocese of Perugia. The constitution and rules were modified to meet the altered circumstances of the times and country. It was described by the founder as "a union of priests, having for its purpose the study of the works of the Angelic Doctor." The precedent was a noble one, and was promptly imitated in Spain and Italy. It was also copied in other countries of Christendom when Cardinal Pecci, become Leo XIII, made the philosophical method of St. Thomas the guide of all Catholic teachers.

The Sixth Centenary of St. Thomas, occurring, as it did, in 1874, gave a fresh impulse to the Perugian Academy, which that year issued the first volume of its "Scientific Transactions." This publication and those which have since followed gave consoling evidence of the high culture which the great prelate's efforts and example had introduced among his clergy.[4]

[4] These "Transactions" were published by Santucci, of Perugia. We can form some estimate of the scientific and practical value of the labors of the academicians by naming the foremost of the matters treated. There is an "Essay on Anthropological Investigations in accordance with the Principles of St. Thomas." This is dedicated to the Angelic Doctor on the recurrence of his Sixth Centenary, 1874 (vol. I.) In this first volume are the constitution and rules of the Academy itself. In 1878 the second volume was published. This contains "Discussions of the Academy of St. Thomas Aquinas of

Thus labored he to raise high the level of the truest science in the souls of those who were soon to become the teachers of his flock, the bright lights of the Church of Perugia. But he was far more anxious and labored far more strenuously to raise higher still in these same chosen souls the level of sanctity. For they were to be guides of the people in all goodness and purity; and their lives were to mirror forth to Italians in the dark and troublous times which were swiftly coming on the land the virtues without which Christianity could not live in the country where Peter and Paul had labored and died, the country of St. Gregory and St. Leo, of Francis of Assisi and Thomas Aquinas, of Dante and Tasso, and of Christopher Columbus.

To return to the subject of education, his solicitude for the observance of strict discipline in all his schools was only a part of his endeavor to promote and secure the highest degree of excellence. He was very particular in supporting the authority of both directors and professors, knowing, as he did by experience, that without authority there can be no discipline, and without discipline no education.

But in his seminaries a severe discipline, to be what it ought to be—a willing, loving, conscientious compliance with rules—must proceed from higher motives than mere outward respect for superiors or a decent submission to a necessary order of things. The discipline of a seminary, a training-school for the priesthood, must be founded on the spirit of self-denial practised in the preparatory stage by men whose lives, to be worthy of their calling, must be one long self-sacrifice.

of the academicians by naming the foremost of the matters treated. There is an "Essay on Anthropological Investigations in accordance with the Principles of St. Thomas." This is

---

Perugia."

Cardinal Pecci's purpose was to demonstrate that all the discoveries and investigations of the ripest and most careful modern science could and should be examined and judged in the light of the sound Christian philosophy of Thomas Aquinas.

dedicated to the Angelic Doctor on the recurrence of his Sixth Centenary, 1874 (vol. I.) In this first volume are the constitution and rules of the Academy itself. In 1878 the second volume was published. This contains "Discussions of the Academy of St. Thomas Aquinas of Perugia."

Cardinal Pecci's purpose was to demonstrate that all the discoveries and investigations of the ripest and most careful modern science could and should be examined and judged in the light of the sound Christian philosophy of Thomas Aquinas.

It was one of the most admirable features in the life of the Cardinal Archbishop of Perugia that he made it both a pleasure and a duty to mingle with his seminarians in their daily and weekly devotions, especially in the solemn exercises of their annual spiritual retreat,[5] which have such wonderful efficacy in purifying men's souls, in lifting them to God and setting them well forward on the road to all self-denial.

"He knew well what a delicate and difficult thing it is to give the souls of the young a right direction—of the young especially who aspire to the service of the sanctuary. To make sure of this he took every pains to have them from their earliest years solidly grounded in piety, in that humility which accepts the rules of discipline willingly, and in that practice of recollectedness which springs from both. He was extremely jealous of having the disciplinary rules in both college school and theological seminary strictly observed. This it was that often brought him into the corridors, into the recreation-halls,

---

[5] A "Spiritual Retreat" is a recess of eight or ten days, given, generally under the direction of a priest of superior virtue and learning, to the meditation of the Eternal Truths—the Destiny of Man, Heaven, Hell, Sin, Judgment—the meditation of the Mysteries of Christ's Life, and all the duties of the Christian man, the priest, and the apostle. The little book of "Spiritual Exercises" composed by St. Ignatius Loyola was the text used by his companions in the sixteenth century to work the wonderful change they effected in Europe as well as in the East Indies and America. Since their time the custom of these yearly Spiritual Retreats or Revivals has become general in all Catholic lands.

and into the chapel.

"He placed at the head of the Seminary well-known and prudent men, men of approved virtue, from whom he wished to receive daily reports. He frequently admitted the seminarians to his presence, and always showed them great affection in order to win their confidence and give them good counsel.

"On the other hand, he knew how to temper this kindness with a just severity toward such as showed themselves indocile and fractious. But he was careful not to use toward them anything like harsh words or bitter reproofs, which only irritate the ill-disposed and drive them to extremities. He reserved to himself the treatment of the most stubborn cases. ...

"It was his habit twice or thrice a week to go to a room specially reserved for him, during the study-hours, and to send for such of the young men as the rector considered to be disobedient or disedifying. There, all alone with each culprit, the Cardinal, with words which united real affection with fatherly severity, told him that he felt himself obliged to tell him that he must correct himself. To render this admonition more effective he usually gave to each of these thus sent for a sheet written by himself and containing, side by side, the faults and defects which it was indispensable to get rid of, as well as the most efficacious means of overcoming them. He insisted that this sheet should remain on the student's table, so as to be continually under his eyes as a reminder.

"This method produced the most excellent results; the most headlong, undisciplined, and passionate were known to change totally for the better. The Cardinal recommended above all things the spirit of obedience, of docility, and the resolute will to subdue self-love and pride, the twin-sources of moral disorder.

"Then, to plant these practical virtues still deeper in the souls of his seminarians, he wrote and published a little book on 'Humility,' which he dedicated to them, and in which he sets forth the means of acquiring this most necessary of all virtues in the priest, the one which should be his distinctive characteristic."[6]

Was all this careful husbandry, with its unceasing labor of love during thirty-two years, rewarded by abundant and worthy fruit? Yes. Cardinal Pecci "had the sweet consolation of forming in his Seminary not a few churchmen worthy of such culture, and who at this day fill high positions and offices of great trust, whether as pastors of souls or as professors, and who are justly regarded as the honor of the Church of Perugia. Among many which might here be mentioned it will be sufficient to name Monsignor Rotelli, formerly Bishop of Montefiascone and now Delegate Apostolic in Constantinople, and Monsignor Boccali, the Pope's special auditor or judge; besides the two brothers the Professors Satolli, Professor Monsignor Ballerini, Professor Brunelli, the Archpriest Boschi, the Archdeacon Salvatorelli, and the two Canons Carnicchi.

"We could say much about the watchful solicitude with which he ever attended to the interests of the Seminary, and of the great expense he incurred in improving it materially and in financial management, especially after the losses and the disasters occasioned by the converting of the patrimonial property of the establishment into government funds. At first he alone had to support the schools and pay the board of poor scholars, to keep the house in provisions in seasons of distress, to meet all the expenses of repairs and improvements, to provide all kinds of school furniture; so that it can truly be said that his forethought and generosity alone saved the establishment, after the conversion just mentioned, from the greatest disasters, not to say certain ruin.

"In fine, people were forced to admire the practical good sense and judgment displayed by him in 1872 when the government issued their Programmes of Studies. He had the tact to draw up a plan and rules of direction for the Seminary, embracing all the new subject-matters to be taught and the

---

[6] MS. This work was published in Perugia in 1871, and republished in Lucca in 1882.

discipline enjoined, in such a manner as not to imperil the solidity and seriousness of the old curriculum, which had given so many distinguished men to the Church and to lay professions. At the same time he was careful that his seminarians should get full instruction on all the subjects required by government examiners of candidates for academical degrees."[7]

[7] MS. With the approbation of the Cardinal Bishop, they printed in 1872 the "Normal Programme of Studies in the Episcopal Seminary of Perugia." This was signed by the prefect of studies, Canon Luigi Rotelli, D.D.; it was that drawn up by the Cardinal.

CHAPTER XI

PREPARING FOR THE BATTLE
II. TRAINING HIS CLERGY:
LEADING THEM IN THE PATHS OF SANCTITY

CAREFUL AS ARCHBISHOP PECCI was of the training of his seminarians—the candidates for the priesthood—he was, if possible, more so for the advancement of his priests in all knowledge and holiness. This was the double armor which alone could protect them and render them invincible in the long and relentless warfare begun against the Church, religion, and society. While, there fore, following with unwearied watchfulness the progress in clerical life and learning of every one of his seminarians, both in the college school and in the philosophical and theological department, he omitted no pains to ascertain how it stood with every one of his priests both as to intellectual acquirements and as to moral conduct and edification of life.

We must not weary the reader by repeating it, but it is none the less true that Monsignor Pecci felt, on taking charge of his diocese, like a general sent to defend a central position in a country threatened with invasion, with a formidable hostile force massed on the frontiers, and secret allies within the land ready to co-operate with the foe. It behooved him, therefore, to look well to his own means of resistance, to inspect the forces at his command, and to examine their state of efficiency.

It may be said here that his long episcopate of upwards of thirty-one years in Perugia was one continuous effort to lift his priests up to the sublime height of intellectual and spiritual perfection demanded by their calling, and more particularly required by the crisis through which are passing, at the present time, all the institutions of Christianity.

Let us listen to one who had the privilege of being both an eye-witness of these episcopal labors and a sharer in the Archbishop of Perugia's admirable system of education, as regarded both seminarians and priests engaged in the ministry.

"Every year he never failed to have several courses of spiritual exercises given to his priests, so that every three years all the members of his clergy, rectors, confessors, and simple priests, could in their turn enjoy the benefit of this holy repose. He restored by reiterated ordinances the practice of holding monthly conferences for the solution of questions or 'cases' of moral theology. He presided in person over those held in the city of Perugia. Elsewhere in the diocese these conferences were presided over by the local dignitaries. ... In 1851 he published an ordinance with wise regulations concerning all clerical students living outside of the Seminary. He selected one of his oldest and best priests to be their immediate superior and to watch over their conduct. In 1856 he published the Diocesan Catechism, to which he added instructions replete with practical wisdom and exhortations to parish priests on the teaching of Christian Doctrine. In 1857 he had printed a precious 'Manual of Practical Rules,' addressed to the parochial clergy, as a guide in all external discipline and the exercise of their ministry.

"For the greater facility of catechising little children on all holydays, and to keep them away from all dangerous amusements, he established, in 1858, under the direction of the Oratorians, and with the help of the younger clergy, catechism classes.

"In 1859 he inaugurated the Scientific Academy of St. Thomas Aquinas, in order chiefly to impel the clergy to cultivate the higher studies and the scholastic philosophy and theology.

"To prevent abuses and profanations in the functions of the public worship on the occasion of the political revolution with its changes, he issued in 1861 an injunction to his clergy recalling the obligation of following to the letter the prescriptions of the liturgy for all extraordinary ceremonies and the internal regulation of their churches.

"In 1863 he sanctioned the establishment of the Conferences of St. Vincent of Paul for all his priests, and approved the rules of the same. In 1866 a circular addressed to them laid down the line of conduct they had to follow in the midst of the sad circumstances of their country, so as not to depart from the dictates of evangelical prudence and priestly moderation.

"As soon as the law on military conscription was published, in 1869, he employed all his zeal and industry in purchasing the liberty of the poorer clerical students drafted, establishing a commission for that object, and appealing, not without success, to the charity of his people for the same purpose.

"The confiscation by the state of all Church property and revenues having reduced a multitude of priests to great poverty, the Cardinal, in 1873, founded the Society of St. Joachim, as a mutual relief association for the benefit of indigent and infirm priests.

"In 1875, feeling keenly the great gaps created in the ranks of the active priesthood by the dispersion of the regular clergy, he founded the Pious Union of Preachers for the better diffusion of Christian instruction among the city population and the country parishes. Missions, pious exercises, catechistical explanations, First Communions—for all of which he had made special rules in 1873—were once more urged by him as the great means of breaking to the people the word of God, and a greater degree of solemnity was given to them everywhere in order to make them more attractive and more fruitful.

"Already in 1872 he had, in accord with the city rectors and parish priests, established for all the churches of Perugia a fixed time-table regulating the hours for Mass and all other divine offices, for preaching, catechism, etc., so that on every Sunday and holyday the people of the neighboring districts should have all facility for fulfilling their religious duties and satisfying their piety. In 1872, as well as by his ordinance of 1875, he urged upon all parish priests and chaplains the necessity of being unwearied in the labor of catechising the little children in the forenoon of Sundays and holydays, and the adults in the afternoon.

"When, in 1877, the government enacted the law of obligatory instruction, one of the articles of which, with well-calculated purpose, forbade the teaching of catechism in the schools, Cardinal Pecci made a fervent appeal to his clergy, pointing out to them the way in which they should act in order to supplement this fundamental defect—that is, by a more general and unceasing use of all means and opportunities to impart religious instruction, and a prudent co-operation to that effect with the teachers of elementary schools. He laid down for that purpose wise practical rules, all bearing the impress of the most enlightened pastoral zeal.

"We ought not here to pass Over in silence his watchful solicitude with regard to the external conduct of his clergy. In his pastoral visitations he was always extremely respectful and courteous toward those hard-working priests. Still, he would not hesitate to reprove them with fatherly frankness and affection if he found them faulty or slothful; he would cheer and praise them when he saw they were zealous and exemplary. As to the parish priests recently appointed, in order that they should not get discouraged in the work of their mission, rendered such a difficult one by the political changes, he summed up in their behalf, in a special pastoral letter, the most salutary advice and precious reminders furnished by his long experience. These he reduced to three points, priestly spirit, an exemplary life, and priestly knowledge, under which heads he gathered together the obligations and prerogatives of a good pastor.

"Lastly, a word must be said of the beautiful order and discipline which he caused to prevail in the celebrations in his cathedral church. He was always on the best of terms with the chapter. Hence in performing his regular pastoral visitations, and on extraordinary occasions, he found the canons most ready and generous in providing all that was needful for the well-ordering of the cathedral clergy, for the exact regulating of the Psalmody, and all that could contribute to the splendor of divine worship and to the repairs and decoration of the great temple itself.

"No wonder, therefore, that both Umbrians and foreigners, on assisting there at divine service, were wont to express their admiration not only at the rare architecture and precious materials of the edifice, but at' the concourse of worshippers and the solemn order of the sacred functions."

This is a bird's-eye view of the Archbishop's labors. Before dwelling more at length on some points indicated in the above summary, the reader will be glad to pause and consider how the private life of so great a teacher corresponded with what he exacted of others.

He was simple in his habits, indefatigably laborious in the employment of his time, as eager and as keen as any young student for the acquisition of new stores of knowledge, blameless and most exemplary in his private life, and ever accessible to priests and to people, to high and lowly who required his ministry. Firm, calm, and unmoved as an antique statue in presence of the persecutors of his clergy and the perverters of his flock when they threatened him or attempted to browbeat or to overawe him, his words could be words of living flame when kindled by the wrong done to others.

The Piedmontese authorities had soon found out that Cardinal Pecci was not one that they could intimidate or circumvent, or draw into the doing of a single deed or the utterance of a single word which could be construed by the most unscrupulous of them into anything that seemed like concession or compromise or compliance. In their contests with him they were always baffled; for he was one who studied to be in the right, and who made sure that his adversaries were in the wrong. They learned, at their cost, the wisdom of letting him alone.

His learning, joined to a conscience of extreme sensitiveness, never allowed him to yield to any of the snares laid for him by men who sought to buy acts of toleration or kindness to the suffering clergy and people of Perugia by some slight advance to the ruling powers or some act of deference which might bear the seeming of acknowledging their rightful sway. They were the mightful, not the rightful, masters in Umbria. He did not by word or act of his sanction their presence or their pretensions. But he did not provoke them. His dignified courtesy, even when his words conveyed a refusal and a rebuke, inspired respect or calmed irritation.

Such as we have described him, such he wished his priests to be—men of God, His worthy ministers; to be looked up to by all, to be looked down on by none.

In 1866, after six years of Piedmontese misrule and of trials the bitterness of which no words can describe, Cardinal Pecci found it necessary to relieve his own heart by laying down for his faithful priests such common rules of conduct as might guide them safely through the difficulties and perils that were thickening around them.

1866 for Italy and for the Church was a memorable year. It was that in which the French garrison was withdrawn from Rome, and the Pope was left to his own resources to create an army to maintain order within the provinces still left to him. But we all know at present that the famous September Convention between Napoleon III and Victor Emmanuel covered only a skillfully devised plan, on the part of the latter at least, to enable him to possess himself of Rome at the first opportunity. It was for his ministers and allies to create it.

On June 29 also they celebrated in Rome the eighteenth centenary of the martyrdom there of SS. Peter and Paul. It was a glorious solemnity; but the bishops who came to the Eternal City from every shore, and the laity who flocked thither after their bishops, were, during the celebration, like children in the house of a parent suffering the keenest affliction. Their joy was tempered by unspeakable sadness; their rejoicing was mingled with tears.

Mazzini and Garibaldi had both issued their manifestoes, and both clamored for the possession of Rome and the extirpation of priests and Papacy. So there was in the portions of the Peninsula already subject to the Piedmontese rule a renewal of the worst outrages against religion, of the worst oppression against the priesthood, even though some of the exiled bishops were allowed to return. In the former States of the Church the position of the clergy became daily more and more intolerable, the moral pressure put upon them to side with the Revolution being like the torture inflicted formerly on prisoners subjected to the "question": human endurance was tested to its utmost limits.

This was more particularly the case in the Umbrian provinces, on account of their proximity to Rome and the close bond which had so long united the people to the Holy See.

It was in these circumstances that Cardinal Pecci addressed himself to his dear fellow laborers. Dear they were indeed to their hard-working and devoted chief, who had taken such unceasing pains in forming by word and example the young among them, and in stimulating and encouraging the holy ambition of their elders.

"No matter how much difficulties and dangers multiply in our path from day to day," he says, "a true and fervent priest must not on that account lose his way, nor fail to perform his duties, nor pause from the fulfilment of his spiritual mission for the welfare and salvation of the human family and the maintenance of that holy religion of which he is the herald and minister. For it is in labors and trials that priestly virtue waxes strong and gets purified; the blessed and all-restoring action of his divine ministry shines forth more resplendently in times of great need and amid social revolutions and transformations."

The terrible changes to which Italy is subjected happen, the Cardinal says, by the permission of Him who is the Eternal Pontiff and the Supreme Ruler of the universe. It is from Him that the priest must seek for light and aid amid the darkness and the throes of the earthquake. In that light it behooves the minister of God to meditate on his own imperfections and to cherish a spirit of humility and compunction.

He then holds up to his priests, as a summary of all the virtues which present circumstances demand that they should practise in a more perfect manner, the admonition of St. Paul to Titus: "In all things show thyself an example of good works, in doctrine, in integrity, in gravity, the sound word that cannot be blamed."[1]

"An exemplary and laborious life," the Cardinal goes on to say, "a life animated by the spirit of charity and guided by the dictates of evangelical prudence; a life of sacrifice and fatigue, spent in doing good to others, consumed in the midst of the world for no earthly views or transitory reward; and that frank, noble, and powerful language, the sound word that cannot be blamed which confounds human contradiction, appeases the old hatred of the world, and wins even the respect and esteem of our adversaries themselves. At all times it is the sacred duty of the man who dedicates his life to the sanctuary to make himself the living and visible mirror of good example; but this is sovereignly necessary when social commotions place God's minister on rough and slippery ground where he may meet at every step snares and pitfalls."

And so the wise guide of the Perugian and Umbrian clergy continues to hold up the lamp before his followers in the priesthood. They must be learned. In our day "it is strictly the charge of the priest to defend doctrine assailed, morality perverted, justice ignored. He must stand like a wall of brass in the path of inundating error and heresy spreading like a pestilence."

His luminous words point out to the preachers of God's word what are the things on which their doctrine can be, in our day, bestowed to the best advantage: the teaching and training of the young, in which "their solicitude should be industrious and indefatigable"; the careful and regular preparation of their Gospel lessons for the people, "and the scrupulous development of the maxims of sound morality." As to religion itself, the preacher must insist on a luminous

[1] Titus ii. 7, 8.

exposition of her divine prerogatives, her extraordinary and lasting services to mankind, in every condition of society and under every aspect, especially in what pertains to true civilization and real progress.

So on the other heads of his instruction the same fatherly and experienced hand marks out the line of conduct to be followed by the priest. Beautiful are his words on the "moral integrity" which should ever adorn the priestly character. "The moral conduct of the priest is the mirror into which the people look to find a model for their own demeanor. ... Every shadow, every stain is remarked by the vulgar eye; and the mere shadow is enough to make the people lose their esteem of priestly worth. ... It is impossible that a priest who lays himself open to such reproaches or suspicions, who has the name of being self indulgent, interested, and of irregular life, should give forth that fragrance of a pure life, that sweet odor of Christ which witnesses to our worth and to our doctrine, as well in the estimation of those who are saved as in that of those who perish."

"Behold," he says in concluding, "the path which, according to my judgment, should be followed by the clergy in our age. This path will lead them to the sure attainment of the two great means which the Divine Master declares to be indispensable in our holy ministry—holiness and knowledge. Let every priest be by his example a pure and brilliant light, let him be by his teaching the salt of the earth, and no difficulties can prevent his fulfilling his ministry of reparation."[2]

Now let us see how, when the conflict came, the Archbishop of Perugia could wisely direct his clergy and protect their dearest interests.

It is a page of history but little known outside of Italy and deserving of everlasting remembrance.

---

[2] "Scelta," pp. 109-116.

CHAPTER XII

HOW CARDINAL PECCI LED HIS BROTHER BISHOPS TO THE BATTLE: III. DEFENDING AND DIRECTING THE CLERGY IN THE BATTLE

ON SEPTEMBER THE 24th, 1869, Cardinal Pecci addressed to his diocesans a touching pastoral letter on the "Redeeming poor Clerical Students from the Military Conscription." It was a delicate, almost a dangerous, subject to write upon. But there was an imperative need of filling up, in the ranks of the Umbrian clergy, the great gaps made by the suppression and banishment[1] of the priests belonging to the monastic orders, as well as the yearly voids left by the conscription law and the sad falling off in the number of seminarians and candidates for Holy Orders. In a circular to the clergy of October 22 following the Cardinal designates with graphic touch the working of that law as "the pitiless axe laid at the roots of the Church's nursery."[2] It was striking the tree of the priesthood in its very roots, and with the priesthood annihilating the Church in Italy. This is precisely what such Italian statesmen as Prime Minister Depretis now openly confess to be the purpose of

---

[1] In a note to the Protest on the Royal *Exequatur*, mentioned on p. 138, it is said : "Omitting the mention of many other instances of banishment and concentration, ... [we take that] of the *instantaneous* expulsion and deportation to Sardinia of the Capuchin Fathers of Todi, of the Reformed Franciscans of Massa, of the Observantines and Reformed of Orvieto, which took place in last May [1563], without any judicial process, and under military escort, as well as the general upsetting and exiling of all the Mendicant communities of Umbria which has just been accomplished ("Scelta," p. 369).

[2] *La scure inesorabile che é messa alle radici del vivaio della chiesa* (ibidem, p. 519).

their legislation and policy.

From 1859 to 1869 statistical figures show, as the Cardinal states in the beginning of his pastoral, that the number of deaths among his clergy exceeded by thirty the number of ordinations to the priesthood.

"It is easy to see from this moment forward," he says, "that the burden of military service must inevitably fall on all young men who have devoted themselves to the clerical career. We are deeply saddened by this; we are tortured by the thought that so many parishes will ask us for pastors, while we shall have none to give them; that so many pious populations will ask for the food of Christian instruction and the comfort of the sacraments, and that no one will be found to minister to them; and that, such a state of things continuing, there is nothing to prevent religion from dying out in these country-places for the very lack of hands to cultivate it."

Then, with a simple and earnest eloquence in which one feels the loving pastor's heart in every phrase, Cardinal Pecci goes on to say how an appeal should be made to the people of the diocese in order to create a fund for purchasing the freedom of poor young clerics whose talents and virtues hold out the promise of their being worthy and efficient priests.

"This work," he says, "is eminently religious and charitable. ... Even considered in its social aspect it has a value and an importance that are unquestionable. For there can be no doubt but that the lack of priests would seriously injure the religious and moral culture of the people, on which depend order, tranquillity, and the well-being of the entire community. We expect, therefore, no one among sincere Catholics, no matter how straitened and burdened financially, will refuse to do what he can and what piety and religion suggest. Above all, we trust to the zeal and solicitude of our clergy. ..."

This to his diocesans. Then he lays down the statutes for the commission which he establishes for such a noble object.

A month after the pastoral letter he addressed a circular to his parish priests, urging on them the greatest zeal and generosity in forwarding the labor of the commission.

"I know the straits to which the clergy have been reduced," he writes, "but I also know the spirit of sacrifice and charity which animates them. Christian charity does not know and should not know what difficulty is, in a work especially such as the present, which aims at keeping off the pitiless axe with which they strike at the roots of our young trees in the nursery of the Church. ...

"If we see lay societies of mutual help making such strenuous efforts to succeed in their purpose, how can we help making equal efforts to rescue so many young men who were being educated and trained for the priesthood, and who are dragged away to the ranks of the army and the exercises of a military camp? If the good work we have taken in hand should not succeed, then we may be sure that the education of the priesthood and the seminaries will be given up altogether."[3]

The commission did succeed, thanks not only to the excellence of the charity which it advocated, but thanks as well to the hearty zeal with which Cardinal Pecci pleaded the cause of these young students—a zeal which his words and example communicated to both people and clergy.

Thus appealed he in 1869. But there were other needs among the clergy which touched his fatherly heart no less deeply. Foremost among these was the utter destitution to which so many ecclesiastics had been reduced since 1860 by the sequestration of all Church property and revenues, and the conversion of the little left to the clergy into slate bonds. The whole system of this legislative plunder was devised, calculated, wrought out scientifically either to extinguish the clergy altogether by deterring young men from joining the ranks of a hopelessly degraded and impoverished priesthood, or by making of all priests thus dependent on the wretched pittance irregularly and grudgingly dealt out by the state treasury the abject slaves of an inhuman and anti-Christian power. The miserable dole obtained from the government of Victor Emmanuel—and the same applies to King Umberto's

[3] "Scelta," pp. 516-5 520.

administration—barely kept the recipients from starvation, if they would with it keep a roof above them and decent clerical raiment on their backs. When sickness and old age with its infirmities came to them no words can describe their destitution. A poor priest, in sickness and old age, is everywhere one deserving of tender commiseration. But in once beautiful, fertile, and bountiful Italy the Revolution has contrived to make the lot of the poor, sick, and aged priest one of indescribable hardship.

Cardinal Pecci exhorted and encouraged the clergy of his diocese to establish a private Relief Fund and a Sodality to administer it. The Sodality was composed of the members of the clergy. It was called the "*Pious Union of St. Joachim for Needy Ecclesiastics.*" Every member paid into the fund an annual fee of five lire (one dollar, or four shillings English money). These regular contributions, together with the donations of benefactors and the voluntary offerings of the faithful, brought timely and indispensable relief to many a lowly roof where poor priests, born in opulence, devoted from their youth to the holy ministry, after having lost their position and being stripped of their own lawful patrimony, were left to pine away unhelped, unpitied, unnoticed by the spoiler.

We cannot refrain here from denouncing to the indignation of the civilized world the crowning cruelty and meanness of the Italian government, established, forsooth, in the name of liberty, of progress, of civilization! Not satisfied with sequestrating all ecclesiastical property, seizing upon the residences of the bishops and the revenue (mensa vescovile) established for their permanent support, it refused to allow any but those whom, for one political reason or another, it approved of to take possession of their residences and to enjoy what the government thought fit of their revenues. This was the working of the royal *exequatur* mentioned elsewhere. To the eternal honor of the bishops of Italy be it said that most of those who were appointed by the Holy See could not be brought to truckle to the usurping government, or to come to any compromise with the new principles and the new masters of Italy, and so were refused the use of the episcopal residence and the enjoyment of their salaries.

The Holy Father, thanks to the liberality of the Catholic world, to the Peter's Pence contributed by every land, was able to bestow on these bishops a temporary allowance barely sufficient to provide for their necessities. Well, the Depretis government found that this was defeating their darling purpose—to make bishops and clergy, so long as any such remained in Italy, entirely dependent on the state. Forthwith a law was passed compelling bishops and all other religious persons thus receiving from the Pope a regular help or stipend in the way of money to pay into the treasury a tax of one-third of the whole until such time as they could prove that such aid in money had ceased to be given to them!

We doubt if Nero, or Diocletian, or Julian the Apostate would have condescended to so base a device.

It is due to the reader who is interested in the public acts of the great personage whose life we are sketching to show, ere concluding this chapter, how nobly Cardinal Pecci could defend the interests of his persecuted clergy and inspire his brother bishops with his own courage and determination.

We have from the pen of the Archbishop of Perugia one of those outspoken and fearless protests addressed to King Victor Emmanuel, and signed by all the bishops of Umbria and the Marches. It is dated August 1, 1864, and is directed against the law which compelled the members of the clergy without distinction, and the clerical students in the seminaries, to serve in the army or navy the regular term imposed on laymen.

It was a vain appeal. As well might they have pleaded to the famished tiger to let go its prey and forego the opportunity of satiating its rabid hunger, as ask Victor Emmanuel, or rather the man who ruled and used him, to forego the opportunity, now that he had the power, of degrading and extinguishing the Catholic clergy, and with them the Church itself. This was precisely what the Revolution aimed at, what the kingdom of Italy, its legislature and administration, were organized for.

Surely they must do their own proper work.

None the less eloquent, courageous, and victorious is this noble remonstrance:

"Sire: With souls deeply grieved we come once more to bring before your majesty our respectful but serious complaints about the evils which are heaped unceasingly on the churches given us to govern: we are willing to hope that our voice may yet be listened to and that justice may be done. During each of the last four years we have raised our voices with increasing frequency, and have given utterance to the grief of our holy religion, afflicted and oppressed in so many ways—by the setting aside ecclesiastical immunities; by depriving her ministers of the necessary means of subsistence; by preventing all free intercourse between the Head of the Church, the pastors, and the people; by withdrawing from all dependence on the bishops both schools and institutions of piety which these same bishops had themselves founded, or which had been placed under their care and government by the pious founders; by profaning, or even destroying, the sacred temples; by expelling from their homes the Religious Orders, and by so many other acts which it would be too long and too sad to enumerate.

"The fact that no heed whatever was paid to our complaints would have induced us to remain silent, contenting ourselves henceforward with lamenting and praying. But a new wrong which is about to be committed against the Church compels us to have recourse to your majesty and to unite our voice to that of our flocks.

"Very limited as is at the present moment the number of young clerical students who may, at the request of their bishops, be exempted from military conscription, nevertheless by a new law it is proposed to annul all these exemptions—a measure which would go very near to extinguish altogether the priestly ministry. They allege, to excuse this law, the singular pretext that all citizens are equally obliged to support the burdens of the state, no matter how these may happen to be felt. But without desiring to recall to mind here how little this reason availed to save the clergy in other cases where they were made the subject of injurious and odious exceptions, we must press upon your consideration that the choice of her ministers was not imposed upon the Church by any human law, but that it is a sacred right which comes to her from her Divine Founder. Wherefore, instead of suppressing such right, it should in no wise be either restricted or diminished. ...

"... If the holy ministry could be abolished the Church would be destroyed; and this was exactly what Julian the Apostate vainly attempted to accomplish by commanding that all the subjects of the Empire, without any distinction whatever, should be compelled to bear arms. ... This tyrannical law was soon repealed by Valentinian, who, like the great Constantine, recognized the right of the Church to choose freely her own ministers. ...

"We shall not stop here to recall to your mind, sire, what long and important studies are necessary, besides the qualities of the heart, to enable young ecclesiastics to be thoroughly prepared for their most important functions—studies which usually have to be made at the very age when young men are called away by the conscription law. Hence it is that it would be almost impossible for a young man, even if he should during his long term of military service keep his soul pure, and not lose amid so many obstacles and seductions the spirit of his vocation, to afterwards undergo a long training in order to enter the sanctuary. ... The life of a cleric is incompatible with that of the soldier.

"... Statesmen are solicitous that a single family should not become extinct in the state; will there, then, be no care taken that the hierarchy of the Church shall be maintained, supremely and vitally important as its existence is to the entire Christian family? ..."

"... Whether it come from the pursuit of temporal interests, or from bad education, or from the little respect paid in our day to the priestly character, the greater number of candidates for the ministry come, in our times, from poor families; and they have only the means to persevere in and follow out their vocation given them by their bishops to return to the seminary. And these means are so restricted that we often see, with a real pain to our fatherly heart, young men very dear to us taken away from the seminary in the very midst of their course. ... We are only allowed to purchase the exemption of one student for every twenty thousand inhabitants; and so these young men are forced into a profession entirely opposed to their character and wishes. In the grief of our souls we could not persuade ourselves that, with all we hear about individual liberty, such liberty should not be allowed in the most serious affair with which man has to deal in this life—the choice of his own profession, and the full liberty to consecrate himself to God."

The Cardinal pushes aside the vulgar objections drawn from "a too great abundance of priests, far above the spiritual needs of the people." That reason does not hold at present. "Where, not many years ago, there were many assistant priests, now the rector is left alone to face the manifold duties of his office. Besides, vocations are injuriously influenced by the spirit of the age, by irreligious maxims, the corruption of morals, the anti-Christian education given to youth. ... Then there is the taking away from the clergy of their means of honorable subsistence, the attraction toward lucrative secular avocations, the outrageous persecution of the priesthood by falsehoods, calumnies, ridicule, sarcasm, insults offered in the house of God itself, by lawsuits, fines, imprisonment, all inflicted even on persons occupying the highest stations in the Church.

"For all these reasons, if at all times it was an act of virtue and self-denial to consecrate one's self to the service of the altar and to embrace the clerical profession, it is a thousand times more so in our day. ...

"Sire, the supreme good of a nation is its morality, and this only comes from religion and from the salutary influence of its ministers. What would an army have to defend in a people without faith, without morals, in a people sunk in corruption? If you take away Christian instruction, the preaching of the

Gospel, the frequentation of the sacraments, the worship and fear of God, can the fear of armed men keep the multitude faithful to their duties? And in the army itself will not morality be the result of that created in the nation by the influence of religion?

"We beseech you, sire, to consider well to what depths of corruption a community would descend if, on the one hand, all the restraints of good morals were relaxed, and, on the other, all the avenues to evil were thrown wide open! It is a sad avowal that we are compelled to make, and that from the evidence of facts. A libertine press no longer spares any holy person or holy thing; the theatrical amusements are full of impiety and obscenity; infamous resorts are opened to enable the sinner to sin safely; blasphemers assail with impunity God, the Virgin Mother, the Saints—nothing restrains the sacrilegious tongue; the sacred images are insulted; crosses are torn down; churches, even such as are consecrated, are turned into market-houses or are pulled down; the ministers of God are persecuted even in the church itself, even in the very functions of their ministry which regard the conscience. And now, as if all this were little or nothing, is the sacred ministry itself to be abolished? Our mind is confounded and our heart is torn with grief when we think that, besides all the calamities that we here indicate rapidly, the priesthood itself shall fail, and with it all remedy, all comfort.

"What will become of the Christian people when they are deprived of the necessary teachers of childhood, of the men who comfort the widow and the orphan, of those who soften the pains and labors of the present life by the thought and hope of the life to come, who wipe away the tears of the afflicted, who direct the doubting and hesitating by words of good counsel, and cheer the last hours of the dying?

"And if our own people lack priests for their need, where shall we find those generous ministers of God who, breaking the dearest ties of the human soul here below, go forth among savage peoples to preach the Gospel, and to plant there the seeds of civilization with the truths of Christian faith?

"We are not exaggerating, sire: such would be the results of this unblessed law, of which it would be impossible to predicate whether it is more hurtful to the Church or to the state itself.

"After this, it is not surprising that no civilized nation in Europe, even the most warlike and in the time when they most needed soldiers, ever thought of enacting such laws. And will it be Italy, Catholic Italy, which will give the world so unhappy an example?...

"For pity's sake put, once for all, a stop to all these laws which succeed each other, tread upon each other, and are heaped up one on the other, all injuring the Church—an injury which invariably redounds as well to the injury of the state."[4]

---

[4] "Scelta degli Atti," pp. 373-80, Aug. 1, 1864.

CHAPTER XIII

THE BENEFACTOR OF PERUGIA; SOWING AND PLANTING BEFORE THE STORM AND THE EARTHQUAKE; A BIRD'S-EYE VIEW OF THE FIELD

EVEN in the political and in the material orders Archbishop Pecci's enlightened and active charity found means and opportunities of benefiting Perugia and her citizens, as well as his entire diocese. In the very beginning of his episcopal administration—in the autumn of 1846—the same unquiet spirit which was already playing the tyrant in Rome stirred up a riot in Perugia. The excited crowds were attempting to break open the prisons and to liberate, together with all persons detained there for political of fences, all the criminals of the country. Already they had taken up arms to resist the Pontifical troops, and the city was threatened with bloodshed and arson, when the Archbishop appeared upon the scene, interposed his pacific authority between the combatants, and put an end to the conflict.

Worse calamities threatened Umbria and its capital in 1849, when, after the taking of Rome by the French troops, the bands of Garibaldi, under the command of the notorious Arcioni and Forbes, committed all kinds of outrages around Perugia and in the city itself. No priestly influence could soften the fanatical ferocity of these brigands, whom English and American anti-papal prejudice has exalted into heroes, whereas they were only lawless free-booters delighting especially in sacrilege and in insulting, persecuting, and massacring (whenever they could) defenceless and harmless priests and monks.

When the Austrians under Prince Von Lichtenstein advanced to repel these bands and to protect the Pontifical provinces from their raids, Monsignor Pecci, who knew the temper of his people well and their rooted dislike to these foreigners, deemed it vital to the peace of Perugia to prevent the city from being occupied by them. He therefore went to meet the Austrian general, and his wise counsels once more prevailed and saved his people from new calamities.

In 1854—made remarkable in Perugia by the celebration in February of Monsignor Pecci's elevation to the Cardinalate—the whole of Central Italy suffered severely from dearth, amounting almost to a famine. To this were added earthquakes, filling the people with terror, as if the divine anger were about to let loose all its plagues against an ungrateful and guilty country.

Cardinal Pecci's fatherly forethought had already suggested the establishment of Monti Frumentari, or "Deposits of Grain," in every country parish, which would, in seasons of scarcity, render the poor country-folk the same services which the Monti di Pieta, or Popular Loan Banks, so long known and so heartily appreciated in Italy, had ever rendered to the laboring classes.

When, in the beginning of 1854, the scarcity began to be most distressing, and the bread, which is the staple of food for the masses of the Italian population, was either at famine prices or could not be obtained at all, the Cardinal showed both his unbounded charity and his wonderful executive skill.

He gave the example to the rich and to Religious Communities by opening in the episcopal residence itself a free kitchen for the poor, with daily doles of unprepared food. The son of Countess Anna Pecci was mindful of the examples of the mother on whose tombstone it is inscribed that she was "the feeder of the needy."[1] Nourishing, substantial soups and broths were every morning dealt out to the needy as long as the distress lasted. It seemed to cost the good Archbishop no effort to deprive himself of all but the strict necessaries to himself and his household when Christ's poor were suffering—so few were his own personal wants, so frugal and

---

[1] *Altrix pauperum.*

self-denying the life which, in truth, resembled, that of an Eastern ascetic.

But he also made his clergy and all the wealthy members of his flock his zealous co-operators at this season. The revolutionary societies always found in the periodical returns of scarcity a ready argument against the Pontifical government: the scarcity and the consequent popular distress, they said (and they were believed), were caused by the authorities, who bought up and hoarded the grain and speculated upon it, unmindful of the starving people.

Cardinal Pecci thought that the best answer to this was to take counsel with the provincial government and the municipal magistrates in providing food for the really needy, in getting profitable labor, sufficient wages, and cheap provisions for all who were able to work.

On January 7, 1854, he published a short and eloquent pastoral letter, appealing to his people to exert themselves in the reigning distress as true Christians, and organizing a "Commission of Charity" under his own personal direction, the membership of which embraced clergy and laity, extending its branches all over the diocese, and effectually meeting all the needs of the population.

The motives suggested in his urgent appeal to his diocesans, and the active measures which he prescribed in the: rules of this Commission of Charity, are alike admirable,, showing how little the Cardinal wished to encourage mendicancy or idleness, and how anxious he was to stimulate all able-bodied persons to work by finding remunerative labor for them in their distress, and preventing little traders from speculating on it.

"To give to the poor," he says, "from out our superabundance is a duty imposed by the Divine Master on all Christians, without exception of times or persons. But to help them with something more than what is superfluous,, by limiting our desires and what we make use of to live upon, when it is required by their extraordinary necessities, that we should do so; to help them so because they bear the image of our Heavenly Father and their condition touches our brotherly hearts as if it were our own; to aim, in fact, at enabling them to bless God's fatherly providence in their distress, because it is His hand which is reached out to them in ours, ... this is what shows in its proper light the greatness and helpfulness of Christian beneficence."

On February 25, 1854, immediately after the festivities on the occasion of his promotion, he urged the active prosecution of this noble charity on his parochial clergy by a circular letter, in which he warmly pleaded the cause of the distressed, and laid down the most practical rules for making the Commission of Charity a success everywhere. He again presses them to establish the *Monti Frumentari* in their respective localities.[2]

"Our zeal and charity," he writes, "which should be the soul of our pastoral mission, can neither be inoperative nor indifferent in presence of the manifold miseries which now afflict our flock, and which come this year from the failure of the harvests and the scarcity of provisions. If our Lord, after having been so long irritated, and having so long waited patiently and in vain that we should amend our lives and correct our evil conduct, has at length lifted the scourge over our heads, ... our people should not therefore be left without the comfort and help of religion. ...

"Explain to your people what are the real causes of the present distress. ... Take away from the minds of the fearful or the unwary the exaggerated and deceptive illusions which the evil-minded propagate, that their sufferings come from the selfish schemes of speculators or the negligence of the government."[3]

During the troublous times of 1859 and 1860 Cardinal Pecci had abundant opportunity for "giving other proofs of his pastoral and patriotic charity toward his flock. He employed the warmest and most fatherly exhortations to dissuade the

---

[2] "Scelta," p. 506.

[3] *Ibid.* p. 508.

leaders of the insurrection from the acts which led to the fatal conflict of June 20, 1859, which was afterward painted as the 'Massacre of Perugia.' But the gentle voice of the Archbishop, unhappily, was not listened to, and was overborne by the secret impulsion given to the insurgents by the prime movers in the rising. Saddened by his ineffectual attempts to prevent the bloody scenes which followed, he bestowed all his kindest efforts on assuaging the bitter suffering which followed. He succeeded in obtaining pardon for the guilty subjects of the Pope, as well as compensation to all those whose property had been injured."[4]

At length came the invasion of 1860.

We prefer to give what followed in the words of our manuscript authority:

"The Swiss garrison, attacked unexpectedly by the Piedmontese in the early morning, after having several times endeavored to repel the assailants, were overborne by numbers and took refuge in the Pauline Fort. There they entered into negotiations for a suspension of arms. While these were going on, and under the pretext that bands of Pontifical troops had found a retreat there, the episcopal residence, that of the canons, and the seminary were taken possession of by the military, who broke open gates and doors with their axes. Meanwhile the bulk of the [Piedmontese] army, with a formidable artillery, which was even posted in the porch of the cathedral, was preparing to bombard and assault the fort, which [by replying to this fire] would have filled the city with ruin and death.

"Thereupon the Cardinal-Archbishop, with the gonfaloniere [mayor], asked to see the general-in-chief, Fanti, who was the Piedmontese Minister of War, with the intention

---

[4] MS. It was a misfortune that in putting down the insurrection in Perugia they did not employ the French contingent which then garrisoned Rome, instead of the Swiss troops in the Pontifical service. It was a part of Napoleon's policy to make it appear that the Pope employed his foreign mercenaries to massacre his Italian subjects; whereas if the French army had been employed no one would ever have heard of the "Massacre of Perugia."

of beseeching him not to carry out his design. His pastoral solicitude only met with a rude repulse, for the bombardment and the assault began with great vigor at the expiration of the brief truce. Still, the Cardinal's interposition had no little influence in preventing the assailants from taking offensive measures against the citizens; it prevented also the effusion of blood, and helped to obtain more favorable conditions for the besieged.

"Deeply pained as Cardinal Pecci had been by the dreadful scenes of the 14th of September, he had another cause of anguish on the morrow in the unhappy fate of Don Baldassare Santi, one of the city rectors. This excellent man was falsely accused of having borne arms in repulsing the Piedmontese, and had been condemned to death by a court-martial during the night. The Cardinal heard of the sentence early in the morning of the 15th, and lost not an instant in seeking the general in command, De Sonnaz, and asking for a more careful and formal investigation of the charge, for a revision of the acts of the court-martial, and a suspension of the hasty death-sentence. The accused had in his favor a well-known reputation for virtue and other presumptions of innocence.

"But even in this second act of intervention the Cardinal was grieved to see his mediation rejected and all the efforts of his fatherly charity fail in their purpose.

"From that day dated for him the beginning of a long series of bitter trials and vexations arising from the establishment of a new dictatorial power ruling all Umbria, and from the sudden transformation and overturning of all ecclesiastical institutions."[5]

So the battle with the Revolution had begun in earnest.

But before describing in other chapters the chief incidents of this momentous struggle we may continue to take a rapid survey of what this good shepherd did for his flock.

No sooner was all Umbria in possession of the Piedmontese than Perugia was filled by swarms of political Italian exiles

---

[5] MS.

who had found a refuge in Piedmont. They had long lived in poverty and were hungry for the spoils of the Pontifical government and its adherents. These men were all supported at the public expense—that is, the expense of the conquered provinces and peoples. Of course those among them who were natives of these provinces had more than one sort of accounts to settle with their fellow-countrymen. The numbers of these famished place-hunters were further increased by the members of the former volunteer bands of various descriptions who had fought under Garibaldi and his lieutenants, had followed the Piedmontese army of invasion, and had been "living on the country."

"One may imagine how the coming together in Perugia of all these elements contributed to put an end to good order, to ruin public morality, and, above all, to destroy all respect for religion and the priesthood. All of a sudden they proclaimed all the subversive laws enacted in Piedmont, and with them was issued, on October 31, 1860, a commissarial decree imposing on all Umbria the institution of civil marriage, with penalties which affected also parish priests, who were at the same time compelled to surrender the sacramental registers.

"Then it happened that, while abundant favors were bestowed on bad and renegade priests, who had also come back from banishment, the good priests, on the contrary, and such as had ever been faithful to their duty, were continually threatened and placed under surveillance; they were made a butt for slander, for malignant denunciations; they were indicted, arrested, interned, imprisoned, and banished the country.

"Not even the Cardinal-Archbishop of Perugia was saved from this species of persecution. In 1862 he was sued in the courts of justice for having opposed the established institutions, because he had officially admonished some of his priests who had subscribed an address to the notorious Padre Passaglia. But he not only came triumphantly out of this suit, but with a vigorous and judicious zeal he defended the interests of religion, and gave a wise direction to the conduct of his clergy amid the perilous circumstances of the times.

"A long series of episcopal acts and remonstrances "which passed between the Cardinal and the functionaries of the new government from 1860 to 1878 bear an illustrious testimony to the truth of what has just been said. Many of these acts are now in print, and several of them bear the signatures of all the bishops of Umbria.[6]

"Besides this he displayed the most efficient zeal in pleading before the new men in power the innocence of his parish priests, wrongfully persecuted and imprisoned, as well as to save from measures of violence and instantaneous expulsion religious communities, among which were Dominicans, Barnabites, Camaldolese Hermits, Missionaries, Oratorians. He acted in the same way to save cloistered communities of nuns from expulsion and concentration (in one house), to prevent the closing and profanation of churches and the opening of heterodox temples.

"On all these occasions the tone of his correspondence with the civil authorities was uniformly dignified and moderate, while being also full of vigor and convincing, such as to compel the respect of these officials, and to prevent measures of greater harshness and destructiveness from being

---

6 In the collection entitled "L'Episcopato e la Rivoluzione in Italia, Atti Collettivi dei Vescovi Italiani," Mondovi, 1867, two vols., are printed the following acts of the Umbrian hierarchy:
1864. Against the "Conscription of Ecclesiastics"; against "the Interference of the Government in Ecclesiastical Seminaries"; against the "Decree subjecting the Nomination of Spiritual Administrators and Parochial Vicars to the royal *placet.*"
1865. Against the projected law abolishing Religious Orders and sequestrating ecclesiastical property.
In the "Scelta di Atti Episcopali del Card. Gioacchino Pecci" are found *nine* Collective Acts signed by him and other bishops, and *nine* official remonstrances addressed to the Royal Commissioner for Umbria, to King Victor Emmanuel, to the President of the Council of Ministers, to the Prefect of Umbria, all directed to the defence of the religious interests threatened by the Piedmontese reforms (?).
Note of the MS.

enacted against his diocese.

"Such was also the character of the many sensible and practical instructions addressed to his clergy in the most difficult conjunctures, especially on the confiscation of the parochial records, on civil marriage, on the abolition of tithes, on the suppression of the ecclesiastical courts, on the national feast, as well as on the enclosure of nuns, on the compilation of inventories, and on the order of public worship in the churches after the dispersion of the regulars."[7]

We have allowed one who was intimately acquainted with all the circumstances he relates, and who himself took a part in the events and labors enumerated, to present the above cursory narrative. It is like a voice, an authorized voice, calm and conscientious, from Perugia, sketching out for us the outlines of a busy life. On some of the acts which he merely points to we shall have to dwell at greater length on account of their intrinsic importance and lasting interest.

But, although surveying thus rapidly the events which followed each other in Perugia and Umbria from 1846 to the invasion of the Pontifical dominions by Piedmont and the firm establishment of the Revolutionary sway in Central and Southern Italy, we have only glanced at a portion of what Cardinal Pecci undertook and accomplished for his people.

In speaking of education we have only mentioned in detail what concerned his seminarians and his priests. He was, from the beginning of his episcopate, no less zealous for lay instruction. Pius IX, who appreciated his learning as well as his zeal and fitness to promote it, appointed him Apostolic Visitor of the University of Perugia. With his wonted intelligence and zeal, that restless energy which pauses not till it has overcome every obstacle in the path of a great design, and which Americans call "push," the new Archbishop Bishop went about doing for the university what he was doing for his own seminary—he remodelled and reorganized it, called to its faculties the best talent he could obtain, reformed, elevated,

---

[7] MS.

completed the whole programme of professional and scientific studies, and endeavored in every way to make of this ancient seat of learning what it had been in mediaeval times when it rivalled Bologna and Pavia. He rendered similar services to the Collegio Pio della Sapienza, of which he was also appointed Visitor, and to the College of Todi, which he soon placed on such a footing that the best families of Umbria and the Marches sent their sons there to be educated.

Female education was no less indebted to his zeal and enlightened liberality. While enlarging and improving his Seminary and reorganizing the University of Perugia he was also carrying out another design for the better education not only of the daughters of the noble and burgess classes, but of those of the laboring masses as well. The Conservatorio Pio, which became under Monsignor Pecci a great high school for female education, had its first origin in 1816, when, at the petition of the then Bishop of Perugia and the municipal authorities, Pius VII appropriated to the establishment of an elementary free school for girls, as well as an academy for the daughters of the better classes, the patrimony of two monasteries suppressed by the former French government in Italy. The institution was placed by the Pope under the care of a board of four directors.

The free day-school for little girls was opened in 1819; the want of necessary means prevented the establishment of the superior school till 1846, when Monsignor Pecci was appointed Archbishop of Perugia. He, with his wonted determination, resolved that the original design should be carried out. Writing to King Victor Emmanuel in November, 1861, when the government had laid its hand on the beautiful and flourishing institution, Cardinal Pecci relates how it had its second birth:

"Poverty, the want of a proper site, and other obstacles had for a long time frustrated the desires of the public, when the Holy See sent me to Perugia. The whole city knows how, within the space of a few months, we succeeded in making a beginning, having obtained perfect unity of purpose and brushed aside all delays. We saw in a short time a vast and remarkable edifice built up from the foundations in the most lovely and happy site, and of a style and .beauty of form that can compare well with any similar provincial establishment. Assisted by the unanimous and unwearied co-operation of the four directors, and by the encouragement given by the reigning Pontiff (who took it under his special protection), I had the satisfaction, in 1857, to see the wishes of the public realized, and to give to the country this new school, so long desired and so useful. Some Sisters of the Sacred Heart were called to take charge of the interior discipline and the instruction of the pupils." The Cardinal placed the house under the patronage of St. Ann, doubtless in remembrance of his mother. The Ladies of the Sacred Heart are obliged by their rules to have a poor school attached to their establishments whenever that is practicable. Their wishes were fulfilled here, for the Cardinal had opened a large and spacious day-school for little girls of the laboring classes, so that their devoted mistresses could satisfy all the yearnings of their hearts in rearing to all goodness and useful knowledge the children of every class in the city.

But the equally devoted Pastor would have every child of his flock receive the boon of a truly Christian education. The daughters of the poor in every land are exposed to peculiar dangers; and Cardinal Pecci knew well that in the Italy of his day every one of the little girls who went forth daily, in town and country, from the poor man's hovel, needed special care and special grace to become in due time a true Christian woman, the mother of true Christian men. Such he would have all these poor little ones of his flock. For their education and reception he founded the Conservatorio Graziani, a protectory school worthy of any city. He next founded a Magdalen Asylum, a no less noble charity. Both of these houses he placed under the Belgian Sisters of Providence, whom he sent for to Champion, in the province of Namur. Other protectory schools already in existence received a new impulse and arose to new life under the touch of his pastoral zeal. He had the gift of making every establishment he took in hand a financial as well as an educational success.

The same all-embracing charity which protected the innocent and lifted up the fallen soon provided the Antinori Foundling Asylum, which he placed under the care of the Sisterhood of the Stigmata of St. Francis, as well as the Donnini Hospice for incurable and chronic diseases.

He did not forget night-schools for children who had to work all day, especially for young artisans. He would have these receive all the instruction necessary to become really superior in their respective crafts.

We have already mentioned the pleasure gardens of St. Philip Neri, under the care of the Oratorians, who had also the co-operation of the young clergy. There, on Sundays and holydays, boys and youths found delightful recreation, facilities for attending divine worship, Christian instruction, safe and agreeable companionship, and protection from the many snares laid in the world outside for unsuspecting youth.

So that no sex or age or class, or pressing need of mind, of heart, of soul or body, was left uncared for, unprovided for by this good shepherd of Christ's flock.

No, not even the industrial and commercial wants of the struggling, laborious, and thrifty classes. Cardinal Pecci founded, revived, improved, or developed the *Monti di Pieta*, the poor man's blessed resource in the Catholic Italy that was, where for the money loaned to those who wished to rise from poverty to independence, or to increase their thrift, no interest, or nothing approaching to modern interest for money, was ever asked.

It was he who inspired the Perugians to found their savings-bank, furnishing himself a good part of the capital.

One of the chief duties of a bishop is to visit regularly, at brief intervals, every portion of his diocese, examining personally everything that pertains to the interests of religion, the instruction of the flock, the condition of public worship, the state of public morality, and the prosperity of parochial institutions of every kind. The bishop goes as the chief pastor, to see to it that his subordinates perform their duty, to listen to the complaints of the people, to correct abuses, reprove indiscipline, and uproot all scandals. It is an arduous task, but one most necessary to be undertaken and performed in the right spirit.

Monsignor Pecci was too anxious to ascertain for himself what was to be done for the good of souls, and the advancement of religion in every corner of his diocese, not to set about visiting it soon after taking possession of his see. And he renewed these visits with the most scrupulous punctuality every fourth year during his long stay in Perugia. Nor was his visitation a hasty, perfunctory, and superficial one. It was the work of a man who believed, and acted on the belief, that he had to answer on his own soul for the soul of every single human creature confided to his care.

On thus visiting in succession each parish a bishop ascertains whether the word of God is duly explained to the people from the pulpit, or whether their children are carefully instructed in the Christian doctrine. It is certain that Monsignor Pecci took every precaution to have these indispensable duties of the pastorate performed by his priests.

We have omitted to mention one of his own favorite and beneficent reforms.

He had in his diocese an orphanage for boys which sadly needed improvement. He at once resolved, while making it an asylum for these waifs of his flock, to make of it an industrial school as well as a loved home for these little ones. He had seen, during his stay in Belgium, the Brothers of Mercy at work and effecting some such wonders as the Irish Christian Brothers at the orphanage of Glasnevin, near Dublin, and at the great industrial school of Artane. A colony of the Brothers of Mercy was, therefore, called from Belgium and placed in charge of the orphanage of Perugia, which soon became a beehive filled with happy and healthful toilers.

The same wise and provident methods were adopted for these boys which worked so admirably in the case of the orphan girls of the Graziani Protectorate; it was the Cardinal's aim to make of these orphans of both sexes, when they had to leave their temporary homes, children so well reared and grounded in Christian principle that they should remain ever after true to God, and children so industriously trained that they were prepared to be self-supporting and most useful members of society.

For both the one institution and the other, when they sent forth their charges to begin life in earnest, other pious organizations were ready to give a helping hand and find the children safe and lucrative employment.

We have seen how zealous he was to build up in men's souls the spiritual temples of the Most High God; he was no less zealous and liberal in building, repairing, beautifying the material house of God.

Of course, in a city where the traditions of high art are so constantly cherished as in the capital of Umbria, the cathedral church, the creation of the mediaeval city in the days when liberty and religion walked hand-in-hand, was the object of the Archbishop's loving care. The Perugians had been so proud of the beautiful structure, their Duomo, their house of God! The misfortunes of more than half a century had left their mark on both interior and exterior; the wanton vandalism of impiety and the forced neglect of an impoverished people left not a little to be done. When Archbishop Pecci had attended to the most pressing needs of his diocese, he ordered, in 1849, the laying of a new marble pavement in the Duomo; and later, when he felt sure that he had conscientiously provided for the other wants of his people, he began to restore now one part of the cathedral, and now another, spending on these repairs some twenty thousand crowns. One of his last cares in this respect, before leaving Perugia for ever, was to have the chapel of Sant' Onofrio adorned with frescoes.

In an age, too, when conspicuous writers both in France and Germany labored to destroy in the Christian mind all belief in the supernatural by making of Christ Himself a mere man, Monsignor Pecci encouraged among his people the most fervent devotion to her whom they and their fathers before them had reverenced as the Mother of God. He built, at the very gates of Perugia, the church of Our Lady of Mercy,[8] a favorite resort of pilgrims in these times of doubt and dread. He began with what was most needful, by building churches where there were none, and supplying them with zealous priests. In doing the work of God he always thought and said that the workman should trust in a great measure to God for the means. His trust never failed to be rewarded. During his administration no less than thirty six church edifices were built from the foundations, and six already in course of construction were completed. Those enlarged, repaired, and beautified are in far greater number. "The example of the Archbishop's generosity," says our manuscript guide, "stimulated the faithful to imitate him in the measure of their own ability. Thus for the church of San Martino in Campo more than twelve thousand crowns were spent; for the great church of Castiglione del Lago more than twenty-five thousand;[9] and so on for many others which it were too long to mention here, but which will be mentioned by the chroniclers of that fortunate period during which Perugia had for pastor and father Joachim Pecci."

Elsewhere we have mentioned with what perfect order, piety, and splendor divine worship was celebrated there, so that strangers who came to admire in Perugia the remains of

---

[8] Note in the MS. "To him it is due that we see near Perugia the sanctuary of Ponte della Pietra in honor of Our Lady of Mercy. Her picture had long hung in a poor niche near a torrent, and had moved the popular veneration by several extraordinary favors bestowed on poor people in their need through the intercession of Christ's Blessed Mother. The pious generosity of the faithful induced the bishop to begin the present beautiful temple, which became the center of a new parish." This recalls the piety shown by Joachim Pecci at Carpineto toward another sanctuary of the Madonna.

[9] When the reader, crossing the Vale of Chiana from below Cortona to Chiusi, comes upon the borders of Lake Thrasymene, he will see, in autumn, from amid the brown foliage of the groves of oak, the snow-white cupola and classic outlines of the Duomo of Castiglione projected, like a fairy vision, on the intensely blue waters of the lake. This is the beautiful church mentioned above.

the mediaeval architecture and the masterpieces of painting which the school of Umbria had accumulated there, remained to witness the "beauty of holiness" in the service of the altar. Cardinal Pecci took especial pains to regulate and cultivate the sacred music which Pergolese had made so entrancing, as well as the sublime Gregorian chant, so well adapted to Catholic worship and congregational singing. He loved all the arts, and, born in the sanctuary as they were, he made them minister to the grandeur and glory of the God of the Temple.

What he did for his cathedral he also did for all the churches of his diocese. He insisted that everything in the celebration of the divine office should be worthy of God, in harmony with the reality of Catholic belief, and such as to instruct, strengthen, and edify his people.

Intensely devoted as he was to all that could advance the interests of his people, temporal as well as spiritual, he wished that every institution of beneficence, like every educational establishment, should yield to the utmost the advantages for which they had been founded. Not the least of his many great qualities was his clear and practical judgment in all business matters. Where the most experienced sometimes were puzzled to find their way out of financial difficulties, his instinct enabled him to perceive at once a solution.

This was very apparent on many important occasions. "He was well aware that the great hospital of Santa Maria della Misericordia owed its birth to the pastoral zeal of the Bulgarian Bishop Montemelini, who had given it canonical existence by his decree of 1305, and built it with the co-operation of pious citizens of Perugia, lay as well as clerical. Cardinal Pecci thought it his duty to offer this institution his help, reaffirming thereby the tight of the bishop to interfere in the good government of an establishment of public charity of such importance. In this way, and by employing the most discreet prudence, he revived the visiting authority of the bishop with regard to several confraternities which believed themselves exempt from all ordinary episcopal superintendence. This exemption was declared in every way unfounded by a decree of the Sacred Congregation of the Council on August 26, 1854. He thereupon wisely established the 'Tutelary Congregation of Holy Places,' composed of the ablest and most experienced clergymen and laymen, who rendered him the greatest assistance in governing and protecting the interests of all pious foundations and establishments. He issued rules for keeping their accounts, and a general law regulating all pious associations and confraternities in his diocese. This reform did so much good that the bishops of even remote parts of Italy hastened to imitate it in their respective dioceses."[10]

Thus labored he while the field he cultivated was still under his control. But the enemy was nigh and watchful; and the harvest so lovingly and hopefully prepared was destined to be trodden under foot and ravaged by the flame of hostile fires.

Assuredly, in placing Joachim Pecci in the see of Perugia, Gregory XVI felt sure that he was not hiding this great light beneath a bushel.

---

[10] MS.

CHAPTER XIV

IN THE BATTLE

I. He Defends the Temporal Sovereignty of the Holy See

THE episcopate of Archbishop Pecci in Perugia, coinciding as it did with the long reign of Pius IX, fell assuredly upon evil days. The greatest calamities which befell Italy from 1846 to 1878 were not, perhaps, the assaults delivered in such quick succession against the Temporal Power of the Papacy, and battering it down in the end, as the anti-Christian and anti social principles and practices propagated in Italy by the triumphant Revolution. Monsignor Pecci was too well acquainted with the hostile intentions of some of the great European Powers, with the indifference of others, and the helplessness or selfishness of the so-called Catholic governments, not to foresee, from the day Louis Philippe was dethroned and Pius IX besieged in the Quirinal, that the Papacy could expect no effective support for the preservation of its sacred and time-honored rights from what was, in 1848, only the decayed and tottering framework of the Christendom built up by the Middle Ages.

It did not escape the notice of a statesman so well conversant with the political intrigues of the day that English public opinion, as indicated or influenced by the *Times*, the *Daily News*, and the *Standard*, was bitterly hostile to the Pope and clamorous for the downfall of his principality, while the leaders of the two great political parties[1]—Palmerston and Gladstone especially—conspired actively and openly with Piedmont for the destruction of the existing governments in

[1] Disraeli's sentiments can be gathered from his "Lothair," in which the heroes and heroine are the embodiment of Italian anti-papal fanaticism.

the Italian Peninsula, the extinction of the Temporal Power, and the unification of Italy under the sceptre of the house of Savoy. The unprincipled and shallow adventurer who succeeded in 1848-49 in confiscating to his own profit the French liberties he had sworn to protect, was, at bottom, like Carlo Alberto and his son, Victor Emmanuel, only the tool—a half-unwilling tool, it may be —of the revolutionary societies to which he had been early affiliated. Whether knowingly or unwittingly, he in fact only interfered in Italian affairs to betray the interests of the Papacy, to help despoil the Pope of his provinces, one after the other, and then to hand over Rome and its Pontiff to Piedmont, just as the Fates or the Furies who pursued him handed him and his empire over to the tender mercies of Prince Bismarck.

Monsignor Pecci was not blind to the policy which dynastic ambition or the overmastering revolutionary conspirators, marshalled under Cavour, dictated to the Savoy princes. Still less blind was he to the anti-Christian character of the now secret, now open agencies which the Piedmontese leaders employed to compass their ends. Political and social Italy was, like the wooden house, eaten through and through by the terrible termites of Mazzini and Garibaldi, and ready to collapse, one part after the other, without any serious resistance.

The Archbishop of Perugia, foreseeing the storm and calculating correctly its destructive effects, omitted no precaution, no effort, no labor to preserve the minds and hearts of his people against the evil influences of the spirit which ruled that storm. It may be instructive, at this stage of our narrative, to show how prophetic was the mind which conceived and produced the various pastoral letters published by him as Archbishop of Perugia. They forcibly remind one of the trumpet-toned instructions delivered, during a cyclone at sea, by the watchful captain of a vessel to crew and passengers. Every note of warning and command tells of the progress of the tempest, the fury of the elemental war, and the courage or dismay of the ship's Company.

One of the means employed by the revolutionary societies, both in France and in Italy, to attract the curious and unwary to their secret meetings, was magnetism, or "spiritualism," with its exciting revelations. In Great Britain and the United States the main attraction of these spiritualistic or mesmeristic gatherings was curiosity. Politics had nothing to do with them. Yet we know what mischief all this charlatanism and imposture did to religion and morality.

In France and Italy, where faith undermined was replaced by superstition and a morbid craving for preternatural knowledge, there was in these meetings not only the moral danger to the conscience, but the revolutionary passions and the hatred of the existing religious belief, which were fostered sedulously by the spirit of the place. Cardinal Pecci, in 1857, issued a pastoral instruction on "The Abuses of Magnetism." He avoided touching on the political aspects of the question, as his title indicates. He was also too well read in all that pertains to natural science to deny the existence of natural magnetic forces, of which observation has only revealed very limited effects. But religion and morality must condemn the use made of these mysterious agencies by unprincipled, irreligious, and interested persons.

Then, while in 1859-60 Cavour, following up the effect produced on the unheroic spirit of the French emperor by the Orsini bombs, got him to cross the Alps, fight the Austrians, hold up for a moment to the sceptic Neo-Guelphs the mirage-vision of an Italy confederated under the Papacy, the Frenchman, half-crazed by his own personal dangers at Magenta and the fearful havoc of Solferino, withdrew beyond the Alps, after allowing his unwarlike namesake and cousin to invade and dismember the Papal dominions and create insurrections in the adjoining States.

It was the second violation by France and the Bonapartes—in alliance, this time, with Piedmont and the Occult Force—of that peaceful and unarmed principality which Charlemagne had bestowed on him whom all in the ninth century, even the Greeks, called the Vicar of Christ, the

Teacher, Guide, and Parent of all Christians. As around the Church the formative force, the glorious Christendom of our fathers arose, they confirmed and secured to the Popes this sovereignty, to make them independent of any one power or nation in the exercise of their great spiritual office of Universal Pastors. Their freedom in this was the inalienable right of all Christian nations and peoples.

The first Napoleon seized upon Pius VII and carried him off to Fontainebleau, while declaring his States an integral part of the first "Kingdom of Italy." But this Kingdom of Italy, with the first Napoleonic empire and its emperor, soon vanished like the splendid show of a dissolving view. The third Napoleon, ere he died in exile like his uncle, and under the British flag, saw the ninth Pius, whom he had betrayed into the power of the Revolution, stripped of all his dominions and left only a shadow of freedom with the mockery of a nominal sovereignty in the Vatican. His empire, too, had gone down, suddenly, frightfully, like one of those seemingly invincible armed vessels devised by modern science, which the first blast of the tempest and the first assault of the waves overwhelm, burying the mighty ship and her crew in the depths of ocean.

The second Kingdom of Italy has its throne in the Quirinal; for how long?

Just as Cavour and Napoleon III were planning their Italian campaign, and while Garibaldi was summoned to Turin to co-operate against the Austrians, Cardinal Pecci wrote his pastoral "On the Temporal Dominion of the Popes." One would almost think, on reading over this pastoral letter now at the beginning of 1887, that he who wrote it must have been inspired by Him to whom there is neither past nor future, but one ever-present knowledge of all human events; so accurately are described as mere possibilities then, the realities of which Pius IX and his successor had to endure—the tyranny at the hands of the Piedmontese usurpation and the domination of the Italian Radicals. Our readers will find even in the brief extracts we here submit a clear and luminous explanation of the present "Roman Question," of the free exercise of the

spiritual jurisdiction of the Holy See as a thing, under present circumstances, inseparable from the Pope's absolute independence in temporals of any sovereign power whatever.

The document is dated February 12, 1860. It was written, consequently, before Garibaldi's expedition to Sicily and the Piedmontese invasion of the Marches and Umbria. After reciting the ancient errors, dating from the *third* century of our era down to the fifteenth, which denied the right of the Church or of ecclesiastical persons to possess property or exercise temporal power of any kind, Cardinal Pecci, in view of the anti-Catholic and revolutionary propaganda then so active in Italy, declares it his bounden duty to instruct his people "on the temporal dominion of the Holy See."

"To discharge before God the strict obligation I have as a bishop to watch over the dangers which threaten the souls of his flock, and not to have one day to reproach my conscience with the terrible *Woe is me, because I have held my peace*, I address myself to you, O my beloved people, with all the warmth of my heart, all the zeal of my soul, begging you, amid the present dreadful upsetting of all notions, the present fearful and fateful circumstances, to hear the voice of your pastor with your wonted docility, inspired as it is solely by that charity which compels him to prefer the salvation of your souls to all human considerations.

"It is all the more needful that I should do so that, on the one hand, people are more earnest in their endeavors to persuade you that this 'temporal dominion' has nothing whatever to do with the real interests of Catholicism; and that, on the other, there are very many persons who, either on account of their simplicity of character, or their lack of knowledge, or their weakness of intellect, do not even suspect the existence of the wicked purpose which is concealed from their eyes with such a criminal skilfulness. 'There is no question here of religion,' they say; 'we want religion to be respected. But the Pope must be satisfied with the spiritual government of souls; he has no need of a temporal sovereignty. Temporal power turns away the mind to worldly cares; it is injurious to the Church, opposed to the Gospel, and unlawful'—with many other silly assertions of this kind, of which it is hard to say whether they are more insulting than hypocritical."

Such is the opening of this address. The Catholic world has long known the admirable publications of Bishop Dupanloup on the Roman question and the temporalities of the Holy See. The French language and the perfect literary forms of modern French controversial composition, which the great Orleans prelate used to such good purpose, have familiarized us all with his polemical writings. But Cardinal Pecci's pastorals, written in his native Italian, were but little known outside of the Peninsula. This was much to be regretted. For they are scarcely less racy and vigorous in style than those of the French apologist of the Papacy, and they are more solid in their doctrine.

"Let us omit to dwell," the Cardinal continues, "on the new ground on which it is proposed to strip every proprietor of all that he does not strictly need for his sustenance. What a farce it would be to say to him that by so doing the despoilers were relieving him of the trouble of taking care of his superfluous goods! Let us say nothing of the August right, consecrated by eleven centuries of possession, of the most ancient and venerated of European monarchies: if such rights are not sufficient to insure respect, then there is no kingdom, no empire, in Europe which may hot be destroyed.

"Let us say nothing of the open robbery of these possessions which the piety of the faithful and of sovereigns bestowed on the Roman Pontiff and on the Catholic body; let us pass by in silence the victory of the Revolution over the most sacred and venerable authority which was the corner-stone of European society, as well as the sad state of abasement to which it is proposed to reduce the Common Father of the faithful, the Supreme Pontiff of the Catholic Church.

"Let us pass over in silence the nefarious work of destroying that temporal principality which has been at all times the August school of the sciences and fine arts, the well-spring of civilization and wisdom for all nations, the glory of Italy by that moral primacy which it secures to her, and which is all the more noble as spirit is superior to matter; this bulwark which protected Europe from the waves of Eastern barbarism; this power which, by restoring the ruins of ancient greatness, founded the Christian Rome; this throne before which the most powerful monarchs have bent low their heads in reverent obeisance, to which from all the courts of Europe, and from Japan at the extremity of the East, have come solemn embassies proffering homage and respect.

"Let us, I say, omit all that, and all else that might be said of a design which contemplates the committing of an accumulation of crimes; let us limit ourselves to the consideration of the close connection which the spoliation of the Papal temporal power has with the interests

of Catholic doctrine, with the mischievous results sure to follow for the Catholic religion."

There are no captious statements, no suppression of the truth, no exaggeration of the rights and claims of the Papacy.

"It is false," the Cardinal says with a manly indignation, "that any Catholic holds the temporal dominion to be a dogma of his faith; such an assertion can only have come from the ignorance or the wickedness of the enemies of the Church. But it is most true, and must be evident to any intelligent mind, that there is a very close connection between this temporal power and the spiritual primacy, whether we consider the latter in the very conception of its nature or in its necessary exercise."

Then follows a clear and rapid exposition of the Catholic doctrine on the divine institution of the Supreme Pastorate in the Church, and of the end for which this supreme teaching and governing power in spirituals was made a concrete, living, and immortal organism on earth.

This "divine principle of holiness and truth," incarnate in a manner in the Roman Pontiff, cannot be the subject of any human power. For it is this living, ruling principle which "maintains in their unity and integrity the Church and religion. Besides, can it be intelligible that the living interpreter of the divine law and will should be placed under the jurisdiction of the civil authority, which itself derives all its own strength and authority from the same divine will and law? ..."

"The Church is the Kingdom of Christ; ... can the head of this kingdom, without unreason, become the subject of a mere earthly potentate? ..." The Church has for its function to direct humanity toward its supernatural destiny, its last end; the civil power is only charged with providing and securing the immediate purpose of the present life—peace, security, order, plenty. Is it in accordance with the dictates of reason that what is final should be made subordinate to what is intermediary—that the end should be made to accord with the means, not the means with the end? "It is a truth attested by faith, by reason, by our own experience, that the happiness of the present life, over which preside the kings of the earth, ... is only a means for procuring the life eternal. ... For procuring the sure attainment of this life eternal watches evermore this High-Priest, who hath received from Christ the mission of guiding humanity toward the everlasting felicity. ... See, then, what upsetting of ideas it would be to make of this High-Priest of the Catholic Church, the Roman Pontiff, the subject of any earthly power."

This is a most admirable sketch of the development of the temporal power of the Papacy. Christ wished to make the world understand that the foundation and propagation of His Church was not the work of any human power. Hence in the early ages "the Popes had not the independence of sovereignty, but that of martyrdom only. ... During the first centuries they were in fact the subjects of lay sovereigns; but we cannot conceive a single instant during which this state of subjection was imposed on them by right. The supreme spiritual power of the Pontificate bore within itself from its very birth the germ of its temporal power. With the spontaneous development of the former, the latter also continued to develop itself in space and time, in accordance with the external conditions amid which it grew. ...

"We see in history how the ample donations, the vast possessions, and the acts of civil jurisdiction exercised by the Roman Pontiffs are things which are traced back so far as to bring us to the first centuries of our era. In no other way can we explain the extraordinary phenomenon of a power which came to be placed in their hands without their knowing it, against their will even, as the celebrated Count de Maistre expresses and proves it.[2] Wherefore those who would have the Pope stripped of his civil principality would like to see the Church brought back to her infant condition, to the first stage of her existence. And this they would have done without considering that, in their conception, the ordinary condition corresponding to the nature of Christianity is that first initial stage which developed into that grandeur fore-ordained by Providence, who from out the Catacombs and the prisons led the Popes through the bloody path of martyrdom to the throne of the persecuting Caesars."

Passing from a right conception of the spiritual primacy of the Popes to its free and full exercise, Cardinal Pecci shows that this at present is not possible without the possession of a temporal sovereignty rendering the Pontiff independent of the influence of any one superior.

"The Pope has to guard intact in its integrity the deposit of the Faith; he must preserve revealed truth from error and corruption among the faithful peoples. ... He must be free to communicate without impediment with bishops, sovereigns, subjects, in order that his word, the organ and expression of the divine will, may have a free course all over the earth, and

---

[2] De Maistre, "Du Pape," 1. I. c.vi.: "Il n'y a pas en Europe de souveraineté plus justifiable, s'il est permis de s'exprimer ainsi, que celle des Souverains Pontifes. Elle est comme la loi divine, *justificata in semetipsa.* Mais ce qu'il y a de véritablement étonnant, c'est de voir les Papes devenir souverains sans s'en apercevoir, et même, à parler exactement, malgré eux."
See also in this connection Count Murphy's "Chair of Peter," 2d ed., pp. 158 and following.

be there canonically announced.

"Now, imagine the Holy Father become the subject of a government, and deprived for a time of the liberty to exercise his apostolic ministry. Whenever his *non licet* or any decision of his sounded harsh to the ears of whoever was sovereign over him, or was opposed to that sovereign's views, or to what they call 'the reason of state,' forthwith should we hear of threats, of decrees, of imprisonment, of exile, in order to strangle the voice of truth at its birth.

"Need we recall Liberius, sent into banishment by the Emperor Constantius for refusing to sanction the sentence against St. Athanasius? or John I, imprisoned by Theodosius for not favoring the Arians? or Silverius, exiled by the Empress Theodora because he would not receive to communion the heretical Anthimus? or Martin I, torn away from the Basilica of the Saviour in Rome, and sent to die among the barbarians of Pontus by the Emperor Constans, a Monothelite? or, in fact, all the Pontiffs of the first centuries,, who had no other way to fulfil their ministry than the courage to endure martyrdom?" Then come the recent instances of Pius VI and Pius VII

"But, in truth, there is .no need of prisons or decrees of banishment to bind the hands of Popes who have become the subjects of another power. Everybody knows how easily a government can, even by indirect means, close up every avenue to publicity, cut off all means of communication, put all sorts of obstacles in the way of truth, and give falsehood a free field. In such a situation how is the Pope to superintend the affairs without number of all the churches, to promote the extension of God's kingdom, to regulate worship and discipline, to publish bulls and encyclicals, to convene councils, to grant or to refuse canonical institution to bishops, to have at his command the congregations and courts which are necessary for the management of so many weighty affairs, to keep off schism, to prevent the spread of public heresies, to decide religious disputes, to speak freely to rulers and peoples, to send nuncios and ambassadors, to conclude concordats, to employ censures, to regulate, in fact, the consciences of two hundred millions of Catholics scattered all over the earth, to preserve inviolate dogmas and morals, to receive appeals from all parts of the Christian world, to judge the causes thus submitted, to enforce the execution of the sentences pronounced—to fulfil, in one word, all his duties, and to maintain all the sacred rights of his primacy?

"Here, then, is what they are aiming at by taking from the Pope his temporal power: they mean to render it impossible for him to exercise his spiritual power."

The demonstration is a complete one. But there is another side to the question. If the Pope, as the supreme teacher and ruler of the Church in spirituals, has both his rights to maintain and his duties to fulfil with respect to the Christian world, Christians, in part, have also their indefeasible rights with regard to the free exercise of the Papal Primacy.

"From the Sovereign Pontiff proceed decisions which directly concern what is deepest and most sacred in our Consciences, our faith, our hope of eternal felicity. Every Catholic has a right, in matters of such an exalted nature, which transcend all the things of earth and of the present life, which nearly touch the interests of his own immortal soul, that the sentence of the judge who is to guide him toward eternal life shall come freely from his lips—so freely that no one may hint at the possibility of such a decision having been obtained through the dictation of another, or forced from the giver by sheer violence.

"Every Catholic, therefore, demands that the Pope shall be placed in such a well-known condition of freedom that not only he shall be independent, but that it shall be clear to the eyes of all that he is so. Now, how can the Catholics of all nations believe that the decisions of their parent and guide are thus free when he is the subject of an Italian, a German, a French, or a Spanish sovereign?"

To complete this triumphant demonstration Cardinal Pecci quotes from the acknowledged leaders and organs of the long conspiracy against Christianity and the temporal power of the Papacy in the last and the present centuries. Mazzini, writing to the London *Globe* in August, 1850, says: "The abolition of the temporal power manifestly carries along with it the emancipation of the human mind from the spiritual power." This, the Cardinal remarks, Mazzini frequently repeats in his "Pensiero e Azione." Frederick II[3] wrote to Voltaire: "All the potentates of Europe, being unwilling to recognize the Vicar of Christ in a man subject to another sovereign, will each create himself a patriarch in their own dominions. ... Thereby every one of them will by degrees fall away from the unity of the Church, and end by having in his kingdom a religion of his own, just as he has a language of his own."

To clear away the last vestige of doubt on this point the Cardinal quotes the official declaration of the Central Lodge of Carbonarism in Italy: "'Our final purpose is that of Voltaire and the French Revolution—the total annihilation of Catholicism and of the Christian idea itself.' This is the result aimed at by the anti-Christian schools opened in various Italian cities; this is what is meant by the hostility fostered against the clergy; this is what is intended by freeing (as they say) from all theocratic tyranny[4] the legislation, public instruction, marriage—the entire social body, in a word. This is the real significance of the resurrection of the country, of progress, and of liberty, as they understand them: to abolish Catholic worship, to suppress the religion of Christ, to stamp out from all hearts the Christian faith, and to plunge us once more in the darkness of heathenism.

"The conspirators' plan is no longer a thing to be doubted of, except by such as wish to remain wilfully blind. But in what way is it to be carried out? In this—and note it well, if you would not fall into the snares of these evil men: by giving loud assurances, protestations, and solemn oaths that in no wise whatever do they intend to touch or to injure religion."

The conclusion is a most eloquent appeal to the ancestral

---

3 "Correspondence of Frederick II.," vol. xii. p. 99.

4 Montanelli, "L'Impero il Papato," etc., Florence, 1859.

faith and the ancestral devotion of the Perugians to the Holy See and its Pontiffs:

"There is no middle course. Either we have to stand faithful to Christ, to His Church, to that Church's visible Head, and against the enemies of our religion, or to take part with these against God and His Church.

"It is no longer a matter of policy; it is a matter of conscience. We cannot continue to hesitate between Christ and Belial. ...

"Would any one among you prefer to espouse the cause of the enemies of Christ's Vicar? This would be to deny the traditions of your forefathers; it would be, to use the words of the Perugian Statute-Book,[5] 'to become degenerate sons of ancestors of the noblest blood.' Not only were these ancestors of yours most devoted to the Faith, but they resolved that their own bodies should be a bulwark to defend the temporal dominion of the Holy See.

"When the Ghibelline and Guelph factions had arisen in Italy, Perugia remained ever faithful to the Popes. When these were obliged by popular turbulence to leave Rome they found in Perugia a secure abode,[6] and a place where the conclaves

---

[5] The Cardinal in a note refers to the year 727, when the Emperor Leo the Isaurian, in his insane war against the Holy Images, attacked and persecuted Gregory II. The Perugians spontaneously and unanimously espoused the cause of the Pope, and bound themselves "by a solemn oath to defend the Pontiff's life and his State for the future, and to place themselves and all their interests under his care"—*Solemni sacramento se Pontificis vitam Statumque in perpetuum defensuram, ejusque in potestate rebus omnibus futuram curavit* (MS. in Dominicini Library, Perugia).

[6] See Sigonio, *De Regno Italico*, 1. iii. "This," Cardinal Pecci says in a note, "is made remarkably clear by what one reads in the proemium to each of the Statutes of the Colleges of Arts (Assemblies of Guilds), and especially in the Public Statute-Book of (Republican) Perugia, where, among other things, is the following declaration: "Dimissis igitur alienigenis et privatis affectibus, Guelphis et Sedi Apostolicse contrariis, quicumque intra Augustae Civitatis moenia, illiusque excultum et fecundum agrum, se parentesve suos ortos esse dixerit, hanc Guelpham partem et Sanctam Sedem Apostolicam profiteatur, illis adhaereat, ipsas amplectatur et foveat, et *ab*

could be held in perfect liberty.[7] This fidelity shone forth wonderfully during the reign of Alexander IV, who was wont to call your ancestors 'the stout champions and the chosen defenders of the Church, the rivals in courage and constancy of soul of the generous Maccabees.'[8]

"Your history," the Cardinal goes on to say, "is full of the splendid deeds done to combat the enemies of the Church and to reduce to obedience her rebellious possessions. So deep were in these men's souls the spirit of religious faith and the love for the Papacy! Oh! if these could only come forth from the peace of the tomb, with what contempt they would treat the advances of whosoever should be planning the spoliation of the Common Father of the faithful and the suppression of all liberty for the Church!"

On October 26, 1861, the Piedmontese Minister of Worship, Signor Miglietti, issued a circular letter to the bishops and clergy, the object of which was either to frighten or to bribe them to renounce their allegiance to Pius IX, to give up the cause of the temporal power, and to declare for the Kingdom

---

antiquo nobilissimoque Perusinorum sanguine non degeneret.'—Wherefore, setting aside all foreign and private affections opposed to the Guelphs and the Holy See, whosoever can say that he or his parents were born within the walls of this city of Augusta-Perugia or within her well-cultivated and fertile territory, must openly declare himself for, attach himself to, embrace, and cherish this Guelphic party and the Holy Apostolic See, and not degenerate from the ancient and most noble blood of the Perugians" (vol. I. of the Statutes, Rub. 473).

[7] *Conclaves in Perugia.*—Innocent III having died in Perugia, Honorius III was there elected to succeed him; so after the death there of Urban IV, Clement IV was elected there; again, Martin IV died there, and there Honorius IV was elected in his place. In 1294 was chosen in Perugia the successor of Nicholas IV (St. Celestine V). Finally, after the death there of Benedict XI, Clement V was chosen in the same city to succeed him.

[8] Alexander IV (1254-61) addresses his letter of praise "to the Podestà, Captain, Council, and Communi of Perugia." They had on the present occasion defended the Pontiff and the Holy See against Manfred, Duke of Tarentum; the Pope gives their constant fidelity and valor extraordinary and merited praise.

of Italy.

II. FIDELITY TO PIUS IX

It was simply a provocative to political treason as well as to religious schism.

Cardinal Pecci and his brother-bishops were not to be caught by such flimsy artifices, nor to be overawed by any penalty the triumphant Revolution could inflict. Their answer was a joint letter, drawn up by the Cardinal, signed by himself and his colleagues, and sent to the Holy Father. It was a document which would send a thrill of religious pride throughout the length and breadth of Italy.

This was one of the first acts of noble and resolute resistance which the Cardinal and his colleagues opposed to the progress and power of impiety and revolutionism.

"Most Holy Father," they said, "in the fierce and protracted storm which at this time agitates the Church so fearfully, and which causes so much anxiety to the great heart of your Holiness, we, who are the copartners of your solicitude and the sharers of all your pain, have had to bewail, as we do still bewail, the unceasing efforts made to cause the ruin of our populations, to separate them from your fatherly rule, and to divide them still more from the center of Catholic faith. To carry out this purpose no sort of seduction or deceit has been left untried. After promoting or openly favoring irreligion and libertinism by the unrestricted diffusion of pestilential books, of erroneous doctrines and heterodox teachings, they are now plying the clergy with provocatives and enticements aiming to detach them from their lofty duties and from the obedience due to their prelates, so as then to use them as instruments for their own guilty designs.

"And as all these attempts met with an insurmountable obstacle in the firm and unanimous zeal of the episcopal body, they have now again made these the object of new assaults, undiscouraged by the partial endeavors made to break down the constancy of many of our venerated brethren in the revolutionized provinces of Italy. Defamations, insults, threats, confiscation, imprisonment, banishment having failed, they have had recourse to the disloyal pens of prevaricating priests to plead, in their turn, the cause of the present Revolution. And seeing how little heed was paid to the apologetic declamations of these men, which died away and were lost like the last sounds of a brass bell, it has been lately deemed proper that an official act (of the minister) should be directed toward weakening the fidelity of the bishops. It aims to detach them from you and from the cause of the Supreme Pontificate, and, setting forth old accusations, it seeks to pledge them to acts of approbation and adhesion toward all that has been accomplished against the inviolable laws of justice and religion, and against the rights of the Holy See.

"They pretend, in fact, that the clergy should recognize both in right and in fact the boasted restoration of a nationality. as understood by the revolutionists, and which is the result of conspiracy, deception, injustice, and sacrilege. They demand that the clergy, like every other social class and institution, should be subject, in the discharge of their mission, to the dictation of the state—just as if the priesthood was the offspring of the political power, and that from it and not from God was derived the mission to preach the truth and teach the nations.

"They take it as a crime that the clergy should show such patient resignation in enduring such storms of misfortune, so many humiliations and oppressions of every kind, taking it for granted that they ought to be the panegyrists and co-operators of a policy which their conscience reproves, which the law of God condemns.

"The clergy are promised, in order to bribe and attract them, pledges and assurances of being left at peace in the exercise of their religious ministrations—as if the sad succession of hostile measures and usurpations consummated up to the present moment did not sufficiently unmask the hideous illusions and disloyalty of such promises. ...

"They are offered, as the basis of reconciliation, to accept the condemned and fatal system of the separation of Church and state, which, being equivalent to divorcing the state from the Church, would force Catholic society to free itself from all religious influence. ...

"The tendency of this last intrigue is patent enough. It is calculated that the clergy of Italy, violating their own duties, and separating themselves from their lawful pastors, and from you principally, Most Holy Father, who are their Supreme Chief and Ruler, should abase themselves to legitimize and sanction the acts accomplished by the Revolution, and thereby become the advocate and accomplice of the total spoliation and destruction of the sacred sovereignty of the Church, which they are now planning so noisily.

"We, perceiving with deep grief what refined artifice the conspirators have had recourse to during these last months in order to mature their design, have felt the necessity of examining and fortifying our relations of subjection and union with Your Holiness and with the Apostolic Chair. And therefore it is that, while others among our venerable brothers in the episcopal office, either by acts or by their writings, manifest openly their rejection and abhorrence of this governmental act, we, on the other hand, have rather followed the impulse of filial affection by lifting toward you our eyes and voice in this new calamity, to signify anew most solemnly our perfect adhesion to your teachings and to the glorious resistance which you, although saddened and opposed in so many ways by unworthy children, have made so courageously for the triumph of religion, of justice, and of the sacred rights of the Holy See.

"This declaration of our sentiments and purpose, by which we glory to be always with you and for you, being thus made public, shall be an eloquent argument, giving a peremptory answer to every flattering advance, solicitation, and threat. Faithful to the obligations which we took on ourselves with our episcopal trust, faithful as well to the oath taken on the day of our consecration, we protest that in you, the successor of St. Peter, the Vicar of Christ, the visible Head of His Church, we venerate with unchangeable respect the center of unity of the faith, the depositary and the infallible teacher of all revealed truth which pertains to the spiritual destinies and the eternal salvation of mankind. From this divine teaching authority Christian society derives its light and its form. And when the overbearing might of the world, in order to supplant it, presumes to enter the sanctuary and to impose on men a fictitious and deceptive morality, it is time that it should hear us repeat: 'We must obey God rather than men.'

"In you [we also revere] the supreme regulator of the discipline of the Church, on whom alone the episcopal body and the inferior clergy have to depend in all that regards the exercise of their mission and the relations of the Church with civil society. We therefore sovereignly deplore both the pretension of our modern politicians, who endeavor to subject to their bondage all ecclesiastical offices, and the blindness of those priests who, forgetful of their August calling, allowed themselves to be won over by blandishments, and, dazzled by the false promises of the world, have strayed away from the sheepfold of Christ.

"And with regard to the sacred sovereignty and the temporal dominions, against which so many conspiracies and expeditions are planned, we accept no other sentiments and declarations than those of the Church herself, attested even in our day by the unanimous suffrage of the Catholic episcopate, and proclaimed by ourselves in our pastoral letters to our diocesans and in many addresses on the same subject laid before the pontifical throne. While, in the sense of the definitions of the ecumenical councils, we acknowledge the inviolability of sacred endowments and ecclesiastical possessions, we also consider this sacred sovereignty to be a special ordinance of divine Providence which no human power may lawfully assail– an ordinance directed toward protecting the independence of the Church, toward securing to her visible Head the fulness of the liberty necessary for the proper exercise of the supreme authority bestowed on him by God over the whole Catholic world. ...

"In the profession of such principles and convictions, and in fidelity to the Apostolic See and to your August person, we desire to be, with the divine help, ever firm in the face of whatever may befall us, of dangers and contradictions to which we may be exposed; nay, more, the greater these may be, the more do we feel the duty of standing at your side, Most Holy Father, and to find in your invincible constancy, in your serenity of soul amid all the tribulations which press upon you, inspiration and increasing comfort in the fulfilment of our pastoral office."

When Pius IX will have passed away, and Piedmontese rule will restrict, even within the Vatican, the liberty and jurisdiction of his successor, how sweet it will be to that successor to receive such encouragements from his brother-bishops all over the world as are contained in the brave and noble sentiments we have just been reading!

CHAPTER XV

THE BATTLE WITH IRRELIGION RAGES FIERCELY; CARDINAL PECCI HEADS THE EPISCOPAL BODY IN DEFENSE OF (I) THE LIBERTY OF THE CHURCH.

DURING the first fourteen years of Cardinal Pecci's episcopal labors in Perugia he had been most zealous, as we have seen, in preparing both priests and people among his flock for the trials which he feared, if he did not foresee, were inevitable in the near future. The foremost position among the hierarchy of Umbria, given him, from his first appointment, by his learning and his great reputation, and afterward confirmed by his elevation to the cardinalate, threw upon him the labor, if not the responsibility, of leading his brother-bishops in every public movement made for the defence of religion and the authority of the Holy See.

What has been said in the last chapters may enable the reader to judge how difficult, not to say morally impossible, it was for the pastors of souls to fulfil their appointed duty or exercise their needful authority in spirituals in the face of the tyrannical and minute restrictions imposed upon them in every direction and at every step by the Piedmontese invaders.

Let the readers of this book not feel surprised that we should use the word "invaders" here. In the English-speaking world, during the years 1859, 1860, and 1861, non-Catholics, elated by the prospective downfall of the Papacy, rejoiced at every step in advance of the revolutionary forces under Garibaldi, or the Piedmontese arms on land and sea against the States of the Church, garrisoned by a few thousand men, barely sufficient to maintain order and to repress the perpetual outbreaks caused at almost every point by the secret societies. There had been for the Pontifical government but little trouble in keeping its own populations quiet, if England and France had not been either urging on Piedmont to seize on all the States of the Peninsula or encouraging directly Cavour and Victor Emmanuel to invade the neighboring independent and sovereign principalities, in a time of peace, without any provocation, and to carry out the plans of a dynastic ambition, cloaked over by the pretence of Italian patriotism and the satisfaction of the national aspirations.

Cavour—as his published Life and Memoirs now amply prove—used Mazzini and Garibaldi, with their formidable and wide-spread organization of revolutionary clubs, as the forerunners and auxiliaries of the Piedmontese army and navy in this unholy and unblessed war. These dark associations, with the revolutionary, anti-social, and irreligious passions with which they had filled every portion of the Peninsula, every city and town, were like the dynamite placed in some mighty reef beneath the waves which the hand of the engineer had scientifically mined and prepared. Mazzini had made all ready for the explosion ere, in May, 1860, Garibaldi had landed a single soldier at Marsala, or before, later in the season, Fanti had sent his army toward the Marches and Umbria, or Persano had received orders to co-operate by bombarding Ancona. Napoleon III had his troops in Rome, feigning to protect the independence of the Holy See and the inviolability of the territory still left to it, while he was helping Cavour to carry out effectively the Piedmontese plans, and betraying into the hands of the invading generals the little Papal army, commanded by the most heroic and accomplished soldier France had known since the first Napoleon.

It was an unholy war and a cowardly war, carried on by base intrigues and by means as unhallowed as those which Antiochus of old used to subjugate the reunited remnants of the Twelve Tribes and to crush out in the souls of a small but brave people their faith in the living God.

It is impossible to understand either the times or country amid which Cardinal Pecci lived and battled for religion without understanding the enemies he had to contend with, the ends for which these fought, and the weapons they used against the Church, her chief, her priesthood and faithful people.

On November the 21st, 1860, the archbishops and bishops of the Marches sent to the Piedmontese governor or commissary-general an eloquent remonstrance enumerating the effects of the regime introduced by him and his subordinates, and the means taken by them to alienate the people of these provinces from their allegiance to God and the faith of their fathers. A few extracts will paint the situation.

I. How the Enemies of God and Man Go to Work in Italy

"Our hearts," they say, "cruelly wounded and torn, are filled with grief and desolation by the thought of the spiritual ruin which threatens our children, our flocks, purchased by the blood of the Lamb without spot. Nevertheless, after all the contradictions, the trials, the obstacles we have had to encounter, not one spark of charity, of zeal, of pastoral and fatherly solicitude has been quenched in our souls—we solemnly affirm it, with our anointed hands on our hearts; and, with the help of God's grace, these sentiments shall never depart from us through fault of ours.

"We scarcely believe our own eyes or the testimony of our own ears when we see or hear of the excesses, the abominations, the disorders witnessed in the chief cities of our respective dioceses, to the shame and horror of the beholders, to the great detriment of religion, of decency, of public morality, since the ordinances against which we protest deprive us of all power to protect religion and morality or to repress the prevailing crimes and licentiousness.

"The public sale, at nominal prices, of mutilated translations of the Bible, of pamphlets of every description saturated with pestilential errors or infamous obscenities, is permitted in the cities which, a few months ago, had never heard of these scandalous productions. ... The impunity with which the most horrible blasphemies are uttered in public, and the worse utterance of expressions and sentiments that breathe a hellish wickedness; the exposition, the sale in public, and the diffusion of statuettes, pictures, and engravings which brutally outrage piety, purity, the commonest decency; the representation in our city theatres of pieces and scenes in which are turned into ridicule the Church, Christ's immaculate Spouse, the Vicar of Christ, the ministers of religion, and everything which piety and faith hold to be most dear; in fine, the fearful licentiousness of public manners, the odious devices resorted to for perverting the innocent and the young, the evident wish and aim to make immorality, obscenity, uncleanness triumph among all classes—such are, your Excellency, the rapid and faint outlines of the scandalous state of things created in the Marches by the legislation and discipline so precipitately imposed on them by the Sardinian government.

"We appeal to your Excellency, ... could we remain silent and indifferent spectators of this immense calamity without violating our most sacred duty?"

Such was the courageous and indignant voice which arose from the episcopal body in the Marches. It soon had a worthy echo on the other side of the Apennines. There the bishops of Umbria found an eloquent mouthpiece and intrepid interpreter in the Cardinal Archbishop of Perugia. Undismayed by the outrages and sufferings which his old schoolmate and friend, the saintly Cardinal de Angelis, Archbishop of Fermo, was made to undergo for his resistance to Piedmontese rule, Cardinal Pecci concentrated all the energy of his character, style, and convictions into the impressive document from which we are about to quote. It sounds like the solemn act of men who know that by publishing to the world this grand protest they are drawing on themselves the worst penalties which unlawful and unrestrained might can inflict.

Let the reader judge whether or not Cardinal Pecci was defending the Christian religion, assailed in its very essence:

"In the year of salvation one thousand eight hundred and sixty, in the month of December:

"We, the undersigned, to whom, albeit unworthy, the Eternal Priest and Pastor Christ Jesus, through His Vicar on earth, the Roman Pontiff, has committed the care and government of the churches over which we are set, in consequence of the proclamation, which has just been made in these provinces of Umbria in the name of the Sardinian government, of certain decrees which bear on religious interests and ecclesiastical discipline, find ourselves impelled by our pastoral office to make freely and solemnly the following declaration of our sentiments:

"It is a grievous error against Catholic doctrine to pretend that the Church is the subject of any earthly power and bound by the same economy and relations which regulate civil society. The Church is not a human institution, nor is it a portion of the political edifice, although it is destined to promote the welfare of the men among whom it lives. It affirms that from God come directly its own being, its constitution, and the necessary faculties for attaining its own sublime destiny, which is one different (from that of the state) and altogether of a supernatural order. Divinely ordered, with a hierarchy of its own, it is by its nature independent of the state.

"This native independence, this condition, so vital to the Church, of being able to extend the blessings of its heavenly mission, is a thing which has ever been respected in the midst of the illustrious populations of Umbria whom God placed under our episcopal care. Beneath the overshadowing protection of the Pontifical government, which we shall ever acknowledge as the work of Providence, created for the indispensable and free exercise of the power of the Church, it had not to dread the obstacles and fetters imposed on it elsewhere by a secular policy either suspicious or unbelieving.

"Wherefore most painful to our hearts and most baneful to the spiritual interests of our flocks is every innovation which, under the name and glitter of modern civilization, without any dependence on the Supreme Pastor, people pretend to introduce among us by these recent decrees, which gravely wound the liberty of the Church, which make no account of ancient, most sacred, and ever-revered interests, which set aside and annul inviolable prerogatives and institutions.

"Whosoever considers the spirit of these decrees must perceive at the first glance that here in our country also it is resolved to make the Church the slave of the state, and to subject and co-ordinate her divine mission to the low views of a worldly policy. ...

"We observe, besides, with a sad surprise, that these innovations are proclaimed in the name of a government which holds by its fundamental law 'the Catholic, Apostolic, and Roman religion as the sole religion of the state,' and which, when it ordered its armies to occupy these provinces, declared its purpose to be 'to restore in Italy the principles of the moral order!

"A Catholic government contradicts itself every time that it lays its hand on the sanctuary and invades the sacred province of the priesthood; every time it changes by its own arbitrary act the external conditions of the Church, and so straitens the latter as to reduce it to a state of bondage. Nor can the purpose of reforming the discipline of the Church give a color of legitimacy to such an unrighteous undertaking.

"Determined not to give up the guardianship of the sacred rights entrusted to our keeping, we lift our voices, and in presence of God and of men we protest loudly against all and every the innovations and ordinances which wound the rights and liberties of the Church, as embodied in the recent decrees. In especial, moreover, ...

"We protest against such as regard the persons belonging to the Church, by the suppression of ecclesiastical tribunals. ...

"We protest against such as are adverse to the institutions of the Church by subjecting to the censure of the state every ecclesiastical provision and disposition; by withdrawing from the direction and care of the bishops the pious foundations, even when deriving their origin from the Church itself or entrusted to the Church by the will of the donors; by prohibiting all care and interference of the bishops with the establishments of education and instruction, compelling the rectors of parishes to do without sacramental registers and the books necessary to their pastoral ministry. ...

"We must deplore the vexations committed against priests, accompanied by reprimands, threats, arrest, imprisonment, and banishment. We deplore the violation of the cloister, the taking possession of sacred asylums, the sequestration and suppression of religious communities. We must deplore the occasions given so frequently to the clergy to engender dissension and scandal, and the seductions held out to them to tempt them away from the due subjection to their superiors. We must deplore the licentiousness of the theatre and the press, and the continual snares laid to surprise pious souls, to undermine faith by circulating infamous pamphlets and heterodox writings, and by the declamations of fanatical preachers of impiety. ...

"And we make these declarations in order not to betray the most sacred rights, which we are bound to protect by the solemn oaths we have taken, and by the strict duties prescribed by our office and our conscience, inasmuch as our silence would take the scandalous color of connivance or of criminal weakness; and because at the sound of our voice, at the publicity given to this remonstrance, the faithful will take heart, for they deplore bitterly in their secret souls the wrongs and the ruin caused to their mother.

"Christian charity bids us never to despair of the repentance and amendment of our neighbor, and to oppose the armor of prayer to those who attack us. We do pray for them, and offer up our petitions that their repentance may help to render more glorious the certain triumph of the Church, to which faith teaches us the divine protection can never fail, and that even the gates of hell shall never prevail against her."

Signed by the Cardinal Archbishop-Bishop of Perugia, the Archbishop of Spoleto, the Bishops of Terni, Foligno, Città di Castello, Assisi, Nocera, Città della Pieve, Gabbio,

Todi, Amelia, Narni, and Rieti.[1]

The war against God, against Christian society, against the dearest, truest interests of humanity and country, had been inaugurated by the Italian Revolution. This was the coup d'essai by which the anti-Christian and anti-social combined forces were trying their power, first, against the Papacy and Catholicism in the very seat of their authority, before they tried their hand, as they are now doing in Belgium and in France and in Switzerland; Germany and Great Britain are to follow.

II. THE NOBLE DEFENCE OF DOMESTIC SOCIETY

Cardinal Pecci stands forth at the head of his brethren, organizing and leading the resisting forces, whose only arms are truth and justice. It is a sublime struggle; it cannot be a doubtful one.

One of the most baneful innovations introduced by the Piedmontese invaders into a country where for so many centuries no religion had prevailed save the Catholic religion alone, regarded marriage, which was entirely laicized, being made a civil transaction subject to the sole laws of the state, and independent in every way of any religious consecration or formality. Indeed, among a population which had been exclusively Catholic for fifteen hundred years, the subversion of all Church discipline and regulations was so sudden and so thorough that, with a stroke of the pen, the pastors of souls were forbidden to keep parish registers, and the records of births, marriages, and deaths were transferred to the municipal officers. The whole sacramental system of the Church, the entire order of priestly duty in its most sacred ministrations, were set aside as abruptly and as peremptorily as if the change were taking place in one of the Fiji Islands, where the inhabitants had been fetichists and cannibals in the

[1] "Scelta di Atti Episcopali del Cardinale Gioacchino Pecci, Arcivescovo Vescovo di Perugia, ora LeoneXIII, Sommo Pontefice," Roma, 1879, pp. 301-305.

last generations, and their present conquerors imposed anew the old ancestral customs.

The archbishops and bishops of Umbria had thereupon issued a declaration drawn up by Cardinal Pecci, and which remains one of the noblest and most eloquent monuments of episcopal independence and courage of that dark period. But the Cardinal did not rest satisfied with this joint action of himself and brethren. He addressed himself directly to the king.

"Sire," he writes, "the extraordinary anomaly of civil marriage imposed on the populations of Umbria by a decree of the Sardinian commissary, the Marquis Pepoli, dated October 31, 1860, was not then fully understood and appreciated in its entire reach and consequences. The Umbrian hierarchy, after witnessing for more than a year a lamentable succession of sacrilegious usurpations and shameful acts, could have drawn from these alone a sufficient reason for mourning and trembling for the fate of their people. ... They did not delay to raise their voice in deploring it, and in the joint protest sent to the government in December, 1860, they denounced the innovation as one of the most baneful among the many carried out to the detriment of religion and the sacred rights of the Church.

"Enlightened, moreover, by the guilty results of this deplorable change, the bishops, after an experience of several months, have published lately a doctrinal 'Declaration,' in which the innovation is submitted to examination, its irreligious character is laid bare, and the capital points of its discordance with Catholic doctrine are placed in evidence.

"Your Majesty will permit me to place in your hands a copy of this 'Declaration.' For it is exceedingly important that you should know and see in its full light an act of such serious consequence, done by the caprice of an extraordinary official, who came hither, after the military occupation of these provinces, to make laws in your royal name. It is an act which still works out its effects, corrupting consciences and the public morality; it now requires a remedy, which can only come from the power from which it emanates.

"Your Majesty must bear with me if I, who, though the last in merit among my venerable colleagues, am bound by stricter ties to the Catholic cause and the Holy Roman Church, the universal teacher and guardian of the divine rights, do now endeavor to place briefly beneath your eyes the inconsistency and deformity of this anomaly, considered in its civil and religious bearings. ...

"... As to its religious aspect, which is the most important, your Majesty needs only, in order to weigh well the gravity of this act, to remember what you witnessed yourself in 1851 and 1852 while the projected law of civil marriage was discussed in the Piedmontese Chambers. ...

"If your Majesty will only now take the trouble to read calmly the few pages of our 'Declaration,' you will feel certain that this projected law, which it is pretended is a boon to Umbria, is of this (anti Christian) character. ... This is shown by the fundamental conception of the law itself, which is based on the theory of the separability of the contract from the sacrament. By dissociating marriage from every religious element it is given features of a merely human character. And by overlooking the divine institution and economy which regulate marriage in its very essence, the law takes upon itself exclusively to arrange what is most intimate in the matter as if it regulated only an ordinary transaction of civil origin and competence.

"This anti-Christian character is shown by the source itself from which the law derives. For it must either come from pagan naturalism, which knew nothing of the fact that God had raised the matrimonial contract to the dignity of a sacrament; or from the heretical corruptions of Protestantism, which, having troubled the very springs of revealed truth, rejected the sanctity of the matrimonial union as belonging to Christian dogma; or, again, from the systematic unbelief of our modern Socialists, who aim at overturning from the foundations the entire social and religious orders.

"This character is also shown by the motives on which the

law is based, which are not only futile and insufficient, when there is question of justifying an act of this moment, but reveal a purpose sadly out of accord with Catholic doctrine.

"They pretend to assert thereby the fulness of the state jurisdiction, and, under the cloak of 'civilization' and 'progress,' to set about transforming God's own work: they command men's consciences to accommodate themselves to a factitious tie which Christian doctrine declares to be illicit and most criminal apart from the sacrament.

"With treacherous phrases about liberty of conscience and separation of the state from the Church, it takes advantage to weaken the bonds of religion, to accredit indifferentism, and to please the heretic and the unbeliever by a fashion of marriage suited to their minds.

"Under the specious and lying color of abuses and restraints it censures the venerated rules of Christian jurisprudence, the wise discipline of the Church, confirmed by the decrees of councils and by the uninterrupted practice of so many ages.

"Therefore it was that Pius IX, writing to your Majesty on this projected law, concluded his letter with these memorable words:

"'We wrote to your Majesty that the law is not Catholic; and if the law is not Catholic, the clergy are obliged to tell the people so, even at the risk of incurring the threatened penalties. Your Majesty, we also speak to you in the name of Christ Jesus, whose Vicar we are, how unworthy soever; and we say to you in His Name, Do not sanction this law, which is pregnant with a thousand disorders. ... We give ourselves up willingly to the hope of seeing you support the rights of the Church, protect her ministers, and free her people from the peril of being subjected to certain laws which bear on their face the decay of religion and of the morality of nations. ...'

"As to the consequences of this law, ... cases of legal concubinage frequently come to our notice, to our grief and the ruin of souls. And it is supremely painful to reflect that the more easily such things happen, the more difficult is it to

repair the evil, on account of the condition of state bondage and interdiction to which the priestly ministry is condemned in our day. For it is the law itself which frequently causes and authorizes such things. ...

"Have we not seen the abuse and prevarication of legal might carried to the point of compelling the parish priests, under threat of fine and imprisonment, to bestow their sacred offices in giving the sacramental consecration to the marriage immediately after the civil ceremony, without taking any account whatever of the forms and discipline of the Church?

"Have we not seen the officials use a studious or inconsiderate precipitancy in admitting parties to the civil ceremony, and then, having discovered thereafter impediments which nullified the contract, have they not displayed a careless connivance in tolerating that the incestuous couples, so ill-united even with respect to the civil act, should continue together in their unlawful intercourse?

"Have we not also seen attempts made to subject the administration of the sacraments and the direction of men's consciences to the official censure and the dictation of the state?

"These are dreadful facts, of which I speak of my own certain knowledge!

"Assuredly a law of this kind, and bearing such pernicious fruits, is not a Catholic law. The natural dictates of moral honesty are offended by it; and, in the long run, it must end in degrading Christian society and cause that 'religious and moral decadence' which our enlightened Pontiff deplored in predicting it to your Majesty. ...

If this law, therefore, which is so manifestly anti-Catholic, comes to be promulgated in your royal name, and by a governor sent by royal ordinance to rule these Pontifical provinces, the Catholic hierarchy has an evident right to expect that your Majesty will apply a remedy to the grievance, and to press you to repair it.

"... There is only question here to insist on the observance of the rule that a delegate is inferior to the power which

delegates him, and that all acts are void of juridical validity which the delegator had neither the right nor the intention to perform or to commission his subordinate to do,

"Let your Majesty do this act of justice to the Catholic religion, the only true religion, the only one acknowledged as such, and the only one professed in all Italy. Have Christian marriage restored speedily to its religious liberty and its superhuman grandeur. Let the annoying exceptions cease which are so grievous a burden to the conscience of our people, and suppress that heterodox innovation which, by desecrating an August sacrament, vitiates in their principle the domestic and social relations, and is a great danger to the purity of faith and morals."[2]

To this eloquent appeal we do not fear to add the conclusion of the united Remonstrance of the archbishops and bishops of Umbria, also the work of the same well-inspired hand. Statesmen and churchmen in America, warned by the fatal facilities of our divorce laws, will do well to read and ponder these pregnant considerations:

"After these considerations our conscience cannot rest satisfied, nor can the zeal which we are bound to cherish for the Catholic cause and for the well-being of Christianity in our midst, if we did not make our words, with evangelical freedom, reach the ears of those who have bestowed their labors in this reform, or who are to give it their care and support. It is still but a project. God grant that the truth, shining forth in its full light, may penetrate and convince every mind before such reform is sanctioned!

"We say, therefore:

"A civil reform regarding marriage which takes on itself, as does the present project, to regulate the validity of matrimony in a manner quite independent of and differing from the dictates of religion, necessarily involves a violation of Catholic dogma, an oppression of the Catholic conscience.

"The sanctity [*l'onestà*] and force of the conjugal tie, in the

---

[2] "Scelta." etc., pp. 470-78, Sept. 27, 1861.

estimation of Christians, are based on the law of nature and that of the Gospel, not on the formulas of the civil law. This is a truth of the divine, the absolute order, from which the Church can never depart; and the conscience of a Catholic people can never be convinced of the contrary. It is not a matter of discipline, about which transactions might be made, or a question of form, about which one may lawfully disagree.

"Under the pretext of claiming its own rights (*rivendicazione*) the state in our day is compelled to repudiate this dogmatic principle, to turn its back on its own traditions, and to violate the consciences of its subjects.

"Can a reform of this character ever be reconciled with the profession of the Catholic faith, of which the whole nation is so proud? Can a wise policy ever consent to accept an institution so hostile to the dominant religion and to the prevailing belief—an institution which, discussed formerly in the Piedmontese Chambers, had there so unhappy an issue, and which elsewhere turned out to be a source of miserable troubles, contentions, and corruption?

"The state has its own duties with regard to marriage, but these only concern the external bearings of marriage connecting it with the civil society. The Church does not pretend to an exclusive fulness of jurisdiction, confining her claim to what God has committed to her as her indefeasible right in her nature as the minister of His religion and the ruler of man in his relations with the Godhead—that is, the validity of the marriage tie, which belongs to the spiritual and divine order.

"... Does the state wish to co-operate in preserving from the abuses of individual licentiousness the purity or legitimacy of marriage? There is a way of doing so without invading others' rights. Let it combine with the Church that precious and sadly needed harmony of action which arranges and secures so admirably the social and religious interests of a nation; let it show itself to be an ally, not an arbitrary master; let it accept and sanction the sacred laws of the Church, impose their observance on its subjects, even in externals, and

it will thus infallibly attain its true purpose. ...

"But let the state beware, and we beg it to beware, of putting thorns and fetters on the Catholic conscience, and of putting itself as a teacher in the place of the Church, the divine and only guide from whom Catholics obtain the rules of morality and justice."[3]

The Archbishop of Perugia could not, in the perils which daily and hourly grew around the Christian homes of Umbria, rest satisfied with demonstrating to the civil authorities the enormity of the evil they were committing; he made his voice heard in every one of these homes, instructing them on these dangers and their own Christian duties.

III. CARDINAL PECCI ENLIGHTENING CHRISTIAN HOMES AND FORMING CHRISTIAN HEARTS

In 1864 Cardinal Pecci, who had been the soul and the mouthpiece of the episcopate of Central Italy during the calamitous years which followed 1860, issued in the form of his usual Lenten pastoral a most remarkable, pregnant, instructive, and eloquent work, worthy of a great and zealous bishop. It bears for title "On the Current Errors against Religion and Christian Life."

The works of mind, and more especially so those which treat of the dearest religious interests of mankind, are like the rare and most precious gems which have their value in every civilized clime and win the admiration of all true men. From this production of the Cardinal Archbishop of Perugia we detach a few passages, which our readers will prize as they would the most beautiful pearls of Coromandel taken from a full casket and held up to them to examine. Here is the preamble:

"The priceless treasure of a frank profession of Catholic faith is a thing too much to be envied and hidden away out of

[3] June, 1861. "Sul Proget to di Matrimonio Civile, esaminato nell' interesse religioso. *Dichiarazione, Scelta*, pp. 308-342.

sight, in our days, that we should not guard it jealously against the traps and plots which are laid to steal it from us. ... To a people like you, who had the fortune to be born Catholics, and who have ever had it at heart to remain so, the free and loving voice of your pastor must surely be grateful when it is raised to warn you of the dangers which your religion runs, and to point out to you the ready means to avert them.

"There is no need that we should spend many words to prove to you the existence and the magnitude of these dangers, and the unceasing labors bestowed to implant even among you unbelief and heresy. The designs and proceedings of the propagators of irreligion are quite well known to you. They profit by the present conditions of our country to make war on the Catholic faith; they endeavor to pervert radically its principles, and to upset all the practices of Christian life. ...

"See how these men would have you throw off from your minds all the dictates of faith, all bonds of subjection to God. They go about writing and proclaiming aloud:

"'Man is free in his own conscience; he can embrace any religion he likes. Natural religion, that which reason dictates to each of us, is all that we want; we do not need either revelation or mysteries. Religion is a purely internal act; it should exist in the heart and confine itself to the sphere of our spirit. It is quite enough for a man to behave himself like one who is honest and honored among his fellow-men; as to religion, he can square his actions on his belief. Religion does not enter into the sphere of external conduct or into the social order; the interests of our spiritual being should be entirely separate from those of our corporeal being.'

"These theories are widely taught even among us, and, let us confess it, they not infrequently meet with favor and welcome. Thank God if the number be small indeed who renounce, to embrace them, their Catholic profession! Nevertheless there are numbers of the hesitating and the deceived who, thinking these theories to be comfortable and plausible, caress them in practice, give them their assent, and, without perceiving it, live according to them. Hence ... a

mortal indifferentism in matters of religion, a blind neglect and contempt of all that concerns the soul and regards the life to come..."

Taking up in succession each of these capital errors, the Cardinal refutes them in a masterly way:

"To all who speak to you of 'liberty of conscience' say that without God there is no liberty. He made man free and gifted with reason, but in so doing He imposed on His creature obligations and dictated laws for him, in order to prevent that native liberty and reason from leading him astray. Among these obligations, among these laws, stand first those that pertain to religion—namely, the worship and obedience which are due to God as the Supreme Author and Repairer of human nature. He has Himself determined and made known to us in what manner we are thus to honor and serve Him. Nor is it left to the free will of man to refuse it, or to fashion for himself a form of worship and service such as he pleases to render. That worship, that religion alone is true, is good, which God Himself has manifestly willed us to practice. After that it would be not only impious but monstrous to maintain every form of worship is acceptable and indifferent, that the human conscience is free to adopt whichever form it pleases and to fashion out a religion to suit itself.

"What! are they then things indifferent, dependent on our choice and good pleasure, these matters which we call truth and error, the divine glory, and God's dishonor?

"What! can it then be a matter of indifference to man to know God or to ignore Him, to revere Him or to worship His creatures, to serve Him, as He bids us, or to refuse His service? ..."

Every one of the *effata* of irreligion or scepticism is then made the heading of each successive section of this noble treatise, and utterly confuted. For instance:

"The religion of the heart is enough for man.—Remark, I pray you, that this false axiom which cloaks the shame of the unbeliever serves also to the cowardly Catholic as a pretext for sacrificing the duties of his religion to the idol of human

respect. God deserves and demands that man's whole being shall confess, worship and serve Him, the Creator. This cannot be accomplished by the heart alone, and by mere interior acts which remain concealed in the depths of the human soul. ...

"The new law of the Gospel, while teaching us to worship God in a manner more perfect and more worthy of Him, 'in spirit and in truth,' also establishes and commands special external observances—sacrifice, the sacraments, prayer—not only as means of personal sanctification, but as a solemn expression of religious worship.

"Besides, honor is due to God, not merely as He is the Creator of individual man, but as He is also the Author and Ruler of the human race as a whole. For if man in his individual capacity derives from Him as from the First Cause, is sustained by His providence and directed by Him toward his proper destiny, even so is every human society.

"So deeply rooted in the universal sentiment and conviction of mankind is the obligation of an outward and public manifestation of such worship, and the persuasion as well that no society can subsist without religion, that no people, how barbarous or degraded soever, has existed who did not confess this debt to the Godhead by erecting temples, instituting feasts, offering sacrifices, and decreeing honors."

In the same lucid and convincing way does he dispose of the next axiom, that "It is religion enough to behave well and to do good to others." And so on to the end of this chain of capital errors.

"We have until now," he continues, "discoursed to you of the principal errors which are propagated against our holy religion. ... Now we feel ourselves impelled to place beneath your eyes the principal points on which is remarked in our day the decay of Christian morality. ..."

"Blasphemy" comes in the first place. It is treated with brief and masterly eloquence. Then the "Profanation of the Sunday and Feasts of Obligation," "Public Immorality," "Bad Books," and "Defective Education."

This last section deserves more than a passing mention:

"We should have too much to say on this subject, on which depend the direction and welfare of the present and of the coming generation. We need not lose time in proving the obligation and the importance for parents to educate their children well; the voice of nature, the precepts of religion, and the sense of all mankind agree in affirming and inculcating this duty.

"Still, to confess the truth, who is it that does not perceive and deplore the neglect and falling-off in the discharge of this duty which are evident in many Catholic families at this time, and that does not thence draw sad auguries for our future? Unwise and lazy parents do not know how to estimate the nobleness of the mission en trusted to them. They generally measure according to the calculations of a low and selfish interest the blessing of having children; they do not at all think of the great debt which they contract toward God, from the first day they become parents, to increase in their offspring and to continue the number of His true adorers; of that which they contract toward themselves to prepare and transmit an honored inheritance of good example and virtues; of the debt contracted toward society to rear for it members laborious, moral, and edifying.

"It is true that in our day another maxim is current bearing on this same subject—namely, 'To the state belongs the training of youth.' Does this maxim avail to excuse the lamentable negligence of parents in our time?

"The duty of education, inculcated by natural reason, is so essential to the parental character and authority that they cannot decline its performance. The state authority, by its place in the order of things, is not called upon to discharge this great parental duty, but to help the natural educators in their work, and to watch and protect the interior discipline and good direction of the family.

"What are, in reality, the relations in which man is placed from his birth, as one of the beings in the order of creation? He comes into the world as God's creature, who has brought him into existence; he is the child of those who have given him temporal life; he is ordained first toward religion and then toward his family; his first duties are subjection and service to God, and dependence on his parents. The family is neither the creation nor the emanation of civil society (or the state); the power of parents is not a concession of human law. The relations and duties which obtain between parents and children are anterior and superior to all human aggregation.

"Man is indeed born sociable; but belonging, before all, to the domestic and religious society, he only comes into the society of the state through the family and already prepared by the teaching of religion and under the guidance of parental authority. Therefore is it that as in the matter of education only an auxiliary part can be attributed to the state authority, so is it evident that the charge of educating remains as a burden they cannot decline on the conscience of the parents, who for that work are the representatives of God the Creator, and are invested with His authority.

"If in our days all parents understood their duties in this light, and if, conceiving an adequate notion of the work they are commissioned to do, they instructed their children in time on the elevated duties and relations which every human being has to fulfil both in the domestic and the religious society, assuredly the state would be much the better for it. For no one can doubt that children who are submissive to parental authority and devoted to their family, that men who have the fear of God and who are obedient to their religion, cannot fail to be also honored citizens and serviceable to their fellow-men."

Then comes up the question of colorless or undenominational education, which so many parents are satisfied with. Cardinal Pecci's luminous explanation leaves here no room for hesitation:

"You must distinguish between 'education' and 'instruction,' between the moral training and moulding of the heart and the simple cultivating of the intellect. Instruction, as such, ordinarily consists in filling the minds of the young with a furniture of knowledge that can help them, according to their years, to turn to a useful account their intellectual and bodily powers.

"The moral training, on the contrary, should be a foundation for the development and the application of the great principles of morality and religion as bearing on men's conduct within the family and in the social sphere.

"Scientific instruction will give you learned and clever young men and women; religious education will give you, on the contrary, honest and virtuous citizens. Instruction, separated from education properly so called, serves rather to fill young hearts with vanity than to discipline them aright. It is quite otherwise with a right education; such a training, under the guidance of religion, which is the regulator of the heart of man and the inspirer of pure and generous affections, knows how to implant and to cultivate virtue in the most illiterate souls without the aid of much scientific polishing or instruction.

"... Then, again, and to speak the truth, do parents pay attention to the nature, the solidity of the instruction given to their children? Do they see to it that it is sound, useful, well ordered, and fit to prepare and help an education such as is fit for Christian children and members of a Catholic community; that those who give such instruction have the necessary gifts of religious conviction, of virtue, of learning, such as may win them the respect and obedience of their pupils; that, above all, the study of religion, so essential to the education and the virtuous life of young people, should hold the foremost place among all other studies, should have a proper and adequate development, and be carried on under the direction of the Church, the depositary and teacher of religious doctrines?

"You see, therefore, that in this respect alone there cannot be (in a neutral school) a sufficient guarantee for a right and complete education, nor any relief for parents of the great burden on their conscience."

Coming to the current sayings in our day, "that both instruction and education should be in harmony with the age and free from prejudices," the Cardinal increases in vigorous remonstrance:

"Have you ever understood the real significance of these words, which are too often heard from the lips of some unwary parent, as well as from those of self-esteemed educators? No one denies that all the arts advance with time, and on all methods of human education a new light is cast by experience and a new increase obtained. Nor would the modernizing processes we hear people talk of meet with any opposition when they only affect the form, when they are really beneficial, and do not affect injuriously either Christian principles or Christian duties.

"These men, however, have in view a far different conception and purpose. Instruction and education, void of prejudices, in the language of the day, mean simply that they should be such as to befit promiscuously families of all shades of religious faith, worshipping at the altars of every creed, whether the creeds be those of Protestantism or that of the Hebrew. It is an education devoid of all the external practices and duties of the Christian faith, and calculated to familiarize young people with 'freedom of conscience' and indifferentism. It is such as to accustom themselves to make such compromises as are incompatible with the immutability of Catholic dogma and Gospel morality each time that such compromises seem demanded by what people call 'social exigencies,' and civilization, and the superiority of the age, and such worldly considerations. It is, in fine, such as to make a man live a gay life in this world, as if here were for him the end of all and his own supreme destiny.

"And although this system of education does not openly exclude every religious element, such as it contains is so superficial and diluted that it is anything but fit to fill the souls of the young with a perfect knowledge, a true love, an exact practice, a hearty profession of the Catholic faith to which they belong.

"There is another great evil resulting from this, as they call it, impartial or unprejudiced education. Do you know what it is? It is to take no account of the powerful influence of the examples of the home-circle, and to afford the children of the household all facilities for finding themselves, from their early years, in the midst of the most powerful seductions of worldly society.

"No! it is not a prejudice, but an undeniable truth, continually demonstrated by the experience of every day, that the school of example has more power to form the minds of the young than mere oral teaching. Nay, frequently what causes the failure of an education well wrought out by the zealous pastor and the skillful schoolmaster are the evil examples given at home.

"It is no prejudice, but a most pressing duty and an earnest of true fatherly love, which guards the young against the dangers and snares with which the road of worldlings is sown—against licentious conversations, pestilential books, obscene spectacles, evil companions, perfidious friendships, and dark associations. It is rather lamentable blindness and inexcusable folly on the part of parents to pretend to accustom their children for a while to the ways of the world, to make them know everything, open the way to the gratification of every passion, allowing their dear ones to be their own masters, exposing them to every temptation, in which their innocence receives wounds which no time can cure."[4]

---

[4] "Scelta."

CHAPTER XVI

CARDINAL PECCI BATTLING FOR HIS CLERGY

I. CONTENDING FOR THE SACRED RIGHTS AND LIBERTIES OF THE SECULAR PRIESTHOOD

IT is not to be denied that among the very worst enemies of religion in Italy from 1846 to 1886 were some of her own ministers. Among these may have been men of unimpeachable moral conduct, who, carried away by the powerful current of ideas and sentiments running resistlessly in favor of Italian nationality, independence, and unity, and with wilful blindness deemed the established religion an obstacle and an enemy, and combated it with all their might. If such pure patriots could be counted in the ranks of the Revolutionists we certainly know them not.

Others there wore, on the contrary, who, finding the obligations of their priestly vows an intolerable yoke, cast it off and sought liberty in the profession of creeds in which they did not believe. We know how bitter is the hatred of such men for the faith they have abjured, and to what extremes they will go to satisfy it.

Others again—and the names of many such have acquired a European and even an American notoriety—had been, while still within the pale of the Catholic Church and holding a position in her ministry, found guilty of various crimes, sometimes of public notoriety, of the most scandalous nature, and punished for the same. Punished again and again, and at last excommunicated, suspended, interdicted, these men found a refuge in Piedmont, or in England, or the United States, justifying the crimes which they did not and could not deny by accusing the Church which had cast them out. We need only recall to the reader the terrible indictment of Cardinal

Newman drawn up against this class of reprobates in the person of one of their cleverest and most notorious representatives.

The old, popular, inveterate prejudices against the Church of Rome, her pretended "errors and corruptions," the perpetual war-cry of the most fanatical and least enlightened sectarians against the Pope as "the Man of Sin," against the Papacy as "the Kingdom of Satan," were too wide-spread on both sides of the Atlantic forty years ago, and are too prevalent even at this day, not to find a ready echo in the pulpit, the press, and the interested portions of the religious community. We know how these men were received, petted, lionized, set up as glorious conquests of the Gospel truth over the corruptions of Popery, and listened to as eagerly by gaping church-audiences and packed lecture-halls as if every one of them was a Luther sent down expressly from heaven to help demolish utterly Papal Rome and to free Italy and the world from the incubus of that grand system of intellectual domination—the Papacy

So with the emissaries of the secret societies, and with the bands of Garibaldi, and with the fleet of Persano and the armies of Fanti and Cialdini, these men returned to Italy, to the Pontifical States. They had—and they knew it —many like themselves, deposed, degraded, despised, who had remained behind in city and country place, looking forward to the coming of the Revolution as to the dawn of that liberty in which evil should be good, wrong should be right, error should be truth, the corrupt heart should have its full satisfaction; in which the lawless should be the lawgivers and judges, and the disrobed priest should be free to pick up the mud in the gutters and cast it in the face of bishop, and cardinal, and Pope.

At length the dawn of this liberty came in Central Italy in 1859-60. In Piedmont it had come in 1848, when the famous Siccardi Laws, inspired by these unpriestly and unhallowed refugees, did away, as a first step toward the emancipation coveted, with the ecclesiastical courts which had tried the prevaricating ministers of the altar, found them guilty, punished them, and branded them with a stigma of indelible

infamy.

As they did in Piedmont in 1849, so did they in Umbria in 1860. And they were evidently in a great hurry to do it. They began by abolishing the ecclesiastical courts; by taking away from the Church the right to judge her own ministers, and for notorious prevarications committed in the fulfilment of their sacred functions, for the public transgression of laws which were the very bulwark of priestly virtue, the guarantee to the faithful priest of the reverence and unbounded confidence of the people to whom he ministered.

There were so many of these "returned, patriot priests," as they called themselves, who wanted to see the Church stripped of every vestige of freedom, of authority, and bound hand and foot by the new political power! And then there were so many others—at least it was hoped so —in Umbria and elsewhere who were to be won over to the new order of things by being made independent of episcopal reprimand or control, by being rewarded for the favor they had shown to the now dominant ideas!

Then simultaneously with the arbitrary decree abolishing ecclesiastical courts came one taking away from churches and all ecclesiastical edifices their sacred character and all the immunities enjoyed from the birth of Christianity almost. Then again was fulminated, with the same hot haste, another edict taking away from the ecclesiastical authorities all control and jurisdiction over establishments of education of every grade. These edicts were published respectively on the 25th and 28th of September, 1860, consequently within less than two weeks after the first Piedmontese soldier had passed the frontiers of Umbria.

Cardinal Pecci, who had reason to remember the sanguinary scenes which followed the needless storming and bombardment of Perugia, as well as the brutal discourtesy shown to himself by the Piedmontese generals, was not to be deterred by any personal considerations from doing at once what he thought to be his duty. He remembered the long imprisonment and exile with which were visited on the bishops of Piedmont acts such as that he was now about to perform. Yet he did not hesitate an instant.

On September 30 he wrote to the Royal Commissary, who, authorized or unauthorized, had taken on himself thus to overturn by a stroke of the pen the foundations of the religious order which had subsisted for so many ages.

"If your first decree," he says, "deprives the Church of the power to judge her own ministers, the second forbids her in a great measure to fulfil her mission of preaching truth and instructing the peoples. This is a mission which she has received, not from man, but from God—a mission which, extending to all the nations of earth, should much the more fully have its free exercise in a Catholic community through the instruction of youth.

"The decree admits that religion is inseparable from a wise instruction and education. But then it excludes in the most absolute manner the direction and superintendence of the religious authority from the institutions in which youth is instructed and educated, and substitutes for it privately those of the government.

"It is easy to measure the scope and consequences of this measure. By it you violate the constitutional right of the Church; you alter the solemn agreements which accompanied the erection of these institutions; you violate and set aside the last will and testament of the generous benefactors who founded them and endowed them on such formal conditions; you ignore the origin of these foundations and the property of the Church in those which, under her direct auspices and with her own substance and means, she called into existence.

"See yourself, sir, if I have not good reason to protest against all this, and, in my position of a bishop and a guardian of the sacred interests of the Church, I can help expressing my formal reprobation and the profound pain these measures have caused me."

No steps were then taken to arrest or imprison the courageous prelate. He felt, no doubt, that his remonstrances would be vain; nevertheless he thought it his duty both to write and to act. He was not one to make a public parade of his opinions and sentiments on any occasion. He always acted for a purpose, and waited until Providence, to whose good pleasure he solely looked, furnished him the fitting opportunity. Even then he implored the divine help as fervently as if all depended on the lights vouchsafed to him from on high.

He was busy consulting his brother-prelates and consulted by them, counselling with his priests on the difficulties which were fast gathering around them, when, in the autumn, another fatal blow was dealt the clergy and Catholic people of Umbria by the suppression and dispersion of the Monastic Orders of men and women and the confiscation of their property, even of the dower which the members had brought with them into their respective communities. In Perugia, from its first occupation, the Piedmontese troops had taken possession of the convents and monasteries. One magnificent establishment in particular, the most ancient and the most beautiful of all, the Benedictine monastery and church of San Pietro Cassinese, was horribly ill used by these barbarians, who, under the cross of Savoy and in the army of a Catholic king, behaved like the Huns of Attila or Genseric's Vandals, and defaced the exquisite frescoes of the cloisters and refectory. Even Protestants who since then visited the place have expressed their reprobation of this gratuitous, purposeless, and wanton destruction.

But what was all that as compared with the wrong done to the communities themselves, who had made the house of God so glorious, and the walks and community-rooms in their monastic homes an image of the everlasting home?

These establishments were blessed by the people, for they belonged to the people, who found there at all times spiritual counsel and aid, and in seasons of distress and affliction help, and medicine, and food, and loving words, and kind looks—doors and hearts never closed to the voice of the needy.

But it was the secular clergy who were to be, in one way, the greatest sufferers. The regular priests, members of these

Monastic Orders, were their ever-ready, efficient, and most generous helpmates in the ministry in every work that regarded the sanctification and salvation of souls. They had made the holy places of Umbria, and in these holy places had been born, and had grown, ripened, and borne such delicious fruit, all that is fairest and best in Italian art, literature, and science, without mentioning that sanctity of life which left its fragrance everywhere.

Cardinal Pecci, with a heavy heart, but with his soul all aflame with righteous indignation, again wrote to the Royal Commissary, who, backed by the anti-Catholic spirit which ruled in the Piedmontese Cabinet and Parliament, set at naught, in promulgating and executing his decree, the restrictions and limitations imposed by the king. They were merciful dispositions tempering the rigor of the law of suppression. But the men of the Revolution knew not what mercy or moderation was.

"The decree published by your Royal Commissariat," he writes, "... suppressing the monastic families together with many other institutions, and sequestrating their property, fills up to overflowing the cup of bitterness held to the lips of all the bishops of Umbria. This decree, starting from considerations as false as they are insulting to the clergy, evidently aims at wounding religion and social justice itself.

"It is a Catholic maxim that it appertains solely to the supreme authority of the Church to found and approve Religious Orders nor, independently of that same authority, may any temporal power order even their partial dissolution or suppression. How can you juridically justify the spoliation and confiscation of properties already sacred both by their nature and destination, the right to possess which and the inviolability of which are guaranteed by all natural reason and positive social law?

"Then this spoliation is accomplished in the name of a Catholic government—of a government which, a few days before[5] this decree, had been obliged to acknowledge and confess in an official act that the ecclesiastical nature of property does not in any way weaken the right of possession.

"You put in force for these provinces of Umbria, by an exceptional measure, the modern Sardinian legislation which called forth the censure and opposition of Catholic sentiment, and met with the loudest remonstrances throughout the Piedmontese kingdom—a legislation afterward formally condemned by the Supreme Head of our religion in his consistorial allocution of July 26, 1855. And, moreover, these laws come to be applied here with a harshness and a sweeping extension all the greater that the religious corporations suppressed are more numerous, and that the poor religious are nowhere allowed to remain in their cloisters.

"Wherefore, seeing all this, Mr. Commissary, I cannot refrain from complaining, and from condemning with pastoral liberty the decree itself in all its parts."[6]

The cruelty—not harshness merely, but wanton cruelty —with which these laws of suppression were enforced have elicited from non-Catholic writers severe and just animadversion. Not all Protestant writers nor all Protestant educated men are willing to condemn as useless or as injurious to society these wonderful organizations of self-sacrificing and devoted men who were, in the middle ages, the greatest benefactors of European society. The cruelty with which they were driven out in Italy from the desolate and barren mountain solitudes which they had made their abode was all the more purposeless that the government had no use for the dwellings which they left behind.

These remote monastic houses amid the barren summits of the Apennines were the real providence of the country-folk far and near. This was peculiarly the case with one monastery in Umbria, the Camaldolese of Monte Corona.. The Cardinal

---

[5] Note of Count Cavour to the Swiss government on November 20, 1860.

[6] "Scelta," p. 464.

Archbishop of Perugia, in his indignation, again appealed to the king against the extreme rigor of his commissary in Umbria, who seemed to have but little regard for the royal wishes.

"The case," he says, "which now happens under my eyes touches the Hermit-Congregation of Camaldolese monks situated at Monte Corona. These virtuous recluses, to whom an illustrious ancestor of your Majesty, Charles Emmanuel, Duke of Savoy, at the solicitation of the venerable Father Alexander di Ceva, gave an honorable abode in his states about the close of 1601, are now made the object of ignoble and rancorous calumnies. ... Dispersed within the space of eight days, they were compelled to tear themselves away from the famous sanctuary which they had themselves founded.

"Men of stainless life, of unbounded popularity among our country-folk, whom solitude, silence, and prayer perpetually separated from all worldly pursuits, they were accused of mixing themselves up with politics! Men whom the world never saw coming down from the lonely peak of their inaccessible mountain, except when the offices of brotherly charity compelled them (and whose convent was the refuge of the pilgrim, the infirm, and the needy)—these were held up as persons who imperilled the interests of the nation! ...

"If, at least, they had been allowed the time and facility to justify themselves! But testimonies in their favor, and intercessions, though never so numerous, availed not to clear them. Nor were the members of the municipal councils allowed to give any expression to their opinion in their favor. They are already undergoing the hard lot to which inexorable fate condemns them in spite of the temperate restrictions of your royal decree. So that, in the era of Italian suppressions, they are condemned to endure the extremity of misfortune from which, under the foreign domination of the French, by an honorable exception, was saved the sacred Hermit-Monastery of Monte Corona, as our history testifies. ...

"Thus, O Sire, every temperate precaution taken by your Majesty was frustrated, the very will of the sovereign was defeated by the disloyalty with which the law was executed. And thus the fate of so many most worthy religious persons comes to be decided by the harsh and oppressive measures of your commissioners. For besides the fact that this oppression has not been so exercised in the other provinces, these measures are too manifestly in opposition to the rights of religion and the social order.

"... In denouncing these incidents to your Majesty I cannot help allowing to overflow, in words of lamentation, the bitter grief which tortures the soul of a bishop at the sight of the repeated shameful outrages committed against the venerable rights of the Church, and at the pitiful condition to which the interests of religion are daily brought in our midst."[7]

All these eloquent and statesmanlike documents were only the echo outside the Italian Parliament in Turin of the admirable and exhaustive speeches delivered there by the illustrious Cesare Cantù—speeches which would have been listened to with respect and admiration of the speaker at Westminster and Washington, but which produced no effect on a revolutionary assembly bent on blotting out from Italy all trace of past legislation and institutions.

Just as little effect had Cardinal Pecci's letters or memoirs on the mind of the king. Nevertheless neither he nor his brethren in the episcopate ceased to protest and remonstrate. No less than nine of these eloquent remonstrances, made in his own name, were addressed to the Piedmontese authorities, and in nine others his name is found with those of his brother-bishops.

He lifted his voice in this solemn manner, however, only when forced to it by an imperious sense of duty. In submitting to the new domination he did not accept it or conceal his opinion of its unlawfulness. Ceasing to struggle against resistless might, he labored without ceasing to save the souls of his people, counselling the moderation which he practised himself, inducing all who obeyed him to practise more

---

[7] Perugia, June 24, 1861, "Scelta dei Atti Episcopali," pp. 466-69.

fervently than ever before the duties of prayer with all the Christian virtues, avoiding in word and deed all that could give offence to others or afford a pretext to the ill-disposed to annoy or to persecute.

While openly and immovably opposed to a government which discarded the legislation, institutions, and traditions of the Christian past, Cardinal Pecci never forgot, in dealing with those in power, the courtesies of life and that gentle dignity of manner which adds so much to superior station. He was careful not to offend where his conscience would not permit him to conciliate. And he never sought to communicate with the new authorities save when he wished to serve the private or public interests of his flock.

In truth, it would have been worse than useless to attempt to conciliate the spirit which ruled the government, the administration, the legislature, or the revolutionary press during all these fateful years. Conciliation, so far as they were concerned, meant more than to compromise on the most sacred principles; it meant virtual, if not formal, renouncement of one's most cherished and conscientious convictions. It was something like apostasy.

As to the lower classes of the men who swelled the revolutionary party and sought a reward in some form or other for the deeds done to serve the cause, it was impossible to conciliate them. Their anti-clericalism and intolerance of everything religious and priestly was and is the blind, blasphemous, unquenchable rage of Garibaldi, their ideal hero. Every city in the annexed Papal States swarmed with these Sbirri of the "sects" or secret societies as soon as they fell under the Piedmontese rule.

These unsatisfied and insatiable servants of the Revolution were evermore on the watch for opportunities and pretexts to display their patriotic zeal and anti-clerical passions. They found a very plausible pretext in the severity shown by Cardinal Pecci in censuring three of his priests who had openly set themselves in opposition with the authoritative teaching of Pius IX. He was denounced to the civil magistrates as having committed a punishable offence by "exciting men to contemn the laws of the kingdom." The court decided that the accusation was groundless; but the case was appealed, and the higher court in its turn declared the Cardinal innocent.

II. CONTENDING FOR THE RIGHTS OF MONASTIC CLERGY

Among the cruel anxieties of his position none was more painful than to see, in the suppression of Monastic Orders, the sequestration of their property, and the breaking up of so many homes of peaceful piety, poverty, prayer, and labor, the number of helpless men and women—many of them infirm and aged—cast upon the world without a roof above them or any adequate means of support. All of these, in choosing to enter religious life in their youth, had devoted their entire existence to the community of which they became members. Very many, if not most, of the communities of men were made up of persons who had brought a goodly share of their worldly substance to their new home. What they brought was their own; they had a perfect right to dispose of it, just as they had an unquestioned right to select their own way of living. This was the case especially with the contemplative orders. As to the communities of women, all brought their dower. Their parents gave to them, on selecting a life of celibacy and retirement, what they would have given them in worldly bridals. These transactions were sanctioned alike by the laws of the Church and the civil laws. It was natural justice as well as religion which presided over the establishment of the monastic home, over the contract formed with it by parents and children. Such homes and their property could no more belong to the state nor be subject to sequestration than the home and property and revenues of the prince, the peasant, or the mechanic. And then to come all of a sudden, and by the brutal right of superior force to turn these men and women, living in accordance with the most ancient and revered laws of the land, out on the street, penniless, homeless, and incapacitated from following any lucrative calling—it was a monstrous injustice, calling down reprobation on a government which ought to be Christian, but which was, in this as in all else, doing the work of Antichrist.

What could Cardinal Pecci do to alleviate such misery? The new masters of Italy seized his income as well as that of his clergy. He and they would get just as much or as little as it pleased the minister of Victor Emmanuel to give—that is, nothing at all to those esteemed unfriendly to the new order of things, and a pittance, sadly diminished and very irregularly paid, to all the others. But the good Cardinal could find resources even in his poverty; for he spent but little, very little indeed, on himself, frugal and austere as he had ever been. And now he would fain refuse himself even the necessaries of life to have something to give to that crowd of wanderers whose hearts had so long been set on that other and better world.

On March 5, 1863, King Victor Emmanuel published a royal edict requiring that all appointments to positions in the clergy and all acts relating to the same should be submitted to the civil authority, and should have no effect or practical validity till confirmed in the king's name by what is known as the royal placet or exequatur. In this decree the Holy See, to which it appertains to nominate and provide for all ecclesiastical dignities and benefices, is spoken of as "a foreign power."

The right here claimed and arrogated by the usurping Piedmontese government is unblushingly described as "one of the supreme rights of the civil power," whereas in all past European jurisprudence the right of royal *placet* or *exequatur* was only granted by the Holy See to certain sovereigns, for a certain time and within certain limits, as a reward for certain extraordinary services rendered to Christendom. In other kingdoms this right was used by the governments in spite of the Church, which never ceased to protest against it as a usurpation. In the former dukedom of Savoy and kingdom of Sardinia the concordats with the Holy See most explicitly affirmed the nature of such right as being a concession and favor of the ecclesiastical or spiritual power.

Hence the unblushing boldness of the minister who spoke in the king's name. But, in truth, Right had very little to do with all the proceedings of Victor Emmanuel and the Revolution in Central Italy. Might alone prevailed. It was needless hypocrisy to seek to color usurpation and oppression by the fair name of justice or right. It was worse than hypocrisy, a pitiful falsehood, to speak of the supreme power in the Church as being "a foreign power" in Italy, and, above all, in the very provinces which had, since the eighth and ninth centuries, acknowledged the Pope, even in the times of the Free Republics, as the suzerain power.

Again the bishops of Umbria had recourse to Cardinal Pecci as their counsellor and mouth-piece, and another magnificent remonstrance was drawn up by him and sent, with his own and his colleagues' signatures, to Victor Emmanuel on June 8, 1863.[8]

There does not exist a nobler monument of episcopal independence and noble Christian liberty in asserting the rights of God and of His Church as against the pretensions and usurpations of the secular power.

Such a pretension "can in nowise be made by a government which is and would continue to be Catholic. Mayhap the divine commission given to Peter and his successors to feed the whole Christian flock, to loose and to bind upon earth, had annexed to it the condition that they should begin by obtaining the placet, or consent of the powers of this world? And the divine mission imposed on the Apostles to preach to all nations and to instruct them in the divine commandments was perchance subordinated to the good pleasure and the restrictions of the civil magistrates?

"Far from it. Peter and the Apostles, and so many other illustrious pastors following their example, struggled and endured martyrdom for no other reason than that they proclaimed the New Law of Christ, no matter how rigorously forbidden by the world, in spite of the prohibitions and

[8] "Scelta di Atti Episcopali," pp. 357 and following.

persecutions of mere human politicians. The independence of the power divinely entrusted to the Visible Head of religion and to the other lawful pastors for the spiritual government of the Christian society has its origin from God; whosoever attacks or ignores it denies the work of God in founding and organizing His Church. To oppose impediments or put restraints such as those in question on the exercise of this power is just to place a human institution above the divine, and to make an earthly power the judge and reformer of a divine commission. ...

"... Modern theorists will not or know not how to distinguish the two well-defined paths along which, by divine ordinance, both the civil and the ecclesiastical powers have to travel toward the end assigned to each respectively. The modern theory will have the much-desired harmony between Church and state considered as a right of inspection (on the part of the latter), whereas this harmony is only greatly recommended for the sake of the reciprocal advantage of the respective subjects of both societies. It thus transforms into a legal patronage and mastery the obligation which each power is under toward the other of assisting and protecting it, in order that each society may fully enjoy its due proportion of utility. Hence it is that, instead of affirming the original independence and superiority of the spiritual power, people endeavored to make of the Church a ward and servant of temporal monarchies."

The remonstrance then deals with the history of the practice called exequatur. The first trace recorded of it occurs in the pontificate of Urban VI (1378-1389) during the great Western schism. The concession, aiming at verifying the authenticity of the papal rescripts and other such documents in a time of calamitous doubt and division, was only given to certain Church prelates and judges in such churches as were most in danger of schism. And the concession was only a temporary one. When there were no more anti-popes or danger of intrusion into pastoral offices this exequatur ceased.

In so far as the house of Savoy is concerned, the concession of exequatur, or all favors granted by the Popes in the matter of benefices or patronal rights, is not one of doubt or obscurity. Such favors that were granted for a time were then claimed as a right, made the subject of grave abuse, gave rise to long and complex negotiations, which were all settled by that great canonist, Benedict XIV, on January 6, 1742. But even he distinctly asserted, what the Piedmontese government of the day recognized, "the independence and inviolability of all papal instructions issued for the spiritual government of that Catholic country."

The remonstrance thereupon contrasts with these facts of past history what has just happened in Central Italy. "The dispositions announced in the ministerial circular of March 22 [1863] depart altogether from these rules, and, setting aside the economy of the conventions concluded in former times [between the Sardinian and Pontifical governments], they arrogate to themselves an absolute and lordly power of registration on all the acts without distinction of the ecclesiastical power."

This, of course, is what the Holy See never could in any supposition tolerate.

The ministerial circular promulgating the new law affirmed that the government only did what always had been done hitherto. This was a palpable falsehood.

"For these dioceses of Umbria," the remonstrance says, on the contrary, "a comparison with the past is too eloquent not to convince any one that the passage from a condition of perfect religious liberty to that of registration and bondage to the state is not only a *novelty*, but a novelty all too real and baneful.

"Is it not a novelty, a novelty in principle, to consider the authority which the Supreme Head of the Church exercises in the midst of the Catholic fold as a foreign authority?

"Is it not a novelty that lay officials should intrude themselves as spies and judges of the spiritual relations between the faithful and their pastors, and of what it is either expedient to do or to permit for the protection and increase of religion?

"Is it not a novelty to give to a single functionary of the treasury the authority to inquire into all ecclesiastical pensions, to receive all opposing documents, to judge appeals, to incite people to refuse, and to confiscate the documents or petitions relating to the refusal?

"Is it not a novelty, in giving the exequatur to revenues for sacred functions, to seek at the same time to fulfil financial transactions, imposing on ecclesiastical bodies which have no legal existence the obligation to convert their property into bonds on the state?"[9]

And so the terrible arraignment went on, enumerating such acts of inconceivable oppression and meanness as would, if made known, have ruined any government in a country where people read the newspapers. But in Italy the masses are not a newspaper-reading people, and the government presumed on the fact to tyrannize with impunity.

"It was the old art of heterodox innovators," the Cardinal elsewhere says to the king, "to make people Relieve that the spiritual power might be always laying traps for the civil power. Their object was thereby to put an end to any beneficial mutual influence or understanding between the Church and the state, and thus to introduce the baneful theory that there should exist between them systematic distrust and aversion. ..."

There is a disheartening picture of the working of this mean and tyrannical interference with the government of the Church in the minutest details, and the spy-system introduced into this state superintendence of all Church accounts and ministerial functions. These are things never till now heard of in the English-speaking world, and will account for the reiterated and indignant remonstrances of Pius IX, and the no less indignant but equally inefficacious protests of his successor.

---

[9] Our readers will doubtless remember that thus was confiscated the property of the Propaganda.

"In the official scales it is not always the conscientious judgment of the bishop, nor the results of the canonical concursus, nor the precedent merits and services, nor the exemplary priestly life which have the greatest weight in obtaining for a candidate the civil possession of the prebend conferred on him; but certain complacencies for the world, the sympathy of political parties, the merits, in fact, of modern patriotism, are the only things which too often are taken into account.

"It is painful to think of it, deplorable to have to say it! The collation of ecclesiastical livings, trammelled by the governmental *placet*, appeared to people to have been changed into a monopoly of political interests, and into a focus of hateful undertakings against the Supreme Pontificate and the Church. To prevent the installation in the charges obtained by them of hard-working and blameless priests who had received canonical investiture and the approbation of their bishops, men were found to pry into the secret thoughts of the candidates, to have recourse to a systematic distrust of them, to the theories current about suspected persons; they opened up the door to secret denunciations, to low party intrigues. At the same time all kinds of favors are showered on disobedient and worldly minded priests;[10] such obtain charges, honors, pensions, assigned to them most frequently at the expense of the revenues of the Church, as a reward for having turned their backs upon her. There has been no lack of official encomiums and encouragements given to certain clerical factions who, led away by ambition, by self-interest or false liberty, endeavored to upset in the sanctuary itself all order and discipline, and to raise there the flag of emancipation and schism. Abundant subsidies were bestowed on suspended priests. ... Generous presents were set apart for the benefit of

---

[10] By a decree of the Royal Commissary of Umbria, November 30, 1860, "... a monthly pension of sixty Italian lire [twelve dollars] is granted to all priests of these provinces who, for their deeds in favor of liberty or patriotism, have been suspended *a divinis*." (Note added to the text)

unruly priests, at the expense of the Clerical Fund and against the spirit of its founders, while so many cenobites and nuns, stripped of their own lawful patrimony, had not wherewith to buy their daily bread."

One's amazement and indignation go on increasing as the courageous Cardinal enumerates the terrible grievances to which the Church and the clergy are subjected "in the name of liberty and patriotism."

"The fact is," he continues, "that here the assent pf the civil authority is necessary for the execution of every episcopal act, every ecclesiastical arrangement, which does not rigorously regard the interior conscience.

"Here you find proscribed all interference of the bishop with instruction and education, even such as are moral and religious, whether in schools or in boardinghouses, in hospitals and asylums; and that in spite of the formal requirements of the testaments of founders and of the conditions imposed by the foundation.

"Our hearts will not permit us to continue this painful enumeration," the prelates say in concluding. "When the Church is thus ill-treated in a Catholic country it is easy to conjecture what ruinous results follow for the religious interests of a people. We hope that our words may not be altogether without fruit, if your Majesty will only weigh the importance of the subject with which their remonstrance deals in the same balance in which you weigh your duties as a Catholic sovereign."

CHAPTER XVII

A PAUSE IN THE CONFLICT: A FAMILY FEAST

I. Celebrating the Archbishop's Elevation to the Cardinalate

IN DESCRIBING the indefatigable labors of the Archbishop-Bishop of Perugia, although we gave him again and again the title of Cardinal, we could not pause to give to the reader the details of his elevation to the dignity of the Roman purple. In some published biographies of Leo XIII it is positively affirmed that Gregory XVI before his death had created Monsignor Pecci Cardinal, and that some sinister influence prevented Pius IX from giving effect to the act of his predecessor. We think the authentic statement we here make will set all doubts on this point at rest.

"The honor of the sacred purple had already been decreed to him in the intention (nella mente) of Gregory XVI from the moment that the latter recalled him from Belgium; and the proof is that the Pope before his death said to a revered member of the Sacred College who en joyed his confidence—Cardinal Bianchi—that he was so much pleased by Monsignor Pecci's prompt acquiescence in accepting the bishopric of Perugia that he was thinking of promoting him in the next consistory.

"This cardinal, on seeing Monsignor Pecci afterwards in 1847, embraced him affectionately, and, making him sit down by his side, 'The Church has experienced a great loss,' he said, 'in the death of Gregory XVI. I am sorry for it for your sake also, Monsignor; for I can now assure you that were it not for that death you would be already a cardinal.'

"The long and difficult series of political changes which unfolded itself after the death of Pope Gregory was the reason why his gracious purpose was not carried into effect and had to be delayed for several years. Pius IX, who was aware of the promises made on this point in the reign of his predecessor, and mindful of the services rendered by Monsignor Pecci to the Holy See in the charges which he had held, resolved to preconize him in the consistory of December 19, 1853, assigning to him the presbyteral title of St. Chrysogonus. During the festive ceremonies of the promotion, and in receiving the cardinal's hat, he had for companion the illustrious Cardinal Brunelli, just returned from the nunciature of Spain. The entire diplomatic corps, the Roman nobility, and many strangers of distinction visited, on this occasion, the new cardinals. Among the visitors was the present Prince Imperial of Germany, Frederick William, who offered them his most courteous congratulations. From Perugia also came select deputations of all orders of citizens to escort their Cardinal Archbishop on his return, and to lay at the feet of the Pope their respectful thanks for the honor done their city and diocese."[1]

In Perugia, meanwhile, they were making great preparations to celebrate, on his return, his elevation to the cardinalate. It was a family feast, at which holiest love presided—the grateful love of a whole people for a pastor and a parent, for a man of God who has been in their midst the visible image of the divine goodness and beneficence.

In the beginning of 1854 Cardinal Pecci's great family could be said to be a united one. During the dark years of 1848, 1849, and 1850 the Archbishop of Perugia had made superhuman efforts to prevent the outbreak of the evil revolutionary passions which had been fanned into so fierce a flame. Where he could not quench these unholy fires he exerted himself to save his people from their fury and to cure the mischief they had done. When the whirlwind and the flame had passed away for a time he besought the Pontifical government to restore to their families such of the insurgents

[1] MS.

as had been more sinned against than sinning, who had been led away by the artifices of the revolutionary propaganda.

So that the Cardinal had, even among those most bitterly opposed to the Pontifical authority and to the Church itself, not a few who regarded him with respect and who gratefully remembered his kindness.

Let us, therefore, rest mind and heart awhile by assisting at the family feast held by the ancient Etruscan city on her hill-top in honor of her benefactor. It is like being present at a real banquet of the soul, in a lull between two awful convulsions of all the elements of earth and air.

Sunday, February 26, was chosen for these solemnities. From early morning along all the winding roads which led up to Perugia from the surrounding valleys the Umbrian populations could be seen streaming upward in their picturesque costumes. A hard-working, industrious, intelligent, and virtuous people, they had responded heartily to the culture bestowed on them for the last seven years by one whose every thought and care were for their dearest interests. If the revolutionary and anti-Christian propaganda had done them no little harm, the good pastor's watchful and fatherly zeal had done them no little good. They loved him, and they were proud of him; and well might they.

The city is adorned everywhere—a quaint and wonderful old city throughout, with her walls, like those of Siena, scrambling up and down and around a group of enormous crags or hills, on which houses have got built, no one knows how, and the crooked, narrow streets find their way in spite of all the laws of gravitation and symmetry. It is—or rather must have been in the days of Perugino and Raphael—a most picturesque and beautiful city. Christian architecture, sculpture, and painting had made of that old Christian republic nestling on these lofty crags a thing of resplendent beauty; and the glory and the joy thereof have not yet departed altogether, despite the anti-Christian hate of the present masters of Italy and the desolation and destruction of her holy places.

The old, lovely mediaeval Free City was the creation of the

labor-guilds, who, protected by the Popes and protecting these in their turn, made the prehistoric Etruscan stronghold a beehive and a temple to religion, to the arts, and to science, and made of the surrounding territory, wild and mountainous as it is, a very garden.

They are a proud race, these Perugians, and have they not a right to be so? And how they love their native soil! It is so full, for them, of most sacred and most thrilling memories! So on that Sabbath morning of February 26, 1854, they have streamed into the city through Perugia's ancient gates—men, women, children, the old and the young, all who could come to share in the common joyous celebration. They stop on their way to hear Mass in some one of the numerous churches. Perugia was still under Papal rule; the monastic communities had not been suppressed and expelled; and there was in every church and at every altar a succession of priests, who afforded the people an opportunity to gratify their devotion and fulfil the religious obligation of the day. The streets are gaily decorated. The Cathedral Square in particular, with its antique and picturesque palaces, is hung with tapestries and streamers. The disfigured front of the Duomo is concealed by the scarlet and gold drapery; and over the great central door is an inscription—a truth-telling inscription in honor of the man and the day.[2]

---

[2] One remarkable feature of the external decorations of the cathedral was the following inscription, placed above the principal entrance amid rich hangings of scarlet and gold. We give it, deeming that more than one of our readers may take a lesson from classic Italy in getting up either civic or religious celebrations:

"Sancta Perusinorum Ecclesia—*Joachimo Pecci*—Antistite suo perillustri ac spectatissimo—munere SS^{mi} Patris Pii Papae IX—in amplissimum Cardinalium S. R. Ecclesiae Senatum—laetatur adscito—eumque nova hac splendentem gloria—vix dum gratulantium civium vota—bene auspicato fortunat reditu—dulci prosequitur amplexu—Deumque Optimum Maximum—solemni ritu pro diuturna purpurati pontificis incolumitate—Precatur—effusa omnium frequentia et laetitia—IV Kalendas Martii MDCCCLIV"—"The Church of Perugia rejoices that her illustrious and most revered Bishop, Joachim Pecci, has been raised, by the favor of our

The clergy had labored to make of the religious part of the festivities one worthy of their chief, of their city, and of themselves. In truth, the spectacle in the interior of the cathedral was one never to be forgotten. The decorations were all that Italian taste and skill could make them. The multitude of worshippers now fill every available space. All the authorities are present in full official costume, and the clergy crowd the sanctuary. The Cardinal himself fulfils to-day the functions of high-priest, and offers the Mystic Sacrifice which is the center of Catholic worship.

After the Gospel, as is his wont when he pontificates, he delivers a homily to the immense audience. His voice, strong and resonant even at the present time, has its full and vibrating tones, every syllable penetrating to the remotest corners of the sacred edifice.[3]

The circumstances of the times and country needed prayer, and at the end of the Pontifical Mass the Blessed Sacrament was exposed, remaining so all day, this being the most solemn form of supplication in the Catholic Church; and all through afternoon and evening priests and people succeeded each other before the mercy-seat.

In the afternoon there was a session of the great Umbrian Academy of the Filedoni in honor of the Cardinal, and which he honored with his presence. Sixteen of the most accomplished and renowned writers in Umbria read exquisite compositions, all of which were afterwards collected and printed. In the evening there were at the cathedral Pontifical

---

Holy Father, Pius IX , to the dignity of Cardinal of the Holy Roman Church; and, while her citizens have just felicitated him on his happy return, she receives him with a loving embrace, and prays with solemn pomp for the long life of her Cardinal Bishop, together with the overflowing and joyous multitudes of people."

[3] The local journal which describes this family feast says that his discourse touched principally on the earthquake shocks which had occurred during the Cardinal's absence in Rome, and which had done great damage and caused widespread alarm. He exhorted his people to appease the divine anger, and bade them put their trust in the Infinite Mercy.

Vespers, followed by the Te Deum. The music, both in the morning and in the evening services, was in keeping with the artistic renown of Perugia.

Most touching it was at the solemn procession to and from the cathedral, forenoon and afternoon, to witness the sincere veneration of the dense multitudes for their pastor. There was no mistaking this outpouring of the popular heart. More than anything else the eagerness of the children to approach the Cardinal and get his blessing or kiss his hand bespoke the love entertained towards him in the homes of the people. On the route of the procession, also, the city band of music discoursed its sweetest and its most triumphal strains. But sweetest music of all was the voice of the citizens of every class which was heard on all sides, and in no suppressed tones, praising and blessing the man whose whole life and strength were devoted to the good of his flock. The municipal authorities, besides generously paying the expenses of this feast, caused abundant alms to be distributed among the poor who had come to the celebration; and, what was more significant, they gave a marriage-dower to five poor and respectable young women to be selected by the Cardinal in the five wards of the city. In the evening Perugia was magnificently and spontaneously illuminated. During the evening also "the Cardinal had the satisfaction to see in his residence all the authorities, all the most distinguished persons of every rank and condition, enjoying the delightful entertainment to which he had invited them. ... Any one who is acquainted with the character of our people, and who could have been in Perugia both at the time of the elevation of our Bishop to the dignity of Cardinal and at the celebration of last Sunday, must have seen how flattered the Perugians were by the favor conferred on the city in the person of our prelate."[4]

---

4 *Osservatore dell' Umbria*, March 1, *1854*.

II. PERUGIA CELEBRATES HER ARCHBISHOP'S SILVER JUBILEE, 1871

It was in the midst of the gloom which settled on all true Catholic hearts in Italy, after the Piedmontese occupation of Rome, that the time came round to celebrate the twenty-fifth anniversary of Cardinal Pecci's appointment to the see of Perugia. His soul, oppressed as it was by the calamities of the Holy Father, by the manifold spoliations which the Church had almost daily to undergo in every diocese of Italy, and by the means openly taken to choke up and destroy all the springs of Christian life in the land, was but little inclined to joyous celebrations. The church of Perugia, which he had taken to his heart twenty-five years before, and which he had loved with a love so true and so devoted, was also subjected to the same Babylonian bondage. He had labored so hard, after the example of the Master, to make her a glorious church, crowned with the beauty of holiness, and rejoicing in children worthy to be truly called the children of God; and lo! his labors seemed doomed to come to naught. The enemy had come into the field where, with the good grain cast so abundantly into the furrows, the sweat and the tears of the father of the family had fallen, and he had ploughed up the growing corn and sown tares and the seeds of all lawlessness. It was a season for weeping, fasting, prayer, and humiliation before the Most High. How could he consent to rejoice or to listen to the glad voices of his people?

The people would not allow his year of jubilee to pass, nevertheless. They had determined to make him feel that, even though the enemy had come in amongst them in the night and done what havoc he could, the generations whose minds and hearts he, the man of God, had cultivated so lovingly, would bear him plentiful fruits of gladness in the season of need.

Clergy and citizens, therefore, assembled in spite of his reluctance, and resolved to celebrate the occasion with as much solemnity and even more profuse demonstrations of love and gratitude than on the occasion—long ago, across the dark gulf of evil days—of his elevation to the cardinalate. The Cathedral of San Lorenzo again put on her most splendid vesture. Pens whom the Cardinal had trained to emulate his own exquisite culture of the Latin tongue composed commemorative inscriptions, for the portal and other parts of the beautiful edifice, which Cicero and Sallust would have admired.[5] Prelates and dignitaries from the neighboring dioceses, and from Rome itself, came to Perugia to testify their love and admiration for one who, next to Pius IX himself, had been the champion of the oppressed Italian churches, the spokesman of the episcopacy, their model and guide in withstanding evil and upholding the sacred rights of the pastors and their flocks, without ever allowing the watchful invader to discover a word or an act which Christ Himself would not have avowed.

The Holy Father sent his congratulations.. Day by day some new merit revealed itself in the life and actions of the Cardinal-Bishop of Perugia which raised him higher in the esteem of the much-tried Pontiff. The festivities in Perugia were, therefore, a sort of national feast, in which all Umbria, Rome, and Italy joined.

Even the Piedmontese masters of Umbria thought it best not to thwart the popular will on that memorable 17th of January, 1871. The procession to the cathedral was even more magnificent than in 1854, when Perugia, still Papal, and the country population round about filled the beautiful Piazza and the adjoining streets. The inscription above the great central door spoke of "the Acts and Prayers of the Clergy of Perugia" on this solemn anniversary.[6] The omission of the word "people" or "citizens" was significant of the great change which had taken place, and of the prudence imposed on the ministers of religion. But far more significant of the temper of

---

[5] See Appendix D.

[6] *Acta et vota—Cleri perusini.*

the times and of the trials religion was then undergoing is the fact that all day, from early dawn till evening, the Blessed Sacrament was exposed in the cathedral as on occasions when there is some great and urgent need of supplicating the divine mercy. All day priests and people succeeded each other before the mercy-seat.

At ten o'clock in the morning the Cardinal celebrated Pontifical Mass. At noon there was a meeting of clergy and citizens at the episcopal residence; a joint address of congratulation was read to the good pastor, and a joint testimonial of gratitude and veneration presented in the form of a bronze statue of Mary Immaculate, a work of the sculptor Cecchini, a Perugian, which had obtained the first premium in Rome the year before.

In the afternoon there were Pontifical Vespers, a sermon on the Christian Priesthood, Te Deum, and Benediction. The *vota* or prayers recorded for the Cardinal-Bishop are too remarkable to be omitted here:

"Mary, Mother of Grace,[7] who art the protectress, honor, and joy of the people of Perugia, do thou some day repay with a crown of glory Joachim, our Cardinal-Bishop, in return for the golden diadem which his filial hands formerly placed around thy virginal brow.

"Holy Lawrence, thou who art given a command over nature, be propitious, we pray thee, to Joachim, our Cardinal and pastor; grant him to the end of his life that strength with which thou didst appall thy executioners whilst consumed by the slow tortures of thy red-hot gridiron, in order that the men who are continually torturing the Church by their plots may

---

[7] The Virgin Mary is called in the Litany "the Mother of Divine Grace" because she gave birth to the Redeemer, the Author and Fount of grace. A votive church near Perugia bore also the title of Our Lady of Grace. In it was a picture or statue of Our Lady which Cardinal Pecci had crowned on a former occasion.

admire him in spite of themselves."[8] How prophetic of the years following 1878!

"Constantius and Herculanus, bishops and martyrs, since to you once fell the care of this church, bid our Cardinal-Bishop Joachim to govern the clergy and people of Perugia, under your guidance and protection, for many times five years more."[9]

III. Made Protector of the Franciscan Tertiaries

Pius IX about this time, when the infirmities of old age, the sorrows heaped upon the Religious Orders and the secular clergy of Italy, and the perplexities of his situation in Rome rendered the counsels and presence of such men as Cardinal Pecci a need of the heart as well as a political necessity, urged on the latter the acceptance of the see of Frascati, one of the suburban sees of Rome. The change would have enabled the Cardinal to live in the Eternal City, and to be thus within call of the Sovereign Pontiff.

But Cardinal Pecci was bound by so many strong ties to the church of Perugia that he could not think of separation from it so long as the Pope allowed him the freedom of choice. Besides, during these troublous and perilous years the bishops of all Central Italy stood sadly in need of the friendly sympathy and timely advice of one so universally revered as the Bishop of Perugia.

The Holy See, as in all cases where an accurate knowledge of ecclesiastical law and usage, a great experience in dealing with vexed questions, and consummate prudence were necessary, commissioned Cardinal Pecci to settle the

[8] The Roman deacon, St. Lawrence, was treasurer of the church, or the depositary of the fund destined to the poor. He was roasted on a gridiron over a slow fire, to force him to give up the moneys which he had already distributed to the needy.

[9] These early martyrs were, under God, the parents of Christianity in Perugia. Herculanus was a disciple of St. Peter.

difficulties occurring. Together with these frequent and delicate negotiations, he had his share—no light share—in the heavy and manifold labors imposed on all the members of the Sacred College. They have to assist the Pope in governing the universal Church; the congregations or permanent committees into which they are divided are charged with all the various and complex matters pertaining to so vast an administration.

Cardinal Pecci was a member of no less than six of these congregations, and the matters referred to him in this connection alone were more than sufficient to tax the time and abilities of no ordinary man. But his life of austere simplicity and well-regulated laboriousness enabled him, seemingly, to despatch with ease any amount of business.

Rising before the dawn, even in the longest summer days, he was early at the altar, and had paid his debt of worship and devotion when the ordinary occupations of the day claimed his attention. His frugality was that of a hermit; for, while doing nobly the offices of hospitality to invited guests or passing strangers, he allowed himself no indulgence. But these habits of personal austerity and almost monastic asceticism were the hidden secrets of his interior life, known only to the few admitted to his utmost intimacy. To all others whom he received and entertained with the dignity and courtesy of a prince, the rigor with which he treated himself could only be guessed from the atmosphere of sweet spirituality which surrounded the man.

That he inspired sincere affection and deep attachment mingled with veneration has been well proved by the numbers of those who still cherish his memory in Perugia, and who emulate both his stainless life and his scholarly qualities.

In 1875 Pius IX, aware of the life-long admiration of Cardinal Pecci for St. Francis of Assisi and the great family of men and women who for the last six hundred years follow in his footsteps, appointed him Protector of the Third Order of St. Francis—an organization established by the saint to enable all persons living in the world to combine and help each other in practising the cardinal virtues of the Gospel.

To help in any way toward restoring the Franciscan institutions to all their primitive vigor and splendor, to make known all over the earth the heavenly spirit of the Saint of Assisi, the passionate lover of Christ crucified and the devoted follower of Christ's poverty, was to Cardinal Pecci a labor of love, one into which he could throw himself with all the ardor of youth.

He proceeded to Assisi as soon as he possibly could, and there, on November 26, in an assemblage of all the Franciscan Tertiaries, of the clergy regular and secular, and a great crowd of people, he took formal possession of his new charge. The address which he delivered on that occasion was only the prelude to more solemn and authoritative utterances in later years, as we shall see.

"When, a few days ago," he said, "His Holiness Pius IX was pleased to appoint me Protector of the Confraternity of the Third Order of St. Francis, which sprang up so many centuries ago in this very city, my heart overflowed with joy. From my infancy I was devoted to this great saint, and have been ever an admirer of his heroic virtues; and I have always looked upon the Third Order founded by him as upon an institution springing from divine inspiration, one replete with Christian wisdom and fruitful in most blessed results for religion and the entire human race.

"To employ one's self in favoring and spreading such an order is to foster a work of the highest benefit to religion, to morality, and to civilization; it is to supply a salutary remedy for the enormous evils which afflict society, and to restore upon earth the reign of holy charity and every virtue. Oh! may God grant that amid all the disasters which sadden our souls, and the misery amid which we are compelled to live, we may see with our own eyes a mighty multitude hastening to take refuge under the protection of the poverty loving Saint of Assisi! Then we should, without a doubt, see those men becoming, in the hand of God, so many instruments employed in re-establishing on earth the quiet we have lost and the peace for which men pray so ardently."

Although the most popular writers of our age in the English language, those most bitterly opposed to the Catholic Church, have bestowed praise on him whom Cardinal Pecci calls in his text the Poverello d'Assisi, no man has been held up to so much contempt by French Voltaireanism, by the Revolutionists, Radicals, and Socialists, who so clamorously profess their love for democratic simplicity, equality, and liberty. In the invasion of Italy and Spain by the revolutionary armies under the Bonapartes no monastic order, no religious establishments were the objects of such fanatical hatred or subjected to such horrible profanations and wanton destruction as the Franciscans, their churches and convents. And the men who to-day misgovern both countries under the banner of liberalism have inherited this same blind, inconsistent, and unreasoning fanaticism.

Since the Divine Author of Christianity was born in a cave by the roadside, brought up in the laborious obscurity of the carpenter's shop, and evangelized Judea and Galilee, without possessing a roof of his own, a bed to repose upon, or a second garment for his use, no man has appeared upon earth who more sincerely, ardently, effectively labored to make the poverty of the Gospel, its practical equality and brotherly love—all the divine charities which blossom and ripen upon the cross of Christ—to be loved truly and embraced heartily than Francis of Assisi.

His dream, his aim, the object of his entire life was to bring back the Christendom, the society of the thirteenth century to that democracy, that society of all mankind become children of God and living on earth, according to Christ's doctrine and example, in the practice of all brotherly virtues.

If this was a dream it was a sublime, a beautiful dream, one which should render the name of the dreamer dear to all lovers of humanity, all believers in the possibility of establishing here below a society in which order and freedom, equality and justice, charity and religion shall be no visions of the brain, no subjects of idle aspiration or bootless quest, but a mighty, ever-present *Reality*!

And how amiable, in every noble sense of the word, was that voluntary mendicant of Assisi, who called around him men born, like himself, to wealth and station, but who aimed only at practising anew upon earth the absolute and perfect poverty practised by Christ and His Apostles and Disciples, their meekness, patience, and unbounded charity, in order that the Spirit which made their own poor cells so fragrant of paradise might penetrate into the palaces of the great, the homes of the wealthy, the cottages of the laboring poor, and be like the attraction of a divine magnetism drawing all men and women, not, indeed, to become monks and nuns, but to band themselves together for the purpose of despising the pride of earthly riches, the enjoyment of sinful luxury and pleasure, of seeking out the needy, the suffering, the heart-sore, and the captive, and of making of brotherly love the law of life for Christian society.

The men who wanted to be Christ-like in poverty, in self-denial and self-sacrificing devotion to their fellow-men, followed Francis in his manner of living. The women, under fit. Clara, or Clare, the towns woman of Francis, emulated the poverty and virtues of Mary, the Mother of Christ, whom He on the cross gave to the fisherman, John, the son of Zebedee, to be cared for as a mother, homeless and shelterless as she was.

Men and women living in the world who desired, in the measure possible to them, to imitate Christ and His Mother, and to bring back among the late Christian society the brotherly love, the gentleness, the spirit of prayer, the tender care of the poor and sick, which the Acts of the Apostles describe as existing in the first Christian community in Jerusalem, became members of the Third Order. Within the saint's lifetime it counted more than half a million of persons of every condition of life, from kings and queens to peasants and shepherds. St. Louis, King of France, and his cousin, St. Ferdinand of Castile and Leon, with their mothers and their queens, with many a heroic noble and knight in their service, and many a noble matron and maiden in their courts, and

crowds of their subjects, undertook to practise the evangelical morality and all its divine virtues more faithfully under the protection of that lowly mendicant of Assisi.

Let us not be turned aside from the contemplation of noble ideals because men have failed to make of them permanent and widespread practical realities. We should never effect any reform or improvement in our own lives or in the world around us if we allowed ourselves to be cast down by the inconsistencies and failures of men who had begun well and then fallen away. Let us listen rather to the men who, in the present need of society and the whole moral world, endeavor to revive in themselves and to restore wherever their influence extends the divine spirit of heroic perfection which animated men long ago, and which, like the seeds of the noblest plants, God never allows to perish utterly from the face of the earth.

Such a man was and is Joachim Pecci.

From his earliest boyhood his feet had trodden the bare cloisters of the Franciscan Observantines near his mother's home in Carpineto. His admiration for these faithful followers of the Saint of Assisi had grown with his growth. As a youth, a priest, the governor of provinces, the honored diplomat, the bishop, and the cardinal, he had known these Franciscan lovers of evangelical poverty—known them thoroughly—and his veneration had gone on increasing. The Third Order of Seculars, or persons living in the world, had become extinct, or nearly so, under the joint action of Voltairean ridicule and revolutionary violence. Honestly, conscientiously Joachim Pecci believed that to revive the spirit and the rule of St. Francis of Assisi, to propagate this Secular Third Order among all ranks of the Christian people, would be the providential means to renew the face of the earth.

We believe that in our day practice is more potent than preaching, example than mere profession. We believe, if ever the countries of ancient Christendom are brought back to Christ, it must be, not by the eloquence of a St. Paul, a St, Bernard, or a Bossuet, but by diviner examples of poverty, purity, self-denial, and self-sacrifice than even those beheld in the Apostolic age.

Men who remember how prepotent feudalism had marred, at the end of the twelfth and the beginning of the thirteenth century, the fairest fruits of the Christian culture of preceding ages, and how military might, violence, and licentiousness were the only forces, apparently, which controlled, or aimed at controlling, European society-will not be astonished that Providence, in seeking to restore the Christian ideal, should have inspired the Poverella of Assisi to become in his life and person a living image of the Divine Master.

We have followed his footsteps in Italy and Spain from the hills above Bologna to Florence and Rome, and from Rome to Barcelona and all along the pilgrim's road to Galicia and the sepulcher of St. James. Men like Charles Dickens and Ruskin can understand and appreciate the beautiful legends which weave themselves around the supernatural life of a man so divine–how the blood gushing from his self-imposed austerities and falling on the thorny shrubs in winter, forthwith was transformed into flowers of supernal hue and fragrance; how, in the province of Vichi, a barren tract to which the saint withdrew to meditate and pray became a land of flowers, while the fountain at which he cooled the ardor of the consuming fire within him became a fount of healing waters. No wonder that beneath those feet, which he yearned to stretch out to the nails that pierced his Master's, our earth, athirst for Christ-like holiness, meekness, and charity, should spontaneously put forth flowers unseen before.

We need such men now; we shall need them more in the evil days the world has to pass through till from out the extremity of ill shall come the salutary reaction.

CHAPTER XVIII

1877—THE LAST YEAR IN PERUGIA

I. Cardinal Pecci at the Golden Jubilee of Pius IX

THE Catholic world is not likely to forget that the year 1877 was celebrated in both hemispheres as the Episcopal Jubilee of Pius IX. He had been consecrated bishop in Rome on June 3, 1827. His fiftieth anniversary, in spite of the occupation of the Eternal City by the Piedmontese, was celebrated there with a solemnity and an enthusiasm such as even Christian Rome had never witnessed.

Foreseeing the spontaneous and irresistible outburst of Catholic sentiment all over Italy on the coming anniversary, the revolutionary Parliament sitting in Rome brought in "The Clerical Abuses Bill," enacting the severest penalties against all persons, clergymen especially, of every grade, who under any circumstances, in public or in private, should give utterance to words censuring the acts of the government. A priest in the confessional or called to administer the last sacraments to the dying, by the mere refusal of absolution to the worst criminals, to the plunderers of the Church or the direct authors of the worst calamities under which she was suffering, would, on the complaint of the false penitent, be liable to fine, imprisonment, or banishment from Italy. It was one of the objects of this law, as its authors did not hesitate to avow in the legislature, that, although they could not punish the Pope himself without violating the Law of Guarantees, yet they could punish any inferior ecclesiastic who should dare to publish or print the Pope's utterances censuring the acts of the government.

The celebration of the Golden Jubilee all over Italy, together with the manifestations and addresses which it would give rise to, naturally would afford the enemies of the Papacy the opportunity of reaping a rich harvest in fines and vindictiveness.

But Pius IX, though grieving for the consequences of this tyrannical law to the Italian clergy, was not to be intimidated by the threats of the triumphant Revolution. In the consistory of March 12 he denounced the bill and the government to the whole civilized world. The infirmities which bent his aged frame could not bend that invincible spirit of his. "By this law," he says to the assembled cardinals, and through them to all Christendom, "the words and writings of every description uttered by the ministers of the altar in the discharge of their sacred office, and expressing disapproval or censure of any act or decree of the civil authorities, though such act or decree may be never so opposed to the laws of God or of His Church, are equally liable to punishment."

The ordinary civil courts alone have a right to decide whether or not a priest is justified in refusing absolution to a penitent under sentence of excommunication, even when the priest has no power to absolve him, or whether he may rightly withhold the sacraments from the sick and the dying, irrespective of the dispositions and fitness of these to receive them. But this, as well as the penalties imposed on all who dare to promulgate the judgments of the Holy See on its own inalienable rights and the wrongs it endures at the hands of the oppressor, was intended to intimidate the Sovereign Pontiff himself in the exercise of his spiritual power.

"How is it possible for us," Pius IX exclaims in his righteous indignation, "to govern the Church under the domination of a power which continually deprives us of the means and protection needed for the discharge of our apostolic office? ... We cannot sufficiently wonder that men can be found who ... endeavor to have the world believe, and to persuade the popular masses, that the present position of the Sovereign Pontiff in Rome is such that, even situated, as he is, under the domination of another power, he is in the enjoyment of full freedom, and is able peacefully and unrestrictedly to discharge the duties of his spiritual primacy."

There was a disposition in government and parliamentary

circles to oppose efficacious obstacles to the approaching celebration in Rome by closing the entrance of Italy to the numerous bands of pilgrims from foreign lands, and to forbid the railway companies from transporting Italian pilgrims and deputations to Rome. In that city itself the anti-clerical clubs only demanded that the government should look on without interfering while they took on themselves to prevent or to mar all displays in honor of the Pope's anniversary. But although in some places pilgrims and deputations were treated somewhat roughly, the movement was too general and too mighty to be stopped all of a sudden; besides, the influx of strangers was to bring to the railroad companies and to Rome itself too bountiful a harvest not to be acceptable in the great penury of gold from which Italy and the government were suffering.

So self-interest prevailed over political passion and anti-Christian intrigues, and the Golden Jubilee ran its course of unparalleled enthusiasm.

By a singular and unusual oversight no mention is made in the narrative in another work of the Author[10] of the part taken in the celebration by the hierarchy of the Papal States—the Æmilia, the Marches, and Umbria. And yet among the imposing pageants which succeeded each other in the Vatican in June, 1877, none exceeded in importance and effect that in which figured the cardinals, the archbishops and bishops belonging to the former States of the Church, having at their head the venerable figure of the Cardinal-Archbishop of Perugia.

He had been requested by his colleagues in the pastoral office to draw up and deliver in their name the address of felicitation. This, for him, was a labor of love.

On the morning of the 3d of June Pius IX could have imagined that the bishops of all Italy surrounded him, for all who could come and were privileged to be there on the occasion accompanied the glorious gathering at whose head

[10] "Life of Pius IX," New York, 1877.

shone Cardinal Pecci. This assemblage was the chief and central one in the long series of the Jubilee demonstrations. One might have thought that the entire episcopate of Italy was there, and that its spokesman was the Archbishop-Bishop of Perugia, every one of whose public utterances for the twenty past years had sounded like a trumpet-note through the Peninsula, warning pastors and people to prepare for the impending battle with Revolution and anti-Christian corruption. So there, at the head of cardinals, archbishops, and bishops, stood the white-haired prelate who was to be called Leo XIII and *Lumen in Coelo* ere another June had come with its flowers, and who now poured out the warm tribute of his soul at the feet of Pius IX, *Crux de Cruce*, already in the last agony of his long crucifixion. Let us listen:

"MOST HOLY FATHER: Surely it is by an admirable design of God's providence that while under your Pontificate the worst enemies of the Catholic Church and of her Divine Head, Christ, were permitted to wage against both the most bitter war which the memory of man can recall in the past ages as well as in the present, we should, on the other hand, be given to behold a succession of happy events bringing into the most prominent light the ardent love of the Christian world for the Church and the most faithful obedience toward the Apostolic Chair.

"More than that, the more skillfully devised were the plans of our adversaries, the more successful did the assaults of the revolutionary sects prove—thanks to the connivance or the aid of the temporal powers—the more closely, on the other hand, did faith and charity draw souls together among the Catholic nations, the nearer did the bonds of union draw the flock to the shepherd, the children to their parent, the firmer appeared the faith of all in the Pontifical authority, the more constantly, O Most Holy Father, shone forth the love of the whole world for your person.

"We cannot help feeling that events are directed toward a happy and prosperous issue when we see the faithful of every land pouring as pilgrim-crowds toward the Vatican, or laying their liberal offerings of Peter's Pence at your feet, uniting in solemn and public prayer or giving vent in some other way to the common joy, all striving in concert to celebrate the happy anniversary of that day on which, fifty years ago, God gave you to be consecrated a bishop.

"Therefore it is, Most Holy Father, that we, the pastors of your provinces, especially those of the Marches, Umbria, and Æmilia, and the flocks confided to us, can yield in fervor to none both in our dutiful obedience to you, in our reverence for the supreme power of Peter, and in our enthusiasm in celebrating this most happy day. You were born in the Marches, of the noble blood of Sinigaglia; happy Umbria first received you as a bishop, and first of all the church of Spoleto had the benefit of your labors and was graced by your virtues; and, last, Æmilia, glorified by your pastoral care and the splendor of your Roman purple, sent you to Rome to ascend the sublime chair of Peter.

"Hence, while in our own name we again and again renew to you to-day the solemn profession of our inviolable union with this same Apostolic Chair of Peter, and of our loving devotion to your person, we also declare, in the deepest joy of our hearts, that both our priests and our people share with us this same solemn profession and heartfelt sentiments. Manifold as are the frauds and the violence by which ungodly men unceasingly try to shake their constancy in the Christian religion, they nevertheless ever remain bound to you by unswerving obedience, and from their inmost soul accept the teachings which your infallible authority sanctions. They unite with us in beseeching humbly and fervently the Divine Prince of Pastors to pour down on you with unsparing hand the fulness of His choicest gifts, comforting and directing you in the bitter trials which press upon you, saving and preserving you for the honor and increase of religion, for the defence and support of His Church. That you may have also some visible proof, though never so small, of the most dutiful love and reverence which we and they bear you, we pray you to accept,

Most Holy Father, the little offering they freely make to relieve your own need, and which we beg you to estimate from the love of the givers, not from its material amount.

"It only remains, Most Holy Father, that you, who love us all, bestow on ourselves and on all the faithful people of our dioceses, who have so much to contend with in the present difficult times of revolution, the Apostolic Benediction, which shall bring them wisdom and strength. This we ask for all the more readily that we have good reason to hope that God, at your prayer, on this day of great joy to yourself and your children, will pour down forthwith on all of us the plentiful streams of heavenly blessing."[11]

Pius IX, touched not only by the sentiments expressed in this noble address, but the dignified and reverent bearing of the venerable speaker, could not refrain from expressing his gratification and his thanks. It was, indeed, as if the churches of the Marches, of Umbria, and Æmilia, so unspeakably dear to him, surrounded him, broken by extreme old age and suffering, to lift up their voices to bless him, and their hands to pray for him, their Pontiff and Parent. The members of the episcopal deputation present also expressed their sentiments of admiration. But Cardinal Pecci was little moved by praise, even when coming from the lips of the most revered of Popes, and from those of his most respected brother-bishops.

While in Rome he was privileged to consecrate the new coadjutor-bishop given to him by the Holy Father. This was Monsignor Charles Laurenzi, who had been his vicar-general ever since 1847, sharing his labors, his solicitude, and his trials, deserving and enjoying the Cardinal's unbounded confidence. The episcopal consecration took place in the ancient church of St. Chrysogonus, one of the oldest in Rome, situated in the Transtiberine quarter of the city, and the Cardinal's own titular church.

As the summer passed away the crowds of pilgrims continued to flock into Rome and to press onward to the

[11] "Scelta," p. 403.

Vatican. It was a sight which the Rome of the Popes had not beheld, and may never again behold. But the Revolutionists could not bear the sight of this spontaneous homage of love and veneration paid to an infirm old man whom their usurpation had forced to confine himself to the walls and gardens of the Vatican. There was a tumultuous meeting held by the leaders in the Apollo Theatre to protest against the pilgrimages and the presence in Rome of all these strangers. But they forgot only one thing—that these men and women from every Christian land were not strangers in Rome, in the Rome which Christendom and the Popes had created, and which was the home of the Common Parent. They forgot, too, that many a barbarous dynasty and tribe had ere then possessed themselves of Rome and believed that their possession of it would last for ever. History has told how soon their throne and their sway had vanished. And, besides, Christendom has not yet set the seal of its unanimous and formal international sanction on the present usurpation. There are those who persist in thinking that Rome will be again the City of the Pope-King.

II. THE OLD CAMERLENGO AND THE NEW

Death was busy among the most illustrious cardinals in 1877. We have seen that while Monsignor Pecci was yet in the College of Nobles one of his dearest companions there was Duke Riario-Sforza, afterward Cardinal-Archbishop of Naples. This descendant of the great warrior chief who had placed himself on the throne of Milan, and had been on the point of subjecting all Italy to his sway, was one of those men who, called to the priesthood by divine inspiration, justify the divine choice by a life of supernatural devotion to God and man. A Roman by birth, ranking with the highest, but lifted above all earthly ambitions and sentiments by his ardent desire to serve God, His Church, and Italy to the best of his power, nothing could ever induce him to sanction by act or word of his the designs of the Italian liberals.

He accepted with gratitude his appointment to the see of Naples, because he had been led to believe that in that city he would be free, far away from the theatre of conspiracies and revolutions, to devote all his energies, under a Catholic conservative government, to the advancement of the spiritual welfare of a large, needy, and neglected population.

How that good archbishop labored in Naples; how he spent his fortune, his strength, his life in seeking the lost sheep of the flock, in bringing them back to the fold and tenderly caring for them; how he sought out souls suffering from sin and sorrow, and lifted them up into newness of life; how the poor, the sick, the plague-stricken were dearer to him than children to their mother—contemporary history has told. Some day, perhaps, this holy archbishop, whom even the pens of Protestants and unbelievers have canonized because of his unearthly goodness, will receive the honors due to God's acknowledged saints. At any rate, in 1877 this great and good man, equally dear to Pius IX and to Cardinal Pecci, was taken to his rest. Both the Pontiff and the Cardinal envied him while sincerely mourning his loss.

But "Riario-Sforza had been preceded in the tomb by Cardinal Philip de Angelis, Archbishop of Fermo, who had presided at the Council of the Vatican, and died on July 8. Of the other four cardinals who had shared with him the honor of presiding over that August assembly, the only ones who survived the year 1877 were Cardinals Bilio and De Luca, Cardinals Bizzari and Capalti having succumbed during this year of Jubilee. The loss of De Angelis was most keenly felt by the Holy Father. They were both natives of the Marches, born within a month of each other on that same sunny shore of the Adriatic; raised to the purple, the one in 1838, the other in 1839; brought still nearer to each other by their passionate devotion to the interests of the Church and the unworldly spirit which animated their whole lives. During the conclave of June, 1846, De Angelis was the man to whom Cardinal

Mastai[12] gave his vote, and Cardinal Mastai was the choice of De Angelis for the dangerous honor of the Pontificate. While the one friend (the Pope) was forced to seek in the kingdom of Naples the liberty needed to govern the universal Church, the other was assailed by the revolutionists in his residence at Fermo, dragged like a malefactor to the prisons of Ancona, and there, during forty days, subjected to the most horrible brutality, attempts having even been made to destroy his life by poison. Later, in 1860, the Cardinal-Archbishop of Fermo was once more carried off to prison, this time in Turin, and endured a six years' captivity."

Such were the men—great in everything which constitutes moral grandeur—to whom Cardinal Pecci, like the Pope, was bound by ties of a friendship that is not all of earth. How many such stood around Pius IX in the solemn sessions of the Council of the Vatican!

How many on that memorable morning of June 3, 1877, surrounded the aged form of the Pontiff, on whose brow the first radiance of eternal day already rested, on whose spirit, amid the benedictions of the Old World and the New, the sweet shadows of the peace everlasting were falling fast!

Cardinal de Angelis was one to whose heroic devotion, saintly virtues, and tried prudence Pius IX could trust, as to an own brother, in the greatest emergencies, the dearest interests of the Church. This unlimited confidence had induced him to select the Cardinal-Archbishop of Fermo for the important charge of Camerlengo of the Roman Church—a charge involving, during the vacancy of the Papal Chair, the supreme authority to administer the temporalities of the Holy See.

Cardinal Pecci's ill-health compelled him to remain in Rome all through this memorable summer. He returned to Perugia toward the end of August to superintend the last examinations in the seminary and to preside at the distribution of premiums. Thus to the last was he faithful to his old love for his church and the young clergy. In the midst of September

---

12 "Life of Pius IX," pp. 521-22, eighteenth ed., New York, 1878.

came the tidings that it was the intention of the Holy Father to proclaim him Camerlengo of the Holy Roman Church in the approaching consistory. Thus was he to inherit the trust of Cardinal de Angelis. The letter which brought him this announcement also conveyed an invitation from Pius IX to take up his residence in Rome, leaving Monsignor Laurenzi to administer the diocese of Perugia.

III. THE SHADOW OF THE CROSS FALLS ON CARDINAL PECCI

The Pope, who felt that the end for him was nigh, felt also that he bequeathed to his Cardinal Camerlengo a responsibility beset by unprecedented difficulties. In choosing Cardinal Pecci he seemed to be ratifying the choice of the united bishops of all Italy. To no more firm or prudent hand could the direction of affairs be committed when his own last hour had come.

While the summer and autumn of 1877 passed slowly away, the Jubilee still drawing crowds of pilgrims to the feet of Pius IX, the strength of the venerable invalid was slowly but surely waning. Winter came, and the Catholic world kept its eyes and its heart fixed on those rooms in the Vatican where the self-sacrificing Pontiff daily received his children, causing himself to be carried through their ranks, blessing, consoling, and strengthening them with words which all treasured ever after in their memory.

Meanwhile, and undeterred by the cares of his new charge and the unceasing occupations attached to his position in Rome, Cardinal Pecci was preparing to do for his beloved flock in Perugia what he had ever done yearly since he had been their bishop: he was about to address them for the Lent of 1878 a second pastoral letter on "The Church and Civilization." Such were the lofty arguments he chose to treat in instructing his people on the prevalent errors of the day, and the truths which were the surest antidote to the intellectual poison.

Now that we are acquainted with the solid Christian instruction on all points of doctrine and practice which

Cardinal Pecci had been unwearied in giving .to his flock for thirty-two years, we can admire the wisdom of the man in lifting up priests and people to the attentive study of such living and momentous questions as that which he undertook to treat in the three last Lenten pastorals which he composed for them: in 1876, "The Catholic Church and the Nineteenth Century" in 1877 and 1878, "The Church and Civilization."

IV. THE LIGHT STILL SHINING BRIGHTLY ON PERUGIA

In his pastoral for the Lenten season, 1877, we have, both in the logical treatment of the subject and the simplicity with which the argument at every stage is presented to the intelligence of the ordinary peasant and workingman, a model for all churchmen dealing with such matters. As to the exquisite elegance and harmony of the original Italian we cannot say too much.

"The duty which our pastoral ministry," he says, "has always imposed on us to preach the truth to you has become more pressing at this moment, because of your own increasing need in the midst of an unhappy age. We must speak to you to enlighten your minds, which others are trying to darken by fallacious and seductive doctrines; and we must put you on your guard against certain sayings which are scattered abroad, and which are found to be dangerous in the extreme. Above all, we need to speak to you in order to do away with the confusion which is so dexterously introduced in the popularized ideas that one does not know clearly that which has been condemned as false from that which, being true and correct, is adopted as such.

"Wherefore, dearest children, the war carried on against God and His Church is all the more formidable in this, that it is not always waged loyally, but conducted with fraud and treachery. If the impious men who live in our midst would only speak out and tell us what they are aiming at, our task would be a very easy one; while, on the other hand, the faithful, perceiving the enormity of their guilty intentions, would be easily dissuaded from lending an ear to these deceivers. This, however, is not the way they go about their work; they, on the contrary, use terms which flatter their hearers, which not bearing any one precise meaning, these men throw, without explaining their sense, as food to the curiosity of the public. ...

"We might quote here many instances of these artifices; but, to mention only one word which misbelievers make such abuse of, who does not know how great a noise is in our day made about civilization, as if between it and the Church there existed an intrinsic repugnance, an irreconcilable hostility?

"This word, which in itself is a vague term, one which those who use it are careful not to define, has become a kind of scourge which they hold over our shoulders, an engine for levelling our most sacred institutions, the means of paving the way to the most deplorable excesses.

"If people turn into ridicule the word of God and of him who represents God on earth, it is because civilization requires it.

"It is civilization which demands that a limit should be put to the number of churches and of the ministers of worship, and which, on the contrary, asks to have the dens of sin multiplied.

"It is civilization which calls for theatres without good taste and without any respect for modesty. In the name of civilization they give usurers liberty to exact the most enormous interest, and speculators to realize the most dishonest gains.

"It is in the name of civilization that an immoral press poisons souls; that art, prostituting itself, defiles the sense with hideous figures, and thus opens up the way to corrupt the heart.

"All the while, beneath the charm of this spell-word, held on high as an honored banner, the pestilential ideas it covers are disseminated freely, and between the loud clash of ideas and the noise which confuses and deafens this impression is produced: that we are to be blamed if civilization does not spread more rapidly and does not rise to more splendid destinies.

"Hence the beginning of that struggle (Kulturkampf) which its authors call the battle for civilization, but which with greater propriety should be called the violent oppression of the Church."

In the pastoral of 1878, addressed from Rome to his beloved flock, his deeply cherished attachment for them breaks forth, as it were, against his will. He is about to begin his sixty-ninth year; is it not time for him also to lay down the burden of care he has borne so long, instead of contemplating with dread the possibilities of the future? He says to his Perugians:

"Closely connected with you, as we have been, during all these long years by the holy bonds of the pastoral ministry, and by mutual relations which have ever begotten an interchange of affectionate sentiments, we feel now, dearest children, how heavy is the weight of a separation which, however justified by reasons the most imperative, is still grievous to us. In this state of mind we look forward, as you can well imagine, with no little satisfaction to the near approach of the holy season of Lent, when we can break our enforced silence and address you words of pastoral instruction.

"Since, therefore, we may not return to your midst in person, we do so by this letter, in order to converse with you and to gather mutual comfort from the interchange of our common sentiments of faith. These are the consolations which God keeps in store for bishops to make up for much sorrow and bitterness. For what can be more grateful to us than to hold converse with the flock who are our crown, our dearest joy; than to speak to them of God, and of His Christ, and of His holy Church, of the duties of our religion and of its immortal hopes, and to repeat to them the apostolic words: 'Therefore, my dearly beloved brethren and most desired, my joy and my crown, so stand fast in the Lord, my dearly beloved'?"

Christian Rome—and in Christian Rome the Vatican—

offered, as the year 1878 dawned upon the world, as January slowly passed away and found the gentle spirit of Pius IX still hovering on the very borders of the peace eternal, a spectacle never before beheld.

"Around the aged Pontiff had been dropping off day by day the men whom he had most loved and trusted, who had passed with him through the flood and the flame. He and three or four members of the Sacred College were left standing, all stripped and scarred by storm and lightning, like those venerable trees of the Californian forest towering on the hillside in their weird and solitary grandeur, while at their feet lie the fallen trunks of their former contemporaries, and around stand a younger growth, dwarfed only into comparative inferiority by their giant elders, the sole survivors of a remote age.

"Not long, however, in spite of the fervent prayers of the Catholic world, did the heroic old man survive the friends of his youth and his intrepid associates in peril and persecution. The joys which flooded his soul, as well as the cruel apprehensions caused by the steady triumph of extreme and undisguised radicalism in the Italian cabinet, much more than the superhuman fatigues of the Jubilee receptions, were too much for a man in his eighty-sixth year."[13]

Conspicuous among the few venerable cardinals who thus gathered around the couch of the long-lived Pontiff, the most trusted and not the least beloved was the Cardinal Camerlengo. Death had come to close the eyes of the weary old man, for whom the long Pontificate of thirty-two years had been little less than the agony of a prolonged martyrdom. He had almost designated his successor to the choice of the Sacred College.

And when this death had happened Cardinal Pecci had not yet concluded the pastoral letter quoted a few pages back. He hastened at once, while his own soul was under the effect of this saintly ending to an eventful life, to conclude his Lenten

[13] The Author's "Life of Pius IX," eighteenth edition, p. 522.

instruction, dating it from the 10th of February.

"And here, dearest children," he says, "having come to this point, our heart must give vent to the grief which oppresses it, having to recall to your mind the sad event which has plunged the Catholic world in mourning, and has befallen us at a time when the evils heaped on the Church were at their heaviest. When I began to write this letter I was far from thinking that our glorious Pontiff and most loving Father would be so suddenly snatched away. I was hoping, on the contrary, that he would be restored to better health, that I might once more ask his Apostolic benediction for you, and beg you in return to pray for your chief and parent. God in His designs has deemed it better that it should not be so. He has hastened for His servant the reward merited by the long and precious labors undergone for the Church, our common mother, by his immortal deeds, by the sufferings endured with such constancy, dignity, and firmness.

"Dear fellow-laborers, do not forget to make mention, in the Holy Sacrifice, of this soul in which God had printed so vivid an image of Himself. Speak to your flocks of his merits, and tell them how much this great Pope had done not only for the Church and for souls, but also to promote the reign of Christian civilization. ... I beseech you, dearest brethren and beloved children, to ask earnestly of God to grant soon a Head to the Church, and to cover him when he is chosen with the shield of His power, in order that the Bark of Peter may be safely guided through the surging waters to the wished-for haven."

POPE PIUS IX

GIUSEPPE GARIBALDI

GIUSEPPE MAZZINI

Camillo Benso, Count of Cavour

Victor Emmanuel II
First King of a United Italy

NAPOLEON III
EMPEROR OF THE SECOND FRENCH EMPIRE

PRINCE CHLODWIG HOHENLOHE
PRIME MINISTER OF BAVARIA

Joseph Ignatius von Döllinger

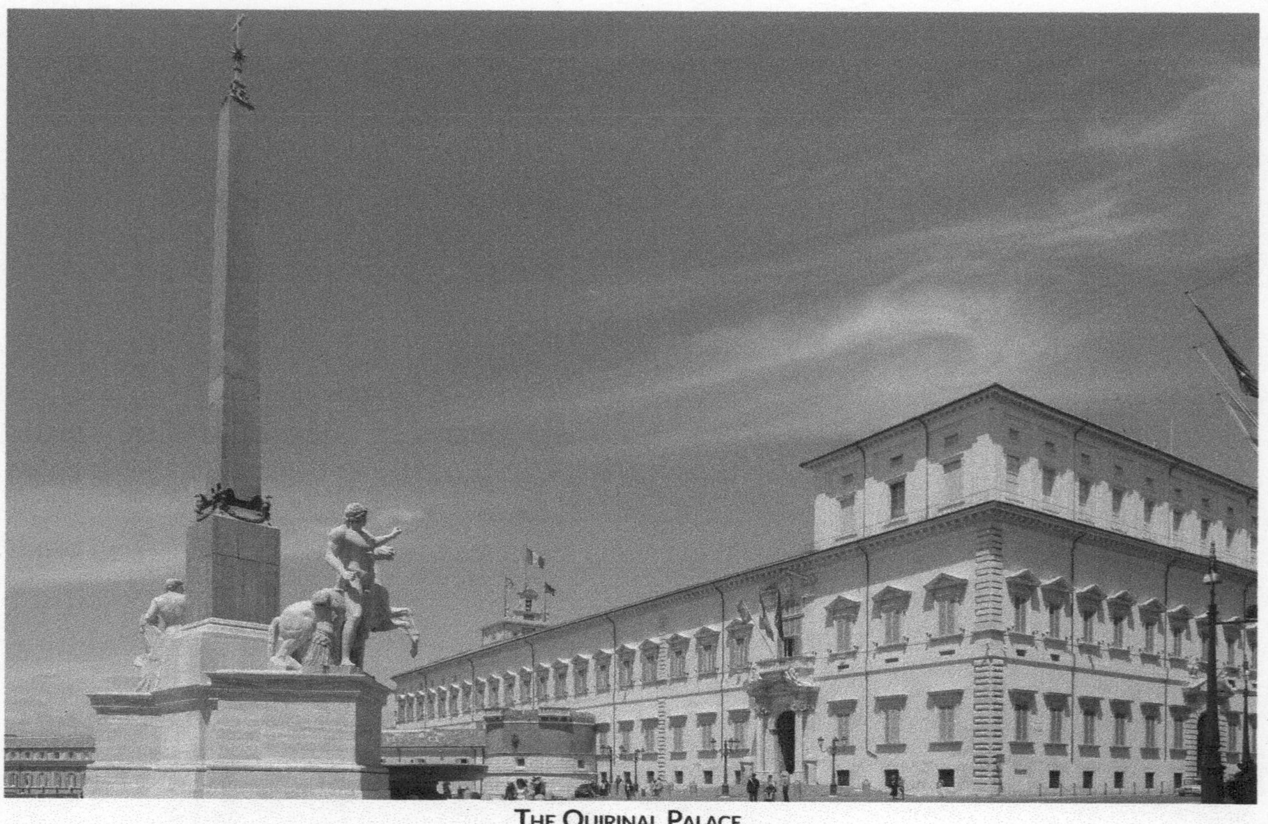

The Quirinal Palace
Papal Residence from 1826-1870

First Vatican Council

TOMB OF PIUS IX. IN THE CHURCH OF SAN LORENZO, OUTSIDE THE WALLS OF ROME.

Museo Chiaramonti,

Vatican Gallery of Ancient Sculpture.

Garden of the Pope, Vatican.

Recreation Place of His Holiness.

Museo Chiaramonti,
Vatican Gallery of Ancient Sculpture.

GARDEN OF THE POPE, VATICAN.

RECREATION PLACE OF HIS HOLINESS.

HIS HOLINESS TAKING RECREATION IN THE GARDEN OF THE VATICAN.

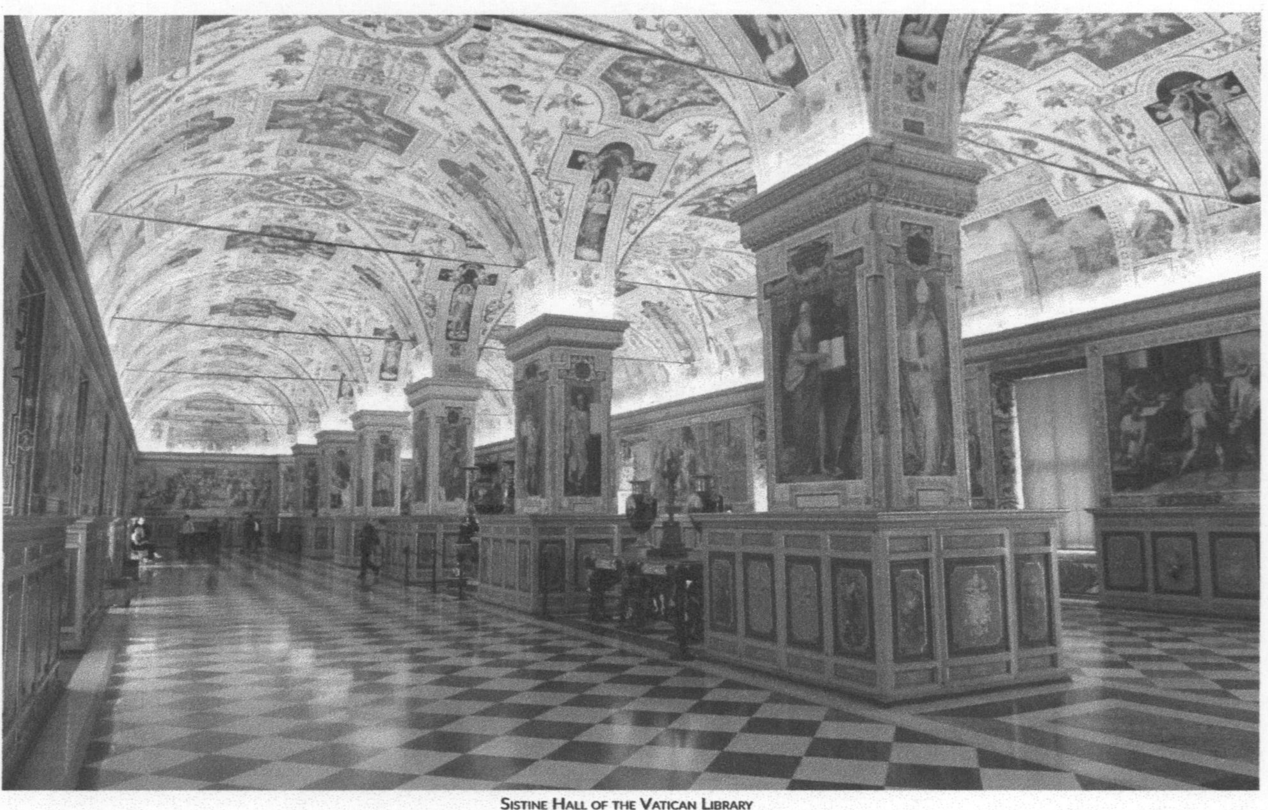

Sistine Hall of the Vatican Library

PART FOURTH

THE PONTIFICATE—LUMEN IN CŒLO

CHAPTER XIX

THE CONCLAVE;
LEO XIII

ONE OF THE LAST ACTS OF PIUS IX was a solemn protest sent in his name by the Secretary of State, Cardinal Simeoni, to the representatives of the Holy See at the various courts. It bore the date of January 17, 1878, the eighth day after the death of King Victor Emmanuel in the Quirinal Palace. Umberto I had succeeded to the throne thus founded by the Revolution and placed in the habitual residence of the Popes. The Pontiff, who was so soon to follow the persecutor and spoliator to the judgment-seat, and who was so conscious of his dread nearness to it, protested in this document "that he maintained intact, as against the iniquitous spoliation, the right of the Church to her most ancient domains." This, he said, was for the purpose of removing all ground for present or future misinterpretations or doubts concerning the pretension set forth by the successor of the late king "in taking the title of King of Italy to sanction the spoliation already consummated."

To all who have read of the fatherly and merciful spirit manifested by the venerable Pontiff not only when the tidings of the mortal illness of the king reached the Vatican, but when all were startled by the announcement of his death,[1] the thought cannot occur that, by so protesting in the face of all the Powers of Christendom, the dying Vicar of Christ was animated by any feeling of personal resentment. Such feelings were alien to the gentle, loving, and Christian spirit of the all forgiving Pius.

The protest was the act of one who, having received in trust, on his election to the Papal Chair, the temporalities guaranteeing its sovereignty and thereby its independence, felt

[1] See "Life of Pius IX," eighteenth edition, New York, pp. 527-28.

bound, as he was to appear before Christ Himself to render an account of that trust, to assert more solemnly that he was suffering violence at the hands of the oppressor, and that he persisted with his dying breath in asserting the imprescriptable right of the Church. His coronation oath had bound him to transmit the patrimony of the Holy See intact to his predecessor. To protest was all that he now could do in the face of overpowering might.

No sooner had the ocean telegraph flashed the news of the death of Pius IX all over America than even the Protestant press began to ask the questions: "Will the Piedmontese government not take possession of the Vatican and St. Peter's? ""Will they, can they, allow the cardinals to assemble freely in conclave and elect a successor to Pius IX?" "Is not this a golden opportunity for the kingdom of Italy to secure, even at the risk of a schism, a Pope of its own—one disposed to recognize and sanction accomplished facts—and thus put a stop to the ruinous conflict between the two powers in the Peninsula?"

Indeed, for months before January 7, 1878—the date of Pius IX's decease—such questions as these were seriously discussed by the public journals on both sides of the Atlantic. Many Catholics were fearful lest some such steps might be taken by the new masters of Rome; nor were there wanting in the Italian press and among Italian statesmen those who would enthusiastically applaud such steps and give effective aid toward their consummation.

Ay, that would have been the consummation of the cherished designs and deeply laid plans of Mazzini, of the anti-Christian Revolution of which he was the prophet and lawgiver. It would have filled with joy inexpressible the soul of Garibaldi and of the men who had steeped themselves in blood and sacrilege to blot out the Catholic religion from the soil of Italy.

Be it said, too, without any offence to the great mass of English and American Protestants who had clapped their hands with transport and sung their loud paeans of thanksgiving when the Porta Pia was breached and the Piedmontese entered Rome and hoisted the flag of Savoy on the Quirinal and Castle Sant' Angelo, their exultation would have been complete if, ere the remains of Pius IX had been cold in death, that same cross of Savoy had floated from the topmost point of the Vatican and the dome of St. Peter's.

Legge relates, in his work on the Pontificate of Pius IX, a fact which is eloquently suggestive. When, after this Pope's flight to Gaeta, a proclamation was issued by the Provisional Republican government in Rome calling a Constituent Assembly, the Pope, on January 1, 1849, issued a counter-proclamation protesting solemnly against all acts tending to a usurpation of the temporal power of the Holy See. This was both his right and his bounden duty. This proclamation, Legge informs us, was torn down by the populace, carried in procession, and then buried with every circumstance of ignominy. Then a public meeting of all the rascality in Rome was called, and the notorious Cicernacchio, the leader in all these demonstrations, moved a resolution to the effect that the Pope be then and there excommunicated, the sentence to be sent to him with an address concluding thus:

"When you, Sir Pope, left the city by one gate, the Bible entered into it by the opposite gate, and now there is no room for you!"[2]

We know—why remind American or English readers of the disgraceful fact?—that it was the boast of some of the modern Biblical evangelists that the Bible again entered Rome in triumph with the Piedmontese army through the breach at the Porta Pia.

So much the worse for the Bible as these men regard it. But we are only speaking at present of the unaccomplished purpose of the Radical Revolutionists, and of the unfulfilled but ardently expressed wish of those societies in league or in sympathy with Garibaldi.

The Italian government, by the invisible control of an

[2] Legge, "Pius IX," vol. ii. p. 139.

overruling Providence, either had no thought or no will to interfere with what was happening inside the Vatican, or with the actions of the Cardinal Camerlengo, on whom it now devolved to administer the Church and to dispose all things for the election of another Pope.

His first determination, when Pius IX had yielded up to the Redeemer and Judge his long-chastened spirit—dying, as dies the humblest Christian, consoled and purified by the sacraments of his faith, confessing his sins with a heartfelt and most touching simplicity, reciting, with a fervor and presence of mind that moved to tears all around him, the act of contrition, of loving sorrow for all offences against the Divine Majesty, and then receiving the last absolution—was to give no pretext to the Italian authorities to cross the threshold of the Vatican.

The custom, when the Pope died in the Quirinal, was to have the corpse lie in state in the Pauline Chapel, where the people were free to come and pray around the bier. If the death took place in the Vatican, then the body lay in state in the Sistine Chapel. But the Sistine being within the precincts of the palace—the only spot over which extends at present the very uncertain and shadowy sovereignty left to the Popes—if the remains of Pius IX were exposed there to the public veneration, the love which yet remained so deep in the hearts of the great majority of the Roman people, as distinguished from the revolutionary multitudes that had flocked to the city after the Piedmontese, would have brought such throngs to the Sistine and through the Vatican as might have justified the municipal authorities and the government in interfering.

Cardinal Pecci wisely resolved to afford no such pretext for violating even the semblance of sovereignty left to the Holy See. He ordered the remains to be laid out in state in St. Peter's, taking also there every means to preserve order and to cut off every pretext for municipal intrusion.

The first official act of the Sacred College, assembled in conclave on Tuesday, February 19, 1878, was to confirm by their united protest that issued by Pius IX on January 17. The cardinals in conclave are the depositary of the Papal sovereignty; the exercise of their right of suffrage in electing the Pope is only the use of that sovereign right. They therefore declared, through the Secretary of State, to all the Great Powers:

"That they thereby renewed all the protests and reservations made by the deceased Sovereign Pontiff, whether against the occupation of the States of the Church or against the laws and decrees enacted to the detriment of the same Church and of the Apostolic See"; all unanimously declaring themselves "determined to follow the course marked out by the deceased Pontiff, whatever trials may happen to befall them through the force of events." This document was signed by the deans of the three orders in the Sacred College—cardinal-bishops, cardinal-priests, and cardinal-deacons.

Every step, every incident in the proceedings of these days, so full of anxious expectancy and half-dread, marked the diplomatic skill, the prudent tact, and the conscientious sense of right and duty characteristic of the man, Joachim Pecci, who stood in the foremost place at the head of his brethren.

It is customary to have funeral services performed in every church and chapel in Rome for the repose of the soul of a deceased Pope during nine days before his burial. It is a touching and instructive custom, reminding Christians of every degree that the higher one's office on earth the greater is the responsibility, the more searching and awful the judgment to be undergone before Him "who searcheth the hearts and the loins," and the more pressing is, therefore, the need of pleading for the departed spirit.

The Vatican Palace and the space adjoining the Sistine Chapel are much less convenient for the purposes of a conclave than the corresponding locality in the Quirinal where Pius IX had been elected. Cardinal Pecci resolved that no delay that could possibly be avoided should take place by any fault of his, so that all should be in readiness for the conclave at the end of the nine days' devotions.

He summoned the architects Vespignani and Martinucci, and bade them get a sufficient body of workmen, with the requisite materials, and set to work at once to prepare lodgings for all the members of the Sacred College, with their attendants and the officers designated by law. On February 10 five hundred workmen at least were busy at their appointed task. Lodgings, furniture, all things needful even for a protracted election, were got in readiness. For, once the conclave is declared in session, all communication with the outside world ceases, and the door of the strictly guarded enclosure only opens to admit some tardy member of the Sacred College.

The Pontifical laws regulating everything that regards this, the highest body of electors in the Church, leave no room for doubt or indecision.[3] It is expressly enjoined that the cardinals present in Rome shall wait for ten days after the death of a Pope, and that then they shall enter into conclave and proceed to the election of a successor without waiting for the arrival of their absent colleagues.

On Sunday, February 17, the Novena, or nine days' devotions, were concluded in the Sistine Chapel by a solemn Pontifical Mass for the Dead, celebrated in presence of all the cardinals. On Monday, the 18th, the Solemn Mass of the Holy Ghost was sung in the Pauline Chapel in the forenoon, and in the afternoon all the ceremonies for the beginning of the conclave were performed.

At the election of the four last Popes, the conclave being held in the Quirinal, Rome being then governed by the Pontifical authorities, and the Sacred College being free to carry out, in public and in private, every part of the ceremonial prescribed, the custom was, on the day for entering into conclave, to proceed in state in the forenoon to St. Peter's, where the Mass of the Holy Ghost was sung by the cardinal dean of the Sacred College, and a sermon was delivered reminding the electors of their duty to consider the divine

[3] See the Author's article, "Conclave," in the "American Cyclopaedia."

glory and the good of the universal Church as their guiding motive in what they were about to undertake.

They then went in state to the Quirinal. It was an impressive scene. The cardinals had laid aside the usual scarlet robes for purple, the sign of mourning. The necessary attendants of the electors opened the march; after them came the Papal choir singing the hymn Vent, Creator Spiritus. A master of ceremonies, bearing aloft the Papal cross, preceded the members of the Sacred College, who advanced in the order of their dignity and seniority. They were followed by the prelates and officials taking part in the conclave.

The governor of Rome walked by the side of the cardinal dean, the people lining the streets and joining in the sacred chants invoking the divine light on the Papal electors.

Of course, on that Monday morning, February 18, 1878, there was no procession to St. Peter's, no solemn High Mass sung beneath its sublime dome to call down the divine blessing on the men about to give a Pope to the Church, and no return in state to the Quirinal. The Quirinal was in the hands of the deadliest foes of the Papacy.

The solemn Mass celebrated to call down the aid of the Holy Spirit was sung within the Vatican, in the Pauline Chapel Cardinal Amat, the dean of the Sacred College, was borne in a litter up the grand staircase of the palace, and from the Pauline Chapel to his sick-bed within the conclave enclosure, and his sick-bed he left not till borne back again to his residence, the election over. Another cardinal, Morichini, was but little better; he had to be supported by two assistants as he slowly and painfully mounted the palace stairs. And Cardinal Càtterini, the head of the Order of Deacons, was only kept up and enabled to take part in the proceedings by his indomitable will.

They were no ordinary body of men, these sixty-one cardinals who met that morning in the Pauline Chapel. Three only of the entire body of electors were missing—Cardinal Broussais de Saint-Marc, who was lying at death's door; Cardinal Cullen, Archbishop of Dublin, detained at first by illness, and who hastened to Rome only to find the Pope elected; and the sole American cardinal, McCloskey, Archbishop of New York, who was on his way, but only came to do homage to the successor of Pius IX.[4]

In the altered circumstances of the political world, and the voluntary or enforced indifference of the so-called Catholic Powers to the cruel position of the Holy See, it was at least fortunate that the Sacred College was no longer to be subjected to the oppression exercised on its members in the last century and the preceding ages.

The electors were thus left free to choose the man whom they knew to be in every way the most worthy and the best fitted to rule the Church. This freedom of election—so often tampered with by the house of Bourbon, as well as by all the other royal dynasties whom mediaeval feudalism had made the arbiters of Christendom—was one of the precious liberties which Providence had restored to the Church as the reward for the bitter trials of more than a century. Who knows but that the perfect independence of the Holy See is only to be the outcome of the present social and political convulsions, which, in upsetting what remains of that same feudalism, will sweep away more than one throne, enfranchise the millions of Italians to whom the Revolution just accomplished has refused the right of honest suffrage, and enable the majority of a people not yet de-christianized to make the Vicar of Christ freer than in the days of the first or the tenth Leo?

---

[4] In the conclave which elected Leo XIII were the following cardinals: Amat, Di Pietro, Sacconi, Guidi, Bilio, Morichini, Schwarzenberg, Pecci, Asquini, Carafa di Tiaetto, Donnet, Antonucci, Panebianco, De Luca, Pitra, De Bonnechose, Von Hohenlohe, Bonaparte, Ferrieri, Berardi, Moreno, Monaco la Valletta, Moraes Cardoso, Regnier, Chigi, Franchi, Guibert, Oreglia di Santo Stefano, Simor, Martinelli, Antici Mattei, Giannelli, Ledochowski, Manning, Dechamps, Simeoni, Bartolini, D'Avanzo, Franzelin, Benavides y Navarrete, Apuzzo, Garcia Gil, Howard, Para y Rico, Caverot, Di Canossa, Serafini, Miha'ovitz, Kutschker, Parocchi, Moretti, Caterini, Mertel, Consolini, Borromeo, Randi, Pacca, Nina, Sbarretti, Falloux du Coudray, Pellegrini.

So thought in February, 1878, and so think to-day some of the far-seeing men who entered the conclave which gave to the world Leo XIII

The sixty-one Princes of the Church who from the Pauline Chapel, the Mass of the Holy Ghost ended, went in solemn procession through the magnificent Sala Regia (the royal hall of the Vatican) to the Sistine, there to perform the first ceremonies of the conclave, were men whom no outside influence turned aside from the one grand purpose of their corning together. Nor was the pontifical tiara, in the present condition of things, a crown that could tempt even the worldly-minded, if such there were among them. The Papal cross was borne aloft before them, to tell them now, as never before during many an age, that he whom they would place in the chair of Peter must, like Peter, share his Master's crucifixion. The voices of the Papal choir made the storied walls and ceiling of the hall resound with the majestic strains of the *Veni Creator.* Every one joined heartily in the sublime words of the prayerful hymn. No open-air pageant could equal the earnestness of spirit pervading the place and the assemblage. All genuflect to the hidden Presence on the altar as they enter the precincts of the Sistine. The senior cardinal bishop, at the foot of the altar, chants the prayer *Deus, qui corda fidelium.*[5] There is silence, and all kneel for a few moments. When all are seated the cardinal sub-dean reads aloud the pontifical laws regulating conclaves, and every one of the electors takes the oath binding him to observe the same. Then comes the turn of the governor of the conclave, the prince-marshal, the secretary, and all the other officials to be sworn to fidelity and secrecy.

This ends the ceremonial of the first part of the day. The afternoon is devoted by the cardinals to the transaction of such business as requires immediate despatch, to the reception

---

[5] "O God! who hast taught the hearts of the faithful by the illuminating grace of the Holy Spirit, grant us in the same Spirit to relish what is right, and thus always to enjoy the sweetness of His consolation."

of such personages as is customary on such occasions, the members of the diplomatic body accredited to the Holy See, the Roman nobility, and foreigners of distinction.

With the Ave Maria closes the Roman business day. When it has ceased tolling a bell sounds in the corridors around the Sistine Chapel, and the master of ceremonies is heard giving in a loud voice the signal for all strangers to depart: *Exeant omnes!* Many a hearty wish had been expressed within these historic walls, as the hours of the afternoon passed slowly away, that such or such a cardinal might fill the place left empty by him whose body had been yesterday laid to temporary repose yonder in St. Peter's.

That place was now to be filled, not by the ambitious, but by the self-sacrificing. God was directing it all.

Prince Chigi, Hereditary Marshal of the Holy Roman Church and Guardian of the Conclave, charged, in virtue of his office, with seeing that all outward precautions for the perfect enclosure of the conclave should be taken, went at the appointed hour from the apartments of the maestro di camera to fulfil his duty. It was a stately pro cession in itself: the prince in his full uniform, attended by his four captains or aids, an escort of the Noble and Swiss Guards, and a body of servants in state liveries bearing torches, advance through the lofty corridors to the great door giving entrance to the conclave. On the threshold of this entrance, and waiting for his arrival, was Cardinal Pecci, the Camerlengo, with the three cardinals, heads of orders. After the usual salutations the great door is closed, the Cardinal Camerlengo locks it on the inside, the prince-marshal locks it on the outside and places the keys in a crimson velvet bag, which he thenceforth safely keeps in his own custody.

This done, Monsignor Ricci-Parracciani, Governor of the Conclave, walks round the enclosure, examining scrupulously every part, and assuring himself, in compliance with his oath of office, that there is no possibility of communication with the outside world. An imperfect enclosure would entail the nullity of any choice made by the electors, even though every other formality had been strictly observed.

The Cardinal Camerlengo this time has taken measures never before practised. A kitchen was by his orders in stalled within the enclosure, with a sufficient number of cooks and other servants. Thus every article of food was prepared within what was properly the conclave, and no occasion or pretext was left for transgressing the sacred rules of isolation and secrecy rendered necessary by the long experience of ages.

On both sides of the chapel, down along those walls on which true Christian art has left its masterpieces, sixty-four lofty screens have been erected, and in front of these are seats for the cardinals, every seat being numbered. There is before each seat a small square table with writing materials. Each seat is canopied, the canopy being the emblem of sovereignty, and all these Papal electors are now co-equal sharers in that sovereignty which they will place, undivided, on the head of the Pope of their choice. Four of these seats, with the overhanging canopies, the tables, and the screens behind, are draped in green cloth; the remaining sixty are draped in purple. What is the reason of this distinction?

The green is the color distinctive of the cardinals created by Gregory XVI, the only four surviving of all those who in June, 1846, had sat among the electors of Pius IX. The other sixty cardinals are of the creation of the long-lived Pius. Think you, when, but a few hours ago, these few cardinals who had voted in the conclave of 1846 found themselves, at so long an interval, called again to give to another the cross which Pius had borne, that their souls were not oppressed with the holy sadness wont to come, in the Catacombs, on the men called to elect the successors of the first Clement, the first Sixtus, and the first Pius, slain by the rage of the persecutor?

There is no electoral assembly known to the civilized world and to all history like these conclaves in which are chosen the men who are, like Simon Peter, charged to feed Christ's entire flock, and destined, like Peter, to lay down their lives for the sheep.

Now let us see how these electors go about their work.

The morning of Tuesday, February 19, has dawned on Rome—a balmy morning, rising cloudless and golden-tinted beyond the Quirinal and the Esquiline, and flooding the lofty masses of the Vatican and the dome of St. Peter's with its first beams. Few there are, if any, within the Vatican and the conclave who have not been beforehand with the dawn. And to-day there is more need than usual in their being early before the mercy-seat. And ere yet the early morning hours have passed, the voice of the master of ceremonies, who is here the organ of the Church, is heard, as he passes along the corridors where the electors are lodged, pronouncing the sacramental formula, *In capellam, domini*—"To the chapel, my lords!" And to the chapel, with the docility of school boys obeying a summons to morning prayer, the venerable train of purple-robed prelates go at once. There they take the seats allotted to them, the Camerlengo, Cardinal Pecci, taking that marked "number nine" on the Gospel side, and not far from the altar. The sub-dean celebrates a Low Mass, after which all take their seats. Now begins the real work of election.

Three cardinals are chosen by vote as scrutineers: their business is to examine every schedule, billet or vote, and to note and announce the result. To each elector is given a schedule, or voting-paper, prepared after a given form. In the center he writes the name of the person for whom he votes.

At the top of the sheet he writes out the first part of the form: "I, N. Cardinal N., elect for Sovereign Pontiff my Most Reverend Lord Cardinal."

The part containing the name of the elector is folded and sealed, leaving visible in the middle space only the name of the candidate he votes for.

At the lower end of the sheet he then writes a text of Scripture of his own choice, which is also sealed up, like his name at the top, and serves, in case of doubt, to verify his vote and signature.

These papers have been carefully distributed, one to each of the electors, by the secretary of the conclave; and each cardinal having duly filled the sheet and sealed it, all is ready for the balloting.

On the altar stands a large chalice with its paten, made and consecrated for this special purpose. The cardinals in due order advance one by one in succession to the altar-steps. The elector, kneeling, pronounces in a loud and distinct voice the solemn words: "I call Christ our Lord, who will judge me, to witness that I elect the person who before God I think should be elected, and which I shall make good in the accessus." Then, ascending the platform of the altar, he lays the folded schedule on the paten, and from this drops it into the chalice.

While cardinal after cardinal is thus giving his vote in the chapel, the vote of Cardinal Amat has been taken in his cell, according to the strict formalities enjoined by the pontifical decrees.

All the bulletins having been thus deposited in the chalice, the three scrutineers ascend to the altar. One of them takes the chalice, covers it with the paten, and shakes it well. A second then takes them out and counts them, one by one, into another chalice. There are exactly sixty-one; had there been one more or less the schedule must all have been burned and the balloting must have been begun again.

The scrutineers now take the second chalice with its contents, and carry it to a large, square table draped in purple, and so placed that the scrutineers seated at it are plainly in view of all the electors. The senior scrutineer draws from the chalice the first folded paper his hand touches, reads the name written in the open middle space, then hands it to the scrutineer next in seniority, who also reads the name aloud and takes note of it. The third does the same—each name being thus thrice proclaimed aloud.

Meanwhile each of the other electors, seated at his own table, has a printed list of all the cardinals before him, and makes a mark opposite to the name thus read out. Twenty-three times the name of Cardinal Joachim Pecci is thus announced. No other member of the conclave receives anything approaching this number of votes. As the name of the Camerlengo thus comes up with ominous frequency, he is seen to be greatly disturbed. His pale, intellectual, ascetic countenance is overcast by an expression of mingled dismay and grief. Still the number twenty-three is not that of half the electors present, and an absolute two-thirds majority is necessary to an election.

Thus the first morning session of the conclave passed without any result. The balloting papers are therefore, according to rule, burned, and the blue smoke issuing from the slender stove-pipe thrust through a window in the chapel tells the expectant crowd on the square of St. Peter's that no Pope as yet has been chosen.

Joachim Pecci with a heavy, foreboding heart retires to his cell, praying fervently that the burden of the Pontificate may not be laid on his aged shoulders.

The hour for the afternoon session has come, and the voice of the master of ceremonies falls on the ears of the Cardinal Camerlengo with a startling sound: "To the chapel, my lords!"

The purple-robed procession of venerable men glides in silence into the Sistine; the silence is deeper still as all kneel before the mercy-seat and the sub-dean of the Sacred College recites aloud the first verse of the Vent, Creator Spiritus, his brother-cardinals taking up the alternate stanzas. This invocation to the Spirit of truth and light being ended, they prepare for the second ballot, the ceremonial being quite the same as in the morning.

During the recess each elector has been reflecting on the eminent qualities of the man for whom the twenty-three votes were cast in the forenoon. Cardinal Pecci has been lifting up his soul to the Searcher of hearts, and beseeching Him to avert from himself the dread honors which threaten him.

What have his brethren been resolving meanwhile? Let us see.

Cardinal Pecci's turn to vote comes early, his seat being near the altar and bearing the number nine. At length the last bulletin has fallen into the chalice on the altar, and the scrutineers have begun to announce and count out the names of those voted for. Again Cardinal Joachim Pecci's name is repeated with even more significant frequency than in the morning. He soon has to mark twenty-three opposite to his own name on the printed list before him; again and again his name occurs till the number reaches thirty—one-half of the electors present; and on, on the number swells till it is increased to thirty-eight!

But when the number thirty has been reached and passed, the trouble, the emotion, the terror of the humble-minded Camerlengo have become uncontrollable. Cardinal Donnet, Archbishop of Bordeaux, whose seat was next to Cardinal Pecci's, describes what he then beheld in a discourse from his cathedral pulpit on his return home from the conclave:

"I remarked that, Cardinal Pecci hearing his own name mentioned so often, and that everything pointed to him as the successor of Pius IX, great tears rolled down his cheeks, and his hand shook so violently that the pen it held fell to the ground. I picked it up and gave it to him, saying: "Courage! There is no question here of you; it is the Church and the future of the world that are in question.' He made no reply, only lifting his eyes to heaven to implore the divine assistance."[6]

Thirty-eight votes, however, did not constitute the two-thirds majority demanded by the canons. So again the voting-papers were all burned, and again the anxious crowd of spectators outside in the piazza dispersed, their curiosity unsatisfied.

It was now most probable that the majority in favor of the Cardinal Camerlengo would, in the session of Wednesday morning, the 20th of February, be so increased as to secure his election. If his emotion in the chapel was such, in spite of his long habits of self-command, that he could not conceal it from the eyes of his colleagues, one may guess that in the privacy of his cell he gave free vent to his tears and pleaded with his whole soul to have the bitter cup removed from him.

Another French cardinal, De Bonnechose, Archbishop of

---

[6] Translated from the "Cenni Storici."

Rouen, gives us a graphic and authentic account of the Camerlengo's appearance and behavior on the morrow.

"Cardinal Pecci," he says, "to whom on the afternoon of the first day a majority of the votes were given, looked, on Wednesday morning, pale and frightened. Just before the voting began he went to one of the most revered members of the Sacred College, 'I cannot control myself,' he said; 'I must address the Sacred College. I fear that they are about to commit a sad mistake. People think I am a learned man; they credit me with possessing wisdom; but I am neither learned nor wise. They suppose I have the necessary qualities for a Pope. I have nothing of the kind. This is what I want to say to the cardinals.' Fortunately the other said to him: 'As to your learning, we, not you, can best judge of that. As to your qualifications for the Pontifical office, God knows what they are; leave it all to Him.' Cardinal Pecci obeyed him."[7]

The third ballot began at the appointed hour. The Cardinal Camerlengo's distress must indeed have touched his brethren deeply. It was, in their eyes, only a further evidence of his worthiness. He was, they thought, the man needed to guide the bark of Peter amid the tempest then raging—a tempest to which no human foresight could fix a term. Acknowledged superiority of learning, with pre-eminent virtue, and experienced skill in managing diplomatic intercourse when international law and international relations were as unsettled, as changing, as complicated as the direction and currents of winds and waves in the center of a cyclone—such were the high and rare qualities these men, assembled to elect a Pope on Wednesday morning, the 20th of February, 1878, believed Joachim Pecci to be possessed of. So, as the balloting proceeded, and he sat prostrated at first, then calmer, resigned, and prayerful, his name was announced with the same prophetic frequency till the preceding number, thirty-eight, was passed, and forty-four votes were recorded in his favor. It was more than a two-thirds majority, and left no room for

---

[7] Translated from the "Cenni Storici."

further scrutiny. Will Cardinal Pecci accept? He sits mute, pale, with closed eyes, as if his spirit were far away from the place and scene.

The master of ceremonies, accompanied by the subdean, the senior cardinal priest and cardinal deacon, approach the seat Number Nine. "Do you accept the election canonically made of you as Supreme Pontiff of the Catholic Church?" asks the sub-dean amid a stillness so painful that one might almost hear one's heart beat. Cardinal Pecci rises; his whole frame shakes with uncontrollable emotion. With a quivering voice, but steadily and distinctly, he affirms his own unworthiness. But seeing them all of one mind and determined in this matter, he bows to the divine will.

The sub-dean kneels thereupon before him; the master of ceremonies claps his hands, and at this signal all the cardinals rise and remain standing in homage to the new Sovereign. Instantly all the canopies above the seats are lowered save that above the seat of the Pope-elect. The sub-dean then asks: "By what name do you wish to be called?" "By the name of Leo XIII," is the prompt answer.

And so Pope Leo XIII stands forth in history to begin a new era for the Church, for Catholicity, for civilization.

Let us conclude our narrative.

The prothonotary-apostolic forthwith makes a minute of these final proceedings, bearing his own signature and those of the prince-marshal, the master of ceremonies, the secretary, and assistant secretaries. While these documents are drawn up the enclosures are removed, the great door is unlocked, and proclamation is made that the conclave is ended.

The Pope-elect allows himself to be conducted behind the altar between the two senior cardinal deacons. There he is divested of his cardinalitial robes and clad in the traditional white vesture worn by his predecessors—cassock, cincture, rochet, hood, white berretta (or scull-cap), and stole; the scarlet stockings are replaced by white. The embroidered shoes alone are scarlet, with a golden cross. Meanwhile they have placed upon the platform of the altar the portable Papal throne—sedia gestatoria—and all is in readiness for the first solemn ceremony of doing homage to the newly-elected Vicar of Christ. This is called "adoration," from the Latin word *adorare*, the ceremony by which the ancient Romans testified their reverence to any superior being or person, by turning their face toward the object of their homage and carrying the right hand to the lips. Here the act of reverence shown is to the person representing on earth the Redeemer and Guide of mankind, and, indirectly, to Christ Himself

Leo XIII, attired in the insignia of his dignity, now advances from behind the altar and takes his place on the throne. The sub-dean, in the absence of Cardinal Amat, is the first to approach the throne. He takes from the Pope's hand the sapphire cardinalitial ring and puts on his finger the Ring of the Fisherman; then he bends low and kisses the feet of His Vicar on earth who in the Last Supper washed and kissed the feet of His apostles; he then kisses the Pope's hand, while Leo in his turn gives him on both cheeks the kiss of peace. So do all the cardinals in succession, and then the officers of the conclave.

This first homage, or "adoration," over, the senior cardinal deacon, Catterini, asks the Pope's permission to announce the election to the outside world. Ill and faint, Catterini is nevertheless too much overjoyed at the result of the election to allow any one else to fulfil the duty of first proclaiming it. There is a great crowd in the square beneath. They have been long waiting; the old ones among them knew at what hour very nearly the morning ballot must have ended. The blue smoke had not made its appearance at the time expected: the election was then an accomplished fact, and the fever of expectancy grew and grew.

At length on the interior gallery of the Vatican, looking down into the vast nave of St. Peter's Church, the Papal cross appeared, with the acolytes, master of ceremonies, mace-bearers, etc., followed by Cardinal Catterini, who, turning his face toward the piazza, where the crowd were waiting, pronounced these words:

"I announce to you tidings of great joy. We have a Pope, the Most Eminent and Most Reverend Joachim Pecci, Cardinal Priest of the title of St. Chrysogonus, who hath given himself for name Leo XIII"

At this the bells of St. Peter's rang forth a merry peal, taken up by all the churches of Rome, the tidings of the election with the name of the new Pope spreading with lightning-like rapidity through Rome, while the electric telegraph bore them as rapidly to every quarter of the globe.

No cannon thundered from the Castle Sant' Angelo— there the usurping flag of Savoy floated; and no universal illumination in the evening proclaimed the joy of the citizens. The majority of the Roman nobility did, however, illuminate their palaces, and very many of the citizens did the same, even though by so doing they were marking themselves out to the violence of the triumphant anticlerical mob which sometimes terrorized over the government itself.

In the New World the name of Leo XIII was hailed by Catholics with delight, with satisfaction by all. The fears of Piedmontese interference were now found to be groundless. And then there was the old prophecy relating to Lumen in Coelo, to which even scholars, who did not believe in its authenticity, still attached, with the people, a half-belief that was not all superstition.

And, sure enough, the ancient shield of the Pecci family displays in the upper part, on an azure ground, a star shedding a stream of light on all beneath. Then there are a tall cypress, the emblem of strength and tenacity, and two flowering lilies, the symbol of sanctity and learning.

It remains to see how Leo XIII will justify this prophetic trust. And in Perugia—how was the news of Cardinal Pecci's election received there?

On that very morning of February 20, as on the 19th, there had been a solemn function held in the cathedral: a solemn High Mass pro eligendo Summo Pontifice was celebrated, in accordance with the prescriptions of the Church, to call down the light of the Holy Spirit on the electors assembled in conclave at Rome. This is the custom in all parts of the Catholic world on such occasions. While the solemn rite was carried out in Perugia, he who had passed so many years of his life in the picturesque old mediaeval city was raised by the suffrages of his peers to the Supreme Pastorship. Not long after noon the whole city was startled by an official telegram from Rome announcing the elevation of their Bishop to the chair of Peter. It was a sudden and a most joyous surprise. Instantly, Monsignor Laurenzi issued a circular announcing the change to the clergy and people of Perugia.

"We perfectly understand," the auxiliary bishop said, "with what joy this providential event must fill our clergy, so long the object of his wise and loving care, and all our people, who on so many occasions and in so many ways have had opportunities to admire his rare gifts of soul, his pastoral virtues, and the exalted wisdom of his administration, whether as our civil Governor long ago, or as the Bishop of this illustrious diocese, which he loved as his own native land, as a choice vineyard confided to his husbandry." The local Catholic organ spoke of the event as follows:

"Our city heard with incredible joy of the exaltation of our revered Bishop to the see of St. Peter. We have witnessed unusual emotion on this occasion—tears of joy in the eyes of many; persons of every rank calling on Monsignor Laurens to offer their congratulations; all the bells sending forth a glad peal, and houses illuminated. They are now forming a deputation of distinguished ecclesiastics and laymen charged to go to Rome to offer the Holy Father the felicitations and best wishes of the entire city."[8] On the following Sunday, February 24, in the cathedral of Perugia and all the city and country churches throughout the diocese, there was a solemn service of thanksgiving, with exposition of the Blessed Sacrament. There was need to thank God for such a Pope; but there was still greater need to beseech God to guide him and his flock through the coming storm and darkness.

---

[8] MS.

CHAPTER XX

LEO XIII—LUMEN IN CŒLO

"Amen, amen I say to thee: When thou wast younger thou didst gird thyself and didst walk where thou wouldst. But when thou shalt be old, thou shalt stretch forth thy hands, and another shall gird thee, and lead thee whither thou wouldst not."—St. John xxi. 18.

THERE were not wanting in the public press, at the very moment when the civilized world was startled by the sudden election of Leo XIII, voices calling on the four Powers once recognized as Catholic—Austria, France, Spain, and Portugal—to veto the election of the new Pope; that is, not to recognize him officially.[1] But the ambassadors of these Powers near the Holy See were among the first, on the day after the election, to offer in the name of their respective sovereigns heartfelt homage and congratulation to the new Pontiff. From every portion of the civilized world, from every shore connected with Rome by the electric telegraph, came to the Vatican, day by day and hourly, messages of felicitation, reverence, love, and thanksgiving. The two hundred millions of Catholics who, spread all over the globe, look to the Pope as the Vicar of Christ, felt instinctively that Leo XIII had been freely, lawfully chosen by the Sacred College, and their hearts went out to greet him at the beginning of a reign which they knew must be one of bitter trial and struggle.

Reign! What a word to use in speaking of the conditions under which the long Pontificate of Pius IX ended and that of his successor began!

Pius, in June, 1846, was hailed by all Rome and by all Italy with such an outburst of enthusiasm as had never been

[1] See Appendix F.

witnessed before. What a scene it was when he, over whose head all thoughtful minds read in characters of light inextinguishable *Crux de Cruce,* gave his first solemn blessing from the historic balcony above the principal door of St. Peter's! What a delirious scene was that presented by the great square with its exultant crowds! But far more triumphant was the "progress" of Pius IX when he was crowned and went in solemn procession through the streets of Rome to take formal possession of his cathedral, the church of St. John Lateran.

Archbishop Pecci, just returned from Belgium, and then in his thirty-sixth year, beheld these splendid pageants and heard the hymns of joy which the multitudes sang day and night to the praise of their new Pontiff.

Thirty-two years well-nigh have passed, and the young Nuncio of 1846 is Pope in 1878.

Will he dare to give his first Pontifical benediction "to the city and the world"—Urbi et Orbi—from the balcony above the portico of St. Peter's?

On the afternoon of that memorable 20th of February, 1878, thousands of the simple folk of Rome, who reasoned but little about politics, and remembered only the reign of the Popes as the time when the poor man's bread and wine were cheap, when the laboring man's industry was not taxed and his son was not taken away forcibly from the field or the fireside, crowded the square of St. Peter's, hoping that Leo XIII would bless them from yonder balcony.

Others, the more knowing ones, in great numbers too, filled the interior of St. Peter's, and waited patiently in the immense nave, their eyes fixed on the interior balcony communicating with the Vatican palace. Many a heartfelt prayer was said at the Shrine of the Apostles, where evermore "flame the lamps of gold," or in front of the beautiful Chapel of the Blessed Sacrament, for the new Pope and for the Church, both beset by such dangers. The afternoon wore away, and it was a little after half-past four when, all of a sudden, the window closing the interior balcony above; he great nave was opened. An electric thrill passes like lightning through the expectant crowd, and, with a great murmur of joy, all instantly kneel.

Then is seen advancing to the railing of the balcony a tall, white figure, the hair as white as the robes he wears, and the countenance almost as white as the hair. Behind him and on each side stand cardinals and prelates. A great silence has fallen on the crowd beneath, while, with a voice clear and distinct like that of a trumpet, Leo XIII utters the sacramental words of the Apostolic Benediction—the first blessing of a parent to his family, of the Supreme Pastor to the wide flock the eyes of his love behold kneeling there before him.

His last words are still echoing through the vast spaces of the basilica, and the hand of the Pontiff is still raised in benediction and prayer, when all that crowd, as if moved by one instinct, rise to their feet, and a mighty shout, "Long live Leo XIII!" rings along the nave of St. Peter's. It is repeated again and again. There speaks the heart of the entire Catholic world.

It is the first time that this second "Prisoner of the Vatican" looks upon his people. He understands them, appreciates their devotion, and retires.

And the coronation? The Pope had appointed for the ceremony Sunday, March 3. It was thought—and even he, old and experienced as he was, fancied—that within the area of the great church of St. Peter's, and the great square which is in reality an integral part of the chief temple of Catholicity, a Sovereign Pontiff might, without let or hindrance, be allowed to perform the necessary and solemn function of his coronation and enthronization.

But he did not know yet the brutal and overmastering force which ruled Rome and its government.

Great preparations had begun to be made in St. Peter's for the ceremony of March 3. Scaffoldings were erected, and the usual magnificent draperies were begun to be hung along the nave, when of a sudden they were taken down again. No precautions would be taken by those in authority to prevent interruptions, or to secure order either in the square outside

St. Peter's or even in the church within.

So on the day appointed, after solemn High Mass in the Sistine Chapel, the ambassadors of the Catholic Powers attending in the name of their governments, the coronation ceremony is performed in the loggia or balcony overlooking the interior of St. Peter's, and from which Leo XIII had given his first blessing to his people. There again he showed himself, bearing his tiara, his triple crown of sharp thorns, and blessed them. But no force, invisible or visible, could prevent them, and all Catholicity with them, from crowning that venerable head with a threefold diadem of love, of reverence, and of undying devotion.

One significant incident had meanwhile occurred in Spain, one which the Catholic world will never fail to remember with gratitude. The Spanish senate, in its sitting of February 26, spontaneously and unanimously adopted a resolution offering to Leo XIII their respectful felicitations, moved, as they said, to this act of public homage by their own religious feelings. The young king had already written his own hearty words of reverent duty and congratulation.

And ere that king had closed his brief career, marked toward its ending by such heroic devotion to his people, was he, as well as they, not blessed a thousandfold for this affectionate homage of the sovereign and his senate? For Spain Leo XIII truly proved to be what a German publicist called him, "the Prince of Peace f saving her from the horrors of war.

The consolation thus given by the kingdom and people of St. Ferdinand to the heart of the new Pontiff, and all the additional testimonies of affection, loyalty, and devotion which every mail brought to the Vatican, were needed by Leo XIII even at the first stage of his government.

On retiring from the loggia where he was crowned, and with the blessings of his people echoing back his own solemn benediction, an affecting ceremony terminated, in the Sistine Chapel, the proceedings of that day. When the Pope had laid aside the pontifical vestments, he received, as is customary on such occasions, the homage of the Sacred College. Cardinal di

Pietro, the sub-dean, in the name of his colleagues renewed the oath and the promises of fealty made in conclave on the day of the election, and then in a brief address expressed their common sentiments toward the new Sovereign. "Behold, we shall be thy mouth and thy flesh," he said, in the words of Scripture. The Pope answered in terms of deep humility, saying that the very rites they had just fulfilled impressed him more and more with the sublimity of the station to which they had raised him, and made him continually repeat with King David: "Who am I, O Lord God, that Thou hast brought me unto this?"

When night came there was a spontaneous illumination. All classes of the true Romans, the old population of the city, as distinguished from the masses whom the government had invited or encouraged to come to Rome from all parts of Italy, lit up their windows. The palaces of the nobles were especially conspicuous on this occasion. But the men who had resolved that the Papal coronation should not be performed with the usual solemnities in St. Peter's were on the lookout for this manifestation of Catholic feeling. They soon had well-organized bands in all the streets, provided with stones, and smashing every window in every house they could reach and that dared to show a single taper or lamp. The palaces along the Corso fared ill on that night. The police were there; but the police took care to encourage the rioters by exhorting them "not to go too far."[2] It is sufficient to know that the Minister of the Interior was then the notorious Crispi.

On the 4th of March, the very day after his coronation, Leo XIII completed the work which Pius IX had been prevented by death from finishing: he promulgated the bull *Ex Supremo Apostolatus Apice*, reconstituting the Catholic hierarchy in Scotland. This work of reconstruction seemed, as he expresses it in his exquisite Latin, "a happy omen with which to begin

[2] English and American readers will recall the classic recommendation of the officer to his men "not to put the bailiff under the pump and not to toss him on a blanket."

the exercise of the Supreme Pastorate, which we have taken on ourself with fear and trembling amid the .calamities of the present times." It is with extreme satisfaction that, remembering the history of the ancient see of St. Andrew's, Leo XIII "recalls it from the tomb and bestows on it metropolitan rank, with the title of the See of Edinburgh." In his first consistorial allocution, on the 28th of the same month, the Pope again alludes to the restoration of the Scottish hierarchy. "We trust," he says, "that the work thus brought to an end by the Holy See shall be productive of abundant fruit, and that, through the intercession of the patron saints of Scotland, the mountains in that country shall put on peace for the people, and the hills righteousness."

Did the watchful eyes of the Common Father not look beyond the shores of Scotland and the isles blessed by Columbkille long ago to that kindred land from which, in Europe's darkest days, light, righteousness, and the peace of the Gospel had come for both Scotland and England, for the adjoining Continent, for the mountains above St. Gall and Lake Constance, for the Ligurian hills where Bobbio arose around the monastery of St. Columbanus? Can he, Leo XIII, will he bring back peace with justice to the Green Isle so unspeakably dear to both Columbkille and Columbanus? We shall see.

On the 11th of that same month, amid all the anxieties and occupations which pressed upon him, Leo XIII found time to reply, with more even than his wonted warmth, to a society founded in Paris for the protection and encouragement of young artisans. It was the creation of a man well known to the author, one of those simply heroic Christians who find it quite natural to devote themselves in life to the most arduous self-denial and self-sacrifice for the good of others, and who face imprisonment and death in the performance of duty with the calm intrepidity of souls that never knew either guilt or fear. This was Father Olivaint, one of the victims or "hostages" of the Paris Commune.

He and his brethren had done wonders to save the

working men and women of the French capital from the temptations of poverty, as well as from ignorance, vice, and the meshes of the socialistic organizations. When Olivaint fell, and his brethren were expelled in 1880 from their own houses, they either remained in obscurity and isolation near the scene of their labors, so as to continue their noble work, or other noble men took it up after them.

It was work such as Leo XIII sympathized with from the bottom of his soul; for he had been careful in Perugia, and indeed wherever he had labored, to watch tenderly over the interests, material as well as spiritual, of the children of toil. And this most fatherly solicitude for the welfare of the laboring classes all over the world has inspired some of his most magnificent encyclical letters, as we shall soon see.

A month later the Pope wrote another beautiful letter to Prince Eugene de Caraman-Chimay, who, with many of his brother-noblemen, were devoting themselves in Belgium to found and promote societies in aid of workingmen. In France there was no less activity in this direction on the part of distinguished laymen, and Leo XIII seized upon every occasion to praise and bless their exertions. How needed were the efforts of the noble sons and the praise of the parent the world will soon see.

In truth, as we shall have occasion to observe in a future chapter, his great mind had long before clearly perceived the utility and necessity of reviving in our age and in every civilized land associations of workingmen and tradesmen after the model of the free labor guilds of the early and later Christian ages, of those of Italy in particular, which had in very truth been the creators of that glorious Italy which the Revolution is now fain to destroy.[3]

[3] The *Riforma* of Rome, the organ of Signor Crispi and the revolutionary party in Italy—the organ, in fact, of what we have designated in this volume as the *Occult Force*—published on March 9, 1886, an editorial article containing a plan for the complete destruction of the Church in Italy, and quite identical with that which is now so effectually carried out in France: "To array the inferior clergy against their superiors; to take away in every

We have just mentioned Leo XIII's first consistorial allocution, pronounced on March 28. Many things contributed to make this discourse remarkable apart from its being the first solemn utterance of the new Pontiff. His former colleagues in the Sacred College and brothers in the pastoral office were well acquainted with the scholarly accomplishments of Cardinal Pecci. But these, great and unquestioned as they were, could only be accounted a secondary merit. They had raised him by their suffrages to the Chair of Peter in the most evil days known since those of Nero or Julian the Apostate, because of the magnificent administrative abilities of which he had afforded so many and such splendid proofs as Bishop of Perugia from 1846 till 1878. They placed on him, well nigh a septuagenarian, the triple crown, because they firmly believed that he, in the necessarily few years he could rule the Church, would guide her bark safely through the fierce storm that raged around it, through the breakers which beset it on every side.

In 1886 we see how gloriously their expectations and trust are realized. But we may not anticipate. It is right that we should give ear to the beautiful words of wisdom addressed to the Sacred College and to the Christian world on that 28th of March:

"Venerable Brothers: When your suffrages called us last month to take on ourselves the government of the universal Church, and to fill on earth the place of the Prince of pastors, Christ Jesus, we did indeed feel our soul moved by the deepest perplexity and perturbation. On the one hand we were filled with great fear by the sincere conviction of our own

---

parish, village, and hamlet the influence and authority of the priest, and transfer them to the atheistical schoolmaster and schoolmistress; to take the complete control of ecclesiastical revenues of every kind, so that no parish priest, no clerical functionary shall receive a penny save from the hand of the government." Such is the Italian Kulturkampf. The letter of Hermann Grimm in the *Deutsche Randau* on the "Destruction of Rome" points to another part of this campaign against Christianity, Christian art, and civilization, and they are putting it into execution with right hearty zeal!

unworthiness, as well as by our utter inability to support so great a burden; and this sense of infirmity was all the more increased by the remembrance of how much the fame of our predecessor ... shone the brighter and more glorious through the whole earth. That great ruler of the Catholic fold had always contended for truth and justice with such invincible courage, and had labored so long and with such exemplary fidelity in administering the affairs of the Christian world, that he not only shed a lustre on this Apostolic See, but filled the whole Church with love and admiration for his person, thereby perhaps excelling all his predecessors in the high and constant testimonies of public respect and veneration paid to him, as he surpassed them all by the length of his Pontificate.

"On the other hand, we were filled with deep anxiety by the very sad state, in our days, of civil society almost everywhere, as well as of the Catholic Church itself, and especially of this Apostolic See, which, violently stripped of its temporal sovereignty, is reduced to a condition in which it can in no wise enjoy the full, free, and unimpeded use of its power.

"Such, Venerable Brothers, were the reasons which moved us to refuse the proffered honor of the Pontificate. But how could we resist the divine will, which was so manifest in the unanimity of your decision, and in that most loving solicitude felt by you for the sole interest of the Catholic Church, urging you to elect, as soon as possible, a Sovereign Pontiff?

"We, therefore, deemed it our duty to take on ourselves the office of the Supreme Apostleship, and to yield to the will of God, placing our whole trust in Him, with the hope that He who had imposed on us the high dignity would also give to our lowliness the strength to sustain it.

"As this is the first time it is allowed us to address your Eminences from this place, we desire first of all solemnly to assure you that in the fulfilment of the service of our apostolate we shall have nothing so much at heart as to bestow all our care, with the help of God's grace, in sacredly guarding the deposit of the Catholic faith, in watching faithfully over the rights and interests of the Church and the

Holy See, and in laboring for the salvation of all; ever ready, for all these purposes, to undergo any fatigue, to draw back from no discomfort. ...

"In the discharge of these duties of our ministry we trust that we shall never lack the benefit of your counsels and your wisdom—nay, we ardently beseech you never to allow them to fail us. And in saying this we wish you to understand that it is not a mere expression of official courtesy, but a solemn declaration of our affectionate desire. For we are deeply impressed by what the Holy Scripture relates of Moses—that, namely, when recoiling from the weighty responsibility of governing a whole people, he, by God's own command, called to his aid seventy men from among the ancients of Israel, in order to have them bear the burden with him, and thus to make them, by their help and counsel, lighten his cares in governing the people of Israel. This is the example which we, who have been made the guide and ruler of the entire Christian people, in spite of our unworthiness, set before our eyes; wherefore we cannot refrain from seeking and finding in you the seventy men of all Israel in the Church of God, a help in our labors, a comfort in our cares.

"We know, moreover, as the word of God declares, that there is safety where there are many counsels; we know that, as the Council of Trent admonishes us, that the administration of the universal Church depends on the counsels given to the Roman Pontiff by the College of Cardinals; we learn, finally, from St. Bernard, that the cardinals are called the Pontiff's colleagues and counsellors. And therefore it is that we, who for nearly twenty-five years have enjoyed the honors of your order, have brought with us to this sovereign seat not only a heart full of affection and zeal for you, but the firm resolve to use chiefly those who were formerly our associates in rank as our fellow-laborers and advisers in transacting ecclesiastical affairs.

"And now a most happy and timely occurrence permits us to share with you the first sweet fruit of consolation which our Lord permits us to gather from the first great work accomplished for the glory of religion. Our saintly predecessor, Pius IX, in his great zeal for the Catholic cause, had undertaken what such of you as belong to the Congregation of the Propagation of the Faith had definitely decreed—to re-establish the episcopal hierarchy in the illustrious kingdom of Scotland, and thereby add a new lustre to that Church; this we have been able to bring, with the divine aid, to a happy termination by the apostolic letters (bull) which we had published on the 4th of this month.

"It was indeed to us a subject of holy joy that in so doing we were fulfilling the ardent wishes of our dearly beloved, the clergy and faithful people of Scotland, of whose great devotion to the Catholic Church and the Chair of Peter we have many striking proofs. We therefore hope sincerely that the work thus accomplished by the Apostolic See shall be crowned with happy results, and that, through the intercession of the patron saints of Scotland, throughout the length and breadth of the kingdom the mountains shall put on peace for the people, and the hills righteousness."[4]

Such was Leo XIII's first official utterance from the Apostolic Throne.

On the 21st of April appeared his first encyclical letter, *Inscrutabili*, on the evils which torment society in Christian countries and endanger its very existence, as well as on their causes and their remedy.

It foreshadowed all the teachings of the magnificent series of encyclicals which were to issue in succession from his pen. He seemed to feel, while penning this first great doctrinal epistle, that the burden of old age was heavy on him, as well as the terrible load of care imposed by his charge. He therefore put all his thought and strength into this first letter, warning, with the voice and the authority of a prophet, governments and peoples of the fearful causes of social disaster and ruin which were at work in their midst.

Every word and act of Leo XIII had, during the first month

---

4 "Leonis XIII Pont. Max. Acta," vol. I. pp. 37-41.

after his election, been watched with a keen if not with a friendly interest by the liberal press of Italy and all Continental Europe. The rumor had been industriously circulated that he had made up his mind, if not to depart entirely from the line of policy pursued by Pius IX, at least to modify it deeply.

The Italian revolutionists identified, or pretended to identify, the wholesale political, legislative, and irreligious changes which they had brought about in the Peninsula with what in other lands was called "progress "and "modern civilization." They wished the Pope, and all Catholics with him, to accept the usurpation of the States of the Church, the occupation of Rome, the suppression of the Religious Orders, the sequestration of Church property, the laws on matrimony, on education, and those even which degraded the priesthood and deprived both the Pope and the bishops of the liberty essential to their office, as the natural consequence of the development of that "modern civilization," and, by accepting "accomplished facts" as done and over, to be reconciled with the existing state of things.

This iniquitous and impossible "reconciliation" Pius IX had denounced, exposed, and stigmatized with an eloquence and a truth which commended themselves to the judgment of all real statesmen, sound politicians, and true Christians. Just as well, in the days of Mohammed II, had the Turks succeeded in conquering Vienna and Rome, and with them the Austrian Empire and the Italian Peninsula, could the victor have demanded of the then existing Pope to accept the change of governments as "progress," and have expected the Church to become reconciled to the Koran and to such toleration and liberty as Constantinople met with in 1450, and Seville and Toledo in 715.

It was persistently asserted, and was believed in some quarters, that Leo XIII would yield to the force of events and endeavor to devise a *modus vivendi* with the masters of Rome and Italy.

So, in spite of the formal and solemn declarations to the

contrary contained in the Pope's first allocution, in spite of the confirmatory statements to be found in other utterances of his, the liberal press still continued their tactics of contrasting the new Pontiff's moderation of mind, high culture, liberality of sentiment, and knowledge of modern society and its exigencies with the "unyielding and uncompromising" spirit and temper of his predecessor. They were impatiently expecting the first encyclical, which, like the discourse of a prime minister at the opening of Parliament, or the first message to Congress of a newly elected American president, is taken as a programme of his future policy.

The encyclical at length appeared, dated on Easter Sunday, the 21st of April, 1878, and it did show in the most remarkable manner that Leo XIII had a perfect "knowledge of modern society and its exigencies," a thorough insight into Christian civilization, its principles and benefits to mankind. But it woefully disappointed all who fancied or hoped that a Pope could reconcile the revealed truth of which he is the divinely appointed guardian, the righteous ness, justice, and divine morality which flow from the revealed law of life, with the awful errors, the unbridled licentiousness of thought and word and deed, the iniquity and the immorality, which are cloaked over by their pretended civilization.

If we have been able in the preceding chapters to convey to the reader the conviction or the impression that Joachim Pecci, while Bishop of Perugia, in giving to his people the magnificent instructions mentioned by us, was giving them the light of revealed truth as he conceived it, and dealing out to them full draughts of Christian wisdom, the philosophy which builds up and perfects and preserves states, then we shall find the same light shining now with greater splendor. From the hill-top on which is throned Perugia the zealous bishop could only speak to Umbria, or at most to Italy. From the sublime elevation of the Chair of Peter, Leo XIII speaks with authority to all mankind; the light imparted by his teaching illuminates both hemispheres.

We say it with the deepest and most intense conviction of

the truth of what we say, that in defending Catholic truth, the institutions and morals of Christian society, Leo XIII defends the dearest, deepest, most vital and sacred interests of every Protestant country on the face of the globe, the essential liberty, morality, and happiness of every Protestant home in existence.

Once more we affirm it: the battle which is now raging in Italy and in Spain, in France and Germany and Belgium, in Great Britain and even in our own United States, is not so much a battle against Catholicism as the most powerful, wide-spread, compact, and ancient form of Christianity, as against *Christianity itself*, against the very notion of religion, the very existence of social order, the very foundations of that glorious civilization which has given to Europe the leadership of the world.

If any man doubt this, then let him read this first encyclical letter of Leo XIII We can only give a few extracts. But these will satisfy the earnest and the candid minded that the world has rarely heard such eloquent and pregnant lessons fall even from the Chair of Peter. It is addressed in the usual form to all the bishops of the Catholic world, by the Supreme Pastor to his fellow-laborers in the fold of Christ:[5]

"As soon as, by an inscrutable design of God, we were, albeit unworthy, raised to the sublime height of this apostolic dignity, we felt impelled by a strong desire and by a kind of necessity to address you by letter, not only for the purpose of expressing our heartfelt affection for you, but for that of discharging the duty of our divinely entrusted office by encouraging you—you who are called to bear a part in our care—to continue with us the battle for the Church of God and the salvation of souls.

"From the very beginning of our Pontificate we have before our eyes the sad spectacle of the evils which assail mankind from every side. There is a wide-spread subversion of

[5] An encyclical letter, like a papal bull, is always designated by the two or three first words. This is termed the encyclical Inscrutabili.

the cardinal truths on which the very foundations of human society repose. There is a wicked disposition of men's minds which is impatient of all lawful power. There is a perpetual foment of dissension, begetting internal strife, cruel and bloody wars. There is a contempt of the laws of morality and justice, an insatiable yearning for the transitory goods of earth, and a forgetfulness of the eternal, carried to the insane pitch of causing so many unhappy persons to lay violent hands on themselves. There is an inconsiderate administration, a squandering, an upsetting of the public property and revenues; and there is the brazen impudence of men who, when they deceive their fellows most, make them believe that they are the promoters of patriotism, of liberty, of right of every kind. There is, in fine, a pestilential virus which creeps into the vital organs and members of human society, which allows them no rest, and which forebodes for the social order new revolutions ending in calamitous results."

No one who is at all acquainted with the social condition of the civilized world but will admit the truth of this diagnosis. Now, what is the nature, what the source of this universal distemper?

"As to the cause of all these evils, we are persuaded that it lies principally in this: that men have despised and rejected the holy and August authority of the Church, which, in the name of God, is placed over the human race and is the avenger and protector of all legitimate authority. The enemies of public order were fully persuaded of this when they found no means of destroying society to its foundations so efficacious as persistent attacks on the Church of God, by assailing her with the weapons of shameless calumny, by odiously accusing her of being the enemy of true civilization, by daily damaging her authority and influence in some new way, and subverting the supreme power of the Roman Pontiff, who is the asserter and protector on earth of the eternal and unchangeable interests of goodness and righteousness.

"Hence the origin of these laws which overturn the divine constitution of the Catholic Church, and which we lament to see in vigor in most countries; hence came the contempt of episcopal authority, the obstacles opposed to the free exercise of the ecclesiastical ministry, the destruction of religious communities, and the public sale of the property which supported the ministers of the Church and fed the poor; hence came the withdrawing from the salutary control of the Church of the public institutions of charity and beneficence; hence sprang the unbridled liberty df teaching and publishing all manner of evil, while, on the other hand, the right of the Church to train and to educate the young is violated and suppressed. Nor is any other purpose to be found for the usurpation of the civil principality which Providence conferred, many ages ago, on the Bishop of Rome, to enable him to exercise freely, without let or hindrance, the power given him by Christ for the eternal salvation of the race."

To be sure, some of our non-Catholic readers will not, perhaps, be ready to grant that the primal and chief source of modern social evils springs from the successful conspiracy organized against the Catholic Church and her institutions, especially against the Papacy and the Temporal Power. But, unfortunately for their view of this great question, we have the recorded utterances of the head-con spirators themselves—of Weishaupt and Frederick II and Voltaire, without mentioning so many others of the so-called "philosophers" of the last century—of the recognized leaders of the sceptic, rationalistic, scientific, and socialistic schools of the present age. They now proclaim it openly in France, in Belgium, in Germany, in Switzerland, as well as in Italy, where they have carried out to the letter the old programme of the anti-Christian leagues.

They are not afraid of Protestantism, because it is not a unit like the Catholic Church, and because the Protestant sects, with their Bible and proselytizing societies, are useful and energetic allies in battering down the bulwark of the common enemy—the Church of Rome.

None the less true is it that all the forces of infidelity and revolution are marshalled against Christianity as embodied in that grand old Church. And equally evident is it that as in Perugia, so in Rome and from his seat of authority in the Vatican, he whom we call Leo XIII leads to battle the forces of those who fight for Christ and revelation and social order.

In addressing himself to the Catholic hierarchy, dispersed all over the globe, he does not, he says, mean to sadden them by depicting the sad social condition of Christian peoples, but clearly to point out to them toward what purpose their common zeal must be chiefly directed.

And then, as if to furnish them a rich theme for the instruction to be given to their flocks, intellectual weapons for the campaign which he wishes them to begin against the enemies of order and humanity, he sketches true civilization with a masterly hand:

"It is well known and self-evident that we cannot conceive of a community in which true civilization is not based on the everlasting principles of truth and the immutable laws of rectitude and justice, and in which men's hearts are not united by sincere love, and where such love does not sweetly regulate the interchange of duties and relations.

"Now, who will dare to deny that it is the Church, which, by preaching the Gospel to the nations, has borne the light of truth into the midst of savage races plunged in hideous superstition, and has thereby led them to acknowledge the Divine Author of the world and to reform their lives? that it was the Church which did away with the miseries of slavery and lifted up mankind once more to their sublime native dignity? that she it was who, planting the sign of redemption on every shore, brought thither at the same time or took under her protection the sciences and the arts, founded and fostered the admirable institutions of charity in which every form of suffering was assuaged, and everywhere instructed and elevated the populations, delivered them from squalid poverty, and labored in every way to make them live in a manner suitable to the dignity of human nature and to its hoped-for destinies?

"If any sensible man in our day will compare the age in

which we live, so bitterly hostile to the religion and Church of Christ, to those blessed ages when the Church was honored as a mother by the nations, he will surely find that the society of our day, so convulsed by revolutions and destructive upheavals, is moving straightway and rapidly toward its ruin; while the society of the former ages, when most docile to the rule of the Church and most obedient to her laws, was adorned with the noblest institutions and enjoyed tranquillity, riches, and prosperity. If the many blessings which we have enumerated, springing as they did from the ministrations and salutary labors of the Church, are the characteristic works and ornaments of true civilization, then, far from being averse to it or repelling it, the Church of Christ, on the contrary, claims that to her belongs the glory of having given birth to it, nursed and developed it.

"More than that, the kind of social civilization which is so hostile to the doctrines and laws of the Church is found to be only a hollow imitation of the reality, a mere name without the substance. You have the proof of this in the peoples on whom the light of the Gospel never shone, in whose manner of living there appeared, indeed, a certain false semblance of true civilization, but the solid and substantial fruits of its culture were not there.

"Assuredly that is not to be deemed the perfection of civilized life which boldly contemns all lawful power; nor is that to be esteemed liberty whose wretched progress is marked by the unrepressed propagation of error, by the unbridled gratification of evil desires, by the impunity allowed to guilt and crime, and by the oppression which weighs on good citizens of every rank. All these are wrong, are bad, are absurd, and cannot, therefore, avail to perfect the human race or to bless it with prosperity, for sin maketh nations miserable;[6] on the contrary, they must, by corrupting both minds and hearts, drag down by their very weight nations into

---

[6] Proverbs xiv. 34. The Protestant Version says: "Sin is a reproach to any people."

every crime, ruin all order, and at length bring the condition and peace of a commonwealth to extreme and certain destruction.

"Now, if we consider the labors of the Papacy, what can be more unjust than to deny the great and glorious services rendered to the whole civilized world by the Bishops of Rome? Our predecessors, in securing the good of the nations, never hesitated to face struggles of every kind, to undergo any amount of labor, to expose themselves to bitter troubles. With their eyes fixed on heaven, they did not quail before the threats of the wicked, nor allow either flattery or bribes to elicit from them an assent which would prove them to be degenerate and unworthy of their office.

"It was this Apostolic See which collected and built up together again the remains of ancient society fallen asunder; it was the Apostolic See in whose friendly beacon light shone forth the civilization of the Christian ages; it was the anchor of salvation which held the bark of humanity amid all the fearful storms that assailed it; it was the sacred tie of concord through which the most widely separated nations, and the most opposed in their manners and customs, were bound together in one great society; it was, finally, the common center at which the nations sought not only the doctrine of faith and religion, but the means to bring about peace and the wise counsels for administering their affairs.

"Why say so much? It was the glory of the Popes that they placed themselves, with inflexible constancy, like a wall and a bulwark to prevent human society from falling back into the ancient superstition and savagery.

"Would to God that this salutary authority had never been neglected or repudiated! Then, assuredly, civil sovereignty itself would not have lost that August and sacred character which religion had bestowed upon it, and which alone gave to the obedience of the subject its worth and nobility; nor should we have witnessed so many rebellions and wars which have filled the earth with blood and misery; nor would realms formerly most prosperous and powerful be now fallen down to the depths of helplessness and oppressed by-calamities of every kind. An example of this is afforded by the Eastern peoples, who, breaking asunder the sweet ties which bound, them to this Apostolic See, have forfeited the splendor of their primitive glory, their fame for the culture of the arts and sciences, and their rank among the nations."

The Pope here enumerates the special benefits for which ungrateful Italy is indebted to the Papacy. He points to the great names shining like stars of the first magnitude along the illustrious line of his predecessors—great, good, and glorious Pontiffs, who were the parents and protectors of Italy and the benefactors of the human race. "This great city itself, the seat of these Pontiffs, bears witness to the countless benefits conferred by them; it became the strong citadel of the faith, the refuge of all the arts of civilization, the abode of wisdom, winning for itself the admiration and reverence of the whole world. As the greatness of all these services is recorded for eternal remembrance in the monuments of history, it is easy to understand that only by bitter hatred and unworthy falsehood, uttered for the purpose of deceiving the unwary, and published from pulpit and press, could this Apostolic See have been represented as an obstacle to the civilization of Italy or to the happiness of her peoples.

"If, therefore, the hopes of Italy and of the Christian world are founded on the influence attached to the authority of the Holy See, an influence so salutary for the advantage and welfare of all; if they also are placed in that close bond of union by which all Christ's faithful people are held in communion with the Roman Pontiff, no duty for us is greater than to maintain secure and inviolate the dignity of the Roman Chair, than to strengthen more and more the connection of the members with their Head, of the children with their Parent.

"Wherefore, first of all, in order to assert in the only way now possible the rights and the liberty of this Holy See, we declare that we shall never cease to contend for the full obedience due to our authority, for the removal of all obstacles put in the way of the full and free exercise of our ministry and power, and for our restoration to that condition of things in which the provident design of the Divine Wisdom had formerly placed the Roman Pontiffs.

"And in demanding such restoration we are moved by no ambition, no desire of domination, but only by the best interests of our office and by the sacred oaths we have taken; and, besides, not only because the civil sovereignty is necessary for the protecting and preserving of the full liberty of the spiritual power, but because, moreover—a thing in itself evident—whenever there is question of the temporal principality of the Holy See, then the interests of the public good and the salvation of the whole of human society are involved.

"Hence it is that in the fulfilment of our duty, which obliges us to defend the rights of holy Church, we renew and confirm by this letter all the declarations and protestations which our predecessor, Pius IX, issued and reiterated both against the occupation of his civil principality and against the violation of the rights belonging to the Roman Church.

"At the same time we address ourselves to sovereigns and to those who are the supreme rulers of states, and implore them again and again, in the August name of the Most High God, not to reject at this needful time the aid offered them by the Church, and that they unite in friendly zeal in favor of that great source of authority and salvation, and seek to be united to her more and more by the ties of hearty love and reverence.

"God grant that, discovering the truth of what we have been saying, and being themselves convinced that the doctrine of Christ, as Augustine was wont to say, is a mighty safeguard to the state when it finds obedient observance[7] and that in the safety of the Church and dutiful obedience to her are to be found the interests of the public surety and tranquillity, they would bestow their thought and care in alleviating the evils which afflict the Church and her visible Head! Thereby would it come to pass that the peoples whom they govern, entering

---

[7] Ep. 138, alias 5 ad Marcellinum, n. 5.

on the paths of justice and peace, would enjoy a golden age of prosperity and glory."[8]

Such was the impressive appeal to the governments of our day, reminding them that those who had the temerity to touch and to change the great principles on which the God whom all Christians adore has established the Christian order in society were moving the foundations of the earth, letting loose the earthquake, the whirlwind, and the flame, and opening up an abyss in which peoples and rulers will be surely engulfed.

He therefore adjures them by the August name of the Most High God to listen to the warning words of the Vicar of Christ. It was the warning of a prophet.

Then, remembering that the family is the organic element from which the state springs; that domestic society is the nursery in which, together with all Christian virtues, are fostered all the solid and noble qualities and habits which alone make great citizens; that on the Christian training of children from their tender years must spring, as the ripe and full fruit from the flower, the education—Christian in its aims, its principles, and its methods—which is the formative force of the modern world, he thus addresses himself to the bishops on the family, its institutions and its education:

"In the next place, desiring to draw more closely day by day the bonds which unite the entire Catholic flock with the Supreme Pastor, we here address ourselves to you, Venerable Brothers, with especial affection, and earnestly beseech you to display your priestly zeal and pastoral vigilance in kindling in the souls of your people the love of our holy religion, in order that they may thereby become more closely and heartily attached to this chair of truth and justice, accept all its teachings with the deepest assent of mind and will, and unhesitatingly reject all opinions, even the most wide-spread, which they know to be in opposition to the doctrines of the Church.

"On this point the Roman Pontiffs who have come before

[8] "Acta," vol. I. pp. 44-52.

us, and, last of all, Pius IX, of saintly memory, especially in the Council of the Vatican, had present to their minds the words of St. Paul: Beware lest any man cheat you by philosophy and vain deceit according to the tradition of men, according to the elements of the world, and not according to Christ;[9] hence they lost no needful opportunity to condemn spreading errors and mark them with the apostolic censure. All these condemnations we, following the example of our predecessors, confirm and renew from this apostolic seat of truth, beseeching fervently, at the same time, the Father of lights that all the faithful, being perfectly of 'one accord and agreeing in sentiment,' should be of one mind with us and speak the same thing.

"Your duty it is, Venerable Brothers, to bestow unremitting care on scattering the seeds of the heavenly doctrines broadcast over the field of the Lord; to make Catholic teaching penetrate, in good time, into the minds of the faithful; to plant it deeply there, and to keep it safe from admixture with corrupt doctrines. The more active the enemies of religion are to teach the unlearned, the young especially, what clouds their intellect and corrupts their morals, the more should you exert yourselves to establish not only a well-adapted and solid method of instruction, but a method in every way, both in letters and in discipline, in conformity with the Catholic faith, especially as regards mental philosophy, on which the right teaching of all the other sciences depends in a great measure—a philosophy such as shall prepare the way for divine revelation instead of aiming at overturning it; which shall defend revealed truth, as in their writings did the great Augustine, the Angelic Doctor, and the other teachers of Christian wisdom.

"The best way of training youth, however—that which conduces to preserve the integrity of both faith and morals—should begin from early childhood and in the Christian home. Unhappily, the Christian family in our times has been

---

[9] Colossians ii. 8.

sadly disturbed, and can only recover its proper dignity by being governed by the laws under which it was placed in the Church by the Divine Author of both. By raising the matrimonial contract, in which He willed us to see the sign of His own union with the Church, to the dignity of a sacrament, He not only sanctified the union of husband and wife, but also provided most efficient helps for both parents and children to fulfil their mutual and respective duties, and thereby the more easily attain to everlasting life and the happiness of the present.

"But impious laws, taking no account of the sacredness of this great sacrament, placed it on the same level as all merely civil contracts; and the deplorable result has been that citizens, desecrating the holy dignity of marriage, have lived in legal concubinage instead of Christian matrimony; the married pair have violated the fidelity pledged to each other; the children born to them have refused them obedience; and, what is most scandalous and most baneful to public morality, very often unhallowed love was followed by fatal quarrels. All these unhappy and deplorable results must move your zeal to warn your faithful peoples assiduously and fervently to have a reverent regard for the doctrine of the Church on holy matrimony, and to observe scrupulously the laws of the Church regulating the mutual duties of parents and children.

"From this we shall obtain one blessed fruit—that every member of Christian society will reform his own conduct and outward manner of living. The decayed or degenerate trunk of a tree puts forth shoots that are worse still and bear unhappy fruit. So does the moral evil which infects the tree of domestic life become a contagion which communicates its virus to the community and yields a baneful harvest for public life.

"On the contrary, where Christian families are governed by the law of Christ, all their members are habituated by degrees to cherish religion and piety, to look with horror on false and pernicious doctrines, to practise virtue, to obey their superiors, and to control that tendency to self-seeking which is the root of human degeneracy and degradation.

"Toward this purpose not a little help will be found in the proper encouragement and direction of the pious associations which have sprung up in our day to the great benefit of Catholic interests.

"These are lofty objects, requiring superhuman efforts, which we hope and wish to see realized. But God has made the nations of the earth susceptible of healing, since He founded the Church for the salvation of mankind, and promised that His help should not fail her to the end of time; we therefore firmly trust that by working together we shall enable the human race, warned by so many evils and calamities, to seek for salvation and prosperity in obedience to the Church and in listening to the infallible teaching of this Apostolic Chair."[10]

A few months later Leo XIII will seize an opportunity for outlining his doctrinal plan: "From the very first days of our pontificate, and from the elevation of the Apostolic Chair, we turned our eyes toward the society of our day, to ascertain its condition, investigate its needs, and to counsel the remedial measures. ..."

And what principally arrested the Pontiff's attention? "... The waning of truth—not only of the truths of the supernatural order which are known by the light of faith, but of natural truth, both speculative and practical; the prevalence of the most baneful errors, ... disorders everywhere increasing. ...

"The most potent cause of such moral ruin is the separation, the attempted apostasy, of actual society from Christ and from His Church, in which alone resides the virtue sufficient to repair all the enormous evils done it." The conviction that, under God, the Church alone established by Him was able to cope with the manifold evils which were desolating society, makes him, almost at the outset, renew the solemn protest of Pius IX on his deathbed against the usurpers of the temporal principality of the Holy See. Then he unfolds his plan for combating the dominant anti-social errors.

---

[10] *Ibidem.*

CHAPTER XXI

LEO XIII FACE TO FACE WITH ANTICHRIST IN ROME

TO CARDINAL SIMEONI, who had been Pius IX's last and trusted Secretary of State, Leo XIII had substituted, on March 5, Cardinal Alexander Franchi, for several years the prefect of the Congregation de Propaganda Fide, in one respect the most important charge in the Church. The new Secretary of State, whose position at the head of the Propaganda had brought him into personal contact with the bishops of four-fifths of the globe, and who was thoroughly acquainted with the affairs of all the churches outside of Italy, Spain, and France, was a man of singular ability. His vast experience, his quick tact, sure judgment, and amiable disposition enabled him to overcome obstacles and to settle difficulties which had defied all the skill and labor of others.

One of his first acts was a hurried journey to Ireland, where the question of university education, the first startling alarms of an approaching famine, and the reappearance of secret societies begotten of starvation and coercion were rendering the labors of the bishops one of extraordinary difficulty. His brief visit is still gratefully remembered by the Irish; for it testified to the Holy Father's intense desire to know the true condition of things in that unfortunate land of unrest and misgovernment.

Certain it is, as we shall see, that Leo XIII had a clear conception of the just claims of Ireland to self-government and to a full and practical religious liberty, and that his efforts thenceforward aimed at keeping the Irish Catholics and the National party within the strict bounds of constitutional agitation, legal, orderly, and peaceful methods, while seeking for the justice which so many illustrious Englishmen acknowledged to be due to them. Cardinal Franchi had no little share in Leo XIII's solicitude for the Asiatic missions, with whose every need he was thoroughly acquainted. The Pope's generous policy toward the Eastern peoples, and his warm sympathies for the forlorn condition of the Christian populations, were those of his Secretary of State, who seconded in every way the superhuman activity with which the Holy Father pushed forward every detail of the vast administration of the Church. But he was stricken down by a fatal illness on July 31, in the very beginning of his career, just when Leo XIII had initiated him in his grand plan for advancing among the nations the cause of Christ, of His Church, of society and civilization, as against all their united and powerful enemies in our day.

Cardinal Lorenzo Nina was chosen to succeed Cardinal Franchi. To set at rest at once and for ever all doubts and hypotheses about his principles and policy, Leo XIII addressed to the new Secretary of State a letter, dated August 27, which contains a retrospect of the first six months of his Pontificate, and defines luminously the lines on which he intends to govern the Church, and to labor for the interests of Christianity and the nations.

"It was a great misfortune and a great grief for us," he says, "to have so suddenly lost Cardinal Alexander Franchi, our Secretary of State. We called him to this high office because of the confidence inspired by his uncommon gifts of mind and heart, and the long services he had rendered to the Church. He so fully answered to all our expectations during the short time he labored by our side that his memory shall never by us be forgotten, and among those who come after us, as among the living, his name shall remain ever dear and blessed.

"As, however, it has pleased our Lord to subject us to this trial, we adore with submissive will His divine counsels. And turning our attention to the choice of a successor, we have cast our eyes on you, my Lord Cardinal, whose skill in conducting affairs was well known to ns, as well as your firmness of purpose and the generous spirit of self-sacrifice

vigilance; there the great events which are just now in course of accomplishment are, perhaps, preparing a better future for religious interests. Nothing shall be omitted by the Apostolic See to promote these; and we cherish the hope that the illustrious churches of these regions shall at length come to live a fruitful life and to shed abroad their ancient splendor.

"These brief remarks reveal sufficiently, my Lord Cardinal, our design of extending largely the beneficent action of the Church and the Papacy throughout modern society in all its degrees. It is, therefore, necessary that you also should apply all your lights and all your activity to carrying out this design which God has inspired us with.

"Besides that, you shall have to give your serious attention to another matter of the highest importance—that is, to the very difficult condition created for the Head of the Church in Italy and in Rome when they had despoiled him of the temporal power which Providence so many centuries ago had bestowed on him to protect the freedom of his spiritual power.

"We do not wish to stop to reflect here that the violation of the most sacred interests of the Apostolic See and of the Roman Pontiff is fatal also to the welfare and the tranquillity of the nations, who, seeing the most ancient and August rights violated in the person of Christ's Vicar, feel their deep notions of duty and justice seriously weakened, their respect for law weakened, and thus the way is opened to destroy the very possibility of living together in society.

"Nor shall we delay you to consider that the Catholics of the different States can never feel at rest till their Supreme Pontiff, the supreme teacher of their faith, the moderator of their consciences, is in the full enjoyment of a true liberty and a real independence.

"We cannot, however, help observing that while we need for our spiritual power, both on account of its divine origin and superhuman destination, and for the needful exercise of its beneficent influence in favor of all human societies, the fullest and most perfect liberty, on the other hand the present conditions in which we are placed so hamper and limit it that we find it most difficult to govern the universal Church. The thing is notorious and proved by daily occurrences. The solemn complaints uttered by our predecessor, Pius IX, in the memorable Consistorial Allocution of March 12, 1877, may with equal reason be repeated by us, with the addition of many other grievances arising from the new obstacles opposed to the free exercise of our power.

"We have not only to deplore, as did our illustrious predecessor, the suppression of the Religious Orders, which deprives the Pontiff of a precious aid in the congregations which transact the most important affairs of the Church. We grieve that divine worship sees its ministers taken away by the law on military conscription, which compels all, without distinction, to serve in the army; that they withdraw from our control and that of the clergy the institutions of charity and beneficence founded in Rome by the Popes, or by Catholic nations who confided them to the watchful care of the Church. We grieve, with the intense, bitter grief which fills our heart as a father and a pastor, to find that we are compelled to see beneath our eyes in this Rome, the center of the Catholic religion, the progress made by heresy, heterodox temples and schools built freely and in a great number, and to have to observe the perversion which is the consequence, especially among young people, who are given an anti-Catholic education. But, as if all this were nothing, they are endeavoring to nullify the very acts of our spiritual jurisdiction.

"It is well known to you, my Lord Cardinal, how, after the occupation of Rome, wishing to calm to some extent the consciences of Catholics who felt very uneasy about the fate of their Chief Pastor, the government publicly and solemnly declared that they would leave the nomination of the bishops of Italy entirely in the hands of the Pope. Then, under the pretext that the acts of their canonical institution were not submitted to the government *placet,* not only were the new bishops deprived of their revenues—thus throwing on the Holy See the heavy burden of supporting them—but, moreover, to the great spiritual injury of their flocks, the government would not even acknowledge the acts of episcopal jurisdiction performed by them, such as the nomination of parish priests or other beneficed persons.

"And when, to obviate all these serious evils, the Holy See tolerated that the newly-elected bishops of Italy should present their bulls of nomination and of institution carried out in due canonical form, the condition of the Church was in no whit improved thereby. Notwithstanding this act of presentation, for one futile reason or another many bishops continued to be deprived of their revenues and to have their jurisdiction ignored. Those who can obtain their object see their petition sent from one office to another and subjected to endless delays. Men of the highest merit, distinguished by their learning and virtue, deemed by the Sovereign Pontiff worthy of filling the highest degrees in the ecclesiastical hierarchy, are forced to see themselves subjected to the most humiliating and prying disquisitions, as if they were vulgarians under the ban of suspicion. The venerable man designated by us to administer the Church of Perugia in our name, although placed already at the head of another church, and legally acknowledged therein, after a long period of waiting still vainly expects an answer. Thus it is that, with a paltry cunning, they take away from the Church with the left hand what mere policy feigned to give her with the right.

"To render this state of things still more painful, they lately began to assert the rights of royal patronage in several dioceses of Italy, with such exaggerated pretensions, accompanied by such odious measures, that the Archbishop of Chieti was judicially informed that they denied his jurisdiction, declared his appointment null, and ignored even his episcopal character!

"It is not to our purpose to insist on the nullity of such rights, which besides was confessed by not a few of our adversaries. It is sufficient to recall the fact that the Apostolic See, to which is reserved to provide for all episcopal sees, was only in the habit of granting the right of patronage to such sovereigns as had deserved well of the Church by supporting her interests, promoting her extension, increasing her patrimony; and that all who combat her by impugning her rights, appropriating her possessions, become by that alone, in accordance with the canons, incapable of exercising such patronage.

"The facts touched upon so far evidently indicate the purpose of continuing in Italy a system of ever-increasing hostility toward the Church, and clearly show what sort of liberty is kept in store for her, and with what kind of respect they intend to surround the Head of the Catholic religion.

"In this most deplorable condition of things we are not ignorant, my Lord Cardinal, of the sacred duties imposed upon us by our sacred ministry; and, with our eyes fixed on heaven, with our soul strengthened by the assurance of the divine help, we shall study never to be unfaithful to them..."[1]

We have rather anticipated the order of events to submit this official programme of Leo XIII's policy to the judgment of the reader. It discloses clearly the grand purpose of his reign: to make rulers and peoples acknowledge the Church as their divinely appointed guide and their safeguard against social errors and anarchy.

The first encyclical of Leo XIII was, indeed, a disappointment to the Italian Radicals and to all others who hoped or fancied that the new Pope would deviate from the policy of his predecessor, shake hands with King Umberto, and become reconciled with Antichrist and the Revolution in the persons of those who, in the cabinet of the Quirinal or in the Parliament of Montecitorio, were incessantly plotting and planning to make Rome intolerable to the Pope, to see it rid of the last cardinal, the last monk, the last priest.

No doubt on that memorable Easter Sunday, April 21, 1878, when the encyclical *Inscrutabili* was published, the prime minister, Depretis, and his associates of all revolutionary and anti-Christian hues, were firmly convinced that the German

[1] "Acta," I. pp. 103-111.

emperor and his powerful arch-chancellor were the firm and devoted allies of the new Italian kingdom, and that they, like all the Great Powers, had as good as set their seal of sanction on the "facts accomplished "in Rome and in Italy We shall see how Leo XIII defeated all their hopes.

Certain it is that Leo XIII, as we read in his own words quoted above, seems to have taken the initiative in his peaceful strategy against the Kulturkampf by writing himself to the Emperor William. It is also certain, from the discourse delivered at what may be called and what is regarded in Germany as the end of this war against the Church, on April 14, 1886, by Prince Bismarck himself, that he was quite disposed to meet the Pope. Why the religious peace was not then concluded was due to misunderstandings on both sides, but principally, if not solely, to the national anti-Catholic and anti-Papal sentiment in the German Reichstag and the nation, which persisted in regarding the Papacy in the Franco-German war as being "the rear-guard of the French army."

In another chapter we shall have to discuss fully the Kulturkampf, and study the strategy with which Leo XIII sought its extinction and succeeded. We can only say now that even when diplomatic relations were taken up and suspended and renewed, and then seemed about to fail utterly in their object, the Pope pursued his glorious plan of enlightening peoples, rulers, and governments on their dangers and the only way out of them, till it grew on the mind of the German emperor, his chancellor, ministers, and his enlightened, conservative aristocracy, that Leo XIII was God's prophet, sent to enlighten and to save the modern social world, and that Catholicism, where it is left free and fostered by the civil authorities, is the great conservative, vital force of the nations.

The Pope also wrote to the Emperor Alexander II of Russia and to the president of the Swiss Confederation; for in both of these countries Catholics were sorely oppressed, and the Holy Father trusted to make both of these governments understand that their interest as well as their duty lay in protecting, not enslaving, the Church. How far he succeeded the sequel will also show.

What he purposed doing for the Christians of the Turkish Empire we have just seen. But no mention is made of the great American continent. In the Canadian Confederation, however, as well as in the United States, the Sovereign Pontiff was left absolutely free to govern the Church as he chose. In Portuguese and Spanish America, the secret anti-Christian societies had long made their home. In the last century they had planted their offshoots in the then flourishing colonies dependent on the two kingdoms of the Spanish Peninsula, and had cast deep roots in that virgin soil, waxing strong and spreading with the vigor and rapidity of tropical vegetation. When the great Catholic teaching communities were suppressed there by the two metropolitan governments, society and education were like the palm and date trees left without the care of the husbandman. The terrible parasites of scepticism and unbelief had soon held them in their deadly clasp, and there was no one to lay the axe to the root of these creepers.

The only hope for religion in Mexico, as in Brazil and all South and Central America, would be in annexation to the United States, in the introduction of American institutions and a plentiful injection of American blood, American practical sense, political conservatism, reverence for religion, and the full liberty for the Holy See to regulate the Catholic interests of the southern, as it does that of the northern, continent.

But the Depretis cabinet had their strategy—a very radical and thorough one, too—by which they meant to destroy not only the educational and missionary resources of the Church in Rome and in the kingdom of Italy, but the very idea of Christianity in the minds of the people, and thereby the very groundwork on which rests the possibility of the existence of the Church among a people.

Further on we shall come to the quasi-confiscation of the Propaganda property. Now let us see the war in Rome itself.

Whether the encyclical *Inscrutabili* had convinced the anti-Christian societies dominating both Italy and France that Leo

XIII thoroughly understood the war carried on by them against the Church, the very structure of Christian society, and the civilization which had sprung therefrom, or whether they had made up their minds to declare open war against the Pontiff and the Church of which he was the head, the year 1878 offered them a most favorable opportunity of solemnly proclaiming their purpose.

It was the centenary year of the death of Voltaire.

The conspirators against the Christian order on both sides of the Alps announced that they would meet at Rome in the month of May, and there celebrate the death—the apotheosis, as they termed it—of the man whose lifelong watchword against Christ had been, *Écrasez l'infâme—"Crush the man of infamy!"*

It is well to recall this occurrence, because it places the civilized world face to face with the reality, with the true enemy whom Leo XIII has had to contend with. It will enable all who still believe in Christ, even though they do not acknowledge Leo XIII as their spiritual guide, to appreciate the nature of the struggle in which he is the central figure.

And so Rome, under the cross of Savoy, beheld those who administered her government, sat foremost in her legislative halls, on the judicial bench, in all the public offices; the *littérateurs* who had been the apostles of incredulity, of revolution, and the apologists of impiety; the journalists who upheld the spoliation of the Papacy, and those who advocated in no uncertain tones the abolition of the existing royalty—all joined together in solemn conclave and in the orgies of intellectual licentiousness, within sight of the Vatican and the Quirinal. And with them were the men who were fast turning France into the Republic of 1793, or aiming at one vast Commune for their country on the model of that of 1871.

This meeting accentuated, to use a current expression, the fierce hostility of the French and Italian *Liberal* (!) press against the Holy See and the reigning Pontiff. There were sessions after sessions held in the halls where the Roman youth had been formerly taught the sublime truths of the

Christian religion and the benefits it had conferred on mankind. It was a carnival of blasphemy and of cowardly outrage against the Pontiff shut up helpless in the Vatican, and against all that the Catholic and the Christian world held to be most sacred or most venerable.

In the English-speaking world these occurrences were not heard of or only received a passing notice. The significance, the deadly importance of these anti-Christian manifestations was understood only by the few. And what could the few do to awaken public attention to the designs and progress of that power which threatens the destruction of the moral world? It is only when such fearful outbursts of the spirit of disorder as the riots in London' and in Belgium, and even the labor troubles in the United States, happen to startle us from our lethargy, our dream of fancied security against socialistic revolution, that we begin to reflect upon Leo XIII's warnings and lessons. But surely the Voltairean and anti-Christian centenary feast at Rome in May, 1878, should, even now at eight years' distance, make us think seriously on the fault committed by the civilized world when they permitted Victor Emmanuel to take possession of the city of the holy apostles.

But we must not imagine that the true Rome—the Rome and the people who remained faithful to Christ and His Vicar, as distinguished from the new Rome, the Piedmontese, with the scum of all Italy whom they had gathered into it—did not resent the insult to their religion and to its Pontiff.

They felt these satanical festivities to be directed against Christ Himself, and they spontaneously set about repairing the outrage by solemn devotions in the churches and by no less solemn protestations addressed to the Holy Father. Rome has been for many centuries renowned for her admirable guilds and charitable societies. These comprise the very highest nobles as well as the simple artisan. They combined, in the last years of Pius IX, in a great union called, after him, La Federazione Piana. They extended their labors to the protection of Catholic interests, as well as to charity and beneficence.

The union chose the feast of the Ascension of our Lord, which happened on May 30, to present themselves before Leo XIII and enter a solemn protest in the name of all true Romans and all patriotic Italians against the desecration of the Eternal City by the disciples of Voltaire and Antichrist. It was a touching scene, and the Pope, as well as all who were present on the occasion, felt it. To their address he answered, impressing on them and on all Christians the importance of repairing the outrage offered to the Divine Majesty by this unparalleled outpouring of blasphemy. He especially felicitated them, the representatives of the Christian Rome, on their courage and determination.

It was not the only counter-demonstration which showed the Holy Father how deeply all classes of Romans and Italians resented the abominable impiety which had run riot in Rome during the month especially dedicated to recalling the memories of the Incarnate Son of God and His Blessed Mother. But to every deputation which waited on him he repeated his courageous words of advice and exhortation. The days of trial had come for them all; they must take their share in the general persecution, and not refuse to suffer for truth and for Christ.

On June 6, while Rome was still filled with the evil atmosphere left behind by the Voltairean celebration, General Kanzler and the veteran soldiers of the Pontifical Army came in a body to offer their homage to the new Pope. He was just the man to appreciate their sentiments. For he was resolved to abate not one jot of his sovereign prerogatives in Rome, nor to forego the hope of seeing Providence restore in time the temporal dominions indispensable to the free exercise of his spiritual power. This was the hope he held out to the brave men who had remained true to the Pontifical flag. "To you," he said, in concluding his stirring address—"to you, glorious defenders of right and justice, we shall say in conclusion: Persevere; remain faithful to your duties. Let no act in your future life ever stain your honored career. If it please God to shorten the days of trial by granting us happier times, you shall be found at your post, ready to protect the sacred interests of the Church. Should it turn out otherwise, you will have the consolation of having shared with us our ill-fortune and to have cast your lot with us."

They were brave words, and he meant them, and those who heard them treasured them up as a hope and as a reward.

But there was another army whose soldiers were ever engaged in the terrible conflict, and who could not, like General Kanzler and his men, lay by their arms and wait for the day of battle. The battle for priests in Rome, in Italy, on every point of the European Continent, never ceases to rage, and no true man can leave the ranks or skulk away from the perils of the contest. The Piedmontese government had woefully thinned the battalions of this spiritual militia by suppressing, dispersing, banishing the Regular Orders. Rome has, ever since Christianity has extended its influence to all the nations of the earth, been a training-camp for the priesthood, for the apostleship to be exercised in all countries. This the Revolution understood right well when it seized upon the great central monasteries, novitiates, and schools of Rome. This was obliterating the very springs of Christian life, learning, and zeal.

Pius IX, though deprived of the revenues of the Papal territories, made every provision his limited resources and the charities of the faithful enabled him to carry out for educating his clergy, for recruiting their ranks, and for keeping education and learning up to the highest levels. His successor was not the man to neglect such a blessed and necessary work, to leave it incomplete. He threw his whole strength into enlarging it rather, extending the sphere of clerical and lay education, and raising the standard of literary and scientific excellence far above that which governed the secular schools. And we shall see that he succeeded.

VISIT OF STUDENTS

On June 13 the students of the Seminario Romano and

Seminario Pio, which were the special nurseries of the Pontifical secular clergy, were admitted to the presence of Leo XIII Never does the personal character of the Pontiff show itself in such an amiable light as when he is surrounded by bands of seminarians or school-children. The memory of all his goodness to the young generations he reared in Perugia will live for ever in the hearts and on the lips of the people of Umbria.

With his seminarians, however, the Pope loves to put in his speeches and conversation all the graces of the purest classic Latin. He delights in encouraging them to aim at perfection in everything. He loves to set ever before them the high ideal of the priesthood, praecelsa sacrorum ministrorum dignitas—"the sublime dignity of God's ministers"; to exalt, amid the present abasement of Rome, the singular privileges of its clergy—*Romani cleri nomen ac decus, nostrorun temporum conditio, quibus ingens errorum ac pestilens corruptionis lues undique grassatur*—"and the sad condition of the present times, when error and corruption like a twin stream of pestilential waters overspread the land."

The men who composed the Italian government were well aware to what extent they had crippled the Church in her clergy by the suppression and banishment of the Monastic Orders, by the law of conscription compelling clerical students to serve their term in the army, by the hopeless, helpless poverty to which the great mass of priests were condemned, by the degrading treatment to which both bishops and priests were subjected in their enforced relations with the civil authorities, and by a thousand-and-one petty means at the use of those in power to make life a burden to an odious class of citizens.

Still, the source of clerical vocations was not dried up among the Italian populations, although the supply was reduced alarmingly. The government resolved to go to the very source itself, and to render the Christian family giving priests to the Church an impossible thing. They would seize on all elementary schools, and banish from them all Christian spirit, all Catholic teaching, the very adored names of Christ and of God.

And they did it in Rome, perhaps to honor the centennial celebration in honor of Voltaire. But they did it! On June 26 the Pope addressed to Cardinal Monaco la Valletta, his vicar-general in Rome, a letter, admirable in every sense, on religious instruction in the schools of that city. The Piedmontese government had not been ashamed, in the city where St. Peter and St. Paul had preached and planted the faith, not only to forbid in all schools under their control the giving of any religious instruction whatever, but they had banished from elementary schools frequented only by the children of Catholic parents the Catholic catechism.

And yet, while still claiming the name of Catholics, these men allowed all other denominations to have their schools, to teach their catechism, and to take every means to entice Catholic children to attend them. It was not even fair play. But their immediate purpose was to destroy the Catholic Church and religion. The rest would easily follow.

Those who rejoiced at whatever event might upset the power of the Papacy, temporal as well as spiritual, and who even now clap their hands at seeing the revolutionists destroying every distinctive feature of Papal—that is, of Christian—Rome, ought to remember that the men who sought to banish the Catholic catechism from the schools of the Eternal City, while permitting non-Catholic sects the fullest liberty of religious instruction and proselytism, are the deadliest, the sworn, the professed enemies of Christianity itself, of all religion indeed.

What Paul Bert did in France, in open pursuance of a design he never attempted to conceal, that Doctor Baccelli, appointed Minister of Public Instruction in 1880, openly avowed as his purpose and carried out faithfully. He declared that from all schools in Italy should be systematically, carefully excluded all religious teaching, even that of the simplest Theism.

Is it right, is it honorable, is it in accordance with Christian principle to be, even indirectly, the allies and auxiliaries of such men in dechristianizing Italy? Is it consistency to have the Bible—the Bible in the Italian tongue, and unauthorized by the Pope or the Italian bishops—ranked with the most blasphemous anti-Christian literature, and with the obscene and utterly abominable books and pamphlets, and flying illustrated sheets, which are studiously circulated in Italy to corrupt the hearts, the minds, the morals of the people?

Surely, where the means employed by the present masters of Italy and of the Eternal City to blot out the notion of God, and to make the very name of Christ our Lord odious and ridiculous, are such as Beelzebub and Belial would avow, men and women who have sincerely at heart the triumph of Gospel truth and morality should ask themselves in what company they are. It is not likely that demons would conspire to overthrow the empire of falsehood and vice. And where they and their visible agents are found arrayed against a venerable and widely-spread creed and order of things, the presumption is that that creed and that order are from God.

From the very beginning of his Pontificate Leo XIII set his heart upon counteracting, by every agency which he could command, the effects of the irreligious and immoral education given, of set purpose, to the children of Roman parents and the youth of the great public schools ever since 1870. Cardinal Monaco la Valletta gave the Pope effectual aid in this; and later, when Cardinal Parocchi, then Archbishop of Bologna, became cardinal vicar, he threw into the work of organizing a thorough system of secular and religious instruction in the primary schools of Rome all his intelligent zeal, experience, and characteristic energy. But, as the government had taken forcible possession of all primary and intermediate secular schools existing at the time of the occupation of Rome, the Pope had to create out of his own crippled resources a system of schools able to counteract the influence of the others.

This was one great object of solicitude. We shall see further on what Leo XIII effected in this direction.

CHAPTER XXII

DIFFICULTIES;
PILGRIMS;
SOLICITUDE FOR FRANCE AND GERMANY;
ENCYCLICAL ON SOCIALISM
1878-1879

WE HAVE not enumerated all the difficulties which from the outset beset the path of Leo XIII, nor have we described their magnitude. To their solution the aged Pope brought a clear head, a firm purpose, an indomitable courage, a rare knowledge of men and of the age in which he lived, consummate prudence and tact in dealing with sovereigns and statesmen as well as with churchmen and laymen of every class. Add to all these qualities an unbounded confidence in the God whose cause was entrusted to him, and the simple faith, the living, ardent piety of the lowliest of Christians, refreshing and strengthening his soul in his gigantic labors.

Formidable as were the obstacles opposed to the fulfilment of his mission in Germany, France, and Belgium, as well as in Russia and the Turkish Empire, there was some hope of removing them by degrees. But in Italy and in Rome itself no diplomatic skill, no concessions, compromises, or transactions, could avail to conciliate or change the fell spirit of the revolutionary and anti-Christian government, which, under the name of a monarchy, moved as steadily, as scientifically, as fatally onward to the annihilation of the Church and the Papacy as a locomotive at full speed on a perfectly safe road, and directed by a skilled and experienced hand, moves on toward its goal, crushing beneath its iron wheels the puny obstacles the hand of a child would oppose to its progress.

We have seen, stripped of all disguises and fair names, the Voltairean, the anti-Christian power which is at present master of Rome, and presides in the councils of the municipality as it does in those of the government.

Outwardly, to all human seeming, judging things from the standpoint of mere human wisdom and experience, and apart from some superhuman intervention of Providence, in May, 1878, there appeared not one ray of hope for the Papacy, for the preservation of the Church and of the Catholic religion in Italy, as against the irresistible domination of the established civil power and the fatal advance of the radical and irreligious spirit.

The Italian prime minister could at any moment he chose order a company of chasseurs to occupy the Vatican, and to put Leo XIII and his secretary, with their breviaries and travelling-suits, into a hackney coach, as Napoleon I ordered the seventh Pius, and have them conveyed to the fortress of Fenestrelle or across the frontier. And not a European or American power would have sent a fleet or an army to prevent the outrage.

Thus it was in 1878.

We see how bravely the Pope faces his enemies and prepares to solve every difficulty, to ward off every danger, while neglecting not one detail of his vast administration, or the urging forward of a single one of the mighty missionary enterprises begun or pursued under his direction in every known land.

Follow him in a few of the cares and labors, the joys and consolations also, which continue to fill up his days as the summer of 1878 passes into autumn.

The government had devised a plan for "renovating" and "reforming" the external aspect of Rome within and without the circuit of the ancient walls. It was intended, under the pretext of laying out new streets, of widening the old, and of providing room for the increasing population, to blot out all the features of the mediaeval and Papal city; in a word, all the characters of the Christian Rome, the capital of the Christian world. The uninhabited quarter on the Esquiline was laid out and united to the Quirinal by avenues intended to rival those of Paris or Berlin or Vienna—as if the torrid climate of Rome in summer was compatible with broad, glaring, sunburnt, and wind-swept thoroughfares! No provision for Catholic worship was made in this new quarter. Indeed, it was openly said in official quarters that none would be made by the government or the city authorities. The municipal council, like the cabinet and the legislature, was now under the control of the revolutionary clubs.

But from the Vatican the Holy Father watched the gradual destruction of the Rome of the Popes and the rapid increase of the city population. He could not leave the new comers devoid of all spiritual succor and comfort, and on August 11, calling before him the chapter and clergy of St. Mary Major, he entrusted to their priestly zeal and generosity the care of this new district.

But with the summer also came bands of pilgrims from distant lands—men who felt the need of renewing at the feet of Christ's Vicar their pledges of fidelity to the law which it was sought to banish from the face of the earth, and to return home, comforted and strengthened by his blessing, to continue the battle with scepticism, with open and professed unbelief, and with the terrible secret associations which pushed on their warfare on religion and all authority.

The German Catholics, so fearfully tried by the Kulturkampf, or by what Prince Bismarck later called "the battle with the Church," sent a noble band of representative men to enter their protest against the Voltairean Congress. They were presented to the Pope on May 23, and the words of filial love, reverence, and sympathy uttered by them to the Common Parent were a sweet consolation amid the hideous atheistic revelry covered by the sanction of the new masters of Rome. And he in return, whose heart went out to suffering Germany, found glowing words of praise and admiration for the pilgrims and their absent brethren.

And here, as if pausing between two of these glorious pilgrim receptions at the Vatican, we come upon a letter addressed on July 24 to the mayor and municipality of Cork, in answer to their address of congratulation and filial homage sent to the Holy Father on the preceding nth of March. Their homage was most grateful to him, he says. "It clearly showed us the reverence and filial piety you entertain toward us, which unite your own hearts together and do not fear to express themselves publicly. It also commended to us the religious sense and wisdom of your illustrious city, which found in you sons worthy of being entrusted with the administration of its affairs. To you therefore, beloved sons, we gladly express in this letter our gratitude and affection; and, ready as we are ever to give you every proof we can of our fatherly love, we pray God from our heart to be evermore your protector and helper, and so to inspire your counsels that your labors may procure His glory as well as the welfare and prosperity of your fellow-citizens."

Simple, sincere, and loving words, which Cork will treasure up in her records, and which found their echo in Ireland as if addressed to her long-suffering millions, promising them that "God would also be their protector and helper," and the Pontiff who had succeeded to Gregory XV and Urban VIII, after an interval of more than two centuries, "would be ever ready to give them in their need every possible proof of his fatherly love and care."

But here comes Spain in the beginning of autumn to have the representatives of all her provinces present in Rome and at the feet of the Sovereign Pontiff on the feast of St. Teresa, October 15. The steamer Santiago had been retained to take the fifteen hundred Spanish pilgrims from Barcelona to Civita Vecchia, so as to avoid all delays and troubles on the road. The Bishop of Huesca was at the head of these sons of Catholic Spain, and everybody had reason to feel that nothing would happen to mar the expectation of the pilgrims.

But they had not taken into account the spirit which now ruled the political affairs of Italy. Pilgrimages of every kind were the special abomination of the men who wished the Pope at the antipodes, and who had intended in 1848-49, during the siege of Rome, to blow up St. Peter's and the Vatican.

Pilgrimages the anti-clerical masters of Rome considered to be a kind of foreign invasion. They kept up the idea of the Pope-King. Had they not killed the "King," and did they not hope soon to extinguish the "Pope," and have an Italy and a Rome entirely after their own heart?

The authorities were fearful for the public health if such a crowd of Spaniards were landed all at once upon the Italian shore; they kept the Santiago at quarantine for four entire days in the bay of Civita Vecchia, although no contagious disease reigned either in Barcelona or in any part of Spain. It was in vain that they demanded to be in Rome before the 15th. The authorities were fully determined that in Rome they should not be on that day. They hoped that the Spaniards would profit by the lesson, and that the Bishop of Huesca would tell his brother bishops that no more Spanish pilgrimages would be welcome in the Rome in which they had been celebrating the apotheosis of Voltaire.

Not before the 17th, two days after the feast, were the Spaniards able to be presented to Leo XIII That he suffered keenly at seeing such an indignity put upon hundreds of the best men of Spain, and led by one of her noblest bishops, we may well imagine. It convinced the pilgrims, if other proofs were absent, of the untenable position of the Supreme Pastor of the Catholic world, living in his own episcopal city under the domination of a power all the more relentlessly hostile and anti-Catholic that both king and queen persisted in calling themselves Catholics!

It was short-sighted policy on the part of the Piedmontese and their subordinates. For we Catholics from every land, thronging to the Tombs of the Holy Apostles and to the home of our Common Father, bear back with us to our own land the memory of the humiliation he endures, of the restraints put upon his liberty, of the rudeness and insults offered to ourselves; and we resolve that the day shall come when the Pope shall be again sovereign of Rome.

That is a hope and a vow registered in many a home of many a land as well as Spain, and the numbers of those who register these vows increase with each passing year. In Germany, hostile as it was in May, 1878, the hope and the vows of its returned pilgrims have been growing like seed in a blessed soil, till we see in May, 1886, what a formidable crop of sympathy for the Pontiff, indignation against the destroyers of Rome, and threatening hostility toward its Voltairean government have sprung up all of a sudden to face usurpers and evil-doers.

And in Spain, and wherever the Spanish language is spoken, how ready the Spanish heart would be to catch fire and espouse the cause of the Pontiff whenever a brave leader and God's golden opportunity appeared! Even in our own great republic will not the quick American sense, and the instinctive love of justice, and the passion for freedom of conscience soon be made to perceive that the dearest religious rights of our millions of Catholics, the dearest interests of civilization among the heathen, demand that the Pope, the great international peace-making power of the world, should be sovereign in the city where he has reigned for eleven hundred years?

All these pilgrims brought with them, together with their filial reverence and affection, their offerings of Peter's pence, the contributions of all the members of Christ's great family toward the support of His Vicar, now despoiled of his patrimony. They were timely and much needed offerings these, for in Italy alone there were many thousands of priests, monks, and nuns stripped of their lawful property by the usurping government, and left destitute of all earthly means of adequate sustenance.

The month of February, 1879, concluding the first year of Leo XIII's Pontificate, witnessed in Rome a very momentous gathering. It was a congress of Catholic writers and journalists, who had come, representative toilers of the pen, from all countries to take advice from the Holy Father on the line of conduct to be followed by the Catholic press in treating of politico-religious questions. No assemblage, apart from an ecumenical council, could wield a greater influence over the course of public opinion, the direction of all intellectual currents, and the peace and prosperity of the Christian commonwealth than such a gathering.

Leo XIII knew it, and sad experience had taught the truth of it to the men who gathered to hear Leo XIII on February 22, 1879. In France and in Spain, as is well known, political opinion among Catholics had divided the very best and most influential into opposite and bitterly hostile camps. In France this division had been still more complicated by theological and philosophical discussions. People in such cases, when they are conscientious and ardent—and they were so on both sides of the Pyrenees—would naturally wish to have Rome on their side. Men who defended religion and the dearest interests of the Church against rampant Caesarism, or no less rampant liberalism and demagoguism, would too often take on themselves to dictate to priests, bishops, and Pope the line of conduct they ought to pursue even in ecclesiastical matters, but more especially in the domain of politics. The peculiar circumstances of the Holy See, the opportuneness or the inopportuneness of making concessions to the foreign invaders who had come from the foot of the Alps in time of peace to attack a defenceless and almost unarmed power hitherto held sacred and inviolable by Christendom—all these were made the continual subject of newspaper discussion, greatly to the injury of religion, to the scandal of the people, and to the detriment of the Papacy, whose interests it was sought to advance.

On the question whether Italian citizens should throw themselves into the new current of political life, and thereby recognize the legitimacy of the existing government, the validity of the spoliations and suppressions accomplished in Rome and throughout the Peninsula, lend an indirect sanction to the sacrilegious restrictions and violations of the Papal and episcopal spiritual jurisdiction daily and hourly taking place even in the Eternal City itself—these were subjects which set men's hearts and heads aflame, and made their pens write words that burned like fire. Who could control these mighty forces of the press? Who but the Vicar of Christ?

When this select body, representing the great host of the soldiers of Catholic truth, stood before him on that same 22d of February, he had but tender words of fatherly gratitude and blessing for them. What had he been himself in Perugia, during the thirty-two long years of intellectual combat with error and wrong, but a soldier of the truth, a toiler of the pen? And so his whole heart went out also to those champions of God and his Church.

Those who insisted on coming to terms with the Revolution received, however, a stern rebuke: they "must not presume to decide in their own name and by their own light public controversies of the highest importance, bearing on the circumstances of the Apostolic See, nor seem to have opinions in opposition to what is required by the dignity and liberty of the Roman Pontiff."

But here in the following words speaks the heart of the Pontiff:

"Beloved sons, who are supremely devoted to the Apostolic See, and show yourselves so ready to sustain its liberty and its honor, be also courageous and unanimous in employing both voice and pen in upholding the necessity of the temporal sovereignty for the free exercise of our supreme authority. With the records of history in your hand, show that there is no power on earth which can pretend to be superior or equal to it in the legitimacy of the right and title from which it sprang. If any one, in order to draw on you the hatred of the multitude, should go about repeating that this temporal sovereignty is incompatible with the welfare of Italy and the prosperity of states, you, on the other hand, should rejoin that the safety and the prosperity of nations has nothing to fear from the sovereignty of the Popes and from the freedom of the Church. ... Add this, which all know, that the Roman Pontiffs at all times bestowed the greatest pains in fostering the letters and sciences, that they were the generous protectors of the fine arts, and that with a just and paternal sway they made their people happy. Proclaim, in fine, to the world that the public affairs of Italy will never prosper nor enjoy permanent tranquillity until provision has been made, in accordance with all sorts of reasons, for the dignity of the Roman See and the liberty of the Sovereign Pontiff."

On the 9th of September, the Pope issued a new code of regulations for the use of the Vatican Library. Already he felt the necessity of stimulating Italian scholars to explore the rich mine of historical lore laid up in Rome, for so many centuries the head of the Christian, as it had long before been that of the pagan, world. In spite of the literary treasures taken away from time to time by those who had possession of the Eternal City, there still remained enough behind to tempt the ambition of the student. In the Vatican particularly, where are the archives of the Christian Church, the records of Christianity itself, it is important that those who would know what the Church did in the world should seek authentic information at its very source.

That same month of September, 1878, had witnessed the establishment of a Council of Cardinals, whose special labor should be to select fit persons to fill the episcopal sees of Italy. The importance of this new act of Leo XIII will at once strike all readers acquainted with the political and religious condition of the Peninsula. At any rate, the Pope, who, from his lofty seat in Perugia, had watched the struggles of the Italian hierarchy with the Piedmontese revolutionists, and the desperate measures resorted to by the latter to bend the bishops to their own will, now resolved that every precaution which the divine wisdom of the Church can suggest should be employed to fill the vacant sees of Italy with none but the best men—men of God, men of superior learning and superior virtue, men of inflexible principles and indomitable courage. Leo XIII wanted to do all a Pope could do to make the hierarchy of Italy the light of the world.

Later, in November (21), the venerable Archbishop Gastaldi, of Turin, who is still so gratefully and affectionately remembered by the Catholics of Great Britain and Ireland, received from the Holy Father a warm letter of thanks and praise for the acts of his Diocesan Synod.

The same month witnessed the creation of the new diocese of Leeds in England.

The trials of German Catholics, particularly in Prussia, were still bitter in the extreme. The Archbishop of Cologne had written to the Holy Father, giving an account of the sufferings endured, but rehearsing the glorious tale of the people's constancy to their baptismal faith, of the priests' fidelity to their flocks and obedience to their bishops, of the perfect union of hearts and minds which reigned among the bishops themselves, and of their devoted attachment to the Vicar of Christ.

On December 24 the Pope answered the archbishop in one of those thrilling letters which sound like the address of a commander-in-chief to troops in battle array and facing the enemy. Bishops, priests, and people get their meed of praise. Glancing at the efforts made all through Germany by the Occult Force to inculcate errors the most pernicious to religion and society, and ever conscious that governments can have no efficient aid against this ubiquitous and destructive enemy save from the Church, he informs the archbishop that he has raised his voice to the rulers of Germany to be at peace with the Church instead of combating and crippling her. While endeavoring to conduct to a successful termination the efforts made toward a lasting peace between Prussia and her Catholic subjects, he will continue to do the work which will, in the end, be most advantageous to the state, by denouncing error, exposing the magnitude and the causes of social disorders, and by pointing out the remedy.

The Pope knew that every line of his letter would be eagerly and attentively read and studied by the Imperial government, by Prince Bismarck above all. He calculated, not without reason, on the effects which his own conservative teaching, which is that of the Church, of Christianity itself, would have on minds that felt the need of such principles, and must end by respecting the Church which upholds and practices them.

Then comes a vivid picture of what that Church has to endure at the hands of the Prussian and Imperial authorities.

Evidently the mind of Leo XIII was then full of the encyclical which he was preparing to issue on Socialism, the one topic which, before all others, was at that moment sure to obtain the undivided attention of both the Emperor William and his prime minister. It was published on December 28:[1]

"As the very nature of our apostolic charge required, we did not fail to point out to you from the beginning of our Pontificate, in an encyclical letter, that mortal poison which circulates in the vital organs of human society and reduces it to the most extreme danger. At the same time we explained to you what were the most efficacious remedies by the application of which society may be restored to health and the grave perils which threaten it may be averted.

"But since then the evils which we deplored have so rapidly developed that we are again obliged to address ourselves to you. It is as if the prophet thundered in our ears: Cry out, cease not, lift up thy voice like a trumpet![2]

"You will easily understand, Venerable Brothers, that we are speaking of that class of men who, under various and strange names, are known as Socialists, Communists, or Nihilists, and who, spread over the globe and bound together closely by a criminal bond, no longer seek the friendly shelter of their secret conventicles, but come forth boldly into the daylight, and seek to carry out their long-cherished purpose of subverting civil society to its foundations.

"These are the men who, as the word of God attests, defile the flesh, and despise dominion, and blaspheme majesty.[3] They spare nothing, leave nothing untouched of all that divine and human laws have devised in their wisdom for the protection and adornment of life. The highest powers, to which, as the

---

1 Encyclical *Quod Apostolici muneris*, Dec. 28, 1878.

2 Isaiah lviii. I.

3 Jude 8.

Apostle teaches, every living soul should be subject, and which hold of God the right to command, they refuse to obey, and preach a perfect equality of all men, both with regard to their rights and to their duties.

"They profane the natural union of husband and wife, which even barbarous tribes hold to be sacred; and as to the marriage bond, which is the chief foundation of domestic society, they either weaken it or make of it the plaything of passion.

"Then, carried away by the greed of actual wealth, which is the root of all evils, which some coveting have erred from the faith,[4] they deny the right to hold property sanctioned by the law of nature; and by a savage audacity, under the pretext of providing for the needs and desires of all mankind, they aim at dispossessing people of all that they have lawfully inherited, or gained by their talents or industry, or hoarded from their savings. These monstrous opinions they proclaim in their meetings, teach in their pamphlets, and spread through a host of organs in the press. From all these lessons such hatred sprang among the seditious crowd against the majesty and authority of rulers that criminal traitors, impatient of all control, have several times within a brief interval made impious attempts on the lives of heads of states."[5]

The Pope then gives the history of modern Socialistic error, tracing it back to the sixteenth century, when "a bitter war was declared against the Catholic faith, gaining strength continually down to the present time, and having for its aim to set aside all revealed truth, all the supernatural order; to pave the way to reason with its discoveries, or its dreams rather. This error, wrongly taking its name from reason, flatters and stimulates man's natural desire of lifting himself above others, gives a free rein to all the passions, and thus naturally found adepts in most men, and spread among the social classes.

---

4 I Timothy vi. 10.

5 "Acta," vol. I. pp. 170-173.

"Hence, an impious thing never dreamed of even by the old pagans, states were founded without any regard to God or to the order by Him established. It was given as a dictate of truth that public authority derives from God neither its origin, nor its majesty, nor its power to command, all that coming, on the contrary, from the multitude; and that the people, deeming themselves free from all divine sanctions, consented only to be ruled by such laws as they chose to enact.

"The supernatural truths of the Christian faith, as a thing repugnant to reason, were denied and rejected, while the very Author and Redeemer of the human race was eliminated from the matters of study in the universities, colleges, and academies, and was finally banished by degrees from the whole intercourse of life.

"In fine, the rewards and punishments of the life to come were put out of mind and sight, and the ardent wishes of the human breast for happiness were limited to the narrow compass of the present life.

"By spreading such doctrines far and wide, such an unbridled licentiousness of thought and action was begotten everywhere that it is no wonder if men of the lower classes, disgusted with their poverty-stricken homes and their dismal workshop, are filled with an inordinate desire to rush upon the homes and fortunes of the wealthy; no wonder is it that tranquillity is banished from all private and public life, and that the human race seems hurried onward to its ruin."

In his first great doctrinal letter or encyclical Leo XIII had spoken of certain doctrines, sedulously and widely inculcated in our day, which poisoned men's minds, inflamed their worst passions, and created ever-increasing disorder and convulsions in the body politic wherever they were allowed to prevail. These doctrines and their effects were happily compared to some such poison as strychnine, which attacks the nervous centres and causes fearful spasms and convulsions.

By this poison he meant Socialistic error; and this it is which the Pope makes the subject of this most important letter.

Two countries in particular were, at the close of 1878, a prey to Socialism—France and Germany. In the former Socialism was openly in close alliance with the secret societies. The latter were now at the head of the government, counted among their adepts the majority in both houses of the French legislature, and were slowly but surely advancing toward the realization of their ideal—a Socialistic republic without any form of religious worship and totally adverse to the influence of religion, its ministers and professors, on any department or function of the state or in any walk of public life.

The Communists and Anarchists, who were the most "advanced" and exaggerated forms of Socialism, were clamorous for a greater share in the management of public affairs. The Communists in particular, who had been imprisoned or banished after their excesses in 1871, were pardoned, recalled, brought back to France at the public expense, and received as brothers and as sufferers for a common cause by the men in power. They constituted one impelling force in France, ever urging the government and legislature to more radical, revolutionary, anti-Christian measures. We see, in 1887, how wonderfully they succeeded.

The Anarchists, though only more consistent Communists, were looked upon with suspicion, if not with dread, by the rulers of France, They dared to draw from Socialistic and Communistic principles their legitimate consequences: they said and say, "Two and two make four."

In Germany Socialism was more in its doctrinal and theoretical stage. It had not penetrated the masses through and through. The laboring classes, to whom the contrast between wealth and extreme and wide-spread poverty was brought home by daily suffering, were ripe for a violent solution of the labor question; but the doctrines of Socialist had not yet got entire hold of the schools or been adopted by the educated. The landed aristocracy formed a great barrier in Germany to the spread and practice of these theories. Still Socialism was daily gaining ground.

Nor had the secret societies obtained among the

conservative and practical Teutonic races the same success which they had achieved among the Neo-Latin peoples. Both the Socialists and the Occult Force had had no little share in preparing the public mind in Germany for that national unity which arose out of the war of 1870-71. But they had far more to do with creating and fostering the public opinion which represented the Papacy and the Catholic religion, as such, as the natural and irreconcilable enemies of the new German Empire.

Fast following on the first persecuting laws enacted against the Prussian Catholics came Socialistic conspiracies, disturbances, and attempts against the life of the sovereign.. These were attributed to Catholics, whether maliciously or not we do not stop to ask; and Catholics, therefore, were made a theme for fiercer denunciation by the Kulturkampf organs. The highest officials, however, could not long acquiesce in such belief. The reports of their own police had convinced them of the contrary.

Very soon both the emperor and the prince chancellor had good reason to know that the great danger for the empire they had built up, for religion and social order in Germany, came from the doctrines and plots of Socialism—not from the intrigues of the Jesuits, the doctrines or practices of Catholicism, or from the fancied hostility of the Holy See.

It was impossible that this second great doctrinal pronouncement should not have made a deep impression on the aged emperor and his far-seeing minister.

The masterly exposition of Socialistic error and its effects on the entire framework of society could be verified in every detail by what was daily happening all over France and in parts of Switzerland, and by what was attempted in Germany and Belgium.

The genesis and history of Socialistic error as given in the encyclical was warmly, angrily even, discussed and disputed. But the great fact asserted by the Pope, that with the spread of the sixteenth-century "doctrines," the supernatural, and with it Christ Himself, was gradually banished from the university schools of non-Catholic countries, could not be denied. Germany had experience enough of it. Then it was that the life to come began to be laughed at and left out of men's calculations. There was nothing for them but the present—no heaven, no hell. Nothing was left to the disinherited classes in society to compensate them for the misery and wretchedness of their present lot; nothing to make them satisfied with their poverty and their ill-requited toil; no force to withhold the passions, excited and maddened by Socialism, from rushing on the wealthy and the great, and gratifying both their revenge and their greed.

The great doctrine on the origin of social power and social authority was still more striking as formulated in the Pontiff's terse and classic Latin. With the Socialists and all who adopt the modern theory of civil society God is nothing and He has nothing to do with the state. The people alone are the source of power; they commit it to whom they please. The depositories of their power are responsible to the people only for the discharge of their trust; beyond the people we need not, cannot go. So that, after all, social man in obeying state authority is only obeying his own freely chosen representatives; in obeying the law he was only submitting to be bound by the act of his own will.

To statesmen, magistrates, rulers—to all men who seek to place social order on a solid and sacred basis—the solemn utterances of the encyclical were like the second promulgation of the law on which rest the foundations of the moral world.

That they made a deep impression where the Pope wished and hoped to make it we shall not say at present.

One by one all the errors of Socialism are confuted and the opposite doctrines clearly defined and admirably formulated.

The parallel which certain writers would fain establish between the humanitarian doctrines of Socialism and those of the Gospel is shown to be illusory. The equality of all men, as set forth in the latter, is founded not only on the same human nature derived from the same parentage, but from the same sublime supernatural destiny in the life to come.

The inequality which exists among men living in society arises from nature and its Author, just as from Him comes in the magistrate the right to rule, and in the subject the duty to obey.

Power—right and legitimate power in the social body—is from God. Human society is, like the angelic, a hierarchical gradation of orders subordinated one to the other in beautiful harmony. So is it in the Church.

Touching with a rapid and masterly hand on the use of power, which should ever be fatherly, like that of God Himself, and directed solely to the good of the subject, the Pope shows how Socialistic error saps the foundation of domestic society by destroying the sanctity and unity of marriage, by denying the authority of parents.

Property, its division and its rights, is next described.

On February 28, 1879, Leo XIII held a consistory, in which he had the great consolation of detailing to the Sacred College the pains he had taken to restore union in the Eastern churches, and the success which had attended his efforts. Monsignor Aboliona, a man in every way devoted to the Holy See, had been duly elected to the metropolitan chair of Babylon; the pallium had been sent him by Rome.

So a brighter light was breaking on the Christians of the East.

But a little more than a month later, on March 25, the Pope, in another letter to the cardinal vicar, denounces once more the systematic warfare which the Piedmontese government in Rome, in conjunction with the anti-Catholic sects favored by the municipality, are carrying on against the religious education of youth.

In order to counteract the labors of this propaganda the Holy Father institutes a Council of Education for Rome, composed of prelates and noblemen, whose duty it will be to watch carefully over all primary schools and to establish new ones wherever needed. The Pope has given generous aid to this enterprise, and exhorts all good Christians to use a like generosity.

Thus the first year of Leo XIII's Pontificate had been fruitful in unexpected and most blessed results.

Not all unexpected, however; for those who were well acquainted with the man and with the qualities which he had displayed as a diplomat, an administrator, and a teacher of men, had confidently hoped that he, if any one could, would bring about peace where peace had so far appeared impossible.

CHAPTER XXIII

LEO XIII AND THE EASTERN PEOPLES

EARNEST as was the desire felt by Leo XIII to reconcile with the Roman Church the various communions in the East which the schism of Photius had wrested from the center of Catholic unity, or to enlighten on their errors the followers of the ancient heresies of Nestorius and Eutyches, there seemed, in the beginning of his Pontificate, but slight prospects of such reconciliation. We shall see, however, how far his endeavors were blessed with success.

At present, to judge aright of his praiseworthy labors in this regard, it will be instructive to glance successively at each of the empires to which they extended, and to estimate the difficulties which the Holy See had to contend with.

I. Leo XIII and the Slavonic Races

During the four last years of the reign of Pius IX we find the Emperor Alexander II, who risked so much of reputation and popularity among his own upper classes by emancipating the serfs, displaying, on the contrary, toward his Catholic subjects a rigor which it is hard to find words to qualify.

In the Parliamentary papers laid on the table of the British House of Commons in April, 1877, a series of persecutions are disclosed, the proceedings of which would seem incredible in themselves, and impossible in any Christian land in this nineteenth century, were it not that they are vouched for by the British officials resident in Russia.

In the province of Chelm, for instance, the government used all manner of threats and seduction to induce the clergy to bring over their flocks into the Russian or Orthodox communion. Even where a few priests yielded to fear and thus prostituted their sacred ministry, the people were too firmly attached to their ancestral faith to follow their erring shepherds. All this strange system of pression and propagandism only filled the country with strife and violence.[1] This was in 1871.

In 1873 and 1874 the provinces of Siedlce and Lublin were the theatre of a like proselytizing campaign. The people revolted against the violent methods used to coerce them into apostasy, and drew on themselves the rigors of military law, all this "resulting in bloodshed, loss of life, and the most barbarous treatment inflicted on the peasants." The British consul-general who furnishes these details gives one instance which will enable the reader to judge of this novel process of "converting" souls. At a place in the district of Minciewicz the priest had apostatized, and the people would not permit him to enter the church and officiate for them. He appealed to the military authorities, who sent a body of troops to enforce obedience on the part of the people. These filled the church and surrounded it to preserve it from desecration. They were hemmed in by the military, and were offered the choice "of signing a declaration accepting the priest, and on their refusal fifty blows with the *nagaika* (Cossack whip) were given to every adult man, twenty-five to every woman, and ten to every child, irrespective of age or sex—one woman, who was more vehement than the rest, receiving as much as a hundred."[2]

Finding that bodily punishment could not avail to shake the constancy of these heroic peasants, the authorities tried what a system of fines would do. But the people suffered everything to be taken from them while remaining true to conscience.

In the summer of 1874 Alexander II visited Warsaw in person. The Uniates, or Catholic United Greeks, attempted to

---

[1] Letter of Lieutenant-Colonel Mansfield, Consul-General in Poland, to Lord Granville.

[2] Letter of Colonel Mansfield, Jan. 29, 1874.

approach him with a petition begging him to examine into their grievances. He would not permit them to approach him. From that moment, says Colonel Mansfield, "the massacres "increased in ferocity, and the Cossacks received orders to "hunt down" the Uniates and to destroy their crops, all of which were ruthlessly carried out.

In 1875 the official press in St. Petersburg triumphantly announced that forty-five parishes, containing fifty thousand persons and twenty-six priests, had abjured the Roman communion and joined the Russian official church. We remember the sensation such an announcement produced in Great Britain and the United States. The thing was believed till the Blue Book published a despatch of Lord Augustus Loftus, the British ambassador in St. Petersburg, dated January 29, 1875. His recital of the truth was a hideous revelation:

"The passing over," he says, "of these fifty thousand United Greeks has been effected by various means, in which physical maltreatment has formed a not inconsiderable element. ... The details of the different degrees of compulsion in the various villages would take too much space to relate, but I cite as a specimen what I heard from a gentleman, of whose veracity I have no reason to doubt, of what took place in a village on his property. The peasants were assembled and beaten by the Cossacks until the military surgeon stated that more would endanger life. They were then driven, through a half-frozen river up to their waists, into the parish church, through files of soldiers, and there their names were entered into the petition as above, and passed out at an opposite door, the peasants all the time crying out: You may call us Orthodox but we remain in the faith of our fathers."

Is this not the heroism of the early martyrs?

In the government of Lublin the authorities registered 250,000 persons as "converted" by similar methods. This went on all through 1875. But in January, 1876, Colonel Mansfield reports that the "converts" repudiated the idea of having changed their religion, steadily refusing the services of any priests but their own, themselves baptizing their own babes, burying their dead, and declining to enter the Russian churches.

In New York and elsewhere in the United States we cannot have forgotten the harrowing narratives of some of these victims of a cruel and unchristian zeal who had succeeded in escaping from Siberia. There, they said, whole districts were peopled by the unhappy but most honorable exiles, laymen and priests, whose only crime was their unshaken fidelity to God and country. For we must not overlook this fact, that antipathy of race entered more into this persecution than antagonism of creed.

Pius IX, in his last years, had not ceased to protest and remonstrate against these atrocious persecutions. They had, in 1845, when the Emperor Nicholas visited Rome, formed the subject of a stirring personal appeal, if not a denouncement of divine judgment, from Gregory XVI to the omnipotent ruler of Russia.[3] The emperor issued, pale, disturbed, terrified, from the Pope's presence.

Pius IX failed not to warn the successor of Nicholas of the terrible wrongs inflicted by him on the Catholics of Poland, as well as on those of the other provinces of the Russian Empire. Did the fall of the temporal power embolden the autocrat to continue his cruel methods of effecting religious unity in his dominions?

We do not like to think so. But in 1877, in the first days of June, the Russian representative in Rome laid before His Holiness, together with the compliments and congratulations of his imperial master, the outlines of a plan for adjusting all differences between the Vatican and St. Petersburg. This was when it was politic to conciliate the Catholics of the Turkish Empire during the terrible Turko-Russian war of 1877. At any rate, on July 26 Cardinal Simeoni, Secretary of State, placed in the hands of Prince Ourousoff, the Russian charg6 d'affaires, an official statement on the grievances of the Holy See with regard to the Imperial government, as well as an enumeration

---

[3] See Cardinal Wiseman, "Recollections of the Four Last Popes.

of the special remedies demanded. This was addressed to the czar. Two weeks followed, and no acknowledgment of having received the memoir was sent to the cardinal. Then it was returned most insultingly. Cardinal Simeoni, in a letter dated August 19, resented with dignity and proper spirit this proceeding, without a single precedent in the history of diplomatic intercourse. The Holy Father dismissed Prince Ourousoff without granting him a farewell audience.

Of course all this did not turn away the Cossack whip from the shoulders of the poor Uniates or close up the road to Siberia for Russian Catholics.

Leo XIII on his accession endeavored to restore friendly relations with the Russian court as well as with the German. In 1880 a favorable opportunity presented itself to the Holy Father of reaching the heart of the czar. The twenty-fifth anniversary of the latter's accession to the throne was celebrated with great rejoicings in St. Petersburg, and the Pope sent his congratulations through the internuncio in Vienna. This was so well received that later, on April 12, the Holy Father was encouraged to write the following letter to Alexander himself:

"SIRE: All the prosperity which, through our cardinal pronuncio in Vienna, we wished your Imperial Majesty on the occasion of the twenty-fifth anniversary of your accession to the throne, we now wish anew in this letter, praying from our heart that the King of Kings and Lord of Lords may fulfil our prayers.

"We cannot, however, forbear to profit by this opportunity to appeal to your Majesty, beseeching you to bestow your thoughts and attention on the cruel condition of the Catholics belonging to your vast empire. Their state fills us with unceasing pain and anxiety. The deep zeal which moves us, in the discharge of our office of Supreme Pastor of the Church, to provide for the spiritual needs of these faithful Catholics, should, it seems to us, impel your Majesty, in the midst of so many political revolutions, of so many convulsions produced by greedy human passions, to grant to the Catholic Church such liberty as would assuredly create peace, beget fidelity, and bind to your person the trusting hearts of your subjects.

"Your Majesty's sense of justice and right moves us to hope that we can both bring about an accord entirely to our mutual satisfaction. For, your Majesty cannot be ignorant of the fact that the Catholic religion deems it her duty everywhere to spread the spirit of peace and to labor to preserve the tranquillity of kingdoms and peoples.

"Trusting, therefore, that our wishes in this regard shall be happily fulfilled, we meanwhile pray with our whole heart Almighty God to keep you long safe from all ill, to inspire you with salutary counsels, and to unite you to us in perfect charity."

The letter has a prophetic significance in view of the tragic death of Alexander, which startled the entire civilized world ere another twelvemonth had elapsed. That the Sovereign Pontiff's words, so different from the empty expressions in which sovereigns exchange compliments, did strike the emperor, is attested by the fact that two of his sons, the Archdukes Sergius and Paul, were sent to Rome before the end of the year, and were instrumental in reopening friendly intercourse between the Vatican and St. Petersburg. The author met these princes by chance in Siena as well as in Rome, and conceived, as did most people, the hope that the cordial understanding of which the Pope spoke in his letter would be brought about between the two sovereigns. But death came to mar this prospect. And the persecution still continues to rage.

Leo XIII, while addressing himself directly to sovereigns and the statesmen who administer great empires, did not neglect another means of staying the progress of persecution, of preparing an antidote to widespread error, and of sowing broadcast the seeds of truth—that is, public opinion. No statesman in modern times has formed a truer estimate of its power, or seen more clearly how its influence should be cultivated and used for the best interests of religion and society.

His encyclicals, allocutions, and other public utterances are all calculated and directed toward the one immediate purpose of enlightening the public mind and preparing a public opinion favorable to the changes he wishes to effect. Thus his letter to the Emperor Alexander II might have remained unknown to all save the comparatively few who possess and read the "Acta" of Leo XIII's Pontificate. But the Pope had even a grander object in view than the mitigating of the hard lot of the Russian Catholics: he wished to raise the flag of reunion with the Church of Rome in the sight of all these Eastern churches so sadly fallen away from their ancient freedom and their ancient splendor.

To the Slavonic populations within the Russian, Austro-Hungarian, and Turkish Empires the names of the great brother-saints, Cyril and Methodius, are deservedly dear. They were for the Slavs what Peter and Paul were to the Romans, Patrick to the Irish, Augustine to the English, and Boniface to the Germans. But Cyril and Methodius lived, labored, died in the communion of the Holy See, and in strict subordination to its authority. Indeed, Cyril died in Rome and was buried there. He it was who invented the alphabet still in use among the Slavs. He is, therefore, in a manner, the parent of Slavonic civilization.

The two brother-apostles had from the ninth century been revered as saints both by the Roman and the Eastern churches. The return of their centenary in 1880 offered Leo XIII one of those happy opportunities for winning still more the affection and respect of the wide-spread nationalities who worship the memory of Sts. Cyril and Methodius as their apostles. The Pope wrote an encyclical letter, extending to the universal Church the duty of honoring the two saints by a solemn office. Dated on September 23, this magnificent encyclical, in every way worthy of the head and heart of Leo XIII, recounts the reasons which induce him to pay such honor to these illustrious brothers.

There is a rapid and pregnant biographical sketch, such as Leo XIII knows how to fill up, like the frame of a miniature painting, with the most exquisite details, finished with a master's hand. He insists on the lifelong relations of the two apostles with the Holy See, and recites the unceasing solicitude of the Roman Pontiffs, after the death of these holy men, to maintain the Slavs in the Catholic faith and to promote their material prosperity as well.

"Wherefore," the encyclical says, "we thank God for giving us an opportunity to do a grateful thing to the peoples of Slavonic race, and to help contribute to their welfare with a zeal in no whit less than that shown by our predecessors. Our sole aim, our only wish, is to use every exertion to provide these peoples with a greater number of bishops and priests. These will confirm them in the profession of the true faith, in dutiful obedience to the true Church of Christ, and daily experience will teach them more and more what blessings accrue from Catholic institutions to families as well as to all classes in society. These Slavonic churches are to us an object of especial care. There is nothing we desire more ardently than to promote their welfare and prosperity, and to bind them to us by the ties of perpetual concord, which to them means a bond of perpetual safety."[4]

The Slavs responded with great enthusiasm to the encyclical of the Holy Father. The centenary was everywhere celebrated with great solemnity. A numerous pilgrimage of representative men of Slavonic origin from Austria-Hungary, Bulgaria, Servia, and other Turkish dependencies came to Rome to express to Leo XIII the gratitude of the various nationalities. It was one of those spectacles which consoled the heart of the Pontiff for the bitter cup held to his lips by Italians. It should have opened the eyes of the purblind Piedmontese government to the absurdity of maintaining in Rome a rival sovereignty with a power which extended its spiritual sway and its incomparable influence beyond the Peninsula, beyond the Adriatic and the Mediterranean, to every Eastern as to every Western land.

4 "Acta Leonis XIII," September 23, 1880.

All through the remaining months of 1880 and during 1881 letters from bishops and addresses came continually to the Vatican, thanking the Pope for his encyclical and the honor done to the Slavs in the persons of their revered apostles. From Bohemia, from Croatia, these expressions of gratitude were particularly significant. Replying to Cardinal Prince Schwarzenberg, Archbishop of Prague, and the bishops of Bohemia, on July 14, 1881, the Pope gives vent to his joy. The Slavonic pilgrimage, and all that he sees and hears about the symptoms of reunion and religious revival, fill him with gratitude to God and with well-founded hopes for the great future of these peoples. He will omit nothing which can help to promote among them the divine honor. The bishops must labor strenuously to promote education, to promote in particular that of the clergy, who are to lead the van of all true progress.

On July 5 of that same year Leo XIII gave a specimen of his practical love for the Slavs and his enlightened interest in their spiritual welfare by doing for Bosnia and Herzegovina what had been done for England and Scotland—establishing, namely, a regular hierarchy in these regions. He rejoices, he says in the bull of institution, that he has been enabled to accomplish what so many of his predecessors had in vain yearned to do.[5]

The movement toward reconciliation and reunion has gone on ever since, and is not likely to die out, in spite of the opposition, secret or open, of the powerful schismatic Greek churches.

It was the Roman Church which sanctioned the mission and the acts of the two brother-apostles; it was to Rome that they referred all they did for blessing and approval. They came thither in 869, Cyril bringing with him the remains of St. Clement, Pope and martyr, from the Crimea, whither he had been sent to labor in the mines and had suffered death for Christ. Cyril, wasted by his apostolic labors, died there and

[5] Bull *Ex hac augusta*, July 5, 1881.

was buried with the most solemn pomp in the church of St. Clement, by the side of the martyr-Pope—that "Clement whose name is written in the book of life." Methodius returned to labor alone among his Slavs, bearing now in his heart a double charity and heroism, bent on running his race and winning the crown to which his loved companion had attained. He performed prodigies of labor more astonishing than any miracle, dying in Moravia, which he had converted and civilized, in September, 880.

To these two the Slavonic races owe not only the possession of the Gospel truth, but their literature and the very characters they use down to the present day.

Well may they reverence their names!

Leo XIII, therefore, did a wise and a politic thing in publishing his encyclical, and giving to this centenary celebration the extraordinary solemnity which won the Slavonic heart.

But he did not confine this policy to that race alone among the Eastern peoples.

II. THE EASTERN GREEKS, AND THE PEOPLES WHO CLING TO THE GREEK LITURGY OUTSIDE OF GREECE

Gregory XIII, whose great mind first conceived the idea of founding the Congregation de Propaganda Fide and colleges for educating in Rome missionaries for all nations, began by founding on January 23, 1577, the Greek College of St. Athanasius, which was destined to be, for all the nationalities who used the Greek language in their liturgy, what the College of Propaganda became later for all nations.

This college prospered wonderfully and became a nursery of great scholars and apostolic men.

Leo XIII conceived that it was not sufficient to guard the faith of the Slavonic races over whom Panslavism and the schismatical Greek Church seek to establish an exclusive domination, but that the light of Catholic truth should be carried into the very strongholds of that same Greek Church itself.

He therefore, from the beginning of his Pontificate, bestowed the greatest attention on the Greek College. He reorganized its studies, enlarged and elevated their standard, selected the most illustrious Greek scholars to teach the students their native literature, and more especially to perfect them in rhetoric, in the most perfect art of the preacher. For classic Greek and all the other languages, ancient and modern, these young men frequent the classes of the Seminario Romano and other great schools which the present Pontiff has done so much to improve.

Besides this, knowing how fondly the Greeks cling to their liturgy, the Pope has founded in the college two special chairs—one for the teaching of everything pertaining to the history, theory, and practice of the Greek liturgy, and another for the teaching of ecclesiastical chant. Church music is a desideratum in the East, and Leo XIII has made up his mind that the young men who go forth in future from the halls of St. Athanasius shall bring with them not only all the graces of accomplished oratory for the pulpit, but a knowledge of the best Church music known in Rome.

The growing fame of the Greek College attracted so many pupils that the Pope, in spite of his limited means and the many calls upon his generosity, has just completed a new wing to the building, enabling it to face all the demands for room made on it.

This was solemnly inaugurated and blessed on May 2, 1886, the feast of St. Athanasius, when the best musical critics in Rome were equally surprised and charmed by the splendor of the morning and evening services and the vocal performances of the students.

Now think for a moment of the various countries from which these young men come, and say if it be not a divine thought thus to bring together men born so widely asunder and often separated by national antipathies which a unity of liturgy is not sufficient to overcome without the aid of divine charity.

The former Greek colonies in Italy itself and the islands once belonging to her are not only permitted by the Holy See but obliged to celebrate the Greek liturgy. So there are students from Sicily, Calabria, Naples, Leghorn, Malta, and Corsica. Besides these Italo-Greeks there are the Hellenes, or Greeks proper, the Roumanians, the Bulgarians, the sons of the vast Ruthenian branches, and the Melchites.

There is a vicariate-apostolic in Greece. But there the Russian influence is all-powerful, and it is only by slow degrees that the old prejudices and antipathies cherished so fondly in the nineteenth century by a far-seeing but unscrupulous policy can be overcome, and a way made for the entrance of truth into minds and hearts.

III. PEOPLES OF THE OTTOMAN EMPIRE

Brief as has been the reign of Leo XIII, his enlightened zeal and prudent policy have already done as much to revive Christianity in the Turkish and Persian dominions as the insane ambition of the republican rulers of France has done to ruin its best interests in the far East. Let us gather from the lips of Leo XIII himself what estimate he had formed of these venerable Eastern churches, and what measures he adopted to aid them in their straits and to build up among them the edifice of religion and civilization:

"Everything pertaining to the Eastern churches," he says in the allocution of February 28, 1879, "because of the supreme ministry entrusted to us, we deem to be deserving of peculiar solicitude and zeal; we, indeed, find it to have been so held by our predecessors in every century. ... For they knew the pristine pre-eminence of these countries, in which the Sun of Justice arose for mankind, as well as the glory of these ancient churches which produced men who were the shining lights of heavenly wisdom and wonderful holiness.

"Wherefore, from the very beginning of our Pontificate, seeing the sad troubles to which the churches of the East were a prey, we endeavored to give what help we could to each one of them in its need. Finding a favorable opportunity for taking measures, through the ambassadors of the chief European sovereigns, to restore peace to the East, we employed every possible means to have full liberty publicly guaranteed and sanctioned for the exercise there of the Catholic religion. Having happily succeeded in this, it is now our firm purpose to take every pains to have the right thus guaranteed fully upheld in practice. ...

"We trust, on the other hand, that those who carry on the government of the Ottoman Empire shall easily understand that it is their interest to grant in the fullest measure to the Catholics of their jurisdiction all that right and justice demand; and this all the more readily that they have lately had splendid practical proofs of the loyalty of these Catholics, of their devotion to the state, on both of which their enemies endeavored to cast odious suspicions by calumnies that did them supreme injustice.

"... We recall to your minds that last year the Church of Chaldea became widowed of her patriarch in the person of our venerable brother, Joseph Audo, whom Pius IX had confirmed and instituted in that dignity on September n, 1848. This prelate, ... in the last years of his life, carried away by the advice of evil counsellors, forgot his duty toward this Apostolic See. But, admonished by the apostolic authority, he returned to his duty, gave evidence of his obedience to the Sovereign Pontiff, incurred and bore with Christian fortitude on that account many annoyances from those of his nation, and on his death-bed, with his latest breath, expressed his sorrow for his fault, bore witness to his love and devotion to the Chair of Peter and the Vicar of Christ, and left a great example of edification behind him.

"After his death the bishops of the Chaldaic rite met in council at Alkosh, as the canons require, and in the usual form elected, on July 26 last past, Peter Elias Abolionan, Bishop of Gezir, to fill the office of patriarch of Babylon of the Chaldeans..."

The Sublime Porte was not one of the last powers to feel and to acknowledge the truth of Leo XIII's affirmation that the Catholic Church is everywhere a mighty element of peace, order, security, unity, and stability to the nations and their rulers. It acknowledged that the successful efforts to bring about concord between the Holy See and the Eastern schismatics, or between the rival Christian denominations themselves, proved to be a great benefit bestowed upon the empire.

The Sublime Porte confirmed the election of Monsignor Abolionan as patriarch of Babylon, and granted him the firman ratifying the Holy Father's approbation of his election. This was an official acknowledgment of the patriarch as the head of his nation—the Chaldeans—and a solemn 'guarantee of full religious liberty to himself and his people.

It was a great and peaceful triumph won by Leo XIII.

This was followed almost immediately by the healing of the deplorable schism which had taken place in another diocese of Mesopotamia, Zachan. The bishop who had intruded himself into the see, and his followers among the clergy, the monks, and the laity, submitted in all humility to the patriarch and asked for absolution from the Holy See.

"From all this," the Holy Father says in his allocution of May 12, "we conceive well-founded hope of seeing the baneful schism which has so long afflicted the Catholics of Mesopotamia entirely extinguished."

A new joy was added to these, as the Pontiff expresses it, by the appeasement of the long and bloody feud between the Jacobite Nestorians of Syria and the Catholics of the Syrian rite. There had been a brief misunderstanding between the Syrian Catholic patriarch and the government, and the Nestorians, under pretence of supporting the civil authority, had taken forcible possession of the Catholic churches, refusing, on any account, to give them up. The Holy Father, having, through his delegate in Constantinople, obtained the ear of the Imperial government, had the question of right submitted to the arbitration of the British and French ambassadors in that capital.

The decision was in favor of the Catholics. But so judicious and conciliatory was the conduct of the Catholic officials that a number of Jacobite families renounced their sect, and numbers of others seemed disposed to follow their ex ample.

A like happy termination concluded the deplorable schism which had taken place among the Armenians. These are very powerful in Constantinople, where their wealth exercises great influence.

Among them, too, the definition of the dogma of the Pontifical Infallibility in 1870 had been taken advantage of by the evil-minded to stir up the jealousy of the government against the Holy See, and to produce some such scandalous and absurd division as that caused in Bavaria by Döllinger and the Old Catholics. But as in Germany, so in Turkey, the prejudices and misconceptions begotten by heated and one-sided theological discussions and by latent national jealousies and antipathies passed away, and people began to see that they had acted rashly and irrationally.

The Armenian Archbishop of Diarbekir, Monsignor Bahtiarian, and the Armenian Bishop of Cyprus, Gasparian, were both ambitious men, who thought that the stir made in Germany and all over Continental Europe by the dogma of Papal Infallibility offered them a favorable opportunity for advancing their own interests. They won over to their designs a number of secular priests and monks, and a large following among the laity. One of these monks, Kiupelian, caused himself to be elected in a conventicle as civil patriarch of the Armenians, and Bahtiarian himself was therein chosen as religious patriarch or Catholicos of Cilicia. Now, Monsignor Antony Hassun had been for many years the acknowledged patriarch and catholicos of the Armenians of Cilicia, the civil and religious head of the nation therefore. But as he, an old pupil of the Propaganda, humble, conscientious, devoted, and too well informed not to know the utter falsity of the charges made against the Pope, remained firm in his attachment to the Holy See, the government, deceived by Bahtiarian and

Gasparian, was prevailed on to banish Monsignor Hassun from Constantinople.

Kiupelian was consecrated by the two schismatical bishops, and officially recognized by the government as civil patriarch of the Armenians. But these refused to acknowledge the division of authority, and would not obey Bahtiarian as *catholicos* or the religious patriarch. Disgusted or threatened, the disappointed schismatic withdrew to the Armenian convent on Mount Lebanon.

Meanwhile Monsignor Hassun was subjected to many indignities, but his virtue and patience were proof against the most bitter trials. And so things went on among the Armenians, the schism even spreading to Egypt, till the accession of Leo XIII

On March io, 1879, Archbishop Kiupelian, urged by remorse, wrote to the vizier renouncing his episcopal and official rank, expressing his sorrow at the wrong done to the Holy See and the lawful patriarch. He cast himself at the feet of the latter, who forthwith urged him to go to Rome and there seek forgiveness from the Holy Father. Arriving in Rome at the beginning of April, he at once wrote to His Holiness. The Pope received him with the greatest kindness, and allowed him to retain the title and insignia of bishop, although the culprit had received them so unworthily.

But the Holy Father calculated the effect which this clemency would have in bringing back the other schismatics. He was not mistaken. On November 26 following Monsignor Gasparian came to cast himself at the feet of the Pope, and was received with a like tender charity. In the summer of 1880 the schismatic Armenian bishop at Cairo, Davidian, also returned to the fold, and at length Bahtiarian himself asked for absolution for his sin.

In April, 1880, the Pope wrote to the sultan, Abdul Hamid, to thank him for his prompt readiness to recall and reinstate Monsignor Hassun. The latter was presented by the delegate, Monsignor Grasselli, and was received with extreme pleasure by the sultan.

Thus was this dangerous and wide-spread schism healed and a great triumph won by the conciliatory temper and wise clemency of Leo XIII

In the public consistory of December 11, 1880, the Pope was happily inspired to reward the patriarch, Monsignor Hassun, by giving him the Roman purple. The first Oriental ever created cardinal was the illustrious Greek scholar Bessarion, whom Eugenius IV raised to the purple after the Council of Florence (1439-1442). So, after an interval of nearly four centuries and a half, the same distinction was granted to an Armenian. There was great rejoicing in Constantinople. The sultan felt the promotion as a personal compliment. Everything in his empire thus promised well for Catholicism.

But Leo XIII, seeing how much could be done for Christianity through the Armenian nation, placed in the very heart of Asia Minor, carried out at once, regardless of his own poverty, the noble idea of Gregory XIII, who had decreed the foundation of a college for the Armenians in Rome, as he had for the Greeks, but was prevented by death from carrying out his purpose in this latter respect.

On March 1, 1881, he issued the bull *Benigna hominum parens Ecclesia*, founding a special college for the Armenians. The bull is one of the most beautiful and eloquent compositions which have come from the pen of Joachim Pecci.

The college is now in full operation.

But the Pontiff, two years before, had sent among the Armenians a colony of Jesuits to open a college there, and another of Christian Brothers to establish popular schools. Both are prosperous beyond the hopes of the founders.

The Chaldeans were not neglected in this respect. The Holy Father sent to the patriarch, Monsignor Abolionan, a colony of learned Dominicans, who have now a flourishing seminary at Mossoul, on the banks of the Tigris, at the very seat of the ancient Babylonian power and civilization. To this seminary flock the Chaldean youth from every part of Mesopotamia. The Roman official journals, as this page is written, are full of the most cheering accounts from this new school, this other advanced post of Christianity and civilization, planted by Leo XIII near the frontiers of the Persian Empire, at the mouth of the Persian Gulf, and in the birthplace of Heber, of Abraham and Sarah.

Note.—This is the proper place to mention one of the grandest projects of Leo XIII—that, namely, of creating two great central schools, one in Athens and the other in Constantinople. For that he needs and should obtain the generous support of the entire Catholic world.

CHAPTER XXIV

LEO XIII AND THE EASTERN PEOPLES (II): PERSIA, CHINA, AND JAPAN

THE ARMENIAN STUDENTS of the Propaganda, like Cardinal Hassun, were the men who since the sixteenth century had kept the faith alive among their fellow-countrymen throughout the Turkish Empire. They were also anxious to spread it among their Mussulman neighbors. But, even had this not been a most perilous kind of proselytism, it was not a very promising one in itself.

The old Moslem populations away from the great cities are simple folk, but sincere and steady believers in Allah; and in their conception Allah is the one, true, living God, the God of Abraham, whom all Christians adore. Of the extravagances or contradictions of the Koran or of its commentators they know or care little or nothing. They are not to be moved from their ancestral faith by the ignorant and tepid Christians who are in their midst. It is only when these shall have been instructed and lifted up by their clergy to a higher intellectual and moral level that the examples of superior virtue first can impress these honest country-folk and open the way to instruction.

The Emperor of Persia, Nasr-ed-Din Shah, is a man of progress, liberal and large-minded. During his tour through Europe newspaper reporters were more eager to collect all the wretched gossip they could pick up here and there from hotel servants and valets about the royal traveller's personal habits and peculiarities than to obtain serious information about his many great qualities. That he made up his mind to travel at all outside of his own dominions and in Christian countries, and that for the avowed purpose of observing what he saw and benefiting thereby his own people, proves that he is a man of no ordinary character.

He is sincerely desirous of improving in every way he can the condition of his country. But its central position on the Asiatic continent, and its remoteness from the ordinary highways of commerce and civilization, render improvement a matter of great difficulty.

The shah is quite awake to the ambitious designs of Russia, and so far he has had the skill to avoid a collision with that power.

From his tour through Europe he has also brought back a great spirit of toleration toward Christians; and this he has communicated to his three sons, who govern the empire under him.

The oldest of these, Prince Zel-el-Sultan, is governor of the central provinces, whose capital is Ispahan. He is not the presumptive heir to the throne, because his mother was of inferior rank. But he is a man of rare intelligence. His confidant and counsellor is Baghi-Khan, rector of the University of Ispahan, a man of culture and exceedingly favorable to the Christians. Both the prince and himself first contracted a warm friendship for Father Arakelian, the superior of the Armenian Catholics, and afterwards with Father Pascal, the local superior of the French Lazarists, to whose care the vicariate-apostolic of Persia is entrusted. Prince Zel-el-Sultan has shown himself a kind protector to the Catholic missionaries and their people.

The third or youngest son, Prince Naïb Sultaneh, is Minister of War and governor of the province of Teheran, with his residence in that city. He is no less tolerant and liberal, and has done much to protect and help the missionaries.

The second son, who bears the title of Wali-Ahed, is the heir presumptive. He is the governor of the important frontier province of Azerbaijan, and is rather reserved and retiring, probably on account of the greater popularity of his two brothers.

The delegate-apostolic in Persia is also a Lazarist, Monsignor Thomas, Archbishop of Adrianopolis, who was appointed by Leo XIII in 1883. Things prospered so well with

Catholics a hard-working, peaceful, law-abiding, and loyal people; expressed his admiration for Father Pascal, the superior of the mission in his province, and said that he was proud to wear the distinction sent him, would write to His Holiness to express his gratitude, and hoped one day to visit Rome and pay his homage in person to the Pope.

These events are only forerunners of greater success. Persia is destined to play a great part in the Eastern drama, whose first acts are already passing beneath our eyes—If Christian civilization—not the mere material civilization, but the culture of the mind, and the elevation of the heart to nobler virtues and nobler aims, and the refining of life and manners—could only prepare the people to receive the improvements in the mechanical and industrial arts made by Christian nations, and to guard against the defects and dangers which we ourselves acknowledge and deplore, then ancient Iran might take a proud place in Asia.

But Leo XIII's keen and practical judgment also saw the necessity of establishing a friendly intercourse between the courts of Pekin and Tokio and the Vatican. He therefore resolved to place himself in direct personal relations with the two great emperors of the far East.

On February 1, 1885, Leo XIII wrote to the Emperor of China for the purpose of warding off from the Christians of the Celestial Empire the outbursts of popular wrath which had already produced bloodshed in more than one city. The invasion of Tonquin by a French army, and the progress of that power in Cochin China, had excited the fiercest national hatred against all foreigners, and threatened to cause everywhere an indiscriminate massacre of Christians.

"We follow the example of our predecessors," [the]
writes, "who have more than once besought the p[rotection of]
your powerful ancestors in favor of the European [missionaries]
and their flocks. We are led to hope much from [your Majesty]
in this, from the fact that, in spite of the br[eaking out of]
hostilities, your Majesty has given many evide[nces of kindly]
feeling toward Christians. We were informed [that from the]

beginning of the war you had given orders forbidding all to trouble the Christians in any way, and not even to molest the French missionaries. In that your Majesty has shown a spirit of justice and humanity worthy of a great sovereign. We acknowledge this all the more gladly that all the priests of European nationality who are in your Majesty's empire have been sent thither by the Roman Pontiffs, from whom they hold their mission, their office, their instructions, and all the spiritual authority they exercise.

"These missionaries do not belong to any one single nation; Italy, Belgium, Holland, Spain, and Germany claim each a large number of missionaries who labor in ten of the provinces of your Majesty's vast empire. The priests of the Society of Jesus and of the Society of Foreign Missions who exercise their ministry in the other provinces belong to divers nationalities.

"This is the special characteristic of the Christian religion: it has not been founded for one people in particular, but for all; and it receives them all into the fellowship of a common brotherly love, without any distinction of race or of country,'"

The Pope then states clearly and briefly the great truth on which he insists so strongly and so unvaryingly in his letters to the emperors of Europe as well as to those of Asia, in his communications with the republics of the New World as well as with those of the Old:

"The labors of those who preach the Gospel are of the very greatest utility to states themselves. For they are enjoined to abstain from meddling in mere political affairs, and to bestow all their zeal in preaching and cultivating among the people the wisdom of Christ. Now, the chief precepts of that wisdom are, to fear God and to have in all things a supreme reverence for justice. Hence it follows that we must be submissive to the magistrates, obey the laws, honor the king, not through fear only, but for conscience' sake. Than these virtues nothing can be more efficacious to keep the multitude within the bounds of duty and to secure the public safety."[6]

The Holy Father then appeals to the emperor, asking him whether the missionaries have not at all times been most exemplary in obeying the laws of the empire, as well as most efficient in procuring the public welfare.

The action of the Holy Father in opening direct communication with the Emperor of China has given rise to some untoward discussions in the French and Italian press. Catholic France, up to the present time, has deemed that both her interest and her national pride were involved in standing forth in China as the protector of the Catholic missions. All negotiations between the Holy See and the court of Pekin were carried on through the French ambassador. That the Pope should himself write directly to the emperor was construed by some officious public journals as at least a slight on the government of the French Republic. Others went further and said that Prince Bismarck had urged the Holy Father to make himself in the East quite independent of the now worthless French protectorate. These discussions, and the national feelings to which they appeal, were most untimely and unfortunate. Happening just when Leo XIII was bestowing on Prince Bismarck a high mark of pontifical gratitude at the happy conclusion of the mediation between Germany and Spain, and coinciding with the strong personal efforts of the German chancellor to end the Kulturkampf and bring about a perfect religious peace in Prussia, the sensitive national feeling in France was quick to take alarm, to accept false statements, and to resent anything like a concordant action in China of the Holy See and the German chancery.

But the cloud which gathered, borne by the winds of misrepresentation, has vanished before the light of truth. The Pope is left free to follow in the East as well as in the West the promptings of his own well-directed genius.

The letter of Leo XIII to the Emperor of Japan was an act of that same far-seeing policy. The Pope knew what deep roots

---

6 "Acta," v. 10-12.

the Catholic religion had left in Japan when Taīco-Sama deluged the land with the blood of so many thousands of martyrs. It was found during the late persecutions among the Christians[7] that Catholicity had survived in many places, although no priest could be found to minister to its professors. One of the vicars-apostolic officially states that the Catholics in his district number at least 25,000. In the *Missionary Herald*, the organ of the American Protestant Board of Foreign Missions,[8] is published a letter from Rev. J. H. Pettee, of Okogama, entitled "A New Peril in Japan," and sounding a loud note of alarm about the manifest leaning of the Japanese nation toward Catholicism. The writer says there is a strong movement among local officials favoring the acceptance of the Roman Catholic religion. The most progressive secular paper in the kingdom has openly advocated baptizing the emperor and a few of the nobles, in order that Japan may be considered a Christian nation.

We give these signs of the times in Japan as observed and noted by an opponent of Catholicity, to enable the reader to appreciate some at least of the circumstances under which Leo XIII wrote his letter of May 13, 1885, to the mikado.

"Great as is the distance in space which separates us," the letter begins, "we have heard of all that your Majesty is accomplishing in order to increase the prosperity of your states. What your Majesty has done to improve the civil administration and to raise the level of public morality are not only evidences of your provident forethought, but most worthy of the commendation of all men who are desirous of seeing nations make a true progress in prosperity and in the interchange of all the best fruits of civilization. For it is gentleness and urbanity of manners which predispose peoples to listen to the teachings of wisdom and to receive the light of truth. This is why we beseech your Majesty to accept with

---

[7] See article "Missions (Catholic)" in last edition of the *American Cyclopccdia* (Appleton's).

[8] April, 1886.

your great kindness the assurances we give you of our sincere affection.

"Indeed, it is gratitude which prompts us to write to your Majesty. The kindly interest which you may take in every one of the missionaries and Christians in your wide empire we shall take as shown to ourselves personally. We know from their own testimony how gracious and kind your Majesty has been to them.

"You could not, assuredly, do anything more in conformity with the principles of justice nor more conducive to the welfare of your states. For you can hope to find in the Catholic religion no little help toward promoting and securing their welfare.

"For the foundation of all states is justice, and there is not one duty which derives from it that is not made obligatory for Christians.

"This is why all who are true Christians are not men influenced by the fear of punishment, but rather by the voice of conscience, in reverencing the majesty of the sovereign, in obeying the laws, in seeking to promote only the public peace and' honor. This also is the reason why we so ardently desire that your Majesty should bestow on Christians the greatest possible measure of freedom, and that you should extend to their establishments your continued favor and protection."

As Leo XIII wrote to these great potentates of the most ancient empires in the world, so wrote he to the king of the Shoa Gallas in Abyssinia, who, in the first years of the Pope's Pontificate, favored the missionaries among his people. Since then, and as we write, this prince's suzerain, the King of Abyssinia, has compelled him to adopt a different policy. The English wars in Upper Egypt and the Italian expedition to Massowah have, not unreasonably, alarmed and irritated both Abyssinians and Gallas. The expeditions of European powers, when undertaken from purely commercial or ambitious motives, are not conducive to the interests of Christian civilization. Italy has started on her new national career with the openly avowed purpose of doing without God and of seeking none of the interests of religion. Even should the new kingdom last a century, we should be curious to peep into the future and know how many colonies she may plant in this way and how they are likely to prosper.

Not so did France, and Portugal, and Spain, and England herself attempt to leave God and all religion out of their calculations when they planted their flag and settled their colonies along the shores of the Indian, the Pacific, and the Atlantic oceans.

Leo XIII's recommendation to nations and their rulers, both in their home and in their colonial policy, is that of the Master: "Seek ye first the kingdom of God and His justice, and all the rest shall be given to you over and above."

CHAPTER XXV

LEO XIII AND GREAT BRITAIN; RESTORATION OF THE SCOTCH HIERARCHY; SETTLEMENT OF DISPUTES BETWEEN THE BISHOPS AND REGULARS

WHEN one reflects on the persecutions to which the Church has been subject in countries which were once the glory of the Christian name; on the many restrictions the governments in these same countries place on the liberty of the bishops in governing their flocks, and on the very freedom of the Holy See in communicating with the bishops and exercising over the local churches the supreme jurisdiction essential to the pontifical office, it is not to be wondered that both Leo XIII and his predecessors looked with grateful affection to Great Britain and the United States, where so much of true liberty is allowed to the Church, to the Popes, and to the clergy of every rank.

The establishment of a regular English hierarchy by Pius IX gave, it is true, occasion for an outbreak of the old anti-Papal and anti-Catholic spirit. It was only a passing storm, however. Public opinion was soon enlightened on the real nature of this restoration, and people were ashamed of having been hurried along by the current of blind popular prejudice into expressing sentiments unjustified by truth or reason or religion, or into acts more blameworthy still.

When the last mutterings of this sudden tempest had died away it was found that the Pope had committed no aggression on the constitutional prerogatives of the crown or the legislature, and that the cardinal-archbishop of Westminster and his brother-bishops were the most devoted of subjects, an ornament to their country by their learning, their eloquence, and their virtues, and with their faithful flocks one of the strongest bulwarks of law, order, liberty, morality, and religion.

And so from 1850 to 1877 the Catholic Church in England grew and prospered. Colleges, convents, monasteries,, stately cathedrals, beautiful parochial churches with their schools, hospitals, orphan asylums, homes for the aged, protectories for the young, and refuges for the fallen, sprang up with surprising rapidity. Every one of the newly erected dioceses became a center of extraordinary religious activity, and it was soon discovered even by the bitter opponents of Catholicism that the revival and the progress of the ancient faith of Alfred and Edward the Confessor, of St. Bede and St. Dunstan, boded nothing but good to the constitution which was the growth of the old Catholic ages, or to that spirit of manly liberty which had written Magna Charta with a Catholic pen, or to the progress of science and civilization of which Roger Bacon had been the prophet and Cardinal Wiseman was then the exponent.

So, although in political life, in the parliamentary struggles of the present century, English Catholics have never exercised or seemingly cared to exercise any controlling action or influence, Catholic life all over the land, like a beautiful and vigorous undergrowth in' one of its own forests, was spreading and waxing strong, and rising steadily and reaching upward to the air and the sunlight. God's appointed time would come for its full stature.

In Scotland, too, that land which Scott's magic pen has rendered classical the wide world over, the wild, beautiful, heroic land of St. Margaret and her husband, Malcolm Canmore, and their son, St. David, the old faith was also spreading and growing. It had held its ground invincibly in more than one part of the ancient kingdom, as among the MacDonalds and the Frazers; and although these clans, whose romantic history has never been written, were forced to migrate to Nova Scotia, Prince Edward's Island, and Upper Canada, the remnants which clung to the native soil, like their own mountain pine and oak, were germs reserved for the glorious revival now beginning. Other germs, from a kindred and well-tried stock within view of their southern and western shores, the storm-winds of misfortune had borne along the track once followed by Columbkille's bark, and they fell on the Caledonian shores, to take root there, and blossom, and bear fruit, also in God's good time.

And time had been, long ages ago, when the apostles from green Erin were welcome on every inch of the soil of Great Britain, and when Britain's greatest and best, like Dunstan himself, were wont to repair to the schools of Erin. How hospitably they were received and entertained there St. Bede himself has attested. Religion and its charities, the knowledge of Christ and the civilization which sprang from it, drew the islands together and all hearts within them. Though the sea ran as now between them, brotherly love bridged it over. Will the faith which the countrymen of Columbkille carry with them across the Channel, hidden, as it were, in the folds of their garments, not grow up on the land, in its length and breadth, as the promise of the coming age when that faith will unite all once more, as in the days of Bede and Dunstan, and the bitter, unnatural passions of to-day will have passed for ever, as passes the violent delirium of a fevered brain?

It surely is the hope of Leo XIII It is the hope of every man and woman who loves Christ, and prays for a greater triumph for His Gospel than in the days of Constantine.

With what glad avidity Leo XIII seized upon the opportunity offered him by the uncompleted work of Pius IX to do for Scotland what the latter had done for England—give her back her episcopal hierarchy! One cannot help feeling, after weighing attentively the heartfelt expressions which he uses both in the bull *Ex Supremo Apostulatus apice* and in his first consistorial allocution, that the Pontiff is drawn by a special affection toward these Western isles, from whose teeming bosom have gone forth the founders of mighty empires beyond the seas—the founders as well of that new and greater Christendom which is to compensate the Church for the decay of faith nearer home.

This is a happy augury for Leo XIII, that the first solemn act of his Pontificate should be to build up again the ecclesiastical edifice at which St. Margaret and her royal husband had labored so many ages before.

"From the highest summit of the apostolic dignity "—so he begins—"to which, by no merit of our own, but by the disposition of the Divine Goodness, we were lately raised, the Roman Pontiffs who preceded us were wont unceasingly to survey, as from the top of a mountain, every portion of the field of the Lord, so as to discover whatever was most needful to the actual condition, the beauty, and the stability of all the churches; wherefore their first and principal solicitude was, in proportion to the aid given them from on high, either to erect episcopal sees all over the world or to recall to life such as had perished through the misfortunes of other times. For as it is the Holy Ghost who hath established bishops to rule the Church of God, therefore, as soon as the state of our holy religion in any country permits the establishment or the restoration there of episcopal government, it is proper that all the benefits which naturally flow from such a divinely constituted order of things should be at once conferred on that country.

"Now, our predecessor of blessed memory, Pius IX, whose death a few days ago we all still deplore, having noticed at the very beginning of His Pontificate the progress made by the Catholic missions in the prosperous kingdom of England—a progress permitting the restoration of the regular form of Church government therein as it exists among other Catholic peoples—gave back to the English their regular episcopal hierarchy. ... And not long thereafter, seeing that Holland and Brabant were in a condition to enjoy the same benefits, he delayed not to restore to them also their episcopal hierarchy. ...

"Passing over the re-establishment of the patriarchate of Jerusalem, all these restorations were evidently acts of wise forethought; for their results, with God's blessing, fully corresponded to the expectations of the Holy See, for everybody knows what benefit the Catholic Church in all these cases derived from the restoration of the episcopal hierarchy.

"It pained the loving heart of that good Pope that Scotland could not then share in the common benefit. And his fatherly pain was increased by the reflection that Catholicism in former times had made such fruitful progress in Scotland. All who know Church history are aware that the light of the Gospel shone there at an early period. For, to pass over what tradition says of the apostolic missions sent in ancient times to that kingdom, we read of St. Ninian having preached there at the close of the fourth century, after having, as the Venerable Bede testifies, obtained in Rome the gift of faith and the knowledge of its mysteries; and of St. Palladius, a deacon of the Roman Church, who followed Ninian in the fifth century, both of them being consecrated bishops. Then there was the Abbot St. Columba, who landed there in the sixth century, and built a monastery which was the parent of many others.

"And although from the middle of the eighth to the eleventh century historical documents tell us almost nothing about the ecclesiastical condition of Scotland, still it is a tradition well remembered that many bishops lived there, though some of them had no fixed sees. But after the accession of Malcolm III in 1057, at the instance of his queen, St. Margaret, he set about restoring and extending the Christian religion, which had suffered no little injury both from the incursions of foreign nations[1] and from intestine political revolutions. The remains, still extant, of church edifices, monasteries, and other religious structures bear splendid testimony to the piety of the ancient Scots.

"But, to come to what more especially relates to our subject, it is certain that in the fifteenth century the episcopal sees had so increased as to number thirteen in all—namely, St. Andrew's, Glasgow, Dunkeld, Aberdeen, Moray, Brechen, Dunblane, Ross and Caithness, Candida Casa or Whithorn, Lismore, and Sodor or the Isles, and the Orcades—all of which

[1] Danes and Northmen.

were immediately subject to this Apostolic See. It is also certain—a circumstance of which the Scotch are justly proud—that the Roman Pontiffs took the kingdom of Scotland under their special protection and bestowed on these churches marks of peculiar favor."

The Pontiff then sketches the hierarchical changes in the Scottish churches down to the Reformation, with the measures taken during the next three centuries to provide for the spiritual needs of the scattered and persecuted Catholics.

In 1877, during the Episcopal Jubilee of Pius IX, Bishop Strain, at the head of a distinguished band of Scotch Catholics, petitioned for the restoration of the hierarchy—a thing which the venerable Pope was most anxious to grant. He committed to the Congregation of Propaganda the labor of making the necessary inquiries, resolving to satisfy as soon as possible the pious wishes of his Scotch children. "But," says his successor, "while he was congratulating himself on the speedy accomplishment of a purpose long and fervently entertained, he was called by the Just Judge to his reward.

"What our predecessor, therefore, was prevented by death from doing, God, so plentiful in mercy and glorious in all His works, hath permitted us to do, in order that we should inaugurate by a happy beginning the Pontificate accepted with fear and trembling in these unhappy times. Wherefore, having informed ourselves thoroughly of this important matter, we have gladly resolved to accomplish forthwith what Pius IX had already decreed. ...

"... After these preliminaries, of our own accord, with certain knowledge, and by the authority which we possess over the universal Church, to the greater glory of Almighty God and the exaltation of the Catholic faith, we constitute and decree that in the kingdom of Scotland the hierarchy of ordinary bishops be hereby recalled to life in accordance with the prescriptions of the canons, these bishops to be named from their sees, which by this our constitution we create and constitute into an ecclesiastical province. ..."

All through this memorable document there are passages

in which the Pontiff's affection for Scotland and his knowledge of her religious glories in the past manifest themselves in glowing language.

"Remembering," he says, "the illustrious memories left behind by the ancient Church of St. Andrew, and taking also into account the rank of this capital city, as well as other reasons, we cannot help calling forth, as it were from the tomb, this celebrated see, and raising it or restoring it to metropolitan or archiepiscopal rank, adding to it the title of Edinburgh. ... As to the see of Glasgow, considering the antiquity of that city, its size and fame, and having especially before our mind the flourishing condition there of our holy religion, and that Innocent VIII had bestowed upon it archiepiscopal privileges, we have deemed it most befitting to give to its bishop the archiepiscopal title and insignia, as we do by these presents. ...

"We have no fear but that the new bishops, following in the footsteps of their predecessors, who have rendered by their own worth the name of the ancient Church of Scotland glorious, will labor with all their might to make the Catholic name more glorious still in that country, and that the good of souls and the worship of God shall be promoted by all possible means."

The new hierarchy is still to remain subject to the fostering care of the Congregation of Propaganda, to whom the bishops are bound regularly to report.

"Let the bishops," he says further on, "be well assured that we shall ever aid them willingly with our apostolic authority, bestowing on them our assistance in all that regards the promotion of the divine honor and the spiritual welfare of their people. ... And inasmuch as, in the present circumstances, the faithful in Scotland are unable to provide sufficiently and becomingly for the support of their clergy and the needs of their respective churches, we cherish the hope that our beloved children, the Scotch Catholics, to whose most urgent solicitations we have yielded readily in restoring their hierarchy, will continue to supply with even a more liberal generosity, by their alms and donations, the means by which the pastors we give them may provide for the restoration of the bishops' sees, the beauty of their churches and the splendor of divine worship, the maintenance of the clergy, the relief of the poor, and the other necessities of their Church.

"And now, addressing our prayers to Him in whom it hath pleased God the Father, in the dispensation of the fulness of time, to restore all things, we beseech Him, who gave the beginning to this good work, to perfect the same, to confirm and strengthen it, and to grant to all those to whom it pertaineth to execute our present decrees the light and energy of divine grace, in order that this restoration of the episcopal hierarchy in the kingdom of Scotland may redound to the prosperity of the Catholic religion.

"To this end we also invoke near the Restorer of all things, our Lord Jesus Christ, the intercession of His most holy Mother, of St. Joseph, his putative father, of the blessed Apostles Peter and Paul, of St. Andrew, whom Scotland especially honors, of the other saints, and in particular of Scotland's queen, St. Margaret, the glory and bulwark of her realm, that they may all extend to this Church in her newness of life a loving and continued favor."[2]

And so in the land of the Bruce, to which her sons and daughters cling with unspeakable fondness and pride, the ancient faith and worship of the generations led to battle by Bruce were reviving anew in all the promise of a glorious springtide. Old prejudices are waning fast, and brotherly love—that true charity begotten of truth, of mutual knowledge and appreciation, and blessed of God and man—is fast bringing minds and hearts together. The spirit of St. Margaret is abroad. The Catholics of Scotland cannot yet rebuild or restore from their ruins the beautiful places of the ages of faith; but other convents and monasteries, schools and colleges, with great institutions of charity and beneficence, are springing up and multiplying. The monastery-bell and the ancient chant of the

---

[2] "Acta," vol. I. pp. 1-16.

Matins and Vesper office are heard in more than one romantic spot among these hills and along loch and stream, so that, in the words of Leo XIII in his first consistorial allocution, "the mountains of Scotland are clothing themselves with peace for the people, and her hills are putting on righteousness."

But the spirit which Margaret had brought with her from her native home on the Thames, that spirit tried and chastened by long suffering, is working powerfully all through her own paternal kingdom, like the vital warmth of sun and earth and atmosphere in May and June. What cannot be hoped of that land and that people when all will once more be governed by that spirit?

Leo XIII in 1881 found a fitting opportunity to place on record his opinion of the Catholic England of the past, and the high hopes he entertained for the future of a thorough revival of Catholicism, and of the mighty influence the Three Kingdoms and their vast colonial empire are destined to exercise on the social and religious future of the world.

This opportunity arose from the peculiar relations in which in Great Britain the members and houses of the old Monastic Orders stood with regard to the newly restored hierarchy. These orders, their members and houses, had been subject immediately to the jurisdiction of the Holy See, and only indirectly subject to the ordinary jurisdiction of the bishops. The bishops themselves, ever since the days of Elizabeth down to the middle of the present century, had lived and labored in Great Britain as vicars-apostolic, immediately dependent themselves on the Propaganda, and partaking of the extraordinary and exceptional conditions of a persecuted religion.

The Religious Orders, the Benedictines and Jesuits in particular, had braved suffering and death in every form, and lived among their tried people as best they might during the dark days which seemed to know no end while century succeeded to century. They lived by twos, by threes at most, generally all alone, and wandering about from house to house when the persecution was at its height. Not before the present century did their residences, their schools, their churches dare to show themselves above the ground, like timid shoots fearful of the frost when the winter has been long and the spring is delayed.

These modest houses and churches and schools of Benedictine and Jesuit throughout the length and breadth of the land had been the sanctuaries and nurseries of the proscribed faith for the heroic generations, who were born and lived and died without seeing any ray of hope brighten for them the western sky as they went down to the grave.

Necessarily these temporary abodes of the Monastic Orders could not be subject to the ordinary prescriptions of canon law during the days of trial; and when the trial ceased and the hierarchy was restored, questions arose concerning the Monastic Orders so situated, in their relations with the secular clergy and the bishops, now restored to the ordinary status, which it required the authority and all-seeing wisdom of the Holy See to settle once and for ever.

This happened in 1880-81, when a special committee of cardinals, aided by the most experienced jurists in Rome, examined the whole matter in all its bearings, submitted each point to be adjudicated upon to the Sovereign Pontiff, and enabled him to issue the constitution *Romanos Pontifices*, which was at once accepted by all parties as God's own oracle.

"That the Roman Pontiffs who have gone before us," the Pope says, "have cherished a fatherly love for the illustrious English nation we know from the records of history, and from the solid proofs enumerated by Pius IX, of happy memory, in his bull, *Universalis Ecclesiæ*, of September 29, 1850. As that bull restored the episcopal hierarchy in England, he thereby crowned the measure of benefits conferred by the Holy See on that nation. For by this restoration of diocesan government that portion of Christ's fold already called to the wedding feast of the Lamb, and become a member of His mystic body, acquired a fuller and more stable possession of the truth and order through the rule and government of their bishops. ...

"The subsequent events wonderfully corresponded to this

wise design [of Pius IX]; for several provincial councils were celebrated, which passed salutary laws for the regulation of diocesan matters; the Catholic faith received thereby daily increase, and many persons distinguished for their rank and learning returned to the unity of the Church. The clergy were much increased in number; so was increased the number of religious houses, not only of those belonging to the Regular Orders, but of those belonging to more recent institutes, and which rendered great services to religion and the state by educating the young and practising works of beneficence. Many pious lay sodalities were founded, new missions were established, and a great number of churches arose, splendid specimens of architecture and magnificently decorated. Then numerous asylums were created for orphans, together with seminaries, colleges, and schools in which a multitude of children and young people are trained to piety and the knowledge of letters.

"The great merit and praise of all this are due to the character of the people of Great Britain, which is one of invincible constancy in misfortune, easily accessible to truth and to reason; so that not undeservedly did Tertullian say of them: *Britannorum inaccessa Romanis loca, Christo subjecta*–The Britons made their regions inaccessible to the Romans, but subjected them to Christ.'[3] But what is most to be praised in Great Britain is the unwearied vigilance of the bishops, the ready disposition to obey of the whole body of clergy, and their prompt and diligent activity."

The points in controversy between the bishops and Religious Orders are then exposed, discussed, and decided with a fulness of detail, a clearness, a grasp of the principles and interests involved, and a spirit of moderation, justice, and fatherly love, which made the sentence on every point most acceptable, as it was final.

Few documents in the annals of the Roman Pontificate are more creditable and more deserving of a canonist's study than

---

[3] "Adversus Judaeos," c. v.

this constitution.

"Having thus solved the disputes laid before us," the Pope says in conclusion, "we trust that the care we have bestowed in settling them shall avail not a little to promote the peace and increase of the Catholic religion in England. We have based our sentences carefully and scrupulously on the rule of justice and equity, and we entertain no fear but that the same diligent care and scrupulousness will guide the parties interested in carrying out our decisions. Thus shall it happen that, guided by the authority and wisdom of the bishops, the members of the Religious Orders, who have deserved so-well of the English missions, will continue to labor strenuously and cheerfully, and to reap therefrom the most abundant and happy fruits of salvation; and that both bishops and religious (to use the words of Gregory the Great to the bishops of England), with common ... accord and united action, shall be unanimous in arranging together what is to be done for Christ's glory, that they shall think aright, and that whatever they have thus thought out they shall carry into effect without, differing from themselves.[4] The fatherly love of the bishops for their fellow-laborers, as well as the reciprocal respect of the clergy for their bishops, alike demand that such concord shall reign. Such concord is also required by the common purpose of both—the salvation of souls, which they have to secure by united zeal and efforts. It is also required by the necessity of resisting those who are the enemies of the Catholic name.

"Concord is a source of strength, and it enables even the weak to accomplish great things; it is also a sign by which the true followers of Christ are known from those who only pretend to be so. To observe this concord we earnestly beseech all and every person concerned, asking them with Paul to fulfil our joy, being of one mind, having the same charity, being of

---

4 *Apud Bedam, "Hist. Ang.," ii. 29.*

one accord, agreeing in sentiment."[5]

The fatherly exhortation fell upon docile ears and loving hearts. The constitution was issued on May 16. Ere the month had passed Cardinal Manning wrote to the Holy Father that he, for his part, cordially acquiesced in the decision of the Holy See. So did the other prelates, and so did the venerable religious whose predecessors had lavished their sweat and their blood on the field they were cultivating. No weeds of discord or uncharitableness could take deep root there.

---

[5] "Acta," ii. 227 and following.

CHAPTER XXVI

LEO XIII AND IRELAND

THE PROBLEM OF IRISH misery, misrule, and unrest was forced upon the attention of Leo XIII from the beginning of his Pontificate. As the Common Father of Catholic Christendom, the teacher, guide, and judge of all in things spiritual—in all things, indeed, which touch the conscience or regard the performance of duty in the political as well as the purely religious order—the Pope had to form his judgment on the right and reason there was in the persistent claims of Ireland for justice.

Leo XIII is not one incapable of grasping the enormous power of the two great English-speaking peoples at the present time—those, namely, of the British Empire and of the great Republic of the United States. He had well considered the fact that, although the great majority of English-speaking folk are not Catholics, they have nevertheless preserved in their home-life and their whole conduct a deep-seated religious sense. This pervades all their institutions—pervades, in very truth, the whole framework of society among them like the animating principle. This religious spirit, inherited from so many generations, is—and the Pontiff knows it well—one of the most precious germs of the Christian life which it is hoped will reign among the civilized nations of the coming era.

In the United States there is, in the relations between the Catholic millions, the Federal government, and the Protestant majority, no existing cause of dissatisfaction or discontent.[1] The Catholic religion and its institutions exist side by side with other denominations on the solid ground of the common law, protected in its free growth and development by the

[1] The only element of religious strife and political danger in the confederation is Mormonism. Sooner or later this sect, like negro slavery, will come under the arbitrament of the sword.

common magistrate and the liberty-loving spirit of the people. There are no more devoted citizens of the Union than the Catholics, of every race, who thrive and prosper beneath the Constitution.

In the British Empire, where the large-minded Pope desires to see the same union of all creeds and races as the common bond of national strength, no chronic injustice or oppression weakens any one portion of the great colonial possessions in which an English speaking population predominates. The one cause of division, of discontent, of weakness, lies in the very heart of the Three Kingdoms themselves, which are the seat of imperial sway.

Could the Irish be appeased? Could the two islands be ever bound together in a political, a social, a moral union as strong as that which holds the State of New York welded to that of Pennsylvania as two integral portions of the great Republic?

This could only be on a twofold condition—that England should undo the wrong perpetuated by more than seven centuries of misrule, and do for Ireland what simple justice and common sense demand: treat her as her dearest self-interest demands she should treat Devonshire or Wales or Yorkshire; have one common law for Irishman and Englishman; compel the landlords of Ulster and Munster and Connaught to have as much care of the productiveness of the soil, and the health and welfare of the tillers, as the landlords of the English counties have ever shown for their estates, their farmers and farm-laborers. Let the development of every resource—agricultural, mineral, industrial, commercial—which Ireland possesses be as great an object of English statesmen's solicitude as are those of Great Britain.

If England persists in doing quite the contrary, then is it manifest that she does not treat the "sister island" as if it were an integral, essential portion of the empire properly so-called—that is, the Three Kingdoms. Where, then, is the real union between the two kingdoms?

This, then, is the first condition required, that the legal bond connecting the two countries should mean the same measure of justice dealt out equally to both, and the same careful and kindly economy in developing the resources and promoting all the best interests of each without partiality or distinction.

The other condition must be to appease the feuds of race and religion so industriously and systematically fostered in England against the Irish Catholic, in Ireland among the English colony, whom the British government and British public opinion persist in regarding and acknowledging as the only "Irish nation."

The concession to Ireland of the measure of self-government granted to Canada, and enjoyed by Ireland a century ago, would satisfy the claims of political justice, and, if accompanied by the liberty to cherish their home industries and commerce, it would also have the effect of putting an end to the degrading poverty, the misery, as well as the misgovernment, which are the inveterate sores of that unhappy country. With the contentment arising from Home Rule, and the prosperity certain to follow it, would slowly but surely come the breaking down of the barriers which a bad land system, together with the bitter passions of race and religion, had created between the Protestant minority and the great mass of their Catholic fellow-citizens.

In this double appeasement Leo XIII, like all true statesmen not born and interested partisans of landlord misrule, like all impartial and enlightened men, saw the only means of cementing a strong, lasting, real union between the two islands and the two peoples. This union, founded on justice and mutual regard, would—so the civilized world thinks—make England all-powerful in her island home, and enable her to cultivate peacefully and surely, in every portion of her vast colonial empire, the best fruits of Christian civilization and material prosperity.

Thus, while the reign of well-ordered liberty, justice, and religion enabled the United States and the Canadian confederacy to make a whole continent populous, prosperous, and happy, the enjoyment of the same blessings would keep

Great Britain and Ireland the great conservative force in Europe, while revolution, irreligion, and anarchism were undermining and engulfing the old order of things on the Continent.

Anxious to see this long-desired appeasement of the just discontent of Ireland brought about and the power of England thereby increased for good, the Pope was startled, in 1879, to hear once more the periodical cry of famine issue from the Green Isle; and with the fearful distress which such a cry is founded on, the rumors and fears of agrarian or revolutionary violence crossed the Continent to Rome.

It would be a miracle indeed if, in a country where the great mass of the rural population, the tillers of the soil, had been for centuries reduced by the blind antagonism of race and religion, and by the inconceivable unthrift, neglect, and hard-heartedness of the majority of the landlords, to depend for subsistence on a single tuber, the potato, and to live in hovels in which the landlords would not keep their dogs—if rack-renting, and starvation, and eviction aroused a perishing people to resistance and such acts of retaliation as their unarmed condition allowed.

In every country and among every people known to history, oppression, spoliation, the pitiless greed of the wealthy and the powerful, have driven, and must ever drive, the oppressed and starving into secret associations and dark conspiracies organized against the oppressor.

In Ireland there has been no exception to this rule. There, too, rack-renting, eviction, starvation, and the systematic denial of all redress have ever driven the unhappy people to seek the only means of resistance and of redress within their reach—in the secret societies. From the despair begotten of the extremity of distress sprang Fenianism and the Invincibles and the Dynamiters. To agrarian violence, the dark deeds and threats of the societies, a drastic Coercion Act was deemed the only remedy. This, instead of reaching the root of the disorder, only attempted to quell the symptoms. It was like cauterizing with red-hot irons a deep wound when the poison was raging in the blood and throwing its victim into spasms he could not control.

To be just we are bound to say that the great statesman who is at this moment[2] prime minister of England, and who then was also the head of the government, did prepare in 1880 a deeper and more efficacious remedy in the shape of a Land Act. This act, "in itself as well as in the designs of its author a magnificent boon far surpassing in importance anything ever bestowed on Ireland by an English Parliament, would have been hailed with rapture and gratitude by the Irish people had it not been heralded by the most odious Coercion Act known in the dark annals of Irish misery. Before insulting the nation with this atrocious measure the prime minister did not stop to ask the Irish bishops and the political leaders of Ireland whether or not the horrible crimes committed in Dublin or elsewhere were the legitimate offspring of the teachings of the former or of the principles of the latter. Both prelates, priests, and politicians would have answered that these deeds of blood were only the natural consequences of a hatred and a despair begotten by an oppression to which there had been, so far, no let-up."[3]

What was needed at that moment in Ireland itself to prevent the organization and growth of these secret societies, to keep the people out of them, and to repress their deeds of violence and blood, was a cordial union of the bishops among themselves and with their priests, and a thorough understanding with the political leaders who possessed the confidence of the nation. Unhappily, in 1880 and the four following years no such union existed or appeared probable.

We are now describing the social and political condition of Ireland as it would have met the eyes of Leo XIII had he visited the island in the autumn of 1879, when the cry of

---

[2] March, 1886.

[3] "The Cause of Ireland pleaded before the Civilized World," P. F. Collier, New York, 1886. It is still problematic whether the Phoenix Park murderers were not suborned by the Dublin Castle officials.

starvation and the fearful reality appalled the country and startled the world.

We have said that the failure of the crops and the utter impossibility of paying rents where no rent had been produced by the land did not prevent the proprietors from exacting it, and, where it was not and could not be paid, turning the tenants out on the roadside and levelling their cottages before their eyes. It was a cruel thing to do.

Then arose the cry: "Keep your grip on the land!" and the Irish Land League sprang into existence.

It stood between the landlord and the tenant, demanding of the former that he should allow the tiller of the soil to live upon it and by it, co-operating with the latter in making the land productive, and allowing him such a share of the fruits of his husbandry as should make life worth living for. It stood between the rack-renter and his unfortunate and helpless tenant, between the evicter with his crowbar-brigade and the cottage in which the tenant and his fathers before him were born. Irishmen must have means, room, and liberty to live, to labor, and to prosper on a soil which God made fertile, but which man's improvidence and cruelty had made unproductive and barren.

Such was the Land League, soon to be suppressed, only to arise anew and more powerful in the National League and its outgrowth, the Irish Parliamentary Party.

One phenomenon struck sagacious observers from the very beginning of the famine of 1879, from the first appearance of the Land League, and the National League which succeeded it—that wherever its branches existed and were patronized by the bishop and his priests, there no agrarian crimes were heard of, no secret-society clubs could subsist. Wherever, on the contrary, as in Dublin, as in parts of Munster and Connaught, the bishop would not tolerate the existence and interference of the League, or permit his priests to keep thereby touch and control of his people, there the secret societies had it all their own way, and outrage and murder were committed.

It thus became a fact of experience, an undeniable truth of observation, that to keep the people from violent resistance to oppressive laws, from acts of bloody retaliation on rack-renting landlords and their agents, from all illegal and reprehensible deeds in a word, it was necessary that both the clergy and the political leaders should stand by the people, advise, restrain, and support them in the advocacy of their just claims.

The National party in Ireland—and by that I mean four millions at least out of the five who compose its present population—needed organization. Clergy and people had the same aspirations, the same aims, and put forward one identical claim for justice; but they lacked what peoples on the Continent of Europe possessed. In every country where revolution has upset the old order of things and established a new, the change, whether for good or for evil, has been effected by organization. That enabled the secret societies to use the government and arms of Piedmont, in Italy, to change the political, social, and religious conditions of the Peninsula. That enables the same dread Occult Force to level, piece by piece, the entire framework of society in France. That gave the seventeen millions of German Catholics the strength to battle and to withstand the most anti-Catholic and destructive legislation of the Kulturkampf.

This want of organization is the secret of Poland's ceaseless and bootless struggles for freedom and the restoration of her nationality.

Up to the summer of 1885 this, with regard, at least, to the furtherance of the national cause, was the fatal defect of the Irish hierarchy and inferior clergy. Now they are morally a unit, and as such they constitute the main element of strength in the present national movement. But with the Land League, the National League, and the Parliamentary party the people and their political leaders found out the secret, the power, and the success of a perfect and compact organization.

Before this salutary twofold union of the clergy among themselves and with the people and the Parliamentary party had been happily consummated, the recurrence of agrarian outrages and deeds of blood in several parts of Ireland had given the bishops much concern and had deeply pained Leo XIII.

Of his opinion and sentiments in regard to the Irish people and the justice of their claims we have very full and satisfactory evidence in the two letters addressed by him to the Irish hierarchy on August 1, 1882, and January I, 1883, respectively.

"The kindly affection," he says in the former, "which we cherish toward Irishmen, and which seems to increase with their present sufferings, forces us to follow the course of events in your island with the deep concern of a fatherly heart. From their consideration, however, we derive more of anxiety than of comfort, seeing that the condition of the people is not what we wish it to be, one of peace and prosperity.

"There still remain many sources of grievance; conflicting party passions incite many persons to violent courses; some even have stained themselves with fearful murders, as if a nation's welfare could be procured by dishonor and crime!

"This state of things is to you as well as to us a cause of serious alarm, as we had evidence of ere now, and as we have just noticed by the resolutions adopted in your meeting at Dublin. Fearful, as you were, for the salvation of your people, you have clearly shown them what they have to refrain from in the present critical conjuncture and in the very midst of the national struggle.

"In this you have discharged the duty imposed alike by your episcopal office and your love of country. At no time do a people more need the advice of their bishops than when, carried away by some powerful passion, they see before them deceptive prospects of bettering their condition. It is when impelled to commit what is criminal and disgraceful that the multitude need the voice and the hand of the bishop to keep them back from doing wrong, and to recall them by timely exhortation to moderation and self-control. Most timely, therefore, was your advice to your people, reminding them of the Saviour's injunction, "Seek ye first the kingdom of God and His justice.' For all Christians are therein commanded to keep their thoughts fixed, in their ordinary conduct as well as in their political acts, on the goal of their eternal salvation, and to hold all things subordinate to the fulfilment of their duty to God.

"If Irishmen will only keep to these rules of conduct they will be free to seek to rise from the state of misery into which they have fallen. They surely have a right to claim the lawful redress of their wrongs. For no one can maintain that Irishmen cannot do what it is lawful for all other peoples to do.

"Nevertheless even the public welfare must be regulated by the principles of honesty and righteousness. It is a matter for serious thought that the most righteous cause is dishonored by being promoted by iniquitous means. Justice is inconsistent not only with all violence, but especially so with any participation in the deeds of unlawful societies, which, under the fair pretext of righting wrong, bring all communities to the verge of ruin. Just as our predecessors have taught that all right-minded men should carefully shun these dark associations, even so you have added your timely admonition to the same effect.

"As, however, these same dangers may recur, it will become your watchful care to renew these admonitions, beseeching all Irishmen by their reverence for the Catholic name, and by their very love for their native land, to have nothing to do with these secret societies. These can in no wise help a nation to obtain redress for its grievances; and, all too frequently, they madly impel those whom they have ensnared to commit crimes.

"Irishmen take a just pride in being called Catholics—an appellation which, according to St. Augustine, means the guardians of all honor and uprightness, the followers of all equity and justice.[4] Let them fulfil by their acts all that this word Catholic implies; and let them, while vindicating their

---

[4] "Liber de Vera Religione," n. 9.

own just rights, endeavor to be indeed all that their name suggests. Let them remember that 'the highest liberty consists in being free from all crime'; and let no one among them, so long as he lives, have to undergo lawful punishment 'as a murderer, or a thief, or a slanderer, or one who has coveted other people's property.'[5]

"... We deem what you have decreed concerning your young priests to be proper and timely. For if ever there were circumstances when priests should be zealous and energetic in maintaining public order amid popular excitement, such are the present circumstances with you. And just as the estimation in which each one is held by the public is the measure of his influence over others, even so should priests endeavor to win this public esteem by self respect, firmness, and temperate word and deed. They should do nothing that prudence could condemn, nothing that can fan the flame of party strife. ...

"In this way, and by following such rules of conduct, we do believe that Ireland shall yet attain to the prosperity which she seeks, and that, too, without wronging any one. As we have already declared to you, we trust still that the government will conclude to grant satisfaction to the just claims of Irishmen. This we are led to believe from their acquaintance with the true state of things and from their statesmanlike wisdom; for there can be no question that on the safety of Ireland depends the tranquillity of the whole empire.

"Meanwhile, sustained by this hope, we shall lose no opportunity of helping the Irish people by our advice, pouring forth to God for them prayers filled with the warmest zeal and love, beseeching God to look down with kindness on a nation made illustrious by the practice of so many virtues, to appease the present storm of political passion, and to reward them at length with peace and prosperity."

Such were the noble words of fatherly love and advice sent to Ireland at a time when superhuman efforts were needed on the part of the religious guides, as well as on that of the

[5] "Acta," iii. 129-133.

political leaders, to prevent a people driven to despair from having recourse to the most violent and hurtful measures.

There is the outspoken acknowledgment of the justice of the nation's claims and of their constitutional right to seek redress by legal means.

Not in vain was the strong appeal made by the Pope to Irishmen's pride in being called "Catholics," and in the prayer that they would fulfil in their conduct the meaning of the word. Still the agitation continued, the working of Coercion Acts only serving to irritate and inflame where the united efforts of all men of order, of all who loved Ireland truly, should have been used to soothe the angry passions of the masses.

In the autumn of 1882 the difficulties in the path of the bishops seemed to multiply, and again they had recourse to the Sovereign Pontiff for light and guidance (October 4).

"Your letter," he says in reply,[6] "is a new proof of your respect and affection, as it is an evidence of the gratitude you and they feel toward us for our concern in the welfare of Ireland, and for the counsels given in our letter of August 1 last past. ...

"We cannot help congratulating you ... on the zeal displayed in calming the existing agitation. ... We also congratulate these children of the Church, who have listened so obediently to your admonitions, and who, enduring with Christian fortitude the sufferings of adversity, knew how to keep their sense of wrong within the bounds imposed by duty and religion.

"Still, although Irish Catholics continue to give splendid proofs of their zeal for religion and of obedience to the Supreme Pastor, the condition of public affairs requires that they should bear in mind the rules of conduct which our affectionate solicitude for them induced us to lay down for their direction. The secret societies, as we have learned with pain during these last months, always persist in putting their

---

6 "Acta," iii.

hope in the commission of crime, in kindling into fury popular passions, in seeking for the national grievances remedies worse than the grievances themselves, and in pursuing a path which will lead to ruin instead of to prosperity.

"It is, therefore, imperative that you inculcate deeply in the minds of your beloved people, as we have already said, that there is but one rule for what is right and for what is useful; that the just cause of their country must be kept separate from the aims, the plots, the deeds of criminal associations; that it is both right and lawful for all who suffer wrong to seek redress by all rightful means, but that it is neither right nor lawful to have recourse to crime for redress; that Divine Providence enables the just to reap at last a joyful harvest from their patient waiting and their virtuous deeds, whereas the evil-doers, having run their dark course to no purpose, incur the severe condemnation of both God and man.

"While we remind you of all these truths, impelled to do so by our ardent desire to secure some solace, quiet, and prosperity to Ireland, we are also filled with confidence that you, acting in concert and bound together by brotherly love, will continue to bestow your best care in preventing your faithful people from having anything to do with men who, carried away by their own passions, think they are doing their country service when they commit the worst crimes, and who, by urging others to like wickedness, bring shame and dishonor on the cause of the people."

It was worthy of the great heart of the Pontiff, tried as he then was by many sorrows, and burdened by an intolerable load of care, to utter his sentiments regarding Ireland with such solemn emphasis and such fatherly tenderness, while the struggle in Ireland was growing in intensity, and every effort to coerce only increased tenfold the power of resistance, and intensified in the same measure the hatred of laws, law-givers, and law-courts, which to the people meant only the administration of injustice.

No doubt the words of Leo XIII, repeated and commended from every pulpit in Ireland, went far to assuage the public resentment at the passing and enforcement of the "Crimes Act," and still further to prevent many from joining the dark societies which always spring from national misery and thrive on national discord.

The Land League was suppressed and its members imprisoned by the hundred; but this repression only left the secret societies a free field to work, and murders and outrages increased apace. The prison-doors were opened by the government, and it became at once apparent that the Land League, instead of being a source of agitation, outrage, and crime, was the only effective barrier against them.

Then arose the National League, which grew and grew until it counted among its members or its fellow-workers the whole body of the clergy, nine-tenths of the Catholic laity, and not a few of the most enlightened and influential among Protestant clergymen and laymen.

An incident occurred soon after this which chilled for the moment the warm feeling of gratitude and veneration felt in Ireland and among Irishmen everywhere for the Holy Father. We allude to the famous Propaganda circular. But the see of Dublin becoming vacant in February, 1885, by the death of Cardinal McCabe, the Sovereign Pontiff reserved to himself to confirm the choice made of Very Rev. Dr. Walsh, President of St. Patrick's College, Maynooth, to succeed to the deceased cardinal.

The election of this distinguished man was in itself remarkable, as indicating among the clergy of the metropolis an almost unanimous impulse to join the national movement, and thus reverse the policy followed by the two last archbishops. The intrigues, authorized or unauthorized, which thereafter occurred, to have the nomination of Dr. Walsh set aside by Rome, proved ineffectual. The Irish hierarchy had been summoned to Rome before the death of Cardinal McCabe. They repaired thither in May. The Sovereign Pontiff had, therefore, ample opportunity to ascertain the wishes of the Irish episcopate on the subject of this important election, and to be made acquainted with the true significance of the national movement.

In June Dr. Walsh's nomination was confirmed. Thenceforward this prelate was both the organ of his brother-bishops in all public and national matters and the spokesman of his fellow-countrymen. From that moment, too, there was unity of thought, purpose, and action between the clergy and the Parliamentary party.

The passing cloud which had in the Propaganda circular for a moment darkened and chilled the Irish Catholic heart was now forgotten, and Leo XIII became to Ireland and her sons the Lumen in Coelo of their own St. Malachy.

In dealing with the British cabinet the Pope, while considering the interests of Catholic subjects in Great Britain and in Ireland, as well as throughout the colonies, had also to have a regard for the feelings of the Irish race both inside and outside the British dominions. As the settled gloom on the material prospects of the Emerald Isle deepened with every decade that passed, leaving the Irish agriculturist less of resources and hope, and Irish labor no remunerative field or market within the compass of the Irish seas, the best and most religious men in the nation found increasing difficulty in restraining the outbursts of mingled despair and righteous wrath arising from wrongs easy of redress, but to which the government only applied homoeopathic doses of relief, coupled with intolerable coercion.

English statesmanship, Orange fanaticism, and hatred of race cried aloud: Let them starve or emigrate! What could the religious guides or the wise political leaders of a starving and oppressed people say or do to prevent an armed uprising, which would have justified the accusations and the demands of the exterminators? And what could the fatherly heart and the unpurchasable justice of the Roman Pontiff do to save the sufferers, to inspire the misgoverning with a sense of equity and humanity, to refuse to the oppressor a sanction of any of his schemes for redressing the wrong, but what, in the preceding pages, as we can judge from his own letter, he has done?

He has set the seal of his sanction on the justice and righteousness of Irish claims for self-government; he has recommended to the nation and its leaders, churchmen and laymen, obedience to the laws, peaceful and constitutional methods, and he has expressed his hope and uttered his prayer that justice may be done to Ireland.

CHAPTER XXVII

FUNERAL OF PIUS IX
SITUATION OF THE POPE IN ROME

THE SUMMER OF 1881 in Rome was rendered sadly memorable by an incident of which the civilized world heard with equal astonishment and indignation. This was the savage riot got up by the anti-clerical clubs of Rome on the occasion of the translation of the remains of Pius IX from their temporary resting-place in St. Peter's to his own chosen burial-place in the basilica of San Lorenzo outside the walls of Rome. As Leo XIII states in his narrative, the government and the municipal authorities had been duly informed of the intended removal. That they deliberately appointed an insufficient military guard for the funeral procession, knowing that it would be attacked, is now a matter of which no statesman in Europe doubts. That they were glad to see the lifeless remains of the man they had persecuted, despoiled, and hated with an intensity proportionate to the greatness of the wrong they did him, outraged in death, who will gainsay?

It is a pity to strip the allocution which Leo XIII delivered on August 4 following of its own native diction. His pen was inspired by a righteous anger at the inhuman outrage thus committed in the city of the Popes against one who had been beloved by the Catholic world as Pope had never been before.

But let us listen to his solemn recital of occurrences:

"Pius IX, as you know, Venerable Brothers, gave instructions that he should be buried in the basilica of San Lorenzo outside the walls. Wherefore, the time having come for the execution of his last will in this regard, the authorities charged with guarding the public peace were informed, and it was resolved to take the remains away from the Vatican basilica in the silence of the night, at the time when all is wont to be most quiet. It was also determined that the funeral procession should be, not what the dignity of the pontifical rank required or was demanded by the ritual of the Church, but what the present state of the city permitted to be carried out.

"But the tidings having spread all over the city, the Roman people, not forgetful of the benefits conferred by the great Pontiff, as well as his virtues, showed spontaneously that they intended to give a last testimony of their regard and love for their Common Parent. This surely was only a mark of gratitude and piety worthy of the Roman people's dignity and religious feeling, all the more so as they purposed doing nothing more than to follow the procession decorously, or to show themselves reverently and in large numbers wheresoever it passed.

"On the appointed day and hour the funeral train left the Vatican, amid a great multitude filling the square and the adjoining streets. There was a large body of pious men around the funeral car; a still greater number followed it. These, reciting the prayers becoming the occasion, had no thought of uttering a word or a sound offensive to others or calculated to incite in any way to disorder. But from the very beginning of the march a well-known band of bad men set about disturbing the performance of the solemn office by unseemly cries. Then, as their numbers and audacity increased, so they went on increasing in their efforts to create tumult and terror; they uttered the most atrocious blasphemies, hailed with hissing and insults the most respectable persons. The funeral cortege was hemmed in by crowds of angry men, whose looks and voices threatened them at every step, while again and again they attacked the procession with volleys of stones or with blows.

"Worse than all, what no savages would have done, they did not even spare the remains of the holy Pope. They loaded his name with opprobrious epithets, again and again hurled a shower of stones at the hearse, crying out repeatedly that the unburied body should be cast forth.

"This shameful scene lasted all through the long route, during the space of two hours.

"If the last extremity of outrage was not reached it is due to the self-restraint of those who, subjected to all kinds of violence and insult, preferred rather to bear everything patiently than to suffer that worse things should happen during the discharge of so sacred a duty.

"These facts, known to all and attested by the public records, cannot be denied by those interested in doing so, all their efforts to the contrary notwithstanding. Spread abroad by public report, they have everywhere filled Catholic hearts with grief, excited the spontaneous indignation of all men who still have a regard for the name of humanity. From all parts we daily receive letters expressing the execration of the writers for the foul shame of the deed and its atrocious savagery.

"But to ourselves above all others this serious and criminal outrage has been a source of equal concern and anxiety. Our duty impels us to guard the dignity of the Pontificate and to defend the memory of our predecessors; we, therefore, in your presence denounce and deplore this outrage, and cast the blame on those to whom it belongs, who failed to defend against the rage of impious men the sacred rights of religion and the freedom of the citizens. From what has occurred the Catholic world can see how little security there is for us in Rome.

"It was before a matter of notoriety that our situation was for many reasons one of intolerable suffering. The facts which have just happened have made more evident still that, if the present condition of things be bad enough, what we have to expect in the future must be still worse.

"If the remains of Pius IX could not be borne through the city without giving occasion to shameful disorders and violent rioting, who will guarantee that the same criminal violence would not break forth should we appear in the streets in a manner becoming our station—especially if a pretext were taken from our having, as in duty bound, censured unjust laws passed in Rome, or any other notorious act of public wrong-doing? Wherefore it becomes more and more a thing well understood that we can now only live in Rome by remaining a prisoner shut up in the palace of the Vatican.

"Furthermore, if one only reads carefully the signs of the times and remembers that the secret societies have conspired to destroy Catholicism, one can reasonably affirm that the enemy is maturing still more pernicious designs against the Church and the Sovereign Pontiff, as well as against the ancestral faith of the Italian people."

Signor Mancini, then Minister of Foreign Affairs in the Depretis cabinet, felt called upon to write to the representatives of his government at the various courts. Not one fair-minded person on either side of the Atlantic believed his statement, bungling, blundering, and palpably untruthful as it was. He and the men whose spokesman he was flattered themselves that they held undisputed possession of Rome, and could, any moment they pleased, turn the Pope out of the Vatican. Even we in America believed that European diplomacy, speaking in the name of all the Great Powers, had for ever set the seal of their approbation on the usurpation of the Papal States and the occupation of Rome. But Signor Mancini and Prime Minister Depretis knew right well, in August, 1881, and remembered with unspeakable bitterness, that at the Congress of Berlin, on the conclusion of the Russo-Turkish war, the proposal of Count Corti, the Italian plenipotentiary, to obtain then and there a solemn and final sanction of the "facts accomplished" in Italy and in Rome by Victor Emmanuel and the revolution, was indignantly repelled by Prince Bismarck and the other members of the Congress.

So the facts accomplished have not been solemnly recognized and sanctioned by the only court in the civilized world to which it appertains to do so. And as the years pass on the chances are continually lessened for obtaining such a sanction.

The day will surely come in Rome when the memory of Pius IX will be honored by a solemn pageant, a procession through the streets of Rome, from the Vatican to San Lorenzo,

of representatives of every Catholic country under the sun.

It is impossible that the Popes, the Common Parents of all humanity, should not have their own again, and be masters in that Rome where, after the downfall of the Roman Empire and the last invasion of the barbarians, they established the focus of that new, that glorious Christian civilization which their missionaries and their authority extended to every continent and every people.

CHAPTER XXVIII

LEO XIII AND THE UNITED STATES

THE first official act of Leo XIII[1] in 1884 was the issuing of the bull *Rei Catholicæ incrementum*, convening at Baltimore, in the November following, a Plenary Council of the Church in the United States. The twelve archbishops had been summoned by the Sovereign Pontiff to meet in Rome in the preceding November (1883), there to receive from himself and the Congregation of the Propaganda the necessary instructions concerning the new matters to be discussed, and the perfecting in every way of Church organization and discipline within the limits of the Republic.

As the venerable Cardinal McCloskey, Archbishop of New York, was prevented by ill-health from being present in the council, the Holy Father appointed Archbishop Gibbons, of Baltimore, Apostolic Delegate and president of the council. The archbishops returned from Rome as soon as their consultations were ended, and began, in conjunction with their respective suffragans, the examination and discussion of the manifold important matters to be decided in the approaching assembly.

The labors of the prelates, the progress of religion among their flocks, and the prospect of the coming council afforded Leo XIII, amid his many cares, incessant labors, and bitter trials, a subject of unspeakable joy. He had presented to the archbishops before they left Rome a full-length portrait of himself, to be hung in the hall where they were to deliberate, so that, as he said to them, he might, in a manner, preside over this great national council —the greatest till then ever held in the New World.

[1] "Acta," iv. I.

It will not seem to the reader to be here out of place to review briefly the history and condition of the great Western Republic and the marvellously rapid growth therein of Catholicity.

While Joachim Vincent Pecci was still in his childhood, the Republic of the United States, though its independence had been formally recognized by Great Britain, had still to contend against the arrogant ill-will of this power. British men-of-war had but little respect for the stars and stripes, asserting and mercilessly using, on every sea, the right of searching American vessels, and the right as well to press their crews into the military service of England. He was still a child when an English fleet could ascend the Potomac and destroy all that it pleased in the nascent capital of the Union, and when a British force could possess itself of Baltimore and hold the citizens absolutely at its mercy.

During the two first decades of the century the government of Washington had scarcely less cause to be dissatisfied with the rulers of France. It required no little moderation and no small degree of tact to prevent a rupture of intercourse between the two countries and the breaking out of open war.

But no external adversity could long or effectually check the development of a free people amid the unbounded resources of a country which embraced a great portion of a mighty continent, and was destined soon to extend its limits from the Atlantic to the Pacific. For at the bottom of that people's unparalleled prosperity lay a twofold fact—they were a religious people, among whom, though divided into various and hostile denominations, there reigned a deep religious sense, pervading not only private life but influencing and regulating public life; and they were a practical people, to whom the fatherly Providence who had in the mother-country watched over the birth and growth of all their social institutions had also in the New World inspired them with a deep love of the same, and thereby preserved them, from the very beginning of their separate national existence, from the revolutionary changes which have been the bane of the Latin races on Continental Europe, as well as in their great colonies beyond the seas.

Americans themselves, who wonder at the decadence which has fallen, like a blighting frost on a fruit-tree in the glory of its full bloom, on Spain, Portugal, and their colonial empires at their highest pitch of power and pride, have never accounted to themselves for the difference between their own progressive prosperity and the rapidly progressive decay of countries once so prosperous, the utter downfall of peoples once so mighty and so enterprising.

The Anglo-Saxon race in the United States were given the conservative instincts which arose from their thorough knowledge of the laws and institutions which had been in the old country the outcome and expression of their whole social life—a life continued in the new, and there expressed by the same institutions, the same laws, the same forms of government, in so far as the altered circumstances of a new existence permitted their doing so.

The laws, the manners, customs, and governmental forms of a nation, from its early birth to its adult state—if these are hallowed by religion and in conformity with the deep moral sense of the people, as well as the circumstances of clime and soil and geographical surroundings, are as much the creation of Nature—that is, of Him who made this world for mankind, and who directs man in his progress and destiny—as the tree is the growth of the soil, and its fruit the joint product of earth and air and sun.

God gave the Anglo-Saxon race at home, in what, in the fullest comprehensiveness of the word, we may call the British Constitution, this full embodiment of the character, the tendencies, the needs of the race; He gave them with that an enlightened love and a deep attachment to these forms of their social life.

In America these forms, with the very important exception of the feudal proprietary system imported into England by the Normans, were planted and cherished by the early British colonists. It was an invasion of the most sacred constitutional rights of the people of the colonies by the British Parliament which led to the War of Independence in 1775. The war, miscalled a revolution, was entirely conservative. Americans fought to defend their rights, to preserve from usurpation or infraction the dearest privileges of British freemen and citizens. The war over, and even from their solemn Declaration of Independence, their governmental forms, their laws, the entire framework of their social life, remained what they had been. After the war the Constituent Assembly which drew up the present Constitution only tried to adjust the existing forms of State governments to the exigencies of a Confederation or Union, bound together by a strong federal bond, while leaving to the component States or sovereign communities all the freedom competent with the existence, the unity, the undivided strength of one national life.

The Union sacredly preserved everything compatible with the condition of the people in a country where no king, no lords, no landed aristocracy, no privileged classes, no feudalism had ever existed. Thus all the precious elements which belonged to the public and private life of the race had been integrally transferred to its American home; all the best features of the English Constitution and government were sacredly preserved or modified with a reverent hand in the political edifice which arose after the War of Independence. This inborn knowledge of American laws and institutions, this attachment to the customs and usages of the fireside and the forum, this deep-seated reverence for authority and order wedded to freedom, the American citizen and his sons take with them to every part of their native continent covered by the flag of the Union.

Leo XIII watched with deep interest the development of these conservative institutions. Every new territory organized from out the wilderness by these hardy and intelligent pioneers was modelled on the time-honored forms of the State and Federal constitutions, every new State which asked for admission into the Union, was, he observed, carefully

constructed on this same plan. This nation is a beehive, made up of cells built symmetrically on one type, as if the workmen, like the bees, were guided by an instinct antecedent and superior to the mere agency of reflective intelligence.

They have been directed, guided, protected by a Power which looked far beyond the present age and the needs of even a continent or an epoch. They have been inspired, impelled to build for all time, for the benefit, the instruction, the happiness, the elevation of the human race in the era which is now dawning, and in that other era which must come for the human family when the Eternal God will think it time to realize the ideal of His own Son, the God-Man, Christ.

We have been, therefore, preserved in the United States from the frightful convulsion of 1789, which, in destroying from its very foundations the very structure of French society, unsettled in the minds of men the very intellectual principles on which all truth depends, and deposited in men's hearts and men's lives the germs of amoral licentiousness commensurate with the libertinism of thought and judgment inculcated by Voltaire, Jean Jacques, and the French Encyclopedia.

How strange, but how striking, that while the French statesmen of 1789 were thus blowing up the social edifice reared by their fathers, and inoculating all the Latin nations with the virus of their own political and religious madness, the assembled representatives of the American Union should have been laying simultaneously the foundations of a system which preserved all that was best in the political life of their forefathers! French principles and practices have been a social plague spreading over a continent, depopulating cities and country places, and leaving behind desolation, ruins, death, or despair. The principles and practices of the American statesmen of 1789 were like the planting of the Sacred Tree of India, which, spreading wide its branches and sending its shoots into a congenial and blessed soil, has covered the land from sea to sea with communities of law-abiding, God-fearing, and ever-progressive freemen.

Of the original thirteen States which formed the American

Union, Leo XIII could see that one only, the State of Maryland, contained the nucleus of a Catholic population. The colony which bore that name had been founded by Catholic emigrants, with a small admixture of Protestants. This is not the place to speak of the perfect freedom of conscience proclaimed by Leonard Calvert and upheld by the men who shared his fortunes; nor of the persecutions to which these Maryland settlers were afterwards subjected. In the Three Kingdoms at home intolerance reigned supreme: it was one of those social epidemics which arise among a people, are fed by the ambient air and the qualities of soil and water around, preying equally upon men of all classes. The epidemic crossed the seas with the ships of the mother-country and the colonies, and raged along the Potomac, the Wycomico, and the Chesapeake, as along the shores of Narragansett and Massachusetts Bays.

It lasted, with periodical outbreaks of fiercer violence, till the War of Independence, and the alliance with the France of Louis XV and Louis XVI acted like a thunderstorm which clears the overclouded skies and purifies the atmosphere of mephitic vapors.

Among the men who were foremost in devotion to the Union at its birth were the ill-treated Catholics of Maryland. Charles Carroll of Carrollton pledged the largest fortune to the cause of liberty; his cousin, the Jesuit John Carroll, was Benjamin Franklin's associate in a fruitless embassy to the Catholic colonists of-Canada, and he it was whom, at Washington's own request, Pius VI appointed first Bishop of Baltimore.

So began, in 1789-90, to spring up the Catholic hierarchy, which was destined ere a century had elapsed to have its goodly branches in every State and Territory of the Union. As the very names of Carroll and of Baltimore[2] indicate, the

2 Leonard Calvert, Lord Baltimore, took his title from the then Parliamentary borough of that name situated near Cape Clear Island, in southwestern Cork, destroyed by Moslem pirates about 1635, and now

children of the Emerald Isle were amongst the first precious seeds of Catholicism cast into the virgin soil of free America. Catholicism, coming principally in the persons of Irish exiles, would add new strength to the religious element furnished by both Cavalier and Puritan. The easily-accounted-for hatred of all civil authority and law begotten in the Irish heart by long centuries of administrative oppression and organized judicial injustice would, when a quarter of a century later the great tide of emigration from Ireland set in steadily, be changed into love of American institutions and a law-abiding spirit all the more lasting that they are founded on conscientious conviction.

And so in the New World, as the radical and anti-Christian revolution progressed in the Old, the Christian religion was casting such deep roots; faith in the Redeemer worshipped by our fathers, and the loving practice of His precepts, bearing, in the pure air and bright sunshine of freedom, fruits unseen before on earth—fruits such as to gladden the hearts of every successor of the sixth Pius and the seventh, from Leo XII to Leo XIII.

No less important an element to the population of the great Republic of the Western world has been contributed by the Teutonic races of the European Continent. The socialistic and radical notions imbibed at home by non-Catholic Germans die out after a few years of sojourn in the free and healthy air of a country where there is room for all, and where the fear of God and respect for established law and order are inculcated at every fireside. So perish in a great measure the Socialist theories brought over from France by the comparatively few Frenchmen who come to the United States to better their fortunes and then return. These retain their flippancy, their scepticism, and their attachment to the baneful theories learned from their doctrinaire masters. But whereas this last fraction of the quicksand population of the United States

---

restored to life, industry, and prosperity by the noble munificence of the Baroness Burdett-Coutts.

contribute little to the hopeful religious future of the Republic, the German-Catholic citizens show in the country of their adoption the same admirable qualities displayed in the Fatherland: intelligence, industry, and habits of organization for all purposes of beneficence, education, and religion, which render them one of the most progressive, as they are one of the most conservative, elements of the new nation.

Religion, therefore, in its teaching and its practice, and in the two great races which are its professors in the United States, is a principal factor in the estimate which the Christian historian and statesman must form of the great future that lies before the nation founded by Washington.

The month of November came at length, and before its first week was ended a number of prelates and priests were to be seen around the cathedral and the archbishop's residence. The metropolitans had been summoned a few days in advance to consult with the apostolic delegate on the rules of procedure and other matters. Two of these preliminary conferences were held on the 6th and 7th, the latter in the Seminary of St. Mary's, where the Sulpicians placed the house at their disposal during the council. It was in the great hall of this institution, which, together with the Jesuit College of Georgetown, is the most venerable seat of learning in the Union. For John Carroll, on returning to Baltimore as its first bishop toward the close of the last century, brought with him a band of Sulpicians, the parents of a long and venerated line of apostolic men, the educators and models of the clergy of Maryland and the neighboring States.

On Sunday, November 9, the great council opened, a wonderful spectacle even to the citizens of Baltimore, who had been accustomed to these periodical assemblages of the Catholic hierarchy and clergy. On the Saturday Leo XIII, without waiting for the message which the council intended to send him, telegraphed: The Holy Father sends his blessing to the fathers of the Plenary Council which begins to day— Louis Cardinal Jacobini. To which Archbishop Gibbons answered: Eighty-three prelates assembled in council return thanks to your Holiness and assure you of their dutifulness and devotion.

Was not this great ocean cable a type of that Catholic faith and love which bind continent to continent and unite the most distant peoples in constant and loving intercourse with the Holy See, the Chair of Peter, and the fatherly heart of the Pontiff?

Then there was a telegram sent to the Archbishop of New York, the first prelate on the American continent on whom the Roman purple had been conferred: "The prelates of the Third Plenary Council, by unanimous vote, salute your Eminence, and tender to you the expression of their most profound respect and sincere attachment." To which the cardinal replied, through his secretary, that "though absent in body, he is present in spirit, and ceases not to implore the benediction of Heaven on their labors."

Foremost among the eighty-three prelates, the fathers of the Church in the United States, after the apostolic delegate, was the venerable Archbishop Kenrick, of St. Louis, consecrated coadjutor to Bishop Rosati in 1841, and Bishop of St. Louis since 1843—most venerable for his age, his learning, his virtues, and his great labors in the cause of religion. What a retrospect was his, as he looked back over nearly half a century of episcopal toil in that great West, to remember how what was one immense desert fifty years before, traversed only by the wild Indian, the trapper, or the herds of buffalo, was now covered by flourishing States with large cities and an ever-increasing population! And then he could remember the Councils of Baltimore held before 1840, when the United States had only one archbishop, and California still belonged to Mexico and was buried in the slumberous obscurity of the Pacific coast.

There, too, was Monsignor Osouf, Vicar-Apostolic of Northern Japan, who seemed to have come there to read in the marvellous growth of that young Church of America the prophetic forecast of what would be, ere another century had elapsed, the already flourishing Church of Australia and New

Zealand, together with his own church in Japan and the persecuted churches of Cochin China and China.

Of the proceedings of the council we need not say much to the reader. All the matters therein discussed had been printed beforehand, carefully discussed by the archbishops and bishops, assisted by a body of theologians and canonists summoned from all points of the Union. In the decrees thus prepared only certain amendments and corrections were introduced. But as all this was to remain as the law of the American Church, every item, every iota was a thing maturely to be weighed. Then the work and the workmen for every session and private assemblage had been distributed before the council opened, so that everything fell at once into its own place, and the great living organism began its functions without hesitation or jar from the first hour to the last.

The council was closed on the 7th of December. It had thus lasted a month. One remarkable circumstance connected with this solemn event in the history of Catholicism in the United States was, as the historian of the council relates,[3] "the courtesy, the kindness, and the hospitality extended by the citizens of Baltimore, even by such as were not Catholics, to the fathers of the council and to the clergymen summoned to attend it, and who were not few in number. Nor were these sentiments manifested by private citizens only, but by the city authorities, who showed in various ways their respect for the members of the council. The public recorder was especially kind, placing one of his deputies entirely at the service of the prelates. For all this attention the delegate apostolic failed not to make grateful acknowledgment at the end of the council."

The joint pastoral letter issued by the prelates, and prepared with extreme care, is in every way worthy of the source from which it proceeds. Should the reader judge that what we have said in this chapter about the institutions and character of the American people, or about the wonderful progress of Catholicism in their midst, is exaggerated, we beg

[3] "Acta et Decreta," lviii.

him to peruse the following extracts:

"Full eighteen years have elapsed," so this pastoral letter begins, "since our predecessors were assembled in Plenary Council to promote uniformity of discipline, to provide for the exigencies of the day, to devise new means for the maintenance and diffusion of our holy religion which should be adequate to the great increase of the Catholic population. In the interval the prelates, clergy, and faithful have been taught by a wholesome experience to appreciate the zeal, piety, and prudence that inspired the decrees of those venerable fathers, and to listen with cheerful submission to their authoritative voice, whether uttered in warning, in exhortation, or in positive enactment. And the whole American Church deeply feels and cordially proclaims her gratitude for the treasures bequeathed to us by their wise and timely legislation. Its framers, in great part, have gone before us with the sign of peace, and now sleep the sleep of peace. But their work, besides following them to the dread tribunal of the great Judge to plead in their behalf and insure their reward, has remained upon earth as a safe guide and a rich blessing for the clergy and people of their generation.

"Since that time, however, the body of our clergy and religious has grown to wonderful dimensions, our Catholic institutions have been multiplied tenfold, with a corresponding increase in the number of our faithful laity. The territory, likewise, over which they are spread has been greatly enlarged. The land of the far West, that once was desolate and impassable, through God's providential mercy now rejoices and flourishes like the lily. Under His guiding hand it has been taught to bud forth and blossom and rejoice with joy and praise. The wilderness has exchanged its solitude for the hum of busy life and industry; and the steps of our missionaries and Catholic settlers have invariably either preceded or accompanied the westward progress of civilization. Forests have given way to cities, where Catholic temples re-echo the praises of the Most High. ... In view of this great progress of our holy religion, ... it has been judged wise and expedient, if not absolutely necessary, to examine anew the legislation of our predecessors. ...

"Such, too, has been the express wish and injunction of our Holy Father Leo XIII, happily reigning, to whom, as Supreme Pontiff and the successor of the Prince of the Apostles, by inherent right belongs the power of convoking this our Third Plenary or National Council, and appointing, as he has graciously done, an apostolic delegate to preside over its deliberations."

Speaking of the religious errors against which the council has to provide the safeguards and remedies, the pastoral letter says:

"We have no reason to fear that you, beloved brethren, are likely to be carried away by these or other false doctrines condemned by the Vatican Council, such as materialism, or the denial of God's power to create, to reveal to mankind His hidden truths, to display by miracles His mighty power in this world, which is the work of His hands. But neither can we close our eyes to the fact that the teachers of scepticism and irreligion are at work in our country. ... Could we rely fully on the innate good sense of the American people, and on that habitual reverence for God and religion which has been so far their just pride and glory, there might seem comparatively little danger of the general diffusion of these wild theories which reject or ignore Revelation, undermine morality, and end not unfrequently by banishing God from His own creation. But when we take into account the daily signs of growing unbelief, and see how its heralds not only seek to mould the youthful mind in our colleges and seats of learning, but are also actively working amongst the masses, we cannot but shudder at the dangers which threaten us in the future. When to this we add the rapid growth of that false civilization which hides its foulness under the name of enlightenment—involving, as it does, the undisguised worship of Mammon, the anxious search after every ease, comfort, and luxury for man's physical well-being, the all-absorbing desire to promote his material interests, the unconcern, or rather contempt, for those of his higher and better nature—we cannot but feel that out of all this must grow heartless materialism, which is the best soil to receive the seeds of unbelief and irreligion. ... The first thing to perish will be our liberties. For men who know not God or religion can never respect the inalienable rights which man has received from his Creator. The state, in such case, must become a despotism, whether its power be lodged in the hands of one or of many."

This is very forcibly stated. How truly it applies to what is happening at this moment in France and in Italy! Coming to the iniquitous and hypocritical war made in Europe on Catholics because of the definition of Pontifical Infallibility, the letter says:

"The governments by which, three centuries ago, the new tenets of Luther, Zwingli, and Calvin had been imposed on reluctant peoples by the sword, were the first, indeed the only ones, to again unsheathe it against Catholic believers. ... It was their purpose to exterminate by degrees the Catholic hierarchy, and to replace it by a servile priesthood. ...

"But the Catholics of Prussia, clergy and people, while proving themselves most devoted and faithful to their country's laws, stood up like a wall of adamant against the tyranny of its rulers. ... The struggle has now lasted fourteen years, but the very friends of this persecuting legislation have been driven at last to acknowledge that it has proved to be a miserable failure; ... they have had to fall back on the patriotism of the Catholic body to stay the threatening march of Socialism and Revolution. In Switzerland, too, the persecution has yielded to the policy of mildness and conciliation adopted by our Holy Father Leo XIII.

"... A Catholic finds himself at home in the United States, for the influence of the Church has been constantly exercised in behalf of individual rights and popular liberties. And the right-minded American nowhere finds himself more at home than in the Catholic Church, for nowhere else can he breathe more freely that atmosphere of divine truth which alone can make him free.

"We repudiate with equal earnestness the assertion that we need to lay aside any of our devotedness to our Church to be true Americans, and the insinuation that we need to abate any of our love for our country's principles and institutions to be faithful Catholics.

"To argue that the Catholic Church is hostile to our great Republic because she teaches that 'there is no power but from God' (Rom. xii. I); because, therefore, back of the events which led to the formation of the Republic, she sees the providence of God leading to that issue, and back of our country's laws the authority of God as their sanction—this is evidently so illogical and contradictory an accusation that we are astonished to hear it advanced by persons of ordinary intelligence. We believe that our country's heroes were the instruments of the God of nations in establishing this home of freedom. To both the Almighty and His instruments we look with grateful reverence. ...

"No less illogical would be the notion that there is aught in the free spirit of our American institutions incompatible with perfect docility to the Church of Christ. The spirit of American freedom is not one of anarchy or of license. It essentially involves love of order, respect for rightful authority, and obedience to just laws. There is nothing in the character of the most liberty-loving American which could hinder his submission to the divine authority of our Lord, or the like authority delegated by Him to His Apostles or His Church."[4]

Coming to speak of Leo XIII, the assembled prelates show that they can appreciate his great qualities: "While enduring with the heroism of a martyr the trials which beset him, and trustfully awaiting the Almighty's day of deliverance, the energy and wisdom of Leo XIII are felt to the ends of the earth. He is carrying on with the governments of Europe the negotiations which promise soon to bring peace to the Church. In the East he is preparing the way for the return to Catholic unity of the millions whom the Greek schism has so long

[4] Acta et Decreta Conc. Plen. Balt. Tertii." pp. lxviii.-lxxvi,

deprived of communion with the See of Peter, and he is following the progress of exploration in lands hitherto unknown or inaccessible with corresponding advances of Catholic missions. To the whole world his voice has gone forth again and again in counsels of eloquent wisdom, pointing out the path of truth in the important domains of philosophy and history; the best means of improving human life in all its phases, individual, domestic, and social; the ways in which the children of God should walk, that all flesh may see the salvation of God.

"But in all the wide circle of his great responsibility the progress of the Church in these United States forms in a special manner both a source of joy and an object of solicitude to the Holy Father. With loving care his predecessors watched and encouraged her first feeble beginnings. They cheered and fostered her development in the pure atmosphere of freedom when the name of Carroll shone with equal lustre at the head of her new-born hierarchy and on the roll of our country's patriots. ...

"In all this astonishing development, from the rude beginnings of pioneer missionary toil, along the nearer and nearer approaches to the beauteous symmetry of the Church's perfect organization, the advance, so gradual and yet so rapid, has been safely guided in the lines of Catholic and apostolic tradition. ..."[5]

Among the subjects on which the Council expended most care and thought was that of education—education in its widest and most comprehensive sense: the education of the clergy and that of the laity in all their grades. This was also the Holy Father's chief care. The creation of a great National University for Catholics, like the Laval University for the Canadian confederation—a great school where the Catholic youth of the Republic, young clerics and young laymen alike, should find, together with the surest safeguards for faith and morality, the very best masters in every department of

[5] *Ibidem.*

knowledge which the country could supply or who could be tempted to come from abroad—such was the ideal. It was no sooner known to the public than a noble Catholic young lady, Miss Mary Gwendoline Caldwell, of New York, at once gave $300,000 toward the divine work contemplated. Her friend and banker, Mr. Eugene Kelly, gave $50,000. Others all over the Union gave generously. In the future, we doubt not, there will be no lack of generosity. As we write upwards of a million of dollars has already been subscribed.

A spacious property has been purchased not far from the city of Washington, and the foundations of one great branch of the future University have been laid—a high-school for clerical studies, to which young candidates for the priesthood who have finished the ordinary curriculum in the seminaries, and who unite superior talent with superior virtue, can come, there to spend some three or four years more in perfecting themselves in mental philosophy, theology, and their kindred sciences, as well as in such of the physical and mathematical sciences as may enable the students issuing from this school to take their place anywhere by the side of the most accomplished scholars, or to consecrate their acquired knowledge to teaching and training others.

It is a noble beginning. May God prosper it and bless all those whose benefactions forward its progress!

This is the place to state more explicitly than we have done that the Holy Father himself took especial pains in elaborating the preparatory schema of all matters to be treated in the council. This schema was discussed with the archbishops in Rome during the preceding November, 1883. The matter of higher education Leo XIII particularly insisted on.

He, therefore, took a warm personal interest in this, council and its labors, as in a work with which he was identified. Even now he reads and studies with the greatest care all that pertains to the great National University.

While the archbishops were in Rome during the autumn of 1883, the Holy Father had strongly pressed upon their attention his project of creating for the higher education of

Eastern Catholics a great school in Athens and another in Constantinople. They had promised him to make an appeal to their people in favor of this apostolic enterprise.

During the council, however, Archbishop Gibbons was requested by the fathers to write to the Pope and obtain fuller information regarding these two proposed schools or universities. We here give that part of Leo XIII's answer which relates both to the American National University and to the proposed schools at Athens and Constantinople:

"It was a great satisfaction to us to learn that you and your brother-bishops have undertaken the noble work of building as soon as possible a Catholic University in America. Carried out by the initiative, the advocacy, and the watchful care of the episcopal body, this work will render great service both to religion and to your country; it will shed lustre on the Catholic name and will conduce to the advancement of literature and the sciences.

"We are well aware what great expense you must incur in order to carry out your design, and have, therefore, abstained from urging you, Venerable Brother, to send us the pecuniary help which we so earnestly besought of you last year while you were in Rome, and that for an object which is also of great importance. We mean the purpose we entertain, and which we press on you with the greatest insistence, of bringing back the Eastern peoples to the Catholic fold, We think that the establishment of schools both in Athens and in Constantinople would help more than anything else [*maxime*] to hasten this result.

"Now, if the other matters already mentioned so naturally fill your mind and employ your care, Venerable Brother, we desire, nevertheless, that you do not altogether forget this other subject we have been just explaining, and that you be convinced, should our purpose come to have a happy result, that it will greatly contribute to the glory of God, to the honor and increase of the Catholic Church, and that it will redound not a little to the credit of your own generosity and that of the

American people."[6]

Americans will understand the fatherly solicitude which the Supreme Shepherd of Christ's flock entertains for the conversion of these Eastern peoples who have strayed away from the fold; they will help him to create these great Catholic schools at Athens and Constantinople. Their charity will only bring a greater blessing on their own National University, the nursery of all true learning for the America of the future.

The American Church has just contracted another debt of gratitude toward Leo XIII In the consistory of June 7, 1886, he raised to the Roman purple the Archbishop of Baltimore, who had so worthily represented the Holy See in the Third National Council. In him and in Archbishop Taschereau, of Quebec, American scholarship thus receives a supreme acknowledgment.

---

[6] "Acta et Decreta," lxiv. lxv.

CHAPTER XXIX

LEO XIII AND GERMANY

OF ALL the enormous difficulties inherited from his predecessor, no one was of such magnitude as that which resulted from the position of the Church in Germany. It has been generally believed among non-Catholics that Prussia and the newly-constituted German Empire (1871-73), in enacting the rigorous "May Laws" and other proscriptive measures against Catholics, and in suppressing Monastic Orders, fining, imprisoning, and banishing bishops and priests, were only acting in self-defence against the machinations of the Jesuits, and protecting the national government and authority against the practical assumption of supreme and unlimited jurisdiction supposed to be implied in the Pontifical Infallibility decreed by the Council of the Vatican in 1870 (July 18). That no such assumption of jurisdiction was implied in the doctrine of infallibility is now recognized by all scholars, by all educated persons, indeed, who have taken the trouble to examine the doctrine itself. That there never existed any machinations of Jesuits, or any sort of organized opposition among German Catholics to the creation of the empire or against its security or permanence, is an unquestioned and unquestionable fact of history.

That, however, at the first official tidings, in 1867-68, of the intention of the court of Rome to convene a general council, a certain number of high-placed and influential Bavarian Catholics and others did organize a conspiracy, with the sole purpose of setting public opinion in Germany in direct and violent opposition to the assembling of the council, is equally unquestionable.

Two men among these are principally responsible for the persecutions to which German Catholics are subjected since

1871, and these are Dr. Joseph Ignatius von Bollinger and Prince Chlodwig Hohenlohe. The former, as scholars know, had been, down to 1860, a foremost defender of the doctrines of the Catholic Church and the prerogatives of the Pontificate, as well as a notorious assailant of the Reformation and the Reformers. Since 1860 Dr. Döllinger's attitude toward the Church and the Papacy underwent a great change. This is evident in the first work issuing from his pen after that year.[1]

In 1868 these two men were so situated as to be able to use the whole power of the Bavarian government in opposing the projected assembling of the council and in influencing the other Catholic courts for the same purpose. On June 29 of that year Pius IX issued the bull convening the council to open in the Vatican basilica on December 8 of the following year.

The venerable Pontiff's "Sacerdotal Jubilee"—the fiftieth anniversary of his elevation to the priesthood—fell on the nth of April, 1869. It afforded the entire Catholic world a very natural opportunity to testify its love for one whose sufferings and kindly virtues had won him the deep sympathy of his children in every land. The movement for making this celebration a most enthusiastic and universal one originated in Germany—in Bavaria itself, by a strange coincidence with the Döllinger-Hohenlohe conspiracy. Beginning in Bamberg, these filial manifestations spread all over Germany, and from Germany extended to every country where Catholics are found. From the palace to the shepherd's hut went forth pilgrims with such offerings as they could bring to the feet of the Common Father. The King of Prussia, the present emperor, who reverenced in Pius IX the guardian of all great and sound principles, sent him on this occasion a vase of precious material and rarest workmanship.

Meanwhile a diplomatic note signed by Prince Hohenlohe, Prime Minister of Bavaria, and addressed to all the representatives of that kingdom abroad, was circulating in all foreign courts. It was said in it: "The only dogmatic thesis

[1] Döllinger, Kirche und Kirchen, Fapsthum und Kirchenstadt. Munich, 1861.

which Rome desires to have decided by the council, and which the Jesuits in Italy and Germany are now agitating, is the question of the infallibility of the Pope. This pretension, once become a dogma, will have a wider scope than the purely spiritual sphere, and will become evidently a political question; for it will raise the power of the Sovereign Pontiff, even in temporal matters, above all the princes and peoples of Christendom."

This bugbear of "Infallibility" was just the very thing to create alarm and excitement in the minds of non-Catholic rulers and statesmen, who had only very confused notions of doctrinal matters, but who were very decided in their hatred of anything that threatened the supremacy of the state, the omnipotence and infallibility of the civil power.

It was so held up to the governmental and the popular minds as to excite the national and anti-papal feeling also. We all know how mighty a part the natural dislike of foreign interference or jurisdiction of any kind had in gaining to Luther the support of the German princes, and in obtaining for the tyrannic measures of Henry VIII the approval of his English Parliament.

From 1868 till long after 1873 the most powerful organs of public opinion in Germany, following in the path opened by the *Augsburg Gazette,* inspired by Dr. Döllinger, began a journalistic crusade against infallibility, the Papacy, and the Jesuits. It is a sad story. But to those who have studied carefully the events of the last fifty years, none of the startling moral phenomena of the age will be more familiar than the fatal facility with which public opinion is created by journalism on any given topic, even when the current thus set in motion is one which runs contrary to truth and to justice.

The Franco German war came to add its astonishing and tremendous catastrophes to the excitement of political and theological passions caused by the definition of the doctrine of Papal Infallibility. The Piedmontese usurpers of the States of the Church had all along been the faithful and energetic allies and co-operators of Döllinger and Hohenlohe in arousing against the Pope and the Church the storm which was at its highest in September, 1870.

In the first Imperial Parliament assembled in Berlin under the sceptre of the Protestant Hohenzollerns, if Prince Bismarck was High Chancellor, Prince Hohenlohe was Vice-President. The Jesuits and the Monastic Orders had been sedulously painted in Germany as the causes of the temporal decay and spiritual ruin which it was said and believed had fallen on Italy and rendered necessary the occupation of Rome by Victor Emmanuel and the deposition of Pius IX from even his little remnant of temporal power. The Jesuits and the Monastic Orders were assiduously held up by the anti-Catholic press of Germany as opposed to the new empire, as the foes of German unity, as those who, having given to the youth of Catholic countries a wrong, unprogressive, and anti-national education in the past, should in the future be deprived of all faculty of training youth and placed outside the pale of the common law.

Dr. Döllinger and his followers—and he had very many powerful friends and disciples in Germany, men whom he had educated and who looked up to him with veneration—now formed themselves into what is known as the "Old-Catholic" church, which allied itself with the Jansenists of Holland, with the Church of England, and sought, but sought in vain, to obtain from the schismatic Greeks the right hand of religious fellowship. As these lines are written it is known that this movement has ended in utter failure.

But in the enthusiasm with which the Protestant world hailed the birth of the new empire, in the dense mist of the prejudices and passions evoked by the definition of infallibility and the downfall of the Pope's temporal power, this "Old-Catholic" church, assembled in council with the Jansenist prelates and priests of Utrecht, with the representatives of the Protestant Church of England and of the old Eastern heresies, loomed up to the eyes of sympathizers like something very great, very portentous, if not prophetic of the utter ruin, spiritual as well as temporal, of the Church of Rome.

At any rate, in Germany, and in particular within the

kingdom of Prussia, the campaign begun against the Catholic Church and the Papacy soon after the inauguration of the empire and the close of the war with France was represented as one begun in the name and with the forces of civilization against the unprogressive and reactionary forces of Catholicism. This was the way that the conflict inaugurated in Prussia against the Church and the principles supposed to be involved on both sides was described by the one famous term Kulturkampf ("civilization-conflict"), used by Prince Bismarck, and thenceforward applied to his long struggle with the Church and the Holy See.

The crusade of the German press against the Religious Orders, against the Jesuits particularly, had been growing ever in fierceness all through 1871 and up to June, 1872, when a law was passed suppressing the Society of Jesus and "other affiliated orders." It was mercilessly carried out. On January 9, 1873, Dr. Falk, the Prussian Minister of Public Worship, who was, whether unconsciously or knowingly, in all this and the subsequent proscriptive legislation, really doing the work of the secret societies, introduced into the Prussian Chambers a more comprehensive law, made still more so in the following May.

These laws, suppressing all the Religious Orders except those engaged in hospital work, and banishing their members from the kingdom, were called "the May Laws." Dr. Falk added to and completed his code till it left not one vestige of religious liberty to nearly nine and a half million Prussian Catholics out of a total population of between twenty-seven and twenty-eight millions. The laws were a despotic code of Caesarism, asserting the omnipotence of the state both in the civil and the ecclesiastical order. They regarded not only the Catholic Church but the Protestant Evangelical Church of Prussia, aiming at securing to the lay members of the latter greater liberty from the control of their clergy, while proposing to substitute, in the case of Catholics, a national training and a national organization to the "Ultramontanism "so hateful to German rationalists and radicals. This was intended, according to the law-makers, to free German Catholics from the despotism of Rome. Episcopal authority was also to be reduced to a minimum under the pretext of giving the inferior clergy their due share of freedom. And the education of candidates for the priesthood, like that of all Prussian youth, was to be laicized, taken away from episcopal and clerical hands. The state was made the sole judge of the fitness of priests for any ecclesiastical office whatsoever; and the very candidates for holy orders were bound to pass a state examination and obtain a state certificate as a necessary condition before ordination. The seminaries were all closed.

We might omit further details, and have only given the foregoing to enable the reader to appreciate what we stated in beginning this chapter, that nothing in the crushing burden of care transferred in February, 1878, from the shoulders of Pius IX to those of Leo XIII, equalled in magnitude the difficulties inherent in the Prussian and German question. But it is instructive to learn more of this, terrible conflict.

During the seven years which preceded his own elevation to the Papal Chair, Cardinal Pecci, from his watch-tower in Perugia, had followed with intense and sympathetic interest the noble struggle of the German Catholics—bishops, priests, and laymen—against the overwhelming power of a state wielding the mightiest military host of modern ages, and backed in its warfare against Catholicism by the combined forces of the secret societies and the influential and unscrupulous press controlled by the lodges or salaried by the state.

It was a spectacle which was all the more interesting to the sagacious mind of the prelate-statesman of Perugia that he saw on the side of the German Catholics one great element of resistance, endurance, and final success which his own Catholic Italy lacked in her death-struggle with the Revolution—organization.

The tendency to organize, and the faculty for doing it thoroughly, seem innate in the Teutonic race; this time they proved the salvation of the Catholic Church in that empire.

Both in the Prussian Chambers and in the Imperial Parliament the Catholic members formed, from the beginning, a body so numerous and so compact, so well led and disciplined, that they made themselves felt as a third power between the government party and the opposition. Their able and eloquent leader, Von Windthorst, compelled all along the admiration and respect of all sections of the legislature. But the Catholics of Germany had not waited for the stormy years following 1870 to assemble and organize and cheer each other on in every path that could lead them to a perfect union of minds and hearts, to a real progress in intellectual and moral culture.

Ever since the first terrible convulsion of 1848 had warned all Europe that the Revolution was upon them, the German Catholics had made it a rule to assemble yearly in congress. The twenty-first Catholic Congress met in Mayence in September, 1871.

They then and there, under the inspiration of such lovers of true nobility as Bishop Von Ketteler, took every precaution which Christian wisdom and charity as well as the purest patriotism could suggest to perfect still more their work of organizing all the Catholic zeal and activities of the Fatherland against the evils which were agitating and convulsing Christendom.

The noble part which the Catholics of Prussia, of all Germany enrolled under the leadership of King William, had taken in the Franco-Prussian war, was a living, a recent memory. The Catholic soldiers had been foremost in bravery and loyalty; the Catholic chaplains—and none among these more so than the Jesuits—had been heroically devoted and self-sacrificing; so had the Sisters of Charity in hospital and on the battle-field. These memories were a perpetual inspiration to Von Windthorst and his associates.

When bishops and priests were imprisoned, disfranchised, banished, the Catholic laity were true to themselves and to God, without ever doing an act or saying a word which might lay them open to the suspicion or accusation of disloyalty or disaffection toward their country or its institutions. They held their yearly Congress, calmly, resolutely surveying together the situation in which the "May Laws" left each diocese, each parish, and devising the most effective means which patriotism and religion could suggest for keeping their suffering brethren together, for providing a remedy to every ill their zeal could reach, for keeping faith and hope and trust in Providence alive in the hearts of their countrymen.

We resume the thread of our narrative, and return to 1872-73.

To the protestations made in the Prussian Chambers by the Catholic members of Parliament, that the laws of the kingdom guarantee expressly and solemnly the full liberty of the Catholic religion, the government and the Parliament answered by at once repealing these laws. Pius IX, for whom in preceding years the Emperor William had professed an esteem full of reverence, remonstrated with his Majesty against acts which were not only violations of the Prussian law but of the treaties concluded with the Holy See; the emperor replied, in terms doubtless dictated to him by the stern chancellor, that the Prussian Catholics were only required to obey the existing laws, and that obey they must.

The Archbishop of Cologne, Primate of Prussia, the bishops of Münster, Breslau, and Paderborn, together with Archbishop Ledochowski, of Gnesen and Posen, became the special objects of the prime minister's severity, as they were the foremost in resisting the passing and execution of the obnoxious laws. And so things went on from bad to worse, and from worse to the very extremity of ill among the Catholics of Prussia, till in the Catholic Congress held at Würzburg on September 9, 1877, it was said that "the churches of Germany all along the Rhine Valley, from Constance to Rotterdam, had not a single bishop left! "Every one of them had been removed by death or by the hand of the persecutor. In 1873, when the "May Laws" began to be in full operation, the nine millions[2] of Prussian Catholics had 8,439 clergymen engaged in

---

[2] 8,711,535.

ministering to their spiritual wants. In 1881, of that number 1,125 parish priests and 645 assistants had either died or been imprisoned or banished the country, while their places remained vacant. Add to these 1,770 secular priests the members of the Monastic Orders, who in peaceful times are the zealous and efficient helpmates of the parochial clergy, and the reader will be able to judge of the religious destitution thus created; 644,697 souls in 601 parishes had not a single clergyman left to them, while 584 parishes with 1,501,994 souls were in a great measure destitute of all priestly ministrations.

While the Falk legislation was as yet in its preparatory stage, it was sought either to obtain the tacit acquiescence of the court of Rome to the proposed measures, or to find a specious pretext for a diplomatic rupture. Cardinal; Hohenlohe, a brother of Prince Chlodwig, was appointed ambassador of the German Empire near the Holy See. Doubtless the cardinal accepted this mission in the hope of preventing greater misfortunes; the Pope, at any rate, refused to receive him. And so all diplomatic intercourse ceased between the Vatican and Berlin. In the consistory of December, 1872, Pius IX animadverted severely on the suppression of the Monastic Orders in Germany, on the harshness and downright cruelty to which their members had been subjected, on the violation of laws enacted with the formal and solemn concurrence of the Holy See. This allocution, if an incentive or a pretext were needed for further and extreme measures of spoliation and persecution very opportunely served the purpose of Prussian statesmanship. All the blame was cast on the unyielding and unconciliating temper of the Vatican by what had begun to be called "the reptile press "of Germany—that is, by the most powerful journals in the pay of the government, and slavishly devoted to the advocacy of all its measures. It was, in reality, the Kulturkampf press, whose sole aim was to hold up the Papacy, the Catholic Church, and their institutions to hatred and scorn, and to make them responsible for the very wrongs done them in the persons of the Catholic millions of Germany.

And the non Catholic world, for the most part, espoused the views of the "reptile press," and sided with the all-powerful oppressor.

Dr. Döllinger and his associates in the "Old-Catholic" movement lost no time in profiting by the favorable opportunity thus created for them; the Catholic body in Prussia and elsewhere had indignantly and unanimously spurned every threat or seduction used to induce them to become a "national" church independent of the center of Catholic unity. The "Old Catholics" at once demanded to be recognized as the legal Catholic body, as the national Catholic Church of the empire. In October, 1873, Prussia recognized the legal title of Dr. Reinkens, lately consecrated as bishop of the "Old-Catholic" church by the Jansenist schismatics of Holland. He was appointed to receive a regular salary from the state.

It is known what active sympathy the Church of England gave to the Old-Catholic faction, which, in the minds of representative men in Great Britain, promised to separate from the Papacy the great body of German Catholics. In London, as in Berlin, those who were most hopeful of such a result forgot that our age has seen many would-be imitators of Martin Luther, every one of whom has ended in ignominious failure.

This is the age for reunion, not for separation; for reconciliation among Christians, not for further division. To the Piedmontese masters of Rome and rulers of Italy, whose examples in the Peninsula the German government were beginning to imitate and to surpass, this warfare against the Church, and the rupture of all relations with the Vatican, seemed a fitting season for drawing the bonds of friendship with the Imperial government closer. The King of Italy visited Berlin, and the Emperor William visited Milan. It was known all through these unhappy times, or it was strongly suspected, that the conservative Hohenzollern monarch, influenced by his admirable and gentle empress, had a lurking respect for the Roman Pontiff and for that Roman Church which Guizot called "the greatest school of reverence which ever existed." He did not, therefore, pay his return visit at Rome and the

Quirinal, but at Milan, the once capital of the fairest southern province ever conquered and held by Germany.

Certain it is that these visits were hailed by the anti-Catholic press on both sides of the Alps, on both sides of the Atlantic indeed, as indicative of a purpose hostile to the Church and the Papacy.

These hopes or expectations, in so far, at least, as a formal schism in Germany was concerned, were doomed to disappointment. English common sense itself reprobated the cruel and illiberal policy of the Prussian government.

"The coercion by force of a clergy conscientiously and irrevocably pledged to resistance is not justifiable, and is still less likely to prove possible." So wrote the greatest of British newspapers. "It may be necessary for the German government to make the experiment of reforming the Roman Catholic Church within their country; and if they could succeed it would be an admirable achievement. But, for our part, we think it more likely that they will fail."[3]

The Catholic Congress which met in Mayence in mid-September, 1871, gave an earnest of the heroic temper of its members and of that of the millions whom they represented. They protested against the occupation of Rome, by a power hostile to the Church, as a robbery which no law can validate, no lapse of time render lawful; they protested against the acts of every temporal government which pretends to dictate to the Church what doctrine she must teach, which opposes obstacles to the teaching of the Church or encourages rebellion against her doctrine or her discipline; they protested against the recent encroachments on their own liberties and rights. They protested as well against the tyrannical and oppressive conduct of the Protestant and rationalistic majority in Switzerland toward their Catholic brethren. There was a noble and manly address drawn up and sent to the latter.

In every act and utterance of the Congress there was evidence of that free and generous spirit which was resolved

---

[3] The London *Times*, Wednesday, December 11, 1873.

to demand to the full the legitimate measure of civil and religious liberty, and to suffer for right and conscience all that might could do. They accepted a plan for binding into one grand national society of education school-teachers, clergy, and parents. The Catholic press was organized after the same fashion. Catholic journalists inadequately supported were to receive aid from a common fund. Pens, purses, hands, heads, and hearts were to unite in one sacred cause. Every effort and utterance thenceforth was to be worthy of it. Against the advance of the so-called "German science "all were asked and pledged to combine by promoting true Catholic science. There was a solemn denunciation of the Italian "Law of Guarantees "because these guaranteed nothing, and there was, underlying them, the inadmissible assumption that the state has a right to say to the Church under what conditions she shall exercise her office, prepare, appoint, and regulate her ministers in their functions. The occupation of Rome is an international wrong, which all Catholics are bound to denounce and oppose until it is done away with.

So spoke Catholic Germany in 1871. So continued the same bold, courageous voice to thrill Europe year after year, rising clearer and more stirring as the wrongs inflicted on Catholics increased. Such accents moved the Catholic heart so powerfully that in 1874 the government forbade peremptorily the reassembling of these Congresses. But though the public meetings of the representatives of the Catholic body were thus prohibited, the school and press associations continued their unceasing labors in private. The organization was so strong, so perfect, so extensive, and animated by so determined a spirit, that the utmost efforts of the police and detective forces proved unavailing to prevent brother from assisting brother in a struggle where the highest, dearest interests were at stake.

We shall speak further on of the negotiations undertaken by Leo XIII to put a stop to these persecutions and to mitigate the lot of the German Catholics. But the reader can better judge of the persistency of the Prussian policy and of its results by the following passage of a letter from the

Archbishop of Cologne, written on behalf of his brother-bishops in answer to an address of sympathy from the Plenary Council of Baltimore. It is dated March 10, 1885:

"Unhappily," the letter says, "we are far from seeing the end of our afflictions. The chain of the May Laws, which fetters the rights and the liberty of the Church, still weighs upon us; our seminaries and our monasteries still remain suppressed; thousands of parishes are still desolate or deprived of their pastors. The Religious Orders and congregations are still expelled and banished from their native land. The discipline of the Church, the discharge of the episcopal office, and the administration of ecclesiastical property are subject, in many respects, to the management and control of the government, which claims, moreover, to manage the schools. Ecclesiastical students, and even priests, are bound to serve in the army. The archbishops of Prussia still languish in exile under a foreign sky. We are thus deprived of many precious graces which, in the midst of the struggle and the danger, we need to aid us to preserve intact and inviolable our unity and constancy to the end."

But in the very year of Leo XII Ids accession to the Pontificate the leading Conservative journal of the Protestant Evangelical press sums up in the following words the results of the Kulturkampf, or pretended battle for civilization and progress, carried on against Catholicism, but extending its ravages to all positive religion:

"The Evangelical Church has suffered grievously from the Kulturkampf. ... Indifference and hatred toward the Church and toward Christianity have increased to an astounding degree, and the unchristianized masses of the lower orders have enrolled themselves by thousands in the army of social democracy. As a result of the putting aside of the Church and of Christianity, and of the impious doctrine that 'everything is nature,' which has been the outcome, immorality has increased and the number of crimes is multiplied to an appalling extent. The bonds of social order are being dissevered, because the moral factors, authority and religion, have been long since set aside and replaced by rationalistic commercialism; so that we find ourselves in the face of the most serious complications in the social, moral, and ecclesiastical order.

"Of all the promises which were made at the beginning of the Kulturkampf not one has been realized; not that only, but the reverse has happened in every direction. Instead of peace there are everywhere disorder and confusion."[4]

Of course the forcible education of all the Catholic youth of Prussia during the seven last years of the reign of Pius IX must have had most disastrous effects. And these must have gone on increasing over another generation of young people during the seven first years of the reign of Leo XIII. No man could more surely calculate these results than one of his cultivated intelligence and long experience.

But finding himself helpless to bring about a sudden change in Prince Bismarck's baneful and (even to Germany) suicidal policy of persecution, he showed invincible patience and consummate tact in accepting the advances of the all-powerful high chancellor, as well as in conducting the negotiations begun. But while waiting and winning every possible advantage offered to him, the wise and enlightened Pontiff, from the very first months of his reign, set about the slow work of surely winning the confidence and respect of both the emperor and his chancellor by a masterly series of encyclical letters, containing the fundamental lessons of social wisdom so needful to Germany in face of Socialism, Rationalism, and Naturalism; so necessary to all governments and peoples in the present age of revolution.

It is certain that, when the first news of his election was announced, it was asked whether Leo XIII would not succeed in settling the "German difficulty." His reputation as a diplomat, a statesman, and a scholar greatly favored him in Germany.

---

[4] The journal *Reichsbote* for October, 1878, quoted from Count Murphy's "Chair of Peter."

It is a most instructive lesson to hear from Prince Bismarck's own lips an account of the advances made by him to the new Pope. As we already know, one of the first acts of the Holy Father was to write to the Emperor William, notifying his Majesty of his election and expressing his deep regret at the rupture between Germany and the Holy See. Now, what says the German chancellor?

"Never did we lose sight of the fact that the 'May Laws' were 'laws of conflict,' but that, nevertheless, their object was to lead to peace. Now [in April, 1886] the public journals tell me that since the battle of Olmütz no such a disgraceful concession has been asked of Prussia [as the revision of the 'May Laws' and the closing of the Kulturkampf]. They cast up to me that I am going to Canossa. But in the same discourse [of 1875] in which I said we would not go to Canossa—and this I repeat to-day—I explained clearly what should be understood by going to Canossa. ...

"I added that the government owed it to their Catholic subjects to persist in seeking a means, a way of regulating in the most conciliating manner the borders which separate the domain of the temporal from that of the spiritual power, the limits necessary for the interior peace of the realm.

"The hope entertained meanwhile that a Pontiff more disposed to peace might appear was realized three years after this last discourse of mine; and I remember what Leo XIII said, soon after his accession, in one of his encyclicals[5] in 1878:

---

[5] No such words are found in the encyclicals of 1878. But in the letter addressed by the Pope, on December 24 of that year, to the Archbishop of Cologne are these eloquent words: "As it was ... our purpose from the beginning of our Pontificate, so we endeavored to induce both sovereigns and nations to live at peace and friendship with the Church. As to you, Venerable Brother, you are aware that we at an early day bent our mind on obtaining for the noble German nation, after settling all their differences, the blessings and fruits of a lasting peace; nor is it less known to you that, in so far as we are concerned, no pains were spared to attain an end so glorious and so worthy of our care. Whether, however, what we have undertaken and are trying to bring about shall have a successful issue, He knoweth from whom cometh every blessing and who hath given us this ardent zeal and

"'Thus we shall continue to labor for the German nation in the midst of obstacles of every kind; nor shall our soul ever know rest until peace be restored to the Church in that country.'

"I believe, my lords, that the passages I here recall are sufficient to show how baseless is the assertion that we ever considered these laws of conflict against the Church as a basis on which to build up the durable future of the Empire or of Prussia.

"In pursuance of the purpose I was just explaining to you, I began, as soon as the present Pope ascended the throne, to open *publici juris* negotiations with Monsignor Masella [the Nuncio in Munich] which gave hope of a good issue, and which lasted till Cardinal Franchi became Secretary of State [March 9, 1878], and were afterwards suspended."[6]

It is evident from this extract not only that Prince Bismarck was anxious for peace and more than willing to withdraw from the untenable position "on the domain of the spiritual power "in which the May Laws placed the Prussian government—the Imperial government of Germany, in fact—in the eyes of the civilized world. Further on in the same memorable discourse he frankly admits that the results of the Kulturkampf were, if not disastrous to the state, at least unworthy of the conflict itself; "When the action of the

---

wish for peace.

"But, no matter how things turn out, we must yield to the divine will, continuing as long as life lasts to cherish the same intense zeal and to persevere in the fulfilment of the duty put upon us. ... Wherefore none of the obstacles opposed to us on every side shall divert us from the purpose of seeking the salvation of all, and therefore of your nation. *For our heart shall never be able to rest* so long as, to the great loss of souls, we shall see the bishops of the Church condemned (as if guilty) or banished from their country, the priestly ministry surrounded by a network of difficulties, religious communities and pious congregations dispersed, and the training of youth, not even excepting young clerics, withdrawn from the authority and watchfulness of the bishops" ("Acta," ii. 167, 168).

[6] Translated, from the full report of Prince Bismarck's speech in the Prussian House of Lords, April 14, 1886.

government and the administration on the clergy is limited to our becoming the rivals of the ecclesiastical authorities and of the Pope himself, then we fall into the chief blunder of the May Laws, which vitiated this entire system of legislation. We began a great strategic movement with mighty forces and very trifling results; we only created strife and opposition, because, in my judgment, we aimed at achieving what was impossible. This strategy against the clergy will always bring about unpleasantness and leave the government in the rear among the ranks of the minority."

Thus, then, we know that in the war against the Catholic Church, as in that against France a few years previously, Bismarck had pushed into the enemy's territory with overwhelming forces, occupying the very heart of the country, and compelling peace at any price, in so far as he could make the Church surrender everything but what the divine law alone forbade to yield. But he found that in ravaging the "domain of the Church "he was ruining the dearest interests of the monarchy. And, wise man as he is, he only wished for a safe and honorable means of retreating from a position it was a crime in morals and a blunder in politics to have ever occupied.

At any rate, in 1880 the very political and financial necessities of the German chancellor compelled him to make some steps toward conciliation. Concessions were made in the parliamentary sessions of 1880 and 1881. In January of the latter year Von Windthorst introduced into the Lower Prussian Chamber a bill relieving priests from all punishment for saying Mass or administering the sacraments. Both the law thus introduced and the penal law it modified remind one forcibly of the legislation of the two first Stuarts in England and Ireland, as well as of the unrepealed Penal Laws which weighed on Irish Catholics just a century ago. Englishmen at present are rather ashamed of this unchristian and barbarous code; and one may well wonder that in the last quarter of the nineteenth century a man of Prince Bismarck's enlightened mind and liberal professions should not have hesitated to employ such weapons as the Falk Laws, or that a nation like the Prussians, so proud of their culture and their rank in Europe, should have applauded or even tolerated such a policy. It was taking up the antiquated, blood-stained, and rusty instruments of coercion and persecution used by Elizabeth and the Stuarts, by Cromwell and his Commonwealth, and by the successors of William III down to our own times. But as these weapons failed in Ireland in their immediate purpose of conversion or perversion of a people—failed, indeed, in everything excepting in exterminating an ancient race and sowing their hearts with bitter memories—so did they and must they fail in Germany. And so must they in Poland.

As the pacific and conciliatory policy of Leo XIII gained ground in Germany, and the power of the Catholic party, the Center, both in the Prussian and in the Imperial Parliament, became more necessary to the government, the tendency to measures of greater leniency became more apparent. But the European press, the so-called liberal press especially, had early asked the question whether the German emperor and his chancellor would not go to Canossa, as had done the Emperor Henry IV in the time of the seventh Gregory. The question was repeated as a watchword and must have had no little influence on a man of Bismarck's temper.

Be that as it may, on June 5, 1883, a very important law called the Church Bill was introduced by Herr Von Puttkamer, who had taken Dr. Falk's place in the Prussian ministry. The bill contained six clauses modifying the most odious and oppressive features of the existing legislation. It was passed by 224 votes against 107.

The very partial mitigation thus obtained was accepted by Catholics only as some slight evidence on the part of the government of a disposition to yield. But although Dr. Falk had resigned, and some of the law's which bore his name had been, nominally at least, repealed, the May Laws remained like a sword suspended over the head of every Catholic man, woman, and child in Prussia, nay, in all the German Empire.

We have seen, by the letter of the Archbishop of Cologne

quoted above, and dated two years after the passing of this law, how deplorable in 1885 was the condition of Prussian Catholics. The testimony of the Catholic Union of the Rhineland, assembled in congress in May, 1884, leaves no room to question the sad condition of their Church. "The Archbishops of Cologne and Posen have been superseded," the Union state in a brief summary of their grievances, "and the other Prussian prelates are liable at any moment to be dealt with in like manner. Upwards of one thousand parishes are bereaved. In the archdiocese of Posen priests are still deprived of their salaries. ... All the seminaries for priestly education have been closed. The Royal Ecclesiastical Court continues to exist, as a monument of the oppression of Catholics. Priests are still liable to be expelled from their country at a moment's notice. Most of the Religious Orders have been suppressed. The few remaining are oppressed."[7]

In September of the same year, and on the eve of the Parliamentary elections, the Catholic members, led by Von Windthorst, issued an address to the electors, in which they say among other things: "The so-called Kulturkampf is by no means ended. It is true that the flood has somewhat subsided, but the current is still running high. Let Catholics beware when these waters become still and stagnant; their poisonous exhalations would be much more fatal to the national life than when the furious flood was at its highest. This is the real evil, the most formidable evil, from which Germany suffers. To counteract it, to extirpate it, is our chief and most patriotic task."[8]

One great disturbing element contributing not a little to prejudice the cause of the German Catholics, to nourish the hostility of Prince Bismarck and the National party, and to prevent the progress of negotiations with the Holy See, was the Polish question. The Poles were Catholics, and, as such, fell

---

7 Quoted from "Chair of Peter," p. 406.

8 *Ibidem.*

under the same proscriptive legislation. But their unquenchable yearning for a restoration of their own nationality, the calamitous attempts to raise aloft the standard of their lost cause, the covert or open agitation which evermore stirred the populations of the Polish provinces annexed to the kingdom of Prussia—all these sacred feelings and aspirations of a dismembered country with a glorious past constituted, in the eyes of the founders of the German Empire and the assertors of Teutonic supremacy, a permanent danger to the Fatherland and its newly established unity.

The one unpardonable sin in the Catholic Parliamentary party in Germany was, all along, their sympathy with the suffering Poles; this community of religion threw upon all Prussian Catholics the shadow of suspicion that they were not the well-wishers of the empire. This prejudice met the Pope at every turn in his unremitting labors for the religious pacification of Prussia.

Even at our present writing, when the last vestiges of the Kulturkampf are being removed one after the other, like a terrific thunder-storm retiring beyond the Vosges and the Alps to devastate other lands, the noble band of men led by Von Windthorst are to the Prussian government an object of fear and suspicion because they will not give up their generous sympathies for their Polish brethren.

It is a pity that Prince Bismarck cannot learn the truth which has taken possession of Gladstone's great mind and greater heart in his latest but most glorious years, and see that conciliation is more powerful to bind people to people, and race to race than coercion; and that the Pole can be made the generous friend and the devoted ally of the German by equal and just laws, by a large-minded share of religious freedom, by that practical brotherly love and equality which Christianity teaches. Make Prussian Poland the happiest portion of the German Empire, and it will be the most faithful. It will be like an impassable barrier between Germany and Russian aggression.

If you would make the Poles forget their lost nationality,

then treat them as a privileged and favored portion of your subjects, so as to convince them that they have found in your government something better than they could hope for under a separate and independent nationality.

At any rate, we do not believe, after the long and sad experience of Ireland, in the policy of expropriating, directly or indirectly, an ancient and proud race. Their native land is their own. God has given them a right to it. It would be wisdom in their rulers to make life in it prosperous, contented, happy for all its inhabitants. Sow their souls with justice and kindness, and you will reap a rich harvest of love, of gratitude, of eternal fidelity.

The new religious law in Prussia, virtually cancelling the existing anti-Catholic legislation, was finally voted by the Prussian Chamber on May 9, 1886, and sanctioned by the king on May 21.

It was a splendid triumph for Leo XIII.

CHAPTER XXX

LEO XIII AND HIGHER STUDIES

EVERY ONE who had known the extraordinary zeal shown by Cardinal Pecci, as Bishop of Perugia, for the advancement of education and the promotion of the highest Christian philosophy as the basis of all true learning, was prepared to see him, when elevated to the Pontifical throne, lend his supreme authority and influence to the fostering of a solid and complete education in every diocese within the Church. We have already seen what he undertook and accomplished in Rome, from the very beginning of his Pontificate, for the benefit of the laboring classes. Not one portion of the children or of the youth of Rome, not even apprentices and young artisans imperfectly educated, escaped the fatherly solicitude of the Pope. Knowing how determined the governmental and municipal authorities were on possessing themselves of every existing school to which they could lay claim by any legal artifice, or of which they could obtain the direction by the utmost stretch of power, the Pope endeavored to be beforehand with them in establishing day and night schools with teachers on whose religious principles he could rely. In that way he succeeded in saving thousands of Roman children, and numbers of boys and young people in need of instruction and eager to obtain it, from being swept into the nets of the anti-Catholic and anti-Christian proselytism spread in every street of Rome.

We have already mentioned the admirable letter written to Cardinal Monaco la Valletta, his vicar-general in Rome, on this very matter. We shall presently see another brief but pregnant and no less admirable letter to Cardinal Parocchi, who succeeded Cardinal La Valletta in his charge. The letter to

Cardinal Parocchi, however, entirely relates to the higher literary studies of the Roman clergy. And this brings us to see what Leo XIII undertook and accomplished in the matter of higher studies.

What all who knew Leo XIII especially expected of him, in the matter of higher studies, was to see him carry out through the universal Church the design so happily conceived in Perugia, and partially executed there, of restoring to its ancient splendor the Christian philosophy which had its birth in the very first age of the Church, receiving its form and developments from the early Apologists and Fathers, and attaining under St. Thomas Aquinas, in the thirteenth century, its scientific maturity.

The reader who in the preceding chapters has followed with any attention the logical sequence of Cardinal Pecci's pastoral letters must have seen that he traces all the moral aberrations and political disorders of our age and of modern times to the introduction, in the sixteenth century particularly, of a false and anti-Christian philosophy, which ignores any authority superior to individual reason, eliminates all the supernatural order from the domain of the' intellect and of private and social life, and enthrones naturalism, rationalism, and individualism as the law-givers in thought and action of human society.

While, in his first encyclicals, he clearly warns not only his brother-bishops, but governments, the entire Catholic flock, and all civilized peoples whom his voice may reach, of the necessity of returning, if society would be saved from imminent ruin, to obedience to the Church, to the docile acceptance of the teaching of the one divinely appointed authority on earth, he affirms that the false wisdom or philosophy which the last three centuries have followed must be set aside and Christian wisdom and philosophy made the light of all education.

A false and fatal education, in conformity with the naturalism and rationalism above mentioned, has, like the flickering of a "will-o'-the-wisp "in a dark night, led modern society into the marshes in which it is floundering. Religion, Christianity, Catholicism must now come with the steady, unfailing lamp of her divine philosophy, extricate social order from its mortal peril, and lead it back to the old paths.

This false education, this anti-Christian training of more than three hundred years has misled and ruined the Christendom reared by the Church; the old educational methods must be put in use again.

And Thomas Aquinas must once more be enthroned as "the Angel of the Schools "; his method and doctrine must be the light of all higher teaching, for his works are only revealed truth set before the human mind in its most scientific form.

Let there be no misunderstanding in this Leo XIII's teaching. He is not for setting aside as pernicious, or useless, or hostile to revelation what Christian theologians, philosophers, and scientists acknowledge and accept as true science. Writing on February 24, 1880, to the Archbishop of Cologne, he clearly expresses the value he sets on such science, while affirming the necessity of the counter-education we are here describing:

"The pest of Socialism, ... which so deeply perverts the sense of our populations, derives all its power from the darkness it causes in the intellect by hiding the light of the eternal truths, and from its corrupting the rule of life laid down by Christian morality; it can never be extirpated till the minds of its dupes are brought back to a clear knowledge of the supremely true and supremely good. ... To bring them thus back ... is our duty. ... For, albeit in our age such wonderful and incredible progress—as all confess—has been made in the arts pertaining to the comfort of life as well as in the natural sciences, nevertheless the corruption of public manners goes on daily increasing. And as the history of past times has taught us that what brings erring nations back from the wrong path and preserves them from ruin is not progress in the arts or natural sciences, but their fervor in learning and fulfilling the law of Christ, we therefore ardently desire that the Church should everywhere be in the full enjoyment of her liberty, that she may bestow on the nations the benefits of this saving doctrine."[1]

There is in the Pontiff's mind and purpose no antagonism to true progress and the legitimate developments of all the arts and sciences; for these follow naturally, inevitably on the increase in Christian knowledge and Christian morality in all communities. But what he aims at is to make the fulness of truth, natural and supernatural, the very life of the mind by setting both the one and the other before it stripped of all doubt and error, like the pure light presented to the sound bodily eye, entering it of its own accord and giving that organ its life by placing it in the full enjoyment of its proper object. And not that only, but the Pontiff aims at giving to the will, in this perfect light of the natural and supernatural world made known to it the moral law of Christ, embracing not only what God has Written on our hearts in the law of nature, but the supernatural law of love and divine self-sacrifice which the Father has written for us in luminous letters in the words and actions of Christ, His Incarnate Son.

The philosophy of St. Thomas, the philosophy off Christianity, does but place every follower of Christ in the heart of these concentric worlds, the natural and the supernatural orders, and enlighten him perfectly on his relations and his duties to both.

Leo XIII entertained the most firm conviction that all education should be reformed on Christian principles; that all the appliances of modern progress should be used to make Christian truth and Christian morality lovely to the young; that the Christian home should be like that of Nazareth in which Christ was brought up, parents there considering themselves bound in conscience to regard and to rear each child of theirs as "a child of God," whose life was to be modelled on that of the Incarnate Son. What his ideas about instruction and education in elementary and intermediary schools are we know already. What they should be in the

[1] "Acta" ii. 43-46.

university or professional stage he informs us in his encyclicals on St. Thomas Aquinas and the numerous letters written to men of every nation to encourage and stimulate them in their efforts to restore Christian philosophy by making the great works of St. Thomas the basis of their studies and teaching.

Not before the 4th of August, 1879, could Leo XIII find time to complete and publish the wonderful document by which he authoritatively declared that the Thomistic philosophy should in all Catholic schools be the source from which the professors should borrow their doctrine and their method. To the non-Catholic world this encyclical was represented as an attempt to make the modern intellectual world retrograde to the scholasticism of the middle ages, and to put on the mind all the fetters of the old un-progressiveness. This could only be said by the thoroughly ignorant or the deeply prejudiced. Theodore Beza and Bucer were wont to say that if the works and method of Thomas Aquinas were taken from the defenders of Catholicism, its doctors would soon be driven from the field of controversy and their Church itself overturned.

But Leo XIII's purpose was not to arm the controversialists of the Church of Rome with victorious weapons against Protestantism; the needs of the age go far beyond that. In our day it is the whole structure of revealed truth, the whole body of religious truth as such, and as distinguished from a godless, spiritless materialism, that the teachers and preachers of Catholic doctrine have to defend and to hold up to the admiration of the educated intelligence of the age.

"The Eternal Father s only-begotten Son, who appeared upon earth to bring down among men salvation with the light of divine wisdom, conferred upon the world a truly great and admirable benefit when, about to reascend to heaven, He bade His apostles 'to go forth and teach all nations,'[2] and thus left the Church which He had founded to be the common and

[2] St Matthew xxviii. 19.

supreme teacher of all peoples. Mankind, freed by truth, must be preserved by truth; the fruits of heavenly teaching in which man found his salvation should have been but short-lived unless Christ, our Lord, had instituted an everlasting teaching authority to convey faith to all minds. The Church, therefore, thus strengthened by the promises of her Divine Founder and imitating His charity, so fulfilled His commands that she always had for sole purpose and chiefly sought this one thing, to have His religion observed and to make a perpetual war on error. Toward accomplishing this purpose bishops bestow their vigilance and their labors; toward this; councils make laws and decrees; and this is the subject of the daily care of the Roman Pontiffs, to whom, as to Peter's, the Prince of the Apostles, successors in the primacy, belongs the office of teaching and confirming in the faith their brothers."

Such is the beginning of this encyclical, the appearance of which marks what may be called a new era in intellectual philosophy, at least in so far as the Catholic Church is concerned. The Pope, after demonstrating the utility of philosophy, "on which all the other sciences depend in a great measure for their own right constitution," insists on the circumstances of the present age, which requires "a philosophical doctrine that has an equal regard for the rules of faith and the dignity of all human science." "If the intellect is sound and firmly based on solid and true principles, its light will become the source of manifold benefits both to the individual and to the community. ... It is quite in conformity with the order of Providence to ask human science to lend its aid in bringing the nations back to faith and health. This was the wise and clever method of which the most illustrious Fathers of the Church frequently mad-e use, as antiquity attests. These same Fathers considered that reason played a manifold and an important part, which the great St. Augustine defined in these pregnant terms: *attributing to this* [*philosophic*] *science ... the reason why* salutary faith ... is begotten, is fostered, is protected, is strengthened.[3]

The encyclical goes on to show how philosophy (that is, a right and scientific use of reason) prepares the way for faith, demonstrates by her own native power many fundamental truths of religion—such as the existence of God, His creation and government of the world, etc.—the nature and attributes of the Deity, and others which "are proposed for our belief by revelation, or which are closely connected with the supernatural order." The early Fathers made use of this method to show the reasonableness of Christianity.

This scientific use of reason, or of the pagan philosophy in so far as it was based on true principles, so common among the early Christian apologists, is compared by the Pope "to the gold and silver vessels and rich vestments borrowed by the Hebrews from their Egyptian masters. ... These spoils, which till then had been used in shameful rites and vain superstitions, were devoted to the service of the true God." So did Gregory of Neo-Caesarea praise Origen for employing the intellectual armor of the heathen in combating their errors. So did a host of others among the early Christian writers.

"If natural reason could produce so plentiful a crop of good fruit before Christ came to bestow on it fecundity, how much richer will the harvest be when His saving grace restores and increases the native powers of the human mind!

"Is it not, then, evident that this manner of philosophizing opens up a level and easy road to faith?"

Continuing this line of argument, the encyclical goes on to show what truths of the religious order natural reason is capable of attaining to and proving—the existence of God, His perfections and attributes; the miraculous and supernatural origin and character of the Gospel doctrine; the foundation of the Church by Christ, "because (as the Vatican Council has decreed) of its eminent propagation, its surpassing holiness, and its exhaustless fecundity in all places; because of its

---

[3] *St. Augustine,* De Trinit., *lib. xiv. 1:* huic scientia tribuens ... illud quo fides saluberrima ... gignitur, nutritur, defenditur, roboratur.

Catholic unity, its unshaken stability, it produces a great and perpetual motive of credibility, and an irrefragable testimony to its own divine mission.

"Based on these firm foundations, philosophy is called into frequent and perpetual use, in order to impart to theology the nature, the condition, and the character of a true science. The whole body of revealed doctrines must be bound together in its various parts, each fitting in its own place and deriving from its proper principles, so that their coherence and connection may be evident; and, finally, all and each must be supported by respectively proper and irrefutable arguments."

This—passing over the history of Christian philosophy—brings us to the last complete and perfectly scientific form which Thomas Aquinas gave to it in his two great works, the "Summa Theologiae" and the "Summa contra Gentiles," which are the most wonderful treatises of natural theology in existence. In the first chapters relating to Joachim Pecci's labors in Perugia we described the peculiar method of St. Thomas. Here we merely add what Leo XIII says of his eminence as a scholar and teacher:

"Among the doctors of the [mediaeval] schools St. Thomas stands forth by far the first and the master of all. As Cajetan has remarked, *because he had a sovereign veneration for all the ancient doctors, he seems to have united in himself the intellectual powers of them all.*

"Their teachings, which were like the scattered members of the same body, he put together and completed, arranging them in a marvellous order, and giving them such wonderful increase that he is justly held to be the great defender and glory of the Catholic Church.

"A man by nature fond of learning and quick-witted, with a ready and retentive memory, of irreproachable virtue, a devoted lover of truth, with a mind enriched with all human and divine knowledge, as the sun he warmed the earth with the vital power of his sanctity and filled it with the light of his doctrine. He wrote on every part of philosophy with equal penetration and solidity. His disputations embrace the laws of reasoning, God and incorporeal substances, man and all things accessible to our senses, human acts and their principles. And in all these you have never to regret the absence of abundance in the rich accumulation of subject-matters, or of a fit arrangement of parts, or excellence in the method of proceeding, or solidity of principles, or cogency in the arguments, or clearness and propriety in the diction, or facility in explaining what is most difficult.

"To this we must add that the Angelic Doctor extended the sphere of his philosophical conclusions and speculations to the very reasons and principles of things, opening out the widest field for study, and containing within themselves the germs of an infinity of truths, an exhaustless mine for future teachers to draw from at the proper time and with rich results. As he used the same intellectual process in refuting error, he succeeded in combating single-handed all the erroneous systems of past ages, and supplied victorious weapons to the champions of truth against the errors which are to crop up in succession to the end of time.

"Besides this, while very properly distinguishing reason from faith, he binds them both together in friendly accord without violating the rights of either or forgetting what is; due to their respective dignity. In this way reason, in St. Thomas, rises to such sublime heights that human nature can fly no higher, nor can faith hope from reason greater or more powerful aid than she receives in the pages of St. Thomas.

"This it was which, in past ages especially, impelled men most eminent as theologians and philosophers to collect together the immortal writings of St. Thomas, and to devote themselves not merely to study his angelic wisdom but to I feed their souls upon it."

The supreme honor paid to this great man's incomparable merit was the homage paid to his works and authority by the ecumenical councils held since the thirteenth century, from that of Lyons to that of the Vatican. In the Council of Trent the "Summa" of St. Thomas was placed on the altar by the side of the Gospels, as being the most perfect and scientific exposition of revealed truth.

This encyclical created great enthusiasm among Catholic scholars in every land. The intellectual activity which it called forth and promoted in all Catholic schools of philosophy and theology was accompanied by increased efforts to make the accord between reason and faith, so beautifully praised by the Pontiff, still more effective in modern Catholic universities, where Science, in the fullest acceptation of the term, should be shown to be the able and willing auxiliary of revelation.

The Holy Father hastened to establish in Rome an Academy of St. Thomas Aquinas, in which the very best scholars the Church can boast of and her foremost scientists should labor side by side to build up the magnificent edifice of philosophical science as Thomas Aquinas conceived it and as modern times require it. The Sovereign Pontiff commissioned some select scholars to prepare a perfect edition of the works of the saint.

Meanwhile, by the orders of His Holiness, the high schools of philosophy and theology in Rome were so enlarged as to accommodate select youths from the dioceses of Italy, who would receive in Rome the very best culture the capital of the Christian world could afford, and would return to their own dioceses to elevate the intellectual standard there, and to form in their turn superior men, thoroughly grounded in true philosophy, and thereby enabled to rise themselves and to lift up others with them to the highest sacred science.

But the Holy Father's chief zeal was bestowed on the clergy of his own diocese of Rome. Just as he was laboring to make the students belonging to the nationalities of the Greek rite accomplished Greek scholars, writers, and orators, in order to insure greater success to their apostolate among their countrymen, so would he have the Roman secular clergy accomplished men of letters, wielding with the most perfect skill their own native Italian and the purest Latin diction of the ancient Romans, as well as that exquisite Greek idiom which Demosthenes, Sophocles, and Plato made the most perfect vehicle of noble thought ever used by man.

He therefore founded for his seminarians a course of higher literary studies in Italian, Latin, and Greek, to which the most distinguished for talent should be admitted at the end of the ordinary college curriculum. They were to be provided with the very best professors to be found, the execution of the whole project being entrusted to that excellent scholar, writer, and orator, as well as model priest and bishop, Cardinal Parocchi, the Pope's vicar.

The letter in which Leo. XIII's will in this regard is made known is dated May 20, 1885:

"You understand perfectly," the letter says, "what we have often said, and not without good reason, that serious and continual efforts should be made to have the clergy distinguish themselves in all branches of knowledge. The needs of the present age imperatively require it. Intellectual culture advances so rapidly, and the appetite for learning is so insatiable, that the clergy would find themselves at a disadvantage for the proper and fruitful discharge of their duties if they did not merit for their order the same reputation for intellectual culture of which other professions are so ambitious.

"This is why we have bestowed so much care and thought on the best methods of culture for our young seminarians. Beginning by the most serious matters of study, we have endeavored to revive the doctrine and method of St. Thomas Aquinas in philosophy and theology.

"But since literature occupies so large a space in college studies, and contributes such large stores to our knowledge for all the purposes of social life and all its humanities and graces, we have resolved to lay down certain lines on which letters have to be cultivated."

After showing at length the advantages to be obtained from high literary culture, Leo XIII continues: "It is on account of these practical advantages that the Catholic Church, which truly values all that is honorable, all that is beautiful, all that is praiseworthy, has always attached to the culture of letters a due importance and has encouraged it in every way. We see that the Fathers of the Church were adorned with all the graces of the literary culture of their respective times. And there are some of them whose native genius and acquired literary art place them almost on a level with the most classic Greeks and Romans.

"Let us also say that the Church can claim the enviable merit of having saved from destruction the greatest part of the masterpieces of the ancient Greek and Latin poets, orators, and historians. Besides—a thing which every one knows—in the ages when the culture of letters was neglected or impossible, when literary fame was drowned amid the clash and tumult of arms all over Europe, letters found a refuge in the community-homes of the monks or the secular priesthood.

"Nor should we forget that among the Popes who have gone before us there are many who acquired distinguished fame in letters."[4]

Leo XIII mentions last among these cultured Popes Leo X, who was rather a patron of learning and literary men than a man of letters himself. He omits all mention of the glorious names of cultured Pontiffs who came after Leo—men, in our judgment, far more accomplished than even their own great predecessors before the sixteenth century.

Cardinal Parocchi was in his element when occupied in promoting advancement and excellence among the youth entrusted to him.

The Seminario Romano, the great school for the diocesan clergy, is organized on the highest level of culture. There is a department or college for Oriental philology, with a faculty of rare excellence. The dean is the illustrious Monsignor Ciasco, the light of the Augustinian Order, who is professor of Hebrew. The chairs of Greek, Arabic, Armenian, Syriac, and Copt are filled by men of the highest fame. But the "Pontifical Institute of High Literature," which the Pope officially founded by the letter just mentioned, is already in full operation. The students have given to the public specimens of their ability

4 "Acta," v. 61-65.

and progress.

The fact is that the very name of Leo XIII is an incentive to the acquisition of literary excellence. His example, his unceasing labors and generous patronage, have diffused throughout the entire body of the clergy a noble spirit of emulation and industry.

CHAPTER XXXI

LEO XIII AND FRANCE

1878-1886

NO PEOPLE, among all those who were the more special object of Leo XIII's pastoral solicitude during the first eight years of his Pontificate, occupied a greater place in his mind and his heart than the French Catholics—no, not even the populations of Italy, his own flesh and blood, and so closely connected with the name, the glories, and the very existence of Catholicity.

France, in spite of the tremendous changes effected by the Revolution of 1789-93 in the whole framework of French society, and in the very habits of thought, the very language, feelings, and conduct of the people; in spite even of the confiscation by Napoleon of the States of the Church and the imprisonment and exile of Pope and cardinals, was still, in the eyes of the whole civilized world, the foremost Catholic nation, as she continued to be, down to 1870-71, the leading nation in the political world.

But the change in the brilliant capital of France from what it was during the Universal Exposition of 1868-69 to what the government troops found it on wresting it from the Commune in 1872 was not more appalling than the change effected throughout the length and breadth of the country from 1878 to 1886. In the capital of the empire and in the empire itself, its institutions and government, the woeful transformation was not effected by the terrible war through which the country had passed, nor by any foreign might upsetting, destroying, and then rebuilding after its own caprice; the forces which had been at work destroying and removing what the first Revolution had spared of the fair and glorious edifice reared by twelve centuries of Christian civilization were forces from within, not from without—they were the fanatical anti-Christian, anti-social passions of Frenchmen themselves.

Why do we solicit the reader's attention to this unique spectacle in all history of the foremost of Christian nations laying violent hands on herself and extinguishing the very sources of her own life?

Simply to make American and English readers understand what a task Leo XIII, on ascending the papal throne on February 20, 1878, had to undertake in his endeavor to save religion in republican France.

From the days of Pope Stephen III (752-757), who first called in the P"ranks under Charles Martel to save Rome and the independence of the Pontifical office from the tyranny of the Lombards, down to the last years of Pius IX, the devotion of Catholic France to the Papacy was a traditional virtue. For one among her rulers who was harsh or tyrannical in his dealings with a Pope, there were ten at least who deemed it their duty and their glory to protect against all external violence the sacred principality which the sword of the great Charles Martel and that of his greater son, Charlemagne, had won for the Roman Church, and which their solemnly recorded acts and the jurisprudence of all Christendom guaranteed to the Holy See as the bulwark of its independence.

Leo XIII knew that if the wine of Jacobinism, with which the French Revolutionary armies were drunk in 1798-99, made them and their leaders commit such impious excesses, that they did not represent Catholic France. There was a Catholic France, oppressed by the Revolution, which survived, and its love afterward overflowed and flooded Rome, and that missionary world so dear to Rome, with its benefactions and heroic devotedness.

But Leo XIII on his accession found France in a worse and more hopeless plight than the seventh Pius found on his election in 1800. That gentle and saintly Pontiff's conciliatory spirit was able to prevail on Napoleon Bonaparte to set up anew the altars torn down by the Revolution.

But could Leo XIII prevent that same Revolution which

was in 1878 a living, mighty, overmastering spirit in France, from tearing down these altars anew, and making of the work of destruction this time a work as thorough as ungodliness armed with political omnipotence could effect?

All intelligent readers know that I am stating in its simplest terms the Problem—one which is still unsolved, while all Europe and all civilized peoples are anxiously watching if even Leo XIII's prudence, skill, and eloquence will be able to solve it in favor of religion.

And now will the reader be patient with us while we give a brief retrospect of that Catholic France, and endeavor to account for the existence of that mighty problem which at this moment religion and irreligion are both trying to solve, each in its own favor?

No Pope had ever to face such a difficulty as this French one, whose phases are still succeeding each other like the terrible scenes in Wagner s epic dramas, where all ends in the setting for ever of the sun of the old-time religion.

We Americans preserve glorious recollections of French missionary zeal on our continent. The French heralds of the Gospel had been at work among the native tribes in our forests before the Mayflower had touched the shores of New England. Our own Protestant historians have told the story of their sufferings and labors and have glorified the laborers.

How account for this twofold life, so contradictory in its principles, its aims, its deeds? We must, however, account for it if we would understand what is now passing before our eyes, what perplexes the ordinary superficial observer, what is the most wonderful, if not the saddest, spectacle in the history of nations, and what is the heaviest cross which Leo XIII has to bear.

When in 1846 Joachim Pecci, on his way from London to Rome, paused awhile in the French capital, he was much struck by the amazing progress religion seemed to be making in the kingdom in spite of the strong Voltairean scepticism which survived the first Revolution, the First Empire, and the Bourbon Restoration, and had gained in intellectual predominance and social influence what it had lost in its early fanaticism and violence.

It is a lesson to be learned by all Christian peoples, the working of these two adverse principles, whose final struggle now claims all the pastoral care, all the preternatural wisdom and patience, that Leo XIII can bestow upon it.

Whatever mistakes Louis Philippe's government committed in its relations toward the Church from 1830 to 1848, it is certain that, both at home and abroad, the deep; religious spirit of French Catholics displayed extraordinary zeal in creating institutions of every kind for education, charity, and beneficence. The religious revival which had begun under the first Napoleonic Empire and had continued under the restored Bourbons produced marvellous results under the Orleanist monarchy. It was like an arctic springtide, the whole land bursting forth into a miraculous bloom of apostolic fecundity. Religious orders of men and women sprang up everywhere, and the old missionary spirit of the French—one of the mightiest forces at the command of the Church to spread the Christian name—covered Asia and America with bands of heroic men and women solely devoted to the propagation of the faith among the heathen or its extension on the unoccupied territories of the New World.

This admirable missionary spirit was only a new form of the living faith which sent Godfrey de Bouillon to Palestine, St. Louis to the plague-stricken Delta of the Nile, and again to his death among the Saracens. It filled all classes in France during the crusading ages, from the royal family and the highest nobility down to the peasant and the artisan. All were the soldiers of Christ. And this glorious; spirit was not confined to one sex: Frenchwomen had caught the sacred flame as well as the men. St. Louis had his young queen by his side all through that first African campaign when pestilence annihilated his army and left the feeble and sickly remnants with their sovereigns in the hands of the Moslem. The spirit of French womanhood in the following centuries found no unworthy representative in the heroic and saintly Joan of Arc, to whose virtues and true character even English scholars are now beginning to do full justice.

The early colonial history of our own North America is the history, principally, of the heroic missionaries of France. Robertson, Bancroft, Parkman, Kipp have vied with each other in describing the expeditions, the sufferings, the successes, the heroic lives crowned by a still more heroic death, of Jesuits, Franciscans, Dominicans, of the Sulpicians of Montreal and of the priests of the Seminary of Quebec, the advance guards of Christ and civilization on all the mighty continent between the Gulf of St. Lawrence and the long line of the Pacific coast. And if the Christian manhood of France was worthily represented in these far-off times by Jogues and Goupil, by Lallemand, Brébeuf, and Rasles, by Champlain and La Salle and Marquette, French womanhood blossomed forth in such glorious names as Marie de l'Incarnation, the foundress of the Quebec Ursulines, and Marguerite Bourgeoys, the foundress of the Sisters of Notre Dame of Montreal.[1]

There was no intermission in that wonderful apostolic fervor which glowed in French bosoms down to the dreadful days of the Reign of Terror. What sublime heights of heroism the Christian men and women of France displayed all through that period of massacres and persecutions every school-boy and school girl knows at present. Their supernatural virtue shone at home in France while the guillotine was *enpermanence* and mowed down its harvests night and day, and when the prisons were full of the noblest, the purest, the best—the hecatombs whose blood washed away the sins of the three preceding generations. And abroad the exiles who found their way to the shores of Great Britain and of America, were not their very lives the Gospel law in practice? All along our Atlantic seaboard and in the interior, all through the vast regions drained by the Hudson, the Susquehanna, the St. Lawrence, the Ohio, the Mississippi, and the Missouri, the exiled priests of France labored fruitfully everywhere, leaving

---

[1] See "Heroic Women of the Bible and the Church," last chapter.

behind names revered alike by Protestant and by Catholic, names to be ever blessed by those who have succeeded to their labors and glory in being their spiritual children: Cheverus in New England, Dubois and Bruté and Marechal in our Middle States, Flaget and his noble associates in the West, Dubourg and Odin in New Orleans—these are only a few among a host of great and good men who brought with them from France the inextinguishable fire of apostolic zeal and priestly virtue to our shores. In Canada, too, these saintly fugitives found a refuge, a home, and a congenial field. He who writes these lines treasures as one of the dearest recollections of his boyhood the memory and friendship of these French refugees.

The scepticism popularized in France by Voltaire and the Encyclopedists, and the fearful moral corruption implanted in court and castle, in city and country, by the example of Louis XIV and Louis XV, had not quenched in the France of St. Louis the living faith and the chivalrous zeal of the crusader-king.

Yes, truly, the Church of France, much as it had suffered in the great Revolution, profoundly as it had been modified by the changes which the First Consul had exacted from Pius VII, and fiercely as it had been assailed and thwarted and restricted by political parties, by the formidable sceptic press, and by unfriendly governments, was in 1846, when Monsignor Pecci visited the splendid capital of the Orleans monarchy, a majestic edifice with its foundations solidly resting on the reverence and devotion of the masses, and doing its work with an enlightened and exemplary clergy, and through the instrumentality of institutions which had not their equal in numbers nor their superior in excellence in any Catholic country, save, perhaps, in Italy and within the Papal States.

And everything in the Church of France went on progressing in excellence after the downfall of Louis Philippe, during the short-lived Republic of 1848-52, and even under the corrupting and demoralizing reign of the last Napoleon—everything: Religious Orders, establishments of education, charity, and beneficence, schools of every grade, from the infant-asylum schools up to the numerous Jesuit colleges which rivalled on every point of France the lyceum colleges of the French University, and confessedly surpassed them in literary and scientific efficiency, as they most assuredly did in the religious training their great schools gave to Catholic youth. Look back and remember how admirably organized was, in every diocese of France, the methods of pulpit and catechistical instruction devised by the bishop and his clergy for the mental training of all classes of their people. We, who were brought up among a people where Sunday preaching and Sunday-schools and Christian Doctrine Societies were standing and flourishing popular institutions, cannot recall without wonder what we beheld in France during well-nigh eight years spent there, mixing with all ranks of her people as a missionary, speaking their own tongue, and laboring among them in the capital as well as in the provincial cities and country parts. Every bishop vied with his brother bishop in devising every possible method for conveying religious instruction to young and old. Think of the great names which adorned the French pulpit under the last Bourbons, Louis Philippe, and Napoleon. And those whose eloquence shone in the cathedrals outside of Paris were men who must have shone anywhere by their superior gifts. Add to this the glorious Catholic literature which addressed itself to the quick French intelligence in every walk of life, and which aimed at counteracting the terrible propaganda of error, corruption, unbelief, socialism, and revolutionism, of which the French University, independent of the Church and supported by the treasure and the influence of the state, was only one mighty ally, and not by any means the mightiest.

The official teaching in the French University was, as is notorious, leavened by scepticism when at its best in the present century; it always combated the Church, discredited Christianity, ridiculed the clergy, and held them up to hatred or suspicion when it did not hold them up to contempt. The French medical schools taught the baldest materialism; the French law schools a rampant Erastianism; the French scientific and military schools laughed at all religion and turned out practical atheists. French novels and the French theatre, aided by all the charms of exquisite elegance of diction and the fascinations of the stage and the opera, taught and sang but one thing—the triumph of vice. Think of Eugene Sue, and Alexandre Dumas, and Balzac, and George Sand, and a host of others who only lacked a little of the pre-eminence in evil of those we have named. And the French daily and periodical press! With the exception of the few excellent journals which defended the cause of religion, journalistic literature in France, the ablest, cleverest, most fascinating in the world, was in the hands of scepticism, unbelief, and all those then secret and mighty organizations which, by various methods, were working out one purpose—the overthrow in France of the Church and of social order.

Such were, on both sides, the antagonistic forces at work as Joachim Pecci had beheld them on the spot, and continued to watch ever at Perugia. It is in the moral world as in the physical—a tyro can construe what is known as the parallelogram of forces, and deduce from the figure, by a very simple calculation, the resultant. On which side, in France, was arrayed the mightiest sum of moral force? On that of irreligion and revolution. All the power and influence of government, legislature, of the University and the army of professors and teachers in its pay, of the press, the theatre, the clubs, all the training of the great schools which fed the army, the navy, the various departments of engineering in a great manufacturing and commercial country, were on the side of irreligion; on the other there was a sum of active forces far inferior to those controlled by unbelief. The numerical majority, made up of the popular masses in the country, were indeed on the side of religion; but they were mere inert and inactive matter.

When, after thirty-two years, Joachim Pecci became Leo XIII, what saw he?

In what were the leading classes, as well as among the laboring population of the cities, there was a sum of active forces on the side of unbelief which far outbalanced those of religion. The former would hesitate at no violence to carry their ends. The latter could only use moral means; armed resistance, for them, was out of the question.

This was well known to the men who overthrew the MacMahon government and placed Jules Grévy in the presidential chair. They knew that if they could make up their minds to set aside all the laws which protected or favored religion in France, even the Concordat, and suppressed, one after the other, all the institutions of Catholicism, and set up the state, as in Italy, to be the absolute and irresistible master of property, of liberty, of life, that no leader would stand forth to bid Catholics arm and defend their homes, their altars, and their schools.

And, knowing this, they have acted on it, progressing year after year in their career of disfranchisement, confiscation, and oppression.

What could the Pope do? In France—let us say it openly—it was the secret societies which elected M. Grévy, as it was they who had upset Marshal MacMahon. Consequently the Church found itself, under the new regime, absolutely in the power of its deadliest foe. Was it to be thought that the foe who had been striving ever since 1816 to gain this very victory over the Church would forego his advantage? There could be no treaty of peace and amity between the two powers. One must perish, and that was Catholicism, in so far as human might can kill it.

And what was Leo XIII to do? What counsels could he give the French bishops, the French Catholic laity, Catholic journalists, and organized Catholic bodies in France? There was no alternative, since armed resistance was out of the question, but to be patient, to be united, to keep together, to help and sustain and cheer each other in a passive resistance which should make use of all the means of persuasion and all the force of public opinion won by putting all the wrong on the side of the enemy, and leaving it in the power of no man to censure justly word or act of the oppressed majority.

1880 came, and the Church of France found herself and all her glorious institutions, rights, and liberties at the mercy of Jules Ferry and Paul Bert.

Gambetta, the sworn enemy of the Church of his country, had risen to be prime minister, and had fallen; and then came his sudden death. His war-cry had been, Down with the clergy! He had made the term *clérical* as odious as hated as ever the name of Jesuit had been. But cléricalism, with him, meant more than the priest; it meant the religion, the belief, the worship of which he was the minister.

But even Gambetta, it was thought when he took the reins of administration in his hands, would be more conservative than his principles and former professions. So the propelling force behind him—the blind, pitiless, relentless force of the secret clubs—pushed him out of the way, and then came, after his death, the sweeping measures of suppression, confiscation, and persecution devised by the Ferry ministry.

The French bishops in this emergency were not to be silenced by the fear of state prosecutions or by the withdrawal of their salaries. The venerable Cardinal Guibert, Archbishop of Paris, sent to the government an eloquent and energetic protest against the suppression of the Religious Orders in France. It had no more effect, nor had the protests of his colleagues, in shaming the ministers and the legislature into a sense of right-doing than shouting at the rushing waters of Niagara or shaking one's fist at the mighty cataract could arrest for an instant the steady downpour of the great river.

What the nuncio in Paris, Monsignor Czacki, attempted or effected to second the resistance of the French hierarchy we need not detail here. His conduct was the theme of adverse and conflicting criticisms, But in October, 1880, while there still remained some faint hope of making the French government pause in their proscriptive measures, Leo XIII wrote to the French bishops, through the Cardinal-Archbishop of Paris, one of those stirring letters which are at one and the same time an appeal to the calm reason of statesmen, based on the highest principles of national self-interest, social order, religion, justice, and equity, and a plea addressed to the deepest sentiments of the heart—gratitude for past services and respect for the loftiest convictions and the noblest deeds of self-sacrifice.

The Religious Orders of both men and women had, the government pretended, arisen and taken root in France without the sanction of the law or in spite of its prohibitory statutes. The weakness of this plea—a shallow pretext which everybody saw through—was demonstrated by the fact that, when the edict of suppression was brought before the law-courts for their sanction and as a preliminary to immediate execution, upwards of five hundred magistrates resigned their position on the bench rather than sanction even by silent acquiescence the illegal and monstrous iniquity contemplated by the party in power.

To their solemn and indignant protest Leo XIII added his own.

He cannot accept the practical premise on which Jules Ferry and Paul Bert base their action—that the Church, in the full integrity of her vital organism and the full liberty of her action, has not a right to exist in France. She was there before the arrival of Clovis and his Franks; her influence and action were the civilizing and organizing forces which built up the nation; they helped mainly to give it the foremost place among those of Christendom and the world.

"Wherever the Catholic Church freely exists," Leo XIII writes, "there Religious Orders spontaneously grow up; they spring from the Church as the branch from the trunk of the tree. They are the auxiliaries whose help the bishops find to be especially necessary in our days, helping by their skill and industry the secular clergy in their ministrations, and relieving by Christian charity the needs of the poor."

He praises the cardinal for showing, in his eloquent letter to the government, "that there is no form of civil constitution to which Religious Orders are adverse or inimical; that it is for the interest of public order and peace to allow so many inoffensive citizens full freedom to lead a quiet and orderly life; that it does not beseem men who wish well to their countrymen to break in appearance with the religion which all profess, and to persecute the faith received from their parents and ancestors."

The great pretence of the men who are either opposed in theory to the existence of Monastic Orders in the Church, or who, in practice, are in favor of their extinction, is that they are only excrescences on the organism of the Church, and that she is better without them. To this the great teacher of Christendom replies:

"The distinguished men against whom the sword of the law was thus sharpened were the lawful offspring of the Church, carefully trained by her to all that is honorable in virtue and in literary culture. Civilization is immensely indebted to them in more than one respect, for their holy lives were to the people a perpetual exhortation to virtue, and their learning shed a lustre on the spheres' both of sacred and of profane knowledge; their immortal works have enriched every department of the fine arts."[2]

The mind of the Pope travels back to those ages when France was troubled by no religious divisions, when the entire mass of her people were of one religious faith and the laborious zeal of their clergy was taxed to the utmost.

"Whenever," he says, "there was a scarcity of secular priests, from the cloister issued bands of holy laborers, whose extraordinary wisdom and skill helped the bishops to foster piety among the people, to train youth to the knowledge of letters and the practices of a virtuous life.

"Of the missionaries sent to preach the Gospel to barbarous countries, the majority have been furnished by the monastic communities in France. Their labors in the cause of Christianity have spread the name of France with the light of the Gospel to the remotest nations of the earth.

"There is no sort of misery which can befall our common

---

[2] In the France of the nineteenth century it is needful only to mention, in sacred oratory, the names of Lacordaire and Monsabre among the Dominicans, those of De Ravignan and Felix among the Jesuits; in general learning and scholarship the names of Dom Guéranger and Cardinal Pitra, Benedictines, of Fathers Cahier and Martin, the authors of the grandest work of descriptive art of our times, "Les Vitraux de Bourges."

humanity that these religious men and women have not alleviated, no form of calamity known to us that they have not remedied—in hospitals, in asylums for the poorest of the poor, during the periods of peace and leisurely enjoyment in civil communities as well as amid the heat and turmoil of war. And all these ministrations they performed with that pitying gentleness which can only spring from divine charity. Of this charity you have before your eyes illustrious examples in every province and city and village."

The Pope then enumerates the testimonies given by leading men of every class to the merits and services of the Religious Orders. It was all in vain. Vainly also did the magistrates resign their seats upon the bench of justice. Equally vain were the remonstrances and protests of the French bishops. Nothing could save the doomed communities. The Jesuits, the Pope says, were the first expelled. "The nuncio in Paris was ordered to protest, and to declare that the Society of Jesus is not only guiltless of any crime, but deserving of all praise on account of the exalted merit of its members, for their learning, their charity, their zeal in educating youth. All France bears witness to their worth by entrusting its children to their care."

The nuncio's protest having produced no effect on the government, the Holy Father was about to raise his voice in remonstrance, condemning the acts of the persecutor, when it was proposed to him that the Religious Orders might be saved from suppression and dispersion if they would only unite in drawing up and signing a solemn declaration and pledge to the effect that they had no part and would have no part in political movements, and adhered to no political party.

This, the Sovereign Pontiff thought, violated no principle of Catholic doctrine or morality, while it would avert from the Church of France a measureless calamity. It would also wrest from the enemy a ready and powerful weapon of attack.

The proposal of such a pledge, however, fell like a bombshell among the justly alarmed and excited French Catholics. Their organs in the press discussed its opportuneness, its necessity, and its consequences with extreme warmth, the result of strong and sincere convictions.

The Holy See, anxious to save the mighty religious interests so seriously threatened in France, did not look with disfavor on such a united declaration. As a basis on which should repose this profession of neutrality as between mere conflicting political parties and opinions, the Pope sketches the nature and aim of monastic life. Their utter unworldliness in the midst of the world, and the sublime services which their spirit of detachment enables them to render, ought to protect them from the suspicion of worldly passions or political partisanship.

"A thing well and familiarly known to this Apostolic See," he says, "is the purpose for which, in the Catholic Church, men or women unite together to form religious societies. There is, first of all, the desire to promote in the members themselves the practice of spiritual perfection in the highest degree. As to the outward form of active life selected for itself by each order, their only aim is to help to secure the eternal salvation of their fellow-men or to aid in relieving the various forms of human suffering. This twofold course of activity is daily pursued in each order with marvellous assiduity and cheerfulness."

So much for the character of Religious Orders as such. Now, what should or might be their attitude toward the civil constitution and the political parties in the state?

"The Catholic Church neither blames nor condemns any form of state constitution. The institutions of the Church herself, deriving their origin from purposes of public utility, can flourish under any government, whether the executive or judiciary power be exercised therein by one or by more. As to the Apostolic See, which has to maintain relations with governments in the midst of political changes and revolutions, its sole purpose is to secure the interests of the Christian religion. It never intends, nor can intend, to violate the rights of any government, no matter by whom administered. It is, therefore, certain that in all things where we do no injustice to others we should obey those in authority. Nor by so obeying do we sanction whatever is wrong, either in the constitution or in the administration.

"Such being the rules of public conduct enjoined on all Catholics without distinction, there could be no objection to the declaration demanded of the Religious Orders.

"But it is not a little surprising that a proposal of this kind, entertained at a moment when the very weightiest interests were at stake, and for the purpose of saving both Church and state, should have found little favor with men otherwise estimable and known for their talent and zeal in defending Catholicism."

The controversy raised on this point was a sore matter on both sides of the Alps. What rendered the opposition of the journalists alluded to most distasteful to the Holy See was the fact that the declaration in question had the sanction of the French bishops.

It turned out, nevertheless, that this negotiation was only a trap laid by the government to create dissension in the Catholic ranks, to elicit expressions of opinion and sentiment that might enable MM. Ferry and Bert to strike with more visible grounds of justice such communities as would prove to be unyielding.

The Holy Father confesses the failure of this sort of compromise. "It is most sad to say," the letter goes on, "that the French government pursued its intended course. Every day brings us sad news from that country. The remaining Religious Orders are scattered and suppressed. The fresh calamity thus befallen France, and which she herself keenly feels, fills us with the deepest concern, the most intense anxiety. We detest and deplore the wrong done to the Catholic religion."

There was just cause for all the fears of the Pontiff. Nothing could arrest the progress of the decatholicizing spirit in France—nothing but the fear of a civil war. Of this, however, there was no danger. The Catholics—the nominal Catholics at least, who were in overwhelming majority—allowed every constitutional agency for asserting their own will to be taken from them by their determined, sleepless, unscrupulous, and energetic enemies. The public offices, from the highest to the lowest in the state, the ballot-box, the parliamentary representation, the command of the army and navy—all was taken away from them by degrees, and that because they lacked union and organization.

It is one of the saddest spectacles of modern times to see thirty millions of French Catholic citizens virtually disfranchised, oppressed, and deprived of their most precious religious liberties by a small minority, because they did not know how to forget their political dissentiments, to unite like one man to assert their rights, and to use every means allowed by the constitution and by conscience to withstand the usurpations of a godless minority.

What is most saddening in this condition of a nation which had played so glorious a part in Christendom is to see the downward progress of Socialism and Anarchism keep a steady pace with the legislative and administrative measures which, step by step, dechristianize every one of the public institutions of France, and bring the Church within the jurisdiction of the republic to a worse state, in many respects, than it was in 1794 and 1795.

What intellectual and moral poison has perverted the judgment of Frenchmen, naturally so quick and penetrating, or so deadened their naturally noble disposition as to make them form so false a notion of freedom, and to mistake its dictates in practice for an injunction to oppress all who differ from themselves in opinion?

It is a problem. And it is a pity. But it is none the less all too true. And this intolerance, this unnatural, fanatical intolerance, of all that is religious or godly, or morally fair and noble, is at present the bane of France. Liberty interverted into meaning, in practice, the freedom for one's self to think and act as one pleases, but to strangle free thought and free action in others, is bringing on— has, rather, already[3] brought

[3] March, 1886.

on—Communism in France, and will soon bring on anarchy and a second division of France.

If the nations round about had combined and sworn to divide France, ungoverned and ungovernable, as was once done with unhappy Poland, they only have to wait patiently for the outcome of the present mad race to destruction. If things go on, within another decade the former kingdom of St. Louis will be without a single form of tolerated public worship, without a single cathedral devoted to religion; the country which, under Napoleon I, dictated laws to Europe, will have neither an effective army to defend her frontiers nor a fleet to guard her coasts.

That is what the "party of action" in the government and the legislature are bringing the country to, as certainly as the yellow waters of the Tiber will find their way to Ostia and the Mediterranean.

And this is what we Americans—and we Irish-Americans in particular—pray God with all our heart to avert from misgoverned France, so dear to us for many reasons.

Leo XIII has been and is still severely blamed by many French Catholics for what they consider his policy of unwise and fatal conciliation. It is a strange censure, seeing that the Holy See, in the circumstances which we have been describing, must choose between firm remonstrances, representations, and endeavors to conciliate, or band all French Catholics together in a great and compactly organized national league, showing to the government and the radicals behind them a solid and unbroken front, resisting every measure of suppression, of confiscation, of encroachment on religious liberty by determined, united, and constitutional action. But would French Catholics have so united at his bidding?

Who among the Catholic leaders of France, lay or clerical, suggested or initiated the formation of such a league? Now that the mischief has been done, and that all constitutional safeguards possessed by the Catholic Church in France are being swept away one by one, till the very cathedrals are allowed to fall into ruin previous to their being confiscated, it is too late to look back and say what should have been done, when all men knew what MM. Ferry and Bert meant, and what was really intended by the parliamentary majority behind them.

It was for the French Catholics themselves, constituting the great mass of the nation—for bishops, priests, and laymen—to come together, to take counsel, as they did in Germany at the approach of danger. It behooved them in presence of the enemy to forget all private or local differences, all party feuds; to forget that they were Legitimists, Orleanists, Bonapartists, or Republicans, and to remember only that they were Christians. It behooved them, speaking in the name of a Catholic nation, to draw up a declaration of rights, every line and word of which should commend itself to the approbation of Rome and the applause of every civilized man all over the world in favor of liberty of conscience and the sacred laws which guard the family, the home, the school, and the Church.

They should not have waited for any invitation from the Sovereign Pontiff to do so. It was their acknowledged right, and it was the sacred duty of the hour, to do so. There is no use in denying it, the fatal dissentiments and bickerings which had so long divided French Catholics among themselves, and which still found vent in the religious press, kept minds and hearts and men asunder, while the common foe, the enemy of religion and social order was storming the outworks of the citadel of faith. When these had been swept away, did the Catholics unite like one man to defend the very heart of their position?

But after the elections of 1885, when every priest who dared to advise his parishioners to vote for a Catholic candidate in opposition to a Radical or government man was punished by losing his salary, and when a new school-law was passed disqualifying all persons belonging to religious communities for teaching in primary schools, the venerable Cardinal Guibert, Archbishop of Paris, broke silence, and wrote to the President of the Republic the following letter, which describes the exact situation of the Church in France with regard to the so-called Republic:

"Paris, March 30, 1886.

"To the President of the Republic:

"Mr. President: The Church of France is passing through a period of painful trials. She complains of being made the object of rigorous treatment by the state; and the state accuses her of having called forth such rigor by setting herself in opposition to the government which the country has chosen for itself. As the conflict grows daily in bitterness you will not be surprised if the oldest among the French bishops, he in whose diocese the government has its seat, addresses himself to you as the chief executive, and conveys to you, together with his respectful protestations, the just complaints, which are, I doubt it not, in conformity with the general sentiment among my brother-bishops.

"How can we allow the public to give credit, through our silence, to accusations which entirely misrepresent our attitude and can only lead public opinion astray? Up to this moment the French clergy have given proof of a patience and moderation that deserve higher praise than that of being called exemplary. Wishing before all things to maintain peace, and thereby to obey the wise directions given by the Sovereign Pontiff, they have uncomplainingly endured much injustice. They have only raised their voice to defend the spiritual interests of their flocks, the teaching of religious doctrine, the necessities of public worship; and in so doing they have shown temper and moderation,, demanding only of the public authorities that they should be shown the same justice and kindness so honorably granted them by preceding governments.

"They have been reproached with having, during the last elections, been favorable to the opposition candidates. If there be truth in this accusation, we can affirm that politics had no influence on the minds of the electors, who, in voting, only thought of the result the ballot-box would'4 have on the interests of religion.

"There were two classes of candidates—one class composed of persons who wished to preserve religious instruction, to protect freedom of worship, and to favor Christian good works; the other class were those who announced openly their intention of extinguishing at once, or in the very near future, the Catholic faith among us. Who would hold it to be a crime in priests to show a preference for the former? It was a conscientious duty to do so, and a fulfilment of the mission received by them from the Church, and, one might say, from the state itself.

"No; the clergy never have made in the past, nor do they make at present, a systematic and hostile opposition to existing institutions. If they show either coldness or uneasiness, these dispositions so loudly complained of only became manifest when the representatives of the government joined hands openly with the enemies of religion. If the republic would only accept the obligation incumbent on all governments of respecting the belief and the worship of the immense majority of our countrymen, nothing in the teaching of the Church or in her traditions could have justified a priest in distrusting the republic or in opposing it. But if the men who have taken on them' selves to establish these political forms in France have at the same time made it their task to wound all men's consciences, if every year of their sway has been remarkable for some blow aimed at one or other of our Catholic institutions, how, I ask again, can churchmen be blamed for preferring those who protect them to those who plunder them, those who respect their ministry to those who vilify it, those who favor the influence of religion on men's minds to those who labor to destroy it?

"To the prejudiced, who still wonder at the conduct of the clergy, I would say: Read over the records of the last five years. In 1880 the Religious Orders are dispersed on the authority of contested laws and without having obtained judgment from the courts. At the same time treasury laws, which impose a heavier burden every year, fall oppressively on communities of religious women, regardless of the immense services they render to the poor, to the sick, to the youth of the country. In 1882 a school-law blots out religion from the programme of public instruction, and inflicts on Christian France, under the name of neutrality—a name hitherto unknown—the stigma of official atheism. Year after year the budget of public worship is cut down. In the space of five years there is a reduction of seven millions of francs. The salary of the bishops is diminished, those of the cathedral canons are threatened; the burses in the seminaries are stricken out of the estimates; the cathedral churches are refused the subsidies necessary for the dignity of public worship and the repair of their buildings; the assistant pastorships are suppressed by the hundred. In every locality where the municipal officers become the tools of anti-religious passions, the government follow in their wake, tolerating or sanctioning the most unlawful usurpations.

"Thus it is that the ministers of religion are excluded from the hospitals which depend on the state or on the municipality; the funeral of a celebrated writer, who had refused the prayers of the Church, serves as a pretext for profaning a Christian temple bearing the name of the patron saint of Paris; and, lastly, the parish priests, those lowly servants of the people in our villages, are treated with no less injustice. The poor salary which represents the sacred debt of the nation toward the Church ceases to be assured to the priest who faithfully discharges his obscure duties. To denounce him to the authorities—an act mostly inspired by hatred or by private interest—suffices to make him lose it. He is visited by an excessive punishment which no law authorizes, and which is preceded by no trial.

"Five years have sufficed to heap up all these violences. The present year had in store for us a reserve of no less sorrowful surprises. While people are expecting the repeal of the law which dispenses the clergy from military service we are made to follow in Parliament the debates on another law taking away from public instruction every Christian characteristic.

"During these debates we heard the Minister of Public Worship attacking, in his speeches, the fundamental doctrines of Christianity.

"Ten years ago it was said, 'Clericalism is the national enemy,' and beneath the ambiguity of the term the man who used it purposely veiled the intention which he did not dare to avow openly. At this moment such a precaution is needless. The objects of direct attack are the honor paid to the Blessed Virgin and the doctrine of Original Sin. To justify the perpetual exclusion of teachers belonging to communities from all public schools, the government declare that these teachers, precisely because they are Catholics, would teach doctrines which the state cannot tolerate from the lips of masters paid by it.

"In very truth, Mr. President, I cannot help asking myself what we are come to. Has the Concordat been abrogated, or is it still in force? It is easy to see that the Minister of Public Worship favors the separation of Church and state, but that he dreads the consequences for our existing institutions, and wishes to prepare public opinion for it. Doubtless it is because he wishes the better to prepare people for the breaking up of the compact that he begins openly to violate its clauses and its spirit.

"The seventeenth article of the Concordat foresees the case in which the First Consul might have a non-Catholic successor, and stipulates that in this case the rights and the prerogatives mentioned in article sixteen and the nomination to bishoprics should be regulated by a new convention. So, in the thought of the two parties to the Concordat, the prerogatives granted to the chief of the French government were subordinated to the condition that he should profess the Catholic faith. And now here is a minister of this government, the very personage who, on his own responsibility, exercises the prerogatives granted by the Concordat, and he makes speeches against the Catholic belief! If he is to be believed, the state owes it to itself not to permit in its schools the teaching of the dogmas of our faith; and yet the state continues to nominate our bishops, who are the guardians of that faith!

"Mr. President, I appeal to your reason and your impartiality. Have I, in what I have just said, done anything but note facts well known and official? And can any one dispute the conclusion to be drawn from them, and which may be thus formulated: The Catholic clergy have not made any opposition to the government, which, during these last six years, has never ceased to persecute the clergy, to weaken Christian institutions, and to prepare for the suppression of the Christian religion itself?

"It is certain, Mr. President, that the constitution which frees you from responsibility leaves you the full enjoyment of your moral influence. Your age, your great experience, your old devotion to the republican cause, the confidence again pledged to you by the National Assembly—all this, by heightening your authority, seems to ask of you to interfere in the difficult situation which has arisen. It is your right to warn those who share with you the burden of power, and to point out to them the consequences of their dangerous policy; they could not, without betraying levity or rashness, help yielding to your wise counsels and having a regard for your serious observations.

"Allow, then, an old bishop, who has seen, during his own lifetime, the political forms of his country changed seven times in succession—allow him to say to you for the last time what his long experience suggests.

"By continuing on the path it is now pursuing the republic can do religion great harm; but kill it, it cannot. The Church has known greater dangers and has passed through worse storms, and yet she lives in the heart of France. She will be present at the burial of those who flatter themselves with the belief that they will annihilate her.

"The republic has received no promise of immortality either from God or from history. If your influence could induce it to respect men's consciences, to apply the Concordat honestly both in its letter and in its spirit, you would do much to restore public peace and to unite men's minds. If you fail in this attempt, or if you think it cannot be made, then it is not the clergy nor the Church that can be charged with laboring to ruin the political establishment of which you are the guardian; you know that rebellion is not one of the weapons that we use.'

"The clergy will continue to endure patiently; they will pray for their enemies; they will beg of God to enlighten these and to inspire them with more equitable sentiments. But those who are the authors of this impious war shall work their own destruction by it, and great ruins will be heaped up in our beloved country before it can see once more happy days.

"The subversive passions which give many signs of their near awakening will create in your path dangers far more formidable than any of the pretended abuses cast up to the clergy. And God grant that in this fearful storm, where the appetites let loose shall find no moral barrier on their road, we do not see go down together the fortune and even the independence of our native land!

"Arrived at the extreme limit of a long career, I resolved, before having to go before God to give an account of my administration, to remove from my own conscience any share of responsibility in the coming disasters. Still, I cannot close this letter without expressing the hope that France will never permit herself to be robbed of those sacred beliefs which constituted in the past her strength and her glory, and secured to her the foremost rank among nations.

"I confide, Mr. President, these weighty reflections to your wisdom and your lofty intelligence, and beg you to accept the homage of my respectful consideration.

"J. Hippolyte Cardinal Guibert,

"Archbishop of Paris."

Here is a prophetic voice from Paris forecasting the near future of France. It is a description of the imposing' ceremony in the cathedral of Notre Dame on Easter Sunday morning, April 25, 1886, in which some five thousand men received together Holy Communion:

"The Communion of the men, as it is called, in the church of Notre Dame, was as imposing on Sunday last as in the best years of the past. The four or five thousand faithful men who follow the Lenten lectures and receive Communion on Easter Sunday are not of the class who are influenced in the profession of their faith and the accomplishment of its duties by the fluctuations of public opinion. Hence the nave and side-aisles of the cathedral were filled. The singing of the *Credo*, and of the psalm *In Exitu*[4] and of the hymns drowned the mighty notes of the great organ. Need we say that there was deep recollection among this multitude, and that, assembled there for the most part long before the hour for Mass, these men never permitted themselves to speak of politics?

"Nevertheless a feeling of uneasiness betrayed itself in the throng, a feeling with which the state of things outside had something to do, and which was also observable last year. One might think that Father Monsabré gave an answer to this secret thought of every man there when, in the farewell address after Communion, he spoke of persecution and the priesthood,, and foretold the dark future in store for a people without priests! What a parallel was that between the brave and generous nation whose warlike epic could be entitled 'Gesta Dei per Francos,'[5] and that same people lowered, degraded, without God or priests, whom the heel of the barbarian would come to crush in the mire of their own corruption! ...

"Everybody felt it; the truth of these forebodings is all too certain, and this degradation will come sooner than we think, if France continues to countenance the war—a war as disgraceful to the French name as it is impious in its nature—which the Revolution is waging against God!"[6]

---

[4] *Psalms cxiii., cxiv.*

[5] "The Doings of God through the Franks."

[6] *L'Univers.*

together Holy Communion.

"The Communion of the men, as it is called, in the church of Notre Dame was as imposing on Sunday last as in the best years of the past. The four or five thousand faithful men who follow the Lenten lectures and receive Communion on Easter Sunday are not of the class who are influenced in the profession of their faith and the accomplishment of its duties by the fluctuations of public opinion. Hence the nave and side-aisles of the cathedral were filled. The singing of the Credo and of the psalm *In Exitu* and of the hymns drowned the mighty notes of the great organ. Need we say that there was deep recollection among this multitude, and that, assembled there for the most part long before the hour for Mass, these men never permitted themselves to speak of politics?

"Nevertheless a feeling of uneasiness betrayed itself in the throng, a feeling with which the state of things outside had something to do, and which was also observable last year. One might think that Father Monsabré gave an answer to this secret thought of every man there when, in the farewell address after Communion, he spoke of persecution and the priesthood, and foretold the dark future in store for a people without priests. What a parallel was that between this brave and generous nation whose warlike epic could be entitled 'Gesta Dei per Francos,' and that same people lowered, degraded, without God or priests, whom the heel of the barbarian would come to crush in the mire of their own corruptions.

"Everybody felt it: the truth of these forebodings is all too certain, and this degradation will come sooner than we think if France continues to countenance the war—a war as disgraceful to the French name as it is impious in its nature—which the Revolution is waging against God."

[illegible]

The Doings of God through the Franks.

L'Univers.

CHAPTER XXXII

"THE CHURCH FREE IN THE FREE KINGDOM OF ITALY"; LEO XIII AND THE SPOLIATION OF THE PROPAGANDA

LEO XIII's passionate love for higher studies would not permit him to overlook the glorious missionary school of the Propaganda—that *Collegium Urbanum*, so called from its great-souled founder, Pope Urban VIII, to which the select youth of all countries and races are sent to receive gratuitously the highest education, and from which they return to their native land to be the apostles of their fellow-countrymen and the promoters of Christian civilization.

Never since Christianity itself began to gather the nations into the fold of Christ was any institution so admirably devised as this Urban College to typify, realize, and foster the great idea of the brotherhood of all men in Christ, and to propagate this great doctrine and its benefits among every tribe of mankind.

Before the occupation of Rome by the Piedmontese in September, 1870, it was the custom in this great school of practical brotherly love to hold yearly, on the Feast of the Epiphany—regarded as the anniversary of the conversion of the Gentiles—an "academy," in which the students, young men of every race and tongue, were wont, in presence of the Sovereign Pontiff, his court, the Sacred College, the diplomatic corps, and all that was most distinguished in Rome, to give specimens of their proficiency. It was a rare spectacle.

As, however, Leo XIII could no longer go to the College of Propaganda, as in the days when Rome was the free city of the entire Christian world, he resolved that the annual academy should be held in the most magnificent apartment in the

Vatican, the Consistorial Hall.

We give the following account from an eye-witness of the proceedings on January 6, 1880:

"The Consistorial Hall was arranged with a throne at one side, ... and with seats for the cardinals and ambassadors placed in a circle, with rows of chairs extending at either side for the prelates and privileged persons permitted to be present. Mustafa and the gentlemen of the Sistine choir occupied part of the upper end of the room, and sang some beautiful pieces of music with exquisite skill.

"Leo XIII entered the hall at a quarter-past ten, attended by Monsignor Cataldi, prefect of Pontifical ceremonies, his major-domo and master of the Camera, his private chamberlains, Boccali and Castrocane, the Marquis Serlupi and Prince Antici-Mattei, and several cardinals. The seats for the corps diplomatique were occupied by the ambassadors or ministers of France, Spain, Portugal, Monaco, Bolivia, and other states.

"The proceedings commenced by the reading in Italian of a prolusion by the Rev. Michele Camillieri, of Smyrna, and then followed the recitation of poetical compositions in forty-nine different languages, including Hebrew, Chaldaic, Coptic, Arabic, Turkish, Kurd, Cingalese, Tartar, Armenian, Persian, Syriac, Ethiopic, and Akka. Twenty-one languages of Asia and Africa were spoken in the first part of the accademia by young men of color, ranging from the pale yellow of natives of the Lebanon or Mesopotamia to the sooty black of the Nubians and Central Africans. The recitations were interspersed with popular songs in Chaldee, Arabic, Kurd, Cingalese, Armenian, and Syriac.

"The second part comprised recitations and songs in twenty-eight languages of Europe, including Greek, Georgian, Keltic, Bulgar, and Roumanian. The accademia was closed by the benediction given by the Holy Father, and at half-past twelve p.m. the assemblage broke up. To this disputation were admitted deputations from the students of the ecclesiastical colleges in Rome."[1]

Of course this academy, intended to represent the great family of all nations and languages belonging to Christ's fold, does not give any idea of the severe course of sacred and secular studies which the pupils of the Propaganda have to follow during their training in Rome. But the above description affords the reader a glance at the truly Catholic composition of the school itself, and hints at the large and practical humanitarian spirit which presided at the foundation of such an establishment and still continues to watch over and direct its progress.

This is not the place to speak of the Propaganda Library, nor of its presses, which print books in the principal languages of every continent. We were only anxious to place before he general reader's eye one of these great nurseries of the apostolic spirit which have contributed immensely to the Christianizing and civilizing so many barbarous nations, and toward spreading and maintaining, wherever the English language is spoken, the Catholic faith in its purity and integrity.

Non-Catholics, indeed, are not expected to view with sympathy these great seminaries for Catholic missionaries. But Protestants have been most generous in their praise of the Propaganda and its dependent colleges, as well as in

---

[1] Letter in the Dublin *Freeman's Journal*, dated Rome, April 18, 1880, quoted in the "Chair of Peter," p. 39.
The "ecclesiastical colleges" here mentioned, and maintained by the Propaganda, are: the Germanic College, the Teutonic College, the English College, the Collegio Pio-Inglese, the Irish College of Santa Agata, the Irish Franciscan College of St. Isidore, the Scotch College, the Polish College, the Illyrian College, the Collegio Pio-Latino for Spanish America, the North American College for the United States, the Greco-Ruthene College of St. Athanasius, the College of St. Gregory, the College of St. Pancratius for the Discalced Carmelites, the College of St. Peter in Montorio for the Observantines, that of San Bartolomeo on the Island for the same, the College of St. Anthony of Padua for the Minors-Conventual, the College of Capuchins, and that of the Armenians founded by Leo XIII. Add to these a college in course of foundation for the Canadian confederacy.

acknowledging the extraordinary results produced by the labors of an administration which disposes of less than one-fifth of the pecuniary means at the command of the Bible and missionary societies of England and the United States.

At any rate, London or New York would be proud to own such an establishment as the Urban College, although only one of the colleges directed by the Congregation de Propaganda Fide. For the very assemblage of these young students, representing all the tribes of earth, is a something which appeals to our Christian affections and our brotherly sympathy for all the descendants of Adam.

One would also think that the Italian Revolutionists, who are so loud in prating about progress, culture, civilization, humanity, and universal brotherhood, would feel some pride in possessing in the city of the Popes such a cosmopolitan institution as the Propaganda with its glorious schools.

It would seem a liberal, a large-minded, and a wise policy in the men who wish to restore to Rome and to Italy something of the moral, if not of the political, supremacy of former ages, to encourage and foster this missionary spirit and the institutions which embody it, because every one of these sons of Asia, Africa, America, Oceanica, and Australia carries with him to his native land the memory and the name of Italy and of Rome.

If anti-Christian hate did not blind the present rulers of Rome and the Peninsula to the incomparable means of influencing the nations of the earth which they have in the Papacy left sovereign, independent, and free as an integral portion of an Italian confederacy! If they could be made to understand that Italy would be far more powerful, more united, more respected, more secure against all foreign aggression and all intestine divisions if the Papacy were left, as it was hitherto, to represent to the world the divine influence of Christian truth and morality, and if the Pope were allowed to be the teacher of all mankind and the supreme director of consciences, without being trammelled by the action or authority of any rival secular power!

What was happening in 1880 under Leo XIII, and what had happened under Pius IX, to mar the labors of the Propaganda and to interfere with the prosperity of the great missionary schools?

In 1874, just when all these youths of the Urban College were working hard to undergo creditably their severe yearly examinations, the Giunta Liquidatrice, a board established by the new Italian government to carry out the laws sequestrating all ecclesiastical property and securing the proceeds of their sale to the state, seized upon the Villa Montalto at Tusculum, the country-house of the Urban College, and put it up for public auction.

It was a terrible disappointment to these young men, who could not return to their native homes to spend the yearly vacation, and who had always enjoyed their well-earned repose among the cool and breezy solitudes of the Roman hills, instead of being cooped up within the sultry, sunburned circuit of Rome itself.

One would think that, even if the right of the government to seize and sell the villa be conceded, consideration for these foreign youths, who could bring back home with them either hatred of the oppressors of religion and the Papacy or admiration for a large and enlightened appreciation of Catholicism and its power in the world, should have made the Giunta Liquidatrice pause or have induced the government to interfere.

The Propaganda were taken by surprise, for they did not imagine that the new laws of suppression and sequestration were meant for them, and the king, Victor Emmanuel, had solemnly declared that the Propaganda and its property were safe from the operation of these laws.

On August 6, 1874, the Propaganda brought the matter before the Roman courts of justice to test the applicability of the law to their property, while the Sovereign Pontiff appealed to the European powers against this invasion of his spiritual mission in favor of the heathen. But the Giunta, secure of the support of the government, and well knowing that the law-courts would be made to sanction the confiscation, sold out the Villa Montalto without waiting for the issue of the suit.

The Congregation of Propaganda, knowing that it was useless to contend for justice when this act of spoliation was accomplished, did not push their suit. But the Giunta, sure of the decision of the courts, demanded that it should be proceeded with. The king, however, interfered, not to cancel the sale and-to repair the wrong, but simply to stop the suit. But the government and their subordinates, who, in the interest of the Revolution, were loud in honoring the king as a hero, a great man, "the father of his country," made very little of his wishes or his orders in practice. He was only a tool, which could be laid aside or used as the occasion required.

Things were allowed to remain quiet till after his death. But on June 12, 1881, Signor Morena, a royal commissary, set up to be sold at public auction a number of farms in the country and of city lots belonging to the Propaganda. Both the Propaganda and the commissary applied to the civil courts in Rome, and on July 5 a decision was given against the former and condemning the Congregation to pay three-fourths of the expense. It was a hard judgment.

The Propaganda appealed on September 22. This time the court would not even allow the necessary delay to obtain evidence, and affirmed the sentence of the inferior court, besides condemning the Propaganda to pay all the expenses.

It is not to be thought that public opinion in Italy was so utterly perverted, or that Italian lawyers had so entirely lost all sense of justice and all honesty and independence in interpreting the laws, as not to utter any remonstrance against so glaring an iniquity. Many generous protests were heard, but they were of little avail.

The Propaganda this time had recourse to the Supreme Court, which invalidated the last sentence and sent the case to be tried anew before the Court of Ancona. Here the Congregation was again condemned; and on December 14, 1881, the case was laid before the full bench of the Court of Cassation, the court of last appeal in the kingdom.

The court, under what pression it were useless to inquire, did not hesitate to stultify and contradict themselves. Four of the same judges who on May 31, 1881, declared that the Sacred Congregation de Propaganda Fide was an institution apart and by itself, *sui generis*, and unlike any other, and "inspired by a great humanitarian conception," and that all the preceding laws had, *ex proposito*, "of set purpose omitted" to comprise its property within the scope of sequestration or conversion, subscribed the second contradictory sentence of January 29, 1884, without protestation, or giving any sign that they differed from the majority of the court. The names of the other four are missing among the signatures to the second sentence.

The best jurists in Italy openly affirmed that instead of interpreting in a wide and liberal sense the dubious terms of the law in a matter of confiscation and sequestration, the judges in the second decision had so stretched their interpretation, instead of restricting it, as to include every establishment and office connected with the Papacy, without even excepting the Pope himself and his household. It was annulling in advance the Law of Guarantees.

And what did Leo XIII say and do in this emergency? On the 2d of March, the anniversary of his coronation, in answer to the address of the College of Cardinals, presented by Cardinal di Pietro, the Holy Father said:

"The wishes which the Sacred College expresses on this day, doubly memorable for us, and the prayers it offers to Heaven for us, move our heart in a special manner. ... The Sacred College, which shares with us the care of governing the Church, knows best the need we have both of divine and of human aid to strengthen and sustain our weakness. The deep fear which overwhelmed our souls when, without any merit of ours, we were called to the Sovereign Pontificate, again takes forcible possession of us in this sixth year, which closes now after having taken away from your midst some of your illustrious members most dear to us, and after having dealt to the Church new blows.

"For she sees her divine mission beset on every side by

difficulties of all sorts and ever increasing in magnitude. More to be deplored than all the others are attacks made on her here in Rome, for they strike her in the very center of her life, and are directed toward obstructing the action of her Supreme Head.

"Bitter indeed to us it was to see a harsh judgment fall on an institution which is the honor of the Church, of the Roman Pontificate, and of Italy itself. We mean the Propaganda. It is easy to see how this sentence decreases the value of its patrimony, both because its capital is thereby rendered subject to the changes and instability of a public fund, and because it is deprived of the power of disposing of any portion of its capital, even to meet cases of urgent necessity or to augment them by new pious bequests, without the interference of a power foreign to it.

"But, if we rise to loftier considerations, we discern what the Propaganda really is—an institution of an order altogether beyond the common level, and by its nature independent of all lay authority. For it was founded by the Roman Pontiffs in virtue of the supreme apostolic ministry with which they are invested, and it is directly ordered for the purpose of propagating and preserving the faith in the various parts of our globe, and for fulfilling the sublime mission of the Church to save the world.

"For this end the Roman Pontiffs transferred to the Propaganda such an important part of their sublime power; it is by its means that they cause the blessings of redemption to reach the most distant nations. Innumerable regions of Africa, of Asia, of both North and South America, of Oceania, and of Europe itself, are indebted to this blessed institution for the light of the Gospel and for the true civilization which the Gospel imparts.

"And it is precisely to enable the Propaganda to correspond with their lofty purpose that the Popes themselves bestowed on it ample property and abundant revenues, exciting by their example and their exhortations the entire Catholic world to do the same.

"It is no wonder, therefore, that men who were no friends of the Catholic Church have always bestowed unbounded praise on this institution. It is no wonder that its property was spared even by the Imperial French government, and that the conqueror, who then seemed the master of Europe, had only great praise and sure protection for it. Such being, therefore, the character of this Papal institution, any act which aims at subjecting it in any way whatever to a power external to it, and to place obstacles in the way of its proper action, is a crime against the liberty of the Head of the Church in the exercise of his spiritual authority, in the discharge of his apostolic ministry.

"For these reasons of the highest order we feel it to be our duty to lift up our voice and to denounce to the Catholics of all nations, who have so many reasons to be interested therein, the new outrage committed against the Apostolic See.

"Meanwhile we shall endeavor, in the best way we can, to provide for the administrative necessities of this vast and magnificent institution. But in proportion as difficulties increase around us and as our condition becomes more intolerable, the more do we expect the aid of the Sacred College, the more abundantly do we claim from the faithful all over the world the help of their prayers, of their co-operation, of their generosity.

"We thereby hope, my Lord Cardinal, that the wishes you have expressed may be in this way largely fulfilled; that, in spite of all the efforts of the enemy, the Apostolic See may never lack the means to spread the Gospel and to accomplish the work of the apostleship."

While the whole Catholic world was moved by strong indignation against the oppressors of the Holy See, and voices denouncing the thinly disguised robbery of the most sacred institution on earth reached Italy from every shore, Cardinal Simeoni, the venerable Prefect of the Propaganda, was, under the Pope's direction, taking steps to prevent the funds sent to the Propaganda by the pious zeal of Catholic peoples from coming to Rome. The first act of spoliation diminished by fully one-third the revenues in Italy of the great institution. No one could foresee the day when the institution itself would be suppressed, or its revenues so crippled and their management so hampered as to render them unavailable.

A consistory was held on March 24, and, encouraged by the general reprobation with which the decision of the Court of Cassation and the conduct and speeches of Signor Mancini, the Minister of Foreign Affairs, had met with in Europe as well as in America, the Holy Father did not hesitate to stigmatize the act of spoliation and the curtailment of his own spiritual freedom in words to which people listened with respect and sympathy:

"When the storms of rebellion, whose fierce attacks were directed against the civil principality of the Roman Pontiffs and for the conquest of this city, had achieved its purpose, both our predecessor, Pius IX, and ourselves raised our voices and used our utmost exertions to protect and to vindicate the rights of the Apostolic See, in accordance with the strict obligations of our office. With the same firmness of purpose, as the Revolution went on its course, every time we saw injustice committed we took on ourselves to protect truth and justice violated; more especially have we, in so far as our firmly resisting could do so, done our best to beat off the violence so long done to us.

"Nevertheless, by a mysterious permission of God, that terrible storm had but a brief interval of subsidence. We scarcely need say it, especially to you, Venerable Brothers, who have the daily experience of what we describe. Our enemies lose not a moment, in the carrying out of their own plans, to establish themselves here on a firm footing, arranging and disposing all things in such a manner as to make people think that they have taken possession of Rome by the best of rights and that they mean to hold it for ever. To this purpose is directed their well-weighed and clever manner of proceeding; a succession of incidents brought about by a well-calculated series of causes; the care which they take to gain at home the good will of the people, and to obtain friends and allies abroad—in a word, every artifice is used which can serve to enable them to obtain and to keep a firm grasp of their power.

"The more, therefore, these men labor to ruin the interests of the Church and the Papacy, the more are we bound to protect them; and, for this reason, in this solemn assemblage we to-day once more reprove and condemn everything that has been done to the injury of the Apostolic See, and we declare, moreover, that we are resolved to see all its rights preserved undiminished to all future time. Nor in this are we influenced by the ambition to reign or the desire of earthly possessions—motives which some persons attribute to us with equal silliness and impudence. We are only moved by the consciousness of our duty, by respect for our oath, by the examples of our predecessors, among whom were men illustrious for their courage and sanctity, who have displayed, when it was needful, consummate fortitude and firmness in protecting their temporal power.

"In this civil sovereignty, apart from the legitimacy of its origin and the various glorious titles on which it was held, there is a special and sacred form and character, proper to itself and to be found in no other state, arising from the fact that it is the secure and permanent safeguard of the Pontiff's liberty in the exercise of his August office. Everybody knows that no Pontiff ever lost his civil sovereignty without at the same time incurring some loss of his freedom. This is evident in our own person at the present time, subjected as we are to the various uncertain chances of an alien power. The last grievous case in point is that relating to the property of the Propaganda. The affair was intimately connected with the apostolic office of the Sovereign Pontiff, and one so much more important than mere human matters as is the propagation of the divine wisdom and the eternal salvation of mankind. And yet the prevailing violence of the present time did not spare that noble institution, which had its origin in the munificence of the Popes and was fostered by the generosity of the Christian nations. And so severe was the blow dealt it that we were constrained to adopt new measures for its safety in the future.

"These things are bitter enough. But we feel that there are more bitter still in store for us, and we are ready for them. We know that our enemies have resolved so to heap wrong upon wrong against the Roman Pontificate as to drive the Pope to extremity, if they can. It is a hateful and insane project. If it be, on the one hand, quite congenial to the spirit of those who only labor to serve the wicked purpose of the secret societies, and who are anxious to place the Church helpless beneath the feet of the state, such a design, on the other hand, must be abhorrent to all who truly love their country, who look upon the Papacy, its power, and its greatness, not with the eyes of prejudice, but as it is in itself; who consider well the benefits which it has bestowed not only on all nations, but especially on Italians, and which it is capable of bestowing in the future."

Leo XIII was not satisfied with this indirect appeal to public opinion. He had, soon after the sentence of the Court of Cassation had been delivered, prepared a masterly exposition of the whole case to be sent by the Cardinal Secretary of State to all the nuncios and diplomatic agents of the Holy See. It is dated February 10, 1884, and was, therefore, anterior to the two addresses just quoted. This document found its way into the public press in both hemispheres, and was received with marked favor even by the great non-Catholic daily journals. It certainly contributed very much to turn public opinion against the stupid and blundering policy of the Italian government.

The Propaganda, the Pope says through his Secretary of State, as is evident from the authentic documents which recite the facts of its foundation, must be "considered as an emanation of the supreme apostolic office of the Papacy; it must, therefore, in its sphere of action, be considered as an eminently cosmopolitan institution; its purpose is to propagate the faith—that is, the truth; the means generously bestowed upon it should be employed, in accordance with the pious will of the donors, in carrying out such a design. Hence it is that the patrimony of the Propaganda is the property of the entire Catholic family.

"Such considerations easily prove that the Propaganda represents the most splendid and efficient creation of the Papacy for the purpose of preparing ready for use and employing the principal means adapted to the fulfilment of the divine mission given it to propagate the faith and civilization among all nations.

"As to the manner in which the Propaganda has answered to the purpose of its founders, we have proof of it in the annals of the missions it has directed, which record the prodigies wrought by the Catholic apostolate from Thibet to Scandinavia, from Iceland to China, and particularly in the East and West Indies.

"Writers, even non-Catholic writers, have acknowledged that the assimilating action issuing from that center and radiating to the remotest countries has everywhere been productive of the peaceful conquests of religion and of civilization.

"And here, the better to point out the universal character of the Propaganda, we should remark that the Popes labored through that institution for the conversion of idolaters, and also to revive the faith in those Christian countries which the Photian schism and heresy had devastated. ...

"On this point it may suffice to recall the generous endowment of Cardinal Antonio Barberini, who founded in the Propaganda twelve scholarships for Georgians, Persians, Melchites, and Copts, seven for Ethiopians, and six for Indians and Armenians.

"Now, this is the institution which, by its origin, its character, its action, its property, and its history, shows itself plainly to be essentially one which is ecumenical and cosmopolitan, that they wish to subject to the private laws of one government, to the judgment of a local tribunal which, by declaring it incapable of juridically possessing property, strips it of the property which it has!

"It was not enough to compel the Propaganda to continue a long suit before the law-courts and to undergo the heavy charges of a costly trial. It was not deemed enough to have forced it to pay enormous taxes, which absorb nearly the fifth part of its yearly income, thereby withdrawn from its proper destination. The kind offices of high personages were of no avail; of no avail were the efforts to render its juridical and economical position less intolerable. No account was taken of the irrefutable arguments alleged in the judicial decisions favorable to it, ... and which deserved the approbation of all honorable men; even the will formally expressed of an August personage was not respected after his death! It might, in a way, be said that an Occult Force had dictated the spoliation of the Propaganda, precisely because it is the most splendid embodiment of the Papacy; and that before the prepotency of that Occult Force all the arguments founded on right and propriety lost all their relevancy, all the remonstrances had to give way.

"To weaken the force of the foregoing considerations, and to do away with the responsibility of such an odious spoliation, they wish us to believe that the Propaganda will in nowise be injured by the application of the law regarding the conversion of its immovable property, inasmuch as the revenues of the alienated property are to be set against an equal value of the state funds inscribed in its favor, and the Propaganda, besides, being left free to increase in the future its patrimony by accepting new bequests.

"Now, to upset this specious reasoning it is sufficient to remark that by taking away from the Propaganda the right to hold property, its legal status was rendered worse than that of the lowliest citizen. For if the right to hold property is a guarantee of the independence and respectability of all persons living together in any civil community, what an outrage is put upon the Propaganda by declaring it incapable of possessing, and by rendering it dependent on another institution, which pays it, as to a person who has only the use of his property, as it were a half-yearly alms?

"But, aside from these reflections of the moral order, it is contrary to the truth to say that the financial condition of the Propaganda is not made worse by the law of conversion.

"In what a plight would the Propaganda be if the value of the state funds fell far below par, if the government had to suspend payment, as it has happened in other countries! Who could guarantee that the yearly income should be paid punctually and in its entirety in the event of a financial crisis, of warlike revolutions, of sinister accidents? Have people forgotten that for the sole reason of reprisals they suspended for many years the payment of ecclesiastical pensions which burdened the properties sequestrated by the Piedmontese government?

"Moreover, it is of the deepest importance to bear in mind that the Propaganda, by the special conditions in which it is placed, and to face the extraordinary demands of its ecumenical action, is not unfrequently obliged to dispose of a portion even of its capital when its ordinary revenue is insufficient for its need. Thus did it happen when it became imperative, during the late famines, to come to the help of the Christians of China and Tonquin, and when great sums of money were required by the perilous condition of the vicariate of Constantinople.

"Besides all this, the ever-increasing developments of Catholicism among the unbelievers, and the increase as well of the facilities of communication, require the establishment of new missionary centres, and with these of seminaries, colleges, universities, apostolic prefectures and vicariates, with regard to which it will suffice to recall the fact that during the glorious Pontificate of Leo XIII there have been erected eighteen new apostolic vicariates.

"Finally, it should be remembered that in the institution called the Propaganda we have not only to consider the chief center of the Catholic missions, but, moreover, a first-class educational and scientific establishment, in which is a flourishing college with upwards of one hundred students, with the corresponding chairs of literature, of philosophy, of theology and linguistics, and which possesses a very rich library, a very precious museum, and a polyglot printing-office."

The Secretary of State then goes on to refute victoriously the futile assertions of the government officials regarding the security afforded for the collection of the full rental and its increase by new legacies, etc. He then concludes his eloquent arraignment of the spoliators:

"You will avail yourself of the preceding considerations to draw the attention of the Minister of Foreign Affairs to the special gravity of this last invasion of the rights of the Holy See, of the exercise of the Pontifical power, of the free use of the necessary means for propagating the faith. From these violations you will draw a new argument for making him understand the manifold outrages and vexations which daily render more painful and alarming the situation of the Supreme Head of the Church. If reasons of the highest order and influence have been unavailing to prevent a sentence as insulting as it is injurious to the Papacy, and regarded as supremely impolitic by the most enlightened men of all parties, it is but too much to be feared that the boldness and the plans of the Revolutionists shall become the ruling power and reduce the Sovereign Pontiff to the greatest straits.

"We have meanwhile confidence that the government to which you are accredited will take an efficient interest in favor of an institution which is the chief glory of the Papacy and of the Catholic world, and that they will seriously take into consideration whether it can be any longer tolerated that the Sovereign Pontiff should be subjected to such spoliations and violences, which render it for him a matter of extreme difficulty, if not of impossibility, to fulfil his spiritual mission."

Outside of Italy the leading organs in the public press stigmatized this act of the Roman government and its Supreme Court as an unjustifiable act of spoliation. The London *Times* said it was simply and purely an act of confiscation, quoting as an instance of the working of the Italian law of "conversion" an episcopal see whose yearly revenue was 60,000 francs before the government took possession of it, and which the process of "converting "brought down to 18,000 francs. This loss really has already befallen the revenues of the

Propaganda.

In France *Le Journal des Débats* repeated the well-known formula that this "conversion" *paralysed the right arm of the Papacy.*

In Germany and in the United States the great daily papers energetically protested against an act which destroyed a great humanitarian and international institution. *L'Indépendance Belge*, though unfavorable to the Church, said that every state should try to save from "conversion" the college or property belonging to its own subjects. This was done by the United States.

CHAPTER XXXIII

LEO XIII AND SPAIN;
HIS MEDIATION

BEFORE giving a history of the mediation accepted by Leo XIII between Germany and Spain in relation to the possession of the Carolinas Islands it will be of interest to the reader to have a fuller knowledge of the mediatorial office exercised between sovereign and sovereign, nation and nation, almost from the days of Constantine down to those of Gregory XV (1621-1623). The benefits conferred on civilization, on humanity, by the action of the Popes, called upon to arbitrate in the most important emergencies, and to end or prevent sanguinary wars by their decisions, have been fully acknowledged by non-Catholic writers of the greatest eminence during the last three centuries.

And since we are dealing in this chapter with an act of the Imperial government at Berlin, there is a special appropriateness in quoting, in the first place, the words of a Protestant historian, a native of that city, and one of its most illustrious scholars in our day.[1]

"During the middle ages," says Ancillon, "when there was no social order, the Papacy alone, perhaps, saved Europe from total barbarism. It created bonds of connection between the most distant nations; it was a common center, a rallying-point for isolated states. ... It was a supreme tribunal, established in the midst of universal anarchy, and its decrees were sometimes as respectable as they were respected. It prevented and arrested the despotism of the emperors, compensated for the want of equilibrium, and diminished the inconveniences of

[1] Johann Peter Friedrich Ancillon, born 1766, died 1837.

the feudal system."[2]

What Ancillon taught in Prussia, that the Calvinist Guizot taught in France.

"Every one is aware," he says in his sixth lecture on "Civilization in Europe," "that it was by the 'Truce of God' and numerous measures of the same nature that the Church struggled against the employment of force and devoted itself to introduce into society a greater degree of order and gentleness. These facts are so well known that I am spared the trouble of entering into any detail."

To be sure the facts are well known, but our age has a faculty for overlooking or forgetting everything favorable to the Papacy; because ever since Pius VI and Pius VII were carried off to France and imprisoned, while their dominions were confiscated by the unscrupulous conqueror, and since the Revolution consummated in the person of Pius IX the work of spoliation it had twice begun in his two predecessors of the same name, it has become too often the rule to revive only such memories of the Papacy as may help the present generation to consider it as the enemy of popular liberty in the past, and the great obstacle to the progress of humanity.

So did not think one who did, perhaps, even more than Luther to lower the Papacy in the estimation of mankind—the man who has been justly called the parent of the Revolution in its most anti-Christian aspect. Let us hear Voltaire:

"The interests of the human race demand a check to restrain sovereigns and to protect the lives of the people. This check of religion could, by universal agreement, have been in the hands of the Popes. These first Pontiffs, by not meddling in temporal quarrels except to appease them, by admonishing kings and peoples of their duties, by reproving their offences, by reserving excommunications for great crimes, would have been always regarded as the images of God upon earth. But

---

[2] Ancillon, "Tableau des Révolutions du Système Politique de l'Europe," I. pp. 79, 106, Berlin, 1803. Quoted from Count Murphy's admirable book, "The Chair of Peter," 2d ed., p. 620.

men are reduced to have for their defence only the laws and morals of their country—laws often despised, morals often depraved."[3]

Another distinguished French Protestant, the contemporary and friend of Guizot, furnishes an apt commentary on this passage from the philosopher of Ferney:

"In those dark ages," says M. Coquerel, "we see no example of tyranny comparable to that of the Domitians at Rome. A Tiberius was then impossible; Rome would have crushed him. Great despotisms exist when kings believe that there is nothing above themselves. Then it is that the intoxication of unlimited power produces the most fearful crimes."[4]

But superior in learning and in the esteem of the two last centuries is another great German Protestant, whose testimony may aptly conclude these quotations: "I have seen something," Leibnitz says, "of the project of M. de Saint-Pierre to maintain perpetual peace in Europe. ... My idea would be to establish, ay, even in Rome, a tribunal (to decide controversies between sovereigns), and to make the Pope its president, as he really in former ages figured as judge between Christian princes. But ecclesiastics should, at the same time, resume their ancient authority, and an interdict or an excommunication should make kings and kingdoms tremble as in the days of Nicholas I or Gregory VII"[5]

This great man, rising above everything like narrow sectarian views, and having in mind only the general welfare of Christendom, and, through Christendom, the interest and progress in true civilization of the entire human race, thus speaks of the exercise of the Papal supremacy over Christian peoples and their rulers:

"Thus Christ reigns, conquers, commands, since history

---

[3] Voltaire, "Essais," ii. ch. ix.

[4] Coquerel, "Essai sur l'Hist. Génerale du Christianisme," p. 75, Paris, 1828.

[5] Leibnitz, "Opera," v. p. 65. He was the founder and first president of the Academy of Sciences at Berlin; died November 14, 1716.

shows that most of the Western nations have with earnest piety submitted themselves to the Church. Nor do I dispute whether or not these things are of divine right. It is clear that they were done with unanimous consent, that they could be done with perfect propriety, and that they are not opposed to the common welfare of Christendom. For it not unfrequently happens that the care and salvation of souls are identified with the common good.'[6]

Leibnitz, in thus desiring to see the Christian family of nations preserved from the despotism of sovereigns on the one hand, and the awful calamities of war on the other, must have had in mind two memorable instances of appeal to the mediatorial office of the Papacy, at the close of the fifteenth century and toward the end of the sixteenth. The one was the reference to Alexander VI of the dispute between the sovereigns of Spain and Portugal concerning the limits of their possessions in the recently discovered New World; the other was the mediation invoked by Russia in the reign of Pope Gregory XIII (1572-83), and of which we have extant so authentic and interesting a narrative.[7]

Whatever Leibnitz may have thought, Protestant and German though he was, of reviving as one of the weapons of international Christian law the usage of interdicts and excommunications toward refractory princes and their subjects, it is certain that such revival is not wished for at Rome or by the Catholic world. But the restoration, in practice at least, if not in public law, of the mediatorial office of the Papacy would be an unmitigated blessing.

And this conclusion is most eloquently demonstrated by the action of Germany and Spain in the affair of the Carolinas, and the prompt and peaceful solution arrived at by Leo XIII

---

[6] Leibnitz, "Tractatus de Jure Suprematus," part iii.—G. G, Leibnitzii "Opera Omnia," vol. iv. p. 299. 6 vols. 4to, Geneva. 1768.

[7] See in *Revue des Questions Historiques* for January, 1885, Pierling's "Un Arbitrage Pontifical au XVIème Siècle; Mission Diplomatique de Possevin à Moscou."

With prospects of growth and prosperity far otherwise than flattering, the great German chancellor looked out for every foothold he could occupy for his countrymen from the Straits of Gibraltar, all along the African shores, to the Indian Ocean and the myriad islands of the Pacific. Even where the continents offer no room for new ownership, or where the most important islands are already covered by some European flag, any one of the almost forgotten or overlooked coral islets are valuable as stations for the fleets which are beginning to traverse the Pacific in every direction.

England, in the interval between 1870 and 1875, had remarked the importance of the Carolinas and Palaos groups, and so had Germany. In the latter year both powers resolved to occupy the most favorable positions in this archipelago, and formally presented a joint note to Spain declaring that they could not recognize her ownership of islands she had so long abandoned.

German colonists, on the contrary, had established themselves at several points in the archipelago, and formed there flourishing plantations and trading-posts. These facts, coming to the knowledge of the Spanish government and people, did what enlightened self-interest and a spirit of enterprise had failed to do—aroused a determination not to yield to strangers even these remote and certainly forgotten fractions of the vast colonial empire of Philip II. Spain, unhappily, was, like her next neighbor, France, a chronic though it may be an unconscious prey to that terrible and mortal decline implanted by the joint virus of Illuminism and Voltaireanism. The contagion had come from across the Pyrenees. The patient, though her life-blood was poisoned and her strength slowly but surely wasting away, labored under the delusion of all consumptives—that she was strong as ever, that nothing serious was the matter with her. Her popular masses still believe her the most powerful of nations.

Her pride, therefore, was fearfully aroused when the joint note of England and Germany was presented in 1875. It was stirred to a pitch of uncontrollable fury when in the first months of 1885 the German flag appeared in sovereignty over the waters of the archipelago. The island of Yap was formally occupied.

On August 14 the Spanish cabinet decided to address an official protest to the Powers against this occupation; and three days thereafter, on August 17, the German government officially notified them of the act of taking possession. The agitation throughout Spain became intense. In Madrid there was a formidable demonstration, and it required all the energy of the civil and military authorities to repress the attempts at lawlessness and even open insurrection. As time went on, and it was found that Germany would not recede from her position, in which she was supported by England, the effervescence grew apace. The nation, and the opposition press in particular, was clamorous for immediate war. Of course the practical good sense of King Alfonso made him feel that Spain was totally unprepared to wage war, her army being but ill-organized, her military navy utterly useless, and her finances in an almost hopeless state of confusion. Germany was too far away to be reached by land; and were she situated at the gates of the Peninsula, she had nothing to fear from Spain. So negotiations dragged their slow length along, till the tidings reached Madrid of what had happened in the port of Jomil, island of Yap, on August 25, when both a Spanish and a German war-vessel planted simultaneously the flags of their nations and took formal possession of the country.

The tidings of this seeming act of hostility reached Madrid on September 4. On the morrow the entire population apparently descended into the streets, attacked and sacked the palace of the German ambassador, tore down the German arms and trampled them under foot, and burned the German flag with every circumstance of ignominy.

It was a most serious crisis for the brave young king and his government. But his was not a spirit to be frightened by a mob, or to be hurried into a bootless war by the senseless cries of the popular masses. Nevertheless, some satisfaction must be given to the national sentiment wounded in its honor. The Spanish ambassador in Berlin is ordered to hold himself in readiness to ask for his passports at any moment.

Meanwhile, and as the whole civilized world is expecting a declaration of war and the breaking out of hostilities, the happy thought occurs, and is seized upon by both cabinets, of submitting the entire question of the occupation of the Carolinas to the arbitration of the Holy See. On September 24 it is officially announced that the Pope has been offered and has accepted the delicate mission, but one which may lead to an amicable settlement of the difficulty, and prevent the effusion of blood and what, to Spain, would have been a most ruinous warfare.

Leo XIII knew and felt the responsibility thus cast upon him. He was fully alive to the necessity of putting a speedy termination to a crisis which, in Spain at least, was of the most intense acuteness. He deputed to a commission of cardinals, the most eminent jurists and diplomatists in the Sacred College, the examination of the double question of fact and of international law involved in the case, with directions to use the utmost diligence in investigating and reporting.

In less than a month on October 22, Cardinal Jacobini sent to the cabinets of Madrid and Berlin the Pope's decision, which consisted in four points on which both governments were to agree, the fact of Spain's ancient discovery of the Carolinas and of their occupation by her being laid down as one ground for conciliation, and the liberty of Germans in the archipelago to occupy the land, develop agriculture, cultivate industry and commerce on a footing of equality with Spanish subjects being also guaranteed, together with a naval station for Germany and perfect freedom of navigation throughout the archipelago.

Thus Spanish sovereignty and German interests were safeguarded by the terms proposed from the Vatican. It was an admirable decision; it gave satisfaction in both countries to governments and peoples, and all danger of war was averted.

The final articles of agreement, drawn up in the Vatican,

and accepted for the respective sovereigns by the Marquis de Forgores and Herr Von Schloezer, their plenipotentiaries near the Holy See, were solemnly signed on December 17, 1885—a conclusion which was delayed by the death of Alfonso XII on November 25.

The blessing of a peace thus maintained, and of the calamities of a ruinous war from which the nation was saved by the moral courage of the young sovereign, was the last which Alfonso bestowed on his people. He had wished to save them from the devastations of cholera, or at least to sustain and cheer them under its awful visitations, rendered more awful still by the destruction and misery wrought by earthquakes, by exposing his own life to every danger in visiting, consoling and relieving the sufferers. Immortal honor to his heroic spirit! He was no unworthy heir of Sancho-el-Bravo and of Sancho's grandfather, the greatest of Christian kings, St. Ferdinand. May Spain, wearied and wasted, and sighing for the rest and restoration, reap the fruits of such examples and such sacrifices!

But let us glance a moment at this act of mediation of Leo XIII.

The relations of the Holy See with both Spain and Germany in September of 1885 were not a little delicate and complicated. The Spanish government administered by Canovas del Castillo, in spite of its conservative professions, yielded to the radical and revolutionary tendencies of a powerful minority in the legislature and the press, and that on the point most vital to the real warfare of the nation—the education of youth. The Concordat of 1854, in which it was expressly and solemnly stipulated that the teaching in all the government schools of every grade should be strictly in conformity with Catholic doctrine and practice, was openly violated. Indeed, the ministry then in power had gone a step in advance beyond their immediate predeessors in office in this wrong direction. They had sanctioned, in the university and intermediate schools, a system of instruction hostile not only to Christianity but to all positive religion. Besides, the superintendence guaranteed by the Concordat to the Spanish hierarchy over all schools, and the right of visitation inherent in their office, had long been rendered impossible by royal decrees modifying the Concordat—repealing, rather, its most important provisions —and that either without consulting the Holy See or in spite of its energetic opposition.

So were the political guides of a Catholic people giving up to the forces of irreligion which beset them what remained of their institutions round about—the very education of youth, the springs of the national life.

In Germany the admirable wisdom and moderation of Leo XIII had succeeded in winning the esteem of both the emperor and his all-powerful chancellor in obtaining the repeal of the "Falk Laws," in filling the most important episcopal sees, long deprived of the presence of a bishop, and in modifying the hard conditions imposed on the parochial clergy by the civil authorities.

It was only a beginning in a work of conciliation, restoration, and reparation which many had despaired of, but it was a great beginning. Both the Emperor William and the great chancellor had discovered that the worst foes of social order in Germany and of the empire which their joint labors had founded were not the seventeen or twenty millions of Catholic citizens it counted. They had also found out that the dogma of Papal Infallibility contained nothing which need alarm the lawful rights of civil sovereignty; the bugbear held up by Döllinger and his followers to excite the national susceptibilities had long vanished in thin air before the light of impartial truth.

On the other hand, it was found that no denomination of Christians taught doctrines so conservative of social order, so favorable to the authority of the prince and the magistrate, so conducive to an enlightened and generous obedience on the part of the citizen, as the Catholic Church. In the successive criminal attempts made on his life the venerable Emperor of Germany, when the first excitement and alarm were over, had found that the conspirators were neither Catholics nor acting in sympathy with any portion of his Catholic subjects. Catholicism, it gradually dawned on him and his counsellors, was one of the strongest bulwarks of his throne, one of the surest safeguards of his life. He could trust both the one and the other to the conscience, the honor, the devotion of his Catholic subjects.

Moreover, the doctrinal encyclicals successively published by Leo XIII were so admirably conceived, expressed, and calculated that they could not but force on such minds as Bismarck's the conviction that the Catholic Church alone was the great school of social doctrine, and that her Pontiffs were the only authority in the civilized world which laid down the law of belief and of life for the nations with a power which carried with it the conviction that Rome still spoke the words of Christ.

Every encyclical of Leo XIII, every one of his official acts, raised him ever higher and higher in the esteem of the German chancellor—no mean judge of men, of their acquirements, their motives, and their achievements.

Nevertheless, the fact that the Protestant Emperor of Germany and his Protestant chancellor had chosen the Pope as arbiter in this angry dispute about the Carolinas Islands took the whole civilized world by surprise. Would Leo XIII hold the balance with a firm hand between the two powers? Could he help remembering that Spain was still Catholic, no matter what might be the inconsistencies of her rulers or the radical tendencies to which her statesmen yielded? Could he forget the cruel, the gratuitous persecutions heaped by the Prussian legislature and the Imperial government of Germany on bishops, priests, and laymen simply because of their fidelity to principle and their attachment to the Holy See?

The extraordinarily prompt decision of the tribunal, so often appealed to in the past by nations and their rulers, first astonished expectant Europe, and then the almost simultaneous tidings that the decision was acceptable to both the appealing parties completed the surprise.

Let us hear Leo XIII himself giving to the cardinals,

assembled in consistory, an account of the transaction:[8] "We gladly accepted the office thus entrusted to us," he says, "because we hoped thereby to serve the cause of peace and humanity. We therefore examined and weighed in the balance of an impartial and equitable judgment the arguments of both litigants, .and then we submitted to them certain propositions as a basis of mutual agreement, which we hoped would prove acceptable to them.

"Spain brought forward many reasons in support of her right to that distant portion of Micronesia. She was the first nation whose ships had reached those shores—a fact acknowledged by the most distinguished geographers. The very name of Carolinas attested the Spanish title. Besides, the kings of Spain had more than once sent thither apostolic men as missionaries, and of this the records of the Roman Pontificate afford confirmatory proof; for there exists a letter of our predecessor, Clement XI, to Philip V, written in 1706, praising this prince for having equipped and furnished a vessel to convey missionaries to the Carolinas. In it the Pontiff also exhorts the king to continue to help propagate the Christian name and procure the salvation of multitudes of human beings.

"The same Pontiff also wrote to Louis XIV beseeching him not to hinder in any way the carrying out of an enterprise so happily begun by his grandson. Again, Philip V fixed an annual sum of two thousand crowns to be set apart for the support of these missions. Furthermore, no nation but the Spanish ever did anything to bring the light of the Gospel to these islands. And, finally, whatever information we possess of the manner of living and customs of the natives has been furnished by the missionaries.

"From this series of facts, viewed especially in the light of the international jurisprudence then in vigor, it is evident that the right of Spain to the Carolinas Islands is fairly established. For if any claim to sovereignty can be derived from the labor

---

8 Allocution of January 15, 1886. (See Appendix E.)

of civilizing a barbarous country, this claim must be highest in favor of such as endeavor to reclaim barbarians from pagan superstition to the Gospel morality, inasmuch as in true religion are to be found all the most powerful civilizing forces. On this principle were often founded the rights of sovereignty; and this was the case, for instance, of several islands in the ocean, of which not a few bear names given them by the Christian religion.

"Seeing, therefore, that a constant and well-founded public opinion conceded to Spain the sovereignty over the Carolinas, it is not surprising that when the late dispute began about their possession the whole Spanish nation was stirred with such excitement as to threaten not only the internal peace of the kingdom, but to imperil its relations with a friendly power.

"To the arguments brought forward by Spain, Germany on her side opposed others also based on the law of nations—that residence on land is necessary to possession; that, taking into account the facts of recent history, the law of nations sanctions as legitimate the claim to ownership of territory when the claimant occupies and uses it; that where the territory is not so occupied and used the land is accounted as having no owner. Wherefore, considering the fact that the Carolinas had not during a century and a half been occupied by Spain, these islands should have been adjudged the property of the first person taking possession of them. In addition to these reasons it was alleged that some such dispute as the present having arisen in the year 1875, both Germany and Great Britain affirmed they did not at all acknowledge the sovereignty of Spain over the Carolinas.

"In this divergence of opinions we took into account the respective rights and interests of the two contending nations, and confidently submitted a plan which we thought well fitted for bringing about a peaceful settlement of the difficulty. We were guided solely in this by our own sense of equity, and, as you are aware, both parties willingly accepted our proposal.

"Thus was accomplished an event which the present currents of public opinion forbade us to look forward to.

Providence willed that two illustrious nations should do homage to the supreme authority in the Church by asking it to fulfil an office so much in keeping with its nature, to preserve by its action the threatened peace and harmony between them. This is the fruit of that salutary and beneficent influence which God has attached to the power of the Supreme Pontiffs. Superior to the envious jealousy of its enemies, and more mighty than the prevailing iniquity of the age, it is subject neither to destruction nor to change.

"From all this, too, it becomes manifest how grievous an evil are the wars waged against the Apostolic See and the lessening of its rightful liberty. For thereby it is not merely justice and religion that are made to suffer, but the public good itself, since in the present critical and changeful condition of public affairs the Roman Pontificate would confer far greater benefits on the world if, with perfect freedom and rights unimpaired, it could devote all its energies to promoting, without hindrance, the salvation of the human race."

The concluding words of this brief allocution, affirming solemnly, as they do, the benefits to civilization and humanity which naturally flow from the exercise by the Popes of the functions of mediators between nation and nation, deserve the serious attention of both modern statesmen and modern peoples. Had the burning questions pending between the free and slaveholding States of the American Union been submitted to such mediation or arbitration as that of the Sovereign Pontiff before 1860, what bloodshed, what desolation, what commercial ruin, what manifold national calamities might have been avoided! Do not say that the religious sense of a Protestant nation would not have entertained the idea of such arbitration; do not believe that there existed not in Rome statesmen, diplomatists, jurists, men versed in the historical facts and the constitutional aspects of our great slavery problem and of the other territorial, legal, and political difficulties connected therewith.

Rome, as it then existed—the Rome of the Popes, with the Papal sovereignty and freedom unshackled—would have constituted a tribunal of arbitration endowed with qualities and attributes which, for the purposes of an American appeal, could have been found nowhere else. It was the serious interest and the fervent wish of Pius IX, then reigning, of the great statesmen and churchmen who surrounded him (as it was, indeed, of the entire Catholic world, as such), that the Union should be preserved; that nothing should oppose or impair the development of the national life; that slavery should be so gradually extinguished and slave-labor so transformed into free that the South should not suffer in its proprietary or agricultural interests, while the certain prospect of such extinction would appease the anti-slavery sentiment of the free States. Neither Great Britain, nor Germany, nor France, nor any other power which we could name, offered, as mediators, the disinterestedness and the absolute fitness for examining and deciding in our case which all must acknowledge in the Papal tribunal.

England and France were notoriously desirous of seeing the Union dissolved and the growth of the national power thus crippled for ever. There was then no German Empire, no United Germany; Austria never was our friend. Every conceivable interest would have impelled the Pope to settle our differences without any danger of an appeal to arms, without ruin to the South or loss of prestige or influence to the North. It might have been a long negotiation, but no interested or unnecessary delay would have kept the nation in a state of ferment. And such a plan of settlement and concord would have come from the Vatican as to satisfy both the great political parties, both the sections of the country, and to have enabled the patriotic and generous-minded of all opinions to work thenceforward together for the peaceful and gradual removal of the causes of discontent.

Every when nearly two millions of brothers stood facing each other in arms in the terrible conflict, and when Abraham Lincoln was induced to make the steps we know toward peace, had any good angel persuaded the combatants to suspend their mutual carnage and to submit their cause with all its grievances to one man, the acknowledged representative on earth of the Prince of Peace, we should have had that peace with honor to both North and South—a peace that should not have left behind the rankling memories caused by subsequent events.

The same reasons hold with regard to the settlement of the Alabama claims. How little satisfaction the settlement arrived at has given to either nation, how great and ruinous were the delays attendant upon the assembling and the discussions of the absurdly complex tribunal, and how enormous the costs to both governments, neither Americans nor Englishmen are likely to forget.

The concert of praise which, in the English-speaking world and elsewhere, has been heard after the settlement of the Hispano-German quarrel, is an assurance that non-Catholic public opinion is undergoing deep modifications not unfavorable to the Holy See.

The day is not far distant when the government of the United States will find it both wise and politic to imitate Prince Bismarck in his statesmanlike conduct towards the Prisoner of the Vatican, maintain an ambassador near him to represent the interests of our growing millions of Catholic citizens, and do homage to the supreme learning, incorruptible justice, and fatherly love of peace ever to be found in the Vicar of Christ on earth.

Of course the revolutionary press—both in Italy, where it is found necessary to justify the invasion, spoliation, and oppression of the Papacy, and in France, where they are preparing to trample under foot the Concordat—will continue to belittle the importance of this act of mediation. Elsewhere the conviction will grow steadily that, in the words of Ancillon quoted at the beginning of this chapter, there should be "a common center, a rallying-point for isolated states, ... a supreme tribunal, established in the midst of universal anarchy," whose decrees are sure to be "as respectable as respected."

One other remarkable act of Leo XIII relating to Spain was

his bull restoring the pilgrimage to Compostella.

No place on the European Continent, after Rome itself, had more attractions for the Catholic heart in every land all through the middle ages than the reputed tomb of the Apostle St. James the Elder at Compostella, in Galicia. The tradition about his relations with Spain was, briefly, this: At the dispersion of the apostles[9] it fell to the lot of James the Elder to carry the light of the Gospel to Spain (A.D. 41-42). After founding many churches throughout the Peninsula, James returned to Jerusalem with alms for the afflicted Christians of Palestine, among whom a great famine prevailed. Then was held the Council of Jerusalem, in which James took part. His death is briefly mentioned in the Acts of the Apostles. Two of his disciples, Athanasius and Theodore, as was the custom all through the ages of persecution, obtained the dead body of their master, and, taking it in all haste and secrecy to the port of Joppa, found there a vessel—a Phoenician merchantman, very likely—about to set sail for the west coast of Spain. The ocean pathway beyond the Straits of Gades were, as scholars are aware, well known to the Phoenician traders. So they went on their way to the magnificent Bay of Arosa, up which they sailed to Iria Flavia, then an imperial city at the head of the bay, and connected by an imperial highway with Braga, in Portugal, another imperial city. The body rested there for a brief space, and was then carried inland some miles to the site of the present Compostella, where it was buried in a Gallo-

---

[9] Eusebius, the most ancient historian of the Christian Church, states ("Ecclesiastical History," v. 18), what is also stated by the ancient author of "The Preaching of Peter," quoted by Clement of Alexandria in his "Stromata" (vi. 5), that it was Christ's express wish that the apostles should give the benefit of their labors to the land of Israel during twelve years before they dispersed to preach to all nations. The words quoted by Clement of Alexandria from the Κήρυγμα Πέτρου are the following: "Wherefore Peter says that the Lord said to the apostles, 'If any one, therefore, is willing to be led out of Israel by penance, and on account of My name to believe in God his sins will be remitted. After twelve years go forth into the world, lest anyone should say, We have not heard.'" (The substance of this note is taken from "The Chair of Peter," by Count J. N. Murphy.)

Roman tomb, probably that of some neophyte, the inscription on it being in mixed Gaelic and Latin. Naturally, Theodore and Athanasius continued in the district the labors begun by the martyred son of Zebedee, and in due time were gathered to their rest and buried by the side of James and in the same crypt. Then came the barbarian invasions, wave after wave, blotting out almost every vestige of Christianity and civilization from the land. Iria Flavia was blotted out, and the spot where the apostle and his disciples reposed was forgotten, or, the original Gallo-Roman population having been swept away, was unknown to the barbarous Suevi who took possession of Galicia. Not till about the year 818 did Providence recall the attention of all Spain and all Christendom to the spot where the first of the apostles to lay down his life for Christ had reposed for centuries. But, long before the year and date of this rediscovery, the fact of St. James being buried in Spain was mentioned in the Martyrologies and spoken of by Anglo Saxon authors of note.[10] Alfonso the Chaste, who was then sovereign of Galicia, apprised by Theodemir, Bishop of Iria Flavia, of the wonderful discovery of the tomb, hastened to the spot, and took at once every measure to rebuild over the shrine a temple more worthy of it than the primitive *Memoria* ruined by the barbarians and shrouded in oblivion b+y time. Around the new church grew the Compostella of the middle ages, which thenceforth, in spite of the fresh ruin wrought by the cruel but resistless Almansor in that same century, became the most famous place of pilgrimage in Europe, eclipsing for a time Rome itself. Calixtus II, while yet Archbishop of Vienne, in Dauphin6, visited the shrine in the beginning of the twelfth century, and gave a description of the tomb, the church, the city, the prodigious concourse of pilgrims from every Christian land, the splendid ceremonial, the more splendid piety of the great multitudes, and the magnificent charity and hospitality of the clergy-and citizens toward the wayfarers.

---

[10] See the learned work of Father Fita on the Shrine of Compostella.

Raised to the Papacy, he did all that Pope could do to encourage and foster the devotion to the shrine of St. James, and this devotion continued to grow century after century.

But, during the reign of Elizabeth, Essex and Raleigh spread terror among the fleets of Spain. The former sacked Cadiz and committed horrible excesses in the churches. His fleet ascended the Bay of Arosa and then hovered around Coruna. Then it was that the Archbishop of Compostella sent away into the interior everything holy and precious which could be removed. Taking on himself the task of preserving the relics of St. James and his two disciples from the possibility of profanation, he descended by night into the crypt, took out the remains of the three apostolic men and buried them in the center of the apse, in a tomb hastily and rudely constructed, and then obliterated all traces of his handiwork. His secret was well kept and died with him. The terror of the English fleets was like a sword suspended over the coast of Galicia till after the archbishop's death. Meanwhile all access to the crypt had been walled up, and so remained till, a few years ago, the present cardinal archbishop repaired the cathedral, and resolved, with the assistance of a mixed commission of ecclesiastics and laymen, to ascertain officially the condition of the tomb and its precious contents. The perquisitions ended first in discovering that the tomb was empty; and next, after the most careful excavation and search in every direction, in coming upon the rude grave in the apse, together with its confused heap of human bones, without a single writing or clue to enable the commission to pronounce as to whom they belonged. Another sub-commission of physicians and scientific men was now appointed for the purpose of examining, classifying, and identifying if possible, the fragments thus found.

They were pronounced to belong to three different skeletons—skeletons of adult men, one more aged than the others, and all in such a condition and bearing such characters as to warrant the belief that they could date some eighteen or nineteen centuries back. A portion of the cranium of one was wanting, that of the oldest; it was the mastoid bone, or back part of the skull, and this had been given long before the time of Essex as a present to the cathedral of Pistoia in Italy. This relic was carefully examined, and its peculiar characteristics were found to conform with the skull just discovered in Compostella.

The cardinal archbishop, a learned and scholarly man, felt his way carefully, step by step, and then submitted the conclusions which he and his commissions had arrived at to the judgment of the Holy See.

Leo XIII selected the leading cardinals, members of the Congregation of Rites, to examine all the documents transmitted from Spain. After a careful scrutiny they decided that some points demanded still further elucidation, and the Pope, desirous, as his predecessors have ever been in such matters, to leave no tittle of evidence unsifted, despatched to Compostella the Promoter of the Faith, Monsignor Agostino Caprara, with full powers to swear witnesses, etc. He thoroughly went over the whole ground, called around him from Madrid and elsewhere archaeologists, historians, anatomists, and other scientific men, weighed on the spot every fact and circumstance, reconciling seeming contradictions, clearing away doubts, and completing a compact body of evidence, with documentary proofs all classified. With this he returned to Rome, and the cardinals with their consultors again began the examination of the whole matter.

This time they arrived at a unanimous conclusion—that the remaining portions of the three skeletons discovered and examined by Cardinal Paya and his commissions of scientists and specialists were identical with the remains revered in Compostella since the ninth century as those of St. James the Elder and his two disciples, St. Athanasius and St. Theodore.

As the last chapter of this book is written the Queen Regent of Spain has given birth to a son, who was proclaimed under the title of Alfonso XIII The queen besought the Pope to be godfather to the royal infant, to which His Holiness assented. It was thought that the number thirteen was an unlucky number; but Señior Moret, the Minister of Foreign Affairs, replied to the objectors that if Alfonso XIII were only as great a king as Leo XIII was a great Pope, he should consider him very lucky.

And so the young Austrian princess has a long and difficult task before her, to watch over the life and fortunes of her infant child till he is of age to grasp the sceptre which others are now so ready and eager to snatch from a woman's hand.

God save Spain!

CHAPTER XXXIV

THE PRISONER OF THE VATICAN

IT IS THE FEAST OF THE ASCENSION, and there is to be a magnificent celebration at the basilica of St. John Lateran, the cathedral church of the Bishop of Rome, the Christian temple first in rank in the world. All Rome is to be there to-day, all the most distinguished artists in Italy, and the very 61ite of her scholars are all most anxious to take part in the solemnities.

What extraordinary circumstance thus attracts to the Lateran basilica, at the very extremity of the dustiest and most desolate part of Rome, all the aristocracy of rank and intellect in this most oppressive weather? They are throwing open to the public to-day the new apse of the basilica reconstructed, enlarged, and decorated with frescoes and mosaics—a royal work undertaken at the command and expense of Leo XIII, and which, artists say, is one of the most glorious works of restoration in the world.

But, the reader will ask, is not Leo XIII going to officiate in person, in his own cathedral church, on such an occasion? No; the Pope, a prisoner in the Vatican, will never set foot within the walls of the Lateran, never gladden his eyes with the sight of the great work of art due to His munificence.

Besides, on this day—the 3d of May—they are celebrating in Rome the death of Garibaldi, his apotheosis, or deification, as the liberal journals call it. The various revolutionary clubs are in the streets with flags and emblems and garlands, and there are to be grand processions. But should Leo XIII's carriage appear in the streets, or should he by some stealthy way appear in St. John Lateran this day, Heaven only knows the consequences which would follow.

No; the Prisoner of the Vatican could not venture into the streets of Rome—no, not even to officiate publicly in the church of St. Peter's; how much less safely could he pass through all Rome to pontificate in his own cathedral or to assist at the joyous celebration of today!

So we shall go to the Vatican, and spend as much as we can of this same Feast of the Ascension with that venerable man of seventy-seven, who bears so courageously the tremendous weight of an administration which knows not its equal on earth.

Here we are in the vast square of St. Peter's. The two great fountains within the opposite semicircles of the colonnade are throwing high into the sultry morning air their flashing waters—the symbols of the unceasing light for the mind and strength for the will which flow from that Holy Spirit ever abiding in the Church. We can only give a passing glance at the lofty dome, glittering in the golden radiance of the eastern sun, on the stately facade, on the middle of which stands Christ holding His cross, while on each side of Him, extending their lines along the church and the mighty sweep of the encircling colonnades, stand the colossal figures of apostles, patriarchs, prophets, martyrs—all glorified by the same golden splendors of a June morning in Rome.

Our carriage makes the circuit of St. Peter's and lands us in the interior court of St. Damasus. We alight, and, as we prepare to ascend story after story of the magnificent marble staircase leading to the Pope's apartments, we meet our friend Monsignor Macchi, the Maestro di Camera, or high chamberlain to His Holiness. Spare and tall, he greets us, as he does everybody, with the pleasantest words, and we ascend. The soldiers of the Swiss Guard, with their picturesque costume and mediaeval halberds, draw up to salute the high court dignitary. You will notice how grand, how solid, how massive even, everything is in these stairs and corridors. Up we go again, another long flight of the same stately dimensions. All is vast in this palace of the Vatican, where such large hospitality has so often been dispensed by the Popes; all is magnificent in its elegant simplicity. Was this not built to last for ever, as long as the peaceful principality of the

Papacy itself? There are beautiful frescoes here and there, which amateurs take leisure to examine. But we are hurrying to the Pope's early Mass in his quiet private chapel, and so may not tarry to gaze about us.

We enter the Guard-Room—spacious, lofty, gorgeously frescoed. The officers and guard at once rise to receive Monsignor Macchi, and we are in the ante-room, quite close to the Throne-Room, the door of which is open. The attendants, in rich costumes, take our hats and the tickets of invitation, and we pass into the comparatively small chamber which opens into the little private oratory. It is a great feast, and a number of distinguished persons have requested the honor of being present at the Holy Father's Mass and receiving Communion from his hand.

Folding-doors open out in front of the little altar, on which everything is ready for the celebration of the Holy Sacrifice. The priestly vestments are laid on the altar itself, and the Missal stands open at the Epistle side. We are ushered to seats in the middle of the room, where we can best see the Pope during the celebration. All present are absorbed in their devotions; no one seems to notice those who enter.

But where is the Pope?

He is still at his private devotions. This is for him a season of unusual fatigue, if one can so speak of a man who never knows, from year's end to year's end, any cessation from overwhelming labors and wasting cares.

After his long, weary days of never-ending toil, his encyclicals, discourses, or letters have to be written in the quiet hours of the night. And has he not been found by his faithful old valet in the morning with his head on his work-table, where sheer fatigue had brought on unrefreshing sleep?

Leo XIII is an early riser. His valet awakes him at a stated and early hour. The aged priest has not changed the simple habits of a lifetime because he is Pope. He is soon dressed in his cassock of pure white, and spends a few mordents in adoration at the altar of his private chapel. Then there is a half-hour spent in meditation or mental prayer on some of the great Gospel truths or mysteries. This over, one of his chaplains recites with him Prime, Tierce, and Sext—the three first morning "Hours" of the canonical office—and the Holy Father is ready for Mass.

Around his private apartments, meanwhile, all is silence. The wearied spirit of him who is Vicar of Christ soars aloft to the throne of grace, to meditate there in the divine light on his own needs and the needs of his wide-spread flock. Prayer is to him a bath of life, from which he comes forth refreshed and strengthened for the day's labor before him. But prayer is also a preparation for the great priestly rite which is and ever has been Leo XIII's supreme comfort—the Mass.

We were also thinking of The Presence on yonder lighted altar, when there was a slight commotion in the chapel. All of a sudden every one had knelt as if moved by some common electric impulse. A white figure stands before the altar, with his face turned to us and the right hand holding a silver aspersory sprinkling holy water on the assembled worshippers. It is but an instant that he remains fronting us. The face is of alabaster whiteness, and transparent almost, and the eyes are all-radiant with the fire of piety and fatherly kindness. The words of blessing were scarcely audible. It was as if some of Fra Angelico's glorified saints had walked out of the canvas or come down from the frescoes on the wall and shone upon us a moment, lifted his hand in blessing, murmured low words of love and greeting, and then turned away.

Leo XIII then genuflected before the altar and retired a little to our left, but out of sight, to read with his chaplain the psalms and prayers before Mass. There is in the Pope's pronunciation of the Latin something uncommonly sweet and distinct. His utterance is slow and measured. Every word is given out as if the speaker were weighing its deepest sense and enjoying it. No man I ever saw at the altar so impressed me with the idea of one who is face to face with God and uttering every word with infinite reverence and feeling. The first Psalm he read is the eighty-third: "How lovely are Thy tabernacles, O Lord of Hosts! My soul longeth and fainteth for the courts of the Lord." Every now and then some verse in the Psalms moved him more powerfully, and his deep, grave voice sounded more clearly: "Wilt Thou be angry with us for ever? or wilt Thou extend Thy wrath from generation to generation?" Or again: "Surely His salvation is near to them that fear Him, that glory may dwell in our land." Psalm after Psalm is thus recited. Is there not a quiver in the aged voice? "Have mercy on me, O Lord; for I have cried to Thee all the day. ... For Thou, O Lord, art sweet and mild; and plenteous in mercy to those that call upon Thee."

When he came to recite alone the beautiful series of prayers after the preparatory Psalms the silence in the chapel was painful. It was as if every heart there held its own pulsations to throb in that of the great High-Priest of the Church pleading before the mercy-seat.

"Bend down to our prayers, O God of infinite mildness, the ears of Thy fatherly love, and enlighten our hearts with the grace of the Holy Spirit, that we may deserve worthily to minister at Thy mysteries and to love Thee with charity everlasting. ... Oh! we beseech Thee, O Lord, visit and purify our consciences, that our Lord Jesus Christ on coming to us may find there a dwelling prepared for Him."

And now the slender white form is again before the altar; he kneels a moment, rises, and stands ready to be vested. Everything is done so quietly, so reverently, that you look on as if entranced. His chaplains assist him, evidently feeble and seemingly fragile as he is, with a respect all mingled with tenderness.

At last he is vested and begins the Mass. As Leo XIII stands before us in his full priestly vestments, it is painfully apparent how aged is that frame on which rests the awful burden of such responsibility, care, and toil. The shoulders and head are slightly bent, as if in reverence to the tabernacle. Beneath the white skull-cap, or berretta, is a circle of the snow-white hair. Every tone of the priestly voice is now fuller, more measured, and instinct with deeper feeling.

"I will go unto the altar of God, to God who giveth joy to my youth. ... Judge me, O God! and distinguish my cause from the nation that is not holy; from the unjust and deceitful man deliver me. ... Send forth Thy light and Thy truth; they have conducted me and brought me to Thy holy mount and into Thy tabernacles. ... I will praise Thee on the harp, O God, my God! Why art thou sad, O my soul! and why dost thou disquiet me?"

Then came the Confession, and, as the aged form bent lowly before the Presence there, every word seemed to shake it with emotion. He is, in truth, standing before the heavenly court on high, and suing for forgiveness to that Awful Majesty, surrounded by the angelic and the saintly multitudes. "I have sinned grievously, through my fault, through my fault, through my exceeding great fault."

It is the feast of the Ascension of our Lord into heaven. The Mass is one of triumphant joyousness. The priest at the altar is made to stand with the apostles and disciples on Mount Olivet watching the form of the risen Saviour ascending slowly beyond our sphere: "Ye men of Galilee, why stand you looking up to heaven?"

But the eyes of faith follow Him beyond the veil and to where He sits enthroned at the right hand of the Father. Leo XIII has but a step to make to pass behind the veil. His heart has long been there. He recites the angelic hymn, the "Glory be to God on high!" as if he had already joined the exultant throng of blessed spirits.

"We praise Thee! We bless Thee! We adore Thee! We give Thee thanks for Thy great glory, O Lord God, Heavenly King, God the Father Almighty."

One who has written of Leo XIII the most unkind and undutiful things ever put in print about him has also recorded that it is impossible to be present while he celebrates Mass without feeling that this man is nearer to God than any one else, and speaks to Him in a tone of deeper reverence, love, and adoration.

We, who have spent within a few years of half a century in

priestly ministrations, are bound to say that nothing ever so powerfully moved our soul as to see Leo XIII at Christ's altar, his whole soul lifted up as if the Beatific Vision held it and made it plead there and supplicate with great heart-cries for the Church whose dangers, trials, and needs are his especial care.

The holy rite occasionally seems to be too much for him. His frame is so shaken that you fancy he will fall if not supported by his chaplains. But the strong will sustains him, and during the Canon and after the Consecration there is a continual upward movement of head and shoulders, as if caused by a weight too heavy to carry.

One could have wished that a person apparently so feeble and so overworked as the Holy Father should not have to give Communion to the large numbers of strangers and pilgrims who are occasionally admitted as a great favor to hear the Pope's Mass. But that is the supreme consolation of Catholics, to receive Christ's divinest gift from his hand who is Vicar to the Giver.

All approach in turn without the slightest confusion or embarrassment. It is a very touching sight. Leo XIII pronounces the sacramental words with extraordinary emphasis and sweetness as each one kneels before him. He presents his hand, which holds the sacred Host, to be kissed by the communicant before placing the Bread of Life on the tongue. Is it not right? He represents the God "who openeth His hand and filleth every living soul with blessing"; we kiss in his the Hand which bestows on us in Communion the pledge of the life eternal.

At length the Mass is over, and the Pope and all present have heard a second Mass of thanksgiving. When the priest has withdrawn from the altar commences a scene such as can only be beheld in Rome, in the home of the Common Parent of Christendom, and at the foot of the very altar where the High-Priest of our faith has just broken to his children the Bread of life eternal.

They bring an arm-chair to the Epistle side, and the Holy

Father is seated, and all present come once more in succession to kneel at his feet, whose very face and air and all about him remind you of Christ the Lord receiving little children and their parents. Family groups are introduced together by good Monsignor Macchi, who whispers to the Holy Father who they are and whence they come. It is a sight never to be forgotten, so full of that light of charity which is the light of Heaven.

How radiant these sweet, spiritualized features are with fatherly interest and kindness! Here are parents who have brought from afar, from the ends of the earth, their little girl to receive her First Communion from the hand which is now laid in blessing on the child's head. Can she ever forget these wonderful eyes bent on her, and the great fatherly soul looking out from behind that transparent face, and the sweet words of blessing he utters? No wonder children are so drawn to Leo XIII. And why, oh! why can he not go out into the streets of Rome? Why cannot that great father go and collect these little ones around ,him, and by his words, his blessing, his very air, and the virtue which goes forth from him, draw these innocents and bind them for ever to Christ?

Parents and children have gone away with their eyes full of tears of joy and their hearts full of reverence. Then other groups come in turn—the afflicted, the tried; general officers, Frenchmen among them, bronzed in distant climes and by long service, but soldiers of Christ as well. How Leo XIII knows to say brave words to these noble professors of the faith! And how reverently they kiss that fatherly hand extended to them or the embroidered slipper on his feet who has borne the words of the Gospel of Peace over the mountains and the seas to the remotest tribes! But Leo XIII seldom gives you an opportunity to bend down and kiss his feet at these morning receptions in the holy place. And then there are journalists and other soldiers of the truth for whom Leo XIII has an especial regard. These are the men on whom he relies in the great battle with popular error and prejudice. Be sure that his first and last recommendation to such will be charity—charity in all things. For why should truth triumph, if not to make charity reign among men?

Here is our turn. Do not be afraid or ashamed to kneel to that venerable man, even though you be not a Catholic. His blessing, the blessing of one who has battled so long for Christ and who has held His banner aloft in the eyes of the nations, will bring you nothing but good. And as you look into those love-lit eyes and watch the ineffably sweet smile around that mouth, do you not think that somewhat of a warmer love, a deeper interest goes out to you, precisely because you are not one of his flock, although he deems you one of his children?

And now we are invited to be a little longer with the Holy Father. Is he not too fatigued? does he not wish to be left alone awhile? No. He is going to take his morning refection before beginning his terrible round of official labors. Quite near the little chapel is the Pope's breakfast-room. It is simple enough in all conscience. And what is this breakfast? A cup of black coffee with a small roll of bread. Nothing more.

And now the breakfast is ended and the Pope withdraws to his private study, where his enormous correspondence and his secretaries are waiting for him.

Every day in the week and every hour in each day has its own appointed labor. The congregations or standing committees of cardinals, among whom are divided all the matters connected with the vast administration of a Church numbering 200,000,000, report regularly to the Holy Father. Some of them have the Pope for president and hold their sittings in his presence. The Propaganda has now two distinct sections, one of which has the same superintendence over the missions and spiritual interests of the Eastern nations that the Propaganda proper has of all other missionary countries. Its multiplicity of affairs would be alone sufficient to occupy a host of active and devoted men.

Here is another new office which the circumstances of the times in Italy have compelled the Holy Father to create. At its head is Monsignor Gabriel Boccali, one of the men whom Leo XIII reared and trained in Perugia to be bright lights in God's Church. He is *Uditor di Sua Santità*—auditor or judge in the

Pope's own palace. The Holy Father has unbounded confidence in him, for he knows him well. Young, pious, devoted to his duty, learned beyond his years, he is sure to rise to the highest eminence. But he will ever be the true priest and servant of the Church.

The special relations of the bishops of Italy to the Holy See in presence of the Italian government, and the need they have of the Holy Father's support, together with the necessity of choosing the very best and safest men for Italian bishoprics, have imposed on him a heavy load of anxiety. It is on such men as Monsignor Boccali that he puts a part of the labor which this peculiar position imposes.

Innumerable congregations and commissions besides have their special work to do, and to report regularly. And Leo XIII is not one with whom it is safe to be unpunctual, or irregular, or inexact, or slovenly in any way. Great as is his mind, and high as it soars in his doctrinal expositions or his masterly surveys of social conditions, political exigencies, or the relative positions and tendencies of philosophical systems, his is also an eminently practical mind, to which the minutest details are grateful. Nay, sometimes people are surprised to find that the Holy Father, whose solicitude extends to every diocese and mission on the surface of the globe, will be familiar with the smallest particulars of administration and insist on the minutest exactness from all who report to him. His memory and his all-grasping intellect seem to be equal to the most astounding labor.

On all these weighty, intricate, perplexing matters which every congregation, every commission treats, his judgment has always to be given. And it is always a deliberate and enlightened judgment.

The Cardinal Vicar, Parocchi, for instance, every Saturday evening has his special audience to report on the affairs of the diocese of Rome for the week last past. Every detail of administration is gone into. Primary, Secondary Schools, the Seminario Romano with its Institute of High Literature, the various confraternities, the parochial work in all the churches, and many other weighty matters are to the Holy Father, as Bishop of Rome, things of absorbing interest. Even with one so zealous, so entirely devoted, so experienced, and so gifted as Cardinal Parocchi, Leo XIII's conscience will not be at rest till he has known and judged for himself on the ensemble and the details.

We could mention the Congregation of Studies, the Commission of Historical Studies, and other bodies which co-operate with the Holy Father in keeping high and raising ever higher the level of science in the great schools of Rome and Italy; all these have to report regularly. And it can easily be imagined if one of Leo XIII's intellectual tastes and culture will dismiss the cardinals who report to him with a few brief words or be satisfied with a perfunctory examination.

Perfunctory Leo XIII is in nothing. He is thorough, and thoroughly in earnest, in all that pertains to the work of his subordinates or his own.

And then there is the Cardinal Secretary of State and the terribly difficult and incredibly delicate work of dealing with the foreign governments. Look over the entire political and diplomatic field, and think of the hard and long battles the Holy See has to fight, not only with non-Catholic courts but with those that we call Catholic. All this is a matter of daily, sometimes of hourly, concern and labor for the Holy Father.

He has to receive ambassadors, archbishops, bishops, pilgrims, deputations, addresses from the numerous Catholic unions and committees, and from Catholic congresses. All this is a part of the working of the living organism of Catholicity. But it is as uninterrupted as the circulation of the blood in the frame.

Go by permission, about ten or eleven o'clock in the morning on the days when the Holy Father receives, and sit in the Throne-Room for the two hours before noon during which audience after audience is given. You look at Monsignor Macchi's spare and spent figure, and you wonder when this good prelate finds rest. He seems to be ever on foot. But his graceful courtesy knows no change. You look at the Pontiff's own face and form, and wonder how the lamp of life is fed or does not go out in such a frail vessel.

But only think of the work that one man has to go through!

At noon the Pope retires for a walk in the gardens of the Vatican during the cool season. In summer this outdoor recreation is perforce put off till evening. But there are the evening audiences, too, which are the most numerous, the longest, and the most wearing. Then it is that bishops are received to report on the state of their dioceses, and that priests who come with them are granted the favor of an audience.

There are certain occasions when strangers are so numerous that private audiences are out of the question. Then a day is fixed when they are admitted by a ticket from Monsignor Macchi to one of the great halls in the Vatican, and the Holy Father passes through their ranks, blessing them and saying some kind words in French and Italian.

But in times of pilgrimage and jubilee, as will be 1887, the year of the Pope's Golden Jubilee, the whole Catholic world sends its bands of pilgrims from every land to pay their homage of love to the Vicar of Christ, and the stream of visitors to the Vatican seems never to end.

But what a consolation to such a fatherly heart as that of Pius IX or Leo XIII, so tried by the persecutions of the Church and the forced captivity they endure, to see this unending procession of nations and peoples coming and going through the halls of the Vatican, around the seat of the Common Father and the Tomb of the holy Apostles!

Where has there ever been seen anything like what Rome saw in 1877, and what it will again see in 1887 when the whole Christian world will pour forth at the feet of Leo XIII the expression of its reverence, love, and fealty? But think, too, of the addition to the ordinary labors which have to be gone through, no matter what throngs may flock to the Vatican or come and go through the glorious temple alongside.

When, then, does Leo XIII find time for his ordinary

meals? They are solitary and frugal meals. Look at his face and see if there are there any signs of indulgence of any kind. The simplest food, a little wine and water—the beverage of all Italians—a little fruit, such is Leo XIII's ordinary morning fare. At night the repast is also frugal.

The Breviary Office is recited with one of his chaplains. The utter weariness begotten by the terrible round of official duties is lightened or dispelled by the pleasure the Pope finds in prayer, in the recitation of the inspired Psalms of "the Sweet Singer of Israel," in the lessons of Holy Scripture and the brief record of the life of the saint of the day.

After examination of conscience and night prayers the aged Pope is supposed to retire and to rest. His room is but simply, scantily furnished; and his rest, when not broken in upon, is barely sufficient to restore the forces of exhausted nature. And he is an early riser. His habits, as we have said elsewhere, are those of an ascetic. But does he never break in upon his rest? Too frequently, they say.

His magnificent encyclicals; his consistorial allocutions; his addresses to pilgrims, deputations, and societies; his most important bulls or constitutions, like those on the restoration of the Scotch hierarchy, on the settlement of the difficulties in England between the bishops and the regulars, are written or corrected or finished in the quiet of the night, when all in the Vatican enjoy much-needed repose.

But the white-robed figure, so much like a supernatural apparition, watches, works, prays alone in the stillness; He bears the burden of a whole world. His soul is sad with the sorrows, trials, sufferings of the nations.

The lamp in the Pope's room in the Vatican, shining at night when all around is darkness, gives forth the *Lumen in Cœlo,* that supernal light which even now illuminates both hemispheres. No such light, since St. Peter's teaching and virtues shone in that very spot, confounding and appalling the licentious and cruel Nero, ever shed its splendors on the world from the Seven Hills of Rome.

meals? They are solitary and frugal meals. Look at his face and see if there are there any signs of indulgence of any kind. The simplest food, a little wine and water—the beverage of all Italians—a little fruit, such is Leo XIII's ordinary morning fare. At night the repast is also frugal.

The Breviary Office is recited with one of his chaplains. The utter weariness begotten by the terrible round of official duties is lightened or dispelled by the pleasure the Pope finds in prayer, in the recitation of the inspired Psalms of "the Sweet Singer of Israel," in the lessons of Holy Scripture and the brief record of the life of the saint of the day.

After examination of conscience and night prayers the aged Pope is supposed to retire and to rest. His room is but simply, scantily furnished, and his rest, when not broken in upon, is barely sufficient to restore the forces of exhausted nature. And he is an early riser. His habits, as we have said elsewhere, are those of an ascetic. But does he never break in upon his rest? Too frequently, they say.

His magnificent encyclicals, his consistorial allocutions, his addresses to pilgrims, deputations and societies, his most important bulls or constitutions, like those on the restoration of the Scotch hierarchy, on the settlement of the difficulties in England between the bishops and the regulars, are written, or corrected or finished in the quiet of the night, when all in the Vatican enjoy much-needed repose.

But the white-robed figure, so much like a supernatural apparition, watches, works, prays alone in the stillness. He bears the burden of a whole world. His soul is sad with the sorrows, trials, sufferings of the nations.

The lamp in the Pope's room in the Vatican, shining at night when all around is darkness, gives forth the *Lumen in Cœlo*, that supernal light which even now illuminates both hemispheres. No such light, since St. Peter's teaching and virtues shone in that very spot, confounding and appalling the licentious and cruel Nero, ever cast its splendors on the world from the Seven Hills of Rome.

APPENDICES

APPENDIX A

THE ROMAN UNIVERSITIES, like those of Bologna, Paris, Oxford, etc., were a union, chartered by both the ecclesiastical and the civil authorities, and teaching all the branches or sciences needful to the great liberal professions of theology, law, and medicine. They did more than this, however; for they deserved their appellation of "university" by teaching all that was worth learning in human and divine knowledge—*universitas scientiarum et artium.*

This will be fully seen and understood from a brief sketch of the University of Sapienza as it existed under the fatherly and generous government of the Popes. It was founded by Boniface VIII in 1303, a Pope who, whatever be his supposed or real demerits, certainly had the merit of being both a scholar and a most enlightened promoter of the highest scholarship. Besides the Sapienza, which still remains as a national monument to his liberal genius, the traveller will be shown, in the museum of the old University of Bologna, a statue in hammered bronze plates erected to him by the Bolognese professors and people in grateful testimony of his protection of their rights.

The Roman university lived on through the disastrous years of the Papal exile at Avignon, as well as through the vicissitudes of the great schism. It was then enlarged by Eugenius IV (Colonna), Nicholas V, and by the clever Spaniard, Alexander VI The great Franciscan monk, Sixtus V, bestowed on it much care and liberality, and from his time, as is related in the text, it began to be called the Sapienza. His immediate successors continued this munificent protection. Leo X reformed its constitution and organization, gave it new statutes, appointed handsome salaries for the professors, erected the university chapel, and endowed two chaplaincies for its service. Gregory XIII, the Bolognese Ugo Buoncompagni, encouraged still further higher studies by granting to all students taking out the degree of doctor a life annuity of twenty-five crowns. Sixtus V did far more, enlarging, repairing, beautifying the university buildings, and creating a congregation or standing committee of cardinals to superintend its teaching as well as all studies in the Roman schools. Alexander VII completed it, as the inscription in front of the church testifies.

To name the Pontiffs who added to its efficiency, enlarged the sphere of science within it, or enriched by princely contributions some one or several of the university departments would be tedious. One would really seem to be sketching, in so doing, the progress of every one almost of those sciences of which the nineteenth century is as proud as if they had been unknown to preceding ages.

Innocent XI, while persecuted and oppressed by Louis XIV, founded the Theatre of Anatomy at the instigation of the celebrated anatomist Lancisius. Clement XI made splendid additions to the library. Benedict XIV decreed that the professorial chairs should only be obtained by a public concursus. He also made ample provisions for the chairs of mathematics, physics, and chemistry, and provided theatres for experimental physics and anatomy, with suitable apparatus. Later Pontiffs added other chairs according as the progress of science or the needs of the age demanded.

The French under Bonaparte closed all these schools, as they had done to the schools of Milan, Bologna, Pavia, and other Italian cities. Restored by Pius VII and then suppressed, the Sapienza was once more reopened on his restoration in 1814.

But the greatest benefactor of this university was Leo XII,

who, as above stated, renovated this establishment and all the other educational establishments in Rome and the Papal States. Five colleges composed the Sapienza or Roman University—those of theology, philosophy, law, medicine, and philology.

"The academical year," says Dr. Donovan, "commences on November 5 and ends on June 27, during which interval gratuitous lectures are given in Latin, Greek, Hebrew, Arabic, Syriac, and Chaldaic; in botany, chemistry, natural history, anatomy, physiology, pathology, pharmacy, and surgery; in algebra, geometry, physics, mechanics, hydraulics, optics, astronomy, mineralogy, and archaeology; in sacred eloquence, dogmatic theology, and Sacred Scripture; in the law of nature, the law of nations, canon, civil, and criminal law. The schools of the Academy of St. Luke are also attached to the university, forming part of the edifice, and in them the pupils are gratuitously taught painting, sculpture, architecture, geometry, perspective, optics, anatomy, history, mythology, etc., by eleven professors, forming a distinct establishment, under the direction of a president. Pius VII instituted a school of engineering, which was remodelled by Leo XII The number of students ... generally exceeds one thousand."[1]

Besides the University of the Sapienza there was the Roman College, or Gregorian University, still more numerously attended, the various national colleges sending their pupils to its schools. Then there was the Propaganda, a university in itself and the great nursery for heathen and non-Catholic countries.

All these great schools were endowed with more than princely magnificence by the successors of the Fisherman, whose object was to make all sciences the handmaids of religion, the zealous servants of the God of all knowledge. Museums, libraries, collections of all the rarest monuments of ancient and modern art, were at the disposition of students and professors—all these rare treasures and scientific

---

[1] "Rome, Ancient and Modern," by Rev. J. Donovan, D.D., vol. iii. c. 11.

apparatus receiving continual additions from each reigning Pontiff and the cardinals and other prelates, who emulated the enlightened zeal of the popes.

Thus was Rome made the intellectual as well as the religious head of the civilized world, the limited revenues of the Popes permitting them to foster all the arts of peace, while their people, without a great standing army or navy, knew nothing of the load of taxation which at present renders their lot well-nigh intolerable.

The University of Sapienza, like all the schools of Rome, continued to be fostered and developed by Gregory XVI and Pius IX till the Piedmontese occupation of Rome superseded the authority of the Holy Father, to the great detriment of education as well as of literary and scientific progress.

APPENDIX B

Among those who contended for this premium was the Rev. Tobias Kirby, D.D., a young Irish priest, who had come to Rome in 1829 and has lived there ever since. Of course he lost the prize, although his dissertation on the same subject, printed at the request of Leo XIII, and now before us, is a most creditable performance.

"I was not personally acquainted with Monsignor Pecci at the time," said to us the other day this venerable prelate, now Archbishop of Ephesus, "and did not make his acquaintance till long afterwards while he was Cardinal Bishop of Perugia. Meeting him one day in the Vatican, I made bold to introduce myself—not a very difficult thing, for nothing could exceed the affability and unaffected goodness of His Eminence. After exchanging the first sentences required by courtesy, I asked him if he were the same young distinguished jurist who, in 1835, bore off the prize on Appeals to the Supreme Pontiff in person.' He replied, with a smile, that he was; and I told him I had come after a long lapse of years to do homage to him as to my victor in that contest. It was a very pleasant introduction; for the eminent prelate, revered throughout all Italy for his learning, his eloquence, and his many virtues, was not loath to recall the academical struggles of long ago, when young men contended apparently for a paltry sum of money. After the death of Pius IX and the elevation to the papal chair of Cardinal Pecci," Dr. Kirby went on, "I happened to be in the Vatican to pay my homage on a certain occasion. 'Holy Father,' I said, 'I have found the dissertation you were inquiring about, among my papers.' 'Have you, indeed?' he replied. 'Well, I should much like to see it, and you must publish it.' Thus it was my little pamphlet saw the light. But," continued Dr. Kirby, "you can see in this little trait the charming humility and simplicity of the Pope's character. To those whom he is acquainted with personally, or who are in any way admitted to his intimacy, he is on the throne what he was fifty years ago—a man utterly devoid of self-consciousness and self-seeking."

Dr. Kirby dedicates the printed dissertation to the Pope in a graceful Latin address not unworthy of Leo XIII's classic taste. "Deign, Holy Father," he says, "to accept these unscholarly pages as a part of the spoils of those vanquished by you at the beginning of your glorious career. Accept them also as some slight earnest of the ancestral faith and devotion toward your Holiness—that is, the Chair of Peter—which I imbibed with my mother's milk. 'For we Irish,' to use the words of my fellow-countryman, St. Columbanus, 'are firmly attached to the Chair of St. Peter. Rome, in truth, is great and her fame is wide-spread. But in our country she is only great and illustrious through that Chair. Because of the two Apostles of Christ you of Rome are almost heavenly beings, and Rome is by them the head of all the churches on earth.'

"So, kneeling at the feet of your Holiness, I ask a blessing for myself, for this college, and my native Ireland; I also pray God to guide your Holiness by His light in the government of the Church, so that even as you were always the victor in the beginning of your sacred warfare for the truth, so you may continue to vanquish all the enemies of the Church to the end."

APPENDIX C

The cardinals are the immediate counsellors and coadjutors of the Pope, who divide with him in Rome the enormous labor of governing upwards of two hundred million Catholics spread all over the globe, and of transacting in the center of Catholicity the vast business pertaining to this administration.

This complex business is divided into various departments and subdepartments, at the head of which is a "Congregation," or standing committee, of cardinals, assisted by a staff of the most eminent jurists, canonists, theologians, and specialists, who, as consultors and referendaries, thoroughly sift each matter submitted to the congregation before it is pronounced upon by the cardinals in session, and then reported to the Sovereign Pontiff for his sanction. The decision thus sanctioned is then signed by the cardinal president of the congregation and by the secretary, and is final, generally speaking.

These congregations, as one may imagine, are very numerous, the same cardinal often doing service in several—a service so laborious that no one who has not been in Rome and followed attentively the working of this great and complicated administrative machinery can have any notion whatever of the continual and enormous fatigue thus imposed on the resident members of the Sacred College.

Here are the names of the most important of these congregations:

1. *Inquisition*—Not that established in Spain as an instrument of state policy, and often maintained in its cruel and unsparing measures in spite of the remonstrances of the Holy See, but the Roman Inquisition, whose object is to watch over the purity of the Christian doctrine in every part of Christ's flock Its judgments are merely doctrinal.

2. *The Index*—For the condemnation of books contrary to faith and morals.
3. *The Propagation of the Faith,* or *Propaganda*—It does the work of Christ's Vicar by taking all possible means to spread the faith in heathen lands and to restore it in lands distracted by heresy. It has a special sub-congregation for the superintendence of all churches belonging to the Oriental Rites, and a special commission of three cardinals for revising and correcting of Oriental ecclesiastical books.
4. *Examination of Bishops.*
5. *Extraordinary Ecclesiastical Affairs.*
6. *Bishops and Regulars*—Judges appeals from the decisions of bishops, hears causes between bishops and members of religious orders, examines and approves the rules of all monastic orders.
7. On *the State of Regulars or Religious Orders.*
8. *The Sacred Penitentiary.*
9. *The Congregation of the Council*—Interprets the doctrine and disciplinary decrees of General Councils.
10. Congregation of Studies—For the studies within Rome and all Italy. To this the present Pope has joined a commission on historical studies.
11. *Sacred Rites.*

APPENDIX D

THE RIGHT OF VETO IN PAPAL ELECTIONS

The three acknowledged Catholic Powers, France, Spain, and Austria (as well as Portugal, according to some authors), had, by moral compulsion or in recognition of some great service rendered to religion, obtained the right of veto or "exclusion" in a conclave. If a certain candidate happened to be obnoxious to the sovereign of any of these kingdoms, he had a right to protest through his ambassador against the choice of such candidate, thereby "excluding" him from all chance of being elected. This right or privilege could only be exercised once during the conclave by any Power, and that before a two-thirds vote had been cast for any candidate. Once such vote had been given the election was over, and no veto or "exclusion" availed to invalidate it.

There is no instance on record of such right of "exclusion "having been exercised by Portugal.

The last instance of "exclusion "was that exercised by Spain in the conclave which, in January, 1831, elected Gregory XVI The person thus excluded was Cardinal Giustiniani, who on the morning of January 7 received twenty-one votes, within four of the required two-thirds. Thereupon the Spanish Cardinal Marco communicated to the dean of the Sacred College and to Cardinal Odescalchi, nephew to Giustiniani, a note of Pedro Gomez Labrador, ambassador of the King of Spain to the Holy See, dated December 24, 1830, and expressly "excluding"Cardinal Giustiniani.

The note was read to the Sacred College immediately after the ballot which gave Cardinal Giustiniani twenty-one votes. This venerable man at once advanced with a joyous air and step into the middle of the chapel, and, after expressing his surprise at such "exclusion "coming from the King of Spain, who had bestowed on him during his nunciature at Madrid signal marks of esteem and favor, he continued:

"Of all the benefits bestowed on me by his Majesty

[Ferdinand VII], that which I look upon as the chief and the most grateful to me—at least in its consequences—is that he has this day excluded me from the lofty dignity of the Pontificate. Conscious as I am of my own infirmity, I could never have anticipated the danger of being burdened with so heavy a responsibility. Still, perceiving during these last days, to my surprise, that I was thought of in this respect, I was filled with heartfelt grief. Today, as this load of anxiety is removed from me, my peace of mind is restored. ..."

It was no secret that Cardinal Giustiniani was utterly opposed to his own elevation to the Papacy. In this he resembled Cardinal Pecci.

Upon this right of veto in connection with the conclave of February, 1878, we may quote the following words: "This privilege, which so often proved to be injurious to the interests of the Church, would be still more in our times, when governments have become entirely separated from the Church. The grounds on which it was originally granted having thus ceased to exist the privilege itself thereby ceased to exist. A journal said something about this veto. But, whatever may have been the dispositions of those who could have claimed the privilege, it is certain that no move was made in that direction, and that the governments showed that they disclaimed it, or rather that they knew they had lost all right to it. Thus it is that, even in the midst of new persecutions, the Church succeeds in freeing herself from bonds and impediments which she had to bear with in other circumstances, but which were far from being desirable or serviceable to her."

APPENDIX E

"Venerable Brothers: The matter on which we have undertaken to address you is already well known to the public. As, however, it regards the common welfare of all nations and constitutes a revival of a most honorable customary function of the Apostolic See, we have thought that the transaction deserved to be related to you by ourselves on this important occasion.

"In the month of September last we were requested, both by the Emperor of Germany and the King of Spain, to take upon ourselves to arbitrate between them in the dispute arisen concerning the Carolinas Islands. We gladly accepted the office thus entrusted to us, in the hope of helping the cause of peace and humanity. We therefore examined and weighed in the balance of an impartial and equitable judgment the arguments of both parties, and then submitted certain propositions as a basis on which both should agree, and which we hoped would prove acceptable to them.

"Spain alleged many reasons in support of her right to that distant portion of Micronesia. She was the first nation whose ships had reached those shores, and this fact was acknowledged by the most distinguished geographers. The very name of Carolinas attested the Spanish title. Besides, the kings of Spain had often sent thither apostolic men as missionaries, and of this the annals of the Roman Pontificate afford confirmatory proof; for there exists a letter of our predecessor, Clement XI, to Philip V, written in 1706, and praising the king for having equipped and furnished a vessel to transport missionaries to these islands. He moreover exhorts his Majesty to continue to propagate the Christian name and help procure the salvation of multitudes of men.

"The same Pontiff also wrote to Louis XIV beseeching him to oppose no obstacles to the happy issue of an enterprise so happily begun by his royal grandson. Again, Philip V appointed in aid of these missions (to the Carolinas) a sum of two thousand crowns. Furthermore, none but the Spanish nation ever did anything to help to bring the light of the Gospel to the islanders. Finally, none but these missionaries have ever given any information to the world on the manner of living and customs of the natives of the Carolinas.

"From this series of facts, viewed especially in the light of the then existing international law, one clearly perceives that the right of Spain to the Carolinas Islands stands forth well established. For if any right of domination can be justly founded on the fact of enlightening barbarous peoples, it must be granted that those who had endeavored to convert them from pagan superstition to the Gospel truth contributed most to their civilization, since to our holy religion belong all the forces capable of humanizing men. On this principle was founded the right of possession in more than one instance, particularly in the case of islands in the ocean, many of which bear names given them by religion.

"Seeing, therefore, that a long and well-founded public opinion conceded to Spain the possession of the Carolinas Islands, it cannot be wondered at if, when this dispute arose, the Spanish people were so excited that there was great danger for the internal peace of the kingdom and for its friendly relations with other powers.

"To these arguments Germany opposed others, also based on international law: that to hold a landed possession residence is necessary; that, taking into account the facts of modern history, international law sanctions the rightful ownership of unoccupied land by holding it and using it; that so long as such lands are not so held by occupation and use they are to be accounted as belonging to no owner. Wherefore, considering the fact that the Carolinas had not during a century and a half been occupied by Spain, the islands should have been adjudged the property of the first person taking possession of them. In support of this it was alleged that some such dispute as the present having arisen in 1875, both Germany and Great Britain affirmed that they would never acknowledge the right of Spain to the ownership of the

Carolinas.

"Seeing how divided between contrary opinions men's minds were, we endeavored to prevent further dissension; and, taking into account the respective rights and interests of the two contending nations, we confidently laid before them a plan for bringing about a peaceful settlement. We were guided only by our sense of equity, and, as you are aware, both disputants willingly agreed to our plan.

"So then a thing happened of which the present direction of public opinion did not afford much hope. Providence willed that two great and illustrious nations should do homage to the highest authority in the Church by asking it to fulfil an office so much in harmony with its nature, to preserve by its action the threatened peace and harmony between them. This is the fruit of that salutary and beneficent influence which God has attached to the power of the Sovereign Pontiffs. Superior to the envious jealousy of its enemies, and more mighty than the prevailing iniquity of the age, it is subject neither to destruction nor to change.

"From all this, too, it becomes manifest how grievous an evil are the wars waged against the Apostolic See and the lessening of its rightful liberty. For thereby it is not merely justice and religion that are made the sufferers, but the public good itself, since, in the present perilous and changeful condition of public affairs, the Roman Pontificate would confer far greater benefits on the world if, with perfect freedom and unimpaired rights, it could bestow all its energies in promoting, without impediment, the salvation of the human race.

"The discovery made by Spain, in the sixteenth century, of the Carolinas and Palaos Islands, and a series of acts done by the Spanish government in these same islands at different times and for the benefit of the native populations thereof, have, in the opinion of the Spanish government and people, created a title to sovereignty over the same, based on the maxims of international law which were in vogue and followed in that age when such conflicts arose. Indeed, when we take into consideration this series of acts, the truth of which is confirmed by various documents in the archives of the Propaganda, it is impossible to deny the beneficent labors of Spain in favor of these islanders. And it is further to be remarked that no other government at any time extended to these islands a like beneficent action. This explains the unbroken tradition, which cannot be overlooked, and the strong feeling of conviction among the Spanish people respecting this sovereignty—a tradition and a conviction which, two months ago, manifested themselves in such outbursts of warmth and animosity that they seriously threatened to compromise momentarily the interior tranquillity of the kingdom and the relations existing between the two friendly governments.

"On her side, Germany, as well as England, declared expressly in 1875 to the Spanish government that they did not acknowledge the sovereignty of Spain over these islands Far from such acknowledgment, the Imperial government is of opinion that nothing but the effective occupation of a territory can constitute sovereignty over it; and such occupation of the Carolinas by Spain never has been effected.

"It is in conformity with this principle that Germany acted in the island of Yap, and on this point the Mediator is gratified in declaring that the Imperial government acted with perfect honesty, which is also acknowledged by the Spanish government.

"Wherefore, and in order to prevent this divergence of opinions from becoming an obstacle to an honorable settlement between the two governments, the Mediator, after duly considering the whole question, proposes that in the new convention to be agreed upon both parties accept the formulas of the Protocol concerning the Soulou (Iolo) Archipelago, signed at Madrid the 7th of last March by the representatives of Great Britain, Germany, and Spain, and that the following points be adopted:

"'First Point: The sovereignty of Spain over the Carolinas and Palaos Islands is affirmed. Second Point: The Spanish government, in order to render its said sovereignty effective, binds itself to establish, as soon as possible, in this archipelago a regular administration, with a force sufficient to preserve order and protect acquired rights. Third Point: Spain proffers to Germany full and entire freedom of commerce, navigation, and fishing in these islands, as well as the right to establish there a naval station and a coaling depot. Fourth Point: To Germany is also secured the liberty of making plantations in these islands, and there founding agricultural establishments on the same footing as Spanish subjects.'

"Rome, from the Vatican, October 22, 1885.

"L. Card. Jacobini."

www.ingramcontent.com/pod-product-compliance
Ingram Content Group UK Ltd.
Pitfield, Milton Keynes, MK11 3LW, UK
UKHW020631160525
5946UKWH00007B/143

9 781953 746122

LIGHT ON DARKNESS

The Untold Story of the Liturgy

COSIMA CLARA GILLHAMMER

REAKTION BOOKS

For my friend Tristan Franklinos,
fellow lover of the liturgy

Published by
REAKTION BOOKS LTD
Unit 32, Waterside
44–48 Wharf Road
London N1 7UX, UK
www.reaktionbooks.co.uk

First published 2025

Printed and bound in India by Replika Press Pvt. Ltd

A catalogue record for this book is available from the British Library

ISBN 978 1 83639 043 5

Contents

Introduction: Why Liturgy?

It is midnight. Deep darkness covers the church. The doors are closed and not a single candle is burning at the altar. Not even the stars can be glimpsed through the high windows. The darkness lies heavy and the silence seems eternal. But then, suddenly, there is movement. The church doors are opened, and the small flame of a single candle pierces the dark space. Stepping upon the threshold, the candle bearer chants two words upon a simple tune: *Lumen Christi*, 'The light of Christ'. In the light of the small flame, a large number of people can be seen genuflecting behind the candle, dark shapes now illuminated by a golden hue. Many voices resound with the answer, *Deo gratias*, 'Thanks be to God'. Three times the candle bearer sings the same incantation, each time at a higher pitch, followed by the same response. Each time the procession moves further into the church, until the candle has reached the middle of the sanctuary. And now, this single source of light is multiplied. The people are each bearing tapers, which are successively lit from the original candle, the flame slowly passed on through the rows and spreading further and further until the entire church is illuminated by hundreds of small candles. Thus the darkness flees and the shadows recede. Thus the light returns, a harbinger of the dawn which is only a few hours away.

It is the night before Easter Sunday. The location of this particular scene is a small village church in medieval England, but a similar version of the same ritual is being performed at the same hour at countless churches, cathedrals and abbeys throughout England and Western Europe. And for years, decades, centuries, until the present day, the same ritual will continue to be celebrated each year, always using the same words. This is how the Christian Church celebrates Easter. The event that is commemorated is specific – the resurrection of Christ from the dead – but the symbolism of the ritual is universal. Darkness is vanquished by light, night recedes before day, hope glimmers in the hearts of those oppressed by sorrow and grief. The ritual has survived the centuries because it expresses something central to the human experience. Witnessing the new light entering a dark church can have a powerful effect on believers and non-believers alike.

The ritual described here is an example of a vastly rich and diverse body of prayers, songs, gestures and movements, to which we collectively refer as the liturgy of the Christian Church. They are closely tied to Christian theological ideas, but at the same time they express, with astonishing variety and creativity, universal human experiences. They incorporate rituals which precede Christianity, such as those of the Jewish tradition; they generate a vast array of poetry; and they prove inspirational for writers, thinkers and artists over many centuries. Liturgy is at the roots of Western culture. Our music, art, literature and architecture are shaped by and developed out of the liturgy. Without it, Dante's *Divine Comedy* would not exist, and neither would Michelangelo's *Pietà*. Not even *Star Wars* would have its memorable soundtrack had it not been for medieval liturgy.

Liturgy has become strange and foreign to us. It is a form that is little understood and mostly relegated to the realm of private religious observance or obscure scholarship. Perhaps it is one of the best-kept secrets of our time that the liturgy stands at the centre of the cultural history of the West. It deserves our close attention and appreciation. It is a common assumption that liturgy is stuffy and stale, but nothing could be further from the truth. The rites of the liturgy are endlessly rich and imaginative, generating in turn new artistic responses throughout the centuries. Through a number of individual stories, this book tells the larger story of how the liturgy influenced the culture of the West for more than a thousand years. It speaks of extraordinary artistic beauty, expressions of faith and human connection. And it contains an enduring symbolism of hope and renewal, passed down the centuries, much like the return of a lighted candle into a dark church on the night before Easter.

What is liturgy, and why does it matter?

'Liturgy' is a term commonly used to refer to the forms of public worship in the Christian Church. Such forms of worship, in Christianity as in many other religious faiths, are characterized by a prescribed set of words, prayers, songs, gestures and movements. It is these prescribed forms which make liturgical ceremonies meaningful to the followers of a faith, as they express a set of beliefs in symbolic form, allowing congregants to transcend ordinary life and connect with the divine. While 'liturgy' is a general term that can be applied in a broad sense to any service of worship in any branch of Christianity, this book is specifically concerned with Western liturgy, the forms of Christian worship that gained their distinctive form in Western Europe during the Middle Ages (the period from approximately the sixth to the fifteenth century) and are particularly associated with Catholic Christianity under the authority of the pope in Rome. The main language of this liturgy for the majority of the past centuries was Latin. In the medieval period when most of these liturgical forms gained their distinctive shape, no split between Catholicism and Protestantism had yet emerged. In post-medieval and post-Reformation times this strand of medieval Christianity with its forms of worship and theological beliefs is most closely represented by Roman Catholicism, but even the Protestant churches retained, to a greater or lesser extent, many liturgical forms that they had inherited from the medieval tradition. In any discussion of Western liturgy, the Middle Ages therefore loom large, and a great part of this book invokes medieval texts and traditions. But the Western liturgy did not arise out of a vacuum. Many of its distinctive forms were inherited from the very early days of Christianity and are shared between Eastern and Western Christianity. Going back further still, as Christianity was in its earliest days a sect of Judaism, worship in the early Christian Church drew heavily on Jewish scriptures and traditions of worship. This long history can be felt in different places in the texts and forms of Western liturgy, and we will explore these texts in greater detail in the chapters below. But these texts not only tell the story of this history; they above all tell a very human story of how universal experiences of life – love, joy, suffering, grief, death – can be understood, contemplated and transformed into poetry and art.

Before we dive further into these stories, a caveat is warranted. This book is an introduction to the forms of worship rather than a meticulous historical analysis.[1] While it is informed by recent historical research, it is not an academic study but a journey – a journey through time, in order to find out why liturgy matters, and how it has shaped culture in the West for many centuries. For the purposes of such a journey, some generalizations are necessary. The two most blatant of these generalizations are two terms that crop up a lot throughout this book: 'liturgy' and 'the West'. The term 'liturgy' is somewhat of an anachronism: it derives from Latin *liturgia*, which in turn is derived from ancient Greek λειτουργία (*leitourgia*) meaning 'public service, service of the gods, public worship'.[2] While the word itself has a long history stretching back to antiquity, in English it is not applied to Christian worship until after the end of the Middle Ages. The earliest use of the term documented in the *Oxford English Dictionary* dates to 1564, which means that the word 'liturgy' was not actually used during the period most crucial to the development of liturgical forms and texts. In medieval

England people talked about religious services using a variety of terms, such as *office*, *rite* or *observance*. It is worth noting that we are therefore using a modern term to refer to the rituals and rites associated with religious worship, while the liturgy was conceptualized in somewhat different terms in the Middle Ages. Part of this conceptual difference was the fact that there was a great diversity of religious rituals throughout Western Europe: church services could vary considerably according to country, region and community, whereas the term 'liturgy' in the singular may suggest a well-defined unity and uniformity which is not borne out by the historical reality. In a sense it might be more accurate to speak of 'liturgies' or 'rites' in the plural. Nonetheless, these rites fall into groups that share many common features. The most common of these liturgical groups in the Middle Ages in the West was the Roman Rite, which developed in the city of Rome and, due to the central papal authority of Rome, became the dominant rite in Western Christianity. Although there were many local variants of this rite during the Middle Ages, the advent of print at the end of the medieval period precipitated a greater uniformity of these rites, particularly following the Council of Trent in 1545–63, which made the Roman Rite obligatory within the Catholic Church with only few exceptions. It remained the dominant rite in this form until the significant changes introduced in the twentieth century by the Second Vatican Council (1962–5). Many aspects of worship within Protestant churches likewise go back to the Roman Rite, and in some cases present direct translations of texts of the Roman Rite, including many aspects of the *Book of Common Prayer*. Despite the post-Reformation developments into separate traditions, in practice this means that many of the texts and customs that were particularly influential through many centuries of Western literature, art and culture are to be found in the Roman Rite, and this is therefore our focus in this book. Where possible I have used a range of sources on the Roman Rite from the medieval period, but where these sources leave blanks to be filled in, I have at times used some poetic licence in how I describe and imagine liturgical celebrations, sometimes inferring certain details of ritual practice based on later printed sources. In doing so, a certain amount of blurring of chronological developments is inevitable but it is my hope that such an approach can help the reader see the spirit of the liturgy more clearly than a detailed historical account would.

The second caveat concerns the term 'the West', which is likewise a generalization. In today's political discourse this term is often loaded with a long list of implicit assumptions, especially concerning specific qualities that are ascribed to Western culture in opposition to other cultures. To think about 'Western culture' as a uniform whole has many problems, and a closer look at the historical and cultural reality reveals a much greater diversity of views and identities than the term might imply. Over many centuries the geographical area known as Western Europe, along with those countries significantly influenced by it, was defined by Christianity as a unifying cultural force, although other beliefs did exist. Yet what is commonly known as 'the West' today is a largely secularized culture, in which religious beliefs are largely relegated to the private sphere. This idea of a private religion would have been quite alien to people in medieval Western Europe. Our notions of 'the West' are inevitably inflected by many centuries of post-medieval historical, political, ideological and technological developments. The term 'the West', then, suffers from similar deficiencies of generalization as the term 'liturgy', and can only ever refer to majority views and broad developments. Nonetheless, 'the West' is a useful shorthand to describe a broad geographic area and dominant cultural identity, which is, at least from the medieval period to the twentieth century, deeply influenced by Christianity, even if this influence has changed over time. It is a particularly useful term in this sense because this book is concerned with cultural production – literature, art, music – arising from the influence of religious ritual. Despite its usefulness, it has its limits, too, and it is worth keeping in mind the complexities that arise when we zoom in from the general to the particular.

WHY, THEN, WAS THE LITURGY so enormously influential on Western cultural production, identity and imagination? To the modern mind, it may seem rather strange that religious ritual could play such a major role. Ritual and ceremony are often seen as something stiff, cumbersome, uninspiring. And yet, it would be difficult to imagine our lives without a series of rites and rituals in various different shapes. We may have our private rituals, things that we do habitually and that add structure to our day. Many people would describe their morning coffee as a private ritual without which the day would have the wrong shape. Others may have specific ways in which they like to arrange their desks before opening their emails on a Monday morning. We may also have rituals that are not unique to us but which we share with our friends and family at specific occasions. The Sunday brunch at the little place round the corner, the fifteen-minute bedtime story we read to our children, the Christmas tree with the time-worn, familiar decorations we put up on the same day every year. All of these things have a special, recognizable format, which always stays roughly the same and recurs at regular intervals.

Then there are events that occur a lot less frequently, milestones in our lives which are also marked by specific rites: baptisms, graduations, weddings, funerals and the like. Even if many of these types of events happen only once or twice in a human lifetime, they recur regularly and in a predictable way across a community or culture, marking moments of transition and important celebrations with a series of ritual words, gestures, movements, garments, accompanied by traditional types of food and drink, music and so on. Other rites only happen in the lives of very few members of the population who take on a leading role, with some ceremonies so elaborate that they take months and years of planning: the coronation of a king, the swearing in of a president, a state visit. These rites may be religious or secular in nature, and their exact form may vary according to context, and may change over time. A wedding ceremony in the eighteenth century would have looked a little different to one in the twenty-first century, for instance, and it will also vary between different religious backgrounds, cultures and individual couples. Yet despite this variation there will be certain key elements that make it uniquely and recognizably one type of ceremony and not another, elements which will be understood by everyone in a certain culture or community. Few people would be in danger of confusing a wedding with a funeral!

What all of these events have in common is that they recur regularly, either within an individual human life or across a community, and that they follow a specific, prescribed form, though this may vary in its details. Rites and rituals accompany every stage of our lives. And yet, if you were to conduct a spontaneous survey in the street, asking for people's opinions on rituals and rites, you would in all likelihood elicit two types of responses: enthusiasm and strong dislike. It seems that there are broadly two groups of people: those who love formal occasions with a specific protocol that must be followed in minute detail, and those who think this sort of thing outdated, arcane, elitist or simply a waste of time. There is little space in between the two views; few people feel lukewarm about whether they enjoy attending a lengthy formal occasion or not. In the twenty-first century in the West, the latter group seems to form the majority. The prevailing view is that informal trumps formal, that sitting through ceremonies is tedious and exhausting, that prescribed rules are unnecessary, that they may preserve problematic hierarchical structures, or exclude people who are not familiar with them.

And yet, despite this prevailing negative view, rituals remain extraordinarily powerful. In London as many as 250,000 people queued up for days to attend the late Queen Elizabeth II's lying-in-state, many of them moved to tears at the coffin of a monarch whom they had never met in person. The Changing of the Guard at Buckingham Palace is a world-famous tourist attraction. A ceremonial procession through the centre of Oxford, comprising university officials in their striking robes and distinctive caps, will stop passers-by in their tracks, fumbling for their phones. The singing of the national anthem at the beginning of a football match at the World Cup is a deeply emotional experience for many. There is a fascination connected with such ceremonies and rituals that is difficult to describe or explain, yet which can be felt by anyone who experiences it. Such rituals seem, at first glance, to have little to do with the history of worship, the question of how people throughout the ages expressed their religious beliefs. And yet, they fall into the same category in that they are events which are out of the ordinary; they stand apart from the mundane because they follow a specific form that has been in existence for a long time and which must be observed. Although in the modern world we often seem to value spontaneity and informality more highly than a prescribed form, we implicitly rely on form in everything we do. A business meeting would not work if it did not follow a form on which every participant agrees: the presence of an agenda, a chairperson, specific rules of behaviour when asking a question. Activities that we do for fun likewise rely on a certain form in order to work and be enjoyable, whether it is dance, sports or music. Following a prescribed and generally accepted form creates a space of security, in which members of a community know how to behave. This is particularly relevant for things which are difficult to deal with – most people would struggle to mourn their loved ones without a funeral ceremony (whether of a religious or non-religious kind), which lends a form to the act of saying goodbye. Funerals give a shape to mourning just as weddings give a shape to joy. Ceremonies such as these bring together communities, they set important life events apart from the ordinary and mundane, and they connect us with the past in the knowledge that many generations before us have observed the same rituals, whatever they may be.

This connection with the past, the knowledge that a tradition has been passed down to us through the ages and has survived for long periods of time, gives a sense of depth to rituals which may partly account for their fascination even today. This power of tradition is particularly strong in the liturgy, which allows congregations to connect as a community, both in the present and across time. A very pronounced element of Western liturgy is the commemoration of the living and the dead – the saints and all those who have lived and died in the faith before the present moment. The liturgy includes this entire community of the faithful in its prayers, which are connected across time by the same belief and the same ritual practice. This connection was much more broadly felt in the Middle Ages than it is today. While in the modern world church attendance is relegated to the private space and left up to individual preferences and beliefs, or absence thereof, medieval culture was suffused by religion, and more or less everybody went to church on Sundays to hear Mass. And even beyond this, life in monasteries, convents and other religious houses was defined by frequent liturgical prayer at regular hours. There were two main forms of the liturgy: the Mass as the church service that was celebrated daily and attended by nearly everyone on Sundays, and the Liturgy of the Hours as the regular prayers at set hours throughout the day in monasteries and convents: Matins, Lauds, Prime, Terce, Sext, None, Vespers and Compline. This meant that in the medieval period and beyond, the liturgy was part and parcel of daily life. Whether lay or religious, everyone was familiar with at least some aspects of liturgical practice, and this shared knowledge was reflected in literature, art and music, just as much as it was integral to daily life. The year was structured according to the liturgical calendar and its feasts, with the liturgical cycle moving through different seasons with their own moods and modes of worship. In Western Christianity, these are, at a glance:

Advent, the season of expectation in December leading up to Christmas
Christmas, the feast of the birth of Christ (25 December)
Epiphany, the feast of the revelation of Jesus as the Son of God (6 January)
The Feast of the Presentation or Candlemas, commemorating Christ being presented in the Temple (2 February)
Lent, the season of penitence in February and March beginning with Ash Wednesday and leading up to Easter
Holy Week, especially Maundy Thursday, Good Friday and Holy Saturday, commemorating Christ's Passion and death on the cross
Easter, the feast of the resurrection of Christ from the dead (in March or April)
The Feast of the Ascension, celebrating the bodily ascension of Jesus into heaven (forty days after Easter)
Pentecost, the feast celebrating the coming of the Holy Spirit (fifty days after Easter)

Added to this was a multitude of saints' feast days and other solemnities (such as Trinity Sunday, the Feast of Corpus Christi, the Assumption of Mary, the harvest festival of Lammas and so on). In the Middle Ages and beyond, the liturgical cycle thus gave shape to the year for the religious and the laity alike. The liturgy was, and for a long time remained, practically everywhere.

This prominence of the liturgy means that liturgical texts are important if we want to understand Western art and culture. Yet its influence goes beyond its pervasive presence in these periods. It is also connected to its powerful role for a community of believers. Part of the enduring fascination of rituals is the fact that they consist of actions, movements, gestures and words in which we can participate. Rituals are primarily something that we do, rather than something we think or say or discuss. These actions are symbolic in nature, such as the exchange of rings at a wedding ceremony, and we act them out in ritual settings. Being physically present is crucial to these ritual actions: a wedding ceremony conducted on Zoom, for example, just doesn't feel like it works, as many of us found out during the COVID-19 pandemic in 2020–21. In rituals a set of common beliefs is acted out in a symbolic setting, in community with others. For example, in religious ceremonies the congregation pray, kneel, bow their heads, sing together, shake hands or perform a number of other symbolic actions in accordance with their beliefs. These symbolic actions model a certain set of behaviours, which in turn encourages individuals to embody these behaviours in their daily lives. In other words, rituals help members of the community internalize their beliefs. This dynamic is well documented in social psychology and anthropology for rites and rituals across cultures,[3] and has been summarized as follows: 'If one must act as though one believed one ends in believing . . . as one acts.'[4] Within the Christian tradition the same process is hinted at by the motto *lex orandi, lex credendi* (the law of prayer is the law of belief). Worship and belief are in a reciprocal relationship. Not only are religious beliefs reflected in the form of worship, but the inverse is also true. The law of prayer – in other words, the form of worship that we find in the liturgy – is not just a random aesthetic choice, but it actively influences Christian faith. Liturgy is not just a matter of personal preference, but it goes to the heart of religious belief. How we pray, how we express and act out our beliefs, matter deeply for the individual and for the community. The liturgy is thus a personal practice, a way in which individuals express their religious beliefs in ritual prayer, but it is at the same time the manifest practice of a community, in which individuals come together in public worship, which in turn strengthens this community and instils in individuals a sense of belonging.

While Christian liturgy has the same anthropological basis as rituals in other faiths and cultures, it is distinctive in that its focus is not just a transcendental sense of the divine, but a very concrete and historical reality: that of the life and death of Jesus of Nazareth. The centre of Christian belief is that God took on human nature and became man in Jesus Christ, who was born of a human mother, lived as a Jew in the Middle East and was executed around AD 33 by being nailed onto a cross. Christians believe that this historical person truly lived, died and rose again from the dead on the third day after his execution. The spiritual significance of Christ's death is the redemption of humankind from sin and eternal death. This makes Christianity a faith which is rooted in history. The human and the divine merge in the life of a specific person at a specific point in time, within a particular historical context. This is reflected by a focus on dates, names and places in the gospels, but also, more broadly, in the way in which Christianity emphasizes the human in trying to understand what it means for a person to be fully God and fully man. Christian tradition has always been preoccupied with this question, and we find this reflected in the subjects explored in the liturgy and in Christian art: from the heights of love and joy to the depths of grief and suffering. The liturgy is not merely a set of abstract and symbolic words and gestures, but an act that engages with the whole breadth of human emotion. It reaches to the bottom of human experiences because it is an expression of the belief that God himself experienced them during his life on earth. Exploring these questions, the texts, thoughts and themes of the liturgy in turn proved inspirational for Western culture, with artists drawing on the liturgy for their engagement with these very same questions, whether in visual art, literature, drama or music. The story of Jesus of Nazareth is the central story around which the Western artistic imagination has revolved for thousands of years, but for audiences in the modern secular world this tradition can seem inaccessible. The liturgy can therefore provide the key for unlocking this tradition, and with it, the story that has shaped the West.

What do Christians believe?

In order to be able to use the liturgy as a key for unlocking Western culture, we must be aware of certain basic Christian beliefs. For readers who are not familiar with this tradition, this section offers a very brief summary of the Christian faith. Readers who are well versed in Christian theology may prefer to proceed to the next section. The summary uses as its basis the Apostles' Creed, a statement of faith that lists the core articles of Christian belief, printed in italics. Individual articles are accompanied by short explanations.

I believe in God, the Father almighty,
creator of heaven and earth.

Christianity believes in one God in three persons, also referred to as the Holy Trinity: God the Father, God the Son and God the Holy Spirit. The love of God inherent in the Trinity is poured out in the act of the creation of the world. The book of Genesis in the Bible offers an account of God's creation of heaven and earth in seven days. On the sixth day, God creates man in his own image (Gen. 1:26). From this creation account arises a belief in the sacredness of human life and the intrinsic value of each individual person. Genesis also tells the story of the Fall: Adam and Eve, the first humans to be created, are placed in Paradise, but after temptation by the Devil they transgress against the law of God. As a result they are cast out of Paradise, and toil, sorrow, pain and death become part of human existence. According to Christian belief, humankind is redeemed from the Fall through the death of Jesus Christ on the cross as a voluntary sacrifice.

I believe in Jesus Christ, his only Son, our Lord,
who was conceived by the Holy Spirit,
born of the Virgin Mary,

Jesus Christ is the only Son of God the Father and the second person of the Trinity. Christian belief states that the Son was incarnate and became man in Jesus, uniting a fully divine and a fully human nature. According to the gospel accounts, Jesus Christ was miraculously conceived by the Holy Spirit, and his mother Mary was a virgin when she gave birth to him. In her unique role as the mother of the redeemer, Mary has a prominent place in Christian theology and devotion, which is reflected in many ways in liturgical texts, where she is exalted as powerful intercessor and protector of sinners. Christ lived his human life among the Jewish people in what was then the Roman province of Judaea, as a radical preacher, teacher and miracle-worker. Jesus laid claim to being the Messiah, the saviour of the Jewish people who had been promised to them by the prophets of the Old Testament. This understanding of Jesus as the Messiah plays an important role in the Christian tradition, with many liturgical texts drawing parallels between Old Testament prophecies and their fulfilment in Jesus Christ.

suffered under Pontius Pilate,
was crucified, died, and was buried;

The mention of the name of Pontius Pilate is a reflection of how deeply Christianity is rooted in human history. Pilate was fifth governor of the Roman province of Judaea, serving under Emperor Tiberius at the time of Jesus' crucifixion around AD 33. The gospels recount how the Jewish priests and elders object to Jesus' claim of being the Messiah, the Son of God, and want to put him to death. At the trial of Jesus, Pilate gives in to their pressure and orders Jesus to be crucified (a common way of executing criminals at the time). The crucifixion of Christ in the gospels is a story of how the worst possible things – betrayal by friends, protracted torture and death in the most humiliating way imaginable – happen to the best possible man: God incarnate, who is innocent of any crime. According to Christian belief, his death on the cross is a redemptive act through which Jesus takes the sins of humankind upon himself out of love, and reopens Paradise, which had been closed since the Fall.

he descended to the dead.

From the early history of Christianity, Christ's death is associated with ideas about his descent into hell, where he liberates the souls of the Old Testament patriarchs and prophets and leads them into heaven. The descent to the dead is based on only a few passages in Scripture, but exerted a particular fascination on the artistic imagination during the Middle Ages, not least because of the role this idea plays in the liturgy (see Chapter Three).

On the third day he rose again;

The gospels recount that Jesus came back to life on the third day after his death, and subsequently walked, talked, prayed and ate with his friends. The resurrection reaffirms the belief that Jesus really is the Son of God who has conquered death and sin, inspiring his disciples to go out and preach this good news in different parts of the earth.

he ascended into heaven,
he is seated at the right hand of the Father,

After his resurrection, Jesus leaves the earth and is bodily taken up into heaven, where he is exalted as Lord and God, returning to his place at the right hand of God the Father.

and he will come to judge the living and the dead.

An important part of Christian belief is that of a coming Last Judgement at the end of days, where all those who have lived and who are still living will be called to give account of their actions during their lives on earth (see Chapter Seven).

I believe in the Holy Spirit,

The Holy Spirit is the third person of the Trinity. He is associated with the giving of spiritual gifts and inspiring conviction of faith, and in Christian iconography is often portrayed as a winged dove.

the holy catholic Church,

'Catholic' means universal. The Church as the universal community of the faithful plays an important role in Christian theology, and is often described with the metaphor 'bride of Christ' to illustrate his love and care for those who believe in him.

the communion of saints,

Saints are those people who have lived righteous lives in loving God and their fellow humans, and who are now enjoying eternal life with God in heaven. The liturgy frequently invokes the saints in prayer as a sign of the universal community of the living and the dead, sharing in the same belief.

the forgiveness of sins,

Christians believe that God is both just and merciful, and that his mercy is everlasting and abundant. This is why so many texts that we find in the liturgy invoke the mercy of God and ask for his forgiveness of human sins. The Christian understanding of sin refers to all human transgressions, failures and inadequacies in our relationship with God and our fellow human beings.

the resurrection of the body,

Christians believe that at the Last Judgement, all those who have died will rise again and will be given back their physical bodies, just like Jesus rose from the grave. Connected to this is the belief that Mary, as a perfect human being free from sin, was physically assumed into heaven at the end of her life – an event known as the 'Assumption', a prominent feast in the liturgical calendar, celebrated on 15 August.

and the life everlasting.

The message of hope inherent to Christianity is that after life on earth, those who have lived lives that glorify God through love, virtue and good actions will experience eternal life and joy in heaven.

How to use this book

More than anything else, this book intends to be an invitation to explore the extraordinary richness and depth of the liturgy. By its very nature, such an invitation has to be selective. This book is not a historical account of the development of the liturgy over time, nor is it a theological account of its meaning, although aspects of both will be discussed. Anyone looking for a stringent scholarly analysis of these questions will find relevant sources in the Bibliography. Instead, this book invites you on a journey of discovery through a wealth of treasures that are almost limitless in their significance and inspiration. It embarks upon this journey through a series of stories about universal experiences that are common to all our lives. Chapters are arranged according to different themes, each of them focusing on a particular emotion or attitude expressed in the liturgical texts and reflected in art, music and literature. The final two chapters, 'Time' and 'Space', broaden out the perspective to think about how the liturgy influences understandings of time as well as addressing the context of the sacred spaces within which rituals take place. These chapters tell the stories that have deeply moved and fascinated the Western artistic imagination for many centuries, and are still powerful today. More treasures are in store for those who want to understand the liturgy more comprehensively, and this book can only be a starting point.

Before we begin, a few thoughts on questions of language and translation. The majority of liturgical texts take their starting point from the Bible, both from the Old Testament (a collection of books related to the history and tradition of the people of Israel) and the New Testament (the gospel accounts of the life of Jesus Christ and writings of his disciples and followers). While in a modern context we often think of the Bible as a book to be read and studied by individual believers, this was not always the case. In the early days of Christianity, the texts of the Bible were read aloud, chanted and meditated upon by communities of believers, often in liturgical settings.[5] In these settings, excerpts from different parts of the Bible were often merged together or combined with non-biblical material such as poetry, and used in liturgical celebrations alongside music, symbolic gestures and movements. The Bible is therefore fundamental to the liturgy, but the biblical text in liturgical settings has a distinctive shape that can at times be quite different from the way in which it appears in the Bible. The original texts of the Bible are written in Hebrew, Aramaic and Greek. The language of Western liturgy is traditionally Latin. Many of the texts of the liturgy in the Roman Rite were commonly based on the Vulgate, the dominant Latin translation of the Bible in the Western Church. The language in which liturgical texts would have been widely known for the greatest part of the past centuries, therefore, is Latin. To reflect this tradition and for the sake of completeness, all quotations of liturgical texts in this book are given in their original Latin form, together with an English translation. No knowledge of Latin is required to navigate this book, but individual texts are sometimes referred to under their Latin titles. Similarly, the book attempts to give a flavour of the original language where it quotes English texts from the medieval period, but translations are provided where necessary. For English translations, I have let my own taste be the guide; biblical texts usually follow the New Revised Standard Version (*NRSV*),[6] but in other places I have preferred other translations, including my own, for reasons of style, tradition or clarity. Where I do not use the *NRSV* I note this in the footnotes. For the psalms, in particular, I cite Coverdale's translation as used in the *Book of Common Prayer* (1662) because of its wide use and significance within English-speaking contexts. As a result there is a range of styles of biblical translation across this book; my hope is that readers will not see this as an inconsistency but rather as a reflection of the rich history of English Bible translation.

This book makes many references to works of art and music. Not all images could be included in the book, and music is by definition difficult to describe in words. To allow the reader to explore these references further, I have created a website that includes a collection of all images and pieces of music mentioned, as well as further information and a list of recommended resources: www.liturgybook.com.

All other references in this book are equally designed to be accessible, and I have used online sources wherever possible. Using these resources, readers are warmly invited to embark upon their own journeys through the untold story of the liturgy.

1
Petition

The year is 1325. An artist in a monastery just outside Norwich is bent over his desk, carefully illuminating a manuscript page. The skill required is considerable: glue and gold leaf must be applied, precise patterns must be drawn, the colours must be just right. With slow and deliberate movements, which speak to many years of experience, the illuminator paints a figure. A head bearing a crown, with long hair and beard, eyes fixed intently on an object close to his face. After several hours of concentrated work by the artist, the figure finally becomes clear, thrown into sharp relief by the shimmering gold of its background: a king playing a small, delicately curved harp which rests on his knee. He is seated on a throne whose finely carved Gothic decorations mirror the turrets and spires of a cathedral. His clothes are exquisite, with a cloak in colours ranging from the deepest to the lightest shades of blue, half covering his red tunic. His legs are crossed and his hands are raised to the strings, his face focused and intent. We are witnessing a king in the middle of his performance. We cannot hear his song, but its words are written on the manuscript page, surrounding the illustration (illus. 1). The image is placed in the middle of a large, decorated letter B at the top of the page, while the stylized capital letters to the right of the image continue the sentence: *B-EATUS VIR QUI NON* . . ., and the writing below the illustration completes it: . . . *abiit in consilio impiorum et in via peccatorum non stetit, et in cathedra pestilentiae non sedit* ('Blessed is the man that hath not walked in the counsel of the ungodly, nor stood in the way of sinners and hath not sat in the seat of the scornful').[1]

The image portrays the famous Old Testament King David, and the words form the beginning of the Book of Psalms, traditionally believed to have been authored by David. The Greek word ψαλμός (*psalmos*), meaning 'song sung to the harp or another stringed instrument', gestures towards the origins of these texts as songs, originally composed in Hebrew.[2] This idea is reinforced by the image of King David as harpist, which accompanies the psalms in this manuscript so masterfully illuminated in the first half of the fourteenth century, known to us today as the Ormesby Psalter. But the image of King David playing his harp is not unique to this manuscript; it appears, in various forms and sizes, executed by different artists with their individual styles, in a large number of manuscripts containing the same text. These Psalters (books of psalms) were ubiquitous in medieval Europe, and today often make for showcase pieces in libraries

1 King David playing the harp, illumination from the Ormesby Psalter, 1250–1330.

and exhibitions, as they are frequently lavishly illustrated and illuminated. But although the shimmering gold and deep blue and red tones of the illustration in the Ormesby Psalter still impress readers today, they can perhaps make us forget too easily how remarkable this image is in its own right, regardless of the sparkle of gold leaf. A king of Israel who lived around 1000 BC appears here clothed in robes of fourteenth-century England, just as the psalms, which were originally written in Hebrew, appear here in Latin, the language of medieval Christian worship. Texts which were originally written in very different cultural, religious and historical circumstances in the ancient Middle East are here translated, through the language of its words and images, into the cultural context of medieval England. That the psalms should speak, and continue to speak, to a Western Christian audience is in many ways unexpected, given that they make frequent reference to the specific circumstances, place and culture in which they were composed. They speak of warfare, persecution, invasion by heathen nations, temple sacrifice and the tribes of Israel. And yet, as a collection of songs, the psalms exerted a powerful influence on Christian worship, theology and poetic expression through the centuries. More than any other biblical text, the psalms provide the very language and imagery through which prayer is conducted within the Western Church.

The form of the psalms is unusual, too: they are structured according to the traditions of Hebrew poetry, which are quite different from what an English speaker might expect from poetry. Central to this structure are parallel construction of words and poetic lines. The parallel structure of the first verse, which we have already encountered on the first page of the Ormesby Psalter, becomes clearer if we separate the text visually into line segments:

> Blessed is the man that hath not walked in the counsel of the
> ungodly, nor stood in the way of sinners
> and hath not sat in the seat of the scornful. (Ps. 1:1)

Another example is a verse a little further on in the same psalm:

> Therefore the ungodly shall not be able to stand in the judgement,
> neither the sinners in the congregation of the righteous. (Ps. 1:6)

Although the English translation is unable to bring out all of the finer points of the Hebrew original, the parallelism is clear. Individual line segments echo each other in their words and imagery, so that often they appear like a rephrasing more than a new thought. To an English audience, such parallel structuring may appear awkward or repetitive as it does not align closely with English poetic forms, but Hebrew speakers clearly felt differently.[3]

If the poetic, cultural and historical features of the Book of Psalms do not lend themselves easily to an adaptation into different languages and cultures many centuries later, how can we explain the extraordinary and lasting importance of these texts within Western Christianity? Part of the reason for their longevity is, no doubt, their inclusion in the canon of Old Testament texts of the Bible in the early centuries AD. As such they became an important point of reference for Christian interpretations of the Bible. Central to this tradition of interpretation is a method of reading Old Testament texts in the light of the New Testament, with the coming of Christ being understood as the fulfilment of Old Testament prophecies and events. Yet this in itself is not sufficient explanation for the psalms' central role in Christian worship. There are many books in the Old Testament, ranging from histories and chronicles to poetry and love songs, but most of them do not feature in Western liturgy with the same prominence as the psalms. The other part of the explanation, then, has to be connected not only with the circumstances of the psalms' transmission and tradition but with the character of the texts themselves. Despite the specificity of some of their references to the history of the people of Israel, the psalms contain a remarkable range of emotions, attitudes and reflections, which have spoken to readers through the ages in myriad different places and circumstances. The tradition of the Christian Church has used the psalms as an evocative and resonant text with which, and through which, believers could speak to God. Some psalms contain verses of joy, trust and thankfulness: 'Yea, though I walk through the valley of the shadow of death, I will fear no evil: for thou art with me; thy rod and thy staff comfort me' (Ps. 23:4). Others plunge into the very depths of anger, despair and tribulation: 'I am poured out like water, and all my bones are out of joint: my heart also in the midst of my body is even like melting wax' (Ps. 22:14). The voice of the psalmist is powerful, the imagery is compelling, and the poetry has a remarkable immediacy and intensity. The specific historical circumstances may be different, but the emotions expressed in the psalms are universally relevant to a community of believers, which explains their continued use in the Church's official cycle of prayers many centuries after the psalms were originally written.

From the earliest records we have of Christian liturgy, we know that recitation of the psalms played a central part in the Church's public prayer, following Jewish models, where the psalms had a prominent position in ritual worship. By the medieval period the psalms formed the central part of the Liturgy of the Hours prayed at fixed times of the day in monasteries, in which a specific selection of psalms would typically be chanted by the monastic community. The Liturgy of the Hours also proved popular among laypeople and spread far beyond religious communities. A great number of Books of Hours containing the texts of the Liturgy of the Hours that survive from the later Middle Ages were owned by members of the laity, testifying to the ubiquitous use of the psalms in private devotion. The psalms also played an important role in the celebration of the Mass, where they provided material from which fitting sections would be selected for chants and prayers for specific feast days. The Introit antiphon (a chant at the opening of Mass) for the third Mass on Christmas Day, for instance, includes the psalm verse *Cantate Domino canticum novum: quia mirabilia fecit*, 'O sing unto the Lord a new song: for he hath done marvellous things' (Ps. 98:1), a fitting expression of joy and wonder at the birth of the saviour.[4] The set hours of prayer in monasteries were primarily composed of psalms, to which were added hymns, readings from the gospels and other prayers. The exact shape of the canonical hours could vary from place to place, but the psalms were always at the centre of liturgical prayer. The psalms thus shaped and guided daily prayer in religious communities and beyond, as they still do today.

In the daily, weekly, monthly and yearly cycle of these liturgical prayers, the entirety of the Book of Psalms would be sung, moving through a broad range of different emotional states and reflective attitudes expressed in the psalms. Often they also include cries for help from God in times of affliction. Petition for divine intervention is one of the primary reasons why humans turn to prayer. Whether it is a good harvest, recovery from illness, the end of a war – there are countless situations in human life that are outside of our control but which have serious or even life-and-death consequences. In such times of trouble and distress, many people throughout human history have turned to God to ask for help and guidance. The psalms offer a model of prayer expressing precisely this: a petition for help and mercy. Perhaps the most memorable and moving psalms among these are the so-called Penitential Psalms, which take their title from their introspective tone, marked by deep sorrow and remorse for the speaker's past misdoings and petition for God's forgiveness and help. They express the speaker's turning to God for help in a striking way, and it is this quality that made the Penitential Psalms particularly prominent in the liturgy.

This is where we come back to King David, whom our illuminator in medieval Norwich took such great care in painting. The Book of Psalms has traditionally been attributed to King David. There are problems with this attribution: the date of most of the psalms is unknown, and the songs were more likely composed and collected over a much longer period of time than that of King David's reign.[5] But the attribution to David is not spurious. Many psalms contain superscriptions which ascribe authorship to David and allude to a particular incident in his life. It is worth noting, however, that the Hebrew word used in these superscriptions with the royal name can be translated as either 'of David', 'for David' or 'about David', so that they are perhaps best understood as indications of authorship in a looser sense. They may have been references to a context in which David acted as the patron of psalms in ancient Israel and authorized the use of such texts in worship through their association with him. Most interpreters today agree that the superscriptions were not originally part of these psalms, but added later during the process of the compilation of the Book of Psalms. Regardless of whether one believes the traditional view of David's authorship of the psalms, the superscriptions at the very least give an indication of the earliest interpretations of the psalms, in that they often mention a specific historical situation or a moment in David's life as a framework for understanding a particular psalm. As such, they can still provide helpful guidance for the reader, and they certainly help us understand the context within which the psalms were seen by medieval Christians.

A good example is Psalm 51, which has been called 'the greatest of the penitential psalms of the church'.[6] The psalm expresses in a particularly memorable way feelings of sinfulness, remorse and prayerful petition. The psalm has traditionally been read as an expression of King David's remorse after an illicit affair with Bathsheba, as indicated by the superscription: 'A Psalm of David, when the prophet Nathan came to him, after he had sinned with Bathsheba'. In 2 Samuel 11–12 you can find the full story to which the superscription alludes (and modern readers may recognize allusions to this story in Leonard Cohen's 1984 song 'Hallelujah'): in the midst of war with the Ammonites, David sends the Israelite army out to besiege the city of Rabbah, but remains himself in Jerusalem. One evening, while taking a walk on the roof of his palace, he sees a woman having a bath. She is beautiful, and David is inflamed with desire. When he tries to find out her identity, his servants inform him that her name is Bathsheba, and that she is married to a man called Uriah, who is currently fighting in the war. David embarks on an affair with Bathsheba, and she falls pregnant. When David finds out about the pregnancy, he schemes to rid himself of Bathsheba's husband. He sends orders to the leader of his army to send Uriah out to the front line where the fighting is fiercest and then withdraw support from him, so that he will be killed in battle. The army leader obeys, and Uriah falls in battle. David then marries Bathsheba, who gives birth to a son. God sends the prophet Nathan to David, who reproaches him for the evil he has done and prophesies that David will be severely punished. The book of Samuel reports David's reaction as follows: 'Then David said to Nathan, "I have sinned against the Lord"' (2 Sam. 12:13). It is at this point that the tradition places Psalm 51, ascribing to David's voice the expression of deep regret after his adultery with Bathsheba and murder of Uriah, calling to God from the depths of guilt and sinfulness.

Looking at the text of the psalm, it is easy to see why such an identification with this episode in David's life came about, even if it was added by later editors. The psalmist's voice utters the deeply personal prayer of someone who is full of distress and remorse.

Miserere mei, Deus: secundum magnam misericordiam tuam.	Have mercy upon me, O God: after Thy great goodness.
Et secundum multitudinem miserationum tuarum, dele iniquitatem meam.	According to the multitude of Thy mercies, do away mine offences.
Amplius lava me ab iniquitate mea: et a peccato meo munda me.	Wash me thoroughly from my wickedness: and cleanse me from my sin.

Quoniam iniquitatem meam ego cognosco: et peccatum meum contra me est semper.	For I acknowledge my faults: and my sin is ever before me.
Tibi soli peccavi, et malum coram te feci: ut justificeris in sermonibus tuis, et vincas cum judicaris.	Against Thee only have I sinned, and done this evil in thy sight: that Thou mightest be justified in Thy saying, and clear when Thou art judged.
Ecce enim in iniquitatibus conceptus sum: et in peccatis concepit me mater mea.	Behold, I was shapen in wickedness: and in sin hath my mother conceived me.
Ecce enim veritatem dilexisti: incerta et occulta sapientiae tuae manifestasti mihi.	But lo, Thou requirest truth in the inward parts: and shalt make me to understand wisdom secretly.
Asperges me hyssopo, et mundabor: lavabis me, et super nivem dealbabor.	Thou shalt purge me with hyssop, and I shall be clean: Thou shalt wash me, and I shall be whiter than snow.
Auditui meo dabis gaudium et laetitiam: et exsultabunt ossa humiliata.	Thou shalt make me hear of joy and gladness: that the bones which Thou hast broken may rejoice.
Averte faciem tuam a peccatis meis: et omnes iniquitates meas dele.	Turn Thy face from my sins: and put out all my misdeeds.
Cor mundum crea in me, Deus: et spiritum rectum innova in visceribus meis.	Make me a clean heart, O God: and renew a right spirit within me.
Ne proiicias me a facie tua: et spiritum sanctum tuum ne auferas a me.	Cast me not away from Thy presence: and take not Thy Holy Spirit from me.
Redde mihi laetitiam salutaris tui: et spiritu principali confirma me.	O give me the comfort of Thy help again: and stablish me with Thy free Spirit.

Docebo iniquos vias tuas: et impii ad te convertentur.	Then shall I teach Thy ways unto the wicked: and sinners shall be converted unto Thee.
Libera me de sanguinibus, Deus, Deus salutis meae: et exsultabit lingua mea justitiam tuam.	Deliver me from blood-guiltiness, O God, Thou that art the God of my health: and my tongue shall sing of Thy righteousness.
Domine, labia mea aperies: et os meum annuntiabit laudem tuam.	Thou shalt open my lips, O Lord: and my mouth shall show Thy praise.
Quoniam si voluisses sacrificium, dedissem utique: holocaustis non delectaberis.	For Thou desirest no sacrifice, else would I give it Thee: but Thou delightest not in burnt-offerings.
Sacrificium Deo spiritus contribulatus: cor contritum, et humiliatum, Deus, non despicies.	The sacrifice of God is a troubled spirit: a broken and contrite heart, O God, shalt Thou not despise.
Benigne fac, Domine, in bona voluntate tua Sion: ut aedificentur muri Ierusalem.	O be favourable and gracious unto Sion: build Thou the walls of Jerusalem.
Tunc acceptabis sacrificium justitiae, oblationes, et holocausta: tunc imponent super altare tuum vitulos.	Then shalt Thou be pleased with the sacrifice of righteousness, with the burnt-offerings and oblations: then shall they offer young bullocks upon Thine altar.

It is clear from the beginning that the speaker is burdened with the sense of a great evil that he has committed. The first part of the psalm is full of remorse: guilt weighs heavily upon the speaker, who asks God to pardon his offences and cleanse him from his evil deeds. While the nature of the sin is never made more explicit in the psalm other than that it involves 'blood-guiltiness', there is a keen sense that God himself has been offended through the evil which has been committed. The speaker addresses God directly in his confession: 'Against Thee only have I sinned', and acknowledges that God's judgement on him is justified. The sense of guilt is so deep that the speaker feels as if it has been with him from the very first moment of his existence: 'Behold, I was shapen in wickedness: and in sin hath my mother conceived me.' He has not merely committed evil deeds, but his very nature and deepest being is sinful. This verse hints at the fallen nature of humankind more broadly, bridging the personal and the universal: not only is the speaker laden with individual sinfulness, but he is burdened by the propensity to sin common to all humans. Against such depths of remorse, only God himself can provide help. A contrast is set up between the righteousness of God, a God of 'truth', and the speaker's disposition towards evil. The psalmist then turns more intently to a petition that God may cleanse him from his evil deeds and renew him in a right spirit: 'O give me the comfort of Thy help again'. Imagery connected to purification is used figuratively here: 'hyssop' was used in Jewish custom for the ritual cleansing of lepers. This association is also picked up in the use of this psalm in the Christian liturgy, where the ritual sprinkling of the congregation with Holy Water at the start of Sunday Mass as a sign of purification is accompanied by this very verse. The speaker prays for spiritual renewal, asking that God may turn his crushing sense of guilt to 'joy and gladness'. As a result of his restoration to joy and innocence, the speaker will be able to convert others to God. He will praise God and offer a sacrifice to him which will consist not of an animal sacrifice but of 'a broken and contrite heart'. The psalm ends with a prayer that God may rebuild the walls of Jerusalem and accept the sacrifices offered to him. The very last verse appears to contradict the previous statement that God does not desire sacrifice, and for this reason it has often been considered a later addition. Yet it need not be a contradiction; if read in the context of the preceding verses, it may simply strengthen the previous statement that God is not interested in the externals of sacrifices if they are not accompanied by the right inward disposition of humility and penitence. Only if this inward attitude is present will God gladly accept sacrifices.

In a metaphorical sense that is less closely connected with the historical context of Jewish animal sacrifice in the temple, the 'burnt-offerings and oblations' of the last verse can also be understood to represent any personal sacrifice of an internal nature, offered to God with the right attitude. What we often mean today when we say we are 'making a sacrifice' is to forgo the pleasure of the moment, of whatever kind, in order to reap greater rewards in the future. This can apply to non-religious contexts as well as religious ones: a student may decide to sacrifice a night out in the hope of doing well in an exam the next day. The short-term pleasure is seen to be less important than the rewards of the long-term future achievement, and this is exactly the sense in which the Christian tradition has understood the concept of sacrifice: something greater may be achieved if something less important is sacrificed. In more recent Christian readings of the psalms, the last verse has often been seen as a figurative reference to sacrifice in this sense. The 'sacrifice of righteousness', the 'burnt-offerings' and 'young bullocks' may be images of the practice of animal sacrifice which here signify internal dispositions and personal sacrifices of a moral and ethical nature that are offered to God. Such details of interpretation are often dependent on whether the psalm is read in its original historical context or applied to contemporary concerns, whether it is seen as a reference to historical Jewish worship or used in later Christian practices of worship, as a psalm that expresses the experience of the worshipping community or the personal penitence of an individual. Of course these aspects need not be mutually exclusive, but may merely express different approaches to an understanding of this psalm.

Because of its deep engagement with sin and petition for God's forgiveness, Psalm 51 played a central role in medieval liturgical practice. It was said in the Liturgy of the Hours in religious communities at Lauds on every weekday, and it was also the final psalm sung in the office of *Tenebrae* during Holy Week (for more on this, see Chapter Four). Due to this prominent liturgical role, it was one of the liturgical texts frequently set to music in medieval and post-medieval times. In a medieval church, the psalm would have been recited or chanted. The chanting of the psalm typically happened according to a set pattern, in which the first and the second part of a psalm verse alternated between the two sides of the choir. Through the singing, the psalm text was realized by and applied to the present congregation or monastic community. What happens through the praying of the penitential psalm by a community of worshippers in a church is that which is characteristic of liturgy more broadly: in the moment of liturgical performance, the congregation inhabits the text. The words of the psalm are made relevant to the present reality of the lives of the congregation. The 'I' of the psalm is no longer primarily the voice of the psalmist or King David himself, but it becomes the 'I' of every individual worshipper.

Let us for a moment imagine what this experience might be like. In the early hours of the morning, we enter a dark church to sing Lauds, the morning office. The sky outside is still dark, only a golden hue on the eastern horizon and a chorus of birds announcing the coming of dawn. The church is dimly illuminated by candles in the choir-stalls; not enough light to give a clear sense of the size of the building, only an awareness of great vaults and slanting columns above. It is cold inside, and the air smells of candlewax and incense. The office begins: *Deus in adiutorium meum intende*, 'O God, come to my help'. Psalm verses are sung, alternating between the sides of the choir. One side calls, the other responds, echoing and continuing each other's thoughts as the psalm moves from confession of sin to hope of renewal in God's mercy. The words are those prescribed by the ritual, words that are ancient and weighty. They have been said in this manner by countless generations of previous worshippers, and they will continue to be said for many generations to come. But despite their ancient origins, the words are also our words. They are no longer the prayer of an Israelite psalmist only. Through the singing, we inhabit the words. It is we who are burdened with an awareness of our faults, and who are asking God to cleanse us and renew us in the right spirit. It is a communal as well as a deeply personal prayer. As the office progresses, the sky outside grows gradually lighter, dispelling the shadows inside the church. First rays of sunlight fall through the high, arched windows to the east, colourful reflections of the stained glass illuminating the altar as the final verse of the psalm speaks of God's merciful acceptance of offerings.

The liturgy is an experience that involves all senses. An intellectual analysis of the texts and prayers of liturgical practice only describes a small part of what makes it so special. The lived experience is much more difficult to capture. But its enduring power is reflected in the fact that it inspired a multitude of interpretations and adaptations in musical form, and continues to do so today. Composers from the late Middle Ages to the present have expressed their understanding of this psalm in a variety of different musical styles. In a medieval context, psalms would usually have been sung in the style of plainchant (an unaccompanied musical setting sung by a single voice, or several voices all singing the same tune together). This style of music arose in medieval monasteries and was traditionally used in the liturgy of the church. It formed the origin of later developments of music in the West, starting from polyphony, a style of music developed in the Renaissance that was marked by interweaving but independent melodic parts. The influence of plainchant has subsequently been heard in musical composition through to the present day, including very recent choral pieces by composers such as Arvo Pärt and James MacMillan. Throughout this long line of development, composers worked on setting psalms to music.

Certainly the most famous musical setting of Psalm 51 is by Gregorio Allegri (1582–1652), a Catholic priest and composer of the

Italian Renaissance. Allegri wrote his setting of the *Miserere* for the celebration of the Holy Week services in the Sistine Chapel in Rome. Holy Week was celebrated with particular intensity in the Vatican, and Allegri's sublime setting for two choirs, written in the 1630s, was a fitting contribution to this tradition that drew inspiration from earlier models of composition by his predecessors. Allegri's original version was very clearly influenced by plainchant, presenting a harmonized version of the medieval chant, interspersed with simple verses of chant following a specific melody, the *tonus peregrinus*. A call-and-response structure is followed by the two choirs, which finally come together for the last verse – a fitting conclusion to the text, emphasizing the reconciliation and forgiveness achieved by God's acceptance of the sacrifice at the end of the psalm. The version of Allegri's *Miserere* that is most widely known today, however, is the result of a long evolution of the piece over the centuries, which involved added ornamentation and several mistakes of transcription in a long history of transmission and copying by later musicians, resulting in the famous soaring soprano line with a high C – a moment that frequently moves modern audiences to tears.

Many other composers, including Byrd, Bach, Handel, Gounod, Wesley and Brahms set the psalm in its entirety or in parts to music, either in Latin or in the vernacular. Perhaps the most compelling musical setting of the psalm in recent years has been that of 2009 by Scottish composer James MacMillan, whose contemporary setting incorporates references to plainchant and the long musical tradition of the psalm, including Allegri's setting. MacMillan's *Miserere* captures superbly the psalm's movement from guilt and sin to forgiveness and renewal. There is a constant contrast between coldness and warmth, despair and hope. The opening sequence sounds desolate and bare, like a whispered prayer coming from the depths under the heavy burden of sin. A few moments later, the score is marked 'warmer and warmer' on the words *magnam misericordiam* ('great mercy'). The word *misericordiam* is drawn out over a long line, illustrating musically the greatness of God's mercy. A still tentative hope is kindled. The verses starting at 'Wash me thoroughly from my wickedness' are sung by the sopranos with a 'keening, crying' sound, making palpable the anguish experienced in the engagement with the speaker's guilt, culminating in the admission of sin: 'Against Thee only have I sinned, and done this evil in thy sight: that Thou mightest be justified in Thy saying, and clear when Thou art judged.' Gradually, the hope in God's mercy grows stronger, marked by a fortissimo outcry that marks roughly the middle point of the piece: *Asperges me hyssopo, hyssopo, et mundabor* ('Thou shalt purge me with hyssop, and I shall be clean'). The word 'hyssop' is prominently emphasized by repetition in MacMillan's version.

To understand the significance of this repetition, we must understand a basic principle of Christian biblical interpretation known as 'typology'. Christian tradition understands the relation of the Old and the New Testaments to each other as one of prophecy and fulfilment in a figurative manner. In this way, key figures and events of the Old Testament are understood to be 'types' of Christ insofar as they prefigure his coming; for example, Abraham and Moses are seen as forerunners of Christ. The Fall and expulsion from Paradise of Adam and Eve in the Book of Genesis are undone by the sacrifice of Christ on the cross; Christ, therefore, is sometimes referred to as 'the new Adam'. Of particular importance here is the Jewish custom of offering and eating the paschal lamb at the feast of Passover, a tradition to commemorate the Israelites' escape from slavery in Egypt. In Exodus 12 the Israelites are told that they can avoid the destruction that awaits the Egyptians by sprinkling the blood of the paschal lamb on the lintel and side posts of their doors using a bunch of hyssop. The Egyptians are punished, while the Israelites escape into freedom. This is understood in later Christian tradition as a symbol of the Passion of Christ, through which the destruction of death and sin is averted from humankind. Christ is referred to in John 1:29 as the 'Lamb of God', and so the animal sacrifice of the Old Testament becomes an image or a figure of Christ's redemptive death on the cross. The double reference to 'hyssop' in MacMillan's piece, therefore, reinforces a word in Psalm 51 that has traditionally been read as a reference to the redemptive power of the death of Christ. This repetition of the word marks a shift at the mid-point of the piece in the journey from the burden of sin at the beginning to forgiveness at the end. Following this crucial shift, the musical development of the text incorporates harmonized chant melodies, as well as a solo tune which evokes associations with Allegri's famous setting. The piece concludes with a warm and hopeful revision of the desolate opening sequence, this time in a major rather than a minor key. The journey from sin to renewal is complete.

In Allegri's and MacMillan's settings we find two interpretations of Psalm 51 that take different approaches and emphasize different aspects of the text, but which also refer back to the same liturgical tradition of plainchant. In this way both pieces hearken back to their liturgical roots while finding a musical language that builds upon this tradition and incorporates new ideas, in the seventeenth century as well as in the twenty-first. But it is not only composers who have been inspired by the central role of this penitential psalm in the liturgy. The psalm was recited in communal prayer in monasteries, but from the Middle Ages onwards Christians also began reading the seven penitential psalms in private devotion. In the late Middle Ages the psalms were regularly included in handbooks of devotion for the laity, so-called *primers*. The popularity of the psalms was due to their central role in the liturgy, as well as their powerful introspective and confessional qualities, which lent themselves especially to private examinations of conscience and reflection on personal faults. The interest of laypeople in these texts for private devotion meant that from the late Middle Ages the penitential psalms were being translated from Latin into English. Several translations survive from the pre-Reformation period, including by poets such as Richard Rolle (1300–1349) and Richard Maidstone (d. 1396).[7] With their emphasis on penitence and self-examination, the psalms also spoke to later post-Reformation readers. An early English translation of the *Miserere* psalm in the wake of the Reformation comes from Sir Thomas Wyatt (1503–1542), an influential courtier and ambassador of Henry VIII. Wyatt presents a unique interpretation of the persona of King David, as he crafts a dramatic speaker of the psalms marked by introspection, self-doubt and theological subtlety. Wyatt's version of Psalm 51 oscillates between close translation and loose paraphrase of the text, resolving many ambiguities of the Latin version. For instance, the apparent contradictions at the end of the psalm between 'For Thou desirest no sacrifice, else would I give it Thee: but Thou delightest not in burnt-offerings' and 'Then shalt Thou be pleased with the sacrifice of righteousness, with the burnt-offerings and oblations: then shall they offer young bullocks upon Thine altar', is resolved in Wyatt's version in the following way:

> For if thou hadst esteemed pleasant good
> The outward deeds that outward men disclose
> I would have offered unto thee sacrifice.
> But thou delights not in no such gloze [= false show]
> Of outward deed as men dream and devise.
> The sacrifice that the Lord liketh most
> Is sprite contrite; low heart in humble wise
> Thou dost accept, O God, for pleasant host . . .
> Then shalt thou take for good these outward deeds
> As sacrifice thy pleasure to fulfil.
> Of thee alone thus all our good proceeds.[8]

Wyatt summarizes the terms specific to sacrifice ('burnt-offerings', 'oblations', 'young bullocks') under a more general category as 'outward deeds', setting up a contrast between sacrifice offered by mere external actions without the appropriate internal disposition, and those actions in which the 'outward deeds' are accompanied by a 'sprite contrite'. The implication is that God only wants external actions if they are done for the right reasons and out of contrition and humility, not for outward show. In paraphrasing the words of the psalm, Wyatt presents a consistent reading that does away with some of the problems of interpretation that we encounter when reading the Latin text.

Shakespeare, too, makes reference to the Penitential Psalms and uses them for dramatic purposes. The *Miserere* features in a scene in *Hamlet*, when Claudius, having murdered his brother, reflects on the possibility of attaining God's forgiveness:

> What if this cursed hand
> Were thicker than itself with brother's blood?
> Is there not rain enough in the sweet heavens
> To wash it white as snow? (III.3.43–6)

The passage alludes to a section from the psalm, 'Thou shalt wash me, and I shall be whiter than snow'. This connection makes sense when we compare Claudius's situation with that of King David. Like David, Claudius is a king who is guilty of murder. Like David, Claudius has married his victim's wife. The parallel between the two kings which Shakespeare sets up in these lines only reinforces the contrast between them: while David is truly contrite, Claudius cannot bring himself to repent. The allusion, in this case, undercuts what Claudius is saying. While his speech implies that there is rain enough to wash away his guilt, the comparison with David subtly indicates that there will be no forgiveness for Claudius as he does not feel true remorse.[9]

It is not only Old Testament texts like the psalms that have been widely used in liturgical prayer and which have subsequently exerted their influence on literature. Texts from the New Testament as an expression of petition were equally influential in medieval Europe and beyond. An example is a short prayer that occurs as part of the

Mass, just before the communion of the faithful, known as the *Agnus Dei*, 'Lamb of God', a term commonly applied to Jesus. As mentioned above, the term 'Lamb of God' refers to a passage from the Gospel of John (1:29), in which John the Baptist first encounters Jesus and exclaims: 'Behold! The Lamb of God who takes away the sin of the world!' The idea of Jesus as the Lamb of God is foundational to Christian theology, which holds that Jesus as the Son of God willingly chose to undergo crucifixion and death in order to take away the sins of humankind. In an instance of typology, the ritual sacrifice of the Passover in the Old Testament is interpreted as a foretelling of the redemption through Christ, whose death atones for human sin. Christ therefore becomes a metaphorical lamb sacrificed for the salvation of all.

This is the background to which the liturgical prayer refers, when God is invoked three times as the Lamb of God, connected with a prayer for forgiveness and peace:

Agnus Dei, qui tollis peccata mundi, miserere nobis.	Lamb of God, who takes away the sins of the world, have mercy on us.
Agnus Dei, qui tollis peccata mundi, miserere nobis.	Lamb of God, who takes away the sins of the world, have mercy on us.
Agnus Dei, qui tollis peccata mundi, dona nobis pacem.	Lamb of God, who takes away the sins of the world, grant us peace.

As a fixed part of the Mass, the *Agnus Dei* prayer has been set to music countless times by composers, perhaps most hauntingly so in Samuel Barber's 1967 choral arrangement of his *Adagio for Strings*. It is the part of the Mass that is traditionally the most introspective and pleading in many musical settings, expressing hope in God's mercy and uncertainty at the prospect of peace on earth. Yet

2 Lamb frieze, Basilica of Santa Pudenziana, Rome, 11th century, marble.
3 Lamb roof boss, All Saints' Church in Kleinschwarzenlohe, 15th century.

nowhere has the motif of the Lamb of God been more influential than in the visual arts. From the Middle Ages onwards, the Lamb of God is a distinctive iconographical motif. In such representations, the lamb typically stands upright, surrounded by a halo of light, its foreleg tucked around either a cross, or a flag with a symbol of the cross. Its stance is triumphant, representing victory over death and sin: a symbol of the risen Christ. An early example of this mode of representation is a relief in the Basilica of Santa Pudenziana, Rome, which dates to around AD 1000 (illus. 2). Countless churches contain the same image, such as that found on an architectural detail at All Saints' Church in Kleinschwarzenlohe, Germany (illus. 3). But it is not only churches that feature this image as a symbol of Christ as the redeemer. In fact, once you start looking for the lamb, you will soon see it everywhere. Few people will associate traditional English pub signs with Christian art, but if you travel around the United Kingdom you will likely chance upon a pub called the Lamb and Flag in one place or another. Many signs still depict the lamb using the traditional iconography. The long history of the liturgy is present in unexpected places, sometimes even when you are enjoying a pint.

2
Love

'I am a rose of Sharon, a lily of the valleys,' a young woman sings. 'How beautiful you are, my love, how very beautiful!' her lover replies, and praises her beauty: 'Your lips are like a crimson thread, and your mouth is lovely.' It is unlikely that a modern reader would interpret such a scene as anything beyond what it seems on the surface: an encounter between two young lovers. And yet, this is not quite how this scene has been interpreted by the majority of its readers since it was first written more than two millennia ago. This imagined scene is a short version of a much longer dialogue from a poem stretching over several chapters. Let us look at a longer section to get a sense of the poem's language:

1 How beautiful you are, my love,
how very beautiful!
Your eyes are doves
behind your veil.
Your hair is like a flock of goats,
moving down the slopes of Gilead.
2 Your teeth are like a flock of shorn ewes
that have come up from the washing,
all of which bear twins,
and not one among them is bereaved.
3 Your lips are like a crimson thread,

and your mouth is lovely.
Your cheeks are like halves of a pomegranate
behind your veil.
4 Your neck is like the tower of David,
built in courses;
on it hang a thousand bucklers,
all of them shields of warriors.
5 Your two breasts are like two fawns,
twins of a gazelle,
that feed among the lilies.
6 Until the day breathes
and the shadows flee,
I will hasten to the mountain of myrrh
and the hill of frankincense.
7 You are altogether beautiful, my love;
there is no flaw in you.
8 Come with me from Lebanon, my bride;
come with me from Lebanon.
Depart from the peak of Amana,
from the peak of Senir and Hermon,
from the dens of lions,
from the mountains of leopards.
9 You have ravished my heart, my sister, my bride,
you have ravished my heart with a glance of your eyes,
with one jewel of your necklace.
10 How sweet is your love, my sister, my bride!
how much better is your love than wine,
and the fragrance of your oils than any spice!
11 Your lips distil nectar, my bride;
honey and milk are under your tongue;
the scent of your garments is like the scent of Lebanon.
12 A garden locked is my sister, my bride,
a garden locked, a fountain sealed.

13 Your channel is an orchard of pomegranates
with all choicest fruits,
henna with nard,
14 nard and saffron, calamus and cinnamon,
with all trees of frankincense,
myrrh and aloes,
with all chief spices –
15 a garden fountain, a well of living water,
and flowing streams from Lebanon.
16 Awake, O north wind,
and come, O south wind!
Blow upon my garden
that its fragrance may be wafted abroad.
Let my beloved come to his garden,
and eat its choicest fruits.
(Song of Songs 4)

The imagery of the poem is rich and suggestive: the eyes of the beloved are compared to doves, her cheeks to pomegranates, her breasts to twins of a gazelle. Middle Eastern flora and fauna are invoked in order to praise the beauty of an unnamed woman. Within the context of an arid country, the images of life-giving abundance used to express her beauty would have resonated particularly strongly. She is strikingly described as a locked garden containing a verdant scenery of well-water, fruits and spices to which her lover will come to 'eat . . . choicest fruits'. The erotic undertones of such imagery are hardly subtle.

Most modern readers would not associate such sensual poetry with divine or spiritual love. The language seems too concrete, the symbolism too sexual, to suggest a spiritual reading. And yet, in the Middle Ages this poem was used more than any other text as a vehicle for thinking about divine love. It was interpreted as describing, in a symbolic manner, the relationship between God and his people, and between God and Mary, the mother of Christ. Although this may seem surprising at first glance, it helps us make sense of many aspects of Western art and music, whether secular or sacred. The unexpected story of how an erotic poem came to be central to the Christian theological tradition takes us back many centuries, and into the heart of the liturgy.

The poem, with its references to gazelles, orchards and warriors, is merely one chapter in a much longer poem known as the Song of Songs, or the Song of Solomon. The title indicates that the poem was originally intended to be sung to music. It is one of the books of the Old Testament used within a Jewish context for reading on the feast of Passover in the synagogue or within the family. In a superscription in the Hebrew text, the Song of Songs is attributed to King Solomon, the son of King David renowned for his wisdom, although, as with King David's psalms, it is unclear whether Solomon was actually the author of the poem. Many scholars today think of it as a collection of songs brought together over a period of time rather than a single song by a single author. The title Song of Songs can therefore be explained as a reference to a collection of songs, or it might simply indicate the excellence of the text – in other words, the 'most exalted', 'best' or 'all-encompassing' song.[1]

Nobody quite knows how the Song of Songs came to be included in the canon of the Old Testament next to historical books and chronicles. It does have some similarities with other poetic Old Testament texts, such as the psalms, but it is very different in that it presents a dialogue between two lovers, without a single mention of God or religious concepts. The subject matter of erotic love is clear from the outset as the song starts with 'Let him kiss me with the kisses of his mouth! For your love is better than wine' (Song of Songs 1:2). As its inclusion in the Old Testament canon was so curious it consequently prompted discussion in early Jewish sources. In Jewish tradition a specific line of interpretation developed, which helped acceptance of the Song of Songs as a sacred text despite its ostensibly secular nature. The poem was read as an allegory (a tale with a hidden meaning) of the love between God and his people, the Israelites. This allegorical interpretation was developed in great detail by Jewish commentators, and later adopted and adapted by early Christian interpreters, who took the general principle in a slightly different direction. Christian readings sought to explain the apparent incongruity of the Song of Songs with the canon of the Old Testament by reading it symbolically in the context of the New Testament. Typology – the method of reading the Bible that we already encountered in the first chapter – played a role here. If the Old Testament was seen as pointing towards the coming of Christ, what could the role of an apparently erotic love poem be in relation to Christ? A range of interpretations emerged. Taking inspiration from the Jewish tradition, the Song of Songs began to be read as an allegory of the love between Christ and the Church, or between Christ and the soul of the individual believer. According to these interpretations, Christ is presented in the Song of Songs as a passionate lover who pursues his bride – the Church or the soul – using secular and erotic imagery to refer to a spiritual reality. The literary language of sexual love, also known as *eros*, is used to refer to divine love or *agape*.

Critics have seen this allegorical interpretive tradition as a sign of a prurient attitude, but interpreting the Song of Songs in a spiritual vein does not have to be an attempt to evade the presence of sexual language – quite the contrary. Much of the literature of the Middle Ages positively delights in the sensual imagery of the Song of Songs, draws upon it, expands it, and uses it as an inspiration to create new poetry. What engagement with the Song of Songs achieves is not so much an avoidance of erotic language and sexual subject matter as a deliberate and creative use of such language in engaging with religious matters. Human sexuality is incorporated into a celebration of the mystical love between the human and the divine. The identification of the Song of Songs with divine love meant that erotic imagery could be used freely and abundantly in religious writings. A space was opened up for innovative, sometimes daring, engagement with erotic language when talking about God. This is particularly clear in the mystical tradition of the Middle Ages, where writers such as Bernard of Clairvaux, Brigit of Sweden, Julian of Norwich and Margery Kempe explored a range of sensual imagery in describing their deep, spiritual union with God. The writings of twelfth-century Benedictine monk Rupert von Deutz are an example of how the Song of Songs inspired mystical experiences of union with God. Rupert describes how, years earlier, he had experienced the call to priesthood. In a dream, Christ calls him to approach him on the crucifix and kiss him on the mouth: 'I held Him, I embraced Him and kissed Him long and profoundly. I noticed how happily He received this sign of love, for in the kissing, He opened his mouth so that I would kiss Him more deeply.'[2] This passage clearly recalls the beginning of the Song of Songs ('Let him kiss me with the kisses of his mouth') and applies it to an experience of connection with Christ. The kiss described is an expression of a spiritual, mystical union – Rupert experiences it as a call to the priesthood – but it is at the same time described with the language of human desire. The Song of Songs allows the sacred and the sensual to meet.

Given these literary and theological developments, it is perhaps unsurprising that the bridal imagery of the Song of Songs eventually came to be applied to a very particular female subject: the Virgin Mary. According to a Christian theological understanding, Mary occupies a unique position in the divine plan of salvation. Though human like all other human beings, she was uniquely privileged to become the mother of Christ, whom she conceived miraculously by the Holy Spirit. The basis for this belief is the Gospel of Luke, which tells of an angel's visit to Mary to announce that she will become the mother of Jesus.

> In the sixth month the angel Gabriel was sent by God to a town in Galilee called Nazareth, to a virgin engaged to a man whose

> name was Joseph, of the house of David. The virgin's name was Mary. And he came to her and said, 'Greetings, favoured one! The Lord is with you.' But she was much perplexed by his words and pondered what sort of greeting this might be. The angel said to her, 'Do not be afraid, Mary, for you have found favour with God. And now, you will conceive in your womb and bear a son, and you will name him Jesus. He will be great, and will be called the Son of the Most High, and the Lord God will give to him the throne of his ancestor David. He will reign over the house of Jacob for ever, and of his kingdom there will be no end.' Mary said to the angel, 'How can this be, since I am a virgin?' The angel said to her, 'The Holy Spirit will come upon you, and the power of the Most High will overshadow you; therefore the child to be born will be holy; he will be called Son of God.' (Luke 1:26–35)

Through interpretation of this account, Mary comes to be thought of as the bride of the Holy Spirit, and yet she is also a child of God as all other humans are. In her relationship with the three persons of the Trinity, Mary can therefore be described paradoxically as mother, daughter and spouse of God, while remaining a perpetual virgin. The miracle of God's Incarnation collapses normal categories of human relationships. Latin theological writings and liturgical poetry play upon these paradoxes with evocative language. One medieval hymn praises Mary as 'wife, sister, dowry, and daughter of the supreme Creator'.[3]

While later Protestant movements were keen to curb devotions to the Virgin Mary in a reaction against what they saw as idolatry and worship of a quasi-divine Blessed Virgin, medieval Christianity had no such qualms. Mary was venerated as the ideal of all women and the mediator between God and humankind. Many prayers and hymns praised Mary as the epitome of all virtue, beauty and grace. In a tradition of biblical interpretation where God was identified with the male speaker of the Song of Songs, it was only a small leap to identifying Mary as the bride of the Holy Spirit with the female beloved in the Old Testament text. This interpretive tradition goes back at least to the patristic writings of St Ambrose in the fourth century, but it is developed in greater detail in theological writings from the twelfth century onwards. This is a particularly interesting development because it is here where we see the true transformative power of the liturgy at work. While we may commonly think of worship reflecting theological beliefs, what seems to have happened around the twelfth century is exactly the inverse: the association of the female beloved in the Song of Songs with the Virgin Mary is an idea which arises, first and foremost, in and through the liturgy, and it is only later that it is discussed and expanded in a more systematic way in theological and scholarly writings of the medieval period.[4] It is, in other words, an illustration of the *lex orandi, lex credendi* principle discussed in the introduction: the form of worship influences belief. Liturgy comes first, and theology after.

The gospels do not provide us with many details about the life of the Virgin Mary. Apart from crucial moments such as her consent to the angel's message, the texts only give us glimpses of her story. Nonetheless, there is a rich early tradition of stories of the life of the Virgin, based on oral tradition as well as sources that were not part of the canonical Bible. An example of an event that is not mentioned in the canonical gospels, but nonetheless appears in Christian worship very early on, is the Assumption, a belief according to which the Virgin Mary was bodily taken up into heaven at the end of her life. This feast proved a particular inspiration for the creation of liturgical hymns. As the event of the Assumption is not described in the canonical gospels, texts from the Old Testament were used in liturgical celebration which were, through a typological reading, applied to the Virgin Mary. Because of the bridal imagery explored above, the Song of Songs ranked foremost in the texts used for this occasion. We find evidence of this in the earliest sources that tell us how the liturgy was celebrated, such as the Antiphoner of Compiègne, the oldest surviving book that contains the Latin texts of the Liturgy of the Hours, dating to the late ninth century. In this we find a striking antiphon for Vespers on the feast of the Assumption of the Virgin Mary:

Quae est ista quae ascendit sicut aurora consurgens, pulchra ut luna, electa ut sol, terribilis ut castrorum acies ordinata?	Who is she that ascends like the rising dawn, fair as the moon, chosen as the sun, terrible as an army drawn up for battle?

This antiphon is almost identical to Song of Songs 6:10, with the single difference that the biblical text contains the word *progreditur* (comes forth) instead of *ascendit* (ascends). The Song of Songs here praises the beloved in a striking way with celestial and martial imagery. The images of dawn, moon and sun may have prompted an association of this particular verse with the feast of the Assumption. We can see in the liturgical version of the verse how the Song of Songs is applied to the Virgin, and made relevant to the feast of the Assumption by replacing the verb with 'ascends'. In this way, the quotation is turned into a reference to Mary being taken up into heaven. It is this early association of the Song of Songs with the Virgin Mary in the liturgy that later prompted more elaborate theological commentaries, which saw the Song of Songs as referring to the Virgin Mary. The powerful poetic qualities of the Song of Songs lent themselves naturally to a use in liturgical worship, and it is only later that this connection became a fully formed system of interpretation.[5]

The solar and lunar imagery of this verse is a recurring feature of many representations of the Virgin Mary in art since the late Middle Ages, such as an illustration from a 1577 work on the Blessed Virgin by Petrus Canisius (illus. 4). We can see the Virgin Mary and the baby Jesus in the middle, surrounded by a range of objects. The sun and moon to the top left and right cite the words from the same verse of the Song of Songs that is used in the Antiphoner of Compiègne:

4 Woodcut of the Blessed Virgin and child from Petrus Canisius, *De Maria Virgine incomparabili, et Dei Genitrice sacrosancta* (1577).

Electa ut sol ('chosen as the sun') and *Pulchra ut luna* ('fair as the moon'). But there are more symbols surrounding Mary, many of which are references to the Song of Songs. Some of these we have already encountered at the beginning of this chapter. We see a well on the left-hand side of the picture, and a tower, a garden and a fountain on the bottom right. These are references to the 'well of living water' (*puteus aquarum*), the tower of David (*Turris David*), the locked garden (*hortus conclusus*) and the sealed fountain (*Fons signatus*) to which the beloved is compared in Song of Songs 4. The inscription at the bottom cites Song of Songs 4:7: *Tota pulchra es amica mea et macula non est in te* ('You are altogether beautiful, my love; there is no flaw in you'). The application of the praise of the beloved in the Song of Songs to the Virgin Mary is here expressed very clearly in visual form. This image illustrates the Litany of the Blessed Virgin Mary, a long prayer that praises Mary with a list of invocations and asks for her help. The symbols surrounding the Virgin form part of this list of invocations. Yet such imagery is more than just a poetic praise of the Virgin; each symbol is imbued with significance.

The enclosed garden is an example that can help us trace this deeper significance. The illustration emphasizes the state of the garden as locked to such an extent that it looks almost like a cage. This emphasis on locking and enclosing is significant, as the image of the *hortus conclusus* was traditionally read as a metaphor of Mary's perpetual virginity, conceiving Jesus by the Holy Spirit. Impassable to men, Mary is a locked garden into which only God can enter. Numerous liturgical hymns of the Middle Ages use this image in often creative ways to emphasize Mary's virginity, such as this hymn of unclear date, which praises Mary with the following words:

O salutaris	Oh saving
Miserorum portus,	port of the wretched
Ortus	Day-spring
Et conclusus hortus,	And closed garden,

Ex te sol exortus,	The sun came forth from you
Virgo deum paris.	You give birth to God as a virgin.[6]

The Latin original makes clever use of the rhyme between *portus – ortus – hortus – exortus* (port – day-spring – garden – came forth), connecting metaphorical images in praise of the Virgin, including those from the Song of Songs, with the birth of Christ. The rhyme between the first line and the last further emphasizes that she is worthy of being invoked as one who saves (*salutaris*) by dint of the fact that she gives birth (*paris*) to God.

An event where Mary's virginity is of particular relevance is the Annunciation as reported in the Gospel of Luke, as we have seen above. This scene exerted a particular fascination on the creative imagination over the centuries, and became a popular subject in religious art. The metaphorical language of the Song of Songs proved an effective tool to communicate Mary's everlasting virginity in visual terms. In a famous Annunciation fresco by Renaissance painter Fra

5 Fra Angelico, *The Annunciation*, c. 1442–3, fresco, Convent of San Marco, Florence.

6 Tintoretto, *The Annunciation*, 1583–7, oil on canvas.

Angelico (1395–1455), we find an insistence on the fact that Mary is sitting in an enclosed garden when the angel approaches (illus. 5). Mary is seated in a covered outdoor space (in an Italian context known as a *loggia*) with a reverent attitude, her head slightly bowed, as the angel delivers the message. The angel is bowing reverently in return; we get the impression of a conversation full of mutual respect. Mary appears calm and composed as she accepts the role she is to play in the salvation of humankind. In the background we see a strongly emphasized wooden fence, which separates Mary's garden from the outside world. Inside the fence flowers abound, while outside there is a wilderness of trees. Using the symbolic language of this garden, Fra Angelico's fresco thus highlights the tradition of the *hortus conclusus* and its implied theological meaning regarding Mary's virginity.

We also find versions of the *hortus conclusus* symbolism in a large number of Renaissance paintings of the Annunciation, with the enclosed garden emphasized to a greater or lesser extent by different artists. The fact that this tradition was so widespread makes any deviations from it all the more noteworthy. A notable example is Tintoretto's *Annunciation* (illus. 6). In this painting Mary is portrayed as one of the common people, seated in a room filled with old furniture and items required for daily work. She sits on a low chair and has clearly been interrupted in the midst of her work. A dove, a conventional symbol of the Holy Spirit, descends on her from above. But her demeanour is quite the opposite of the calm and composed Mary whom we saw in Fra Angelico's version. She looks startled, even shocked, by the sudden appearance of the angel and the accompanying host, who appear to be flying towards her at great speed from above. Her arms and shoulders are turned away in a gesture of surprise and fear. As in Luke 1:26, this Mary is 'much perplexed' by the angel's visit. Whereas in Fra Angelico's version the Virgin and the angel are separated by a column, there is nothing separating the two in Tintoretto's painting: the angel has passed between two stone pillars at the threshold of her home, breaking into the private space of her humble abode, upsetting the routine of everyday life. And unlike Fra Angelico, Tintoretto also disrupts the traditional iconography of the enclosed garden. Mary's home is not surrounded by a meadow of beautiful flowers, but by a dark and chaotic scene. Bits of broken furniture are spread around the outside of her house in a disorderly fashion. According to the gospels, Mary was engaged to be married to a carpenter, but the chaos outside her home is more than just a nod to St Joseph's profession. It is precisely the contrast with the earlier tradition of the well-ordered beautiful garden that makes the disorder in this painting all the more striking. We get the impression that this is a messy and broken world, into which, unexpectedly, the divine message is brought. Everything is changed in an instant. Tintoretto deviates from the familiar iconography of the *hortus conclusus* only to introduce a different, equally powerful symbolism: a bright dawn is rising over the distant hills on the left, announcing the coming of hope for humankind at the incarnation of its saviour.[7]

At this point in the Renaissance period the imagery of the Song of Songs has come a long way from an apparently secular erotic poem to an allegory of Mary's excellence in the liturgy, only to be negated and disrupted to communicate a different, equally powerful theological idea. But the original context of the Song of Songs, that of a passionate exchange between two lovers, was not completely lost along the way. As we have seen in the mystical tradition of the Middle Ages, the line between secular erotic imagery and a religious, spiritual meaning could be blurry, and in fact it was very deliberately blurred in many texts. In reality, it is difficult to separate the two, and the evocative language of the Song of Songs inspired both secular and religious poetry and song.

Many medieval poems exploit these blurry boundaries between the religious and the secular for dramatic effect. There is an entire group of Middle English lyrics (short poems) that take the form of a love quest, a setting common in secular, chivalric French songs. In their original form these songs typically include a male speaker who, after wandering out into the country, unexpectedly meets a woman and has a conversation with her. This setting is sometimes transferred onto a religious context, in which the speaker has a dream in which he meets a woman who is revealed to be the Virgin Mary. One of these types of poems begins as follows:

In a tabernacle of a toure,	In a niche of a tower,
As I stode musyng on the mone,	As I stood musing on the moon,
A crouned quene, most of honoure,	A crowned queen, of greatest honour,
Apered in gostly syght ful sone.	Appeared very soon in a vision.
She made compleynt thus by hyr one,	She made a complaint thus on her own,
For mannes soule was wrapped in wo,	For man's soul was enveloped by woe,
'I may nat leve mankynde allone,	'I cannot leave mankind alone,
Quia amore langueo.'	*Because I languish for love*.'

'I longe for love of man my brother,	'I long for love of man, who is my brother,
I am hys vokete to voyde hys vyce;	I am his advocate to eliminate his faults;
I am hys moder – I can none other –	I am his mother – I cannot do otherwise –
Why shuld I my dere chylde dispyce?	Why should I despise my dear child?
Yef he me wrathe in diverse wyse,	If he angers me in different ways
Th[r]ough flesshes freelté fall me fro,	Through flesh's frailty fall from me,
Yet must me rewe hym tyll he ryse,	Yet must I pity him until he arises,
Quia amore langueo.'	*Because I languish for love.*'[8]

The trope of love-longing is here transferred onto the Virgin Mary, who languishes for love of humankind, whose state of sin she laments. Every man is her brother whom she patiently helps and for whom she intercedes. Yet the identity of the lady is at first mysterious and is then only slowly revealed in the course of the poem. The text invokes the trope of a noble lady lamenting her lover, which appears in different forms in many secular love lyrics, but this initial impression is quickly undermined. The ghostly vision of the 'crowned queen' takes place while the speaker is 'musing on the moon', and this association with lunar imagery subtly hints at the lady's true identity as Mary. The lady is not waiting for her lover, as we might expect, but expressing her love for 'mankind'. The second stanza makes clear that the lady can only be speaking of spiritual love, as she is lover, mother and sister to the man for whom she laments. The poem plays with these paradoxes to make us reassess our initial understanding of the text in the light of the complex family ties that are mentioned. Like the speaker of the poem who receives a vision, we are on a journey of discovery, trying to make sense of the identity of the initially mysterious lady. Fitting with these paradoxes, each stanza concludes with a refrain that quotes the Song of Songs: *Quia amore langueo*, 'Because I languish for love' (Song of Songs 2:5 and 5:8). Spoken in the Bible by the woman awaiting her lover, the line is here given to Mary as the lover of all human souls. Just like the liturgy, the poem uses associations and connections between the Song of Songs and the Virgin that are traditional, and at the same time plays with this tradition in an innovative way.

A different approach to the Virgin Mary through the language of the Song of Songs is found in a fifteenth-century poem by the friar James Ryman, which celebrates the Assumption of Mary into heaven. According to traditional medieval belief, Mary was crowned as queen of heaven after her Assumption. The poem uses the invitation famously spoken by the lover to his beloved in the Song of Songs, 'Come', and attributes them to Christ himself, who addresses the Virgin Mary when she is taken up into heaven:

Carissima in deliciis, *Iam ueni: coronaberis.*	*Sweetest in delights,* *Come now, you shall be crowned.*
Come, my dere spowse and lady free; Come to thy sonne in heven blis,	Come, my dear spouse and lady free; Come to your son in heavenly bliss,
For why next me thy place shalbe, *Iam ueni: coronaberis.*	For next to me your place shall be, *Come now, you shall be crowned.*
Come, my myelde dove, into thy cage, With ioye and blis replete whiche is; For why it is thyne heritage. *Iam ueni: coronaberis.*	Come, my mild dove, into your cage, which is full with joy and bliss, For it is your heritage. *Come now, you shall be crowned.*

Moost faire and swete, moost meke and myelde,
Come to thy sonne and king of blis.
Moder and mayden vndefielde,
Iam ueni: coronaberis.

Most fair and sweet, most meek and mild,
Come to your son and king of bliss.
Mother and maiden undefiled,
Come now, you shall be crowned.

Thou art alle fayre, my spowse moost dere,
And spotte of synne in the noon is:
Come fro Liban, to me appere.
Iam ueni: coronaberis.

You are all fair, my spouse most dear,
And spot of sin is not in you,
Come from Libanus, to me appear.
Come now, you shall be crowned.

Thy stature is assymylate
To a palme tree and thy bristis
To grapes, spowse inmaculate.
Iam ueni: coronaberis.

Thy stature is to be compared
To a palm tree and thy breasts
To grapes, spouse immaculate.
Come now, you shall be crowned.

Off alle clennes I am the floure,
The felde wherof thy pure soule is.
O virginall floure moost of honoure,
Iam ueni: coronaberis.

Of all cleanness I am the flower,
The field whereof your pure soul is.
O virginal flower most of honour,
Come now, you shall be crowned.

Thy blessed body was my bowre,
Wherefore my blis thou shallt not mys,
And alle seintes shalle the honoure.
Iam ueni: coronaberis.

Your blessed body was my bower,
Wherefore my bliss you shall not miss,
And all saints will honour you.
Come now, you shall be crowned.

With thy brestes so pure and clene
Thou haste me fedde, wherfore, i-wis,

With your breasts so pure and clean
You have fed me, wherefore, truly,

Of heven blis thou shalt be quene.	Of heaven's bliss you shall be queen.
Iam ueni: coronaberis.	*Come now, you shall be crowned.*[9]

Christ here speaks to the Virgin Mary, who is his spouse, mother, lover and queen. He remembers what she has done for him as his mother during her earthly life, and now invites her to come and be crowned in heaven. We once again find here a play with the language of the Song of Songs and paradoxical images that do not map onto human relationships but only apply to God as the Trinity. As in the Song of Songs, God speaking as the lover compares his beloved's breasts to grapes, but later on in the poem this image is related to Mary's feeding of the infant Jesus. Once again, we are brought up short by the paradoxes and incompatible categories of human relationships that shift throughout the poem. By playfully disorienting the reader, the poem encourages us to pause and consider the exceptional role that Mary plays in the divine plan of salvation.

It is not only medieval religious poetry that is influenced by the Song of Songs. We likewise find secular love poetry using the imagery of the Song of Songs in abundance. 'Dû bist mîn, ich bin dîn' ('You are mine, I am yours') begins one of the oldest medieval German minnesinger poems, echoing Song of Songs 2:16: 'My beloved is mine and I am his.' Later on in the medieval period the images describing the beauty of the beloved in the Song of Songs became stock phrases to describe the beauty of the lady in French and Italian love poetry, where they frequently occur in secularized contexts. For instance, Italian poet Guido Cavalcanti (1250–1300), a friend of Dante Alighieri, wrote a sonnet praising an unnamed woman, whose beginning, 'Chi è questa', invokes Song of Songs 6:10, *Quae est ista* ('Who is she'). We have previously encountered this phrase as it is used in the liturgy for the feast of the Assumption of the Blessed Virgin Mary, but here it is used to refer to a courtly lady rather than the Virgin Mary:

Rime, 4

Chi è questa che vèn, ch'ogn'om la mira,
che fa tremar di chiaritate l'âre
e mena seco Amor, sì che parlare
null'omo pote, ma ciascun sospira?
O Deo, che sembra quando li occhi gira!
dical' Amor, ch'i' nol savria contare:
cotanto d'umiltà donna mi pare
ch'ogn'altra ver' di lei i' la chiam' ira.
Non si poria contar la sua piagenza,
ch'a le' s'inchin' ogni gentil vertute,
e la beltate per sua dea la mostra.
Non fu sì alta già la mente nostra
e non si pose 'n noi tanta salute
che propiamente n'aviàn conoscenza.

Who comes this way, that all men stand and gaze,
Who gives a trembling brightness to the air,
And leads Love with her so that no one there
Can speak a word, but all must melt in sighs?
O God, the radiance of those glancing eyes,
Beyond what I can say, let Love declare:
All other women seem but fretful care
Before this lady's modest gracious ways.
There is no tongue that can describe her grace,
Before her all the noble virtues bend,
Beauty's divinity made manifest.
But we were never granted such great bliss,
Nor was our mind so raised as to pretend
To knowledge of her as she truly is.[10]

Even though the context is a secular one, the spiritual resonances invoked by the first line continue throughout the poem. The object of affection is a paragon of all virtue and nobility and the manifestation of a divine kind of beauty. There is an exaltation and idealization of the beloved that we have also seen in religious poetry. Cavalcanti's lady is not the Virgin Mary, and yet she is not unlike the Virgin Mary, who likewise is the epitome of all female virtue, grace and beauty. Indeed, the lady is so exalted that the true extent of her virtues is ineffable: our mind cannot know her 'as she truly is', much like a religious ideal. Cavalcanti is not the only poet to play with this idea: Dante's Beatrice and Petrarch's Laura are described in very similar terms. The line between secular and religious, sensuality and mysticism, is difficult to draw. Many love poems of this period deliberately hover between these two poles, just as the Song of Songs itself can be read along both erotic and spiritual lines.

This rich tradition inspired by the Song of Songs had a long afterlife until modern times. More recent texts that allude to this tradition sometimes use references to the Song of Songs to undermine traditional readings, or to throw up new perspectives. Walt Whitman's *Song of Myself* (first published in *Leaves of Grass* in 1855), a poem which remains among the most acclaimed in American poetry, sets out its key idea at the start: 'I celebrate myself, and sing myself.'[11] Rather than the love between two people, as in the Song of Songs, Whitman's poem celebrates love of the self, but it does so in distinctly biblical language. The parallel structure of the opening line echoes the repetitive structure so characteristic of Hebrew poetry. Whitman's poem is filled with images reminiscent of the language of the Song of Songs. Lines such as 'Houses and rooms are full of perfumes, the shelves are crowded with perfumes' evoke an echo of 'Your anointing oils are fragrant, your name is perfume poured out' (Song of Songs 1:3), and likewise, 'The delight alone or in the rush of the streets, or along the fields and hill-sides' seems to invoke 'Come, my beloved, let us go forth into the fields, and lodge in the villages' (Song of Songs 7:11). In Whitman's poem there is no beloved but the self, which is praised in such terms. As such it is a distinct break from the tradition of biblical love poetry, a deliberately provocative act. But at the same time it is not entirely dissimilar from moments in the Song of Songs where the woman celebrates her own beauty, 'I am a rose of Sharon, a lily of the valleys'.[12] Even in its biblical origins, love of other and love of self are intertwined, inspiring modern poets to take these ideas further. Modern pop music likewise draws inspiration from the Song of Songs, such as Kate Bush in her 1993 'Song of Solomon'. Even after a long and complex history of interpretation and transformation, the Song of Songs has not lost its inspirational qualities for poets and songwriters.

3
Hope

Every story has a beginning. Christian interpretation of the Bible includes many moments of prophecy and foreshadowing, as we have seen with the typology of the Song of Songs. But the Christian belief, at its heart, is centred around the life of a single extraordinary person: Jesus Christ. The life of Jesus begins, according to the gospels, in a stable. His parents have travelled to a small town called Bethlehem, and all available guest rooms are taken. So it happens that Mary has to give birth between farm animals, and uses a manger as a crib for the baby. Countless carols and songs have been sung about this event, and when we celebrate it today as Christmas, the very name of the festival refers to the liturgical celebration: the 'Christ-Mass' said on the day marking the birth of Jesus.

But Christmas is more than just the extended festival starting on the eve of 25 December. In the liturgical calendar it is followed by the closely associated festivals of Epiphany and Candlemas, but preceded by a period of waiting and preparation for the birth of the saviour. It is this latter season that we call Advent, derived from the Latin word *adventus*, meaning 'arrival'. In the liturgy the arrival of Christ is not a sudden event, but it is heralded by a season of expectation. The liturgy of the four weeks of Advent is marked by constant and ever more intense calls for the coming of the saviour. The imagery used for the impending arrival of Christ often draws upon Old Testament episodes that speak of the various exiles of the people of Israel and the long period during which they receive prophecies of the coming of the Messiah. The birth of the baby at Bethlehem is seen as the fulfilment of these prophecies.

A recurring feature of services in the season of Advent was traditionally the *Rorate* verse, so called after the Latin word with which it begins. It cites the opening words of Isaiah 45:8:

Rorate coeli desuper et nubes pluant justum.	Drop down, ye heavens, from above and let the skies pour down righteousness.

The English translation given is widely known through a popular hymn. It is elegant and flows well in English, but it is worth noting that it presents a very specific interpretation of the Latin words. The Latin version is itself a translation of the original Hebrew via Greek, but it is the Latin that is the most influential for liturgical practice. Strictly speaking, the word *rorare* in Latin refers to the falling of dew drops, and *justum* can mean either 'just thing' or 'just man', so the verse can be understood to refer to a person coming to earth from above, rather than the more abstract 'righteousness'. The poetic conceit of the Latin text is unusual and immediately evocative: the first half of the verse speaks of dew drops falling from heaven, while in the second half this image of dew from heaven may be associated with a person. The original Old Testament text is no more explicit than this, but within Christian understanding and liturgical symbolism this 'just man' is associated with the coming of Christ as the Messiah. This verse occurs in the daily prayer of the Church during the season of Advent, where it is accompanied by the response *Aperiatur terra et germinet salvatorem* ('Let the earth be opened and send forth a Saviour'), which is a citation from the remainder of Isaiah 45:8. After the image of a just man being rained down from heaven, the response presents us with the inverse image. Here, the Messiah comes out of the very earth, springing out of the soil like a new tree. Heaven and earth, above and below, are intimately connected in this verse. In this way they mirror the miracle of Christ's birth, which combines the heavenly with the earthly, God with humankind. But the poetic expression of the *Rorate* merely alludes to such complex theological ideas, and instead uses immediately accessible natural images of the dew, the rain and the growing of plants to express the expectation of the coming of Christ.

The verse has also lent its name to a particular kind of service that takes places during Advent: the 'Rorate Mass', a votive Mass in honour of the Virgin Mary. Rorate Masses take place very early in the morning, before sunrise, and are only lit by candles. Let's picture the scene: a dark church, before the break of dawn. The air is wintry cold, and the only sources of warmth are the candles on the altar and the many tapers which the congregation carry. The Mass begins with the *Rorate* verse, praying that the saviour may come down to earth as the dew, bringing justice and peace. As the service proceeds, the sky outside grows gradually brighter – a dark grey at first, then lighter and lighter, until at last the first rays of sunlight fall through the high windows. The church is illuminated by the light of the new day, a symbol of the hope of the coming of the Messiah. We started out in a cold and dark world, but we emerge from the church in the bright light of the dawn which Christ brings.

The *Rorate*, a constant companion of the faithful on their liturgical journey through Advent, was often combined with other biblical passages to form a series of prayers that express the yearning for a saviour, followed by words of comfort spoken by God to his people. In the Anglican tradition this series of prayers was adopted in English translation under the title the 'Advent Prose'. The music to which the Advent Prose is set uses the same plainchant melody as the original Latin text. It is simple, meditative and full of longing, and the musical line reinforces the words: the word 'heavens' is sung on the highest note, followed by a descending line that imitates the falling of the dew from above. The English translation of the Latin prayer is as follows:

Drop down, ye heavens, from above,
and let the skies pour down righteousness.

Be not wroth very sore, O Lord,
neither remember iniquity for ever:
thy holy city is a wilderness,
Sion is a wilderness, Jerusalem a desolation:
our holy and our beautiful house,
where our fathers praised thee.

We have sinned, and are as an unclean thing,
and we all do fade as a leaf:
and our iniquities, like the wind, have taken us away:
thou hast hid thy face from us:
and hast consumed us, because of our iniquities.

Behold, O Lord, the affliction of thy people,
and send forth him whom thou wilt send;
send forth the Lamb, the ruler of the earth,
from Petra of the desert to the mount of the daughter of Sion:
that he may take away the yoke of our captivity.

Ye are my witnesses, saith the Lord,
and my servant whom I have chosen;
that ye may know me and believe me:
I, even I, am the Lord, and beside me there is no Saviour:
and there is none that can deliver out of my hand.

Comfort ye, comfort ye my people;
my salvation shall not tarry:
why wilt thou waste away in sadness?
why hath sorrow seized thee?
Fear not, for I will save thee:

For I am the Lord thy God,
the Holy One of Israel, thy Redeemer.[1]

This series of prayers is suffused with the feeling that the cries of the afflicted people will be heard, creating a call-and-answer structure in which God responds to his people with words of comfort: 'Fear not, for I will save thee.'

Perhaps more than any other text, the *Rorate* encapsulates the atmosphere that fills the period of Advent: a feeling of yearning, of expectation, of hope and of eventual comfort. In contrast with the expected salvation, the present is experienced as barren and desolate; 'thou hast hid thy face from us', the people cry, lamenting that 'Sion is a wilderness, Jerusalem a desolation.' The desolation of the present makes this hope of the coming of the Messiah all the stronger. It is these verses about Jerusalem's desolation that inspired the most famous setting of these words to music, William Byrd's two-part piece *Ne irascaris Domine* and *Civitas sancti tui*. Byrd's setting uses the Latin version of the verse that appears as the second part in the English Advent Prose, complete with an additional line from Isaiah 64:9–10:

Ne irascaris Domine satis,	Be not wroth very sore, O Lord,
et ne ultra memineris iniquitatis nostrae.	neither remember iniquity for ever.
Ecce respice populus tuus omnes nos.	Behold, we are all your people.
Civitas sancti tui facta est deserta	Thy holy city is a wilderness,
Sion deserta facta est, Jerusalem desolata est.	Sion is a wilderness, Jerusalem a desolation.

William Byrd (*c.* 1540–1623) lived during a time of political and religious upheaval in sixteenth-century England, in which he belonged to the much-embattled minority group of recusant Catholics. Born around 1540, a few years after Henry VIII's break from Rome, Byrd saw England's Catholic heritage demolished and traditions broken as the Protestant Reformation sought new ways of religious belief and expression outside the authority of Rome. For most of Byrd's lifetime Catholics were persecuted, and those who remained attached to the old faith often had to follow it in secret or flee abroad. This was only broken by a brief restoration of Catholicism under Mary Tudor, which brought on a persecution of Protestants, followed by Elizabeth I's reinstatement of the Protestant Church, during which those who remained loyal to the old faith had to retreat into hiding once again. The pendulum of history swung between extremes, but nonetheless for a good part of his life Byrd managed to straddle the divide relatively successfully. As a composer who was widely appreciated and embedded in Elizabeth's court and the religious establishment, he wrote music in Latin and English for Catholic and Protestant services and escaped serious persecution, although in the latter part of his life he had to retreat from the court to rural Essex, where he had a room at a noble household in Ingatestone, where clandestine Catholic Masses were said. Although he himself remained relatively unscathed, Byrd was a member of a community deeply aware of the destruction of their heritage: prominent Catholics were tortured and executed, others fled into exile; monasteries that had long flourished were demolished, their windswept ruins a tangible reminder of all that had been lost, as they still are today.

Within this context, the utterly devastating musical image of desolation that Byrd paints in *Ne irascaris* gains an additional layer of significance. The destruction to which the Old Testament text refers is that of the holy city of Jerusalem, and the anguish is that of the people of Israel amidst persecution. Yet in Byrd's music we may also sense a deep grief at the desolation of his own lifetime, in which the old faith to which he belonged was persecuted, old friendships and alliances were broken in the midst of political turmoil, and the monumental buildings that had been great symbols of faith were destroyed. *Sion is a wilderness, Jerusalem a desolation*. In Byrd's setting, the Advent text is about not only the historical affliction of the Israelites, but the barren wasteland that England had become for Catholics. Despite such connections that we might draw, Byrd's music goes beyond an interpretation along denominational divides. It can be applied to any situation marked by loss, destruction and desolation, historical or contemporary. Byrd's musical language is universal; it speaks to the listener in immediate and truthful ways about the reality of grief, which crosses all boundaries. Much could be said about the musical architecture of Byrd's setting, the delicate interplay between upper and lower voices, and changes in texture that make this piece so extraordinary. But as words are a poor substitute for music, it is best to listen to the piece and let it speak for itself. Listen out for two moments in particular: in the first part (*Ne irascaris*), there is an appeal to the Lord to look upon us in mercy (*Ecce, respice*), like a cry from the depths of anguish. In the second part (*Civitas sancti*), pay attention to the moment when the texture of interweaving independent voices is interrupted by all voices singing together the phrase *Sion deserta facta est* ('Sion is a wilderness'). It is an abrupt change in the flow of the piece, which emphasizes a melancholy sense of the city of God as a desolate wasteland. But there is hope, too: even though Byrd's setting does not include the *Rorate coeli* verse, the liturgical context from which this text is taken implies that God's mercy is present even in the midst of destruction. It may appear hidden, as in Byrd's piece, but it is always there in the background. It is no wonder that this is one of Byrd's best-loved pieces of music today, a feeling that was shared by his contemporaries. An anonymous Elizabethan copyist summed it up nicely when he annotated his manuscript of *Ne irascaris* with the comment 'good song'.[2]

The sense of hope and expectation of a saviour who will free his people from the bleak desolation of their present situation becomes stronger and stronger in the liturgy as Advent progresses. In the final seven days before Christmas, this feeling is prominently expressed through the inclusion of a number of antiphons at Vespers, the 'O Antiphons'. They are a series of invocations of the Messiah under a range of titles, all starting with 'O'. The titles are, in chronological order: *O Sapientia* ('O Wisdom'), *O Adonai*, *O Radix Jesse* ('O Root of Jesse'), *O Clavis David* ('O Key of David'), *O Oriens* ('O Radiant Dawn'), *O Rex Gentium* ('O King of Nations'), *O Emmanuel*. The order of these titles is easy to remember with a Latin acrostic, as the first letters of the titles read in inverse order form the words *ero cras*, 'tomorrow, I will be there' – an apt phrase, as the last of the O Antiphons appears on 23 December, the day before Christmas Eve. These are what are known as the 'Great O Antiphons', while there are additional lesser O Antiphons in local liturgical traditions, which extend this list with further invocations. The O Antiphons are thought to be a very early liturgical tradition, dating back to at least the sixth century. Each of the antiphons is composed of quotations from different biblical passages, predominantly from the Old Testament, but also including some New Testament allusions. These quotations are combined in a new way to form an invocation that lends voice to the yearning expectation of the coming Messiah, seen through the eyes of the Old Testament prophets and prefigured in a range of images. These images can be highly symbolic and frequently mysterious to modern readers: what does it mean, for instance, to invoke Christ with the title of 'key' or 'root'? To answer these questions, we must look more closely at the O Antiphons.

O Wisdom

O Sapientia, quae ex ore Altissimi prodiisti, attingens a fine usque ad finem, fortiter suaviterque disponens omnia: veni ad docendum nos viam prudentiae.

O Wisdom, coming forth from the mouth of the Most High, reaching from one end to the other, mightily and sweetly ordering all things: come and teach us the way of prudence.[3]

The first of the O Antiphons invokes the coming Messiah under the title 'wisdom', creating an immediate connection with the wisdom literature of the Old Testament. In the Book of Wisdom and Proverbs, wisdom is praised as the highest good. The phrase 'coming forth from the mouth of the Most High' is a quotation from Sirach 24:3, but at the same time it subtly evokes an association with the beginning of the Gospel of John: 'In the beginning was the Word, and the Word was with God, and God was the Word.' This association implies that Christ is the Word, coming from the mouth of the Most High. Wisdom is personified in Christ. The connection also implies that the Old Testament wisdom books are to be interpreted from a Christocentric point of view, as prophesying and pointing towards the coming of Christ.

The earliest known literary reference to this antiphon occurs in a work from late antiquity that was to become one of the most influential texts in the intellectual world of the Middle Ages: Boethius' *Consolation of Philosophy*. Written in the sixth century while Boethius was imprisoned and awaiting torture and death, the *Consolation* is an imagined conversation with the personified Lady Philosophy, considering the value of philosophy in the face of adversity and death. Boethius himself was a Christian, but the *Consolation* does not take a pronounced Christian view – rather, it turns to Greek philosophy: Boethius consoles himself with Neoplatonist ideas about God as the one and ultimate good, rather than with the story of the redemption through Christ. There are only a few direct biblical references in the work, but the one that stands out is a reference in Chapter Twelve, alluding to Wisdom 8:1, which also occurs in *O Sapientia*: 'So God is the highest good which governs all things powerfully, and orders them sweetly.'[4] It is not entirely clear whether Boethius cites the biblical text directly, but it is thought most likely that he draws upon the Advent antiphon. If this assumption is correct, it indicates that the O Antiphons are very old indeed, going back to at least the sixth century, and that *O Sapientia* was used by Boethius for a very specific purpose, in which the Neoplatonic world of his work meets the veiled liturgical prophecy of the coming of Christ.

O Adonai

O Adonai, et Dux domus Israel, qui Moysi in igne flammae rubi apparuisti, et ei in Sina legem dedisti: veni ad redimendum nos in brachio extento.

O Adonai, and leader of the House of Israel, who appeared to Moses in the fire of the burning bush, and gave him the law on Sinai: Come and redeem us with an outstretched arm.

The second O Antiphon is particularly focused on Jewish history, reaching far back into the Old Testament. Two episodes are mentioned in particular: God appearing to Moses in the burning bush and God giving Moses the tablets of the law on Mount Sinai. The former (Exodus 3) marks the beginning of the Israelites' departure from slavery in Egypt. The story is of crucial importance in the history of the Israelites, both within Jewish understanding as a sign of God's guidance of his chosen people from captivity to freedom, and in Christian interpretation, which sees this manifestation of God as a precursor to the manifestation of God in Christ. Moses, while keeping his flock, comes to Mount Horeb. God appears to him in a burning bush, which is blazing with fire but 'not consumed'

(Ex. 3:2). He names himself as 'the God of Abraham, the God of Isaac, and the God of Jacob' (Ex. 3:4), and proclaims that he is going to deliver the Israelites from slavery in Egypt, with Moses as his chosen prophet who will lead them into the Promised Land.

The giving of the law takes place after the miraculous crossing of the Red Sea, when Moses leads the Israelites to Mount Sinai. There God reveals to him the law of the covenant and gives him two stone tablets on which the Ten Commandments are inscribed. Both events are crucial in the Old Testament. God is revealed as the protector and lawgiver of his people, who communicates directly with Moses and guides the Israelites to freedom. Drawing on both these events, the O Antiphon establishes a continuity between Old Testament history and the coming of Christ. God is invoked with his Jewish title 'Adonai', a Hebrew word meaning 'My Lord', and commonly used in Jewish tradition as a substitution for the holy name of God, which may not be spoken aloud. From a Christian perspective Christ the Messiah, whose coming is eagerly awaited in the Advent season, is the very same God who led the Israelites to freedom and gave the law to Moses. Through the liturgy, the Christian people adopt the voice of the people of Israel. Implied in this O Antiphon is a foreshadowing of the great deeds that the Messiah will accomplish: just as God in the Old Testament led his people out of slavery in Egypt, Christ will lead all of humankind out of the slavery of sin through redemption.

The prayer at the end of the antiphon subtly reinforces this typological connection. 'Come and redeem us with an outstretched arm' seems at first glance a straightforward prayer for the coming redemption, emphasizing God's strength. The reference is a direct quotation from Exodus 6:6, where God instructs Moses: 'Say therefore to the Israelites, "I am the Lord, and I will free you from the burdens of the Egyptians and deliver you from slavery to them. I will redeem you with an outstretched arm and with mighty acts of judgement."' But there are additional layers of meaning hidden within this simple phrase. It is reminiscent of the moment when the Israelites arrive at the shore of the Red Sea, pursued by Pharaoh:

> Then Moses stretched out his hand over the sea. The Lord drove the sea back by a strong east wind all night, and turned the sea into dry land; and the waters were divided. The Israelites went into the sea on dry ground, the waters forming a wall for them on their right and on their left. (Ex. 14:21–2)

Just as God parts the sea through Moses' outstretched hand and saves the Israelites from their enemies, the liturgy prays for the coming of the Messiah who will save the Christian people. God's outstretched arm is a reminder of God's faithfulness towards those who are oppressed and struggling, but in relation to Christ it is also a subtle foreshadowing of how the redemption is going to be accomplished – by a man whose arms are stretched out on a cross.

O Root of Jesse

O radix Jesse, qui stas in signum populorum, super quem continebunt reges os suum, quem Gentes deprecabuntur: veni ad liberandum nos, jam noli tardare.	O root of Jesse, standing as a sign among the peoples; before you kings will shut their mouths, to you the nations will make their prayer: come and deliver us, and delay no longer.

The invocation of Christ as the 'root of Jesse' plays upon a prophecy of the coming of the Messiah found in the prophet Isaiah (11:1–2): 'A shoot shall come out from the stock of Jesse, and a branch shall grow out of his roots. The spirit of the Lord shall rest on him, the spirit of wisdom and understanding, the spirit of counsel and might, the spirit of knowledge and the fear of the Lord.' Jesse is named in the Book of Samuel as the father of King David and one of the ancestors of Christ. The royal lineage of Jesus receives particular emphasis in the gospels of Matthew and Luke, who include lengthy genealogies naming Christ's ancestors (Matthew 1:1–17; Luke 3:23–38). The gospel writers place such emphasis on Christ's ancestry in order to demonstrate that he is truly the Messiah who fulfils all the Old Testament prophecies. In medieval art this metaphorical family tree emerging from the 'root of Jesse' is a popular motif in manuscript illuminations, stained-glass windows and stone carvings.[5] It appears, for instance, in an illustration from the twelfth-century French Bible des Capucins, which shows the family tree at the beginning of the Gospel of Matthew, forming a large illuminated initial letter L of the title *Liber generationis* ('Book of the genealogy of Christ'; illus. 7).

Within this L-shaped illustration, we can see Jesse at the very bottom. The stem of a tree emerges from his loins, branching out in different directions. The person sitting directly above him on the stem is his son David, with a crown to indicate his kingship, followed by his son, King Solomon. Other branches of the tree hold other members of the family, while at the very top we can see an image of Christ, whose divine nature is symbolized by the seven doves surrounding his head as a sign of the Holy Spirit. Below him sits his mother, Mary, who occupies a central position in the tree amidst an overwhelmingly male ensemble. The uniqueness of her position illustrates her role as the virginal mother of Christ: unlike the other figures in the tree, Christ has no human father. Through the Jesse tree, the symbolic genealogy of Christ shows that he is a legitimate descendant of David, but at the same time emphasizes what is extraordinary about his lineage: unlike all others before him, he is miraculously born of a virgin. This iconographical tradition was likely influenced by a pun upon the 'radix Jesse' text from Isaiah: the Vulgate uses the word *virga*, 'shoot, twig', which is very similar to the Latin word for 'virgin', *virgo*. This textual association implied that it is Mary who is the 'shoot' from the root of Jesse, rather than Christ. The medieval tradition varies between these two interpretations. In post-Reformation times the 'root of Jesse' motif

7 *Root of Jesse*, illumination from the Bible des Capucins, 1150–1200.

became a point of contention. Protestant usage of the motif tended to focus on Christ as the 'shoot', while Catholic traditions emphasized Mary to a greater extent, seeing her as the 'shoot' from which grows a flower, which stands for Christ. The two interpretations can be seen clearly in the well-known Advent carol 'Lo, how a Rose e'er-blooming'. The carol is commonly sung to a sixteenth-century tune by Protestant Michael Praetorius, but the English text is a translation of a medieval German text beginning with 'Es ist ein Ros entsprungen'. While the original medieval version interpreted the Jesse tree imagery with an emphasis on Mary and her virginity, Praetorius rewrote the lyrics so as to align better with the Protestant focus on Christ rather than Mary. There are two well-known English translations, one by Theodore Baker and the other by Catherine Winkworth (used by Herbert Howells in his oft-performed setting 'A Spotless Rose'). Theodore Baker's translation stays relatively non-committal on the thorny question of stem and rose, choosing the inclusive translation 'with Mary':

Lo, how a Rose e'er blooming
From tender stem hath sprung!
Of Jesse's lineage coming
As men of old have sung.
It came, a flower bright,
Amid the cold of winter
When half-gone was the night.

Isaiah 'twas foretold it,
The Rose I have in mind:
With Mary we behold it,
The virgin mother kind.
To show God's love aright
She bore to men a Savior
When half-gone was the night.

With carols such as this, the imagery of the *O Radix Jesse* antiphon still regularly features in Advent and Christmas services, regardless of denominational differences.

O Key of David

O Clavis David, et sceptrum domus Israel; qui aperis, et nemo claudit; claudis, et nemo aperit: veni, et educ vinctum de domo carceris, sedentem in tenebris et umbra mortis.	O Key of David and sceptre of the House of Israel; you open and no one can shut; you shut and no one can open: come and lead the prisoners from the prison house, those who dwell in darkness and the shadow of death.

The next O Antiphon invokes the Messiah under the title 'Key of David'. The invocation is a reference to Isaiah 22:22, 'I will place on his shoulder the key of the house of David; he shall open, and no one shall shut; he shall shut, and no one shall open'. In its original context, God speaks of Eliakim, who is to replace a self-seeking royal official in his office. In the antiphon, however, it is applied to the coming Messiah, who is here seen as someone who can open prison doors and lead out the captives. The prisoners who 'dwell in darkness and the shadow of death' are symbolic of fallen humanity, hoping for a saviour to redeem them and release them from their prison of sin and death. But for a medieval audience, this antiphon would also have evoked associations with something more specific than the prison-house of unredeemed humankind: the 'Harrowing of Hell'. This term refers to a belief unfamiliar to most modern audiences. After his death and before his resurrection, Christ was believed to have rescued the souls of those in Hell who had led righteous lives, particularly the Old Testament prophets and patriarchs. Since the Fall of Man and prior to the redemption, all of these souls had been held captive by the Devil in Hell, but through Christ's redemptive death on the cross, they were delivered from the dominion of Satan and heaven was opened for them once more. Some theologians distinguished between Hell and Limbo to differentiate the place of the damned from the place of the righteous who had lived before the time of Christ. It is this event of the 'Harrowing of Hell' that is referred to in the Apostles' Creed with the phrase '[Jesus Christ] was crucified, died, and was buried. He descended to the dead.' This event played a significant role in the belief of medieval Christians in particular, reinforced by non-canonical gospels such as the Gospel of Nicodemus, and was transformed creatively in many shapes in poetry, drama and art.[6] Dante's great vision of the afterlife in the *Divine Comedy*, for instance, identifies the first circle of Hell with Limbo, in which are Virgil and many other souls of those who lived in pre-Christian times but led righteous lives. Virgil, who acts as Dante's guide through the *Inferno*, explains:

> they did not sin; and yet, though they have merits,
> that's not enough, because they lacked baptism,
> the portal of the faith that you embrace.
>
> And if they lived before Christianity,
> they did not worship God in fitting ways;
> and of such spirits I myself am one. (*Inferno* 4:34–9)[7]

When Dante then inquires whether anyone has ever been released from Limbo, Virgil mentions the Harrowing of Hell:

> I was new – entered on this state
> when I beheld a Great Lord enter here;
> the crown he wore, a sign of victory.
>
> He carried off the shade of our first father,
> of his son Abel, and the shade of Noah,
> of Moses, the obedient legislator,

8 Fra Angelico, *Christ in Limbo*, *c.* 1442–3, fresco, Convent of San Marco, Florence.

of father Abraham, David the king,
of Israel, his father, and his sons,
and Rachel, she for whom he worked so long,

and many others – and He made them blessed;
and I should have you know that, before them,
there were no human souls that had been saved.
(*Inferno* 4:52–63)

In Dante's vision it is Old Testament figures such as Adam, Abel, Noah, Moses, Abraham, David, Israel and Rachel whom the victorious Christ led out of Hell because they worshipped the true God, unlike virtuous pagans such as Virgil himself. Jesus is described as a 'Great Lord' who entered Hell wearing a crown of victory as a sign that the redemption had been accomplished. Perhaps the most famous artistic depiction of the Harrowing of Hell is Fra Angelico's fifteenth-century fresco in San Marco, Florence (illus. 8).

We can see Christ with the signs of the nails upon his hands, bearing the banner of triumph, entering a cavernous dark place in which the prophets and patriarchs are being held captive. His light drives back the demons, who flee in terror; the iron gate of Hell has been shattered and lies underneath Christ's feet, crushing a demon with its weight. Christ extends his hand towards a long line of captives, guiding them out of their prison into freedom. First in line is Abraham, depicted as an old man with white hair and a long beard. Behind him are Adam and Eve, followed by Moses. The prisoners being released are those who knew the true God but who were unable to enter Paradise until the redemption, the event which changes everything.

O Clavis David, then, merges the hope of the coming of the Messiah who will release mankind from the darkness of its current state, with a more specific reference to Christ's redemptive deeds during his descent to Hell. Christ is aptly described as a 'key', since he opens the gates of Hell and unlocks the kingdom of heaven. Under its deceptively simple surface, the antiphon contains a wealth of associations that hinge upon the imagery of opening and closing of gates.

O Radiant Dawn

O Oriens, splendor lucis aeternae, et sol justitiae: veni, et illumina sedentes in tenebris, et umbra mortis.

O Radiant Dawn, splendour of eternal light, sun of justice: come and shine on those who dwell in darkness and in the shadow of death.[8]

In the liturgical calendar this antiphon is sung on 21 December, three days before Christmas, which is also the day of the winter solstice, when the day is shortest and the night is longest. It is no coincidence that it is on precisely this day that the Messiah is invoked as the 'radiant dawn' and 'sun of justice'. More than any other of the O Antiphons, this text focuses on light. Christ is the new dawn, the new sun, who will shine into the darkness of those who wait for his coming. The liturgy connects the events of the physical world, the annual pattern of growing and receding darkness, with a spiritual significance. Just as 21 December marks the hope of the return of the light, a turning point in the cycle of the year, the days before Christmas mark the hope of the coming of the saviour who will enlighten those who believe in him. The desire for light and warmth is universal. We can imagine the effect of this text in the gloom of a cold church on the evening of the shortest day of the year: the liturgy draws its power from not only the poetry of its texts and music, but the connections that it creates with the physical world and the concerns of the people who live within it.

The imagery of this antiphon speaks to us directly and immediately, as it has done for many centuries. From the earliest days of the English language survives a translation of *O Oriens* in the tenth-century Exeter Book, in a collection of Old English poems titled by modern scholars (somewhat unimaginatively) *Christ I*. The Old English version is not so much a direct translation of the liturgical text but more of a poetic reflection expanding on the imagery of the Latin antiphon. It begins with the following words:

Eala earendel, engla beorhtast,
ofer middangeard monnum sended,
ond soðfæsta sunnan leoma,
torht ofer tunglas, þu tida gehwane
of sylfum þe symle inlihtes!
Swa þu, god of gode gearo acenned,
sunu soþan fæder, swegles in wuldre
butan anginne æfre wære,
swa þec nu for þearfum þin agen geweorc
bideð þurh byldo, þæt þu þa beorhtan us
sunnan onsende, ond þe sylf cyme
þæt ðu inleohte þa þe longe ær,
þrosme beþeahte ond in þeostrum her,
sæton sinneahtes; synnum bifealdne
deorc deaþes sceadu dreogan sceoldan.

O Earendel, brightest of angels,
sent to mankind over middle-earth,
and righteous radiance of the sun,
splendid above all stars, of your own self
you ever enlighten every age.
As you, God born of God long ago,
Son of the true Father, eternally existed
without beginning in the glory of heaven,
so your own creation cry with confidence
to you now for their needs, that you send
that bright sun to us, and come yourself
to lighten those who long have lived,
surrounded by shadows and darkness, here
in everlasting night; who, shrouded by sins,
have had to endure death's dark shadow.[9]

This is only the first half of the poem, but we can already see how the poem intensifies further the imagery of light and darkness: words abound that describe light, brightness, radiance, stars and the sun. The translation of *oriens*, which in Latin can mean 'dawn' or 'morning star', is particularly striking. Christ is invoked under the title 'Earendel'.

The origin of this word is somewhat mysterious and may have mythological connections, but our best guess is that it is a name the Anglo-Saxons used for the morning star Venus, or another bright constellation.[10] Through its use in the Old English text, the word *Earendel* also acquired a more popular afterlife in the twentieth century. When the young J.R.R. Tolkien, studying Old English as an undergraduate at Oxford, came across the word, he was immediately struck 'by the great beauty of this word (or name)', noting that he felt 'a curious thrill, as if something had stirred in me, half wakened from sleep. There was something very remote and strange and beautiful behind those words.'[11] It was his fascination with this name that struck a creative spark, and Tolkien would later describe these Old English words as the source of the mythology he created. He included a character named Eärendil in his mythology of Middle-earth, as a mariner who is set into the skies as a star, casting light upon the darkness of the world as a token of hope. Tolkien's work is a testament to the power of the words of this antiphon, even if they are so ancient and strange that we hardly know their meaning.

O King of Nations

O Rex Gentium, et desideratus earum, lapisque angularis, qui facis utraque unum: veni, et salva hominem, quem de limo formasti.

O King of the nations, and their desire, the cornerstone making both one: come and save the human race, which you fashioned from clay.

The overarching theme of the penultimate O Antiphon is unity. Christ is invoked under the title 'King of the nations', implying a universal reign that stretches across different countries and continents. But there is a certain ambiguity in the title, as the Latin could also be translated as 'king of gentiles'. The Jewish tradition distinguishes very clearly between those of Jewish and those of non-Jewish heritage and belief, and 'gentile' was the term generally used for a non-Jewish person. The early days of the Christian Church in particular were still marked by this distinction, as the early followers of Christ came from both Jewish and non-Jewish backgrounds. As Paul's letters to the early Christian communities show, there were tensions between those of Jewish and those of non-Jewish heritage, and discussions about whether Jewish laws and customs should be upheld. Eventually the matter was settled: there were to be no distinctions between those of different cultural traditions, as everyone was united in their common belief in Jesus Christ – the sign of a new, truly universal faith. It is this unity that Paul invokes in his letter to the Ephesians, and a short but decisive section of this letter is picked up in the antiphon: 'making both one'. Some translations of this section render the Latin as 'uniting all as one', but strictly speaking the reference is to two factions becoming one. In the original context of Paul's letter, he refers to both Jews and gentiles: 'For he is our peace; in his flesh he has made both groups into one and has broken down the dividing wall, that is, the hostility between us' (Eph. 2:14). At the centre of this antiphon, then, is the thought of the unity that the coming saviour will bring, acting as a 'cornerstone' who will connect divided factions. The antiphon ends with a poignant reference to the communality between all humans, who, according to the account of creation in Genesis, were all 'fashioned from clay' (Gen. 2:7). The faith in Christ unites all those who believe in him, regardless of race, gender and background.

O Emmanuel

O Emmanuel, Rex et legifer
noster, expectatio Gentium,
et Salvator earum: veni ad
salvandum nos, Domine,
Deus noster.

O Emmanuel, our king and our
lawgiver, the hope of the nations
and their Saviour: come and
save us, O Lord our God.

The final O Antiphon on the day before Christmas calls upon the Messiah under the title of 'Emmanuel', a Hebrew name meaning 'God with us'. It is a one-word summary of the expectation of the saviour whose arrival is imminent, as God – become man – who will be 'with us' quite literally and live among us. It is this antiphon that gives its name to the well-known Christmas carol 'O come, O come, Emmanuel', which is inspired by the O Antiphons and recapitulates many of the titles of the Messiah that we have seen. Its first stanza paraphrases the final O Antiphon:

O come, O come, Emmanuel,
And ransom captive Israel;
That mourns in lonely exile here,
Until the Son of God appear.
Rejoice! Rejoice! Emmanuel
Shall come to thee, O Israel.

It is difficult to imagine a Christmas in English churches without hymns such as this, a testament to the continued influence of the O Antiphons and their liturgical tradition. The antiphons are poetic, powerful and immediate. They express the human longing for someone to come and heal the world from its evil, hatred and despair, a desire which is as present today as it was 2,000 years ago, and is renewed every year in the liturgical cycle.

4
Suffering

It is a cold and rainy evening in early spring. The last light of day is slowly fading. Clouds in the west obscure the setting sun. The gargoyles atop the tower cast long shadows, their grotesque faces uncannily dark in the growing gloom. Inside the church, monks in brown robes gather, bowing their heads in prayer in the choir. A large congregation is assembled in the nave, silent, waiting. Outside the wind howls, raindrops patter against the windows, through which now falls only a pale light. In the sanctuary a large candelabrum stands tall, its fifteen candles illuminating the front of the otherwise dim and shadowy church. At the toll of the bell, the monks begin their chant, their voices alternating across the aisle: *Zelus domus tuae comedit me* ('The zeal of your house consumes me'). The ancient words reverberate in the sacred space. After each psalm a candle at the front is extinguished, gradually plunging the church into ever deeper shadows. Only a few candles are still burning when a lone monk moves to the lectern. In a mournful tone that pierces the darkling vaults above, he recites the opening of the Book of Lamentations: *Incipit lamentatio Jeremiae prophetae* ('Here begins the lamentation of the prophet Jeremiah'). Through his voice, the words of Jeremiah the prophet come alive, lamenting the fall of Jerusalem, once beautiful and full of life, now full of sorrow: 'How lonely sits the city that once was full of people! How like a widow she has become, she that was great among the nations! She that was a princess among the provinces has become a vassal. She weeps bitterly in the night, with tears on her cheeks' (Jer. 1:1–2). Jeremiah's words echo through the gloom as the church encounters anew and embraces the weight of his grief.

But this is not Jerusalem. It is a church somewhere in fifteenth-century England. And yet the lament over the destruction of the city is fitting, because today is Maundy Thursday. The congregation is assembled to commemorate the betrayal, capture, torture and execution of Christ. It is something that is almost unthinkable, and must be spoken about in metaphors and poetry: God himself who became a man is put to death. God, immortal and impassible, suffers and dies. He accepts this death willingly in order to atone for the sins of humankind. The best man who ever lived, innocent of any crime, is betrayed by his friend and executed by one of the cruellest methods of torture ever invented. It is an event that is both a theological mystery and an unbearable human tragedy. The voice of the prophet mourning the fall of the holy city becomes the voice of the people mourning the death of their God. Like Jerusalem, they weep 'bitterly in the night'.

The service continues. Darkness has fallen outside. Psalm follows psalm, and ever more candles are gradually extinguished until at last only a single burning candle remains at the top of the candelabrum. When the final psalm is finished, a monk rises from his stall and picks up the last candle. He carries it with him, moves towards the back of the church and behind the altar. Utter darkness now covers the church. The congregation is silent. But then, at once, a tremor runs through the rows. Suddenly a loud noise fills the air. The people are banging upon the wooden pews with their hands, some are slamming their books shut, some are stomping their feet on the cold stone ground. The noise continues until at last the monk returns from behind the altar, the candle in his hand still burning: a single warm flame emerging from the darkness, illuminating the face of its bearer. A flickering source of hope in the midst of death.

Thus concludes the first service of *Tenebrae*, which can be translated literally as 'darkness'. It is the most intense time of the liturgical year, the three days leading up to Easter, when the Church celebrates the day of the resurrection of Christ from the tomb. The so-called Triduum ('three days') of Maundy Thursday, Good Friday and Easter Saturday is marked by long and elaborate ceremonies, which are among the most moving the liturgy has to offer. The power of the texts emanates not only from the words themselves, which create a rich panorama of feelings of mourning, loss, shock and horror at the death of the saviour, but from the way in which the texts are embedded into a liturgical tapestry of music, gesture and movement. The symbolism of light and darkness in the liturgy of *Tenebrae* illustrates this: the gradual extinguishing of candles represents the growing darkness and despair at the suffering of Christ. The congregation is physically plunged into darkness, experiencing the gradual withdrawal of light at first hand in order to reflect on Christ's death. The darkness is full of Scriptural resonances: the gospels report that 'darkness came over the whole land' (Matthew 27:45) when Jesus was on the cross. The single candle left burning at the end, hidden from view behind the altar-stone and finally returned with a loud noise, is a symbolic representation of the death of Christ. According to the Gospel of Matthew, when Christ died on the cross 'the earth shook, and the rocks were split' and the tombs 'were opened' (27:51–2). The noise created by the congregation at the end of the service, also known as a *strepitus* ('loud noise', 'crashing sound'), can be interpreted as a symbolic imitation of the earthquake at the death of Christ. It can also be seen as a reference to the closing of Christ's tomb, into which he is laid on Friday after the crucifixion. In this liturgical drama, we are reliving the events that accompanied the crucifixion. Through visual experience of darkness, the congregation is immersed in the symbolism and its Scriptural resonances, but through the banging and stomping of the *strepitus* the congregation also co-creates this symbolism. This is not a performance we are watching: we are part of the drama, participate in it and make it happen. The return of the candle at the end represents the return of hope as Christ rises from the tomb. A small, flickering candle remains. Darkness has not conquered. Witnessing this return of the light, having lived through the darkness in the ceremony, can be a deeply moving experience. Through the liturgy, the hope of the resurrection becomes our hope.

One of the things that gives *Tenebrae* such a sombre and moving character is the use of a range of poetic reflections on the passion of Christ, which are interspersed between psalms in the liturgy and take the form of responsories – chants which alternate between a small group singing verses and the whole choir or congregation responding with a refrain. These so-called *Tenebrae* responsories are famous for their emotional and immediate engagement with the Passion of Christ. Unlike many of the liturgical texts that we have seen thus far, they do not merely present biblical material in a liturgical context, but often form a free and creative reflection on the events of the Triduum, which is inspired by, rather than a faithful reproduction of, biblical texts. There are nine responsories for each *Tenebrae* liturgy of the three holy days. Originally sung as plainchant in the liturgy, the *Tenebrae* responsories were also frequently set to music of various styles by composers in post-medieval times. Their intensely moving words alongside the dramatic symbolism of darkness and light in the ceremony lent themselves particularly well to musical explorations of these texts. A selection of five responsories from Maundy Thursday to Holy Saturday will help us understand better their poetic and dramatic qualities, and how these are reflected in later musical settings.

The responsories of Maundy Thursday transport us into the setting of the garden of Gethsemane on the Mount of Olives. It is here, according to the gospels, where Christ suffered his agony, foreseeing his passion and death. The second *Tenebrae* responsory on this day, *Tristis est anima mea*, creates an ominous sense of anticipation of the events that are about to occur:

Tristis est anima mea usque ad mortem:	My soul is sorrowful even unto death.
sustinete hic et vigilate mecum.	Stay here, and watch with me!
Nunc videbitis turbam quae circumdabit me.	Now you will see the mob that will surround me.
Vos fugam capietis, et ego vadam immolari pro vobis.	You will run away, and I will go to be sacrificed for you.
Versus:	*Verse:*
Ecce appropinquat hora, et Filius hominis	See, the time draws near, and the Son of Man
tradetur in manus peccatorum.	will be delivered into the hands of sinners.
Vos fugam capietis, et ego vadam immolari pro vobis.	You will run away, and I will go to be sacrificed for you.[1]

This responsory is based on the narrative of the gospels, selecting different passages in order to evoke an emotional response. The first two lines, 'My soul is sorrowful even unto death. Stay here, and watch with me!' cite Matthew 26:38, the words spoken by Jesus to his disciples in the garden, while the rest of the responsory uses different gospel passages more freely. Christ foretells to the disciples what is about to happen: he will be surrounded by the mob and led away to be sacrificed, while the disciples, terrified, will run away. The verse reinforces the sense of urgency: 'See, the time draws near.' We stand on the brink of the most significant event of human history: God himself will be killed at the hands of sinners. But in the midst of the sense of urgency and anticipation of the death of God, there is also a very real and tangible feeling of human sorrow. It is Christ as man who speaks of his mental pain: 'My soul is sorrowful even unto death.' It is the pain felt within the soul that is highlighted here, preceding the physical pain which is to come. Jesus shudders with horror at the thought of being surrounded by a mob, being deserted by all his friends, and only hopes for someone to stay and watch with him in this moment of agony. These are the words of an innocent man who is about to be confronted with the depths of human malice and cowardice.

This responsory uses the words that Jesus speaks to his disciples in the gospel, but the addressees are implied rather than explicitly mentioned here. This allows the text to gain a significance that is both broader and more personal to those who believe in him. Christ speaks not only to the disciples, but to every individual who participates in the liturgy. It is also us who have abandoned him, run away, and who are now invited to stay and watch with him. This is particularly apt for the setting of *Tenebrae*, where the congregation is assembled to pray in the gathering darkness. We too are the disciples, and we too are here to watch with Christ.

Such are the feelings evoked powerfully in just a few lines of the responsory. It is an aid to personal reflection, soul-searching, as well as profound feelings of compassion for the very human sorrow that Jesus endures on the eve of his death. The original chant melody encourages such reflection through its sombre tone. Later composers often attempted to heighten the impact of these words by emphasizing particular aspects through word-painting, such as in the setting of the responsory by Carlo Gesualdo, written in 1611. A controversial and mysterious figure who murdered his wife and her lover, and later in life suffered from poor mental health, perhaps insanity, Gesualdo nonetheless was a musical genius who experimented with the tonal language of the Renaissance in a way that anticipated the musical developments of later centuries. His setting of 'Tristis est anima mea' opens with a slow downward movement, which evokes Christ's desolation in Gethsemane. The 'vos fugam' section, however, forms a complete contrast to the beginning, imitating the running away of the disciples with fast, hectic runs in all voices. This is again followed by a contrasting section as we move from frantic movement into stillness. Clashing chords express the aching loneliness of Christ when he prophesies *ego vadam immolari pro vobis*, 'I will go to be sacrificed for you.'

Francis Poulenc's setting of the same text, written in 1938–9, more than three hundred years after Gesualdo, uses a very different musical language. A soaring soprano solo opens the piece with Christ's sorrowful words. Similar to Gesualdo, Poulenc takes his cue from the text of the responsory and provides vivid word-painting of the flight of the disciples. But Poulenc has a very different interpretation of the announcement of Christ's sacrificial death: *ego vadam immolari pro vobis* is marked by a dissonant intensity that builds up to a climax, perhaps reflecting the outrage and painful wonder at the thought of God himself being sacrificed for the salvation of humankind. It is only the repetition of these words at the very end of the piece that offers a sense of resolution, with the solo soprano accompanied by a full eight-part choir leading the piece to a luminous end in which we glimpse a hope of final salvation.

The third responsory for *Tenebrae* on Good Friday enters more deeply into the emotional world of the crucified Christ. The text itself is, at first glance, somewhat counter-intuitive: it is the song of a gardener lamenting his vineyard.

Vinea mea electa, ego te plantavi:	O vineyard, my chosen one, I planted you.
quomodo conversa es in amaritudinem,	How is your sweetness turned into bitterness,
ut me crucifigeres et Barrabbam dimitteres.	to crucify me and take Barabbas in my place?
Sepivi te, et lapides elegi ex te, et aedificavi turrim.	I surrounded you with a fence; I cleared you of stones, and built a watch-tower in your defence.

An analogy is drawn here between those who crucify Christ, and a chosen vineyard that has turned rebellious despite the gardener's care. The image is connected with Old Testament texts, where the metaphor of a vineyard is commonly used to describe the people of Israel, as in Isaiah 5:1–4:

> Let me sing for my beloved
> my love-song concerning his vineyard:
> My beloved had a vineyard
> on a very fertile hill.
> He surrounded it with a fence and cleared it of stones,
> and planted it with choice vines;
> he built a watch-tower in the midst of it,
> and hewed out a wine vat in it;
> he expected it to yield grapes,
> but it yielded wild grapes.
> And now, inhabitants of Jerusalem
> and people of Judah,
> judge between me
> and my vineyard.
> What more was there to do for my vineyard
> that I have not done in it?
> When I expected it to yield grapes,
> why did it yield wild grapes?[2]

Within the Old Testament world this section is read as the voice of God speaking of his love for his people in spite of their rebelliousness. God, having tended to his vineyard with love and great care, is disappointed by the result of his efforts. Despite his work, the vineyard yields only wild grapes, which are too sour for consumption. The vineyard with its wild grapes can be interpreted as a symbol of the people of Israel, who in their history often reject, disappoint or fall away from their God, who nonetheless looks after them with great faithfulness. In the New Testament Jesus uses the same imagery to speak about himself and his relationship with his people. The idea occurs in the gospels of Matthew and Luke in the 'Parable of the Wicked Tenants', which Jesus tells the people:

> 'A man planted a vineyard, and leased it to tenants, and went to another country for a long time. When the season came, he sent a slave to the tenants in order that they might give him his share of the produce of the vineyard; but the tenants beat him and sent him away empty-handed. Next he sent another slave; that one also they beat and insulted and sent away empty-handed. And he sent yet a third; this one also they wounded and threw out. Then the owner of the vineyard said, "What shall I do? I will send my beloved son; perhaps they will respect him." But when the tenants saw him, they discussed it among themselves and said, "This is the heir; let us kill him so that the inheritance may be ours." So they threw him out of the vineyard and killed him. What then will the owner of the vineyard do to them? He will come and destroy those tenants and give the vineyard to others.' When they heard this, they said, 'Heaven forbid!' But he looked at them and said, 'What then does this text mean:
>
> "The stone that the builders rejected
> has become the cornerstone"?
>
> Everyone who falls on that stone will be broken to pieces; and it will crush anyone on whom it falls.' When the scribes and chief priests realized that he had told this parable against them, they wanted to lay hands on him at that very hour, but they feared the people. (Luke 20:9–19)

In keeping with his usual way of teaching, Jesus tells a story that has to be interpreted, here presenting a metaphor for his relationship with the Jewish people. Without saying so overtly, Jesus draws an analogy between God the Father and the owner of the vineyard. The slaves sent to the tenants can be interpreted as the prophets of the Old Testament, while the son stands for Christ himself, who is cast out and killed by the people. The reference to the cornerstone that Jesus adds to the parable is a quotation from Psalm 118:22–3, which again relates ideas of the Old Testament to the person of Christ. An interpretive thread is therefore drawn from the Old Testament to the New, and the rebellious vineyard (or its rebellious tenants) become an image of God's people who reject and kill him.

It is this tradition to which the imagery of the *Tenebrae* responsory refers. The actions of God that are mentioned in Isaiah are quoted here, but whereas they occur in the third person in the Old Testament, they are here spoken by the poem's speaker in the first person: 'I cleared you of stones' rather than 'He . . . cleared it of stones'; 'I built a watch-tower for your defence' rather than 'he built a watch-tower.' The words here are more immediate, spoken directly to an unidentified addressee. The responsory also makes clear that these words are spoken by Jesus, who asks: 'How is your sweetness turned into bitterness, to crucify me and take Barabbas in my place?' The mention of the crucifixion and Barabbas, a criminal who was released instead of Jesus as mentioned in the gospels, connects the complaint about the rebellious vineyard to Christ's suffering. Christ speaks God's words from the Old Testament, and he is the one reproaching the people for betraying him. The liturgical text is full of references to biblical material, but it also offers a free and poetic reflection on those ideas. This shift means that the application of the text is broader. Originally the verses from Isaiah referred to the disobedient behaviour of the people of Israel, but the responsory does not specifically target them. It is Christ's reproach to his own people, those who crucify him, but it is also meant for everyone. Christ addresses the listeners in the second person, 'you.' The implication is that each individual is involved in the crucifixion, having betrayed Christ through their own wrongdoings.

The liturgy of the Triduum reverberates with this theme of personal accountability and even culpability. It is a notion that often seems odd or perplexing for non-Christians, and yet it is foundational for believers. How could someone living many years after Christ be in any way personally implicated in his death? The notion hinges upon the biblical idea that all humans are made in the image of God, and so every human being bears a reflection of the divine. Consequently any transgression against another person, whether rooted in enmity, envy, lust or anger, is in the final analysis a transgression against God. This idea also has an internal dimension, as there is a reflection of God found within the self. Accordingly, instances of personal failings, such as wrongs committed, lies told, moments of cowardice and weakness, are not mere individual failings, but also transgressions against the divine image within the self. This conception of God is not just a vague spiritual notion, but a very concrete reality, which is anchored in the person of Jesus Christ. Against this background it is easier to understand the sense of personal accountability that the liturgical texts evoke. The liturgical narrative does not merely contemplate the execution of a man in Jerusalem two millennia ago, but emphasizes the lasting relevance of this event. It reminds each participant in the liturgical celebration of their personal responsibility to live a life guided by virtue and integrity. The vineyard of the responsory is not only ancient Israel – it is us in the here and now.

These ideas are variously emphasized in musical settings of the responsory. In Francis Poulenc's version, for example, the piece begins at a slow and meditative pace, full of tender harmonies expressing God's love for his people, but it soon turns to intense dissonance as the speaker reflects on the bitterness of the people's betrayal and the injustice committed against him. Love and betrayal are set in a heart-wrenching contrast.

As *Tenebrae* continues, we enter further into the very depths of suffering. The fifth responsory on Holy Saturday again speaks with the voice of the crucified Christ. Taking its inspiration from the words of the prophet Jeremiah in the Book of Lamentations (1:12) as he sits weeping over the destruction of Jerusalem, the text uses words from the Old Testament and gives them to Christ, who speaks to the passers-by who see him on the cross:

O vos omnes qui transitis per viam:	O all you who pass by the way,
attendite et videte si est dolor sicut dolor meus.	look and see if there is any sorrow like my sorrow.
Versus	*Verse*
Attendite, universi populi, et videte dolorem meum.	Look, all you people, and see my sorrow:
Si est dolor similis sicut dolor meus.	If there is any sorrow like my sorrow.

Using only few words, the responsory conjures up an image of the crucified through an invocation of the passers-by, placing the individual reader or listener in the midst of the scene. Through the liturgy, that which is in the historical past – the event of the Crucifixion – is made present. Golgotha is past, but it is also called to mind powerfully in the ritual. We are on the highway to Jerusalem. The responsory invites us to pause, stand and look. It leaves space for individual thoughts and reflections. It does not tell us what to think or how to relate to the suffering of Christ, except to look and consider if there is any sorrow like that of Jesus.

The responsory's sense of profound sadness and suffering is captured particularly effectively in the setting by twentieth-century cellist, composer and conductor Pablo Casals (1876–1973). The piece starts quietly in the lower voices, almost as if with a whisper. The upper voices then join in gradually as the music builds in volume and intensity, until it reaches a climax with an almost unbearable outcry of pain on the word *attendite*, 'look'. After this it slowly dies away again. The piece ends on an extremely quiet repetition of the opening words 'O all you who pass by the way', which leaves the sentence unfinished, suggesting the last sigh of a man exhausted from his ordeal.

What we see throughout the poetry of the *Tenebrae* responsories is an intense and insistent engagement with the pain and suffering of the crucifixion. Through the texts we experience the emotional depths of a fierce human tragedy, of an innocent man killed in the most horrific way imaginable. What underlies the insistent exploration of these emotions is an emphasis on the humanity of Christ. We do not see a divine figure exalted and removed from human suffering, but a God who shares in humanity, shares in it to the very depths of agony and death. Behind the texts of the liturgy is an invitation to the congregation to engage with this startling, almost unbelievable fact, to consider its relevance to each individual life. And perhaps deeper still, there lies a sense of wordless, silent wonder at a God who loves so deeply that he would die for humankind.

This is what moved, and continues to move, congregations about the liturgies of the Triduum. It is also the context from which we can begin to understand other elements of the ceremonies of these holy days. These ceremonies include not only *Tenebrae*, but an ensemble of Triduum services that commemorate the events around Christ's death. A memorable element of the main Good Friday liturgy, which is traditionally celebrated around the time of Christ's death (3 p.m.), is the so-called *Improperia*, or Reproaches. They form an extended poem which, similar to some of the *Tenebrae* responsories that we have seen, speak with the voice of the crucified Christ, reproaching his people for their cruelty in putting him to death.

To get a sense of the impact of the *Improperia*, we first need to think ourselves into the drama of readings, music, gestures and movements of the liturgical ceremony itself. Details of the ceremony in medieval times could vary from place to place, but they usually converged upon some central elements, which were later unified and prescribed. The Good Friday liturgy is lengthy; its celebration has a sombre and mournful tone. The church is bare, stripped of any decorations. Statues are hidden behind cloths, and even the crucifix on the altar is covered. Towards the beginning of the ceremony the account of the Passion according to John is read or sung, often with roles distributed between three singers, with the voices each taking the narrator, Jesus and other speakers in the gospel. The long account of Jesus' capture, trial, torture and execution comes alive through the dramatic quality of the recitation. The gospel reading is followed by a long list of prayers and intercessions for all members of the church, the society and the world. Through this juxtaposition, a parallel is drawn between the historic event of the gospel account and its lasting effect on the present. The sacrificial death of Christ and the anticipated resurrection, the liturgy reminds us, are the source of all grace for the present, for every single person.

After the conclusion of the intercessions, we move to the veneration of the cross, at the heart of which stand the *Improperia*. The alternating verses of the Reproaches are sung by the priest or deacon and the choir, forming a dialogic structure. During the singing a covered crucifix is carried to the front of the church. Later the cover is removed and the tortured body of Christ is revealed to the congregation with the words *Ecce lignum crucis in quo salus mundi pependit. Venite adoremus!* ('See the wood of the cross, on which hung the salvation of the world. Come, let us worship!'). The choir and congregation then genuflect in a gesture of adoration. Any description of the intricate choreography of the liturgical celebration must needs seem dry and abstract, and it is only in personal experience that the liturgy comes to life. It is clear, however, that the gestures, chanting and recitation of the Good Friday liturgy focus with intensity on the mystery of the cross, and express awe and veneration, mixed with restrained horror at the great paradox that the salvation of the world should be brought about by the death of God, suspended upon an instrument of torture. The liturgy uses words, music, movement, but also absence – the emptiness and silence of the church, the veiling of all religious symbols and statues – in order to reveal with greater clarity why and how the cross has become the central symbol of Christianity.

And in the midst of this symphony of sound, gesture and symbolic veiling and unveiling, Christ himself speaks from the cross. It is his voice that we hear in the *Improperia*:

Popule meus, quid feci tibi?	O my people, what have I done to you?
Aut in quo contristavi te?	How have I offended you?
Responde mihi.	Answer me!
Quia eduxi te de terra Aegypti: parasti Crucem Salvatori tuo.	I led you out of Egypt, from slavery to freedom, but you led your Saviour to the cross.
Agios o Theos.	
Sanctus Deus.	Holy is God!
Agios Ischyros.	
Sanctus fortis.	Holy and strong!
Agios Athanatos, eleison ymas.	
Sanctus immortalis, miserere nobis.	Holy immortal One, have mercy on us.
Quia eduxi te per desertum quadraginta annis:	For forty years I led you safely through the desert.
et manna cibavi te, et introduxi te in terram satis bonam:	I fed you with manna from heaven, and brought you to a land of plenty;
parasti Crucem Salvatori tuo.	but you led your Saviour to the cross.
Agios o Theos.	
Sanctus Deus.	Holy is God!

Agios Ischyros.	
Sanctus fortis.	Holy and strong!
Agios Athanatos, eleison ymas.	
Sanctus immortalis, miserere nobis.	Holy immortal One, have mercy on us.
Quid ultra debui facere tibi, et non feci?	What more could I have done for you?
Ego quidem plantavi te vineam meam speciosissimam:	I planted you as my fairest vine,
et tu facta es mihi nimis amara:	but you yielded only bitterness:
aceto namque sitim meam potasti:	when I was thirsty you gave me vinegar to drink,
et lancea perforasti latus Salvatori tuo.	and you pierced your Saviour's side with a lance.
Agios o Theos.	
Sanctus Deus.	Holy is God!
Agios Ischyros.	
Sanctus fortis.	Holy and strong!
Agios Athanatos, eleison ymas.	
Sanctus immortalis, miserere nobis.	Holy immortal One, have mercy on us.
Ego propter te flagellavi Aegyptum cum primogenitis suis:	For your sake I scourged the firstborn of Egypt,
et tu me flagellatum tradidisti.	but you have given me up to be scourged.
Populе meus, quid feci tibi?	O my people, what have I done to you?
Aut in quo contristavi te?	How have I offended you?
Responde mihi.	Answer me!

Ego te eduxi de Aegypto,demerso Pharone in mare Rubrum:	I led you out of Egypt, having drowned Pharaoh in the Red Sea:
et tu me tradidisti principibus sacerdotum.	but you have delivered me to the chief priests.
Popule meus, quid feci tibi?	O my people, what have I done to you?
Aut in quo contristavi te?	How have I offended you?
Responde mihi.	Answer me!
Ego ante te aperui mare:	I opened the sea before you,
et tu aperuisti lancea latus meum.	but you opened my side with a spear.
Popule meus, quid feci tibi?	O my people, what have I done to you?
Aut in quo contristavi te?	How have I offended you?
Responde mihi.	Answer me!
Ego ante te praeivi in columna nubis:	I led you on your way in a pillar of cloud,
et tu me duxisti ad praetorium Pilati.	but you led me to Pilate's court.
Popule meus, quid feci tibi?	O my people, what have I done to you?
Aut in quo contristavi te?	How have I offended you?
Responde mihi.	Answer me!
Ego te pavi manna in desertum:	I bore you up with manna in the desert,
et tu me cedisti alapis et flagellis.	but you struck me down and scourged me.

Popule meus, quid feci tibi?	O my people, what have I done to you?
Aut in quo contristavi te?	How have I offended you?
Responde mihi.	Answer me!
Ego te potavi aqua salutis de petra:	I gave you saving water from the rock,
et tu me potasti felle et aceto.	but you gave me gall and vinegar to drink.
Popule meus, quid feci tibi?	O my people, what have I done to you?
Aut in quo contristavi te?	How have I offended you?
Responde mihi.	Answer me!
Ego propter te Chananeorum reges percussi:	For your sake I struck the kings of the Canaanites,
et tu percussisti arundine caput meum.	but you have struck my head with a reed.
Popule meus, quid feci tibi?	O my people, what have I done to you?
Aut in quo contristavi te?	How have I offended you?
Responde mihi.	Answer me!
Ego dedi tibi sceptrum regale:	I gave you a royal sceptre,
et tu dedisti capiti meo spineam coronam.	but you gave me a crown of thorns.
Popule meus, quid feci tibi?	O my people, what have I done to you?
Aut in quo contristavi te?	How have I offended you?
Responde mihi.	Answer me!

Ego te exaltavi magna virtute: et tu me suspendisti in patibulo crucis.	I raised you to the height of majesty, but you have raised me high on the gibbet of the cross.
Popule meus, quid feci tibi?	O my people, what have I done to you?
Aut in quo contristavi te? Responde mihi.	How have I offended you? Answer me![3]

The *Improperia* are a very old element of the Good Friday liturgy, dating back to at least the ninth century, and they occur, in different forms, in both the Western and the Eastern churches. It is given here in its longest extant version, which eventually became the standard format, while many early manuscripts contain a shorter version. Modern translations and adaptations in different traditions of Christianity have variously chosen to omit specific verses, but the essence of these Reproaches is always the same. They are a series of rhetorical questions, directed by God at his people, with the repeated refrain *Popule meus, quid feci tibi?* ('O my people, what have I done to you?'). Interspersed with these reproaches in the first part are praises of God as thrice-holy, the so-called *Trisagion* ('Holy is God! Holy and strong! Holy immortal One, have mercy on us.'). This hymn is a regular part of the Byzantine Rite, but its only use in the Roman Rite is on Good Friday, where it occurs in both Greek (*Agios o Theos*) and a Latin translation (*Sanctus Deus*). The *Improperia* thus invoke the Greek tradition, reaching back far in time to the very roots of Christianity. They are often sung antiphonally, alternating between a cantor and the choir. The cantor's verses juxtapose God's love and protection of his people in the Old Testament with their rejection of Christ as the saviour. God, by whom the people of Israel were led out of slavery in Egypt, guided through the desert and fed with manna, led through the Red Sea, given a powerful kingdom, and granted victory over their enemies – this very same God has now been crucified despite his never-wavering faithfulness to his people. The specific acts of God in the Old Testament are contrasted in a moving way with the suffering of Christ, playing upon the similarity of words and concepts: 'I opened the sea before you, but you opened my side with a spear.' The warlike imagery of some of these references alludes to the violence done to Christ, but the Old Testament references are more than mere reminders of military victories of the Israelites over their enemies (with all the violence that this entails). Once again, we encounter the principle of typology: the Old Testament episodes mentioned in the Reproaches are key events that have a rich history of allegorical interpretation. The parting of the Red Sea, which delivered the Israelites from the Egyptians in the Book of Exodus, for example, was traditionally interpreted as a prefiguration of the redemption through Christ, who leads the Christian people out of captivity by the Devil. The sea was seen as a reference to the water of baptism. The drowning of Pharaoh and his troops was understood to represent the victory over the Devil and the forces of Hell through Christ's death. On one level, by mentioning these Old Testament events the Reproaches delve into the emotional landscape of Christ cruelly betrayed by his people. But there is also a deeper meaning, relating events that were seen as prophecies of the coming of Christ to their fulfilment in Christ. The events of the Red Sea point towards the crucifixion, and it is exactly at the moment of crucifixion that the voice of Christ speaks them in the liturgy. The past and the present merge; here is the moment when the prophecies come true.

Within the later history of the *Improperia*, modern audiences have sometimes seen the emphasis on the betrayal of Christ by his people as a sign of a veiled antisemitism within this text. This concern is understandable in view of the troubled history of antisemitic views within Christianity, but it is important to realize the full context and implication of the Reproaches rather than merely picking up on partial phrases of ideas from the text. It is striking that God's address to his people is broad in nature: 'O my people, what have I done to you? How have I offended you? Answer me!' We have seen in some of the *Tenebrae* responsories how the idea of the transgressions of the people of Israel came to stand more generally for the transgressions of the people of God – the Christian people, and therefore each and every individual attending the liturgical ceremony. In fact, the *Improperia* even use the same image of the vineyard yielding sour grapes that we have already encountered in *Vinea mea electa*: 'What more could I have done for you? I planted you as my fairest vine, but you yielded only bitterness.' As in the responsory, the text of the *Improperia* gains a broader application. Its use within the Good Friday liturgy serves as a reminder that every individual present has betrayed Christ through wrongful actions, lack of love and unfaithfulness. The people of Israel and the Christian people become merged. The poetic engagement with the bitterness of betrayal as God's son is rejected by his own makes this pain relevant to each member of the congregation in the Good Friday liturgy.

This sense of each individual being implicated in the Passion is clearly apparent from vernacular adaptations of the *Improperia* from the Middle Ages. From medieval England there survive several close translations of the *Improperia* from Latin into English, but perhaps most interesting are those poems that engage with the tradition more freely, play with the liturgical tradition and merge it with other literary traditions, often to striking effect. Reflected in these innovative adaptations is an interpretation that highlights a sense of general responsibility, in which Christ's reproaches are directed against each and every human being. This becomes particularly clear in a poetic development of the *Improperia* tradition in a poem that scholars have titled 'A Dialogue between Natura Hominis and Bonitas Dei'.[4] What is so striking about this poem is that it is not a one-sided list of reproaches but a dialogue, as it imagines a response from man. The first few stanzas go as follows:

Saluator mundi domine, to þe, Ihesu, make I my mone, to haue mercy Thorow þi pyte; gracius god, now here my bone.	Lord, Saviour of the world, To you, Jesus, I make my complaint, To have mercy through your pity; Gracious God, now hear my prayer.
If I haue done owte of þo way of ryghtfulnes thorow my foly, Or dethe me kache & close in clay, mercyful god, I crye mercy!	If I have strayed from the way Of righteousness through my folly, Before death catches me and returns me to clay, Merciful God, I ask mercy!
Bonitas dei: Man, qwat haue I done to þe? qwy art þu, man, to me vnkynde? Qwy has þu, man, for-sake me? qwy flese þu, man? I am þi frynde.	God's goodness: Man, what have I done to you? Why are you, man, unkind to me? Why have you, man, forsaken me? Why do you run away, man? I am your friend.
ffurst, I þe made to my lyknes & put al þis world in þi bayle, And, for to hele al þi sekenes, I lost my myght & toke mercy.	First, I made you in my likeness, And put all this world under your stewardship, And, in order to heal all your sickness, I lost my power and took mercy.
Natura hominis: Þu maduste me, lord, to þi lyknes, And to þin ymage þu me schape Þo makynge, lord, of þi godnes let not me, lord, thorow fowle warke.	Human nature: You made me, Lord, in your likeness, According to your image you have shaped me. Because of your goodness, Lord, Let me not destroy this work through wickedness.

My flesche is frele & redy to fall,
þo world, þo dele, a grete enmy.

With meke hert þer-fore I cal,
Mercyful god, I crye mercy!

Bonitas dei:
Man, þo rede see I partud in too,
owte of egypte qwen I browghte þe;
I was þi frynde, þu was my foo,
þu in deserte haste for-sake me;
With awngels methe þer I þe fedde,
my luf to þe þu fonde ay redy;

þer þu were worthy hell pyne to haue had,
I left my myght & toke mercy.

Natura hominis:
þat mercy, lord, take þu to mynde,
þat þu wold schewe to Maudeleyn;
Thynke þat þu art of owre kynde,
let noght mane-kynde þoro synne be sleyn.
Opone my synful sole þu rew,
as þu hit boght with þi body.
ffor dedly syne has chawngude þo hewe,
mercyful god, I cry mercy!

My flesh is frail and ready to fall,
The world, the Devil, a great enemy.
With a meek heart therefore I call,
Merciful God, I cry for mercy!

God's goodness:
Man, the Red Sea I parted in two,
When I brought you out of Egypt;
I was your friend, you were my foe,
In the desert you have forsaken me;
With the bread of angels I fed you there,
You always found my love ready for you;
When you were deserving of the pains of hell,
I left my power and took mercy.

Human nature:
That mercy, Lord, call to mind,
That you showed to Mary Magdalen;
Remember that you are of our nature,
Let not mankind be slain through sin.
Have mercy upon my sinful soul,
As you bought it with your body.
For deadly sin has changed your face,
Merciful God, I cry for mercy!

The poem takes its starting point from the *Improperia*, with God's reproach 'Man, qwat haue I done to þe?' ('Man, what have I done to you?') echoing the memorable opening of the refrain from the *Improperia*: *Popule meus, quid feci tibi?* ('O my people, what have I done to you?'). Christ here speaks explicitly to 'man' – all of mankind, rather than only the people of Israel. The ideas behind the liturgical text are here expanded and made more concrete, as the poem includes a series of insistent questions ('Why are you, man, unkind to me? Why have you, man, forsaken me? Why do you run away, man? I am your friend'), followed by a list of God's deeds that demonstrate his mercy and love ('First, I made you in my likeness, And put all this world under your stewardship, And, in order to heal all your sickness, I lost my power and took mercy.'). In contrast to the *Improperia*, however, Christ does receive a response to his questions. The poem imagines an answer from mankind which responds directly to the points which God has raised, and turns it into a plea for mercy: 'You made me, Lord, in your likeness, According to your image you have shaped me. Because of your goodness, Lord, Let me not destroy this work through wickedness.' The next stanza again draws upon the imagery of the *Improperia* as God's reproach invokes the Old Testament exodus. In the liturgical text God contrasts his deeds in the Old Testament with the injustice done to Christ ('I led you out of Egypt, having drowned Pharaoh in the Red Sea: but you have delivered me to the chief priests'), but the poem again takes this as a starting point to broaden out the perspective. God's words here are not spoken to the Jewish people, but to all of humankind: 'Man, the Red Sea I parted in two, When I brought you out of Egypt; I was your friend, you were my foe.' We can see clearly how the words, style and imagery of the liturgical text are used as a source of inspiration in the poem, which expands upon these ideas and makes them directly relevant to the present lives of its readers.

Other Middle English responses to the liturgical tradition transform it equally creatively. In a poem beginning 'In a valley of this restless mind', tropes and images associated with the tradition of medieval love poetry are fused with images derived from the *Improperia* to striking effect.

In a valey of this restles mynde,
I soughte in mounteyne and in mede,
Trustynge a trewelove for to fynde.
Upon an hil than Y took hede:
A voice Y herde, and neer Y yede,
In huge dolour complaynynge tho:
'Se, dere Soule, how my sidis blede,
Quia amore langueo.'

In a valley of this restless mind,
I sought in mountain and in meadow,
hoping to find a true-love.

Upon a hill I then took notice;
I heard a voice – and I drew closer –
lamenting in great sorrow:
'See, dear Soul, how my sides bleed,
because I languish for love.'

Upon this hil Y fond a tree,
Undir the tree a man sittynge,
From heed to foot woundid was he,
His herte blood Y sigh bledinge:

Upon this hill I found a tree,
under the tree a man sitting;
from head to foot wounded was he,
and I saw his heart's blood bleeding.

A semeli man to ben a king,
A graciouse face to loken unto.
I askide whi he had peynynge,
He seide, 'Quia amore langueo.

He was a man fit to be a king,
with a gracious face to look at.
I asked why he was suffering;
he said, 'Because I languish for love.'

'I am Truelove that fals was nevere.
My sistyr, mannis soule, Y loved hir thus:
Bicause we wolde in no wise discevere,
I lefte my kyngdom glorious.

'I am True-love who never was false.
My sister, man's soul, I loved her thus:
because we would not in any way be parted,
I left my glorious kingdom,

I purveide for hir a paleis precious;	I prepared for her a precious palace.
Sche fleyth; Y folowe. Y soughte hir so,	She flees; I follow; I sought her in such a way
I suffride this peyne piteuous,	that I came to suffer this terrible pain,
Quia amore langueo.	because I languish for love.
'My fair spouse and my love bright,	'My fair spouse and my love bright!
I saved hir fro betynge, and sche hath me bet!	I saved her from beating, and she has beaten me.
I clothid hir in grace and hevenli light,	I clothed her in grace and heavenly light;
This bloodi scherte sche hath on me sette!	she set this bloody shirt upon me.
For longynge of love yit wolde Y not lette –	For longing of love I will not cease –
Swete strokis are these, lo!	these are sweet strokes, lo!
I have loved hir evere, as Y hir het,	I have loved her always, as I promised her,
Quia amore langueo.	because I languish for love.
'I crowned hir with blis, and sche me with thorn;	'I crowned her with bliss, and she crowned me with thorns;
I ledde hir to chaumbir, and sche me to die;	I led her to a chamber, and she led me to die.
I broughte hir to worschipe, and sche me to scorn;	I brought her to worship, and she brought me to scorn;
I dide hir reverence, and she me vilonye.	I did her worship, and she did me villainy.
To love that loveth is no maistrie;	To love one who loves you is no hard task;
Hir hate made nevere my love hir foo.	her hate never made my love her foe.

Axe me no questioun whi –
Quia amore langueo.

Do not ask me questions why;
because I languish for love.

'Loke unto myn hondis, man:
These gloves were yove me whan Y hir soughte.
Thei ben not white, but rede and wan,
Onbroudrid with blood. My spouse hem broughte.
Thei wole not of; Y loose hem noughte.
I wowe hir with hem whereevere sche go –
These hondis for hir so freendli foughte,
Quia amore langueo.

'Look at my hands, man:
these gloves were given me when I sought her.
They are not white, but red and pale,
embroidered with blood. My spouse brought them.
They cannot come off; I will not undo them.
I woo her with them wherever she may go.
These hands fought for her so lovingly,
because I languish for love.

'Merveille noughte, man, though Y sitte stille:
Se, love hath schod me wondir streite,
Boclid my feet, as was hir wille,
With scharp naile, lo! Thou maiste waitenails;
In my love was nevere desaite.
Alle myn humours Y have opened hir to,
There my bodi hath maad hir hertis baite,
Quia amore langueo.

'Marvel not, man, though I sit still:
see, love has shod me very tightly,
and buckled my feet, by her choice,
with sharp nails, look! You may know by these nails,
there was never any deceit in my love.
I have opened all my blood to her
and made my body her heart's bait,
because I languish for love.

'In my side Y have made hir neste.
Loke in: how weet a wounde is heere!
This is hir chaumbir. Heere schal sche reste,
That sche and Y may slepe in fere.

'In my side I have made her nest.
Look in, how wet a wound is here!
This is her chamber; here she shall rest,
and she and I shall sleep in company.

Heere may she waische if ony filthe were;
Heere is sete for al hir woo.
Come whanne sche wole, sche schal have chere,
Quia amore langueo.

Here she may wash away anything that befouls her;
here is shelter for all her sorrow.
Come whenever she will, she shall have good cheer,
because I languish for love.

'I wole abide til sche be redy,
I wole hir sue if sche seie nay;
If sche be richilees, Y wole be gredi,
And if sche be daungerus, Y wole hir praie.
If sche wepe, than hide Y ne may –
Myn armes her highed to clippe hir me to:
Crie oonys! Y come. Now, Soule, asay!
Quia amore langueo.

'I will wait until she be ready;
I will seek her if she say nay.
If she be careless, I will be insistent;
if she be disdainful, I will beseech her.
If she weep, then I cannot conceal myself –
my arms are outstretched to clasp her to me.
Cry once, I come! Now, soul, try me!
Because I languish for love.

'I sitte on this hil for to se fer,
I loke into the valey my spouse to se:
Now renneth sche awayward, yit come sche me neer,
For out of my sighte may sche not be.

'I sit on this hill to see far:
I look into the valley to see my spouse.
Now she runs away, now she comes closer,
but she cannot be out of my sight.

Summe wayte hir prai to make hir to flee,	Some others lurk to make her their prey, to make her flee to them,
I renne bifore and fleme hir foo.	but I run before them and drive away her foes.
Returne, my spouse, ayen to me!	Return, my spouse, again to me!
Quia amore langueo.	Because I languish for love.
'Fair love, lete us go pleye!	'Fair love, let us go play:
Applis ben ripe in my gardayne;	apples are ripe in my garden.
I schal thee clothe in a newe aray,	I shall clothe thee in new array,
Thi mete schal be mylk, hony, and wiyn.	thy food shall be milk, honey, and wine.
Fair love, lete us go digne;	Fair love, let us go dine;
Thi sustynaunce is in my crippe, lo!	thy sustenance is in my bag, lo!
Tarie thou not, my fair spouse myne!	Tarry not, my own fair spouse,
Quia amore langueo.	because I languish for love.
'Iff thou be foul, Y schal thee make clene,	'If thou be dirty, I shall make thee clean;
If thou be siik, Y schal thee hele;	if thou be sick, I shall heal thee.
If thou moorne ought, Y schal thee meene.	If thou mourn for anything, I shall comfort thee.
Whi wolt thou not, fair love, with me dele?	Why wilt thou not, fair love, have dealings with me?
Foundist thou evere love so leel?	Hast thou ever found such loyal love?
What woldist thou, spouse, that Y schulde do?	What wouldest thou, spouse, that I should do?
I may not unkyndeli thee appele,	I cannot accuse thee of unkindness,
Quia amore langueo.	because I languish for love.

'What schal Y do with my fair spouse
But abide hir, of my gentilnes,
Til that sche loke out of hir house
Of fleischli affeccioun? Love myn sche is!
Hir bed is maade, hir bolstir is blis;
Hir chaumbir is chosen, is ther non moo.
Loke out on me at the wyndow of kyndenes,
Quia amore langueo.

'What shall I do with my fair spouse,
but wait for her, in my courtesy,
until she look out of her house
of fleshly affection? She is my love!
Her bed is made, her pillow is prepared in bliss,
her chamber is chosen – there is none other such.
Look out on me at the window of kindness,
because I languish for love.

'My love is in hir chaumbir. Holde youre pees!
Make ye no noise, but lete hir slepe.
My babe Y wolde not were in disese;
I may not heere my dere child wepe;

'My love is in her chamber, hold your peace!
Make ye no noise, but let her sleep.
I would not have my babe troubled;
I cannot hear my dear child weep.

With my pap Y schal hir kepe.
Ne merveille ye not though Y tende hir to:
This hole in my side had nevere be so depe,
But Quia amore langueo.

With my breast I shall feed her.
Do not marvel that I tend to her so!
This hole in my side would never have been so deep,
but that I languish for love.

'Longe thou for love nevere so high,
My love is more than thin may be:

'Long thou for love never so much,
my love is more than thine can be.

Thou wepist, thou gladist, Y sitte thee bi,
Yit woldist thou oonys, leef, loke unto me?
Schulde I alwey fede thee
With children mete? Nay, love, not so! –
I wole preve thi love with adversitè,
Quia amore langueo.

'Wexe not wery, myn owne wiif.
What mede is it to lyve evere in coumfort?
In tribulacioun I regne moore riif,
Oftetymes, than in disport –
In wele and in woo Y am ay to supporte!
Than, dere Soule, go not me fro!

Thi meede is markid whan thou art mort, Quia amore langueo.'

Thou weepest, thou rejoicest, I sit beside thee;
but wouldest thou once, love, look to me?
Should I always feed thee
with children's food? No, love, it cannot be so!
I wish to test thy love through adversity,
because I languish for love.

'Wax not weary, my own wife;
what reward is there to live in comfort for ever?
In tribulation I often reign
more fully than in pleasure.
In weal and woe I am ever there to help!
Then, dear soul, do not go from me.
Thy reward is fixed after thy death,
because I languish for love.'[5]

What happens in the poem is extraordinary. Different liturgical and literary traditions are blended together, taking the reader on a roller-coaster of abrupt changes of direction and surprising views. We start out with a setting that we might typically expect from a medieval love poem: the speaker, troubled in mind, goes on a journey to find 'a true-love'. There is a deliberate ambiguity in this word, as it can refer either to a specific kind of flower, which was associated with fidelity, or to the idea of steadfast love itself.[6] The speaker's journey leads to a man sitting underneath a tree on a hill, and the man's lament has much in common with conventional love laments, with the concluding quotation *Quia amore langueo*, 'Because I languish for love'. We have already encountered in Chapter Two the use of this quotation from Song of Songs 2:5 and 5:8 in a poem that plays with and breaks down categories of secular and spiritual love, and the present poem takes a similar approach. The speaker here, however, is Christ himself, 'a man fit to be a king' who is wounded 'from head to foot'. Gradually the poem reveals that this is not, as we may have expected at first, a lovesick knight weeping over his lady, but Christ himself with the wounds of the Passion upon his body recounting his long love affair with 'man's soul'. As we have seen in Chapter Two, the language of the Song of Songs is used liberally to blur the boundaries between erotic and religious, and earthly categories are broken down in the course of the poem. Man's soul is the beloved who is pursued passionately by Christ, described in language that recalls the sensual imagery of the Song of Songs: 'Fair love, let us go play: apples are ripe in my garden. I shall clothe thee in new array, thy food shall be milk, honey, and wine.' But at the same time, man's soul is described as Christ's 'sister', and later on as a child who is nursed by a loving mother: 'Make ye no noise, but let her sleep. I would not have my babe troubled; I cannot hear my dear child weep. With my breast I shall feed her.' The image is disorienting in the context of what has come just a few stanzas before, until in a striking conceit it is revealed that the reference to breastfeeding is an allusion to the wound to Christ's side, which he sustained when the soldiers pierced him with a lance.

The poem is full of unexpected turns like this, leaving the reader with a sense of vertigo. The constant betrayal and unfaithfulness of man's soul, by contrast, is described with a series of antitheses that borrow from the *Improperia*:

> I crowned her with bliss, and she crowned me with thorns;
> I led her to a chamber, and she led me to die.
> I brought her to worship, and she brought me to scorn;
> I did her worship, and she did me villainy.

The liturgical tradition is invoked in the midst of the whirlwind of images of this poem, and yet such oppositions of Christ's love and the soul's disdain occur side by side with words of love-longing:

> My fair spouse and my love bright!
> I saved her from beating, and she has beaten me.

Such conceits are achieved in this poem through the fusion of different liturgical traditions with an exuberantly creative spark that plays with apparent contradiction, paradox and rich layers of meaning, prompting the reader to reflect on the suffering man who is also God. The repertoire of images, words and ideas found in the liturgy of the Triduum have thus proved a sheer limitless source for poets' engagement with the theme of Christ's Passion.

In later periods, too, this influence can be felt. Priest and poet George Herbert (1593–1633), whose writings are associated with the 'Metaphysical poets' who delighted in innovative poetic conceits, alludes to the same liturgical traditions in 'The Sacrifice', which begins:

> *O, all ye,* who pass by, whose eyes and mind
> To worldly things are sharp, but to me blind;
> To me, who took eyes that I might you find:
> Was ever grief like mine?
>
> The Princes of my people make a head
> Against their Maker: they do wish me dead,
> Who cannot wish, except I give them bread:
> Was ever grief like mine?
>
> Without me each one, who doth now me brave,
> Had to this day been an Egyptian slave.
> They use that power against me, which I gave:
> Was ever grief like mine?[7]

The poem takes its cue from *O vos omnes*, framing the first stanza with the central idea of the *Tenebrae* responsory: 'O all ye, who pass by . . . Was ever grief like mine?' Christ is the speaker, and his insistent question subsequently acts as a refrain to each stanza of the long poem, which contemplates the stages of the Passion from Christ's point of view. In various places the *Tenebrae* responsory is merged with the *Improperia* tradition, as in the second and third stanzas, which compare God's acts of kindness to his people with their present malice: 'The Princes of my people make a head/ Against their Maker: they do wish me dead/ Who cannot wish, except I give them bread', with the reference to 'bread' evoking associations with both the manna in the desert and the Eucharist. 'Without me each one, who doth now me brave/ Had to this day been an Egyptian slave' continues this line of thought: God's aid in guiding the Israelites out of Egypt is juxtaposed with their betrayal, once again drawing inspiration from the liturgical tradition. This perspective gradually becomes broader in the course of Herbert's poem, and shifts towards a focus on Christ's suffering as a remedy for the Fall:

> *O all ye who pass by, behold and see:*
> Man stole the fruit, but I must climb the tree;
> The tree of life to all, but only me:
> Was ever grief like mine?

The antithesis used here refers to the Fall. The taking of the forbidden fruit from the tree of Paradise in Genesis is undone by Christ's suffering upon the wood of another tree: the cross. In order to accomplish the redemption and turn the cross into a 'tree of life to all', Christ must die. For him it is an instrument of torture and death; for humankind it is the source of life. The juxtaposed ideas here relate to all of humanity, placing the earlier descriptions drawn from the *Improperia* into a more universal context. Again, as in the liturgical text, it becomes clear that, in a moral and theological sense, everyone is a member of the people who betray Christ. His death atones for all of humankind: 'My wo, man's weal.'

But now I die; now all is finished.
My wo, man's weal: and now I bow my head:
Only let others say, when I am dead,
Never was grief like mine.

In such poetry and many other literary texts we hear the liturgy echoing down the ages, from the medieval period to the seventeenth century and beyond. The liturgical texts provide models of thinking about the Passion and exploring Christ's emotional landscape, but at the same time they are an invitation to poets to transform these models in ever-changing ways. The liturgical tradition remains lively, dynamic and vibrant.

5
Grief

Many of the liturgical texts of Good Friday take the perspective of the crucified Christ, as we have seen. But Christ, though the protagonist, is not the only participant in the events of Good Friday. As the Gospel of John reports, 'standing near the cross of Jesus were his mother, and his mother's sister, Mary the wife of Clopas, and Mary Magdalene' (19:25). John the disciple is also present, and Jesus makes sure that his mother will be looked after by John in the future: 'When Jesus saw his mother and the disciple whom he loved standing beside her, he said to his mother, "Woman, here is your son." Then he said to the disciple, "Here is your mother." And from that hour the disciple took her into his own home' (John 19:26–7). The gospels restrict their laconic narrative to events that can be externally observed. They report what happens and what is spoken as Christ is on the cross, but are mostly silent on the subject of feelings. In every age these blank spaces have been filled by believers' own imaginations. The inner life of the bystanders and onlookers of the crucifixion prompted poetic explorations and re-imaginings. Particularly prominent among these are explorations of the feelings of the Virgin Mary as she sees the events of the crucifixion unfold. Mary is exceptional not only in her singular virtue and status as mother of Christ, but in the singular grief that she had to undergo. What does it feel like to watch your only child dying for the salvation of the human race? This is an insistent question that has long occupied the artistic imagination and that gave rise to the *Stabat Mater* tradition, a term which literally translates to 'the mother stood'. In this tradition, we see the crucifixion through Mary's eyes, empathizing with her bitter grief. The text that gave its name to this tradition is *Stabat Mater dolorosa*, a poem first written in thirteenth-century Italy and known widely throughout medieval Europe. The liturgical history of the text is turbulent: in the Middle Ages it was soon incorporated into liturgical celebrations of the Passion in many places. Its use within the liturgy was later suppressed by the Council of Trent (1545–63) in the attempt to unify different local liturgical uses, only to be restored as a part of the liturgy for the Feast of the Seven Dolours of the Blessed Virgin Mary in 1727. The poem moves from a reflection on the grief of the mother standing before the cross to a direct address to the Virgin, in which the speaker asks Mary for her intercession.

Stabat Mater dolorosa Iuxta crucem lacrimosa Dum pendebat Filius.	The sorrowful mother stood weeping before the cross where hung her son.
Cuius animam gementem Contristatam et dolentem Pertransivit gladius.	Her grieving soul, anguished and lamenting, was pierced by a sword.
O quam tristis et afflicta Fuit illa benedicta Mater unigeniti!	O how sad and afflicted was that blessed mother of the only-begotten one.
Quae moerebat et dolebat, Pia Mater, dum videbat Nati poenas incliti.	She who grieved and suffered, the loving mother, while she looked on the torment of her glorious child.

Quis est homo qui non fleret,	Who would not weep
Matrem Christi si videret	seeing the mother of Christ
In tanto supplicio?	in such agony?
Quis non posset contristari,	Who would not share her sorrow,
Christi Matrem contemplari	seeing the loving mother
Dolentem cum Filio?	grieving with her son?
Pro peccatis suae gentis	For the sins of his people
Vidit Iesum in tormentis,	she saw Jesus in torment
Et flagellis subditum.	and subjected to scourging.
Vidit suum dulcem natum	She saw her own sweet son
Moriendo desolatum	dying, abandoned,
Dum emisit spiritum.	as he gave up the spirit.
Eja Mater, fons amoris	O Mother, fount of love,
Me sentire vim doloris	make me feel the strength of your grief,
Fac, ut tecum lugeam.	so that I may mourn with you.
Fac, ut ardeat cor meum	Make my heart burn
In amando Christum Deum	with love for Christ, my God,
Ut sibi complaceam.	that I may find grace in his eyes.
Sancta Mater, istud agas,	Blessed Mother,
Crucifixi fige plagas	cause the sufferings of the crucified
Cordi meo valide.	to be fixed deeply in my heart.
Tui nati vulnerati,	Share with me the agony
Tam dignati pro me pati,	of your wounded son

Poenas mecum divide.	who deigned to suffer so much for me.
Fac me tecum, pie, flere, Crucifixo condolere, Donec ego vixero.	Make me truly weep with you, grieving with him who is crucified, as long as I shall live.
Iuxta crucem tecum stare, Et me tibi sociare In planctu desidero.	To stand with you beside the cross and to be your companion in grief is my desire.
Virgo virginum praeclara, Mihi iam non sis amara Fac me tecum plangere.	O Virgin, peerless among virgins, do not turn away from me, let me weep with you.
Fac, ut portem Christi mortem Passionis fac consortem, Et plagas recolere.	Let me bear the death of Christ, be a sharer of his Passion, contemplate his wounds.
Fac me plagis vulnerari, Fac me cruce inebriari, Et cruore Filii.	Let me suffer his pain, let me be engulfed by the cross, and by the blood of your son.
Inflammatus et accensus, per te, Virgo, sim defensus in die iudicii.	Lest I be destroyed by devouring flames, Virgin, by you may I be defended at the day of judgement.
Fac me cruce custodiri Morte Christi praemuniri Confoveri gratia.	Grant that I may be protected by the cross, fortified by the death of Christ, strengthened by grace.

Quando corpus morietur,	When my body dies,
Fac, ut animae donetur	let my soul be given
Paradisi gloria. Amen.	the glory of Paradise. Amen.[1]

A reciprocal relationship of compassion is evoked: the speaker contemplates the grief of the mother undergoing the most painful experience imaginable, and asks in turn for her compassion and support. While no actual dialogue takes place between Mary and the speaker, the emotive style of the address to the sorrowful Virgin immediately invites us to place ourselves in the position of the speaker. Mary's experience is described in simple words which are all the more heartbreaking for their lack of elaboration: 'She saw her own dear son, dying, abandoned, as he gave up the spirit.' Even if many aspects of medieval devotion have grown alien to modern sensibilities, it is difficult to remain indifferent to these reflections as they address an experience that, across the ages, has always been one of the most devastating things that can happen to a person: the loss of a child. Mary's experience powerfully resonates with the reader. Despite Mary's unique experience of being the mother of God, her feelings underneath the cross also express a universal experience that is shared by many others – even more so in the Middle Ages, where infant mortality was extremely high. But this text is not only written for parents who have gone through a similar loss; it connects to other kinds of loss and grief. It is easy to empathize with Mary. The poem sets the scene for a heartfelt emotional response from the individual believer: 'Who would not share her sorrow, seeing the loving mother grieving with her son?' Inspired with compassion for the sorrowful Virgin, the speaker then asks for Mary's protection and intercession. Suffering and understanding are connected: Mary's unique position at the foot of the cross also gives her privileged insights into the mysteries of the crucifixion. Because of this privileged position, Mary can act as a mediator between the speaker and her son: 'Let me bear the death of Christ, be a sharer of his Passion, contemplate his wounds,' the speaker asks.

There is, then, a dialogue implied by this poem, even though Mary's response is left to the reader's imagination. This communicative situation is relevant to this text, but the interplay between different perspectives is also an important motif in portrayals of the crucifixion in other media. In visual art, the crucifixion scene is frequently portrayed with at least three people: Christ on the

9 Anonymous, *Christ on the Cross*, *c*. 1400, oil on wood.

cross, the Virgin Mary, and John the disciple underneath the cross. Sometimes other figures are added: Mary Magdalene (one of the women who followed Jesus), Roman soldiers and the other two men who were crucified with Jesus. Although there is some variation in the dramatis personae, communication is always important. Who looks at whom is crucial in crucifixion paintings, guiding the spectator's gaze into the scene and suggesting a range of interpretations. Similar to the *Stabat Mater*, an Austro-Bohemian painting of Christ on the cross by an anonymous artist from around 1400 invites the audience into a dialogue with the sorrowful mother (illus. 9). In this painting Christ's eyes are half closed in silent agony. John looks attentively up at Christ, but Mary gazes straight at the spectator. Her arms are crossed protectively and her head is slightly inclined towards her right. Her body language betrays her sorrow. But the look with which she greets us is lively and direct, perhaps even questioning. Through Mary's gaze, a communication with the viewer is established. We become part of the scene. We too are bystanders at the crucifixion, and Mary's look invites us to consider what our own role in it might be. Are we about to turn away with indifference, or are we going to stay and contemplate this event and its relevance to our lives? Mary's gaze turns this painting of an oft-portrayed scene into something that is deeply personal, to her and to us.

We might see the effect of this painting as the inverse of the *Stabat Mater* poem: whereas in the text the speaker opens up a conversation with the Virgin without receiving a direct response, in this painting it is Mary who initiates the communication, challenging us with her look to respond. The interaction is open-ended and ongoing, and the outcome may be radically different depending on the viewer's response. We don't know whether the anonymous painter meant to allude directly to this poem, which was familiar through liturgical uses, but the work clearly arose from the same tradition and imaginative world. In this way, the *Stabat Mater* tradition creates a space for conversation underneath the cross that includes the individual spectator. Through Mary, it makes the crucifixion personal.

We see this movement towards dialogue reflected in a large number of vernacular poems that stand in the same tradition. There is an entire family of Middle English poems that imagine different kinds of conversations underneath the cross – between Mary and Christ, between the speaker and Mary, sometimes between all three. Many of them take their starting point from the *Stabat Mater* motif. An anonymous fourteenth-century poem, for instance, takes its cue from the liturgical text with the words 'Stond wel, Moder, under rode' ('rode' being an old word for cross), but then takes the idea in a different direction with an imaginary conversation between Mary and Christ.[2]

'Stond wel, Moder, vnder rode,	'Stand well, Mother, under the cross,
bihold þi child wyth glade mode,	Behold your child with a glad mind;
blyþe Moder mittu ben.'	Joyful, Mother, you may be.'
'Svne, quu may bliþe stonden?	'Son, how may I joyful stand?
hi se þin feet, hi se þin honden,	I see your feet, I see your hands
nayled to þe harde tre.'	Nailed to the hard tree.'
'Moder, do wey þi wepinge;	'Mother, cease your weeping:
hi þole þis ded for mannes thinge	I suffer this death for man's sake;
for owen gilte þoli non.'	I do not suffer for my own guilt.'
'Svne, hi fele þe dede stunde,	'Son, I feel the hour of death
þe swerd is at min herte grunde,	The sword is at the bottom of my heart,
þat me byhytte symeon.'	As foretold to me Simeon.'
'Moder, reu vpon þi bern!	'Mother, have pity on your child,
þu wasse awey þo blodi teren,	And wash away those bloody tears,

it don me werse þan mi ded.'

'Sune, hu mitti teres wernen?
hy se þo blodi flodes hernen
huth of þin herte to min fet.'

'Moder, nu y may þe seyn,
bettere is þat ic one deye
þan al man-kyn to helle go.'
'Sune, y se þi bodi swngen,
þi brest, þin hond, þi fot
  þur-stungen –
no selli þou me be wo.'

'Moder, if y dar þe tellen,
yif y ne deye þu gost to helle;
hi þole þis ded for þine sake.'
'Sune, þu best me so minde,
with me nout; it is mi kinde
þat y for þe sorye make.'

'Moder, merci! let me deyen,
for adam ut of helle beyn,
and al mankin þat is for-loren.'
'Sune, wat sal me to rede?
þi pine pined me to dede,
let me deyn þe bi-foren.'

'Moder, mitarst þu mith leren
wat pine þolen þat childre beren

wat sorwe hauen þat child
  for-gon.'

They hurt me worse than my
  death!'

'Son, how could I stop these tears?
I see those bloody floods run
Out of your heart to my feet.'

'Mother, now I may to you say:
Better that I alone should die
Than all mankind should go to hell.'
'Son, I see your body swung,
Your breast, your hand, your foot
  pierced,
No wonder that I mourn!'

'Mother, if I dare you tell,
If I die not, you will go to hell;
I suffer this death for your sake.'
'Son, you are so kind to me.
Blame me not, it is my nature
That I for you this sorrow make.'

'Mother, have mercy! let me die,
Adam out of hell to buy
And all mankind that is forlorn!'
'Son, what would you have me do?
Your pain pains me to death;
Let me die before you.'

'Mother, now you may well learn
What pain they endure who
  children bear,
What sorrow they have who
  children lose.'

'Sune, y wot y kan þe tellen,
bute it be þe pine of helle
more sorwe ne woth y non.'

'Son, indeed, I can you tell,
No sorrow but the pain of hell
Is greater than to suffer so!'

'Moder, reu of moder kare!
nu þu wost of moder fare,
þou þu be clene mayden m(an).'
'Sune, help alle at nede,
alle þo þat to me greden –
m(ay)den, wyf and fol wyman.'

'Mother, pity a mother's care,
Now you know how mothers fare,
Though you are a pure virgin.'
'Son, help all at need,
All those that to me cry
Maiden, wife, and unchaste woman.'

'Moder, y may no lenger duellen,
þe time is cumen y fare to helle,
þe þridde day y rise upon.'
'Sune, y wyle wi'the funden,
y deye ywis of þine wnden,
so reuful ded was neuere non.'

'Mother, I may no longer dwell;
The time is come, I go to hell,
The third day I will rise upon.'
'Son, I will with you go;
I die, indeed, of your wounds;
Such pitiful death was never none.'

When he ros þan fel þi sorwe,
þe blisse sprong þe þridde morewe,
wen bliþe moder wer þu þo.
Moder, for þat ilke blisse,
bisech vre god, vre sinnes lesse,
þu be hure chel ayen hure fo.

When he rose then fell your sorrow:
The bliss sprang up the third morrow.
Joyful, Mother, were you then!
Mother, for that very bliss
Beseech your son, our sins release,
You are our shield against the foe.

Blisced be þu, quen of heuene,
bring us ut of helle leuene
þurth þi dere sunes mith.
Moder, for þat hithe blode
þat he sadde vpon þe rode,
led us in-to heuene lith. Amen.

Blessed be you, full of bliss,
Bring us out of the fire of hell
Through your dear son's might.
Mother, for that selfsame blood
That he shed upon the rood,
Lead us into heaven's light. Amen.

The conversation between Christ and Mary contrasts a divine perspective with an intensely human one. His suffering is necessary in order to save humankind from hell. Christ tries to comfort his mother. But Mary sees the crucifixion through a mother's eyes, horrified by her child's bitter pain. When Christ asks her to wipe away her tears, she rejects this as impossible: 'Son, how could I stop these tears?' The interchange has a dramatic immediacy that draws the reader into the scene. The two perspectives seem irreconcilable because they operate with different time frames. Jesus sees the future victory that his suffering will bring, while Mary is unable to see beyond the unbearable present. It is a very understandable response, giving a voice to the validity of human grief. Despite the necessity of suffering for the greater good in the divine plan, it is nonetheless a thing awful and intolerable. Only in the last two verses does the poem give us a resolution to the two clashing perspectives: 'When he rose then fell your sorrow: The bliss sprang up the third morrow. Joyful, Mother, were you then!' In this poem, a glimpse of the joy of the resurrection only follows after a profound exploration of the reality of pain and death.

This is a reality that is also explored in great depth in religious art through the centuries. Paintings of the crucifixion emphasize, to a greater or to a lesser extent, the suffering which Mary undergoes as she stands underneath the cross. While the anonymous painting earlier in this chapter shows us a calm and composed Mary who focuses on an interaction with the spectator (see illus. 9), we see an entirely different Mary in the *Isenheim Altarpiece* by Matthias Grünewald, which dates to the early sixteenth century (illus. 10). The wings of the altarpiece can be opened up or closed, revealing or hiding a range of scenes on the outside and the inside, but they are never all visible at the same time. The outside confronts us with Christ on the cross in near-complete darkness, which throws into relief the bright red that predominates among the bystanders' clothing and Christ's pale, emaciated body. It is one of the most poignant crucifixion scenes in Western art, depicting the full horror of what it means to be nailed to a cross. Christ is writhing in agony, his skin covered with wounds and his limbs ridden with cramps. His head is bowed, lips parted in a silent scream. There could hardly be a more radical contrast with the serenity that seems to emanate from the Christ of the Austro-Bohemian piece. In the *Isenheim Altarpiece*, Christ is flanked on the left by John, the Virgin Mary and a kneeling Mary Magdalene, while on the right John the Baptist, accompanied by a lamb, is symbolically included, even though his execution preceded that of Jesus. As the forerunner of Christ, he stands here explaining the significance of the event. In a teacher's pose with book in hand he points at Christ, proclaiming: *illum oportet crescere me autem minui*, 'He must increase, but I must decrease' (John 3:30). In this way, Grünewald's version includes both symbolic elements and dreadful realism, expressing both the metaphysical significance and the physical reality of the crucifixion. Mary, in this version, recoils in horror at the scene in front of her, her hands wrung in a gesture of helpless dismay. Her eyes are closed, her face is ashen, her body is swaying backwards, and she has to be supported by John. True to the gospel account, Mary stands – but only just. Her posture is that of a mother stricken to the depth of her soul. We could well imagine this Mary speaking the words of 'Stond wel, Moder, under rode': 'Son, how could I stop these tears?'

A painting by the follower of the Flemish artist Rogier van der Weyden, roughly contemporary with the *Isenheim Altarpiece*, takes Mary's grief a step further (illus. 11). The body of Christ on the cross here does not show the same intense physical agony as in Grünewald's version. His fingers are clutching the nails, but his face looks almost peaceful. Mary, with a look of utter exhaustion, has fainted. She is kept upright by John, whose face shows concern as he supports her, but her knees have buckled under the weight of her anguish. Her body is the very image of grief. Unlike the other paintings, this Mary is falling rather than standing.

10 Matthias Grünewald, *Isenheim Altarpiece*, *c.* 1512, oil on wood.

We have seen a range of portrayals of the Blessed Virgin underneath the cross: from restrained grief to near collapse. The latter is particularly prevalent in the fourteenth and fifteenth centuries, where a large number of paintings portray Mary's emotional state through her fainting or having fainted next to the cross, a motif also known as the 'swoon of the virgin'. It was a deviation from the *Stabat Mater* idea of the liturgical poem following the Gospel of John, a choice made by artists who went to new extremes in order to plunge the viewers into the depths of suffering and grief of Christ's mother. The very point of these images is that Mary does not stand; as we might say, *mater non stabat*. As such, this motif also calls for a compassionate response from the spectator. It intends to move and touch the emotions rather than explain. This focus on a compassionate response is connected to a particular devotional movement of the Middle Ages, known as 'affective piety'. The term summarizes a set of practices rooted in a religious sensibility that focuses on an emotive approach to the mysteries of the faith. Believers are encouraged to meditate

11 Follower of Rogier van der Weyden, *The Crucifixion*, *c.* 1510, oil on panel.

on different episodes in the life of Christ by imagining themselves present at the scene, entering into the same experience as Mary or the disciples. A compassionate response to the suffering of the Virgin Mary could also serve as a model of behaviour to the viewers in their daily lives, encouraging them to act with compassion when encountering those in sorrow or grief.

The fainting virgin, however, was not without controversy. This representation of Mary worried theologians, particularly in the sixteenth century, as it had no biblical precedent, and indeed seemed to contradict the wording of the Gospel of John, which insists that Mary *stood* underneath the cross. Critics of the fainting virgin worried that this might show her as weak, unable or unwilling to bear the immensity of the sacrifice required of her for the salvation of humankind, implying a lack of perfection. For a brief period images of the 'swoon of the virgin' tradition were even subject to official disapproval by the Catholic Church, while many Protestants rejected it outright along with many other images that were not rooted in Scripture.[3] But it seems that the Catholic condemnation of the swoon of the virgin was short-lived, perhaps due to the great popularity of the image, variations of which were found in thousands of churches. Perhaps it was also the artistic integrity and intense humanity of this way of portraying a grieving mother that made this image prevail. We still find the same motif in much later paintings, such as Carl Heinrich Bloch's crucifixion scene from the late nineteenth century (illus. 12). Here we see Mary in a full state of collapse, lying on the ground. She is deathly pale, and at first glance it is difficult to tell whether she is alive or dead. A turbaned male is bent over her and seems to be asking the same question. He has taken her hand; his body language betrays his uncertainty. Mary's head rests in the lap of Mary Magdalene, who has been taken by the sleep of exhaustion. A sorrowful John looks on, seated on a rock in the background. On the left-hand side, men arrive with ladders, ready to take the dead Jesus down from the cross. The great deed has been accomplished.

Christ is dead, and Mary's body stretched out at the foot of the cross mirrors the dead body of her son suspended above.

Bloch's painting captures a particular moment in time, when Christ's suffering is finished and his body is about to be taken down. According to tradition, another moment is to follow shortly after, though not explicitly mentioned in the gospels: Christ's dead body will be cradled by his grieving mother. This motif, known as the 'Pietà', is particularly widespread in sculpture, but also makes

12 Carl Heinrich Bloch, *The Crucifixion*, 1870, oil on copper.

appearances in other art forms. Without doubt the most famous example is Michelangelo's *Pietà*, which he completed at the end of the fifteenth century, when he was only 24 years old (illus. 13). Although the motif of Mary cradling her dead son in her lap had been common in the Middle Ages, Michelangelo's depiction is strikingly different to previous ones. He shows Mary as young and beautiful rather than as the middle-aged woman she would have been at the death of Jesus, who died aged 33. Her features are not those of a woman stricken by sorrow: her face is calm and peaceful; one might almost call her joyful. Reflected in her face is the certainty that the great act of salvation has been accomplished. She looks more like a young mother cradling her baby than a bereaved woman who is going through the most painful experience imaginable. The comparison is apt because Jesus, too, is smaller than he would naturally be. The two figures are out of proportion, with the effect that the fully grown man in Mary's lap looks more like a child or teenager. The statue evokes a faint memory of a much happier time in Mary's life as a young mother; an allusion to Jesus as an infant cradled in his mother's lap underlies the present scene, creating a parallel between the beginning and the end of Jesus' life. There is little emphasis on the Passion in Michelangelo's *Pietà*. In addition to Mary's calm and gentle face, the stigmata (the marks of the nails) on Christ's hands and feet are small and understated. The emotional impact of this sculpture lies not in the emphasis on suffering, but in the haunting suggestion of a soon-to-be-lost innocent childhood scene. This image of the Pietà is unbearably sad precisely because she is so beautiful.

The parallel between the infant Jesus on his mother's lap and Mary cradling his dead body is not unique to Michelangelo but goes back to medieval times, where the two scenes are sometimes juxtaposed in visual art, but also explored in literature, such as the following fifteenth-century carol.[4] A carol in medieval times was not just a song for Christmas, but could address a range of themes. This

13 Michelangelo, *Pietà*, 1498–9, quartz.

text explores the idea of Mary singing to her child, who has foreknowledge of how his life will end. The carol begins:

> So blessed a sight it was to see,
> How Mary rocked her Son so free
> So fair she rocked and sang, 'By, by.'
> 'My own dear mother, sing lullay.'

The innocent childhood scene of a lullaby is soon harshly interrupted, when a few stanzas later, the baby declares:

When I am naked, they will me take
And fast bind me to a stake
And beat me sore for man's sake
My own dear mother, sing lullay.

Upon the cross they shall me cast,
Hand and foot nail me fast,
Yet gall shall be my drink [at] last,
Thus shall my life pass away.

The jarring juxtaposition of the words of a cradle-song and violent images of Christ's death on the cross plays upon the same idea as Michelangelo's *Pietà*, though it is explored from a very different angle here. The poem achieves its startling effect from the baby's unexpected prophecy, so at odds with the imagery of the first stanza that the cruelty of Christ's death is thrown into sharp relief. Even more explicit is this parallel in a poem from the fifteenth century in which Mary speaks to all mothers, which begins:

Of all women that ever were born
That bear children, stay and see
How my son lies before me
Upon my knee, taken from the tree.
Your children you dandle upon your knee
With laughing, kissing, and merry cheer;
Behold my child, behold now me,
For now lies dead my dear son, dear.[5]

Mary addresses those mothers who can still enjoy playing with their infant children, contrasting such happy childhood scenes with her own experience. She speaks these words in the moment of receiving her dead son from the cross; it is almost as if we can hear a Pietà image gaining a voice.

Across the ages, the image of the mother mourning for her only son has deeply resonated with those going through a similar experience. It is not surprising that Pietà images are a frequent feature of war memorials in churches. Some of these memorials take the traditional form of Mary cradling her dead son, full of a pathos that is relatable for the mourners of the countless dead of the two world wars. There are also variations upon this theme, with some artists choosing to take a more secular perspective. A sculpture that is inspired by the Pietà tradition, yet is not overtly religious, was created by Käthe Kollwitz, one of Germany's most celebrated female artists. *Mother with Her Dead Son* was completed in 1937 on the anniversary of the death of Kollwitz's son, who died in 1914 (illus. 14). It shows the large figure of a mother in a meditative pose. Her silhouette is mirrored by that of her son, who is seated in an embryonic posture on the ground between her legs, as if to seek shelter. This portrayal is different from the usual tradition: the son is sitting between his mother's knees rather than lying in her lap. The mother is holding her son's hand, and her draped clothing protectively enfolds his body. He seems like a small child asking for his mother's protection. The sculpture invokes silence and reflection rather than focusing on the outward display of pain. Kollwitz's diary entries suggest that the work was not initially designed to be a Pietà, but rather became one in the course of the creative process: 'I am working on the small sculpture that is the result of my sculptural experiments to portray old age. It has become a kind of Pietà. The mother is seated, her dead son lying on her lap between her knees.'[6] Although Kollwitz clearly draws on the religious tradition, her work is not explicitly religious. The mother and child are not Mary and Christ, but two figures unidentified. They could be anyone – or everyone. This particular interpretation of the Pietà motif takes a distinctly secular perspective, highlighting the universal nature of the experience of a mother mourning her dead child.

As we have seen, the Pietà can take many different shapes. The image still resonates deeply in modern times, and variations upon

14 Käthe Kollwitz, *Pietà* (*Mother with Her Dead Son*), 1937–9, bronze (enlarged copy by Harald Haake, 1993).

the same theme are found in many places. Even popular culture is influenced by the Pietà motif. It is a recurring trope on comic book covers, such as the 1982 graphic novel *The Death of Captain Marvel* by Jim Starlin, which features Death cradling the hero of the story in his lap in the same posture as Michelangelo's *Pietà*.

In films, too, this trope is frequently invoked. Like the comic book cover, visual citation in popular culture often plays with the motif or changes it to dramatic effect. An example is the ending of the Bond film *Skyfall* (2012, dir. Sam Mendes), which has the devastated Bond cradling M as she dies. Within the 007 universe, M has become something of a mother-like figure to Bond, and thus the motif in *Skyfall* exchanges the roles of the two figures: the metaphorical son holding the body of his dying mother. In *The Lord of the Rings: The Return of the King* (2003, dir. Peter Jackson), Sam cradles the exhausted and near-comatose Frodo on the slopes of Mount Doom before making the decision to carry him so that the quest can be fulfilled. The variations upon this theme are near-endless, and the contexts in which the Pietà is invoked are frequently secular, or at least not explicitly religious. And yet the underlying symbolism of the motif lingers. The pose is typically used in popular culture at a particular point in the story, often connected with a heroic moment in which the hero sacrifices him- or herself for the greater good. Fighting this heroic battle, the protagonist either dies or is believed to have died before unexpectedly coming back to life. It is not hard to see parallels with the dying Christ as a sacrifice for the sins of humankind in the underlying symbolism of such stories. The moment of mourning the fallen hero has such a deep resonance because it is a narrative archetype, recurring in a thousand forms in the stories that move us the most.

6
Joy

It is the Easter Vigil. Candles illuminate the dark church. The congregation has come together to celebrate Christ's resurrection from the grave. The deacon stands at the front, prepared to start the reading. A parchment scroll is brought forth and slowly unrolled. The deacon begins to sing the text on the scroll. His voice carries to the furthest crevices and darkest corners of the building, an elaborate melody of keen and ancient beauty.

> Exult, let them exult, the hosts of heaven, exult, let Angel ministers of God exult, let the trumpet of salvation sound aloud our mighty King's triumph! Be glad, let earth be glad, as glory floods her, ablaze with light from her eternal King, let all corners of the earth be glad, knowing an end to gloom and darkness.

As he sings, the scroll is further unrolled and its top is draped further and further over the lectern, so that it becomes visible to the congregation. In the flickering candlelight those at the front of the church are able to glimpse the pictures that are interspersed with the text on the scroll. The images are upside down in relation to the text the deacon sings, allowing the congregation to see them more easily. Scenes from the Old Testament are revealed in the half-light of the church: Adam and Eve, the parting of the Red Sea; scenes from the life of Christ: the crucifixion, Christ enthroned, the paschal lamb.

The images unfurl before the people's eyes, taking their cues from the hymn sung by the deacon, lending colour and substance to the words that praise Christ's resurrection from the dead:

> This is the night when Christ broke the prison bars of death and rose victorious from the underworld. Our birth would have been no gain, had we not been redeemed. O wonder of your humble care for us! O love, O charity beyond all telling, to ransom a slave you gave away your Son! O truly necessary sin of Adam, destroyed completely by the Death of Christ! O happy fault that earned for us so great, so glorious a Redeemer!

These words are from the *Exsultet* (meaning 'rejoice'), the Easter proclamation, which expresses the exuberant joy at the resurrection of Christ. Good Friday is over, and the light has returned. The broken world is healed by the voluntary sacrifice of God become man. Even in the darkest night, there is hope. Hope rises like a flame, conquering the shadows of death and despair. This is the thought that dominates the liturgical ceremonies of Easter. It is the most important feast of the church calendar, the feast without which none of the other feasts would exist. Without it, none of the other practices of the Christian faith would make sense. This is the night of Christ's resurrection, the night when life rises from the grave triumphant. After the abyss of horror and despair of the crucifixion, explored to its very depths by the poetry and music of the Triduum, comes a new day. Christ's tomb is empty. The light of new life radiates from the symbolism of the liturgy. We have already caught a glimpse of this symbolism in the scene that opened this book: the new fire is lit, blessed and carried into the pitch-black church. Each member of the congregation carries a taper, and as the candles are successively lighted, the church is gradually illuminated, a visible sign of the return of life after the darkness of the tomb, and the joy of those who are redeemed. Joy is central to the Easter liturgy. Joy shines through every word, every movement, every gesture. Joy particularly speaks through the *Exsultet*, which is perhaps the most intensely poetic hymn of the entire liturgical year. Its imagery is particularly rich, combining typological references to the Old Testament and complex theological ideas with a tender consideration of seemingly small and insignificant things, such as the bees that produced the wax of the great Easter candle. The great and the small things of heaven and earth meet in this triumphant hymn of praise, which presents its ideas like a kaleidoscope of images. It is a hymn that invokes all senses, an effect that in the Middle Ages was often heightened by the use of colourful illustrations on the *Exsultet* scrolls that the people were able to glimpse, along with the smell of incense and the touch of the wax tapers held by all. The moving power of the *Exsultet* becomes particularly clear in performance. Given here are both the Latin original and an English translation, which are best read while listening to a recording of the hymn as it is sung.

Exsultet iam angelica turba caelorum: exsultent divina mysteria: et pro tanti Regis victoria tuba insonet salutaris.	Exult, let them exult, the hosts of heaven, exult, let Angel ministers of God exult, let the trumpet of salvation sound aloud our mighty King's triumph!
Gaudeat et tellus, tantis irradiata fulgoribus: et aeterni Regis splendore illustrata, totius orbis se sentiat amisisse caliginem.	Be glad, let earth be glad, as glory floods her, ablaze with light from her eternal King, let all corners of the earth be glad, knowing an end to gloom and darkness.
Laetetur et mater Ecclesia, tanti luminis adornata fulgoribus: et magnis populorum vocibus haec aula resultet.	Rejoice, let Mother Church also rejoice, arrayed with the lightning of his glory, let this holy building shake with joy,

	filled with the mighty voices of the peoples.
Quapropter adstantes vos, fratres carissimi, ad tam miram huius sancti luminis claritatem, una mecum, quaeso, Dei omnipotentis misericordiam invocate. Ut, qui me non meis meritis intra Levitarum numerum dignatus est aggregare, luminis sui claritatem infundens, cerei huius laudem implere perficiat. Per Dominum nostrum Iesum Christum Filium suum qui cum eo vivit et regnat in unitate Spiritus Sancti Deus, per omnia saecula saeculorum.	Therefore, dearest friends, standing in the awesome glory of this holy light, invoke with me, I ask you, the mercy of God almighty, that he, who has been pleased to number me, though unworthy, among the Levites, may pour into me his light unshadowed, that I may sing this candle's perfect praises. Through our Lord Jesus Christ His Son, who with Him and the Holy Ghost lives and reigns, one God for ever and ever.
R. Amen.	Amen.
V. Dominus vobiscum.	Deacon: The Lord be with you.
R. Et cum spiritu tuo.	People: And with your spirit.
V. Sursum corda.	Deacon: Lift up your hearts.
R. Habemus ad Dominum.	People: We lift them up to the Lord.
V. Gratias agamus Domino Deo nostro.	Deacon: Let us give thanks to the Lord our God.
R. Dignum et iustum est.	People: It is right and just.
Vere dignum et iustum est, invisibilem Deum Patrem omnipotentem, Filiumque	It is truly right and just, with ardent love of mind and heart and with devoted service of

eius unigenitum, Dominum nostrum Iesum Christum, toto cordis ac mentis affectu, et vocis ministerio personare.

our voice, to acclaim our God invisible, the almighty Father, and Jesus Christ, our Lord, his Son, his only begotten.

Qui pro nobis aeterno Patri Adae debitum solvit, et veteris piaculi cautionem pio cruore detersit.

Who for our sake paid Adam's debt to the eternal Father, and, pouring out his own dear blood, wiped clean the record of our ancient sinfulness.

Haec sunt enim festa paschalia, in quibus verus ille Agnus occiditur, cuius sanguine postes fidelium consecrantur.

These, then, are the feasts of Passover, in which is slain the Lamb, the one true Lamb, whose blood anoints the doorposts of believers.

Haec nox est, in qua primum patres nostros, filios Israel eductos de Ægypto, Mare Rubrum sicco vestigio transire fecisti.
Haec igitur nox est, quae peccatorum tenebras columnae illuminatione purgavit.
Haec nox est, quae hodie per universum mundum in Christo credentes, a vitiis saeculi et caligine peccatorum segregatos, reddit gratiae, sociat sanctitati.

This is the night when once you led our forebears, Israel's children, from slavery in Egypt and made them pass dry-shod through the Red Sea.
This is the night that with a pillar of fire banished the darkness of sin.
This is the night that even now throughout the world, sets Christian believers apart from worldly vices and from the gloom of sin, leading them to grace and joining them to his holy ones.

Haec nox est, in qua, destructis vinculis mortis, Christus ab inferis victor ascendit.	This is the night when Christ broke the prison bars of death and rose victorious from the underworld.
Nihil enim nobis nasci profuit, nisi redimi profuisset.	Our birth would have been no gain, had we not been redeemed.
O mira circa nos tuae pietatis dignatio! O inaestimabilis dilectio caritatis: ut servum redimeres, Filium tradidisti! O certe necessarium Adae peccatum, quod Christi morte deletum est! O felix culpa, quae talem ac tantum meruit habere Redemptorem! O vere beata nox, quae sola meruit scire tempus et horam, in qua Christus ab inferis resurrexit!	O wonder of your humble care for us! O love, O charity beyond all telling, to ransom a slave you gave away your Son! O truly necessary sin of Adam, destroyed completely by the Death of Christ! O happy fault that earned for us so great, so glorious a Redeemer! O truly blessed night, worthy alone to know the time and hour when Christ rose from the underworld!
Haec nox est, de qua scriptum est: Et nox sicut dies illuminabitur: et nox illuminatio mea in deliciis meis.	This is the night of which it is written: The night shall be as bright as day, dazzling is the night for me, and full of gladness.
Huius igitur sanctificatio noctis fugat scelera, culpas lavat: et	The sanctifying power of this night dispels wickedness, washes faults

reddit innocentiam lapsis et maestis laetitiam.
Fugat odia, concordiam parat, et curvat imperia.

away, restores innocence to the fallen, and joy to mourners, drives out hatred, fosters concord, and brings down the mighty.

In huius igitur noctis gratia, suscipe, sancte Pater, laudis huius sacrificium vespertinum, quod tibi in hac cerei oblatione solemni, per ministrorum manus de operibus apum, sacrosancta reddit Ecclesia.
Sed iam columnae huius praeconia novimus, quam in honorem Dei rutilans ignis accendit.
Qui, licet sit divisus in partes, mutuati tamen luminis detrimenta non novit.
Alitur enim liquantibus ceris, quas in substantiam pretiosae huius lampadis apis mater eduxit.
O vere beata nox, quae expoliavit Ægyptios, ditavit Hebraeos! Nox in qua terrenis caelestia, humanis divina iunguntur!

On this, your night of grace,
O holy Father, accept this candle, a solemn offering, the work of bees and of your servants' hands, an evening sacrifice of praise, this gift from your most holy Church.
But now we know the praises of this pillar, which glowing fire ignites for God's honour,
a fire into many flames divided,
yet never dimmed by sharing of its light,
for it is fed by melting wax, drawn out by mother bees to build a torch so precious.
O truly blessed night, which spoiled the Egyptians and made rich the Hebrews! Night in which things of heaven are wed to those of earth, and divine to the human.

Oramus ergo te, Domine, ut cereus iste in honorem tui nominis consecratus, ad noctis huius caliginem destruendam, indeficiens perseveret.

Therefore, O Lord, we pray you that this candle, hallowed to the honour of your name, may persevere undimmed, to overcome the darkness of this night.

Et in odorem suavitatis acceptus, supernis luminaribus misceatur.	Receive it as a pleasing fragrance, and let it mingle with the lights of heaven.
Flammas eius lucifer matutinus inveniat. Ille, inquam, lucifer, qui nescit occasum. Ille, qui regressus ab inferis, humano generi serenus illuxit.	May this flame be found still burning by the Morning Star: the one Morning Star who never sets, Christ your Son, who, coming back from death's domain, has shed his peaceful light on humanity.[1]

The words are rich and evocative. The *Exsultet* is a truly ancient part of the liturgy, going back to the fourth or early fifth century AD. Throughout the Middle Ages there was local variation between different versions of the text and the melody to which it was sung, before it became more standardized. Today it is often sung in the vernacular rather than Latin, but the essence of its ideas and imagery has remained stable over different centuries and in different places. The imagery of light illuminating the darkness and lifting the shadows of death is a central theme throughout the hymn. Christ is the bringer of light to a world in darkness, which is suddenly set 'ablaze with light from her eternal King'. Christ is hailed as 'the one Morning Star who never sets . . . who, coming back from death's domain, has shed his peaceful light on humanity'. With its emphasis on light dispelling the darkness, the hymn echoes the sensory experiences by which the congregation is surrounded in the liturgical celebration. The text makes reference to the dramaturgy of the liturgy as the light of the Easter candle is shared by the tapers of the faithful, 'a fire into many flames divided, yet never dimmed by sharing of its light'. The words reflect the ritual, and the ritual reflects the words.[2] The hymn is loosely structured by the recurring phrase 'This is the night', which exalts the

Easter vigil as a moment long foretold and central to human history. It uses typological readings of key events of the Old Testament, such as the exodus from slavery in Egypt and God leading the Israelites through the desert with a pillar of fire, as prophecies of the redemption through Christ. These promises are all fulfilled in this one night when Christ rises from the tomb. We encounter, as in so many other liturgical texts, an understanding of the Christian celebration as a continuation and fulfilment of the history of the people of Israel, who are described as 'our forebears'. It is striking, too, that the text describes the resurrection as an event not of the past but of the present: 'This is the night', rather than 'That was the night'. In the liturgical celebration, the past becomes the present. We are not merely commemorating a past event but participating in it through the ritual because of its everlasting significance for every individual person. All of humankind is redeemed, including each member of the present congregation. This historical event, which happened many centuries ago in the Middle East, is still relevant, still present, still celebrated through the liturgical ritual: 'This is the night when Christ broke the prison-bars of death and rose victorious from the underworld.'

The understanding of time implied by these words is different from the kind of chronological reckoning of time that we encounter in everyday life. The logic of the text is not based on a progression from hour to hour, year to year, century to century, but rests on a type of thinking that sees time as relative, expressed as a series of relationships between the past and the present, prophecy and fulfilment. This fulfilment in the form of the redemption is so central to human history that it is not bound by the normal daily progression of time; it is continually present, and can be repeatedly made present in the liturgy. On a poetic level, however, these ideas create a rich web of resonances, by which the pillar of fire in the desert becomes a mirror of the lighted Easter candle in front of the congregation's eyes. Everything is interconnected: words, objects and present experience are linked.

The section framed by the repetition of 'This is the night' then shifts to a different mode of expression. Typological references give way to repeated exclamations that express wonder at the abundant love of God for humankind: 'O love, O charity beyond all telling, to ransom a slave you gave away your Son!' This is followed by what is certainly the most controversial idea in the entire hymn: 'O truly necessary sin of Adam, destroyed completely by the Death of Christ! O happy fault that earned for us so great, so glorious a Redeemer!' This is an idea often referred to by its Latin term, *O felix culpa* ('O happy fault'). Embedded as it is in this richly poetic hymn of praise, it is easy to miss just how radical this thought is. The Christian faith rests upon the idea that humankind is fallen, that the world is broken, that things are not as they should be, as expressed in the story of Adam and Eve's expulsion from Paradise. Equally foundational is the idea that in order to repair what has been broken and heal humankind from the consequences of the Fall, Christ became incarnate and died as a willing sacrifice. The *felix culpa* motif turns this narrative upside down: Adam's sin was necessary, it was even a 'happy' event, as it brought about such an inestimably wonderful thing as the incarnation of God himself. Within a Christian framework, to describe the Fall as necessary and fortunate could hardly be more provocative. Indeed it has been controversially debated by theologians through the ages, and has sometimes been excised from the hymn in different churches and traditions, particularly by Protestant reformers who took exception to the idea. Yet the early liturgy boldly makes this claim. The idea is rooted in the writings of the Church fathers, such as St Ambrose and St Augustine, who writes that 'God judged it better to bring good out of evil than not to permit any evil to exist.'[3] The *felix culpa* idea stretches paradox to its limits with its underlying logic that the unexpectedly fortunate outcome of an unfortunate event would not exist, had the unfortunate event not occurred in the first place. By this logic, the unfortunate event itself is redefined as something positive. The 'necessary sin of

Adam' is an idea so radical and paradoxical that it is perhaps only palatable in the liturgical context in which it occurs, accompanied by rich symbolism, and presented not as a sermon but as a poetic song.

Despite, or perhaps because of, the unexpected and provocative nature of this idea, it quickly became part of the fabric of Western thinking about the Fall. We see the motif reflected in a range of medieval texts, such as the carol 'Adam lay y-bounden', which is still sung in church services in the English choral tradition today. Here is a slightly modernized version:

> Adam lay ybounden, bounden in a bond;
> Four thousand winter thought he not too long.
> And all was for an apple, an apple that he took,
> As clerkes finden written in their book.
>
> Nor had the apple taken been, the apple taken been,
> Then had never Our Lady a-been heaven's queen.
> Blessed be the time that apple taken was!
> Therefore we may singen, *Deo gratias*![4] [= 'Thanks be to God']

The carol refers to the Fall as the taking of an apple, a somewhat more tangible version of Genesis, where Adam and Eve eat of the forbidden fruit of the Tree of Knowledge. Adam is described as being 'bounden in a bond' for 'four thousand winter' – according to medieval views, the length of time that was believed to have elapsed between the expulsion from Paradise and the redemption through Christ. Adam's punishment for the taking of the apple ends with the salvation of the world, and hope is restored. In the middle of the carol, after the first two stanzas, there is an abrupt shift: what has previously been alluded to in negative terms suddenly turns into something positive. If the apple had not been taken, if the Fall had not happened, the great mystery of the incarnation would also not have happened. Mary would never have become the mother of God and queen of heaven. Based on this shift of perspective, which looks at the positive outcome of a negative event, the final stanza then paradoxically praises the Fall and declares that the taking of the apple was a 'blessed' event. This poetic text very clearly echoes the *felix culpa* of the liturgy. It is deliberately designed to turn upside down our ideas of what it means to define something as good or bad. The redemption through God's own son is unexpected, shocking, unhoped-for; it stands outside our usual frames of reference, and the texts emphasize this with ideas that are meant to startle and provoke.

The *felix culpa* motif had a long afterlife. John Milton (1608–1674) refers to the same idea in *Paradise Lost*, where Adam praises the goodness of God with the following words:

> Oh goodness infinite, goodness immense!
> That all this good of evil shall produce,
> And evil turn to good; more wonderful
> Than that which by creation first brought forth
> Light out of darkness! Full of doubt I stand,
> Whether I should repent me now of sin
> By me done, and occasioned; or rejoice
> Much more, that much more good thereof shall spring;
> To God more glory, more good will to men
> From God, and over wrath grace shall abound.[5]

In *Paradise Lost* the *felix culpa* paradox leaves Adam personally conflicted. He is unsure whether he should repent of his sin – the reaction which we would see as appropriate under normal circumstances – or in fact do the opposite and rejoice that his sin has brought about an even greater good: 'over wrath grace shall abound'. There is no easy answer to Adam's conundrum. The problem is not one of logic, but one of perspective and timescales:[6] only in hindsight does it become clear whether an unfortunate event has led to fortunate consequences. Milton's Adam is both within and outside of time. He speaks with the knowledge of the coming of Christ, knowledge which stands outside of the timeline of normal earthly chronology, which contends with the perspective of the supposed historical Adam who does not have the knowledge that his Fall will have a good outcome. The historical Adam wants to repent of his sin as he sees its negative outcomes, while the Adam with foreknowledge of the redemption wants to rejoice. Temporal and eternal perspectives are not easily reconciled. A thing can both be bad and turn out to be good in hindsight, depending on one's point of view. As the liturgy indicates, believers have to hold both of these aspects in balance and accept the paradox. The Fall is both unfortunate and, through God's unexpected intervention, the most fortunate thing that has ever happened.

The use of the motif was not restricted to religious contexts and narratives of the Fall and redemption; we also find it, for instance, as a literary motif in an Arthurian romance of the fourteenth century entitled *Sir Gawain and the Green Knight*. The plot of the story is complex, but at its core it revolves around the redefinition of a sign of failure as a sign of victory. Sir Gawain, the hero of the story, is sent on a quest to find the mysterious and monstrous Green Knight at the Green Chapel. In order to keep his honour, Gawain must accept a blow to the neck with the Green Knight's axe. Gawain tries to live up to the challenge, but in fear of his life accepts the gift of a green girdle said to protect the life of whoever wears it. Although he had initially promised to surrender the gift, Gawain secretly keeps the girdle for himself. When he meets the Green Knight, his courage is tested and his life is spared. Gawain has proved himself a worthy knight, but with a single fault: he has not surrendered the green girdle. Gawain returns to King Arthur's court wearing the green girdle around his arm as a sign of his shame at his failure to keep his promise. Happy to see Gawain alive, the knights of the round table absolve him from all blame, and collectively start to wear green girdles on their arms in recognition of Gawain's quest. In this way an unfortunate event – Gawain's failure to live up to his word – is redefined as a token of honour worn by all of King Arthur's knights. Gawain's fault has become a happy fault. The implications of the motif in *Sir Gawain and the Green Knight* are less universal and far-reaching than that of the redemption of humankind, but the same idea of the *felix culpa* echoes through the story.

We also find the idea of the Fortunate Fall expressed in visual art from the Middle Ages and beyond. Medieval representations of the Fall frequently include references to the crucifixion, or juxtapose the two images in a way that makes clear that Christ's sacrifice atones for Adam's Fall. For instance, in the south rose window at Lyon Cathedral, the expulsion from Paradise and the crucifixion are depicted on opposite sides, paralleling and balancing each other in the structure of the window. The parallel between the two scenes was emphasized by the fact that both the Fall and the redemption of humankind came from a tree: the Tree of Knowledge in Eden and the wood of the cross, respectively. The medieval imagination was much preoccupied by this parallel, giving birth to a number of legends that connected the wood of the cross quite literally with the tree of Paradise, whose fruit prompted the Fall. The Holy Cross legend weaves these connections into a story in which Adam's son is given a seed from the tree of Paradise and plants it in his father's grave. From this seed grows a young tree which, after many centuries, is cut down and eventually becomes the cross of Christ. The legend was extremely popular in the medieval period. It seems that a story that created a connection between the two trees, which was palpable rather than merely metaphorical, touched a nerve.

A late heir to this tradition is a stained-glass window at Saint Meinrad Archabbey in Indiana, produced at the beginning of the twentieth century (illus. 15). In the lower half we see Adam and Eve being banished from Paradise. The serpent is curling around the

15 Crucifixion and Adam and Eve, stained glass,
Saint Meinrad Archabbey, Indiana.

trunk of a tree, which appears like a traditional representation of the Tree of Knowledge if we look at the image in isolation. If we look at the upper part of the window, however, the tree grows into the tree of the cross on which Christ is suspended. The expulsion and the crucifixion scene are intimately connected; the tree from which came the Fall grows to be the tree on which humankind is redeemed. Out of death comes life. O happy fault!

The Easter liturgy may abound in joyful paradoxes, but it also teems with other exuberant expressions of joy. Certainly the most memorable and widely known of these is the exclamation 'Alleluia', which also occurs in the spelling 'Hallelujah'. Today the word is used in everyday contexts that often have nothing to do with religion, but still express joy or relief: 'I made it to the meeting on time, hallelujah!' Originally, though, the word was a loan from Hebrew, expressing praise of God in psalms and prayers. It literally means 'praise God', composed of the Hebrew words *hallēl* 'to praise' and *yāh*, a shortened form of the Hebrew holy name of God, Yahweh. The spelling 'Alleluia' mirrors the Greek form, which was also adopted into Latin. Along with 'Amen', it is one of the few Hebrew words taken over untranslated in most biblical translations and in both Latin and Greek liturgies. It is a word familiar to all branches of Christianity, regardless of whether services are celebrated in Latin, Greek, English, Spanish, Vietnamese or any other language. Biblical translators clearly felt that the Hebrew version of the word carried a power or expressed a feeling that a translation simply could not match. The word is melodic and beautiful, including a range of different vowels connected by the consonant 'l', which gives it a flowing sound, almost like water. It is a uniquely singable word in the way in which it rolls off the tongue. Perhaps this is why it was felt to be such an appropriate word of praise. In the Bible the word occurs primarily in the psalms, at the beginning or conclusion of psalms of praise as a kind of acclamation giving glory to God. The word is included in Jewish worship, in a prayer known as *Hallel*, where six psalms of praise are recited at specific feast days, including Passover. Outside of the psalms, Alleluia is a relatively rare word in the Bible. Nonetheless, it is a regular and constant feature of Christian liturgies. As an expression of exuberant joy, Alleluia is associated first and foremost with the celebration of Easter. In the Western liturgical tradition this is particularly marked as the Alleluia is not sung during Lent, the period preceding Easter, only to return triumphantly in the celebration of the resurrection of the saviour. St Augustine explained the significance of the absent Alleluia as follows:

> The season before Easter signifies the tribulations in which we live now, while the time after Easter which we are celebrating at present signifies our happiness in the future . . . This is why we dedicate the first season to fasting and prayer, but now the fast is over and we devote the present season to praise. This is the meaning of the Alleluia we sing.[7]

Lent is a sombre period of fasting and penance, and this fasting is metaphorically echoed in liturgical practice: the church is fasting from the Alleluia. In medieval France various customs arose to make this absence of the Alleluia more tangible. In some places the Alleluia was physically buried in a solemn ceremony at the start of Lent. A hole was dug in the parish garden for a banner or wooden board on which was written the word 'Alleluia', only to be retrieved at Easter. This was not an official church service and the clergy did not officiate. Rather it was the choirboys who took the lead in the burial of the Alleluia, as a fifteenth-century statue book from a church at Toul reports:

> On Saturday before Septuagesima Sunday all choir boys gather in the sacristy during the prayer of the None, to prepare for the burial of the Alleluia. After the last *Benedicamus* [i.e., at the end of the service] they march in procession, with crosses, tapers, holy water and censers; and they carry a coffin, as in a funeral. Thus

> they proceed through the aisle, moaning and mourning, until they reach the cloister. There they bury the coffin; they sprinkle it with holy water and incense it; whereupon they return to the sacristy by the same way.[8]

At the paschal celebration of the resurrection of Christ, the Alleluia was also resurrected, both in physical form in the parish garden and as part of liturgical singing.

The Alleluia appears in the music of the liturgy in many different shapes and forms, with a rich tradition of different chant settings that express the joy of Easter with elaborate melodies. Composers of sacred music through the ages continually came up with new and different ways to voice the joyous character of the Alleluia. The musical form in which the word is probably most widely known today, however, is Handel's setting of the Hallelujah Chorus. Although it was originally written as part of the oratorio *Messiah*, the chorus has become a famous stand-alone piece, used in a wide range of contexts from religious services to adverts and television series such as *South Park* and *The Simpsons*. It is a uniquely memorable and moving piece, and audiences around the world often express their love for it by rising to their feet whenever it is performed. Handel's piece takes its cue from the Book of Revelation, the final book of the New Testament. The Alleluia here occurs in the context of a mystical vision of worship in a renewed heaven, where God is praised with the words 'Alleluia: for the Lord God omnipotent reigneth' (19:6). The word 'Hallelujah' occurs as a memorable, short motif at the beginning and throughout the chorus. Charles Jennens, Handel's librettist, adds to the quotation from the Book of Revelation the lines 'The kingdom of this world is become the kingdom of our Lord and of his Christ, and he shall reign for ever and ever' (11:15). This text is interspersed with repeated exclamations of 'Hallelujah'. Perhaps the most exciting part of the piece occurs towards the end, when the final acclamation 'King of Kings and Lord of Lords' is repeated at an increasingly higher pitch by the sopranos, accompanied by trumpets, raising musical tension until it culminates in a final *Hallelujah* chord as a triumphant, solemn praise of God. It is hardly surprising that many people feel so moved by this piece that they cannot stay in their seats.

The Alleluia has stirred not only concert hall audiences, but entire armies. The Venerable Bede, in his seventh-century historical account of the early years of the Christian Church in Britain, tells the story of the 'Alleluia Victory'. It recounts how in the year AD 430, Briton villagers on the Welsh borders were subject to attacks by the pagan tribes of the Picts and Saxons. Just after Easter, when many members of the army of the Britons had been newly baptized, they learnt that a great host of the Picts and Saxons was travelling towards them, preparing for a violent attack. A Christian bishop named Germanus offered to lead the Britons into battle. Germanus decided to waylay their foes in a narrow valley encompassed by hills, and instructed his army to repeat the words that he would speak, and shout them at the top of their voices. Bede writes:

> as the enemy approached confidently, believing that their coming was unexpected, the bishops shouted 'Alleluia' three times. A universal shout of 'Alleluia' followed, and the echoes from the surrounding hills multiplied and increased the sound. The enemy forces were smitten with dread, fearing that not only the surrounding rocks but even the very frame of heaven itself would fall upon them.

In blind panic, the enemy host took flight and was caught in a nearby river, where many men drowned. The Britons celebrated their unexpected victory, which had been accomplished without shedding of blood.[9] According to the belief of the early Christians in the British Isles, the victory of the risen Christ over sin and death could also give them victory over their pagan enemies – sometimes simply by shouting 'Alleluia'.

7
Death

Somewhere in medieval Europe, in some remote monastery on a cold winter's evening, a monk sitting in his lonely cell decided what death sounds like. He was trying to set a poem to music, a poem to describe the horror, grief and destruction of the Day of Doom in the most evocative language. The poem was gripping, but the music the monk invented was what made it truly haunting. It contained a simple, distinctive tune of just a few descending notes, in a key that sounded hollow and ominous. The tune of death was a stroke of genius. We will never know who the monk was, but his music has survived. It was passed down the ages, first from monastery to monastery, and later picked up by composers writing for general entertainment rather than religious purposes. Whenever they wanted to create a haunting atmosphere of danger, death and despair, this was their favourite tune to use, and it never failed to cast its spell. You can even find it in films today. Were you gripped by the spine-chilling music in Peter Jackson's *The Return of the King* (2003) that plays when the armies of Mordor march forth against Gondor? Or by the music in *Jaws* (1975, dir. Steven Spielberg) when the shark is closing in on its intended victims? Or by the terrifying march that accompanies the Huns' attack in Disney's animated film *Mulan* (1998)? What they all have in common is the same threatening tune that aurally convinces us that something dangerous and sinister is afoot. We are listening to the musical shorthand for death.

Much is unclear about the history of this music. We will probably never know whether it really was one monk in his solitary cell who wrote it, as the tune may have been the product of the creative efforts of several people, perhaps over many years. But what matters more than the historical circumstances under which the music was created is the fact that it survived many centuries and, in Western culture, became almost synonymous with ideas of death and destruction. It is commonly referred to as the musical motif of *Dies irae*, named after the poem that inspired the music. It still is the most frequently invoked motif in all of Western music, and often appears in film scores with grand orchestral settings, in operas and oratorios involving large choirs, with a volume and acoustic force that is not easily forgotten by the audience. The origins of the music, however, are more humble, and start, as all liturgical singing, with plainchant and a simple musical motif, which was to become the defining tune of death.

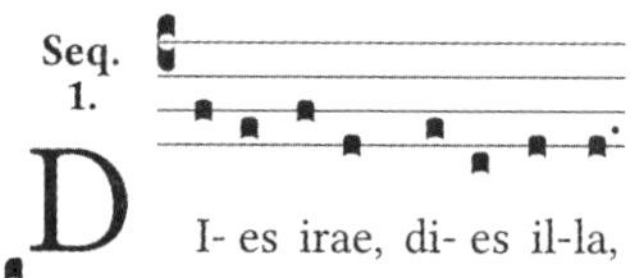

But what was the text that inspired this music and was to become so profoundly influential in expressing a feeling of impending doom and destruction? The Latin poem starting with the words *Dies irae* ('day of wrath') is a text full of astonishing imagery describing the Day of Doom. It features trumpets, dead bodies rising from their graves and a fearsome judge. The ideas are traditional, taking inspiration from the Bible and established Christian beliefs, but nowhere do they find a more powerful expression than in this poem. The text is both gripping in its content and masterful in its form, switching between a descriptive and an intensely personal perspective. It is hardly surprising that this poem would exert a virtually unending fascination on artists for centuries to come.

The poem is most frequently attributed to Thomas of Celano, a thirteenth-century Italian friar. Friars were members of a mendicant religious order: having taken vows of poverty, chastity and obedience, they lived itinerant lives of preaching and apostolic mission in service of the community. This meant that friars were closely connected with the concerns of laypeople, and in the Middle Ages became a driving force in literary activity, particularly in the writing of poetry. Thomas of Celano was a friend and biographer of St Francis, the famous Italian saint after whom the Franciscans are named. A friar as the author of *Dies irae* would certainly be plausible, but other figures have been put forward as potential authors of the poem, including St Bernard of Clairvaux (d. 1153) and St Bonaventure (d. 1274). The number of potential authors who have been named is testimony to the enduring power of the poem, which gave rise to a curiosity about its origins.

To understand the poem in its context and fully appreciate its imaginative power, we have to be aware of Christian views of the afterlife. Like all religions, the Christian faith has a set of beliefs regarding death, including specific ideas about a judgement that awaits the deceased. The Christian idea of judgement after death has two aspects: one is a particular judgement of each person after death, the other is a general judgement at the end of time. Christianity inherits ideas about God's judgement of mankind at the end of the world and the coming resurrection of the dead from the Jewish tradition, although Jewish apocalyptic literature contains a wide divergence of views on this event. Filtered and reinterpreted through a Christian lens, these ideas take on a particular form in the later Christian tradition, particularly during the Middle Ages. Some aspects of these ideas tend to be emphasized more or less in different periods, but their essence has remained stable over the course of many centuries. At its core, Christianity believes in a judgement after death, in which each individual person will be judged by God according to their good and bad actions in life. If the good outweighs the bad, the soul will be rewarded with eternal life in heaven, but evil actions will be punished by eternal death in hell. We are familiar with traditional representations of heaven and hell in art by images of light, sun, clouds, pointing towards a realm of beauty above, in opposition to darkness, terror and fire in a devil-swarmed realm below. In a more abstract theological sense, heaven is understood as the presence of God, who is life, truth, goodness and beauty, whereas hell is eternal separation from God, and by extension the absence of those positive qualities in a realm of death, lies, horror and evil.

This particular judgement awaits each individual soul immediately after their physical death. Even though the outcome of this judgement is heaven or hell eternal, according to the medieval understanding (which is later continued by the Catholic Church) there is a recognition that people are neither straightforwardly saintly nor purely evil, but that in most people's lives good deeds and bad actions are intermingled. Many good people die in a state in which they are too imperfect to enter into the presence of God directly. This intermediate state is represented by the idea of purgatory as a state of purification, which a soul has to undergo after death before it is admitted to heaven, provided that the good actions during a person's life outweigh the bad ones. The outcome of this particular judgement, then, may be the commitment of a soul to purgatory for a certain period of time according to the gravity of the person's faults, until it has been cleansed of its wrong inclinations and deeds. According to the medieval understanding, later contested by Protestant reformers, the progress of a soul through purgatory can be helped and expedited by the living through their prayers for the dead.

This individual judgement is distinct from the idea of a general judgement awaiting all of humankind at the end of time at the Day of Judgement, also frequently referred to as the Last Judgement, the Day of Wrath and the Day of Doom. Once the history of earth has run its course, Christ will come again in glory, the dead will be resurrected and given back their bodies, to stand before the judge on the day of universal judgement. The idea is based upon a number of biblical verses, in particular those in Revelation, in which the prophetic voice speaks of the future judgement:

> And I saw a great white throne, and him that sat on it, from whose face the earth and the heaven fled away; and there was found no place for them. And I saw the dead, small and great, stand before God; and the books were opened: and another book was opened, which is the book of life: and the dead were judged out of those things which were written in the books, according to their works. And the sea gave up the dead which were in it; and death and hell delivered up the dead which were in them: and they were judged every man according to their works. And death and hell were cast into the lake of fire. This is the second death. And whosoever was not found written in the book of life was cast into the lake of fire. (Rev. 20:11–15)

The passage emphasizes the strict separation between those who have done good works and those who will be cast into the 'lake of fire'. Particularly striking here is the image of good and bad works being recorded in books that are brought forth as evidence at the trial, an idea which was frequently echoed in representations of the Day of Judgement in art. There is a key difference between the concepts of universal judgement and particular judgement: at the end of time there will be no more purgatory, but the judgement will be a final and eternal division between those in heaven in the presence of God and those in hell suffering eternal separation from God. The ultimate hope of the Christian faith, then, is the expectation of salvation from the torments of hell in order to have eternal life in the fullness of God's glory. This expectation of the final things, the ultimate destiny of the individual soul and the whole created world – a set of ideas often referred to as 'eschatology' – shaped the imagination of the Christian West from the Middle Ages for many centuries, and is reflected in the art, literature and music of these periods. Perhaps the most famous artistic representation of the Last Judgement is Michelangelo's fresco in the Sistine Chapel in Rome, but the subject goes back far earlier to medieval times and the tradition of 'doom paintings', which display the Judgement on a large scale on church walls. The apocalyptic scene also frequently appears in medieval cathedrals as a tympanum carved above an entrance to the building, which is decorated with reliefs presenting to the viewer the Day of Judgement in all its awful detail. The central west portal at Bourges Cathedral, France, for instance, creates a striking narrative (illus. 16). Christ as judge is enthroned in the middle of the scene. The bottommost panel shows the dead rising from their graves, anticipation and dread written on their faces. Tombstones are upturned and lie scattered about. In the panel above the rising dead, an angel is weighing up the virtues and faults of humankind with a scale. Those deemed worthy of entering into heaven are congregated on Christ's right with blissful expressions on their faces, whereas the damned on the left are attacked by grimacing devils and at last thrown into the terrifying mouth of hell and engulfed by flames. The twisted bodies to Christ's left form a stark contrast to the serene figures of the blessed on his right. On the panel above, Christ is surrounded by angels holding instruments of the Passion, such as the cross, the nails and the crown of thorns (also known as the *arma Christi*, the 'weapons of Christ'). Implicit in the relief is a question for the viewer of this awe-inspiring scene: where will I stand on the Day of Judgement? Will I be called among the saved, or hounded by devils into the depths of hell? At the same time, the scene presents an answer to these questions: the only hope lies in taking refuge in the merits of the Passion of Christ and imploring God for mercy, as modelled by two kneeling figures in the corners of the central panel.

The quality of the scene is highly dramatic; the events of the Day of Judgement are narrated through images that are symbolic and at the same time shockingly vivid. The viewer on the steps of the portal,

16 Portal of the Last Judgement, Bourges Cathedral, *c.* 1195–1240.

about to enter the cathedral, receives a call to action, something akin to: 'Use well the time still left to you on earth, and pray for yourself and for others.' In this way, the present and the future become closely intertwined. The actions of today stand in a close relationship with the events at the end of time, as they determine the ultimate destination of each individual.

These connections between present and future, bound up with ideas of particular judgement and universal judgement at the end of time, make it easy to see why the idea of the Last Judgement took on a special role in the context of prayers for the dead. The medieval church placed an emphasis on prayers and devotions for the souls of the deceased so that they might be released from purgatory. In their ritualized, liturgical form, prayers for the dead occurred in particular in the Requiem Mass, the Mass said at funerals for the repose of the soul of a deceased, and repeated annually on All Souls' Day on 2 November. The texts of the Requiem Mass draw an impactful connection between the fate of the souls of the recently deceased and the coming universal judgement: while we pray for the dead, we are also reminded of our own death and the final realities we will have to face when the judge returns to weigh up our merits and failings. The liturgy encourages us to see an individual's death not just as an occasion for grief and prayers, but also as a memento mori for the living. A few centuries later, Metaphysical poet John Donne in his 1624 work *Devotions upon Emergent Occasions* wrote the famous words 'and therefore never send to know for whom the bell tolls; It tolls for thee.' Donne was a Protestant, but at its core the idea is a similar one: the fates of the living and the dead are closely intertwined.

Part of the Requiem Mass is the *Dies irae*, the most famous and long-lived poetic engagement with the theme of the Last Judgement. The poem picks up on many traditional motifs that we also encounter in the Bible and in medieval visual culture, but it does so in a uniquely impactful way.

1 Dies irae, dies illa
solvet saeclum in favilla,
teste David cum Sibylla.

A day of wrath; that day,
it will dissolve the world into glowing ashes,
as attested by David together with the Sibyl.

2 Quantus tremor est futurus,
quando iudex est venturus,
cuncta stricte discussurus.

What trembling will there be,
when the Judge shall come
to examine everything in strict justice.

3 Tuba mirum spargens sonum,
per sepulchra regionum,
coget omnes ante thronum.

The trumpet's wondrous call sounding abroad
in tombs throughout the world
shall drive everybody forward to the throne.

4 Mors stupebit et natura,
cum resurget creatura,
iudicanti responsura.

Death and nature shall stand amazed
when creation rises again
to give answer to its Judge.

5 Liber scriptus proferetur
in quo totum continetur,
unde mundus iudicetur.

A written book will be brought forth
in which everything is contained
from which the world shall be judged.

6 Iudex ergo cum sedebit,
quidquid latet, apparebit;
nil inultum remanebit.

So when the Judge is seated,
whatever is hidden will be made known:
nothing shall go unpunished.

7 Quid sum miser tunc dicturus?
Quem patronum rogaturus,
cum vix iustus sit securus?

What shall I, wretch, say at that time?
What advocate shall I entreat (to plead for me)
when scarcely the righteous shall be safe from damnation?

8 Rex tremendae maiestatis,
qui salvandos salvas gratis,
salva me, fons pietatis.

King of awesome majesty,
who grants salvation to those that are to be saved,
save me, o fount of piety.

9 Recordare, Iesu pie,
quod sum causa tuae viae:
ne me perdas illa die.

Remember, dear Jesus,
that I am the reason for your journey:
do not cast me away on that day.

10 Quaerens me, sedisti lassus:
redemisti crucem passus:
tantus labor non sit cassus.

Seeking me, you sat down weary,
You have redeemed me, suffering
the death on the cross:
let not such toil have been
in vain.

11 Iuste Iudex ultionis,
donum fac remissionis
ante diem rationis.

Just Judge of vengeance,
grant me the gift of pardon
before the day of reckoning.

12 Ingemisco tamquam reus:
culpa rubet vultus meus:
supplicanti parce, Deus.

I groan like one condemned:
my face blushes for my sins:
spare a supplicant, o God.

13 Qui Mariam absolvisti,
et latronem exaudisti,
mihi quoque spem dedisti.

You who absolved Mary,
and heard the robber,
gave hope to me as well.

14 Preces meae non sunt
dignae:
sed tu bonus fac benigne,
ne perenni cremer igne.

My prayers are not worthy:
but you, of your goodness, deal
generously with me,
that I burn not in the everlasting
flame.

15 Inter oves locum praesta,
et ab haedis me sequestra,
statuens in parte dextra.

Give me a place among the
sheep,
and separate me from the goats,
setting me on your right hand.

16 Confutatis maledictis,
flammis acribus addictis:
voca me cum benedictis.

When the accursed have been
confounded
and sentenced to acrid flames,
call me along with the blessed.

17 Oro supplex et acclinis cor contritum quasi cinis, gere curam mei finis.	I prostrate myself, supplicating, my heart in ashes, repentant; take good care of my last moment!
18 Lacrymosa dies illa qua resurget ex favilla iudicandus homo reus. Huic ergo parce, Deus: Pie Iesu Domine, dona eis requiem. Amen.	That day will be one of weeping on which shall rise again from the embers the guilty man, to be judged. Therefore spare him, O God. Merciful Lord Jesus, grant them rest. Amen.[1]

The poem is one of the finest examples of Latin liturgical poetry. The Latin text is arranged into stanzas of three eight-syllable lines rhyming aaa, bbb, ccc and so on, which is lost in the English translation. This regular pattern changes only towards the end of the poem, in stanza 18, which switches from triple rhymes to rhymed couplets. This has been seen as an indicator that the final stanza may originally have been a different, separate poem, which was appended to *Dies irae* at an early stage. However the poem came to exist in its current form, this is the version that has become widely known through its inclusion in the liturgy.

The poem dramatically imagines the events of the Last Judgement. The first stanza draws the reader in immediately: the approaching dreadful day is a 'day of wrath'. The destruction of the world by fire and its dissolution into ashes is foretold by the two authoritative prophetic voices of David and the Sybil. We have already encountered David in Chapter One as the putative author of the psalms. The psalms contain multiple references to the day of God's wrath, as in Psalm 110:5: 'The Lord at thy right hand shall strike through kings in the day of his wrath.' The reference to the Sibyl, here mentioned as the second credible witness, is somewhat more cryptic. It is not entirely clear to whom exactly the name refers, but the most common interpretation sees her name as a reference to the pagan oracles. Sibyls were virginal prophetesses who prophesied at holy sites in ancient Greece, the most famous of which was Delphi. The reference to a pagan prophetess in this context is likely prompted by visual traditions in Christian art since the thirteenth century, which tended to represent the Sibyls alongside Old Testament prophets. A late example of this tradition can be found in Michelangelo's frescoes in the Sistine Chapel. The implication of this verbal juxtaposition of a Jewish prophet and a pagan oracle is clear: the coming of the Last Judgement is a fact universally acknowledged by both Judaeo-Christian and pagan sources of the ancient world. Nobody can claim ignorance of the coming Day of Wrath.

Stanzas 2–6 turn to a description of the Day of Doom in all its terrible detail. All creatures tremble in anticipation of the coming judgement. Summoned from their graves by a trumpet, the dead rise to stand before God's throne and face their creator. All that was hidden will be brought out into the open, and a book will be brought forth that contains an account of every good and evil work which has ever been done. The striking images in these lines are full of biblical resonances. We have already encountered the idea of the book of life with its detailed record of good and evil in Revelation 20:15. The trumpet calling humankind to judgement is likewise a biblical idea, mentioned in both the Old and the New Testaments, perhaps most memorably in 1 Corinthians 15:51–2, famously quoted in Handel's *Messiah*: 'Behold, I tell you a mystery; We shall not all sleep, but we shall all be changed, in a moment, in the twinkling of an eye, at the last trump: for the trumpet shall sound, and the dead shall be raised incorruptible, and we shall be changed.' The imagery in these lines is traditional, but the way in which this dramatic scene is laid out in the poem is novel and gripping. The events described are so great and terrible that even 'death and nature' themselves marvel to see them. Two of the most fundamental realities of human life become personified onlookers who stare in awe at the judgement as it unfolds. All-important as death and nature may seem to humans now, they will in the end be mere impotent bystanders in the face of such wondrous occurrences. They are not the final facts of human life, as something greater than them, something which even they cannot comprehend, is about to take place.

Having contemplated the scene on a grand scale, attended by death and nature in personified form, the poem then takes a sudden introspective turn. Stanza 7 features the first occurrence of the personal pronoun 'I'. The speaker here becomes an everyman who can stand in for the individual reader as well as for all of humanity. The focus shifts to the speaker's own reaction to the terrible events unfolding: it is a universal judgement, but by implication it is also a highly individual judgement. What will this judgement mean for me? If even those who have only done good during their lives on earth can only just be sure of their salvation, how will the judge respond to me, as I am so far from perfection? These are the questions that preoccupy the speaker. The answer can only be found in an appeal to God's mercy. Stanzas 8–18 contain an extended prayer that juxtaposes images of God as a fearsome and righteous judge with images of Christ's deeds of mercy to save humankind. Jesus is addressed directly here. In conversation with Christ, the speaker reminds him that the reason why he became man and suffered on the cross was to save each individual sinner. This appeal takes the shape of an intensely personal dialogue with Jesus – 'Remember, dear Jesus, that I am the reason for your journey' – culminating in a plea for the remission of the speaker's sins before the fearful Day of Judgement, so that Christ's suffering may not have been in vain. In a personal and emotional turn, two views of Christ – one as the just judge, the other as the merciful friend who dies in order to save humankind – are pitted against each other, so that the latter may prevail over the former.

Stanza 12 heightens this emotional appeal by focusing on the speaker's shamefaced look and feelings of guilt. But the speaker has reasons to hope that all sins may be forgiven; after all, Jesus forgave two of the most prominent sinners he encountered: Mary and the robber. The first is a reference to Mary Magdalene, who was traditionally seen as a symbol of penitence. According to the gospels, Mary of Magdala was one of the followers of Jesus, and was present at his crucifixion and resurrection. Mary Magdalene was later conflated with an unnamed woman who anointed Jesus' feet, mentioned in the Gospel of Luke. A reference to her as having lived 'a sinful life' (Luke 7:37) and an identification with Mary Magdalene led to the widespread belief that Mary had led a life of promiscuity before meeting Jesus, being forgiven by him and becoming one of his closest friends and disciples. As a result, medieval culture understood her as synonymous with a repentant sinner, which explains her being mentioned so prominently in *Dies irae*. The other reference is to one of the two robbers who were crucified next to Jesus, according to the Gospel of Luke. One of the robbers hurls insults at Jesus, while the other is penitent and asks Jesus to remember him when he comes into his kingdom, to which Jesus responds: 'Truly I tell you, today you will be with me in Paradise' (Luke 23:43). The penitent robber is here mentioned as another example of prominent sinners who were forgiven by Jesus, and it is because of these examples that the speaker of *Dies irae* is able to feel hope for the remission of sins.

Stanzas 14–17 expand on this theme of hope. The speaker implores God to be called among the numbers of the blessed rather than cursed to 'everlasting flame' in hell. This separation of the blessed from the damned is reinforced by the image of separating the sheep from the goats. The reference stems from Matthew 25:31–3:

> When the Son of Man comes in his glory, and all the angels with him, he will sit on his glorious throne. All the nations will be gathered before him, and he will separate the people one from another as a shepherd separates the sheep from the goats. He will put the sheep on his right and the goats on his left.

Sheep versus goats, right versus left, thus form a traditional metaphoric way of speaking about the blessed in heaven versus the damned in hell. It is, by extension, also a way of imagining a final state in which evil and good are no longer intermingled, as they are at present on earth. The metaphysical realities after the end of the world are, according to the poem, fundamentally different to anything we know. There will be an eternal separation of good and evil, light and darkness, with no grey areas in between. The realm of evil is described in the poem using images of burning fire and flames. The speaker, however, is humbly asking God to be merciful, with a prayer to be numbered among the saved.

The final stanza not only marks a shift from rhyming triplets to couplets, but shows a change in perspective that accompanies the change of form. From the intensely personal focus of Stanzas 7–17, the last two stanzas once again zoom out to the bigger picture. The speaker is no longer a tangible 'I', but the point of view is a more universal one, recapitulating the events of the day of 'weeping' when 'guilty man' will rise again to be judged. The poem ends with a prayer to spare the speaker on that day of judgement, followed by a prayer that refers more obviously to the present rather than the future: 'Requiem aeternam dona eis, Domine', a prayer traditionally said by the Church to commemorate the souls of the dead in purgatory. Their death is here figuratively imagined as an eternal sleep, and the living implore God to grant the dead eternal rest from their labours. The image of the sleeping dead gestures forward to the coming day of the resurrection, when the dead will rise again to eternal life.

The *Dies irae* paints an awe-inspiring scene of universal judgement. It contains compelling images of death and the resurrection of the dead, fear of being held to account paired with hope in the mercy of God. What makes it particularly successful as a poem is the close connection it creates between the great and terrible events at the end of time, affecting the whole of creation, and their intensely personal application from the individual speaker's point of view.

This connection explains why this poem was incorporated into the liturgy of the Requiem Mass, said for the repose of the souls of the faithful departed. The last stanza makes it clear that the coming Day of Judgement and the present concerns of the congregation gathered together for a Requiem Mass are intricately connected. The death of an individual, the prayers said for their soul, and the hope that they will live eternally in heaven point towards the final Day of Judgement of all humankind that is to come. Through this connection, the prayer to grant the soul of the deceased 'eternal rest' is at the same time a prayer for those who are now living. The members of the congregation are led to meditate on their own deaths, in anticipation of the events that are to come.

If the poem itself is compelling, what gave it an enduring place in Western cultural memory is the plainchant melody to which it was set. Plainchant is monophonic – a single melody sung by one or several voices without accompaniment – and has a less rigorously defined rhythm than later Western music, giving chant its free and flowing character. The *Dies irae* was officially incorporated into the Requiem Mass in 1570, but its use in the liturgy goes back to medieval times. It was sung as a so-called Sequence, a Latin hymn, after the Alleluia chant and preceding the gospel reading. The words *Dies irae, dies illa* are set to a sombre descending motif that forms an instantly recognizable tune, which perfectly captures the ominous atmosphere of the text. The original chant was sung in unison, usually by a small group of either male or female voices in monasteries and convents. The Sequence alternates between different tunes used for two stanzas each, thus creating a call-and-response effect that musically relates two adjacent stanzas closely to each other. The signature tune recurs several times in the course of the Sequence (in stanzas 1/2, 7/8, 13/14), evoking a sense of an inevitable cycle of repetition. The setting of the Latin words is simple and mostly syllabic, with a purposeful progression that feels disconcerting in its determination.

The characteristic setting of the first two words, 'Dies irae', occurs on four descending notes in the Dorian mode, an ancient Church tonality. The motif fills the listener with a sense of foreboding and brings the text to the fore in its declamatory style. Throughout the Sequence, the musical setting responds sensitively to the content of the Sequence: the tune of *Lacrimosa dies illa*, 'Oh that day of weeping', is markedly mournful and establishes a tone that is quite different from the hollow, threatening effect of the opening motif. The sombre character of the opening motif would have been all the more resonant in its original setting as part of the Requiem Mass, in the context of a dimly lit church, with the coffin of the deceased set up in the middle of the church, surrounded by candles. The music is perfectly in tune with such a setting, and connects themes of tears and mourning with dark and threatening references to the future day of judgement in a most effective manner.

Quivering between fear of judgement and hope in the mercy of the judge, the Sequence gives a ritual form to mourning that is personal and yet transcends the personal. The music is more than mere ornamentation of the words of the *Dies irae*; rather, the musical setting is integral to this process of reflection and mourning. Medieval liturgical theory emphasizes the centrality of music to worship, stressing that the meaning of the words of a text is closely connected to its musical expression. It is this interplay of text and music that has a deep emotional and intellectual effect on the individual listener.

This effect was evidently a long-lasting one, with the *Dies irae* becoming the most frequently cited musical motif throughout the history of Western music, and surviving into contemporary music. Over time, its meaning underwent subtle changes, but to the present day it has maintained its association with danger, death and destruction. In modern times plainchant has acquired very distinctive qualities. With its characteristic monophonic sound, it sounds radically different to most other types of Western music. Instantly recognizable as the music of Western Christianity, it is often used in modern culture to evoke a spiritual aura – the sense of something meditative and otherworldly. On the other hand, plainchant can be used in popular culture to construct an image of the 'Dark Ages', evoking associations with sinister-looking monks in dark robes processing round dimly lit Gothic cloisters. Neither association is consonant with the complex historic reality. These perceptions are based on a changing understanding of Christian theology and an increasing secularization of the Western world. As a result of this secularization, themes and ideas originally bound up in a systematic theological system, such as those of divine mercy and judgement at the end of days, became disconnected from this system, while other associations, such as those of doom and death, were retained. This is why we encounter the *Dies irae* motif today in film scores from *The Shining* to *Star Wars* to *The Lion King*, where the invocation of the musical motif tends to be used as a shorthand for death, often without a specifically religious context. The association is so strong that whenever the tune occurs in a film, it 'can arouse in the audience a feeling of imminent danger' even when it is woven into an instrumental composition without accompanying words.[2]

In the first centuries after the medieval period, however, the *Dies irae* motif was still firmly connected to a religious framework. It frequently occurs in polyphonic settings of the Requiem Mass, marked by interweaving independent voices which maintain a close relationship with the original chant, often carefully following the plainsong themes. Jacobus de Kerle (1532–1591), for instance, a Flemish composer of the Renaissance, sets the *Dies irae* as part of his *Missa pro defunctis*. His setting alternates polyphonic stanzas with stanzas in plainchant. We hear a polyphonic setting of the opening of the Sequence, with independent lines of melody that are musically innovative. We have moved far beyond monophony, and yet the piece's inspiration by chant is obvious. At the start of the *Dies irae* the characteristic descending chant motif appears first in the lower voices, then in the upper voices, interlocking and developing to form different harmonies. The musical tapestry is complex, but the original chant melody can still be clearly heard in each independent voice.

Later classical composers setting the texts of the Requiem Mass to music continued to be influenced by the chant motif, but at the same time introduced unique alterations and variations. Mozart's unfinished Requiem in D minor (1791) contains one of the best-known settings of the *Dies irae*, which has in turn been invoked many times in popular culture, such as in *Mad Max* (1979, dir. George Miller) and the superhero films *Watchmen* (2009, dir. Zack Snyder) and *X2* (2003, dir. Bryan Singer). Mozart's approach to the opening of the Sequence is different to what we have seen in Renaissance polyphony. Rather than citing the chant motif directly, Mozart's music evokes associations with the chant through its rhythm and word setting, even if the medieval chant melody is never heard directly. The beginning of the Sequence is sung by the choir and accompanied by a full orchestra at a speed that makes palpable the breathlessness and terror of the Day of Wrath. Mozart's word setting, like that of the chant melody, is syllabic, with each note falling like a hammer to heighten the impact of the words. In a surprising inversion of the descending motif of the original chant melody, Mozart's setting presents an ascending motif, in which the soprano line becomes gradually higher, increasing the intensity of the anguish expressed in the music. Mozart takes his starting point from the chant and its word-setting, but alters the tune in order to achieve an effect of even greater intensity and dread.

The beginning of the Sequence is not the only place where Mozart responds to the vivid descriptions of the text and makes them more explicit in his music. For instance, the third stanza, *Tuba mirum spargens sonum*, inspired the use of an unaccompanied solo trombone at the start of the second movement before the words are declaimed by an expressive bass solo. 'The trumpet's wondrous call' is no longer left to our imagination as it was in the chant. In his setting, Mozart gives the imagery of the Sequence a musical expression.

Later composers of the Romantic period took this musical word-painting to even further extremes. Verdi's setting of the Messa da Requiem (1874) presents us with a veritable abyss of terror. The *Dies irae* movement starts with four abrupt staccato chords from the orchestra, four knife-like stabs followed by a tumultuous swirl of strings. Then, a threatening crescendo from the lower voices ushers in a high descending soprano line on the words *Dies irae*, a line which can only be understood as a wailing of horror. Verdi's interpretation of the Sequence is fundamentally operatic in the depths of its musical expression: every emotion in the text is taken to its musical extreme. Where Mozart took inspiration from the mention of a trumpet in the text, Verdi turns the third stanza of the Sequence into a theatrical moment of epic dimensions, with trumpets sounding from the distance with a mighty crescendo that makes the audience feel as if the Day of Judgement is truly come upon them. Verdi imagines what it would be like to hear the call of a trumpet that 'shall drive everybody forward to the throne' with a power that cannot be withstood. The trumpets pierce the listener through and through with an irresistible force before the full orchestra enters, followed by the choir announcing the end of the world at the top of their lungs. And indeed, the call of the trumpets has pierced even the 'tombs throughout the world': At the end of the third verse, we hear the dead rising from their graves. The orchestra plays an isolated, eerie, stumbling motif evocative of the rattling foot of a skeleton stepping out of a tomb. Breathless fascination and horror intertwine. Verdi takes the text of *Dies irae* seriously and literally, with a setting that quivers between operatic spectacle and inclusion of the audience.

When the trumpets are heard calling behind us, we become implicated in the action of the text, part of the countless living and dead called before the throne of God.

Over time the *Dies irae* motif also increasingly started to appear in classical music in contexts divorced from the Requiem Mass and its religious setting. In Hector Berlioz's *Symphonie fantastique* (1830), for instance, this secularized use of the chant theme appears in the context of a programme piece of orchestral music that charts the life of an artist in five sections. We follow different episodes in the life of a young artist, who desperately falls in love with a woman who represents the ideals of all his dreams. He subsequently becomes haunted by her beloved image, which follows him wherever he goes. The five movements are entitled 'Rêveries, passions' ('Dreams, Passions'), 'Un bal' ('A Ball'), 'Scène aux champs' ('Scene in the Fields'), 'Marche au supplice' ('March to the Scaffold') and 'Songe d'une nuit du Sabbat' ('Dream of a Witches' Sabbath'). The artist's journey of increasing obsession and disorientation finally leads him to poison himself with opium, and the last movements of the symphony consist of strange opium-fuelled visions, culminating in a witches' sabbath. Berlioz's original programme notes describe the scene:

> He sees himself . . . in the midst of a hideous gathering of shades, sorcerers and monsters of every kind who have come together for his funeral. Strange sounds, groans, outbursts of laughter; distant shouts which seem to be answered by more shouts . . . The funeral knell tolls, burlesque parody of the Dies irae, the dance of the witches. The dance of the witches combined with the Dies irae.[3]

Berlioz here uses the *Dies irae* motif to evoke its associations with death and funeral rites, but also places it in an explicitly diabolical scene, filled with ghoulish groans and hollow laughter. We have come a long way from the plainchant warning about the impending day of

God's judgement. Berlioz here exploits the ominous feeling of dread that the tune evokes, while dispensing with its original religious and moral context. Interestingly, Berlioz also relies solely on the music to evoke these associations; the symphony is purely orchestral and does not feature the actual words of the sequence.

Berlioz's use of the theme divorced from its immediate religious context proved groundbreaking for many other composers, in particular because artists of the Romantic period were fascinated with the grotesque and the macabre. Franz Liszt, for instance, used the tune prominently in his piece for solo piano and orchestra entitled *Totentanz* (Dance of the Dead): *Paraphrase on Dies irae* (1849). Sergei Rachmaninov's symphonic poem *Isle of the Dead* (1908) is themed around an image of the dead being ferried across an expanse of water to a desolate island. Rich with symbolic and mythological resonances, the symphonic poem quotes the *Dies irae* motif as an allusion to death, passing it from instrument to instrument as the music builds. The motif also appears in Gustav Mahler's Symphony No. 2 (1894), dubbed 'Resurrection' because of its final movement, which contains a setting of Friedrich Gottlieb Klopstock's poem *Die Auferstehung* (Resurrection). The programmatic theme is that of a funeral, memories of the life of the deceased, and hope of the resurrection. The *Dies irae* motif is heard prominently in the last movement, first quietly, and later as a solemn brass chorale, as a symbol of death that must precede resurrection. The theme seems traditionally religious at first glance, but the emphasis of the text is on the resurrection of the human heart after its manifold trials, a process of transcendent renewal that can be read as symbolic or psychological rather than religious in its narrow sense. At any rate, there is no mention of judgement as accompanying the resurrection, and the hope that is evoked is unequivocally positive, without any sense of fear and trepidation:

> O believe, my heart, O believe:
> Nothing is lost to you!

Yours, yes yours, is what you desired
Yours, what you have loved
What you have fought for!

Gustav Holst's orchestral suite *The Planets* likewise invokes the motif in the fifth movement, entitled 'Saturn, the Bringer of Old Age'. The music begins with a slow, creeping 'tick-tock', suggesting the passage of time. Echoes of the *Dies irae* fill the music with a sense of foreboding as the ticking clock merges with the atmosphere of a funeral dirge. Near the end of the piece, however, this ominous atmosphere gives way to a sense of wonder and final resolution.

What all of these later examples have in common is that they dispense with the words of the *Dies irae* and instead rely solely on the tune as a proxy to evoke a specific atmosphere. Out of the range of themes originally contained in the poem – individual death, universal judgement, second coming of Christ, rising of the dead, plea for mercy, prayer for eternal rest for the souls of the dead – the music of later periods merely actualizes specific associations, usually without embracing their full religious context, which had originally implied a moral directive about doing good works and hope in divine mercy. Increasingly the theme becomes a shorthand for death and an impending feeling of doom, and this is very much the musical usage that survives into contemporary film scores.

The use of the *Dies irae* motif in film goes back to the early days of cinema. Perhaps the first use of the motif was in Gottfried Huppertz's 1927 score for Fritz Lang's silent film *Metropolis*. The theme is generally used in films to evoke an ominous sense of dread and premonition of evil. In this way it lends itself naturally to the horror film genre. *The Exorcist* (1974, dir. William Friedkin, theme comp. Mike Oldfield) is a prominent example, in which the theme contains a modified version of the *Dies irae*. It is subtle, and the scene when we first encounter the theme is innocuous enough – nuns with billowing robes leaving church – but the music warns the attentive listener that there is something sinister lurking in the background. Much less subtle than *The Exorcist*, the soundtrack of *The Shining* (1980, dir. Stanley Kubrick, music comp. Wendy Carlos) opens with a synthesized brass version of the *Dies irae* motif, complemented with ominous electronic sounds, filling us with a sense of trepidation and foreshadowing of the doom to come.

It is not only horror films that use this theme. It occurs in a vast number of films of a wide variety of different genres. Remember the heart-wrenching scene in *Star Wars: Episode IV – A New Hope* (1977, dir. George Lucas, music comp. John Williams), when the young Luke Skywalker finds that his adoptive parents have been brutally murdered on their farm in Tatooine? The Skywalker theme indicates that the young Luke is being called to fulfil his destiny, but at the same time this is overlaid by the *Dies irae* motif harshly played by brass instruments, reinforcing the feeling that a horrible force of evil is at work here. Similarly, in *The Lord of the Rings* trilogy (2001–3), an ominous figure of descending thirds reminiscent of *Dies irae* represents the threat of the realm of Mordor to enslave all the free peoples of Middle-earth. The figure is first heard in the Prologue to *The Fellowship of the Ring* (music comp. Howard Shore) when the armies of Mordor clash with the armies of elves and men, and appears at prominent points in the narrative to reinforce the sense of threat and impending doom connected to the power of Mordor and the Ring. Disney's original animated film *The Lion King* (1994, dir. Rob Minkoff and Roger Allers, music comp. Hans Zimmer) likewise uses *Dies irae* in the context of Scar's evil plot to usurp the throne. In a pivotal scene, when Scar's plan has almost succeeded, he tries to cover up his murder of his brother Mufasa by blaming Simba for Mufasa's death. The high-pitched, fast and relentless repetition of the *Dies irae* motif at this moment leaves us in no doubt that Scar is the epitome of a twisted villain. Modified allusions to the *Dies irae* motif pervade the entire score of *The Lion King*, imbuing it with quasi-religious significance. Not only does Scar represent the ultimate, Devil-like antagonist, but Simba's return to the throne at the end of the film as the rightful heir may, in combination with the insistent use of the *Dies irae* motif, evoke associations with the second coming of Christ.

There are more than one hundred film scores that use the *Dies irae* motif. It is astonishing that the music exerts a profound effect on listeners regardless of whether they are musically trained or even consciously recognize the motif. The dark and foreboding character of the music, perhaps along with subconscious memories of having heard the tune many times before in contexts of death and doom, is enough to evoke in audiences feelings of anxiety, fear and desperation. We are far removed here from the apocalyptic struggle of the Christian Day of Judgement, but the conflicts between good and evil presented in many of these films imply an archetypal struggle that is similar in structure to the original context of the *Dies irae*. The use of the motif can evoke complex religious allusions, or it can be used in a more simplistic manner as a shorthand for doom. What has remained constant since the Middle Ages, however, is the association of the music with death. Invented many centuries ago, the tune of death has remained definitive until the present day.

8
Revelation

The Christian understanding of Doomsday may seem rather gloomy, and it may have a secular equivalent in modern apocalyptic visions such as those of nuclear war, climate catastrophe or asteroid impacts. The negative bent of such visions of destruction has been parodied many times, such as in R.E.M.'s song 'It's the End of the World as We Know It (And I Feel Fine)'. But Christian ideas are not solely about fire and destruction but also about the hope of Paradise. The Book of Revelation abounds in imagery of the remaking of the broken world and the establishment of a new Heaven after the end of days, in which all of the faithful will dwell in the company of God and all angels and saints. This vision of Paradise bears within it the hope that all suffering and death of the present life will in the end be made right, that this world will pass away and a better one will take its place, in which humanity will be healed from its hurts. The justice towards those who in this life have committed wrong is one side of this, as we have seen in the previous chapter, but the reward of those who have done good is the other side of the coin. The Requiem liturgy, which on the one hand contains the *Dies irae*, also expresses this hope in many ways. One of the antiphons sung at burial services prays that the deceased may be taken up into Paradise and may be granted rest eternal with the angels and the saints:

In paradisum deducant te angeli,	May the angels lead you into Paradise,
in tuo adventu suscipiant te martyres, et perducant te	may the martyrs receive you in your coming,
in civitatem sanctam Jerusalem.	and may they guide you into the holy city, Jerusalem.
Chorus angelorum te suscipiat,	May the chorus of angels receive you
et cum Lazaro quondam paupere	and with Lazarus once poor
aeternam habeas requiem.	may you have eternal rest.

This antiphon, most famously set to music by Gabriel Fauré in his Requiem, is usually sung by the choir when the body is taken out of the church and carried to the graveyard to be buried. It contains two references that we encounter again and again in biblical and liturgical texts concerning the afterlife and the end of days: Jerusalem the holy city, and 'Lazarus once poor'. The latter is a reference to a story told by Jesus in Luke 16:19–31 about a rich man and a beggar named Lazarus. The rich man lives in luxury, while Lazarus lies outside the rich man's gate and begs to be fed with the crumbs from his table. When both men die, however, their fates are reversed, and Lazarus is carried by the angels into Abraham's bosom (in Jewish belief the abode of the righteous dead, later interpreted by Christians as heaven), while the rich man is punished by torments. This reversal of fortunes from suffering to eternal bliss in the biblical story is applied to the here and now in the *In paradisum* antiphon, with the prayer that the deceased may be taken up to the same place of comfort and rest as Lazarus.

The reference to the holy city of Jerusalem in the context of the afterlife is one of the most central images for the remaking of heaven and earth. We encounter the metaphor throughout biblical, theological and religious literature and art. Its origin is the Book of Revelation. This book, the last book of the New Testament, is also known as the Apocalypse of John. The term 'apocalypse' has entered common parlance as a word to describe a disastrous event leading to the end of the world, but its original etymology is simply Greek for 'revelation, disclosure'. The Book of Revelation is told by a first-person narrator who calls himself John (in later Christian tradition often identified with the Apostle John, though this is thought unlikely by many modern scholars). John describes a series of prophetic visions, which concern the events that lead up to the Second Coming of Christ. Many of the events in the Book of Revelation have entered our cultural memory and popular culture, and are familiar even to those who have never read the Book of Revelation. Key figures include the Four Horsemen of the Apocalypse, the Seven-Headed Dragon, the Beast and the Whore of Babylon. It is a long and complex series of visions, describing a universal destruction of the earth and subsequent renewal, with a new heaven on earth in which the resurrected dead will live in celestial joy. Its cryptic imagery has led to a wide range of often contradictory interpretations. The liturgy uses the imagery of the Book of Revelation selectively, and this chapter discusses in greater detail a number of motifs that are particularly prominent in the liturgy.

The image of the holy city of Jerusalem occurs towards the end of the Book of Revelation. It is preceded by a description of a range of calamitous events on earth and in the heavens, involving a dragon's attack on a woman clothed with the sun and the dragon's defeat by Michael (discussed below), two beasts, the destruction of Babylon, followed by the marriage-feast of the lamb (discussed below), the Second Coming of Christ and the great battle at Armageddon in which Satan is overthrown and bound. A period of peace ensues, the thousand-year reign of the saints, until Satan is loosed again and overthrown in a second great battle. At the end come the resurrection of the dead and the Last Judgement, after which is found the passage that mentions the heavenly Jerusalem.

> Then I saw a new heaven and a new earth; for the first heaven and the first earth had passed away, and the sea was no more. And I saw the holy city, the new Jerusalem, coming down out of heaven from God, prepared as a bride adorned for her husband. And I heard a loud voice from the throne saying,
> 'See, the home of God is among mortals.
> He will dwell with them;
> they will be his peoples,
> and God himself will be with them;
> he will wipe every tear from their eyes.
> Death will be no more;
> mourning and crying and pain will be no more,
> for the first things have passed away.'
> And the one who was seated on the throne said, 'See, I am making all things new.' (Rev. 21:1–5)

In this passage the holy city, new Jerusalem, stands for the renewed creation and a heaven on earth without suffering or pain, in which God himself will dwell with the blessed souls in everlasting joy. The liturgical antiphon *In paradisum* expresses the hope that the deceased may become an inhabitant of this city.

The tradition of interpreting this section from the Book of Revelation as a metaphor rather than a reference to the historical city of Jerusalem goes back to St Augustine in his work called *De civitate Dei* (The City of God). He interprets the New Jerusalem as the bliss that is to come in the 'immortality and eternity of the saints' after the Last Judgement.[1] This is certainly the interpretation that is behind the inclusion of this reference into the Requiem liturgy. Accordingly, the image of the New Jerusalem, also known as the Heavenly Jerusalem, has often been used in literature as shorthand for the renewal of the fallen world. The celestial city is described in Revelation in very specific terms:

> The wall is built of jasper, while the city is pure gold, clear as glass. The foundations of the wall of the city are adorned with every jewel; the first was jasper, the second sapphire, the third agate, the fourth emerald, the fifth onyx, the sixth cornelian, the seventh chrysolite, the eighth beryl, the ninth topaz, the tenth chrysoprase, the eleventh jacinth, the twelfth amethyst. And the twelve gates are twelve pearls, each of the gates is a single pearl, and the street of the city is pure gold, transparent as glass. (Rev. 21:18–21)

The description of the city as transparent, clear and radiant, adorned with jewels, inspired a fourteenth-century poem known as *Pearl,* in which the narrator falls asleep and has a dream vision of the heavenly Jerusalem. Outside its gates, he meets one of the blessed souls, a girl who might be the dreamer's daughter who died at a young age, although this never becomes entirely clear. Whoever she may be, the dreamer knew her in her life on earth, but now meets her in her new state as an inhabitant of the heavenly city. She acts as his guide in the dream, in which he sees and hears many marvellous things. Although he is not allowed to enter the city, he is able to describe it in great detail, echoing the Book of Revelation:

> Then I did not want to wait any longer, but passed under boughs so beautifully leaved until on a hill I caught sight of the city and, as I made my way onwards, gazed at it, situated beyond the brook, at some distance from me, shining brighter than the sun with beams of light. The form of it is shown in the Apocalypse, as the apostle John describes it. Just as John the apostle saw it clearly, I saw that city of great renown, Jerusalem so new and royally adorned, as though it had come down from heaven. The city was all of bright refined gold, burnished bright like gleaming glass, set beneath with noble gems, with twelve tiers fixed on the base, the twelve layers of the foundation admirably joined; each tier

> was a different stone, as the apostle John splendidly describes this same city in the Apocalypse.[2]

Inspired by the Book of Revelation, *Pearl* fills the description of the city with further detail and incorporates it into a different kind of story, in which the narrator tries to understand how someone whom he knew on earth has changed into one of the blessed souls in heaven. The poem is a reflection on what it might mean for an individual to inhabit the celestial city – the very hope expressed in the liturgy through texts like *In paradisum*. In *Pearl*, however, this is not at all a straightforward or uncomplicated state of bliss. The dreamer struggles to understand the laws of heaven, which are so different from earth. It is a place where the last are the first and earthly hierarchies are irrelevant. In the end, the dreamer is tied to his earthly existence and unable to pass over into the heavenly city, despite its mystical beauty.

The metaphor of the New Jerusalem for heaven is adopted by many other authors throughout the history of English literature, sometimes with an unexpected twist, as in William Blake's 'And did those feet in ancient time', first published in 1808. Today, it is better known as England's unofficial anthem 'Jerusalem', set to music by Sir Hubert Parry in 1916. Blake's poem plays with the idea of the heavenly Jerusalem while applying it to his present time. The first two stanzas allude to the legend that, in his young years, Jesus once travelled to England accompanied by Joseph of Arimathea (the man who buried Jesus after the crucifixion). Blake subtly implies some doubt about the veracity of this folklore idea by phrasing the first two stanzas as a series of questions:

> And did those feet in ancient time
> Walk upon England's mountains green?
> And was the holy Lamb of God
> On England's pleasant pastures seen?

And did the Countenance Divine,
Shine forth upon our clouded hills?
And was Jerusalem builded here,
Among these dark Satanic mills?[3]

Whether Christ's feet really did walk on England's green hills is left up for debate; the speaker is unsure. The imagery, too, implies a certain incongruity of this legend: imagining 'the holy Lamb of God' on 'England's pleasant pastures' and the 'Countenance Divine' shining 'upon our clouded hills' means to transpose traditional epithets of Christ into a distinctly English setting. The second stanza is also where we encounter a reference to 'Jerusalem'. If Christ really did visit England, the poem implies, he must have established a New Jerusalem on these very green hills, a heaven on earth. The speaker is somewhat incredulous that there might once have been a paradise where now there are only 'dark Satanic mills'. This phrase, oft-cited in the English language, has frequently been explained as a reference to the destruction of nature in the wake of the Industrial Revolution with its factories and machinery, which Blake witnessed. The new, industrial, steam-powered, 'dark Satanic' mills stand in stark contrast to the light-filled Heavenly Jerusalem with its gates of pearl. But it is not only the factories' physical ugliness that prompts Blake to use the word 'Satanic'. Perhaps even more than the visible destruction of pleasant landscapes, the word implies destruction of a spiritual kind: of human relationships, dignity and freedom. For Blake, factory work in inhuman conditions under a black cloud of smoke is the very expression of hell on earth. The Heavenly Jerusalem could not be further from the reality of industrialized Britain. This contrast inspires the speaker to fight unceasingly to establish the New Jerusalem in England:

Bring me my bow of burning gold;
Bring me my arrows of desire;

Bring me my spear – O clouds, unfold!
Bring me my chariot of fire!

I will not cease from mental fight,
Nor shall my sword sleep in my hand:
Till we have built Jerusalem,
In England's green and pleasant land.

What this Jerusalem that the speaker envisages would look like remains unclear; it seems to be a physical place, located in England, but at the same time it is also a spiritual state, which can only be gained by 'mental fight'. The weapons that the speaker uses for this fight appear to be metaphorical rather than physical, too: the 'bow of burning gold', 'arrows of desire' and 'chariot of fire' express a mental attitude rather than real-life weapons. This is no call to arms in an ordinary sense. It is a call for radical change from the present state, a change for the better that requires endless dedication. As such, it has a lot in common with traditional religious views of the New Jerusalem, which in Revelation descends from the clouds after much war and strife, but Blake's vision is different in that his Jerusalem is a vision of a better society that has a very strong bent of social criticism.[4] The New Jerusalem is presented as an antidote to the moral ills and social alienation of the present.

The New Jerusalem is not the only image from the Book of Revelation that has had a lasting impact on our liturgical and literary imagination. A large part of the biblical book is concerned with a description of the battles that precede the coming down of the holy city. Perhaps most memorable among these is the war between the great dragon and the woman clothed with the sun:

> A great portent appeared in heaven: a woman clothed with the sun, with the moon under her feet, and on her head a crown of twelve stars. She was pregnant and was crying out in birth pangs,

> in the agony of giving birth. Then another portent appeared in heaven: a great red dragon, with seven heads and ten horns, and seven diadems on his heads. His tail swept down a third of the stars of heaven and threw them to the earth. Then the dragon stood before the woman who was about to bear a child, so that he might devour her child as soon as it was born. And she gave birth to a son, a male child, who is to rule all the nations with a rod of iron. But her child was snatched away and taken to God and to his throne. (Rev. 12:1–5)

Using astrological language, this passage presents a cosmic conflict. The dragon, identified with the Devil, wreaks havoc upon the heavens and pursues the woman and her child. Such imagery is not unique to the Bible: many mythologies contain a dragon-like creature, representing the forces of evil, chaos and destruction. In these stories the slaying of this dragon is usually a pivotal event that restores order and peace. Due to its similarities with such mythological accounts, this passage in Revelation has variously been connected by scholars to a sun goddess in several Near Eastern myths, as well as an ancient astrological idea about the conflict between Scorpio and Virgo. Regardless of its links with other mythologies, in a Christian context the woman clothed with the sun was traditionally interpreted in two different ways: one was to see the woman as a metaphor for the Church of all the faithful, persecuted by the Devil. Another option, however, was to see the woman as an image of the Virgin Mary giving birth to the Messiah, 'who is to rule all the nations'. It is this interpretation that was particularly foregrounded by the liturgy, as the first line of Revelation 12 was sung at the annual celebration of the Assumption of the Virgin Mary into heaven. We have already seen in Chapter Two how imagery from the Song of Songs was used to refer to the Virgin Mary, following liturgical tradition. One picture of Mary shows her standing on the sickle of the moon, surrounded by the beams of the sun, with stars around her head (illus. 4). This way of portraying Mary merges imagery from the Song of Songs with Revelation, showing her to be the apocalyptic 'woman clothed with the sun, with the moon under her feet, and on her head a crown of twelve stars'. In this tradition, the cosmic aspects of the Book of Revelation and the amorous language of the Song of Songs were combined into a single image of the Virgin Mary, who is seen as beautiful beyond all humans and exalted to cosmic significance.

This Marian interpretation of Revelation also appears in literary works, such as Dante's *Divine Comedy.* Near the end of his vision of heaven in *Paradiso*, Dante lifts up his eyes to Mary, the Queen of Heaven. What he sees is a sun that shines brighter than all others, described with luminous language:

> I lifted up my eyes; and as, at morning,
> the eastern side of the horizon shows
> more splendour than the side where the sun sets,
>
> so, as if climbing with my eyes from valley
> to summit, I saw one part of the farthest
> rank of the Rose more bright than all the rest.

Dante goes on to describe the quality of the sun's rays, which are brightest in the middle and then shade off at the sides:

> And as, on earth, the point where we await
> the shaft that Phaethon had misguided glows
> brightest, while, to each side, the light shades off,
>
> so did the peaceful oriflamme appear
> brightest at its midpoint, so did its flame,
> on each side, taper off at equal pace.[5]

17 *The Woman Clothed in the Sun*, illumination from the Getty Apocalypse, *c.* 1255–60.

Dante imagines in detail what it might look like to see a woman who is 'clothed with the sun', describing the light radiating from her using the classicizing term Phaethon, the son of Sol, who lost control of his father's chariot while attempting to direct its course (compare Ovid, *Metamorphoses* 2). It may be a little difficult to imagine the quality of the light described here solely with words, but a look at medieval illustrations can help.

Here we see a thirteenth-century illustration from a manuscript that was illuminated around fifty years before the *Divine Comedy* was begun (illus. 17). In this image, we can see something of the vision that Dante describes. Fiery rays of light surround the woman, flowing outwards in waves as if they were a living thing. The woman, crowned with twelve stars and the moon under her feet, is at the centre of this radiant brightness. Images such as these may be similar to what Dante had in mind when he wrote his exquisite verses.

Later artists found very different approaches to this passage from Revelation. William Blake produced a series of illustrations on this theme, including *The Great Red Dragon and the Woman Clothed with the Sun* (illus. 18). The woman is depicted with circular wings, her hair like flames of fire. The sickle of the moon beneath her feet shines brightly. Her light is all the more powerful in contrast with the stormy darkness that reigns all about her. Her arms are lifted up as she braces herself for the attack of the red dragon swooping down above her. The dragon has features of both reptile and man,

18 William Blake, *The Great Red Dragon and the Woman Clothed with the Sun*, *c.* 1805, pen and grey ink with watercolour over graphite.

the horns on his head invoking a common motif in portrayals of the Devil as goat-like in appearance. Yet in his fall from above, the outstretched arms of the dragon mirror those of the woman below, visually balancing light and darkness. The two forces, Blake's image suggests, act like *yin* and *yang* as good and evil are poised, in conflict and yet in balance.

This mystical dualism of Blake's interpretation takes a specific perspective on the role of good and evil in the world. In this it is unlike the perspective we find in the Book of Revelation as we read on in the same chapter:

> And war broke out in heaven; Michael and his angels fought against the dragon. The dragon and his angels fought back, but they were defeated, and there was no longer any place for them in heaven. The great dragon was thrown down, that ancient serpent, who is called the Devil and Satan, the deceiver of the whole world – he was thrown down to the earth, and his angels were thrown down with him. (Rev. 12:7–9)

Michael the Archangel is here portrayed as the chief adversary of the dragon, who is also named the Devil and Satan. As the leader of an army of angels, Michael defeats the Devil in battle and casts him and his followers out of heaven. Michael, whose name in Hebrew means 'Who is like God?', represents here the spirit of willing obedience to God that conquers the rebellion of the fallen angels. This role as the chief of the angels is assigned to Michael not only in the New Testament but in a number of Jewish works, which are often similarly apocalyptic in nature. It is from this passage in Revelation, however, that Christian tradition took its inspiration in portraying St Michael as the dragon-slayer. The liturgy praises him in these terms on his feast day on 29 September, where the office at Matins contains an antiphon that echoes Revelation:

Factum est silentium in caelo,	There was silence in heaven
Dum committeret bellum draco cum Michaele Archangelo.	When the dragon fought with the Archangel Michael.
Audita est vox millia millium dicentium:	The voice of thousands of thousands was heard saying:
Salus, honor et virtus omnipotenti Deo.	Salvation, honour and power be to almighty God.
Millia millium ministrabant ei et decies centena millia assistebant ei.	Thousands of thousands ministered to him and ten hundreds of thousands stood before him.

This antiphon would have been sung in monasteries before the break of dawn. It contains quite a striking change from how the passage is worded in Revelation. While the biblical text frames the deeds of Michael by emphasizing the context of a war in heaven, the antiphon takes a different approach by emphasizing silence. It invokes an image of all the multitudes of heaven standing silently and awaiting with bated breath the outcome of Michael's decisive battle with the dragon. While Revelation names St Michael first ('Michael and his angels fought against the dragon'), the antiphon delays the mention of his name until the end of the sentence ('the dragon fought with the Archangel Michael'). The phrasing of the liturgical text places its audience in the same position as the multitudes of heaven, as we likewise await the outcome of the battle. The unsettling idea of silence in heaven only reaches its reassuring conclusion at the end of the sentence with the mention of Michael's name. As a religious audience would have known, Michael's presence ensures that good triumphs over evil, but the breathless tension of the moment of battle is reinforced in the liturgy. Michael's victory and the fall of the demons is not explicitly mentioned here, but instead implied in the chorus of praise that follows: 'Salvation, honour and power be to almighty God.' The liturgical text here splices together verses from various books of the Bible, which include not only Revelation but the Book of Daniel. The result is a narrative that is somewhat different in its emphasis from Revelation. After the battle follows the image of an overwhelming multitude of angels, 'thousands of thousands' praising God in triumph.

The vivid imagery and dramatic quality of the narrative in this antiphon are echoed in the most famous setting of this text to polyphonic music by Richard Dering (1580–1630). *Factum est silentium* opens with a quiet, slow, almost static phrase. The silence in heaven is palpable. This only heightens the contrast with the faster rhythmic energy of the next phrase, describing the battle, culminating in the word *draco*, 'dragon'. We get a sense of the fearsome size of the dragon through repetitions of the word at successively higher pitches. Dering's setting of the antiphon uses word-painting so evocative that we can almost see the image of the great dragon before our very eyes. The war in heaven could hardly be more gripping.

The liturgical feast of St Michael on 29 September was memorable for its engrossing descriptions of dragon-slaying as well as its importance in the annual cycle of the seasons. The word 'Michaelmas' (a shortened form of 'St Michael's Mass') is still used to describe the first term of the year, beginning soon after 29 September, at various universities and schools, as well as law courts in England, Ireland and Wales.[6] In medieval England, Michaelmas day marked a quarter-day of the business year, when accounts had to be settled and rents were due. As the feast occurred near the autumnal equinox, it was frequently associated with the beginning of autumn, and the ending of the harvest for farmers. This is why various flowers that bloom around this time of the year are known as Michaelmas daisies or asters. In some places festivities accompanied the liturgical celebrations, with Michaelmas processions and pilgrimages taking place in Scotland and Ireland. The tradition of Michaelmas fairs, at which servants found work, continued until well into the eighteenth century, as described by Sir Frederick Morton Eden in 1797: 'In Gloucestershire,

Oxfordshire, Wiltshire, and Berkshire, servants continue to attend the mopp, or statute, as it is called, (that is, Michaelmas fair,) in order to be hired.'[7] Evidently St Michael was important in slaying the dragons of hunger and unemployment, too.

St Michael, then, is the original dragon-slayer in the Bible. But the slaying of a dragon is a motif that is not unique to the Bible. We encounter it in legends and myths around the world, whether it is Sigurd's fight with Fafnir, Hercules' fight with the nine-headed Hydra or Susanoo's fight with Yamata no Orochi. It is a truly universal idea in folklore across cultures, representing the fight against the cosmic forces of evil to be fought in all ages. Within a Christian context, St Michael has a counterpart in St George the dragon-slayer. According to tradition, George was a soldier in the Roman army, originally from Cappadocia, who was martyred for his Christian faith. Medieval legends surround his great deed of slaying a dragon that was wreaking havoc upon the city of Silene in Libya. In order to keep the dragon at bay, the people of the city were forced to sacrifice to him first sheep, and later humans chosen from among the city's population. George arrives in Silene when the lot is cast again and the king's daughter is selected to be sacrificed. Armed with a lance, George then rides out to meet the dragon and slays it, saving the king's daughter from death. The legend became known in medieval Europe through Jacobus de Voragine's *The Golden Legend*, a collection of saints' lives. The saintly dragon-slayer on horseback appealed to medieval knightly culture in particular, with George becoming a model of chivalry in Arthurian stories, being invoked as the patron saint of chivalric orders such as the Order of the Garter, and eventually becoming known as the patron saint of England. It may be that the idea of slaying a dragon has a fascination that is hard to resist, but it is likely that the prominence of St Michael in the Book of Revelation, in the liturgy, and the importance of the feast in the cycle of the year, helped to further George's popularity.

The Book of Revelation is important to liturgical practice not only as a source of texts and prayers for specific feasts. Beyond these paths of influence, it also provides a symbolic model for the very form of Christian worship. Many of the things that John sees in his vision seem, at first glance, rather odd. The vision culminates in a marriage feast, at whose centre stands the Lamb:

> Then I heard what seemed to be the voice of a great multitude, like the sound of many waters and like the sound of mighty thunder-peals, crying out,
> 'Hallelujah!
> For the Lord our God
> the Almighty reigns.
> Let us rejoice and exult
> and give him the glory,
> for the marriage of the Lamb has come,
> and his bride has made herself ready;
> to her it has been granted to be clothed
> with fine linen, bright and pure' –
> for the fine linen is the righteous deeds of the saints.
> And the angel said to me, 'Write this: Blessed are those who are invited to the marriage supper of the Lamb.' (Rev. 19:6–9)

In Revelation, what concludes the end of the world and marks the beginning of the new heaven and the new earth is a wedding and a banquet. This cryptic imagery of a marriage feast may seem unexpected but it makes sense seen in relation to the Old Testament, where the metaphor of a marriage is repeatedly used to speak about the relationship between God and the people of Israel (for example, Isa. 54:1–8; Ezek. 16; Hos. 2–6). Here we again meet the imagery of Christ as a Lamb. Given this context, the Lamb's marriage in Revelation is often understood to be a symbolic marriage of Christ with the Church or with his people in the New Jerusalem. The motif of a wedding feast or banquet occurs frequently in the New Testament in Jesus' parables, and in the miracle at Cana. There is also an explicitly liturgical implication: Jesus' Last Supper with his disciples on the evening before his death marks the institution of the Eucharist, and this is an event that is celebrated and commemorated through the liturgy of the Mass. The Mass is a Eucharistic feast in which Christ himself gives himself as spiritual food to his people.

From this perspective, the descriptions of the worship of the Lamb in the Book of Revelation can be understood as a cosmic liturgy at the end of time, with its apocalyptic banquet as a reflection and fulfilment of the liturgy of the Mass that is celebrated in the here and now. Many of the elements of the liturgy of the Mass are present, in one form or another, in Revelation. For example, the servants of God standing around his throne in Revelation praise him with the words 'Holy, holy, holy, the Lord God the Almighty' (4:8), a prayer which also occurs as the *Sanctus* in the liturgy of the Mass. The 'Alleluia' that is sung before the proclamation of the gospel likewise appears in the cosmic worship of John's vision, as we have seen in the section from Revelation 19 above. There are references to incense (5:8), an altar (8:3) and many other elements of liturgical practice.[8] The vision of Revelation imagines the new Heaven as an everlasting liturgy, which is at the same time a celestial marriage feast.

This imagery is reflected in the works of many writers who have imagined communication or union with God in terms of a banquet. George Herbert's mystical dialogue with God in his poem *Love (3)* is an example:

Love bade me welcome: yet my soul drew back
Guilty of dust and sin.
But quick-eyed Love, observing me grow slack
From my first entrance in,
Drew nearer to me, sweetly questioning,

If I lacked any thing.
A guest, I answered, worthy to be here:
Love said, You shall be he.
I the unkind, ungrateful? Ah my dear,
I cannot look on thee.
Love took my hand, and smiling did reply,
Who made the eyes but I?

Truth Lord, but I have marred them: let my shame
Go where it doth deserve.
And know you not, says Love, who bore the blame?
My dear, then I will serve.
You must sit down, says Love, and taste my meat:
So I did sit and eat.[9]

The speaker is invited to a feast by God as personified Love. The poem imagines a dialogue between host and guest: the speaker is laden with feelings of sin and unworthiness, while Love is concerned about the well-being of his guest. Through a series of exchanges, the speaker is reassured that God has atoned for all sins, and is encouraged to serve the Lord with love and courage. The poem ends with an invitation to 'sit and eat', which the guest at last accepts. Within the context of Revelation, it becomes clear why this poem images a conversation with God around the theme of food. The imagery of feasting in connection with divine love evokes associations with the liturgy of the Eucharist, and at the same time with the cosmic liturgy at the end of all time. The apocalypse and its heavenly marriage feast is foreshadowed in the liturgy of the Mass, where the faithful are invited to full communion with God by sharing in the Eucharist. Through the liturgy, the apocalypse is now, and the apocalypse is a feast.

9
Time

It is the middle of the Mass. The epistle and gospel have been read, prayers have been said, a homily has been preached. The choir has sung the *Sanctus*. Silence has fallen. But this is not a silence of inaction; it is a silence that is deep and reverent, which speaks of concentration and anticipation. We are approaching the holiest, most central moment of the service: the consecration of the bread and wine on the altar, the very reason for which the congregation have come together. The congregation's attention is focused on the priest at the east end of the church, who stands bowed over the altar, speaking in a low voice the words of consecration. Through these words, the offerings of bread and wine will be miraculously transformed into the body and blood of Jesus Christ. These words are strictly prescribed, echoing the words which the gospels report Christ speaking to his disciples at the Last Supper: *Hoc est enim corpus meum* ('This is my body'). In the midst of the deep silence, a bell rings as a sign that the words have been spoken. The priest genuflects and raises the host high above his head for the congregation to see, small and white and round like a pearl in the gloom of the church. This liturgical dramaturgy makes it easy to see why Latin hymns praise the Eucharist as *panis angelorum*, 'bread of angels'. Moments later, the priest consecrates the wine in the golden chalice: *Hic est enim calix sanguinis mei, novi et aeterni testamenti, mysterium fidei, qui pro vobis et pro multis effundetur in remissionem peccatorum* ('For this is the chalice of my blood, of the new and eternal testament, the mystery of faith, which will be shed for you and for many unto the remission of sins'). The same movements are repeated, and the chalice containing the wine, which has now become the blood of Christ, is lifted up high by the priest while heads are bowed and lips move in fervent prayer.

This is the scene evoked in an illustration from a medieval Book of Hours (illus. 19). The congregation is assembled in silent adoration of the sacrament of the Eucharist. The formula of consecration spoken by the priest speaks of the mystery of faith, and indeed the celebration of the Eucharist is the central mystery around which the liturgy of the Mass is structured, and around which the entire Christian faith revolves. The Latin texts, prayers, hymns and chants that accompany the celebration of the Mass follow a prescribed, poetically and dramatically consistent form, which culminates in the elevation of the host and chalice, and eventually the communion, where the bread and wine are consumed as a sign of oneness with Christ, so that each individual can participate in the divine life. The Eucharist is not only the central mystery of faith, but one of the central points of contention within Christianity: across the history of the Christian West, countless pages have been written, arguments have been had, wars have been fought, countries have been torn apart and people have died over the question of what exactly happens to the bread and wine at the celebration of the Mass. Catholics and Protestants are divided on the question of whether the bread and wine literally become the body and blood of Christ while retaining their external appearance of bread and wine – the Catholic view known as 'transubstantiation' – or whether the bread and wine are merely symbols of the body and blood of Christ, with a wide range of views within Protestantism on the exact nature of this symbolism. Both schools of thought are represented by medieval thinkers, for whom this question was a central issue, which had crucial implications not only for the faith, but for philosophical and scientific thought more broadly. Debate among medieval scholars about this

19 Illumination from a Book of Hours, Use of Tournai, *c.* 1480–1500.

question started around the ninth century, centring around a philosophical and theological question: are the consecrated elements of bread and wine entirely replaced by the body and blood of Christ, do they coexist with it, or do they not change their nature at all? Out of these questions arose the doctrine of the Real Presence, the view according to which Christ's body is truly present in the consecrated bread and wine, and that the substance of bread and wine changes into the body and blood, while the 'accidents' (that is, the external appearance, physical properties, texture, taste and so on) of the bread and wine remain.[1] The Fourth Lateran Council (1215) affirmed the doctrine of transubstantiation, and this remained the dominant theological opinion in the course of the Middle Ages in the West until the great rift opened by the Protestant Reformation at the beginning of the early modern period, which engulfed Europe in religious conflict for the following centuries. The question of the Eucharist was much more than a mere academic difference of opinion: for many people, it was worth dying for.

For Protestants and Catholics alike, then, the Eucharist and its meaning are central to the faith, one way or another. Many histories have been written of the Reformation and its religious, cultural and political implications for Europe, but they are not what this book is about. Instead, we will focus on how the liturgy of the Eucharist understands and conceptualizes time, and why this is important. Our reference point here is the medieval liturgy; not to take sides in a theological debate but because it is the common root of all later developments across religious divides within Western Christianity. The liturgy of the Eucharist today will vary, sometimes significantly, between Catholic and Protestant communities, and will be influenced by different theological understandings. But fundamentally, all of these different liturgies are derived from the medieval tradition (or are marked by deliberate deviations from this tradition), and it is this tradition which has profoundly influenced representations of time in art, literature and music for centuries.

When we talk about time in an ordinary sense, we often tend to think of it as an inexorable movement from minute to minute, hour to hour, day to day, year to year. Each segment of time, be it long or short, is precisely measured out in smaller units, and clocks are ubiquitous to remind us of the passing of time. Through these means, time is often perceived as objective, external, scientifically laid out. We cannot influence it; we can merely try to keep up. But there are various problems with this perception. Ever since Einstein's theory of special relativity, we know that this perception of time as a constant that is forever and steadily moving without interruption is a fallacy: time in a scientific sense can expand or contract; it is dependent on our frame of reference, on the position of the observer. Such theories may be difficult to conceptualize in our daily lives; the relativity of time is of little relevance when one is running late for a train. But apart from the models of modern-day physics, we are very much aware of a different sense in which time is not objective: while an hour can fly by and feel like five minutes when we are engaged in an exciting activity, it can feel like ten hours when we are waiting for a boring meeting to end. Perception of time can be very much subjective and dependent on the emotional state of the individual.

Not unlike the modern world, the Middle Ages had a range of ways of conceptualizing the passing of time. The clock, for us a ubiquitous item that we now carry on our wrists and mobile phones, was much less common in the Middle Ages than the presence of church bells. As in any largely agrarian society, the cycle of the seasons dominated medieval life, and the life of an ordinary peasant looked different in winter time than in the spring or summer, with agricultural tasks dependent on the time of the year.[2] Those members of society who were engaged in trade were equally dependent on meteorological time and changes in climate: a storm could delay the arrival of a merchant ship, for example, with ramifications for commerce. While the natural cycle of seasons was continuously the same, commercial activities required timekeeping of a more precise sort than that of the agricultural labourer. Time in the countryside was measured by the tolling of church bells, which indicated the hours of religious services. The bells tolling these hours were reliant upon sundials, and could be unreliable and weather-dependent. But within urban environments, more complex and precise timekeeping was necessary for the purposes of trade. Clocks were built opposite church towers, fulfilling a secular function that was directed towards the daily business of the merchant, rather than the concerns of the church. Jacques Le Goff has described these two different conceptions of time as the 'merchant's time' and the 'Church's time'.[3] Secular structures of timekeeping directed towards the requirements of urban tradesmen developed around an older system of keeping time that measured the liturgical hours. For the Church, the hours of the day were primarily important in order to maintain the rhythm of prayer, giving thanks to God at allotted times throughout the day. Such astronomical observation of the most basic sort existed alongside highly specialized versions, with a sophisticated apparatus of astronomical and computational tools appearing in many medieval almanacs, prayer books, psalters and Books of Hours.[4]

Despite these different requirements, however, both the merchant's time and the Church's time were closely interlinked with the natural order of seasons. For trade and agriculture, the time of the year dictated activities that had to be performed: the sowing of seeds, the selling of goods, the storing of produce. For the Church, the turn of the seasons in the yearly cycle had an immediate relevance in a different sense. The cycle of feasts in the liturgy repeated every year, thus following an annual pattern that linked into the natural cycle of the seasons. The secular year and the liturgical year were not identical, however: the liturgical year started with Advent (the period of four weeks until Christmas) and ended the day before the first Sunday of Advent, usually at the end of November, with the exact dates variable depending on when Advent Sunday fell in a particular year. Advent, Christmas, Epiphany, Candlemas, Lent, Easter,

Pentecost: the Church's year was marked by important feasts and the seasons leading up to them, with Easter being the most important feast of the entire year. Easter was a 'moveable feast' dependent on the lunar cycle, celebrated on the Sunday following the first full moon after the vernal equinox (the date in spring when day and night are of equal length). In practice, this meant that Easter was celebrated on a different date each year, and as a result many other moveable feasts dependent on the date of Easter took place at equally variable dates. This cycle of moveable feasts was known as the *Temporale*. Alongside these important moveable feasts and related liturgical seasons there was a concurrent cycle of feast days of saints, the *Sanctorale*. Saints' feasts were celebrated on the same fixed date every year. A page from a Book of Hours of Simon de Varie lists the calendar of saints for the first half of the month of July (illus. 20). Saints such as Thibault (Theobald), Thomas and Benoit (Benedict) are mentioned. The presence of French saints' names indicates that this Book of Hours originates from France: a calendar from England, by contrast, would show a slightly different inventory of saints, including some who were of local or regional significance, as well as widely known biblical saints. Despite the universal nature of the Church's calendar, which prescribed the cycle of Sundays, seasons and feasts for everyone, there was room for local variation. People were more inclined to venerate their 'own' saints from a nearby town or at least from the same country, and this preference for the local and the familiar is reflected in the Sanctorale. Believers did not worship saints in the same way that they worshipped Christ, but rather asked them to intercede for them with God or pass on their prayers for specific intentions. The cult of saints may seem odd or arcane from a modern perspective, but the logic behind it was not dissimilar to that of asking a friend to put in a good word for you with their friend (in this case, God). People seem to have felt closer ties of friendship with saints who lived in the same area and spoke the same language than with those from far away, though there were exceptions.

Although the liturgical cycles of the Temporale and the Sanctorale are distinct from the natural cycle of the seasons, they do not exist in isolation from it. We have seen in previous chapters that the texts of the liturgy allude very deliberately to natural phenomena connected to the seasons, such as the return of light in the depths of winter. An example of the interlinking of the natural and the liturgical cycles can also be seen in the calendar in Simon de Varie's Book of Hours (illus. 20): to the right of the list of saints' feasts is an illustration of a man and a woman binding sheaves in the fields. The month is July, and the image points to the importance of the harvest that takes place in this month, an activity of daily life which occurs alongside the Church's feasts. On the manuscript page, the harvest is almost given a greater focus than the calendar itself, occurring as it does in a beautifully executed illustration with careful details, in the middle of a decorative floral border. The miniature of a lion at the bottom of the page represents the sign of the zodiac relating to July: Leo. We have, then, three different ways of measuring time presented side by side in this calendar: the year of the Church, the year of the labourer, and the year of the stars.

Calendars such as this show just how important liturgical time was to medieval life, even to those not in religious orders. The liturgical calendar intersected with and defined the rhythm of daily life. Holy days, feasts, anniversaries and rituals formed the very social fabric of medieval society, and were equally important not only as religious occasions but for such mundane duties as paying rent. A document from around 1440 from the London Guildhall specifies the 'vsuell dayes of Rent paying . . . at Witsonday, Lammasday, alhalowday, and Candelmasday'.[5] 'Witsonday' refers to the feast of Pentecost; 'Lammasday' is derived from the Old English word *hlafmæsse*, 'bread-Mass', and refers to the feast on 1 August, which was observed as a harvest festival in the early church; 'alhalowday' refers to the feast of All Saints on 1 November, and 'Candelmasday' to the feast of the purification of the Virgin Mary on 2 February.

The presence of '-mas' in some of these words (as, of course, in 'Christmas') indicates the importance of religious services on these dates, but evidently the liturgical celebration did not impede transactions of a more secular nature on these festivals. Although terms such as 'Lammas' have fallen out of use, or are relegated today to firmly religious spheres, we find references to them in centuries far beyond the Middle Ages, such as Alfred, Lord Tennyson's 'Youth' (1833):

> I heard Spring laugh in hidden rills,
> Summer thro' all her sleepy leaves
> Murmur'd: a voice ran round the hills
> When corny Lammas bound the sheaves:
> A voice, when night had crept on high,
> To snowy crofts and winding scars,
> Rang like a trumpet clear and dry,
> And shook the frosty winter stars.[6]

Lammas is here invoked as a personification of the harvest, who binds the sheaves of corn. There is no religious aspect to Tennyson's vision of autumn, and yet the use of the word persists, a word whose very form speaks of the liturgical connection that this season used to have.

In the Middle Ages liturgical practice is thus closely interwoven with seasonal activities, trade and commerce. The liturgy is, therefore, in one sense intensely time-bound and time-dependent. Measuring and keeping time are necessary in order to celebrate the feasts of the liturgical year. This time is cyclical: the same feasts recur every year, the same prayers are said and the same hymns are sung on the same day each year. Within the rhythm of monastic life, hours are measured by the tolling of bells, and every day follows the same pattern of prayer. Through the Liturgy of the Hours in religious communities, every hour is filled with significance, through the Mass and eight

20 Illumination from the Book of Hours of Simon de Varie, 1455.

set times for communal prayer. This custom was inherited from the Jewish tradition of praying seven times a day (based on Psalm 119:164: 'Seven times a day do I praise thee'), which was expanded in the Christian tradition to include an additional night office, bringing the total number of liturgical hours to eight: Matins, Lauds, Prime,

Terce, Sext, None, Vespers and Compline, set hours of prayer from the very early morning to evening.[7] The prayers for these canonical hours are set out in medieval prayerbooks called 'Books of Hours'. The survival of a great number of Books of Hours, often sumptuously illustrated and illuminated, shows the significance of this liturgy not only within religious houses but for society more broadly. Judging by the number of surviving manuscripts, Books of Hours were among the most popular and sought-after texts in late medieval England, France and the Netherlands. Many of these books were not intended for monks and nuns, but for pious laypeople, who wished to follow the Liturgy of the Hours as private devotions and prayers in their homes. Some of these books are relatively modest and simple, while others include finely executed illustrations and miniatures with scenes from the life of Christ and lavishly decorated borders, such as the nativity scene in the Arenberg Hours (illus. 21). From simple objects for private prayer to luxury objects often made for members of the nobility, Books of Hours enjoyed a broad appeal.[8]

The nativity scene in this stunningly illustrated Book of Hours is attributed to Flemish illuminator Willem Vrelant (d. 1481). With tempera colours, ink and gold leaf, the illustration shows Mary and Joseph with the Christ-child, set in a rural scenery. God the Father and the Holy Spirit are depicted above the stable, accompanied by angels. But although the image is the centrepiece of the page, and the delicate border decoration certainly absorbs the reader's attention, both are there to embellish and illustrate the text of the Liturgy of the Hours at Prime (with *Ad primam* written in red in the first line): *Deus, in adiutorium meum intende. Domine, ad adiuuandum me festina. Gloria patri et filio et spiritui sancto. Sicut erat in principio et nunc et* . . . (supplied from the next page) *semper, et in saecula saeculorum. Amen.* ('O God, come to my assistance. O Lord, make haste to help me. Glory be to the Father and to the Son and to the Holy Spirit. As it was in the beginning, is now and ever shall be, world without end. Amen.') These words, citing Psalm 70:1, form the introductory prayer to every liturgical Hour. In a religious community, these verses would usually be chanted, following a call-and-response structure. But they would likely have been recited privately by the owner of this Book of Hours, with its lavish illustrations encouraging private meditation on the mysteries of the life of Christ at set hours of the day. The book is an object of great beauty, which is intended to reveal the even greater beauty hidden within the Liturgy of the Hours.

The Liturgy of the Hours focuses on prayers that recur at the same time every day. It is repetitive, cyclical, designed to lead the individual into ever-deeper meditation upon the same words. But there is also another understanding of time expressed in the liturgy, which appears to clash with this idea of cyclical time. Time can be seen as a movement from the Creation to Old Testament history to the birth and death of Christ to the many centuries after Christ until the present, and continuing from the present into the future, with a distinct end, after which will come the resurrection of the dead and the renewal of heaven and earth. In this sense, Christian time can be imagined as teleological, as a straight line rather than a circle, moving inexorably forward towards an end point. The two understandings, though they seem at first glance contradictory, are deliberately brought into conversation in the liturgy. We have seen in previous chapters that the *Dies irae* sequence moves from prayers said for the individual soul of a deceased to prayers for the Day of Judgement at the end of time, and how the idea of eventual renewal of heaven and earth is alluded to in liturgical prayers. Through the liturgy, there is a close connection between the here and now and the future that is to come. The feasts of the present point forward in time, as emphasized in many liturgical prayers such as the prayer after communion (also known as the *Postcommunio*) on the third Mass of Christmas Day: 'Grant, we pray thee, almighty God, that as the Saviour of the world born today is the author of our supernatural birth, so he may himself also be to us the giver of immortality.'[9] The feast celebrated on this particular day is relevant in relation to eternal life that is to come.

21 *The Nativity*, illumination from the Arenberg Hours, early 1460s.

The present looks towards the future, and the liturgical celebration of a feast, dependent upon the measuring of time, invokes a future immortal life outside of time.

The liturgy not only points forward to the future in a teleological sense, however, but draws the past into the present. At its core the Christian understanding of time sees the life of Christ as the central event of all history. It is through the death of Christ on the cross and his resurrection that salvation has been accomplished, and therefore all of human history is dependent upon this one decisive moment in time. Throughout the previous chapters, we have seen the importance of the concept of typology for the liturgy: episodes, characters, and narratives of the Old Testament are interpreted in relation to the life of Christ. The liturgical use of such Old Testament material turns it into a prophecy of the coming of Christ, in which the Old Testament is the prefiguration, and the life of Christ is the fulfilment. In this understanding, time is not so much a straight line, but circles around Christ as the centre of gravity. Such an outlook raises an important question: how can the life of Christ as the centre of all human history stay relevant to those who live many centuries afterwards? How can the death of a Jewish man around AD 33 influence the lives of people in the fourteenth, the sixteenth or the twenty-first century?

The liturgy offers a solution to this question. Among the multiplicity of different understandings of time that we have seen, perhaps the most mysterious, but also the most crucial, is the idea of liturgical presence. This is where we come back to the scene of the elevation of the host and chalice from the beginning of this chapter. When the priest speaks the words of consecration, he uses the very words of Christ at the Last Supper reported in the gospels: 'This is my body' and 'this is the chalice of my blood.' The theological idea behind this liturgical practice is that the priest speaks and acts *in persona Christi* (in the person of Christ), representing Christ in ritual practice. This is why the priest's words are the words of Christ himself, rather than words of a human minister spoken to God. This idea is important in relation to theological ideas about the Real Presence of Christ in the form of bread and wine. According to this idea, it is not the priest who miraculously transforms these elements into the body and blood of Christ, but it is God himself who effects the miracle. The priest is not important in his own right, but rather as an instrument of divine power. What happens during the Mass is not a re-enactment of the Last Supper as if it were a play on a stage; to the contrary, it is an actualization of past events that is anything but a play. Nicholas Wolterstorff explains it like this: 'the celebrant actually blesses; he does not play the role of Christ blessing. We actually give thanks; we do not play the role of the disciples giving thanks.'[10] Although there are significant disagreements and divergent interpretations of these ideas in later Protestant movements, the understanding of the Eucharist expressed by medieval liturgy insists that Christ becomes truly present through the words of consecration.

This idea has implications for the understanding of time within the liturgical ritual. The liturgy collapses time into a single liturgical moment. If the priest speaks the words spoken by Christ at the Last Supper in the person of Christ, this means in turn that within the liturgy the events of Christ's death and resurrection are brought into the present, although they have historically taken place within the past. In other words, the liturgy makes present again the key events of salvation history. What happened in a Roman province around the year AD 33 is again made present in every celebration of the Mass through the ritual. We can see this understanding of time reflected in many ways in the liturgy. When the church calendar commemorates a particular event, the liturgy speaks of it not as a past but as a present event.[11] For instance, the liturgical celebration of Christmas speaks of the birth of Christ as an event of today rather than an event that is being merely remembered, as in the *Postcommunio* on the third Mass of Christmas quoted above: 'the Saviour of the world born *today*'. The *Exsultet* of the Easter vigil (see Chapter Six) likewise celebrates the redemption as an event of the present time: 'This is the night when Christ broke the prison bars of death and rose victorious from the underworld.'[12] But in the *Exsultet*, there are further events that are spoken of as having taken place this very same night: 'This is the night when once you led our forebears, Israel's children, from slavery in Egypt and made them pass dry-shod through the Red Sea.' The parting of the Red Sea in Exodus, which is understood as a prefiguration of the salvation through Christ, likewise becomes mystically present in the liturgy of today. Past, present and future are connected in one all-encompassing liturgical present. Through the words of the ritual, the present expands to include prophecy, fulfilment and vast swathes of historical time. All these things have already happened, but in the liturgy they are still happening, and continuously happening in every church in any place where Mass is said.

In this way, liturgy breaks through the barriers of the linear time of ordinary life, and reorients the congregation towards the Redemption as the focal point of all of human history. Time becomes flexible, malleable, all-inclusive. This stands in sharp contrast to a strict linear chronology, in which one second ticks on into the next, and will never return once it is past. Theologically, liturgy is situated at the intersection between the passing of ordinary time and divine timelessness. God is outside of time, and therefore the historical events of the Redemption can remain perpetually present in the liturgy, not just as a memory or recollection of past events, but as an actualization of that which happened in the past. At the same time, the liturgy points forward to the events of the Last Day and the subsequent renewal of earth and heaven as the completion of salvation history that is still to come. Chronological time is important to the celebrations of the liturgical year, but at the same time liturgy transcends it, merging past and future in an everlasting liturgical presence, which mirrors the timelessness of God.

This mysterious and all-encompassing sense of liturgical time is part of the reason why the Mass is so fundamental to Christian worship. It also helps us to understand why the question of how to celebrate the Eucharist, and how to interpret it, has been so important to Christians of different persuasions through the ages. It explains why Catholics and Protestants alike, in the middle of religious, political and social crises such as the Reformation, were willing to argue, fight and die for it. The mystery of liturgical time is powerful, not unlike the mysterious simultaneity of time to which T. S. Eliot (1888–1965) alludes in the *Four Quartets*: 'Time past and time future/ What might have been and what has been/ Point to one end, which is always present.'[13]

10
Space

We are standing in the magnificent cathedral in medieval Wells. A bell is rung. Its pure, sharp sound reverberates through the high vaults above. The congregation rises as the procession moves up the aisle, a line of white robes slowly advancing towards the high altar. Their steps can be heard on the stone floor, coming closer and closer. First comes a golden cross carried at the head of the procession, shimmering whenever it catches a ray of sunlight falling through the high, arched windows on the side of the nave. The smell of incense fills the church, and the burning candles of the torch-bearers shine through the white cloud around the thurible. The sun casts colourful specks of light through the stained-glass windows; red and blue and green and gold dancing on walls. For a moment the incense veils the vaulted ceiling above, so that all that remains visible are the pillars on either side of the nave, going upwards, ever upwards. The whole building seems to be reaching towards the heavens, stretching its limbs higher, higher. Then, the organ starts, and a low chord fills the building that can be not only heard but felt in the depths of the body. The choir begins to sing the Introit, voices interweaving like the twisted vines that decorate the stonework on the outside of the cathedral. The procession has reached the altar, and the priest genuflects and ascends the steps, his brightly coloured vestments shining in the light of the candles. The choir now changes from Latin into another language: *Kyrie, eleison* – 'Lord, have mercy' in

Greek – reaching far back in time and asking for God's forgiveness with the same words as the earliest Christians. The music is reflective and yet hopeful, directing a heartfelt plea upwards, reaching towards heaven just like the high pillars and the arched windows and the vaulted ceiling.

The preceding chapters have mainly focused on liturgical texts and their role within worship. But although the words of these texts are of crucial importance in the liturgy, it is important to remember that they are not the only important aspects of Christian worship. Liturgy is a multi-sensorial experience; it gains its life through the interplay of spoken word, singing and silence. It includes not only sound but a vibrant display of colour, light and darkness, carved statues and images, the movements of the priest and the servers around the church, the smell of incense, burning candles, the feel of cold air from the stone floor and the warmth of sunlight through the windows. It is a symphony of sound, light and colour. The ritual's significance is enhanced by the space within which it takes place; the liturgical words draw their weight not only from their theological and poetic qualities but from the setting in which they are used. In medieval England, the most impactful settings for the liturgy would have been provided by the numerous Gothic cathedrals, built with breathtaking craftsmanship and considerable sacrifice, sometimes even the sacrifice of human lives lost in the process of construction. Their construction took many decades, often centuries, leaving behind monumental works of art in stone, which have remained in use as places of worship until the present day. Gothic architecture reflects in stone the same attitude towards the divine that we also find in the liturgy. The key to understanding these buildings is to remember that they were built for the liturgy and are an expression of its spirit. They are monuments that speak of what G. K. Chesterton (1874–1936) called the 'battle-beauty of the Gothic', in his poetic vision of Lincoln Cathedral with its spires, gargoyles and flying buttresses, contrasted with the mundane city around it:

> I had climbed the sharp, crooked streets up to this ecclesiastical citadel; just in front of me was a flourishing and richly coloured kitchen garden; beyond that was the low stone wall; beyond that the row of vans that looked like houses; and beyond and above that, straight and swift and dark, light as a flight of birds, and terrible as the Tower of Babel, Lincoln Cathedral seemed to rise out of human sight. As I looked at it I asked myself the questions that I have asked here; what was the soul in all those stones? They were varied, but it was not variety; they were solemn, but it was not solemnity; they were farcical, but it was not farce . . . All of a sudden the vans I had mistaken for cottages began to move away to the left. In the start this gave to my eye and mind I really fancied that the Cathedral was moving towards the right. The two huge towers seemed to start striding across the plain like the two legs of some giant whose body was covered with the clouds. Then I saw what it was. The truth about Gothic is, first, that it is alive, and second, that it is on the march. It is the Church Militant; it is the only fighting architecture. All its spires are spears at rest; and all its stones are stones asleep in a catapult. In that instant of illusion, I could hear the arches clash like swords as they crossed each other . . . The graven foliage wreathed and blew like banners going into battle; the silence was deafening with all the mingled noises of a military march; the great bell shook down, as the organ shook up its thunder. The thirsty-throated gargoyles shouted like trumpets from all the roofs and pinnacles as they passed; and from the lectern in the core of the cathedral the eagle of the awful evangelist clashed his wings of brass.[1]

Regardless of whether or not one agrees with Chesterton's vision of the cathedral at war, his description captures an important aspect of the magnificent buildings erected for the celebration of the liturgy: they are no mere functional spaces for religious ceremonies, but they are an expression of an idea, of a vision of God. Every part of a Gothic cathedral points upwards, directing our gaze and thought towards the divine, beyond the mundane present. But the small and the mundane are not insignificant. Beyond the monumental, the upward movement, the light shining from above, there is room for almost obsessive detail. Intricate decoration – painting, carving and engraving – adorns every nook and cranny of the building, up until the highest tower, where perfectly carved saints stand guard even though they are too far from the ground to be seen by any human eye. Cathedrals are theology made stone. Like the texts of the liturgy, they are dramatic, poetic and almost unbearably beautiful.

Nothing about the architecture of a medieval cathedral is accidental. The building, its form, orientation and decoration – everything is symbolic. Its very geometry, with its intricate relationship between circles and squares, expresses core Christian beliefs about the divine. A medieval cathedral is built in the shape of a cross, the central symbol of Christ's death and resurrection. The building is oriented towards the east, with the High Altar at the east end invoking the rising sun, a symbol of Christ, the light that overcomes the darkness. Accordingly, as we enter the building from the portal at the west end and follow the nave towards the east, our path maps a symbolic journey from darkness towards light. This symbolism is mirrored by many architectural elements, such as the placement of the baptismal font usually found near the main entrance of a church (though sometimes placed in a separate chapel, called a baptistery). Baptism marks the initiation of new members into the church, and therefore the placement of the font at the beginning of this symbolic journey towards the rising sun emphasizes the importance of the baptismal rite as a moment of transition when the newly baptized child or adult enters the community of the faithful. Reinforcing this symbolism, the baptismal rite begins outside the sacred building, before moving inside and to the font placed near the entrance.[2] The baptismal font, then, stands at the beginning of the way into a church building, just as baptism marks the entrance of the individual into the Church as a community, the symbolic body of Christ. Sacred architecture reflects the meaning of the liturgy.

Understanding the liturgy within the broader context of the spaces within which rituals take place means that we have to fill in many blanks with our imagination. Historical research can reconstruct, up to a certain point, which words were said or sung at which point in the ritual, which movements accompanied it, where in a building a ceremony took place, and so on. Nonetheless, we have to imagine many aspects relating to sound, sight and space. This can only be a poor substitute for the real thing, because fully understanding the experience of a liturgical ritual, its effect on all the senses within the astonishing space of a church, requires bodily presence at this ritual. The liturgy, in the way it channels sound, sight, smell and movement, demands to be experienced in a fully embodied form because it demands participation in community with others. In the liturgical celebration, a series of postures and movements are required not only of the priest and the servers, but of the congregation who have assembled – kneeling, standing, sitting, making the sign of the cross, going up towards the altar to make an offering and so on. This participation is encouraged in the Middle Ages even for those who did not understand the Latin texts of the liturgy. A number of texts survive from late medieval England that guide lay members of the congregation in their devotions during Mass and serve to explain what the priest is doing, even if they do not translate the exact words. What is particularly notable about these texts is the way in which they not only describe the priest's movements but instruct the congregation in their movements, with directions such as these: 'When thou thy Creed thus hast done, upon thy feet thou stand up soon'; 'a large cross on thee thou make'; 'take good keep unto the priest, when he him turns, knock on thy breast'; 'kneeling hold up both thy hands'.[3] The lay members of the congregation are encouraged to participate in the ritual, not only by silently saying prayers but by adopting collective postures and gestures that reflect what is happening in the liturgy.

The liturgy thus follows an intricate dramaturgy in which all those present participate, and which becomes a unified whole through speaking to all the senses within dedicated sacred spaces.

The structure of the Mass follows a detailed theological logic, which unites stable parts that are strictly prescribed, and some variable parts that change according to specific liturgical feasts. Its dramatic architecture is representative of core theological beliefs that are embodied, or enacted, in the ritual. Fundamental to these beliefs is an understanding of the Mass as a ritual that makes present again the crucifixion, in which Christ is wholly and truly present in the sacrament of the Eucharist under the appearances of bread and wine, according to the dominant belief in the medieval period, and continued in post-Reformation times in Catholic doctrine. The crucifixion was a sacrifice that Christ willingly underwent in order to atone for the sins of humankind, and consequently the Mass has the character of a sacrifice. This understanding is expressed in a multitude of ways in the dramaturgy of the Mass, in which all liturgical texts, prayers and actions build up to the pivotal moment of the consecration of the bread and wine, which become the body and blood of Christ. The ritual gestures and movements up to and around the altar all express this sacrificial character – the priest stands at the altar facing east, as a sign of directing prayers to God on behalf of the congregation, the altar is incensed as a sign that it is the place where the sacrifice is offered, and the prayers over the offerings of bread and wine implore God to accept them graciously for the remission of sins. This emphasis on sacrifice, though somewhat alien to modern sensibilities, is deep and old. Most ancient cultures had ritual practices that involved sacrifice of some kind, including the slaughter of animals connected with ideas of ritual cleansing, expurgation and renewal. Jewish ritual practices, too, involved animal sacrifice in the temple, and many aspects of the Mass hearken back to Jewish traditions, prayers and psalms. Christian liturgy thus draws a connection between animal sacrifice in the temple and the sacrifice of Christ at the cross, using the metaphor 'Lamb of God' to refer to the idea that Jewish animal sacrifice prefigured the ultimate sacrifice of an innocent man who is also God, laying down his life for the salvation, cleansing and renewal of the world.

The structure of the Mass is complex, and at first glance can merely seem a long list of prayers and readings. One way of approaching this structure is to understand it as a narrative arc that leads us from God's words to God's actions. In the first part of the Mass, we listen to and reflect on the word of God, while in the second half we celebrate the Eucharist, making present Christ's death on the cross. This narrative logic helps us to understand the individual elements of the rite, which construct a dramatic development across both parts of the Mass, culminating in the consecration of the bread and wine. The introductory rites at the beginning of the Mass take place at the foot of the altar, preparing the celebrant and the congregation for what is to come in order to enter into the liturgy in an attitude of humility and reflection, with the recitation of a psalm and a general confession of sins. When the priest has ascended the steps to the altar, the liturgy leads us from prayers for God's mercy in the *Kyrie* and praise of God in the *Gloria* to listening to the word of God in the epistle and gospel readings. The gospel is then expounded and interpreted in the homily, in order to understand more deeply the layers of meaning contained in the biblical text. The first part of the Mass concludes with an affirmation of the articles of faith in the Creed. Broadly speaking, the first part is therefore focused on an engagement with Scripture through listening and exegesis, and in the Middle Ages those members of the congregation who were unable to follow the readings in Latin were still able to gain an understanding of them through the homily, which was often in the vernacular.

After this focus on the word of God, the sacrificial character of the Mass becomes increasingly prominent in the second part. The offering is prepared and the priest washes his hands as a ritual sign of cleansing before performing the sacrifice. The offering is incensed and the sign of the cross is made many times over it. The *Sanctus* expresses a sense of the ineffable divine majesty and power. Prayers are said for the living, and the saints in heaven are invoked, expressing the idea that the sacrifice is offered for the entire community of the faithful. Then we approach the dramatic climax: the consecration of the bread and wine, with the words of Christ at the Last Supper said inaudibly by the priest – creating a silence for the congregation that enhances the mystery and awe of the moment. The host and chalice are lifted up high for the congregation to see, in a symbolic gesture that echoes Christ being lifted up high on the cross. After the moment of consecration, the priest says a number of prayers asking God to accept the sacrifice and commemorating the souls of the departed. Finally, as a means of preparing for communion, the Lord's Prayer is said, reflecting a sense of trust towards God who is 'our Father'. The choir then sings the *Agnus Dei*, which in many musical settings is the most introspective and moving part of the Mass, invoking Christ as the 'Lamb of God' sacrificed for our sins. After the communion of the faithful (or, in medieval times where communion was less frequent, the communion of the priest only), concluding prayers are said, and the final blessing is given.

This summary makes apparent the dramatic development of the liturgy of the Mass, from introduction through reflection on Scripture to the sacrifice, and final conclusion. Within this large-scale narrative framework, many psalms and prayers, which change with the liturgical occasion (also called 'propers'), offer abundant material for reflection. What is not described above is the extent to which this rite varied locally, particularly in the Middle Ages in the West, before the liturgy became more unified after the Council of Trent. Also missing from the description above are those elements that can only be fully experienced in person: the setting within a church with its distinctive architecture and stained-glass windows, the sound and movement and visual appearance of the ritual, the priest's and the servers' movements from one side to the other around the altar, the bowing, genuflecting and elevation of hands, the swinging of the thurible, the liturgical vestments, the alternation between sung and spoken words, all of which are imbued with deeper significance in the ritual. There is a choreography to the celebration of the liturgy that gives it a dramatic sense, and yet the Mass, as we have seen in the preceding chapter, is not like a stage play. The Mass makes Christ's actions present again, rather than merely representing them as a play would. Nonetheless, there are areas of overlap between ritual performance and stage acting, and the two have fruitfully inspired each other.

From the early Middle Ages in the West onwards, a tradition of liturgical plays developed around the liturgy, containing dramatic representations of crucial moments in the life of Christ. The earliest evidence of such plays comes from monastic communities. For example, the *Regularis Concordia*, a manual of rules for houses of the Benedictine order in England compiled by Bishop Æthelwold of Winchester between AD 965 and 975, contains a dramatic dialogue between the women at the empty tomb of the risen Christ and the angel who announces Christ's resurrection, centring on the question *Quem quaeritis*? ('Whom do you seek?').[4] Small 'plays' such as this were designed to accompany major feasts such as Easter and Christmas, and were performed in Latin and usually in plainchant within monastic communities: in this case the Benedictine monks would have taken on the roles of the angel and the women. Other examples of such liturgical plays survive from communities in England and continental Europe. There are, as we have seen in preceding chapters, also texts within the liturgy itself that harness such dramatic elements, such as the *Improperia* of Good Friday, which imagine the crucified Christ reproaching his people. Another example can be found in liturgical processions for Palm Sunday at the beginning of Holy Week, which enact in liturgical form the triumphant entry of Christ into Jerusalem before his passion and death. The Gospel of Matthew recounts these events as follows:

> A very large crowd spread their cloaks on the road, and others cut branches from the trees and spread them on the road. The crowds that went ahead of him and that followed were shouting, 'Hosanna to the Son of David! Blessed is the one who comes in the name of the Lord! Hosanna in the highest heaven!' (Matthew 21:8–9)

The liturgy of Palm Sunday contains many elements of the gospel account and re-enacts them in symbolic form: palm branches are blessed and distributed to the people, and a procession is formed leading to different stations, where readings, prayers and chants take place, before the procession finally enters the church. During the procession, various antiphons and hymns are sung, including one that starts with the words:

Gloria, laus, et honor tibi sit Rex Christe Redemptor: cui puerile decus prompsit Hosanna pium.	Glory, praise, and honour belong to you, O Christ, king, redeemer, to whom the youthful virtue presented the holy Hosanna.
Israel es tu rex Dauidis et inclita proles: nomine qui in Domini rex benedicte venis.	You are king of Israel and the celebrated offspring of David, who comes in the name of the Lord, O blessed king.[5]

Ascribed to Theodulf of Orléans (*c.* 760–821), the full hymn describes Christ's triumphant entry into Jerusalem, with the refrain *Gloria, laus, et honor* repeated after each verse. The hymn takes its cue from the acclamations of Christ as the 'Son of David' and 'the one who comes in the name of the Lord' reported in the gospel, with the jubilant shout 'Hosanna'. The rubrics of liturgical manuscripts indicate that this hymn was sung at Palm Sunday processions by choirs of young boys, echoing the hymn's emphasis on 'youthful virtue'.

The dramatic elements of such processions can be gleaned when we imagine what such occasions would have looked like: the members of the procession clothed in liturgical vestments, the choir, the congregation with palm branches in their hands, the music, the incense, the movement from station to station up to the entrance into the church, the diverse array of prayers and hymns. It is not only a liturgical celebration but a spectacle that speaks to all senses. And yet the drama of the occasion was heightened even further by the ways in which the procession was adapted to the spaces in which it took place. The rubrics of the *Gloria, laus* hymn contain instructions that the refrain was to be sung by the boy choir standing in an 'elevated place',[6] while the alternating verses of the hymn were sung by a choir in a response-and-answer structure coming from different places. Where exactly this 'elevated place' was would have depended on the particular church or cathedral in question; platforms or other devices could have been used. The features of a specific location could be used effectively in order to heighten the dramatic impact of the moment, as the example of medieval Wells demonstrates. Wells Cathedral has an imposing facade, which shows scenes from the heavenly Jerusalem. The facade also hides a secret: behind a row of carved angels is a hidden passage for singers, built around 1220.[7] Openings originally hidden behind statues of angels allowed for singers to stand in the passage and sing to those congregated below in front of the facade. The passage is constructed so that it would function as a resonating chamber to amplify the sound, with the effect that it could be clearly heard across the space outside the portal.[8] The historical evidence suggests, then, that these architectural elements were constructed so that the liturgy could be celebrated in an even more dramatic fashion. In medieval England, the Eucharistic host – the body of Christ – was carried in a golden monstrance during Palm Sunday processions, thus vividly re-enacting the entry of the historic Jesus into the city of Jerusalem.[9] The sacramental body of Christ approached the cathedral whose front depicted the Heavenly Jerusalem. The symbolism of this moment could hardly be more impactful: as the procession moved towards the west door of the cathedral, there would have been a dramatic interchange in the singing of the hymn between the boy choir stationed up in the passage behind the statues of angels, and the responding choir down below. The boys' choir would have been invisible to those below, creating the impression of angels singing from on high, with mankind below responding and joining in a shared song: heaven and earth united in shouts of praise before the carved facade of the Heavenly Jerusalem as Christ entered. The space within which the liturgy took place was used to maximum symbolic effect, acting as a breathtaking stage-set for the Palm Sunday celebrations.[10]

Imagining the liturgy in the spaces within which it took place allows us to catch glimpses of how it was dynamically adapted and developed in order to heighten the effect of the texts, creating rituals that communicated not only through words but through a multitude of sensory experiences. Dramatic elements, and sometimes even plays, could be used to this end. It is difficult to say whether there is a clear line of development from such liturgical drama to what we would these days associate with the term 'drama', such as Shakespeare's plays and more recent modern forms of acting in film and television. But what we do know is that the medieval precursor to Shakespeare's plays was very closely associated with liturgical and religious ideas. This tradition, one of the main forms of medieval theatre, is what we usually refer to with the terms 'biblical drama', 'cycle plays' or 'mystery plays'. Records of such plays survive from a number of medieval towns, including Chester, York and various places in East Anglia. The medieval conception of such plays is quite different from what a modern-day theatregoer might expect. Plays were performed in cycles, and the performances took place as open-air street theatre, with a series of wagons for the pageants set up at stations at key points within the medieval towns. Audiences were able to move from wagon to wagon along the streets in order to watch individual pageants being performed. The subject matter of such plays was religious in nature and spanned the whole of Christian history, representing crucial events from the creation of the world to the life of Christ to the Day of Doom. A complete cycle of plays survives from medieval York, containing 47 plays in total, which gives us an idea of the truly remarkable scale of such performances. The theatrical spectacle of such a cycle was a civic event in which everyone took part, whether as a member of the audience or as an actor in a play. Associations of craftsmen and merchants practising a specific trade (called 'guilds') were in charge of individual plays and all aspects concerning their performance, acting and staging. Guilds were often put in charge of plays that had some connection with the crafts or trade they were practising: in medieval York, for instance, the play about the building of Noah's Ark was under the direction of the shipwrights, while the play about Christ's suffering on the cross was the responsibility of the butchers. Although some other forms of medieval theatre used troupes of professional actors, the biblical drama of the cycle plays was a truly communal endeavour. The religious subject matter might lead us to assume that the cycle plays were a solemn and serious affair, but in reality the plays incorporate plenty of the kind of humour that would appeal to their audiences in such civic settings, with many comical and rowdy moments, not unlike the bawdy humour in Shakespeare's plays. Medieval theatre leaves space for laughter even in the midst of the most serious plays.

In medieval towns, the performance of such biblical theatre was associated with the liturgical calendar. The York cycle was performed on the feast of Corpus Christi, which was celebrated every year on the Thursday after Trinity Sunday (late May or early June, depending on the date of Easter). Corpus Christi was a feast in honour of the sacrament of the Eucharist, during which the consecrated host was carried in solemn procession through the city in order to celebrate and affirm belief in the Real Presence of Christ in the Eucharist. This liturgical occasion was accompanied by the annual performance of the cycle of plays, which allowed the members of the community to visualize and experience the central events of salvation history.[11] In this way, biblical drama was embedded into a liturgical context in how, where and when it was performed. We can see the importance of the liturgy to biblical theatre throughout the individual plays, which take their cues not only from the Bible, but specifically from the liturgy in the way in which characters, themes and ideas are portrayed.

We have already seen above the dramatic elements of liturgical processions for Palm Sunday. The York Corpus Christi play of the entry of Jesus into Jerusalem is closely reminiscent of such liturgical practice in a scene where the town officials of Jerusalem decide to go and welcome Christ:

> Go we then with procession
> To meet that comely [= gracious one] as us ought
> With branches, flowers, and unison,
> With mightful songs here in a row.
> Our children shall
> Go sing before that men may know.[12]

Precisely as in the liturgical celebration, Christ in the play is being welcomed into Jerusalem by singing children. The singing is not just a mention in the text, but an instruction and an action to be performed, as the play includes the stage direction *Tunc cantant* ('They then sing'). The manuscript sources do not specify precisely what was sung, but given the liturgical resonances of the play, it is likely to have been a hymn or antiphon taken from the Palm Sunday liturgy. For the medieval audience of this play, such references would inevitably have brought to mind the ritual re-enactment of the event on Palm Sunday.

Other plays, too, weave a rich web of references to the liturgy. As we have seen in Chapter Five, the human sorrow of Christ's mother under the cross is a subject that was explored with intensity in Western liturgy, literature and art. It is not surprising, therefore, that the portrayal of this moment onstage would have particular poignancy. When we see Mary standing underneath the cross in play 32 of the so-called N-Town plays (a cycle that would have been performed in a number of different towns), the Virgin's grief-stricken address to Jesus can hardly fail to move the audience:

> Alas! Alas! I live too longe
> To see my sweet son with pains stronge,
> As a thief on cross doth honge,
> And never yet did he synne!
> Alas, my dear child to death is dressed!
> Now is my care well more increased.
> A! My heart with pain is pressed,
> For sorrow my heart doth twynne [= break].[13]

This is reminiscent of the *Stabat Mater* (see Chapter Five), which begins:

> The sorrowful mother stood
> weeping before the cross
> where hung her Son.
>
> Her grieving soul,
> anguished and lamenting,
> was pierced by a sword.

Mary's speech in the play contains close verbal echoes of the *Stabat Mater*, such as 'my sweet son', as well as her description of her sorrows, in which her 'heart doth twynne'. The play clearly invokes this tradition, but presents it from a first-person perspective rather than the third person, as the Latin *Stabat Mater* does. Similarly to some of the Middle English poems that we have seen in Chapter Five, the pathos of the mother watching her only son suffer torment is further enhanced in heart-wrenching words when Mary speaks to her own heart, bidding it to leave her body, and wishes for her own death:

> A! Out on my heart! Why burst thou not?
> And thou art maiden and mother and seest thus thy child spill [= die].
> How mayst thou abide this sorrow and this woeful thought?
> A, death, death, death! Why wilt thou not me kill?[14]

What is merely descriptive in the *Stabat Mater* is here imagined as an anguished mother at the brink of what she can endure, wishing for death, and her *cri de coeur* would have been even more haunting in live performance onstage. The crucifixion play in the N-Town cycle also makes reference to the tradition of the swoon of the virgin formed in visual art, with the stage directions specifying that she 'falls to the ground as if dead'.[15] The dramatic performance clearly invokes a larger liturgical and paraliturgical tradition of Mary underneath the cross, and uses it for an emotionally impactful scene onstage.

While the N-Town crucifixion play alludes to the *Stabat Mater* tradition, using it rather freely in order to create an emotionally compelling stage performance, medieval plays frequently cite directly from liturgical texts.[16] An example is the York crucifixion play, which shows us in brutal detail the irreverent Roman soldiers nailing Christ to the cross in a rather incompetent fashion. When at length they have finished, and have hoisted the cross upright, the crucified Christ speaks to the passers-by with the following words:

> Al men that walk by way or street,
> Take tente ye shal no travail tyne [= Pay attention so that you may not miss any suffering]
> Behold my head, my hands, and my feet,

And fully feel now, or ye fyne [= before you go away]
If any mourning may be meet [= equal]
Or mischief measured unto mine.
My Father, that all bales [= sorrows] may beat [= cure],
Forgive these men that do me pain.
What they work wotte [= know] they not.
Therfore, my Father, I crave
Let never their sins be sought,
But see their souls to save.[17]

This speech echoes the *Tenebrae* responsory *O vos omnes*, as we have seen in Chapter Four:

O all you who pass by the way,
look and see if there is any sorrow like my sorrow.

The beginning of Christ's speech directly cites the liturgical text, which in turn draws from the words of the prophet Jeremiah lamenting the destruction of Jerusalem (Lam. 1:12). We have seen how the liturgy brings together Old Testament texts and the events of the Passion in order to emphasize that Christ's redemptive acts are the fulfilment of these prophecies. The York play invokes this tradition but expands upon the idea contained in the responsory, listing the signs of his suffering: 'Behold my head, my hands, and my feet'. Christ then turns to a prayer for his tormentors, following Luke 23:34: 'Then Jesus said, "Father, forgive them; for they do not know what they are doing."' The text of the play thus merges Christ's words from the cross, which the Gospel of Luke reports, and the words that the liturgy uses to contemplate Christ's suffering, creating an emotional appeal which directly addresses the spectators, inviting them to contemplate the crucifixion through their senses, to 'take tente', 'behold' and 'feel'. The speech uses a regular four-stressed metre, with alternating rhymes and numerous alliterations, making Christ's words all the more memorable. It also forms a striking contrast to the Roman soldiers' short, scornful comments that follow the speech:

> I MILES [1st soldier]: We, hark, he jangles like a jay.
> II MILES [2nd soldier]: Methinks he patters like a py [= magpie].

The derogatory comparison of Jesus with a chattering bird could not be further from the reality of his simple yet profound speech through which we hear the authority of biblical and liturgical tradition. But the use of this tradition in a play, the act of transposing these words from a liturgical setting onto a stage, has a very specific effect. While the liturgical *O vos omnes* imagines a situation in which Christ speaks to those who pass by where he is crucified, in a performance in a cycle play this appeal gains an additional layer of meaning and becomes quite literal: since the wagons on which the plays were performed were set up along the main streets of the medieval town, the audience wandering from pageant to pageant literally become the 'men that walk by way or street'. The appeal to the passers-by, inviting them to look upon the crucified Christ and see if there is any sorrow like his, is directed at the spectators of the play. Christ on the cross speaks to the medieval inhabitants of York who are watching the play. The past and the present meet through the words of the liturgy enacted onstage.[18]

These are just a few examples of how liturgical allusions were used in medieval theatre with theological depth and dramatic effect. Biblical drama continued into the sixteenth century and well beyond the Reformation, and Shakespeare's plays show that he was aware of this tradition. Many aspects of his themes, characters and dramaturgy are influenced by medieval dramatic forms. Hamlet expresses his aversion to excessively exaggerated performance and admonishes the players to avoid it, since 'it out-Herods Herod' (*Hamlet* III.2.14), a reference to the portrayal of Herod as a raging tyrant in medieval biblical drama.[19] But Shakespeare's plays are also concerned with the importance of the liturgy in a deeper sense than such passing references. One of the key themes of *Hamlet* is the question of how we remember the dead, and what rituals should be performed at their passing.[20] In the medieval world, this function was fulfilled by the elaborate liturgy of the dead, with Requiem Masses and prayers said for the souls of the departed. The Reformation, with its changes to the old idea of purgatory, heralded changes also to funeral rites, which could vary widely according to local custom in England during Elizabeth's reign.[21] This change in liturgical rites of remembrance is reflected throughout *Hamlet* by a prevailing concern over deaths and burials without full rites. Old Hamlet's ghost is restless, he tells us, because he was

> Cut off, even in the blossoms of my sin,
> Unhouseled, disappointed, unaneled
> No reck'ning made, but sent to my account
> With all my imperfections on my head.
> O horrible, O horrible, most horrible! (I.5.76–80)

In other words, Old Hamlet has died without having received the last rites, consisting of confession, communion and the sacrament of extreme unction, administered to those who are dying. Likewise, Ophelia is buried with 'maimed rites' (V.I.208), on account of her suicide. Laertes, deeply disturbed by this curtailment of the ritual, insistently repeats the question: 'What ceremony else?' (V.I.212–14), only to be told by the priest that no Requiem Mass has been sung:

> We should profane the service of the dead
> To sing a requiem and such rest to her
> As to peace-parted souls (V.I.245–7)

Throughout the play there is a profound sense of disturbance and unrest associated with such absence or curtailment of ritual, which speaks to anxieties about the changes to liturgical ritual in Shakespeare's time. Part of what *Hamlet* seems to say is that the full liturgy of the dead is of crucial importance to both the living and the dead – 'Words must be said over the dead, goodbyes must be uttered, goodnights liturgically chanted.'[22] Disruption of these rites is the road to political, social and spiritual peril.

In its ritual celebration in sacred spaces, and in its influence on performance onstage, liturgy is about presences, both human and divine. Liturgy speaks to the everlasting presence of God across time, and in turn highlights the role that each individual plays as a part of the ritual at a given point in time. Understanding its texts and allusions is only one aspect in a complex experience of liturgy, which can only be grasped if one is fully present in the ritual – the spaces within which it takes place, as well as the music, sounds, gestures, movements and visual cues that accompany it. The liturgy requires the individual to be embodied and present in the space, in the moment. This importance of presence is connected to the liturgy's key function of making present the divine mysteries. As a result, the ritual also serves to create a community that includes both the living and the dead, united in a common ritual practice and belief. The presence of God is at the heart of the liturgy, and as such it also proved richly inspirational for dramatic representation onstage. Shakespeare, in turn, thinks through the importance of liturgical presence by showing the consequences of the absence of rites. Liturgy remains crucial in the changing post-Reformation world, and has continued to inspire literature, art and music for many centuries beyond the Middle Ages.

Liturgy Revisited

There are many sides to the liturgy. As we have seen, the yearly cycle of celebration of feasts explores the full range of human experience, from profound despair to triumphant joy. The liturgy is poetic, expressing these experiences with words of great depth and beauty. The liturgy is inspiring, prompting artists through the ages to engage creatively with its texts and themes, and transform them as part of a living tradition. The liturgy is connective, forging a link between past, present and future in its ritual. The liturgy is immersive, speaking through words, music, gesture, movement, architecture, colour, light. The liturgy is participatory, drawing the individual into the ritual as a member of a larger community. The liturgy is embodied, celebrating the divine mysteries in the physical presence of the priest and congregation. The liturgy is both public and private, an expression of the public prayer of a community of faith as well as an invitation to members of the congregation to listen, reflect and let themselves be moved. The liturgy is a living tradition, and the forms of worship, texts and rites described in this book can still be experienced, in one form or another, in many churches today.

This is why the liturgy has been so extraordinarily important to Christian communities over the centuries. Its profound influence on Western culture as a common frame of reference, whether in literature, music or art, can hardly be overstated. The reasons for the depth of this influence are perhaps best explained if we think of liturgy not as a one-sided monologue – a form to be observed, a set of rubrics to follow, a range of prescribed readings to attend to – but as a dialogue between thoughts and words that have come down to us from previous generations on the one hand, and the responses of the present congregation on the other. The community and the individual, the past and the present, are in conversation with each other in the ritual. Yet these are not the only participants in this conversation: more than anything else, the liturgy is a dialogue between humans and God. This is expressed in the oft-repeated prayer that opens Matins every morning after the Roman Rite, and also occurs in the Anglican tradition near the beginning of morning and evening prayer: 'O Lord, open thou our lips – And our mouth shall show forth thy praise.' Citing Psalm 51:15, this prayer asks God to enable the congregation to praise him in the right way. In a sense, the liturgical prayer opens with a prayer to God to make the liturgy possible in the first place. Without his help, the liturgy is empty and futile, no more than a set of hollow phrases. The liturgy requires the presence of God in order that it may become an active exchange.

Over hundreds, even thousands, of years, countless artists have been inspired by the liturgy. Many lips have indeed been opened to show forth God's praise in word, song, painting, sculpture, architecture. This dialogue with God has continued down the centuries, and it is still ongoing today. It is an involved dialogue with plenty of disagreement. Artistic productions that have engaged with the liturgy have added to its detail, richness and meaning, but also questioned it, provoked it and reacted against it. Such responses are part and parcel of a living tradition, and the fact that liturgical inspirations have proved meaningful in sometimes entirely secular contexts shows the extraordinary stability, yet also the versatility, of this tradition. The liturgy forms the fabric of Western creative imagination; it provides the very images, words and concepts with which we think and tell stories. It is surprising, perhaps, that the story of the liturgy itself is not known more widely. This book can only provide an introduction to this untold story, and there are many more riches to discover in the liturgy for those who wish to take part in the conversation between the divine and the human, between tradition and present moment, which has preoccupied us for many centuries.

How this conversation will develop in the future is difficult to foretell. The liturgy certainly has its own answer to this question: the set formula for the conclusion of many liturgical prayers is *in saecula saeculorum, Amen*. This has in the English tradition often been translated as 'world without end. Amen', referring to God's eternal and everlasting presence. However, the Latin words translated more literally mean something closer to 'unto the ages of ages'. Each age of human history is different and brings its own novelties, challenges and surprises. And yet, *in saecula saeculorum* imagines the praise of God as lasting through all of these changes, from age unto age, for all eternity. There is, it would seem, a bright future ahead for the liturgy.

REFERENCES

Abbreviations

CPDL *Choral Public Domain Library*, www.cpdl.org

ICEL International Commission on English in the Liturgy, 'Music for the Roman Missal', http://icelweb.org

MED Hans Kurath et al., eds, *Middle English Dictionary* (Ann Arbor, MI, 2000), available at http://quod.lib.umich.edu

NRSV *The Holy Bible: New Revised Standard Version* (Cambridge, 1989)

OED *The Oxford English Dictionary*, 3rd edn online, www.oed.com

Introduction: Why Liturgy?

1 There is a sizeable body of scholarship on medieval liturgy. Good starting points are the following: Nicholas Orme, *Going to Church in Medieval England* (New Haven, CT, 2022); Eamon Duffy, *The Stripping of the Altars* (New Haven, CT, 2011); Richard Pfaff, *The Liturgy in Medieval England* (Cambridge, 2012).

2 *OED*, liturgy *n.*

3 Dimitris Xygalatas, *Ritual* (London, 2022), pp. 210–12.

4 E. E. Evans-Pritchard, *Witchcraft, Oracles, and Magic among the Azande* (Oxford, 1977), cited in Xygalatas, *Ritual*, p. 212.

5 J. A. Lamb, 'The Place of the Bible in the Liturgy', in *The Cambridge History of the Bible*, ed. P. R. Ackroyd and C. F. Evans (Cambridge, 1970), pp. 563–86.

6 *NRSV*.

1 Petition

1 All translations of psalms, as well as the psalm numbering, follow *The Book of Common Prayer* as printed by John Baskerville (Cambridge, 1662).

2 *OED*, psalm *n*.
3 For more details on the structure of the psalms, see Walter Brueggemann and W. H. Bellinger, *Psalms*, New Cambridge Bible Commentary (Cambridge, 2013), pp. 1–12.
4 F. H. Dickinson, *Missale ad usum insignis et praeclarae ecclesiae Sarum* (Burntisland, 1861), col. 57.
5 C. S. Rodd, 'Psalms', in *The Oxford Bible Commentary*, ed. John Barton and John Muddiman (Oxford, 2007), pp. 355–404.
6 Ibid.
7 See the edition by George Shuffelton, *Codex Ashmole 61: A Compilation of Popular Middle English Verse* (Kalamazoo, MI, 2008).
8 Thomas Wyatt, *The Complete Poems*, ed. R. A. Rebholz (New Haven, CT, 1981), pp. 208–9, ll. 495–508.
9 Hannibal Hamlin, 'William Shakespeare', in *The Blackwell Companion to the Bible in English Literature*, ed. Rebecca Lemon (Chichester, 2012), pp. 225–38 (p. 253).

2 Love

1 Athalya Brenner, 'Song of Solomon', in *The Oxford Bible Commentary*, ed. John Barton and John Muddiman (Oxford, 2007), pp. 429–33.
2 Rupert of Deutz, *De gloria et honore filii hominis super Mattheum*, ed. Hrabanus Haacke, Corpus Christianorum Continuatio Mediaevalis 29 (Turnhout, 1979), 12.383; trans. J. Arblaster, cited in Louise Nelstrop, 'Erotic and Nuptial Imagery', in *The Oxford Handbook of Mystical Theology*, ed. Edward Howells and Mark Allen McIntosh (Oxford, 2020), pp. 328–46 (p. 336).
3 Joseph F. Mone, ed., *Lateinische Hymnen des Mittelalters, aus Handschriften herausgegeben und erklärt*, vol. II (Freiburg im Breisgau, 1853–5), hymn 548; my translation.
4 A more detailed account is given in E. Ann Matter, *The Voice of My Beloved: The Song of Songs in Western Medieval Christianity* (Philadelphia, PA, 2010), pp. 151–77.
5 Ibid., pp. 188–92.
6 Guido Maria Dreves, ed., *Analecta Hymnica Medii Aevi*, vol. I: *Cantiones Bohemicae: Leiche, Lieder und Rufe des 13., 14. und 15. Jahrhunderts* (Leipzig, 1886), Hymnus 49. On this poem, see also J. M. Salvador-González, 'Hortus Conclusus: A Mariological Metaphor in Some Renaissance Paintings of the Annunciation in the Light of Medieval Liturgical Hymns', *Religions*, XIV/1 (2023), pp. 36–52.

7 Richard Stracke, *A Guide to Christian Iconography: Images, Symbols, and Texts*, www.christianiconography.info, accessed 24 January 2024.
8 Karen Saupe, ed., *Middle English Marian Lyrics* (Kalamazoo, MI, 1998), lyric no. 79; my translation.
9 Translation based on Eleanor Parker's version, *A Clerk of Oxford*, https://aclerkofoxford.blogspot.com, accessed 24 January 2024.
10 Translation by Anthony Mortimer in Guido Cavalcanti, *Complete Poems* (Richmond, Surrey, 2010).
11 Walt Whitman, *Song of Myself with a Complete Commentary*, ed. Christopher Merrill and Ed Folsom (Iowa City, IA, 2016), p. 7.
12 For more details, see Ilana Pardes, *The Song of Songs: A Biography* (Princeton, NJ, 2019), pp. 178–9.

3 Hope

1 Prosper Guéranger, *The Liturgical Year: Advent*, 2nd edn (Dublin, 1870), pp. 155–6. The translation is adapted from *The New English Hymnal*, Melody edition (Norwich, 1994), no. 501.
2 Kerry Robin McCarthy, *Byrd* (New York, 2013), p. 109.
3 This and the following English translations (with the exception of 'O Radiant Dawn') follow the Church of England's *Common Worship*, available at www.churchofengland.org, accessed 24 January 2024.
4 Boethius, *Consolation of Philosophy*, trans. P. G. Walsh (Oxford, 1999), p. 67.
5 Wolfgang Braunfels and Engelbert Kirschbaum, *Lexikon der christlichen Ikonographie*, vol. IV (Rome, 1968), pp. 549–58.
6 David Lyle Jeffrey, *A Dictionary of Biblical Tradition in English Literature* (Grand Rapids, MI, 1992), pp. 332–3.
7 Translation by Allen Mandelbaum, *Digital Dante: The Divine Comedy* (New York, 2014), https://digitaldante.columbia.edu, accessed 24 January 2024.
8 The translation follows Thomas O'Gorman, ed., *An Advent Sourcebook* (Chicago, IL, 1988), p. 138.
9 Translation by Eleanor Parker, at *A Clerk of Oxford*, https://aclerkofoxford.blogspot.com, accessed 24 January 2024.
10 Carl F. Hostetter, 'Over Middle-Earth Sent unto Men: On the Philological Origins of Tolkien's Eärendel Myth', *Mythlore*, XVII/3 (1991), pp. 5–10 (p. 6).
11 J.R.R. Tolkien and Christopher Tolkien, *Sauron Defeated* (London, 2010), p. 236.

4 Suffering

1 This and the following translations are adapted from CPDL.
2 Translation adapted from NRSV.
3 Translation adapted from CPDL.
4 Carleton Brown, ed., *Religious Lyrics of the XVth Century* (Oxford, 1939), no. 107; my translation.
5 Translation by Eleanor Parker at *A Clerk of Oxford*, https://aclerkofoxford.blogspot.com, accessed 24 January 2024.
6 MED, treu-love *n.*
7 George Herbert, *The Complete English Poems*, ed. John Tobin (London, 2004), p. 23.

5 Grief

1 Translation adapted from *The Ultimate Stabat Mater Website*, https://stabatmater.info, accessed 24 January 2024.
2 Carleton Brown, ed., *English Lyrics of the XIIIth Century* (Oxford, 1932), pp. 89–91. Translation adapted from Eleanor Parker at *A Clerk of Oxford*, https://aclerkofoxford.blogspot.com, accessed 24 January 2024.
3 Nicholas Penny, *National Gallery Catalogues: The Sixteenth Century Italian Paintings*, vol. I: *Paintings from Bergamo, Brescia, and Cremona,* exh. cat., National Gallery (London, 2004), pp. 26–8.
4 Richard Leighton Greene, ed., *The Early English Carols*, 2nd revd edn (Oxford, 2019), no. 153, modernized spelling.
5 Karen Saupe, ed., *Middle English Marian Lyrics* (Kalamazoo, MI, 1998), no. 42, modernized spelling.
6 Käthe Kollwitz, Diaries, 22 October 1937, quoted in 'Pietà (Mother with Dead Son), 1937–1939', www.kollwitz.de, accessed 24 January 2024.

6 Joy

1 English translation adapted from ICEL, 'Music for the Roman Missal', http://icelweb.org, accessed 24 January 2024.
2 Aspects of this analysis are based on Nathan Chase, *Contingent Magazine*, 11 April 2020, www.contingentmagazine.org.
3 Augustine, *Enchiridion*, viii, 27, trans. Albert C. Outler in Augustine of Hippo, *Confessions and Enchiridion*, Library of Christian Classics 7 (London, 1955).
4 Carleton Brown, ed., *Religious Lyrics of the XVth Century* (Oxford, 1939), p. 120; modernized spelling.

5 John Milton, *Paradise Lost*, ed. Alastair Fowler, 2nd edn (London, 2013), pp. 469–78.
6 Victor Y. Haines, 'The Iconography of the *Felix culpa*', *Florilegium*, 1/1 (1979), pp. 151–85.
7 Augustine of Hippo, *Enarrationes in Psalmos CI–CL*, ed. E. Dekkers and J. Fraipont, Corpus Christianorum Series Latina 40 (Turnhout, 1956), psalmus: 148, par: 1, ll. 14–21.
8 Francis X. Weiser, *Handbook of Christian Feasts and Customs: The Year of the Lord in Liturgy and Folklore* (New York, 1958), p. 159.
9 Bede, *Bede's Ecclesiastical History of the English People*, ed. Bertram Colgrave and R.A.B. Mynors, Oxford Medieval Texts (Oxford, 1969), Book 1, Chapter Twenty.

7 Death

1 The English translation follows *CPDL*.
2 Kees Vellekoop, *Dies ire dies illa: Studien zur Frühgeschichte einer Sequenz* (Bilthoven, 1978), p. 14.
3 English translation of the programme notes from the Hector Berlioz Website, www.hberlioz.com, accessed 24 January 2024.

8 Revelation

1 Cited in David Lyle Jeffrey, *A Dictionary of Biblical Tradition in English Literature* (Grand Rapids, MI, 1992), p. 546.
2 Malcolm Andrew and Ronald A. Waldron, ed. and trans., *The Poems of the Pearl Manuscript in Modern English Prose Translation: Pearl, Cleanness, Patience, Sir Gawain and the Green Knight* (Liverpool, 2013), p. 22.
3 William Blake, *The Poems of William Blake*, ed. W. H. Stevenson and David V. Erdman (London, 1972), pp. 488–9.
4 Jeffrey, *Dictionary of Biblical Tradition*, p. 548.
5 *Paradiso* 31.118–29; translation by Allen Mandelbaum, Digital Dante, https://digitaldante.columbia.edu, accessed 24 January 2024.
6 *OED*, Michaelmas *n*.
7 Sir Frederick Morton Eden, *The State of the Poor: or, An History of the Labouring Classes in England*, vol. 1 (London, 1797), pp. 32–3.
8 Scott Hahn, *The Lamb's Supper: The Mass as Heaven on Earth* (London, 2003), pp. 66–7.
9 George Herbert, *The Complete English Poems*, ed. John Tobin (London, 2004), p. 178.

9 Time

1 Cristina Maria Cervone, *Poetics of the Incarnation: Middle English Writing and the Leap of Love* (Philadelphia, PA, 2012), pp. 42–3.
2 For further details on the medieval seasons, see Eleanor Parker, *Winters in the World: A Journey through the Anglo-Saxon Year* (London, 2022).
3 Jacques Le Goff, 'Merchant's Time and Church's Time in the Middle Ages', in *Time, Work, and Culture in the Middle Ages*, trans. Arthur Goldhammer (Chicago, IL, 1980), pp. 29–42.
4 For more details on scientific tools in medieval manuscripts, see Seb Falk, *The Light Ages: A Medieval Journey of Discovery* (London, 2020).
5 *MED*, lammasse *n. 2b*.
6 Alfred Tennyson, *Alfred Lord Tennyson: A Memoir by His Son* (London, 1897), p. 112.
7 Glenn Gunhouse, 'Introduction to the Book of Hours', *A Hypertext Book of Hours*, available at https://medievalist.net, accessed 12 April 2024.
8 For further details on Books of Hours, see Eamon Duffy, *Marking the Hours: English People and Their Prayers, 1240–1570* (New Haven, CT, 2011).
9 F. H. Dickinson, *Missale ad usum insignis et praeclarae ecclesiae Sarum* (Burntisland, 1861), col. 62; my translation and italics.
10 Nicholas Wolterstorff, 'The Remembrance of Things (Not) Past', in *Christian Philosophy*, ed. Thomas Flint (Notre Dame, IN, 1990), p. 146. For more on the topic of liturgical remembrance, see also Joshua Cockayne and Gideon Salter, 'Feasts of Memory: Collective Remembering, Liturgical Time Travel and the Actualisation of the Past', *Modern Theology*, XXXVII/2 (2021), pp. 275–95.
11 Roch Kereszty, 'Contemporaneity: The Mystery of Liturgical Time', *Nova et vetera*, XVIII/2 (2020), pp. 505–19 (p. 510).
12 Dickinson, *Missale*, col. 340.
13 T. S. Eliot, *The Complete Poems and Plays* (London, 2004), p. 172.

10 Space

1 G. K. Chesterton, *A Miscellany of Men*, 3rd edn (London, 1920), pp. 211–13.
2 For further details, see Nicholas Orme, *Going to Church in Medieval England* (New Haven, CT, 2022), pp. 302–14.
3 Thomas Frederick Simmons and Dan Jeremy, eds, *The Lay Folks Mass Book or the Manner of Hearing Mass: With Rubrics and Devotions for the People; in Four Texts and Offices in English, According to the Use of York.*

From Mss. of the xth to the xvth Century, Early English Text Society 71 (London, 1879), pp. 10, 18, 24, 38; spelling modernized.

4 Alexandra F. Johnston, 'An Introduction to Medieval English Theatre', in *The Cambridge Companion to Medieval English Theatre*, ed. Richard Beadle and Alan J. Fletcher (Cambridge, 2008), pp. 1–25 (p. 3).

5 Translation by Chris Fenner, 'Gloria laus et honor', *Hymnology Archive*, 6 March 2023, www.hymnologyarchive.com.

6 J. Wickham Legg, ed., *The Sarum Missal* (Oxford, 1916), p. 96 ('pueri in eminenciori loco canentes').

7 Carolyn Marino Malone, 'Architecture as Evidence for Liturgical Performance', in *Understanding Medieval Liturgy: Essays in Interpretation*, ed. Helen Gittos and Sarah Hamilton (London, 2016), pp. 207–38 (p. 225).

8 Ibid., p. 231.

9 Eamon Duffy, *The Stripping of the Altars* (New Haven, CT, 2011), p. 26.

10 Malone, 'Architecture as Evidence for Liturgical Performance', p. 236.

11 'Introduction', in *The York Corpus Christi Plays* , ed. Clifford Davidson (Kalamazoo, MI, 2011).

12 Douglas Sugano, ed., *The N-Town Plays* (Kalamazoo, MI, 2007), Play 25, 'The Entry into Jerusalem', ll. 260–65; spelling modernized.

13 Ibid., Play 32, 'Procession to Calvary; Crucifixion', ll. 222–9; spelling modernized.

14 Ibid., ll. 97–101; spelling modernized.

15 Ibid., l. 269a; my translation ('Hic quasi semi-mortua cadat prona in terram').

16 For a detailed analysis, see Pamela M. King, *The York Mystery Cycle and the Worship of the City* (Cambridge, 2006).

17 Davidson, ed., *The York Corpus Christi Plays*, Play 35, 'Crucifixio Christi', ll. 253–64.

18 For more details, see King, *The York Mystery Cycle*, pp. 144–50.

19 This and all following references follow the edition of *Hamlet*, ed. Ann Thompson and Neil Taylor, revd edn (London, 2016).

20 On this in greater depth, see Gerard Kilroy, 'Requiem for a Prince: Rites of Memory in *Hamlet*', *Downside Review*, CXX/419 (2002), pp. 91–112; and James V. Holleran, 'Maimed Funeral Rites in *Hamlet*', *English Literary Renaissance*, XIX/1 (1989), pp. 65–93.

21 Holleran, 'Maimed Funeral Rites in *Hamlet*', p. 72.

22 Kilroy, 'Requiem for a Prince: Rites of Memory in *Hamlet*', p. 107.

BIBLIOGRAPHY

Primary Sources

Andrew, Malcolm, and Ronald A. Waldron, ed. and trans., *The Poems of the Pearl Manuscript in Modern English Prose Translation: Pearl, Cleanness, Patience, Sir Gawain and the Green Knight* (Liverpool, 2013)

Augustine of Hippo, *Confessions and Enchiridion*, ed. and trans. Albert C. Outler, Library of Christian Classics 7 (London, 1955)

—, *Enarrationes in Psalmos CI–CL*, ed. E. Dekkers and J. Fraipont, Corpus Christianorum Series Latina 40 (Turnhout, 1956)

Bede, *Bede's Ecclesiastical History of the English People*, ed. Bertram Colgrave and R.A.B. Mynors, Oxford Medieval Texts (Oxford, 1969)

Blake, William, *The Poems of William Blake*, ed. W. H. Stevenson and David V. Erdman (London, 1972)

Boethius, *Consolation of Philosophy,* trans. P. G. Walsh (Oxford, 1999)

The Book of Common Prayer, printed by John Baskerville (Cambridge, 1662), available at www.churchofengland.org

Brown, Carleton, ed., *English Lyrics of the XIIIth Century* (Oxford, 1932)

—, ed., *Religious Lyrics of the XVth Century* (Oxford, 1939)

Canisius, Petrus, *De Maria Virgine Incomparabili, Et Dei Genitrice Sacrosancta, Libri Qvinqve, Atq[ue] hic Secvndvs Liber est Commentariorum de Verbi Dei corruptelis, aduersus nouos et veteres Sectariorum errores nunc primum editus* (Ingolstadt, 1577)

Cavalcanti, Guido, *Complete Poems*, trans. Anthony Robert Mortimer (Richmond, Surrey, 2010)

Chesterton, G. K., *A Miscellany of Men*, 3rd edn (London, 1920)

Dante Alighieri, *Digital Dante: The Divine Comedy* (New York, 2014), available at https://digitaldante.columbia.edu

Davidson, Clifford, ed., *The York Corpus Christi Plays* (Kalamazoo, MI, 2011), available at https://d.lib.rochester.edu

Dreves, Guido Maria, ed., *Analecta Hymnica Medii Aevi*, vol. I: *Cantiones Bohemicae: Leiche, Lieder und Rufe des 13., 14. und 15 Jahrhunderts* (Leipzig, 1886)

Eliot, T. S., *The Complete Poems and Plays* (London, 2004)

Greene, Richard Leighton, ed., *The Early English Carols*, 2nd revd edn (Oxford, 2019)

Herbert, George, *The Complete English Poems*, ed. John Tobin (London, 2004)

Legg, J. Wickham, ed., *The Sarum Missal* (Oxford, 1916)

Milton, John, *Paradise Lost*, ed. Alastair Fowler, 2nd edn (London, 2013)

Mone, Joseph F., ed., *Lateinische Hymnen des Mittelalters, aus Handschriften herausgegeben und erklärt*, vol. II (Freiburg im Breisgau, 1853–5)

The New English Hymnal, Melody edition (Norwich, 1994)

NRSV = The Holy Bible: New Revised Standard Version, Containing the Old and New Testaments (Cambridge, 1989)

Rupert of Deutz, *De gloria et honore filii hominis super Mattheum*, ed. Hrabanus Haacke, Corpus Christianorum Continuatio Mediaevalis 29 (Turnhout, 1979)

Saupe, Karen, ed., *Middle English Marian Lyrics* (Kalamazoo, MI, 1998), available at https://d.lib.rochester.edu

Shakespeare, William, *Hamlet*, ed. Ann Thompson and Neil Taylor, revd edn (London, 2016)

Shuffelton, George, ed., *Codex Ashmole 61: A Compilation of Popular Middle English Verse* (Kalamazoo, MI, 2008), available at https://d.lib.rochester.edu

Simmons, Thomas Frederick, and Dan Jeremy, eds, *The Lay Folks Mass Book or the Manner of Hearing Mass: With Rubrics and Devotions for the People; in Four Texts and Offices in English, According to the Use of York. From Mss. of the xth to the xvth Century*, Early English Text Society 71 (London, 1879)

Sugano, Douglas, ed., *The N-Town Plays* (Kalamazoo, MI, 2007), available at https://d.lib.rochester.edu

Tennyson, Alfred, *Alfred Lord Tennyson: A Memoir by His Son* (London, 1897)

Tolkien, J.R.R., and Christopher Tolkien, *Sauron Defeated* (London, 2010)

Whitman, Walt, *Song of Myself with a Complete Commentary*, ed. Christopher Merrill and Ed Folsom (Iowa City, IA, 2016)

Wyatt, Thomas, *Sir Thomas Wyatt: The Complete Poems*, ed. R. A. Rebholz (New Haven, CT, 1981)

Secondary Sources

Braunfels, Wolfgang, and Engelbert Kirschbaum, *Lexikon der christlichen Ikonographie* (Rome, 1968)

Brenner, Athalya, 'The Song of Solomon', in *The Oxford Bible Commentary*, ed. John Barton and John Muddiman (Oxford, 2001), pp. 429–33

Brueggemann, Walter, and W. H. Bellinger, *Psalms*, New Cambridge Bible Commentary (Cambridge, 2013)

Cervone, Cristina Maria, *Poetics of the Incarnation: Middle English Writing and the Leap of Love* (Philadelphia, PA, 2012)

Cockayne, Joshua, and Gideon Salter, 'Feasts of Memory: Collective Remembering, Liturgical Time Travel and the Actualisation of the Past', *Modern Theology*, XXXVII/2 (2021), pp. 275–95

Dickinson, F. H., *Missale ad usum insignis et praeclarae ecclesiae Sarum* (Burntisland, 1861)

Duffy, Eamon, *Marking the Hours: English People and Their Prayers, 1240–1570* (New Haven, CT, 2011)

—, *The Stripping of the Altars: Traditional Religion in England, c. 1400–c. 1580* (New Haven, CT, 1992)

Evans-Pritchard, E. E., *Witchcraft, Oracles and Magic among the Azande* (Oxford, 1977)

Falk, Seb, *The Light Ages: A Medieval Journey of Discovery* (London, 2020)

Guéranger, Prosper, *The Liturgical Year: Advent*, 2nd edn (Dublin, 1870)

Hahn, Scott, *The Lamb's Supper: The Mass as Heaven on Earth* (London, 2003)

Haines, Victor Y., 'The Iconography of the *Felix culpa*', *Florilegium*, I/I (1979), pp. 151–85

Hamlin, Hannibal, 'William Shakespeare', in *The Blackwell Companion to the Bible in English Literature*, ed. Rebecca Lemon (Chichester, 2012), pp. 245–58

Holleran, James V., 'Maimed Funeral Rites in *Hamlet*', *English Literary Renaissance*, XIX/I (1989), pp. 65–93

Hostetter, Carl F., 'Over Middle-Earth Sent unto Men: On the Philological Origins of Tolkien's Eärendel Myth', *Mythlore*, XVII/3 (1991), pp. 5–10

Jeffrey, David Lyle, *A Dictionary of Biblical Tradition in English Literature* (Grand Rapids, MI, 1992)

Johnston, Alexandra F., 'An Introduction to Medieval English Theatre', in *The Cambridge Companion to Medieval English Theatre*, ed. Richard Beadle and Alan J. Fletcher (Cambridge, 2008), pp. 1–25

Kereszty, Roch, 'Contemporaneity: The Mystery of Liturgical Time', *Nova et vetera*, XVIII/2 (2020), pp. 505–19

Kilroy, Gerard, 'Requiem for a Prince: Rites of Memory in *Hamlet*', *Downside Review*, CXX/419 (2002), pp. 91–112
King, Pamela M., *The York Mystery Cycle and the Worship of the City* (Cambridge, 2006)
Klauser, Theodor, and John Halliburton, *A Short History of the Western Liturgy: An Account and Some Reflections*, 2nd edn (Oxford, 2000)
Lamb, J. A., 'The Place of the Bible in the Liturgy', in *The Cambridge History of the Bible*, ed. P. R. Ackroyd and C. F. Evans (Cambridge, 1970), pp. 563–86
Le Goff, Jacques, 'Merchant's Time and Church's Time in the Middle Ages', in *Time, Work, and Culture in the Middle Ages*, trans. Arthur Goldhammer (Chicago, IL, 1980), pp. 29–42
McCarthy, Kerry Robin, *Byrd* (New York, 2013)
Malone, Carolyn Marino, 'Architecture as Evidence for Liturgical Performance', in *Understanding Medieval Liturgy: Essays in Interpretation*, ed. Helen Gittos and Sarah Hamilton (London, 2016), pp. 207–37
Matter, E. Ann, *The Voice of My Beloved: The Song of Songs in Western Medieval Christianity* (Philadelphia, PA, 2010)
Nelstrop, Louise, 'Erotic and Nuptial Imagery', in *The Oxford Handbook of Mystical Theology*, ed. Edward Howells and Mark Allen McIntosh (Oxford, 2020), pp. 328–46
O'Gorman, Thomas, ed., *An Advent Sourcebook* (Chicago, IL, 1988)
Orme, Nicholas, *Going to Church in Medieval England* (New Haven, CT, 2022)
Pardes, Ilana, *The Song of Songs: A Biography* (Princeton, NJ, 2019)
Parker, Eleanor, *Winters in the World: A Journey through the Anglo-Saxon Year* (London, 2022)
Penny, Nicholas, *National Gallery Catalogues: The Sixteenth Century Italian Paintings*, vol. I: *Paintings from Bergamo, Brescia, and Cremona*, exh. cat., National Gallery, London (2004)
Pfaff, Richard, *The Liturgy in Medieval England: A History* (Cambridge, 2012)
Rodd, C. S., 'Psalms', in *The Oxford Bible Commentary*, ed. John Barton and John Muddiman (Oxford, 2001)
Salvador-González, J. M., '*Hortus Conclusus*: A Mariological Metaphor in Some Renaissance Paintings of the Annunciation in the Light of Medieval Liturgical Hymns', *Religions*, XIV/1 (2023), pp. 36–52
Vellekoop, Kees, *Dies ire dies illa: Studien zur Frühgeschichte einer Sequenz* (Bilthoven, 1978)
Weiser, Francis X., *Handbook of Christian Feasts and Customs: The Year of the Lord in Liturgy and Folklore* (New York, 1958)
Wolterstorff, Nicholas, 'The Remembrance of Things (Not) Past', in *Christian Philosophy*, ed. Thomas Flint (Notre Dame, IN, 1990), pp. 118–61

Xygalatas, Dimitris, *Ritual: How Seemingly Senseless Acts Make Life Worth Living* (London, 2022)

Websites and Online Resources

Chase, Nathan, 'This Is the Night', *Contingent Magazine*, 11 April 2020, www.contingentmagazine.org

Choral Public Domain Library, www.cpdl.org

Common Worship, Church of England, available at www.churchofengland.org

Fenner, Chris, 'Gloria laus et honor', *Hymnology Archive*, 6 March 2023, www.hymnologyarchive.com

Gunhouse, Glenn, *A Hypertext Book of Hours*, http://medievalist.net

International Commission on English in the Liturgy, 'Music for the Roman Missal', http://icelweb.org

Käthe Kollwitz Museum, Cologne, www.kollwitz.de

Kurath, Hans, et al., eds, *Middle English Dictionary* (Ann Arbor, MI, 2000), available at http://quod.lib.umich.edu

The Oxford English Dictionary, 3rd edn online, www.oed.com

Parker, Eleanor, *A Clerk of Oxford*, http://aclerkofoxford.blogspot.com

Stracke, Richard, *A Guide to Christian Iconography: Images, Symbols, and Texts*, www.christianiconography.info

Tayeb, Monir, and Michel Austin, *The Hector Berlioz Website*, www.hberlioz.com

The Ultimate Stabat Mater Website, http://stabatmater.info

ACKNOWLEDGEMENTS

I owe thanks to many for helping me make this book a reality. First and foremost, I must thank the wonderful team at Reaktion Books for their help with this book despite its somewhat unconventional nature. My thanks also go to Eleanor Parker for permission to reproduce some of her fine translations of medieval poems in this book. The book was written while I was a Junior Research Fellow at Christ Church, Oxford, and I am most grateful to my college for giving me this opportunity, as well as for many encouraging comments from colleagues, especially Mishtooni Bose. The reproduction of colour images in this book was made possible through a grant by the Research Centre at Christ Church. My students in medieval literature at Trinity College, Oxford, have played no small part in shaping this book through their questions about these texts over the years; this book is an attempt to provide more detailed answers for which there was insufficient time in tutorials. My special thanks go to Minty Plumstead for acting as a student test reader and offering detailed suggestions that have helped me make this a better book.

Space does not permit me to name everyone who has had an influence on the conception and completion of this book but I am grateful for all of the help, support, kind words and criticism that I have received. My heartfelt thanks go to Tristan Franklinos, not only for his detailed comments on the manuscript but for many years of friendship. Katie Bank provided excellent company on a trip to Gladstone's Library, where I first started thinking about this project, challenged me to rethink how I approach terminology, and pointed me towards relevant pieces of music with her impressive mental archive of polyphony. Florence Hazrat's guidance was extremely helpful in navigating how to write a trade book. Jessica Frazier accompanied me on many a trip to Cotswold pubs, making writing all the more productive and enjoyable. Felicity Brown, Will Ghosh and Harry Daniels have been supportive friends and cheerful lunch companions. Rebekah Wallace provided pipes as well as ruminations on the universal and the particular.

The Very Revd Professor Sarah Foot, Dean of Christ Church, prompted me to change the book's title during an engaged High Table conversation; it is much improved as a result. My friends in various choirs over the years have helped me discover, understand and perform many of the pieces mentioned in this book; particularly memorable are long conversations with Martin Heissler about the musical history of the *Dies irae*. Last but certainly not least, I owe thanks to my parents, for introducing me to the liturgy in the first place, and for their constant love and support.

PHOTO ACKNOWLEDGEMENTS

The author and publishers wish to express their thanks to the sources listed below for illustrative material and/or permission to reproduce it. Some locations of artworks are also given below, in the interest of brevity:

Bayerische Staatsbibliothek, Munich: 4; Bibliothèque nationale de France (MS Latin 16746, fol. 7v): 7; Bodleian Library, University of Oxford: 1 (MS Douce 366, fol. 10r), 19 (MS Douce 266, fol. 11v); Gemäldegalerie, Staatliche Museen zu Berlin: 9; photo Jim Grey, all rights reserved: 15; The J. Paul Getty Museum, Los Angeles: 17 (MS Ludwig III 1, fol. 19v), 21 (MS Ludwig IX 8, fol. 85r); Koninklijke Bibliotheek, The Hague (MS 74 G 37a, fol. 94r): 20; Musée Unterlinden, Colmar: 10; Museo del Convento di San Marco, Florence: 5, 8; Museo Nacional del Prado, Madrid: 11; National Gallery of Art, Washington, DC: 18; Nationalhistorisk Museum, Frederiksborg Slot, Hillerød (photo Hans Petersen): 12; Scuola Grande di San Rocco, Venice: 6; Wikimedia Commons: 2 (photo Sailko (Francesco Bini), CC BY 3.0), 3 (photo Wolfgang Sauber, CC BY-SA 4.0), 13 (Basilica di San Pietro, Rome; photo Stanislav Traykov, CC BY-SA 3.0), 14 (Neue Wache, Berlin; photo abbilder (Axel Kuhlmann), CC BY 2.0), 16 (photo Zairon, CC BY-SA 4.0).

INDEX

Illustration numbers are indicated by *italics*